The
BIGGEST
Book of
HOROSCOPES
EVER

The
BIGGEST
Book of
HOROSCOPES
EVER

Learn More About Your Future and Past with
This Extraordinary Collection of Astrological Readings

Trish MacGregor

renowned astrologer, author of *Unlocking the Secrets to Scorpios*
as well as the Sydney Omarr day-by-day yearly astrology books

PAGE STREET
PUBLISHING CO.

PAGE STREET
PUBLISHING CO.

First published in 2016 by
Page Street Publishing Co.
27 Congress Street, Suite 103
Salem, MA 01970
www.pagestreetpublishing.com

Distributed by Macmillan, sales in Canada by The Canadian Manda Group.

19   18   17   16   1   2   3   4   5

ISBN-13: 978-1-62414-293-2
ISBN-10: 1-62414-293-1

Library of Congress Control Number: 2016906106

Cover and book design by Page Street Publishing Co.

Printed and bound in the United States

Page Street is proud to be a member of 1% for the Planet. Members donate one percent of their sales to one or more of the over 1,500 environmental and sustainability charities across the globe who participate in this program.

This one is for Rob and Megan,
with much love always

CONTENTS

Introduction   8

2017   20

Introduction to 2017   20
Aries   23
Taurus   36
Gemini   50
Cancer   62
Leo   75
Virgo   88
Libra   102
Scorpio   115
Sagittarius   128
Capricorn   142
Aquarius   155
Pisces   169

2018   183

Introduction to 2018   183
Aries   186
Taurus   199
Gemini   212
Cancer   225
Leo   238
Virgo   250
Libra   263
Scorpio   276
Sagittarius   290
Capricorn   303
Aquarius   317
Pisces   330

2019   343

Introduction to 2019   343
Aries   346
Taurus   359
Gemini   373
Cancer   387
Leo   401
Virgo   415
Libra   428
Scorpio   442
Sagittarius   455
Capricorn   468
Aquarius   482
Pisces   496

Acknowledgments   511
About the Author   511
Index   512

Introduction

One afternoon at our local dog park, a teacher and performance pianist mentioned that she was interviewing for a new job for the fall and was nervous about the upcoming interview. I asked Estis her birth information and the time and date of the interview and entered the information into an astrology app on my phone.

By placing the transits for the date of the interview into a bi-wheel around her birth chart, I could see which of her natal planets were being triggered by the transits. On the date of the interview, Jupiter—the planet that symbolizes luck, expansion, higher education, publishing, worldview—was forming a beneficial angle to her Midheaven, the part of the chart that represents profession and career. I told her I felt she would get the job.

A few days later, I ran into her again at the dog park, and she said she'd been asked back for a second interview. I did another bi-wheel for the date and time of the second interview. These transits also looked promising. Jupiter would still be forming a powerful angle to her Midheaven, and Mercury—the planet of communication—would be forming a beneficial angle to her sun sign and wouldn't be retrograde. Also, just as importantly, the second interview would occur during a new moon, a time when new opportunities are ushered into our lives.

"The job is yours already," I told her.

Sure enough, a week later, she texted me that she'd gotten the job.

Transits, the daily motion of the planets, impact our lives according to the nature of the planets, the angles they form to each other and to our natal planets. For the purpose of this book, we'll be dealing with the signs and placements of the planets in respect to your sun sign and the angles these planets make to your sun sign. We will also be looking at the new and full moons each month and how they are likely to affect you. Retrograde planets are also taken into account.

When a planet is retrograde, it appears to be moving backward and enters a kind of dormancy so that its energy doesn't function at full capacity. The sun and the moon are the only planets that never turn retrograde, and Mercury turns retrograde the most often—three times a year, for about three weeks a pop. During this time, communication and travel are likely to encounter snafus. It's wise not to sign contracts, or buy electronics or cars because, in all likelihood, you'll end up returning them. It isn't time to launch projects. The common wisdom for a Mercury retrograde is to revise, review and revisit. One of the curious attributes of a Mercury retro is that old friends and formers lovers and spouses sometimes resurface in our lives. If you travel during a Mercury retro, then you may return to the location at a future date.

In the monthly roundup sections, you'll find references to the days when Mercury and other planets turn retrograde and go direct and what it may mean for you. I've also included references to the new and full moons each month as well as the solar and lunar eclipses.

A Mercury Retrograde Story

On November 7, 2000, Mercury had been retrograde since mid-October: first in Scorpio, then it slipped back into Libra and at 9:20 p.m., it turned direct in that sign. When Mercury stations, which means it's about to turn retrograde or direct, the potential for miscommunication is strong. But for that date, the station caused bedlam because it was election day in the U.S.

Astrologers were predicting chaos, and sure enough, at 7:49 p.m. NBC decided they had enough data from exit polls in Florida. Tom Brokaw called the state for Al Gore. With Florida's twenty-five electoral votes, it meant he had won the election.

However, shortly after 10 p.m.—less than an hour after Mercury had turned direct—Brokaw backtracked and said that George W. Bush had won the state and the election. We all know what ensued after that—the endless dispute over the chads on Palm Beach County's ballot and the eventual decision by the Supreme Court that Bush was the 43rd president of the U.S.

So be forewarned! In the introduction to each year, you'll find the dates for that year's Mercury retrogrades.

Some Astrological Basics
The Sun Signs

Your sun sign is the primary archetype that describes who you are. You probably already know whether you're an Aries or a Taurus, a Gemini or a Cancer, but here's a chart that spells out the dates and the archetypal theme for the signs:

SIGN	SYMBOL	DATES	ARCHETYPE THEME
Aries	♈	March 21–April 19	The Pioneer
Taurus	♉	April 20–May 20	The Pragmatist
Gemini	♊	May 21–June 21	The Communicator
Cancer	♋	June 22–July 22	The Nurturer
Leo	♌	July 23–August 22	The Actor
Virgo	♍	August 23–September 22	The Perfectionist
Libra	♎	September 23–October 22	The Harmonizer
Scorpio	♏	October 23–November 21	The Transformer
Sagittarius	♐	November 22–December 21	The Truth Seeker
Capricorn	♑	December 22–January 19	The Achiever
Aquarius	♒	January 20–February 18	The Paradigm-Buster
Pisces	♓	February 19–March 20	The Healer

ARIES
Bold, courageous and fearless, you're the true trailblazer, pioneer, the type who conceived the NASA space program, and who will eventually colonize other planets. Down here on planet Earth, you'll try anything once.

TAURUS
While Aries is busy pioneering and discovering new lands, you're settling it, cultivating the land and using your resources for practical purposes. Your stubbornness and determination keep you around for the long haul on any project or endeavor.

GEMINI

After Aries and Taurus have discovered and cultivated the new land, you come in and create the communication networks: newspapers, books, Wi-Fi. You connect people in this new land. You learn and teach new ways of doing things and communicate your knowledge to others.

CANCER

Now that the first three signs have discovered, settled and connected everyone in this new land, you come along and tame it, civilize it. You create retreats for solitude, put down roots and call it home. You're the nurturer, the one who imagines what might be.

LEO

You bring drama and excitement to these new lands and communities. Your flamboyance and magnetism capture hearts—and break a few!—and you enjoy adulation and applause. Your desire to succeed extends to every area of your life.

VIRGO

If Gemini doesn't start the community newspaper, then you do. Or you write for it. Or blog for it. Your grasp of details exceeds that of any other sign, and your mental agility and quickness is practically legendary. Like Gemini, you're a deft communicator, but delve more deeply.

LIBRA

You're known for your diplomacy, sense of fairness and love of beauty in all its forms. You, like no other sign, can see both sides of an issue, can step into someone else's shoes and see things as that person sees them. You're an excellent strategist and seek harmony in every facet of your life.

SCORPIO

Intense, passionate, intuitive, strong-willed. Where Libra brings beauty and art to this new land that Aries founded, you bring spirituality, a profound transformation and an awareness that other dimensions exist. You're as relentless and stubborn as Taurus and are after the absolute bottom line in whatever you tackle.

SAGITTARIUS

You're nomadic, restless, a seeker of truth. You see the big picture and leave the details to others. You're always outspoken, so the people around you usually know what you believe. You bring philosophy and discourse to this new land and a sense that all people have the right to live freely.

CAPRICORN

You're hard-working, industrious and disciplined. When you're assigned a task, you do it with your eyes pinned to the ultimate goal—the top of the summit where you would like to be. Your common sense keeps this new land organized, humming along at the perfect pitch. And you nearly always succeed at whatever you set out to do.

AQUARIUS

You prize individuality and freedom above all else. You're the original thinker in this new land, the eccentric, the genius who asks *what if* and then goes on to explore what that might mean. You're the rebel who galvanizes the masses to bust the existing paradigm.

PISCES

Emotions and imagination—that's how you explore your world. You're deeply intuitive, creative and compassionate. In this new land that Aries discovered, you may be the village psychic, the extraordinary artist or the musician.

Elements & Modes

The twelve signs fall into two distinct categories—triplicities or elements and quadruplicities or modes.

The elements—fire, earth, air and water—describe the basic energy and conscious focus of a particular sign. Do you see the world primarily through your intellect? Of do you feel and intuit your way through life? Are you an action-oriented individual? A doer? Are you someone who must make things tangible or grounded? The element of your sign is the lens through which you perceive the world. The energies of these elements are manifested through the vibrational frequencies of the modalities: cardinal, mutable and fixed. They express the ways we use this energy. Each sign is classified by both its element and its modality.

The Elements

FIRE: ARIES, LEO, SAGITTARIUS

Fire signs are energetic and passionate, and they zip through life doing stuff. You won't find these people sitting passively on the sidelines, waiting for others to make decisions before they act. They're the leaders, both dynamic and enthusiastic. They tend to be adventurous, and many of them are fearless. They'll try just about anything once. They may lack patience and get bored easily, but the threat of boredom is what propels them forward.

EARTH: TAURUS, VIRGO, CAPRICORN

When an earth sign has an idea, he mulls it over, thinks about it, tears it apart and examines it from every conceivable angle. How can he make it practical? Useful? A fire sign, however, usually takes the idea and runs with it. Earth signs generally enjoy getting out into nature to hike, garden, farm or camp. For a fire sign, nature is something you compete against—hike faster and farther, camp deeper in the middle of nowhere. Many earth signs are excellent cooks who harvest ingredients for exotic recipes from their own gardens. They move at their own pace and cannot be rushed.

AIR: GEMINI, LIBRA, AQUARIUS

♊ ♎ ♒

Air signs are mental and communicative people, and they love ideas. The mind is their domain and the way they explore what they feel. They need to understand what they feel and why they feel it. Present an air sign with anything—a fact, an observation, a feeling, a flower—and he'll ask why, what, where, when and how?

WATER: CANCER, SCORPIO, PISCES

♋ ♏ ♓

Water signs feel and intuit their way through life. It's the lens through which they see the world. When their emotions are especially powerful, they connect to something larger than themselves, to the world of imagination and myth. They are the natural psychics of the zodiac.

The Modalities

CARDINAL: ARIES, CANCER, LIBRA, CAPRICORN

♈ ♋ ♎ ♑

Cardinal signs tend to move in a singular direction. They're focused, intent on the goal, whatever it is. They're initiators and often find unique ways of doing things.

MUTABLE: GEMINI, VIRGO, SAGITTARIUS, PISCES

♊ ♍ ♐ ♓

These people are adaptable and flexible and can camouflage themselves in any situation to fit in. They're the networkers, communicators, the social weave in society. Sometimes, they can be too malleable, too willing to change who they are so that they are accepted by others.

FIXED: TAURUS, LEO, SCORPIO, AQUARIUS

♉ ♌ ♏ ♒

They know who they are and can't be told otherwise. They're stubborn and set in their opinions. They have to be convinced that someone else's opinion is correct before they change their minds. They aren't quitters, and long after the competition has given up, they're still in the running.

The Planets

Each planet rules a particular sign and a certain area of our lives. The inner planets—Sun, Moon, Mercury, Venus and Mars—move the most swiftly. Neptune and Pluto are the snails of the zodiac. Neptune takes about fourteen years to transit a single sign and Pluto takes from twelve to thirty-one years. As a result, these two planets are considered to be generational.

Neptune has been in Pisces since April 2011, where it stayed for four months before it retrograded back into Aquarius. It returned to Pisces in February 2012 and will be there until January 2026. Pluto entered Capricorn in 2008 and won't enter Aquarius until late March 2023. In June of 2023 it retrogrades back into Capricorn and finally enters Aquarius again in late January 2024. Overall, these two planets have the most long-term effects on our lives, while the swifter-moving planets have the most immediate effect.

Jupiter takes twelve to thirteen months to transit a sign. Saturn takes about two and a half years, and Uranus takes roughly seven years. From the table below, you can tell at a glance what sign and the areas of life that each planet rules.

What They Rule

SUN
Rules Leo, the yang principle, the father or a woman's husband, children, occupations of power and authority, the ego and individuality.

MOON
Rules Cancer, the yin principle, intuition, emotions, the mother/nurturing parent, your inner world. It changes signs every two and a half days.

MERCURY
Rules Gemini and Virgo, the intellect, mental quickness, verbal acuity, writing, speaking, communication, short-distance travel, the left-brain, contracts and friends. It stays in a sign between fourteen and thirty days, depending on whether it's moving in direct motion or is retrograde.

VENUS
Rules Taurus and Libra, feminine energy, romance, beauty, artistic instinct, earning capacity, the arts and music, pleasure in all its forms and luxuries. It stays in a sign from four to six weeks, depending on whether it's moving direct or retrograde.

MARS
Co-rules Scorpio and rules Aries, physical energy, sexual drive, aggression, survival energy and male energy. It stays in a sign from six to eight weeks, depending on its motion.

JUPITER
Co-rules Pisces and rules Sagittarius, the higher mind, foreign travel, people, cultures, higher education, expansion, luck, growth and the abstract mind. It stays in a sign for twelve to thirteen months.

SATURN

Rules Capricorn, responsibility, discipline, structure, limitations and restrictions and pragmatism. It stays in a sign for about two and a half years.

URANUS

Rules Aquarius, individuality, sudden or unexpected events, genius, eccentricity, astrology, creativity, originality and inventiveness. It stays in a sign for about seven years.

NEPTUNE

Rules Pisces, the visionary self, illusions, escapism, addictions, delusions, imagination, dreams, psychic experiences, artistic inspiration, flashes of insight and mystical tendencies and experiences. It stays in a sign for about fourteen years.

PLUTO

Rules Scorpio, transformation and regeneration, power and authority, the afterlife and good and evil. It stays in a sign from fourteen to thirty years.

Houses & Rising Signs

In the instant you drew your first breath, one of the signs of the zodiac was just passing over the eastern horizon, at a certain degree. Astrologers refer to this as the rising sign or ascendant. It's what makes your horoscope unique. Think of your ascendant as the front door of your horoscope, the place where you enter into this life and begin your journey.

Your ascendant is based on the exact moment of your birth. If you have Taurus rising, for example, that is the cusp of your first house. The cusp of the second would be Gemini, with Cancer on the cusp of the third and so on around the horoscope circle in a counterclockwise direction. Each house governs a particular area of life, which is outlined on the next pages.

The best way to find out your rising sign is to have your horoscope drawn up by an astrologer. For those of you with access to the Internet, though, you can obtain a free birth chart at www.astro.com.

In a horoscope, the ascendant (cusp of the first house), IC (cusp of the fourth house), descendent (cusp of the seventh house) and MC (cusp of the tenth house) are considered to be the most critical angles. Any planets that fall close to these angles are extremely important in the overall astrological picture of who you are. By the same token, planets that fall in the first, fourth, seventh and tenth houses are also considered to be important.

Here's a rundown on what the houses mean.

ASCENDANT OR RISING:
THE FIRST OF FOUR IMPORTANT CRITICAL ANGLES IN A HOROSCOPE
How other people see you
How you present yourself to the world
Your physical appearance

FIRST HOUSE—PERSONALITY
Early childhood
Your ego
Your body type and how you feel about your body
General physical health
Defense mechanisms
Your creative thrust

SECOND HOUSE—PERSONAL VALUES
How you earn and spend your money
Your personal values
Your material resources and assets
Your attitudes toward money
Your possessions and your attitude toward those possessions
Your self-worth
Your attitudes toward creativity

THIRD HOUSE—COMMUNICATION & LEARNING
Personal expression
Intellect and mental attitudes and perceptions
Siblings, neighbors and relatives
How you learn
School until college
Reading, writing and teaching
Short trips (the grocery store versus Europe in seven days)
Earth-bound transportation
Creativity as a communication device

IC OR FOURTH HOUSE CUSP—THE SECOND CRITICAL ANGLE IN A HOROSCOPE
Sign on IC describes the qualities and traits of your home during early childhood
Describes roots of your creative abilities and talents

FOURTH HOUSE—YOUR ROOTS

Personal environment
Your home
Your attitudes toward family
Early childhood conditioning
Real estate
Conditions at the end of your life
Early childhood support of your creativity
Your nurturing parent

Some astrologers say this house belongs to Mom or her equivalent in your life. Others say it belongs to Dad or his equivalent. It makes sense to me that it's Mom because the fourth house is ruled by the Moon, which rules mothers. But in this day and age, when parental roles are in flux, the only hard and fast rule is that the fourth belongs to the parent who nurtures you most of the time.

FIFTH HOUSE—CHILDREN AND CREATIVITY

Kids, your first-born in particular
Love affairs and romance
What you enjoy
Gambling and speculation
Creative ability
Pets

Traditionally, pets belong in the sixth house. But that definition stems from the days when "pets" were chattel. These days, we don't even refer to them as pets. They are animal companions who bring us pleasure.

SIXTH HOUSE—WORK & RESPONSIBILITY

Day-to-day working conditions and environment
Competence and skills
Your experience of employees and employers
Duty—to work and to employees
Health
Daily work approach to creativity

DESCENDANT/SEVENTH HOUSE CUSP—THE THIRD CRITICAL ANGLE IN A HOROSCOPE

The sign on the house cusp describes the qualities sought in intimate or business relationships
Describes qualities of creative partnerships

SEVENTH HOUSE—PARTNERSHIPS AND MARRIAGE

Marriage
Marriage partner
Significant others
Business partnerships
Close friends
Open enemies
Contracts

EIGHTH HOUSE—TRANSFORMATION

Sexuality as transformation
Secrets
Death, taxes and inheritances
Resources shared with others
Your partner's finances
The occult (read: astrology, reincarnation, UFOs—everything weird and strange)
Your hidden talents
Psychology
Life-threatening illnesses
Your creative depths

NINTH HOUSE—WORLDVIEW

Philosophy and religion
The law, courts and judicial system
Publishing
Foreign travels and cultures
College and graduate school
Spiritual beliefs

MC OR CUSP OF TENTH HOUSE—THE FOURTH CRITICAL ANGLE IN A HOROSCOPE

Sign on cusp of MC describes qualities you seek in a profession
Your public image
Your creative and professional achievements

TENTH HOUSE—PROFESSION AND CAREER

Public image as opposed to a job that merely pays the bills (sixth house)
Your status and position in the world
The authoritarian parent and authority in general

People who hold power over you
Your public life
Your career/profession

ELEVENTH HOUSE—IDEALS & DREAMS
Peer groups
Social circles (your writers' group, your mother's bridge club)
Your dreams and aspirations
How you can realize your creative dreams

TWELFTH HOUSE—PERSONAL UNCONSCIOUS
Power you have disowned that must be claimed again
Institutions—hospitals, prisons, nursing homes and what is hidden
What you must confront this time around, your karma and issues brought in from other lives
Psychic gifts and abilities
Healing talents
What you give unconditionally

In the monthly predictions, you'll find references to transiting planets moving into certain areas or houses of your chart. These houses are actually solar houses that are created by putting your sun sign on the ascendant. This technique is how most predictions are made for the general public rather than for specific individuals. To find out where your transits are actually occurring, have your natal chart handy. You can obtain a free copy at http://alabe.com/freechart. If you don't know your time of birth, use noon. The chart won't be as accurate, but you will be able to see the placements of all the planets except the moon.

2017

Introduction to 2017

The year begins with Mercury retrograde in Capricorn, then moving back into Sagittarius on January 4, and turning direct in that sign on January 8. It means the year may be off to a slow start, with things not falling into place the way we would like. After January 8, the pace picks up. Be sure to check on the specifics for your sign in the monthly roundups.

Jupiter, the planet of luck and expansion, begins the year in air sign Libra—particularly good for all you air and fire signs—and on October 10, enters water sign Scorpio, where it will be for about thirteen months. Check your respective signs and monthly roundups for what that means for you. During that transit, water and earth signs will benefit the most. If you have any planet in Scorpio, Pisces or Cancer, though, that planet's energy will be bolstered and expanded. It will be retrograde from February 6 to June 9.

Since September 2015, Saturn has been in Sagittarius. On December 20, it enters Capricorn, the sign it rules, and will be there for the next two and a half years. During this period, it will be traveling with Pluto in Capricorn, a powerhouse for Capricorn and other earth signs and for the water signs. Remember, Saturn is about foundations and structure and making dreams concrete and real. Pluto is about power and transformation.

Uranus has been in Aries since 2011 and continues its journey through that fire sign until next year, 2018. Neptune has been transiting Pisces since early 2012 and won't be changing signs until 2026.

Dates of Mercury Retrogrades in 2017

When Mercury turns retrograde, it appears to move backward relative to the earth. These retro periods can be especially trying for Geminis and Virgos, signs ruled by Mercury. But, as you can see in the example about the Mercury retrograde in 2000 (see page 9), everyone is impacted in some way.

During this time, miscommunication is often rampant, and appliances and electronics break down. It's wise not to launch any new projects or to sign contracts, since Mercury rules contracts. Try to follow the rule of the three Rs—review, reconsider, revise—rather than launching anything new. Mercury also rules moving parts, so it's smart not to buy a car or electronics during these periods. Travel can be iffy—plans go south quickly and itineraries change without warning. Everything moves more slowly. By following the guidelines above, you can mitigate some of the effects of these retrograde.

The Mercury retrograde periods are noted in the monthly predictions, but here's a quick reference:

On December 19, 2016, Mercury turns retrograde in Capricorn and won't turn direct again until January 9, 2017, in Sagittarius.

On April 9, Mercury turns retrograde in Taurus, travels back into Aries and turns direct in that sign on May 3.

On August 12, Mercury turns retro in Virgo, travels back into Leo and turns direct in that sign on September 5. Notice that Mercury will be in this position on the day of the solar eclipse. If you're planning to travel to a particular location to see the eclipse, be sure to make your plans before Mercury turns retro and give yourself extra time on the day you actually travel.

On December 2, Mercury turns retro in Sagittarius and turns direct in that sign on December 23.

New and Full Moons for 2017

New moons, when the sun and moon are in the same sign, usher in new opportunities. They mark the beginning of a fresh cycle and are great for setting goals, launching projects or starting anything. If you're trying to actualize something, then the new moon is the time to set your intentions, visualize and back your intentions with powerful emotions. This is when creative seeds are planted. The two-week period from the new moon to full moon are the most powerful for new opportunities.

Full moons, when the moon and sun are opposite each other, are times of culmination, harvest and completion. It's a good time to complete what you began under the new moon. Emotions that have been buried often roar to the surface. Issues in a relationship sometimes must be confronted. Emergency rooms often get more than the usual amount of patients. You get the idea here. Full moon lunacy!

These moons are calculated for Eastern time.

NEW MOONS IN 2017
December 29, 2016—Capricorn
January 27—Aquarius
February 26—Pisces: solar eclipse
March 27—Aries
April 26—Taurus
May 25—Gemini
June 23—Cancer
July 23—Leo
August 21—Leo: solar eclipse
September 20—Virgo
October 19—Libra
November 18—Scorpio
December 18—Sagittarius

FULL MOONS IN 2017
January 12—Cancer
February 10—Leo: lunar eclipse
March 12—Virgo
April 11—Libra
May 10—Scorpio
June 9—Sagittarius
July 8—Capricorn
August 7—Aquarius: lunar eclipse
September 6—Pisces
October 5— Aries
November 4—Taurus
December 3—Gemini

Eclipses

A solar eclipse occurs when the moon comes between the earth and the sun. It happens only with a new moon, when the sun and moon are conjunct, meaning in the same sign. If a solar eclipse is visible where you live, then the day turns from bright to partial or full darkness, depending on whether the eclipse is partial or total. If it's a total eclipse, the black disk you see is actually the moon and the aura of light around it, the corona, is light from the sun.

A lunar eclipse occurs when the earth moves between the sun and the moon, cutting off the sun's light to the moon. Usually, there are two lunar and two solar eclipses each year, and they happen two weeks apart.

Astrologically, solar eclipses are the most powerful of the two types, and the degree of the power is determined by the amount of light that's cut off. A solar eclipse is like a double new moon—double the new opportunities—and usually involves external events. A lunar eclipse triggers inner needs and concerns, and we tend to feel things more deeply. Depending on how sensitive you are to eclipses, the effects can be felt for several months on either side of the eclipse date.

The total solar eclipse of August 21 will be the first since March 1970 that's visible in the southeastern U.S. It will also be the first time in nearly a century—since 1918—that an eclipse will be seen across the entire breadth of the continental U.S. It will be at 28 degrees Leo, a fire sign. So Leo and other fire signs—Aries, Sagittarius—born in the latter half of their sign will be powerfully impacted by this eclipse in a positive way. Also, Geminis, Libras and Aquarians born in the latter half of their signs will also feel the effects. Other signs, of course, will also feel the impact of this eclipse, but fire and air signs will feel it most strongly.

As a general guideline, it's best not to make major decisions near or on the day of an eclipse. The energy of eclipses is sometimes extreme and it's best to let things settle down first. That said, though, the purpose of eclipses is to clear out the old to make way for the new. And that's done from the inside out!

Aries 2017

Your sign is ruled by Mars, so pay particular attention to that planet's transits each month. It will be noted when Mars is making angles to other planets and when it changes signs. Mars won't be retrograde at all this year, so it will transit eight of the twelve signs.

If you know your natal rising sign, it's a good idea to keep track of that sign's ruling planet, too. Let's say your rising or ascendant is Taurus. If you look in the introduction, you'll find that Taurus is ruled by Venus, so its various transits and angles it makes to other planets will be significant for you.

In 2017, Venus will be retrograde in your sign from March 4 to April 15, when it turns direct in Pisces. This period may create some bumps in your love life and possibly in your finances as well. But the good news is that you enjoy two periods this year when Venus is moving direct in your sign, always an excellent harbinger of smooth sailing!

The new and full moons, eclipses and various retrogrades are also included in the roundups.

January 2017
Starts slow, picks up speed

The year starts off with the stars lined up in your favor for new business and personal partnerships. If an offer comes your way during the first week of January, don't sign a contract until after the 8th, when Mercury turns direct in Sagittarius. On the 12th, Mercury enters Capricorn and joins Pluto in your career area, bringing great mental resolve and determination.

With expansive, lucky Jupiter in your partnership sector until mid-October, you and a lover may decide to take your relationship to the next level. You might move in together or get married and it all may unfold quickly, suddenly and without warning. But you're a master at flying by the seat of your pants! Jupiter here could also improve your relationship with a business partner and even an enemy! Open enemies fall in this area. It's possible that a little diplomacy could turn an enemy into an ally.

The full moon on January 12 could bring some tension and irritation in your domestic environment. Just roll with the punches, Aries. The new moon on January 28, in the compatible air sign Aquarius, will be more to your liking. It ushers in new opportunities that enable you to reach for your dreams. Your network of acquaintances and friends proves vital.

For much of the month Venus and your ruler, Mars, travel together in imaginative Pisces. This duo heightens your love life and creativity. Your intuition is sharper, so it's smart to follow hunches and impulses. Your dreams may turn lucid and be easier to recall. Keep a notebook by your bedside. During this period, which lasts until the 28th, you may have psychic experiences—telepathic moments with a loved one, a prescient dream or an out-of-body experience. Synchronicity will be your ally.

On the 28th, the same day as the new moon, Mars joins Uranus in your sign and will be there until March 9. During these weeks, you're innervated, enthusiastic and focused on moving everything in your life forward. From the beginning of January through mid-December, Saturn is forming a beneficial angle to your sun, bringing greater structure and commitment to whatever you're involved in.

AT A GLANCE
January 3—Venus enters Pisces
January 8—Mercury retrograde ends
January 12—Full moon in Cancer, Mercury joins Pluto in Capricorn
January 28—New moon in Aquarius, Mars enters Aries

February 2017
Busy, creative and romantic!

There's a lot going on this month in the stars!

It looks as though February is all about romance, love and whatever brings you pleasure, Aries. On February 3, Venus joins Mars in your sign and the two travel together until March 9. This period is particularly favorable for existing romantic/sexual relationships or for the beginning of a relationship. Whenever Venus and Mars travel together, your sexuality is heightened.

With Venus in your sign, you're going to enjoy one of the most romantic and creative periods all year. Your muse is whispering in your ear, and your love life hums along at a pace that suits you. Since Uranus is also in your sign, there may be an edgy, unpredictable quality to your personal relationships that keeps things exciting. The only other period this year that is equal to this one occurs between August 26 and September 19, when Venus transits Leo and the romance/creativity section of your chart.

On February 6, Jupiter turns retrograde in Libra, in your partnership area, and remains that way until June 9. The retrograde may slow things down a bit in your personal and business partnerships, but it's nothing insurmountable. Jupiter's retrograde turns its expansive energy inward, so you are better able to figure out how your personal and business relationships can be improved.

Circle February 7 on your calendar. Mercury, the planet of communication and travel, enters compatible air sign Aquarius and suddenly, your social calendar heats up. You're out there networking, meeting new people and making new contacts.

On February 10, the lunar eclipse in fellow fire sign Leo is likely to bring about sudden insights and you'll feel quite self-confident about expressing your individuality. Sometimes with lunar eclipses, there's a lot of angst because eclipses tend to bring personal issues up front and center, and you have to make quick decisions. However, your creativity is stoked, and you're eager to get moving with a creative project.

Between February 25 and March 12, Mercury transits water sign Pisces, and your conscious mind is exceptionally intuitive and receptive. That heightened intuition will be particularly helpful on February 26, when the solar eclipse in Pisces ushers in new opportunities to work behind the scenes in some capacity, perhaps pioneering some new project that is radically different from what you've done before. Solar eclipses represent new opportunities, but something in your life may end first, making way for the new. Intuitively, you'll grasp what's going on.

Overall, it's a busy month, Aries. Don't run yourself ragged!

AT A GLANCE
February 3—Venus enters Aries
February 6—Jupiter turns retrograde in Libra
February 7—Mercury enters Aquarius
February 10—Lunar eclipse in Leo
February 25—Mercury enters Pisces
February 26—Solar eclipse in Pisces

March 2017
Love life bumps & bruises

Your love life may take a step backward this month when Venus turns retrograde in your sign on March 4. Between then and April 15, when Venus turns direct again, you may have second thoughts about a personal relationship. You and your partner may not see eye to eye on an issue. Creatively, you may have to backtrack on an endeavor, revise and review. It's nothing huge. Just be aware.

Keep an eye on your finances, too. With Mars entering Taurus and your financial sector on March 9, a lot of your physical energy is poured into earning income, perhaps from various sources. You may feel an urge to splurge. If you can afford the splurge, then by all means go for it, and pay cash! Otherwise, play it safe. Since Venus involves money and it's retro in your sign, the Mars transit through your financial area could be a source of discord with a partner. Try not to argue about money. The Mars transit lasts until April 21.

A full moon in detail-oriented Virgo on March 12 may bring a work project to fruition. You also may become more health conscious on a day-to-day basis, making you more aware of the food you eat, the exercise you get, what you think about what you eat and do. If you already have an exercise routine, you may increase the time you spend doing it. If you're a runner who routinely does a mile a day, for example, consider increasing it incrementally. Or, add a yoga or Pilates class each week to your routine. If you have a health app on your phone, keep track of how far you walk just in the course of your daily life.

A day later, on March 13, Mercury enters your sign, where it will be until the 31st. During this period, you're completely in step with who you are. Your conscious mind is sharp, edgy and alert for opportunities. Your entrepreneurial spirit is dominant.

The new moon on March 27 falls in your sign, and that happens just once a year. It sets the tone for the rest of year. You can expect new opportunities to be ushered into your life in whatever area you focus on. One good thing to do before this new moon arrives is to create a wish list. What would you like to see happen in your life this year? Focus on those things, back the focus with emotion and then get out of your own way and let the universe do its job.

AT A GLANCE
March 4—Venus turns retrograde in Aries
March 9—Mars enters Taurus
March 12—Full moon in Virgo
March 13—Mercury enters Aries
March 27—New Moon in Aries
March 31—Mercury enters Taurus

April 2017
A mixed bag

Since December 2014, Saturn has been in fellow fire sign Sagittarius, forming a beneficial angle to your sun. This transit has helped you to fortify your worldview, your beliefs and the structure of your life. Perhaps you have gone to college or grad school or taken workshops in something that interests you. Maybe you've traveled overseas and gained considerable perspective on foreign cultures and people. However this transit has unfolded for you until now, things are about to slow down.

Between April 6 and August 25, Saturn will be moving retrograde in Sagittarius. While it's retro, you may be examining the various belief structures in your life—your spirituality, your worldview, your politics and your fundamental philosophy about who we are as people, as a culture, as a society and as a global community. The retro period facilitates scrutiny of the various goals you have set yourself. Are they realistic? Too small? Too large? Then, on December 20, it's going to enter Capricorn and your professional career area, where it will be for the next two and a half years. So this retrograde helps you fine-tune what you would like to achieve professionally in the next few years. Saturn can help you to establish the proper structures for realizing your ambitions and dreams.

On April 15, retrograde Venus turns direct in Pisces, and your love life begins to straighten out. Things really heat up between April 28 and June 6, when Venus transits your sign again. Your passions are evident in everything you do and undertake, from relationships to creative projects to adventures. This period, like the time between February 3 and March 4, is one of the most romantic and creative for you all year, so if you've planned for it, you'll be able to put the energy to good use!

Mercury enters Taurus and your financial area on March 31, turns retrograde there on April 9 and doesn't turn direct again until May 3. During this period, don't sign contracts, buy electronic appliances, a car, computer or any other item of this ilk. If you have to travel, be flexible. Your itinerary will likely change. Mercury retro travels with Mars in Taurus until the 21st, so there's a kind of push and shove going on with these two planets. *Spend! No, hold back. Sign that contract, invest in that stock.... No, no.* Once Mars enters Gemini and the communication area of your chart on April 21, some of that tension will be relieved.

With the full moon in Libra on April 11, you're in the mood for love and romance, and this moon should bring it in spades. Life is a delicate balancing act, Aries, and rather than rushing ahead in a relationship, take your time, savor the moment, be *patient!* April 26 brings a new moon in Taurus and opportunities for new sources of income. Seize the moment.

AT A GLANCE
April 6—Saturn turns retro in Sagittarius
April 9—Mercury retrograde in Taurus
April 11—Full moon in Libra
April 15—Venus turns direct in Pisces
April 21—Mars enters into Gemini
April 26—New moon in Taurus
April 28—Venus enters Aries

May 2017
Kick back & enjoy

May is a rather chill month, and you should have plenty of time to do the things you most enjoy.

On May 3, when Mercury turns direct in your sign, you'll be ready to hit the road, sign contracts, buy a new computer and do whatever else you've been postponing. On the 16th, Mercury enters Taurus and your financial area, and you'll have plenty of grounded ideas about earning additional income.

With Venus in your sign until June 6, your love life should be humming along at a pace that suits you, and your creative drive is strong. You feel particularly self-confident, which acts as a kind of magnet that attracts interesting people and experiences. The only other period this year that matches this one occurs between August 26 and September 19, when Venus transits Leo and the romance/creativity area of your chart.

For much of the month Venus and Mars, your ruler, form beneficial angles to each other. Mars is in compatible air sign Gemini until June 4, so this is an excellent time to communicate your ideas, verbally and in writing. You might consider starting a blog or writing a book, novel or even a screenplay.

Look to May 10 for a full moon in Scorpio. Something concerning shared resources comes to light. Perhaps your partner or spouse receives a raise, a mortgage or loan application is approved or you gain valuable insight into an issue that has puzzled you. The Scorpio moon can be psychically, emotionally and sexually intense, so be sure to follow your hunches on and around the time of this full moon.

The new moon on May 25 falls in Gemini and forms a beneficial angle with Mars. This combination should usher in new communication opportunities and increased contact with siblings and neighbors. If you've been on the outs with a brother, sister, neighbor or friend, now is the time to heal the rift.

After the 3rd, only two planets are moving retrograde—Jupiter in Libra and Saturn in Sagittarius. Jupiter's retro, as mentioned earlier, turns its expansiveness inward. You may be studying comparative religions, reading philosophy books or traveling abroad, and the goal of all of it is expand your knowledge. Saturn's retro helps you to reevaluate the foundations and structures in your life.

Jupiter turns direct next month, on June 6, which will help to facilitate all your partnerships. Saturn remains retrograde until late August and may be causing delays in an overseas trip or with something concerning college or grad school.

AT A GLANCE
May 3—Mercury turns direct in Aries
May 10—Full moon in Scorpio
May 16—Mercury enters Taurus
May 25—New moon in Gemini

June 2017
Hectic, with bright, stunning moments

Buckle up, Aries! June is a busy month and it's important that you don't allow yourself to become run down. Make sure you get enough sleep and pace yourself. Balance is key!

On June 4, Mars enters water sign Cancer, where it will be until July 20, and this transit brings a lot of activity in your domestic/home life. You may be involved in renovation projects, visitors may arrive from out of town or someone could be moving into or out of your home. You may even be working out of your home during this transit.

June 6 features two planets changing signs. Mercury enters Gemini and the communication area of your chart, and Venus enters Taurus and your financial area. The first transit may cause you to be mentally restless, where you're casting around for ideas, doing research and perhaps building a website or starting a blog. You may feel like getting out of town for a few days, perhaps to a location where you can indulge in all sorts of physical activity—hiking, biking or rock climbing. Even if you leave town, take your computer or a notebook with you. New ideas will occur to you, and you'll want to jot them down. Sometimes, you simply need a different focus for a few days to return refreshed and invigorated.

The second transit could indicate that you're spending money this month on things like art or jewelry or on anything that beautifies your home. If you earn more than you usually do this month, stash it away somewhere. Invest it in a stock or mutual fund that you trust.

On June 9, Jupiter turns direct in Libra for the first time since early February. This movement should facilitate both business and personal partnerships. With all the astrological energy occurring on the 6th and 9th you might want to plan something special with the people you love.

The full moon on June 9 falls in Sagittarius. A spiritual belief may be highlighted in some way. Travel plans for an international trip may come together just perfectly. If you're headed for college or graduate school in the fall, there may be news. This moon in a fellow fire sign is sure to uplift your spirits and put you in a party mood!

June 21 brings Mercury into Cancer, where it joins Mars. With this combination, you're not just doing home renovations, you're actively talking and planning, perhaps with someone you've hired to help you with the job.

The new moon on June 23 joins Mercury and Mars in Cancer. Where the new moon ushers in new opportunities related to home and family, Mars enables you to seize the opportunities, and Mercury enables you to intuitively sift through your options.

AT A GLANCE
June 4—Mars enters Cancer
June 6—Mercury enters Gemini, Venus enters Taurus
June 9—Full moon in Sagittarius, Jupiter turns direct in Libra
June 21—Mercury moves into Cancer
June 23—New moon in Cancer

July 2017
Full throttle, baby!

July may actually be a busier month than June, so strive for balance and pace yourself, Aries!

On July 4, Venus enters Gemini. It's possible that a beautiful chemistry develops between you and a neighbor or someone you met through your brother or sister. If you're in an established relationship already, then you and your partner are in a smooth phase where communication flows easily, and you're on the same page about nearly everything. When Venus slides into Cancer on the 31st, you two may decide to move in together or commit more deeply to each other.

July 5 finds Mercury entering Leo and it looks as if you enjoy the long weekend with your kids and family. You should also find time for working on a creative project. With Mercury forming a beneficial angle to your sun, your communication skills are in tip-top shape. Put them to use! On the 25th, Mercury enters earth sign Virgo, and now you're connecting the dots and details in a work project. You may also be paying much closer attention to your daily nutrition and exercise regimen. Be sure your exercise routine is something you know you won't quit out of boredom!

Mars slips into Leo on July 20, joining Mercury there for five days. This particular period should trigger a lot of creative activity and fun time with kids—yours or someone else's. Once Mercury moves on, Mars continues to stir up activity and adventures that keep you on the move.

The other notable dates this month fall on July 8 with a full moon in Capricorn, and July 23, which features a new moon in Leo. The full moon lights up the professional area of your chart. Something is completed, your work is applauded, you're feeling confident that you're making strides. The new moon on the 23rd is a beauty for you and should bring in new opportunities in creativity, with children and romance and in whatever you do for pleasure and fun. Another possibility? You and your partner discover you're going to have a child.

AT A GLANCE
July 4—Venus enters Gemini
July 5—Mercury goes into Leo
July 8—Full moon in Capricorn
July 20—Mars enters Leo
July 23—New Moon in Leo
July 25—Mercury goes into Virgo
July 31—Venus enters Cancer

August 2017
Eclipses & Merc retro alerts!

Fewer planets are changing signs this month, but before you breathe a sign of relief, be forewarned that August may not be much calmer than the last couple of months. There are two eclipses!

Circle August 7 on your calendar. That's the date for the lunar eclipse in Aquarius. You may feel the effects of this eclipse for several days on either side of it. Issues with friends may surface. Perhaps you gain a sudden insight into a friend's mind and heart. You may have a dream that illuminates a concern or provides an idea that proves to be valuable. You may be evaluating your wishes and dreams, asking yourself if you're on the right track or whether you should change tracks.

The solar eclipse on August 21 is in fellow fire sign Leo which means it forms a strong and powerful angle to your sun sign. On or around the time of the eclipse, you may sell an artistic endeavor, enter a creative venture with a lover or partner or discover that you and your partner are going to become parents. Or you may launch a creative project or find your life's passion. This area of your chart is about enjoyment, whatever makes your heart sing. I mention it right at the beginning here so that you can prepare for it.

You might, for example, plan something special for that day. Or have a particular sacred nature ritual that honors the eclipse. Or, if you live in the southeast U.S., get a telescope and have a solar eclipse party!

This eclipse brings a new opportunity for a creative project or to work with children in some capacity. A new romantic relationship may begin. You might receive recognition for something you've done. Whatever unfolds, the experiences will be positive.

Mercury turns retrograde in Virgo on August 12 and will remain that way until September 5. So sign contracts, finalize travels plans, update your computer and electronics before August 12 and after September 5. Some possibilities for this retrograde? You have to revisit a project at work; a former co-worker or friend you haven't seen for years re-enters your life; or you resume a nutritional or exercise program you've tried in the past.

On August 25, Saturn turns direct in Sagittarius. Any delays you've been experiencing these past months related to higher education, publishing and foreign travel should become history.

Five days after the solar eclipse in Leo, Venus enters that sign, increasing the likelihood of a new romance, new methods of self-expression and a general feel-good time. This transit lasts until September 19.

August 7—Lunar eclipse in Aquarius
August 12—Mercury turns retro in Virgo
August 21—Solar eclipse in Leo
August 25—Saturn turns direct in Sagittarius
August 26—Venus enters Leo

September 2017
Creative adrenaline pumping!

Now you can kick back and chill, Aries. September is much slower astrologically than the last several months, and you may actually have time to take some real time off. Let's take a closer look.

Mercury turns direct in Leo on September 5, always welcome news! This means that any delays or setbacks you experienced the past few weeks—with creative projects, your kids, romance or work—should now straighten out. On September 9, Mercury enters Virgo once again, and you'll have a chance to rectify anything that went wrong in August. This transit lasts until September 29, when Mercury enters Libra.

Also on the 5th, Mars enters Virgo, adding energy to your daily work routine and to your health habits. Mars will be in Virgo until October 22, and the amount of work you can get done may astonish you. You're better at details, complete what you start and are able to stick to any routine you establish.

As Venus continues its journey through Leo until the 19th, your love life and creative adrenaline continue to heat up. You feel good about yourself and your life and the people around you. Then on the 19th, Venus joins Mercury and Mars in Virgo. When this trio gets together in the daily work/health sector of your chart, all sorts of interesting things can happen. Your work may take a decidedly artistic turn. A romance with a co-worker may take off. You may be publicly recognized in some way for your contributions to a project.

The full moon in Pisces on September 6 should stimulate your imagination and intuitive ability, but could make you somewhat indecisive in matters of the heart. An issue you have ignored or buried may surface.

Then on September 20, along comes the new moon in Virgo, adding a fourth planet to the lineup! With this much earth energy now grouped in the same area of your chart, you may become a paragon of pragmatism and a master of details. New work opportunities surface, too—perhaps a job offer or a raise and increased responsibility at your present job. Or, if you have aspirations to become self-employed, you may have a chance to do exactly that.

September 5—Mercury turns direct in Leo, Mars enters Virgo
September 6—Full moon in Pisces
September 9—Mercury enters Virgo
September 19—Venus goes into Virgo
September 20—New moon in Virgo
September 29—Mercury moves into Libra

October 2017
All about you & me

On September 29, Mercury entered Libra and your partnership area. This transit, which lasts until October 17, indicates that you'll be thinking and communicating about relationships. And with Jupiter still in Libra, your personal and business partnerships may be expanding. You could feel a greater need for balance in both professional and personal relationships. You may also be better able to compromise and mitigate disagreements. Once Mercury moves into Scorpio, your conscious thoughts will be focused on finances that you share with others—a partner, bank, mortgage company, even a publisher that pays you royalties. You'll be looking for the absolute bottom line in just about everything you tackle.

A full moon in your sign occurs on October 5. This should be a riveting, adventurous couple of days for you. The full moon highlights all the traits that make you an Aries—a pioneering spirit, passionate and fearless. There could be positive news of a personal nature, too.

Jupiter enters Scorpio on October 10. This transit lasts until mid-November of 2018. It brings luck and expansion to resources you share with others. This means you're fortunate when it comes to mortgages, loans and your partner's income. He or she could receive a substantial raise, or you might inherit money during this year. You may also become more interested in life after death, ghosts, reincarnation and things that go bump in the night. You might travel internationally for research in this area.

Venus enters Libra and your partnership area on October 14. Very nice for all personal and business partnerships. It suggests smooth sailing, a need for greater balance and more socializing and networking. This transit lasts until November 7.

The new moon this month, on October 19, falls in Libra, which is certain to usher in new business and personal partnerships for you as well as new artistic/creative opportunities. Then, on October 22, Mars joins Venus in Libra. You can see how October is shaping up with a cluster of planets in Libra just as September had a cluster of planets in Virgo. Any time this occurs, you experience a surge of energy according to the sign and the area of your chart where the planets cluster.

October 5—Full moon in Aries
October 10—Jupiter moves into Scorpio
October 14—Venus enters Libra
October 17—Mercury enters Scorpio
October 19—New moon in Libra
October 22—Mars enters Libra

November 2017
Buy that lottery ticket

You may be aware now of how Jupiter in Scorpio is impacting your life. Synchronicity is occurring more frequently. Or your dreams may be providing information and insights. An opportunity to travel internationally may fall in your lap. However the specifics are unfolding for you, this transit is a lucky one. That said, Jupiter is also about excess, so be sure to pace yourself, Aries.

November 4 features a full moon in Taurus, your financial sector, and brings a money issue to light. Perhaps you're wondering how you're going to meet your bills this month, then someone repays a loan or you land a raise or receive a refund. This full moon is a good time to state your intentions, visualize what you would like and back it with emotion.

Mercury enters fellow fire sign Sagittarius on November 5 and remains there for the rest of the year. This period includes the last retrograde of the year, which begins on December 3. While Mercury is in direct motion, your conscious mind is focused on the larger picture of everything you encounter. You're asking, *How does this piece fit with everything else? Where am I headed and what's the best way to get there?* This transit adds intellectual fire, so ideas flow.

When Venus joins Jupiter in Scorpio on November 7, where it will be until December 25, your sexuality and capacity for love and romance are heightened. You and a partner may discover that you have more in common than you thought. Your feelings run deep and may prove to be transformational. Your psychic ability is on target.

Mars continues its transit through Libra and your partnership area until December 9, a rather interesting juxtaposition of energies. You strive for balance even while you're feeling things so deeply.

On the 18th, the new moon in Scorpio joins Jupiter and Venus in that sign and suddenly, luck is your middle name. The new moon brings new opportunities that Jupiter expands in unexpected ways and Venus offers her kiss of approval. The opportunity could concern just about anything—a new relationship, a new source of income or a breakthrough in research.

Overall, November shapes up to be an intriguing, surprising month.

November 4—Full moon in Taurus
November 5—Mercury enters Sagittarius
November 7—Venus goes into Scorpio
November 18—New moon in Scorpio

December 2017
One last Merc retro

The last month of 2017 may turn out to be wild and unpredictable, rather like an F5 tornado, but without the destruction. There's a lot going on, including the last Mercury retrograde of the year.

On December 3, Mercury turns retrograde in Sagittarius and remains that way until the 22nd. If possible, do your holiday shopping on either side of these days, particularly if you're purchasing high-ticket items. Be aware that your travel and holiday events may change suddenly and without warning. Rather than get frustrated about these changes, try to go with the flow. Look at it all as an adventure.

Also on the 3rd, there's a full moon in compatible air sign Gemini. This one indicates that you complete a communication or writing project. Even though you're ready to submit, don't do it until after Mercury turns direct on December 22.

You're more sociable now, with invitations pouring in from friends and acquaintances. You may be spending more time with siblings and neighbors.

Mars enters Scorpio on December 9, joining Jupiter in that sign. This combination indicates that as soon as an opportunity presents itself, you seize it and run with it. You're vigilant, motivated and focused. Your physical energy is good, and your ambition is heightened.

The new moon on December 18 falls in Sagittarius. Mercury is now retrograding through that sign, so the new opportunities that come your way may change or may not manifest themselves until after Mercury turns direct. That said, though, these opportunities could involve international travel, publishing or higher education.

Before you barely have a chance to catch your breath, a huge change surfaces: on December 20th, Saturn moves into Capricorn, the sign that it rules. During the next two and a half years, Saturn in your professional/career area brings increased responsibility, more recognition and discipline and a certain focused ambition to achieve your dreams and desires. Earth and fire aren't compatible, and Saturn is technically forming a difficult angle to your sun. But you, Aries, are stimulated and inspired to work harder, and Saturn helps you to reap the rewards.

December 22 brings a cause for celebration: Mercury turns direct! Go holiday shopping now, secure in the knowledge that you won't be standing in the return line on December 26.

On Christmas day, Venus joins Saturn in Capricorn. Now, things get a little easier with your career. You attract the right people at the right time. And, romance may be waiting for you when you return to work!

AT A GLANCE
December 1—Venus enters Sagittarius
December 3—Mercury turns retro in Sagittarius, full moon in Gemini
December 9—Mars enters Scorpio
December 18—New moon in Sagittarius
December 20—Saturn enters Capricorn
December 22—Mercury turns direct in Sagittarius
December 25—Venus enters Capricorn

Reflection
Take a look back at 2017 and reflect on what it was like for you. Did you achieve and experience what you hoped you would? Did some facet of your life pivot in a new direction? Are you happier and more prosperous now? Jot your notes below.

_____
_____
_____
_____
_____

Happy New Year!

Taurus 2017

Your sign is ruled by Venus, so pay particular attention to that planet's transits each month. It will be noted when Venus makes angle to other planets, if it's retrograde or changing signs. If you know your natal rising sign, it's a good idea to keep track of that sign's ruling planet, too. Let's say your rising or ascendant is Virgo. If you look in the introduction, you'll find that Virgo is ruled by Mercury, so its various transits and the angles it makes to other planets will be significant for you.

The monthly roundups also include information on new and full moons, eclipses and the various planetary retrogrades. This year, your ruler is retrograde in Aries from March 4 to April 15, when it turns direct in Pisces. During this period, old issues in a relationship may crop up and have to be dealt with. It's also possible that a former lover or spouse resurfaces in your life.

2017 is a year of innovation, creativity and communication. Set your intentions early. Write them down. Post the list where you'll see it frequently.

January 2017
Creative & lucky

If the holiday season at the end of 2016 wasn't busy enough for you, then January makes up for it! The action starts on January 3, when Venus enters Pisces and the friends/networking sector of your chart. Your social calendar starts filling up quickly. There may be sudden shifts in your schedule, however, because Mercury is still retrograde and has slipped back into Sagittarius. Once it turns direct on the 8th, you can now move forward on mortgage and loan applications, travel plans, contractual agreements and all the other things you postponed doing during the retrograde.

On the 12th, Mercury enters Capricorn once again and joins Pluto in that area of your chart that governs beliefs and the higher mind. This combination confers tremendous mental resolve and determination to succeed. You may be making plans for an international trip, mulling over educational options or researching worldwide spiritual traditions.

With Venus joining Neptune in imaginative Pisces, you have a combination for intense creative activity, the kind of creativity that comes from deep within. And there's an element of luck here, too, where you may meet the right people at the right time.

You'll enjoy the full moon in Cancer on January 12. It highlights your family life, your intuitive ability and your relationship with your mother or other women who are significant to you. Your communication abilities have a strong intuitive component with this full moon and you may find yourself dabbling in divination systems like the I Ching, the tarot or even astrology!

Two significant things occur on January 28. There's a new moon in Aquarius and Mars enters Aries. The new moon should bring new opportunities in your professional life. These could range from a job offer that would entail more income than you earn now, a raise/promotion in your current job or even a chance to strike out on your own on an entirely new career path. The Mars transit, which lasts until March 9, enables you to draw on your own unconscious for creative fodder. Because Mars urges us to act, you may undertake an exploration of your own psyche by keeping close tabs on your dreams, taking a workshop or embarking on a shamanic journey that enables you to consciously enter the realm of dreams. Be aware that your buttons may be more easily pushed during this transit.

January 3—Venus enters Pisces
January 8—Mercury retrograde ends
January 12—Full moon in Cancer, Mercury joins Pluto in Capricorn
January 28—New moon in Aquarius, Mars enters Aries

February 2017
Roller coaster

Months that feature eclipses often seem fraught with strangeness, tensions, opportunities, triumphs and the entire range of human emotions. Lunar eclipses are often more emotional than solar eclipses, which deal with outer events. However, outer events trigger emotional reactions. So, what can you expect with this month's eclipses?

February 10 features a lunar eclipse in Leo, in the home/domestic area of your chart. Someone in your home life—a partner, child, relative—may need additional help or support. You give it gladly, but may feel somewhat stressed about it. Try to go with the flow regardless, Taurus. The quality of this eclipse for you depends, like most things in life, on whether or not you put up resistance.

The solar eclipse on February 26 falls in Pisces, a water sign compatible with your sun sign. This eclipse should bring in new opportunities to attain your wishes and dreams. The opportunities may come from your network of friends and acquaintances, through people you have met on the Internet or through people you hang with. Be alert and ready to seize the opportunities when they knock!

The other planets are busy this month, too. Mercury visits two signs, Venus enters Aries and Jupiter turns retrograde in Libra. Let's start with Venus, the ruler of your sign. Between February 3 and March 4, when it turns retrograde, you may be enjoying a romance or some sort of creative work that occurs behind the scenes. You feel quite passionate about things, and ideas flow out of you. In some ways Venus's transit and retrograde next month are preparing you for Venus's transit through your sign in June, which is sure to be a stellar month! By then, you're going to have a clear idea of what, exactly, you're seeking.

Mercury, the planet of communication, travels through visionary Aquarius between February 7–25, in your career area. During these weeks, you're primed for work, have a million ideas about how to implement or launch a project and may be heading up a team of co-workers. Once Mercury moves into Pisces, where it will be from February 25 to March 13, things calm down a bit. Your imagination ramp ups, enabling you to use some of your ideas creatively. Your intellect turns dreamier.

Jupiter, the planet of luck and expansion, turns retrograde on February 6 in Libra, your daily work and health area. Until it turns direct again on June 9, things may move at a slower pace on a day-to-day basis, which is just fine with you. Its expansion during the retro period occurs inwardly, as your beliefs and spirituality deepen and broaden.

February 3—Venus enters Aries
February 6—Jupiter turns retrograde in Libra
February 7—Mercury enters Aquarius
February 10—Lunar eclipse in Leo
February 25—Mercury enters Pisces
February 26—Solar eclipse in Pisces

March 2017
Active

Spring is typically a busy time, but March may knock your socks off, Taurus, particularly after Mars enters your sign on March 9. This transit is about *doing* and getting things done. Projects you may have postponed can now be achieved efficiently and quickly. Mars in your sign is energizing, and you may be doing more actual physical activity (such as hiking, biking, workouts and yoga) between March 9 and April 21, when the transit ends. In areas where it seems things have stalled, you can now push forward, and obstacles fall away.

Between March 4 and April 15 your ruler, Venus, moves retrograde through Aries, then slips back into Pisces. While it's retrograde in Aries, you may be revisiting issues in a personal relationship and could feel somewhat out of sorts. Don't sample any new financial investments during this phase. Wait until after April 15.

Mercury joins Venus in Aries from March 13–31, and during this period, your conscious focus may be on artistic and creative pursuits, romance and love and finances. All of these thoughts, though, will be percolating through your head and won't necessarily be something you discuss with others. Once both planets enter your sign, however, that will change.

A full moon in fellow earth sign Virgo on March 12 should illuminate a creative project you're working on, something with your children or activities that you do strictly for fun and pleasure. You'll be able to connect the details in a way that has eluded you and should be able to complete what you've started. The Virgo moon may trigger attention to your health—how you maintain it day-to-day and your exercise and nutritional routines. You may decide to make some changes.

The new moon in Aries on March 27 could attract new opportunities, a pioneering project of some sort, an adventure or a passionate romance. Aries is a restless, passionate, active sign, so it's likely that the opportunities will be flavored with a sense of adventure. Follow the cues in your environment. Be alert for synchronicities that act as guideposts.

Once Mercury enters your sign on March 31, you'll have about nine days before the planet turns retrograde. So do whatever you need to do before then—sign contracts, make travel plans and update your computer.

March 4—Venus turns retrograde in Aries
March 9—Mars enters Taurus
March 12—Full moon in Virgo
March 13—Mercury enters Aries
March 27—New Moon in Aries
March 31—Mercury enters Taurus

April 2017
Pace yourself

This month features seven astrological events that are apt to make April a hectic month. The action starts on April 6, when Saturn turns retrograde in Sagittarius. Saturn governs the structures in our lives, limitations and restrictions, responsibility and discipline. It will turn retro in your eighth house of shared resources, so between April 6 and August 25, when it turns direct again, there may be delays or snafus in obtaining mortgages or loans. Your partner's income may be restricted for some reason, and you may have to step up to the plate and make up for the gap.

On March 31, Mercury enters your sign, Taurus. Until the 9th, when Mercury turns retrograde, your conscious mind is grounded, focused and practical. You know exactly what you're doing and why and can accomplish a great deal. The retrograde begins in the early degrees of Taurus, so Mercury slips back into Aries and turns direct in that sign on May 3. You know the rules for this retrograde now, right? Follow the three Rs: revise, review and rethink. Don't sign contracts. If you have to travel, go with the flow. Your itinerary may change suddenly. You'll get to enjoy this planet in your sign, in direct motion, for much of May. Re-read the Mercury retro section in the introduction for other guidelines.

The full moon in Libra on April 11 highlights a work, health or relationship issue. In work, you complete a project or reap the harvest for something you've achieved. In health matters, you reach your desired goal. In relationships, you are reminded of a need to compromise. This full moon enables you to understand other people's points of view.

Venus, your ruler, turns direct in Pisces on April 15, and this suggests that your social calendar heats up again. A romance may begin with a friend or someone you meet through friends. On the 28th, Venus enters passionate Aries. If you're involved with someone, you may keep it under wraps until Venus enters your sign in June.

Energetic Mars enters communicative Gemini on April 21, and things start moving financially. *You* make stuff happen by taking steps to increase your income in some way. Perhaps you take a part time job or a second job, or you may push your boss to give you a raise.

A new moon in your sign happens just once a year and is always something to anticipate. It sets the tone for the rest of the year. So before April 26, think about what you would like to experience and achieve in the next year. Make a bucket list. Back your desires with emotion. Post the list where you'll see it often. Some new opportunities come your way with this new moon that are personally satisfying.

AT A GLANCE

April 6—Saturn turns retro in Sagittarius
April 9—Mercury retrograde in Taurus
April 11—Full moon in Libra
April 15—Venus turns direct in Pisces
April 21—Mars enters into Gemini
April 26—New moon in Taurus
April 28—Venus enters Aries

May 2017
Enjoyable

May is a calmer month, and you'll be able to initiate some of the ideas you seeded in April and store up your energy for a rather demanding summer ahead.

The best news occurs on May 3, when Mercury turns direct in Aries. With Mercury, Venus and Uranus all in Aries now, you may be feeling restless and more impatient than usual. Perhaps it's time to pack your bags and hit the road. Drive to a town you've never seen before, go exploring and poke around in the shops, cafes and museums. That should sate your restlessness for a while. If you're in a relationship, invite your partner on the trip. It may be more romantic than you ever imagined.

The full moon in Scorpio on May 10 heightens your sexuality and illuminates something about a business or personal partnership. It prompts you to ask if you are satisfied in these areas and if not, what would you like to change? What's the absolute bottom line? Your intuition is sharpened, and your dreams may provide insight and information that help you in some way.

Between May 16 and June 6, Mercury transits Taurus. This period is comfortable for you. You're pragmatic and grounded and feel good about yourself and the direction of your life. By late May, Mercury is forming a beneficial angle with Pluto in fellow earth sign Capricorn, and you may be involved in some way in publishing or higher education or could be traveling abroad.

The new moon in Gemini on May 25 falls in your financial area and joins Mars in this area. The combination indicates new opportunities concerning money and your earning power, perhaps with social media, networking and communication.

Overall, May should be an enjoyable month, with events moving at a pace that suits you.

AT A GLANCE
May 3—Mercury turns direct in Aries
May 10 —Full moon in Scorpio
May 16—Mercury enters Taurus
May 25—New moon in Gemini

June 2017
Communicate & network

This month is packed with astrological events. The action gets off to a running start when energetic Mars enters water sign Cancer on June 4 and revs up the communication area of your chart. Between now and July 20, when Mars enters Leo, you'll be doing a lot of writing. You might complete a novel and submit it to your agent. You may be putting together a new project at work that entails considerable emailing, blogging or updating a website. Regardless of the specifics, this period is one in which communication is heightened.

June 6 features two events and is likely to be a hectic day. Mercury enters Gemini, a sign that it rules, and Venus enters Taurus, a sign it rules. Jupiter turns direct in Libra on June 9. The Mercury transits lasts until the 21st and should bring ideas and communication about money—how to earn more, how you may need to budget and what to save. Friends and your network of acquaintances are helpful. You may be busy updating your blog and social media.

Once Mercury enters Cancer on June 21, joining Mars in your communication sector, you are bursting with ideas and ready to take on any writing/communication project that comes your way. Two days later, on the 23rd, the new moon in Cancer ushers in new opportunities related to communication, writing or your family and home. You may be invited to speak at a conference or workshop. Your intuition is so sharp that if you ignore those hunches, you do so at your own peril!

When Jupiter turns direct in Libra on June 9, you may notice how things that were stalled in your daily work routine now move forward with smoothness or a greater flow. You're able to compromise more easily with co-workers and find a better balance between your work and your personal life. And when you feel balanced, Taurus, when your life is without drama, you tend to be much happier.

The Venus transit, from June 6 to July 4, marks one of the most romantic and creative times for you all year. Your self-confidence soars, you feel at peace with yourself and the direction in which your life is going, and you're in the right place at the right time. If you're involved in a relationship, then things should go well during this period. If you're single, then you may meet someone special during this transit.

The full moon in Sagittarius on June 9 illuminates the area of joint finances. Your spouse might land a plump raise that enables the two of you to travel internationally. You might refinance your home for a better interest rate. You could receive an unexpected royalty check or refund.

June 4—Mars enters Cancer
June 6—Mercury enters Gemini, Venus enters Taurus
June 9—Full moon in Sagittarius, Jupiter turns direct in Libra
June 21—Mercury moves into Cancer
June 23—New moon in Cancer

July 2017
Full steam ahead

Seven astrological events make July an extremely busy and hectic month. Be sure to get enough rest. You'll want to be in tip-top shape to take advantage of these energies!

On July 4, Venus enters Gemini and Mercury moves into Leo. The Venus transit, which lasts until July 31, can work in two ways: you earn more money and do so easily, or you spend more money just as easily, or both! You and your partner agree on the fundamental beliefs that are important to you both and enjoy a time of greater communication.

Mercury transits Leo from July 5 to July 25, in the home/family sector of your chart. Any parties and festivities during this time are likely to happen at your place. You take great pride in your home and family and may be spiffing things up around your home and property.

The full moon in Capricorn on July 8 joins Pluto in the worldview and travel section of your chart. This combination can result in power games, if you aren't careful. But it can also urge you to use your tremendous willpower to push through obstacles and meet challenges.

Between July 20 and September 5, Mars moves through Leo and the home/family area of your chart. Someone around you may be overly dramatic during this period, and it leads to some tension at home. That said, this transit is an excellent one for getting stuff done at home, for hanging out with your kids and for generally enjoying home activities. Three days later, on the 23rd, there's a new moon in Leo in the same area of your chart. This one should bring in new opportunities related to home and family. A move? A pregnancy? Someone moves in or out? And because the new moon is in Leo, there may be opportunities related to your creative endeavors.

Between July 25 and August 12, Mercury transits Virgo, which it rules, and your creative life takes a new, improved turn. You're comfortable with the energy of this fellow earth sign, and it prompts you to become more detail-oriented.

Your ruler, Venus, changes signs on the 31st and enters Cancer, a water sign with which you're comfortable. It will be there until August 26 and should facilitate your communication abilities. There could also be a flirtation with someone who lives in your neighborhood or whom you meet through a sibling.

July 4—Venus enters Gemini
July 5—Mercury goes into Leo
July 8—Full moon in Capricorn
July 20—Mars enters Leo
July 23—New Moon in Leo
July 25—Mercury goes into Virgo
July 31—Venus enters Cancer

August 2017
Backtracking

If you thought July was hectic, August may not offer much of a respite. There are two eclipses, two planets change directions and one planet changes signs. The eclipses alone are enough to keep you in perpetual motion, so let's start with them.

The lunar eclipse in Aquarius on August 7 falls in your career/profession area. It indicates that your emotions are running fast and furiously concerning a career issue or a relationship with someone. You may feel pressed to make a decision about something. If at all possible, delay the decision a couple of days. You may feel the effects of this eclipse for several days on either side of it.

The solar eclipse in Leo on August 21 is like a double new moon and presents you with several new opportunities concerning your home, family and perhaps even your creativity and public life. If your home is on the market, then you could get a solid offer. If you're house shopping, then you find just the right place. If you're ready to start renovations on your existing home, then you find the right contractor. Be vigilant for synchronicities that provide insight and guidance.

What about the rest of the month? Well, big ouch! Mercury turns retrograde in Virgo on August 12 and doesn't turn direct again until September 5. During this period, your creative projects may seem to move in reverse, with your having to revamp, rethink and revise them. Use this time to improve the product. These retro periods urge us to slow down, take time for ourselves, clean out closets and garages and get rid of stuff we no longer use or need. If you have to travel during the retrograde, be flexible, try to go with the flow; your itinerary is likely to change. Don't sign contracts or break off relationships.

On the 25th—and this is great news!—Saturn turns direct in Sagittarius. You'll feel the relief almost immediately, as your work schedule straightens out. Relationships with co-workers and others will be more balanced.

When Venus transits Leo from August 26 to September 19, your love life at home picks up steam. If you're single, then you may be hosting friends at your place. You get along well with the women in your life, particularly sisters and female friends, and they are helpful to you.

August 7—Lunar eclipse in Aquarius
August 12—Mercury turns retro in Virgo
August 21—Solar eclipse in Leo
August 25—Saturn turns direct in Sagittarius
August 26—Venus enters Leo

September 2017
Creative & romantic

Circle September 5 on your calendar. Mercury turns direct in Leo, and now you can move forward with ease with your travel plans, contracts, home renovation projects and everything else that was put on hold during the retrograde. Four days after it turns direct, it moves into fellow earth sign Virgo and ramps up your creative adrenaline. You'll be particularly adept at details during its transit through Virgo, which lasts until the 29th, when Mercury enters Libra and the daily work area of your chart. You're able to find greater balance with co-workers during this transit and are more willing to compromise.

Also on the 5th, Mars enters Virgo, so from the 9th to the 29th, Mars and Mercury will be traveling together, a winning combination for any kind of creative work you're doing. Mars energizes whatever it touches. Your intellect is particularly sharp.

The full moon in Pisces on September 6 should bring about a definite uptick in your social life. The Pisces moon also deepens your intuition and artistic sensibilities. You may get involved in a creative project with friends or acquaintances.

The 19th brings Venus into Virgo and the creativity section of your chart, where it joins both Mercury and Venus. This powerful lineup is terrific for all creative work. Ideas flow, Mars confers the energy to make things happen, and Venus ensures smooth sailing. Because the creative area of your chart also rules romance, love, kids and everything you do for pleasure, romance is certainly in the air. In fact, the period from September 19 to October 14, when Venus moves into Libra, is one of the most romantic and creative periods for you all year. The other romantic period occurred during the summer, between June 6 and July 4, when Venus was in your sign. Whenever these two Venus transits occur, your muse is at your beck and call—and so is your partner!

On the 20th, the new moon in Virgo should bring in new opportunities in all the areas mentioned above. Once Mercury enters Libra on the 29th, you're popping with ideas at work and may be socializing with co-workers. You may even be brainstorming with a team of co-workers, so take notes!

September 5—Mercury turns direct in Leo, Mars enters Virgo
September 6—Full moon in Pisces
September 9—Mercury enters Virgo
September 19—Venus goes into Virgo
September 20—New moon in Virgo
September 29—Mercury moves into Libra

October 2017
A Jupiter shift

If you were hoping for a really laid back month—as in *relaxing*—October isn't it. Six astrological events occur and most of them involve the signs Libra and Scorpio. October 5 brings a full moon in fire sign Aries that illuminates issues you may have buried or power you have disowned. You're fired up to get to the bottom of this stuff and feel restless enough to tackle it. The Aries moon also stirs your passions.

October 10 features a major shift for Jupiter, as it moves into water sign Scorpio, where it will be until November 2018. During this thirteen-month period, Jupiter expands your business and personal partnerships. If you're already involved in a committed relationship, then you and your partner may take things to the next level. If you're single, you probably won't be when this transit ends in 2018. In terms of business, you and a partner may decide to branch out on your own. Jupiter is now in opposition to your sun sign and that angle can result in expansion so great that it becomes excessive. You may find, for example, that you have so much work to do that you have to hire help or turn down projects. In many ways, it's a nice position to be in. It means you and your services/company are in demand!

Venus moves into Libra on October 14, and things in your daily work routine smooth out. If you've been having trouble with a co-worker, the relationship finds the proper balance, and peace is declared! In terms of the maintenance of your health, you realize that your emotional health is an intricate component of your physical health and take steps to ensure your happiness from moment to moment, hour to hour. It's possible that an office flirtation blossoms into a full-blown romance.

On the 17th, Mercury joins Jupiter in Scorpio and what a powerful combination this is! You're well-equipped now to plumb the depths of anything and everything you tackle. This combo is terrific for research, especially research on esoteric topics—life after death, the paranormal or reincarnation.

The new moon in Libra on the 19th brings new opportunities in your daily work. A raise? A promotion? A larger office? New assistants? It's also possible that you have an opportunity to become self-employed in some capacity.

Mars moves into Libra on October 22 and stays there until December 9. This transit energizes your daily work and your relationships generally with the people in your environment. It would be a good idea to sign up for a gym membership or for a series of yoga or Pilates classes.

AT A GLANCE
October 5—Full moon in Aries
October 10—Jupiter moves into Scorpio
October 14—Venus enters Libra
October 17—Mercury enters Scorpio
October 19—New moon in Libra
October 22—Mars enters Libra

November 2017
Kick back & chill

Finally! A calm month. There are only four astrological events in November that we should really be concerned about, and the first one is the full moon in your sign on November 4. This one illuminates an issue, relationship or situation in your personal life that you appreciate. Something you've been working on is either near completion or completed, and you have a sense of accomplishment about it. Neptune forms a harmonious angle to this moon, conferring an ease with artistic and creative projects. Your social calendar may get crowded rather quickly.

The next day, the 5th, Mercury enters fire sign Sagittarius and the shared resources area of your chart. It's easier now for you to grasp the big picture in finances you share with another person—like a spouse—and to deal with debt, mortgages and loans. Mentally, you travel far and wide, perhaps because of research in which you're involved. You may be planning a trip abroad and are checking out travel sites for the best deals. Mercury shares this sign with Saturn, which is moving inexorably toward a monumental change next month. But while these two travel together, you tend to be quite disciplined in how you think.

On November 7, your ruler, Venus, enters Scorpio and the partnership sector of your chart. This transit heightens your sexuality, deepens your intuition and confers clear insight into business partnerships. If someone has ulterior motives, you recognize it and back off. Venus will be in Scorpio until December 25.

The new moon in Scorpio on the 18th attracts new partnership opportunities. If you aren't romantically involved with anyone, then this new moon may usher the right person into your life. The right person for a business deal could also be part of the new moon package. Any planet in Scorpio deepens your emotional reaction, so just be careful that you don't overreact!

AT A GLANCE

November 4—Full moon in Taurus
November 5—Mercury enters Sagittarius
November 7—Venus goes into Scorpio
November 18—New moon in Scorpio

December 2017
A new Saturn cycle

As the year winds down, the astrological energies ratchet upward. It's smart to take some time early in the month to consider what you would like to experience or achieve in the new year. Rather than looking at this as New Year's resolutions, think of them as desires. Where would you like to be a year from now? What would you like to be doing?

On December 1, Venus enters Sagittarius, where it will be until the 25th. This transit impacts your daily work and health and should smooth over things at the office. A flirtation is possible with a co-worker.

The last Mercury retrograde of 2017 begins on December 3, in Sagittarius, and doesn't end until December 22. Since this is the holiday buying season, it would be smart to do your shopping on either side of the Mercury retro dates—unless you don't mind standing in the return lines on December 26.

The energy on the 3rd may feel quite strange because in addition to Mercury's shenanigans there's a full moon in Gemini in your financial area. It shines a light on some financial matter—perhaps a check you're expecting doesn't arrive or there's a snafu with a bill payment. Or the check arrives and it's less than it should be.

On the 9th, Mars moves into Scorpio, into your partnership area, and once again, energies rise, fuses may be short. The best way to use this energy is through research, psychical activity and, with the Mercury retrograde, revising and rethinking what you're doing. This transit ends in late January 2018.

The new moon in Sagittarius on the 18th occurs shortly before Saturn moves into Capricorn, so this potent pair could attract serious financial opportunities that will require you to think carefully about your options. Don't sign any contracts until after December 22, when Mercury turns direct.

Saturn enters a whole new phase when it moves into Capricorn, a sign it rules, on December 20. It will be in Capricorn for two and a half years, riding tandem with powerful Pluto. When these two get together in this particular sign, power structures may topple and new paradigms may be born from the ashes. It won't be *your* power structures that are collapsing, Taurus, but structures around you. Since both of these planets now form beneficial angles to your sun, you should be in a very good place as the year winds up and through the next two and a half years. You're able to build powerful structures in your life and to strengthen existing structures in financial, relational and professional matters.

Mercury turns direct on December 22 in Sagittarius. Throw a party in celebration!

On Christmas Day, Venus moves into Capricorn, joining Saturn and Pluto. Wow! You're a powerhouse now, Taurus. Love, money, career: you're in the right place at the right time. Make it count.

AT A GLANCE
December 1—Venus enters Sagittarius
December 3—Mercury turns retro in Sagittarius, full moon in Gemini
December 9—Mars enters Scorpio
December 18—New moon in Sagittarius
December 20—Saturn enters Capricorn
December 22—Mercury turns direct in Sagittarius
December 25—Venus enters Capricorn

Reflection
Was it a great year? Did it meet your expectations? If not, why not? If so, how can you carry this positive energy into the new year? Jot your notes here.

_____
_____
_____
_____
_____

Happy New Year!

Gemini 2017

Your ruler is Mercury, so pay particular attention to what that planet is doing each month. Retrogrades, the angles Mercury makes to other planets and the sign it's in will be noted. If you know your natal rising sign, it's a good idea to keep track of that sign's ruling planet, too. Let's say your rising or ascendant is Scorpio. If you look in the introduction, you'll find that Scorpio is ruled by Pluto and co-ruled by Mars, so the various transits and angles these planets make to other planets will be significant for you.

The monthly roundups also include information on the new and full moons, eclipses and the various transits.

It's a year for building new foundations, forging new relationships and trying new things. You'll be communicating and networking more frequently, so remain positive and upbeat.

January 2017
Career & romance

The year begins with a Mercury retrograde hangover that started in mid-December 2016 and ends, thankfully, on January 8, when the planet turns direct in Sagittarius, in your partnership area. As the planet that rules your sign, Gemini, this retrograde may have messed up your New Year's plans and/or travel plans. That said, perhaps friends you hadn't seen for years returned to your life. Or you resolved an old issue. Retrogrades are simply prompts to slow down.

Venus enters Pisces and your career area on January 3 and sticks around until February 3, a fabulous boost to your professional concerns. You could land a raise or promotion. If you've had trouble with co-workers, things should straighten out. The other nice part about Venus in Pisces is that it enhances your imagination, and in your flights of fantasy, you may bring back ideas you can easily use in a creative way. Mars is also in Pisces, in the same area of your chart, so there may be a romance brewing at work. Mars energizes whatever it touches and prompts you to take action when you need to.

On the 28th, Mars moves into Aries, the sign it rules, and it's likely that your social life heats up in a major way. You may become more active on social media and make new contacts that are helpful to you. You might sign up for an online course or a workshop. Mars remains in Aries until March 9, and because it forms a harmonious angle to your sun, the impact on you is positive.

Jupiter is still transiting Libra, a fellow air sign, and will continue to do so until October 10, when it moves into Scorpio. This transit has expanded—and will continue to expand—your creativity, romantic options and everything you do for fun and pleasure. Saturn continues its transit of Sagittarius until December 20 of this year and brings structure and a solid foundation to both your personal and business partnerships.

January 12 brings a full moon in Cancer, your financial area, and sheds light on some monetary concern or issue. It forms a beneficial angle to Mars in Pisces, so it's likely to be an intuitive and perhaps even emotional day. Also on the 12th, Mercury joins Pluto in Capricorn, in the shared resources area of your chart. The energy of this powerful duo could result in some resourceful way for you to increase your income.

January 28 features a new moon in fellow air sign Aquarius, and proves to be a real treasure for you. An opportunity for international travel may present itself, or you may have a chance to link up with a visionary group of people.

AT A GLANCE
January 3—Venus enters Pisces
January 8—Mercury retrograde ends
January 12—Full moon in Cancer, Mercury joins Pluto in Capricorn
January 28—New moon in Aquarius, Mars enters Aries

February 2017
Surprising opportunities

Months in which there are eclipses are often emotional and tend to draw our focus toward areas of our lives that need attention. The two eclipses this month are no exception. On February 10, the lunar eclipse in Leo stirs emotions about a relationship with a sibling, friend or neighbor or about your public persona, the face you present to the public. Uranus forms a beneficial angle to this eclipse, so there's an element of surprise to how internal events reveal themselves.

The solar eclipse in Pisces on February 26 ushers in new professional opportunities. Neptune is closely allied with this eclipse, so there may be an idealistic, artistic or creative component to these opportunities. Solar eclipses are like double new moons and can be felt several days or even months on either side of the actual eclipse date.

On February 6, expansive Jupiter turns retrograde in fellow air sign Libra, in that area of your chart that governs children, creativity, romance and whatever you do for fun and pleasure. This retrograde tends to slow things down. Creative projects and a romantic relationship may not hum along as quickly as you would like. That said, this retrograde's effects aren't as immediate as those of a Mercury retro. The planet's expansive energy turns inward, prompting you to tackle your creativity in new and different ways.

Between February 7–25, Mercury moves through fellow air sign Aquarius, forming a beneficial angle to your sun. Your intellect assumes an edgy, visionary quality. You're able to spot cutting edge trends before they tip into mass consciousness, and you may associate with individuals who are experts in their fields or who are eccentric in some way.

When Mercury slips into Pisces on the 25th, your focus turns to career and professional matters, and your imagination and intuition deepen considerably.

AT A GLANCE
February 3—Venus enters Aries
February 6—Jupiter turns retrograde in Libra
February 7—Mercury enters Aquarius
February 10—Lunar eclipse in Leo
February 25—Mercury enters Pisces
February 26—Solar eclipse in Pisces

March 2017
Financial focus

This month features enough astrological events to keep you in perpetual motion. That shouldn't be a problem for you, as a multitasker, but don't skimp on your sleep. You'll need to be alert to take advantage of some of these transits.

Venus turns retrograde in Aries on March 4, so between that date and April 15, when it turns direct in Pisces, your relationships with friends and with a romantic partner may hit a few bumps. You often tend to blurt out what you're thinking and feeling, but during this retro period, particularly in the midst of a disagreement, it's wisest to think before you speak. Be sure to check and recheck your bank statements and pay for items with cash rather than by credit card. This way, you'll be aware of exactly what you're spending.

On March 9, Mars enters Taurus and the financial area of your chart. Your expenses may tick upward this month, but you may be earning more, too. A lot of your physical energy goes into generating income, especially if you're self-employed. It's an excellent time to join a gym or sign up for yoga or aerobic classes of some kind. Mars remains in Taurus until April 21.

The full moon in Virgo on March 12 highlights your home and family life. Does someone in your domestic environment need more support than usual? Is your home in need of repairs that you've been postponing? Are you planning to put your house on the market? Pluto forms a wide, beneficial angle to this full moon, so part of the equation may involve resources you share with others—your partner's income, for instance, or taxes that are owed.

Mercury enters compatible fire sign Aries on March 13. Between then and March 31, when it moves into Taurus, you're constantly on the go, meeting this friend for dinner, that friend for a movie. In other words, your social calendar gets crowded quickly. This transit sharpens your wit and your communication skills and adds a touch of daring to your intellect!

The new moon in Aries on the 27th brings new opportunities for networking, meeting people and making contacts that prove valuable to you in some way. With Mercury, Venus retrograde and Uranus all in Aries as well, you may be feeling restless, impatient and like quite the daredevil. Exercise caution when driving. All this fire energy can make you reckless!

Mercury moves into Taurus on the 31st, and your mind is more grounded, calm and pragmatic. This transit is lengthy for Mercury because it turns retrograde on April 9. Mercury doesn't enter your sign until June 6.

AT A GLANCE
March 4— Venus turns retrograde in Aries
March 9—Mars enters Taurus
March 12—Full moon in Virgo
March 13—Mercury enters Aries
March 27—New moon in Aries
March 31—Mercury enters Taurus

April 2017
Hectic & insightful

Buckle up, Gemini! There's so much going on this month that April could be a wild and bumpy ride! But there are opportunities tucked away in all this activity, too. The more vigilant and aware you are, the better equipped you'll be to handle it all and run with the opportunities.

Saturn has been transiting Sagittarius since the fall of 2015, moving through your partnership area. This transit has probably caused you to chafe and rebel against restrictions placed on you by others. But you've been learning to take such things in stride and to appreciate your business and personal partnerships for what they are—solid structures in your life. On April 6, Saturn turns retrograde, and you may be revisiting some of the issues you've been dealing with since 2015. Think of it as a second chance to resolve stuff and clear it up and out so that the new can enter. The retro lasts until August 25.

You'll enjoy the full moon in fellow air sign Libra on April 11, in that area of your chart that rules creativity, romance and children. Jupiter retrograde is also in Libra and the combination should prompt you to get out and enjoy yourself, spend time with your kids and converse with your muse!

Venus turns direct in Pisces on April 15, a welcome reprieve for your love life. It slipped back into Pisces during the retro, and now that it's in your career area, your professional life hums along smoothly. A promotion or raise could be in the offing, or you might even get an offer for an entirely new job. A romance could be brewing with a co-worker.

Once Mars enters your sign on the 21st, you're revved up and ready for action! You may have opportunities for public speaking. Your writing is sharper, and your verbal skills are so good you could sell virtually anything to anyone. Your physical stamina is also excellent, and you may want to consider joining a gym. If you don't have a daily exercise routine yet, now is the time to start one. This transit lasts until June 4.

The new moon in Taurus on April 26 could bring a new opportunity to work behind the scenes in some capacity. Ghostwriter? Set designer? The power behind the throne? Since Mercury is retrograde when this new moon occurs, one possibility is that the opportunity that surfaces is something from the past that you may have passed on.

Between April 28 and June 6, Venus moves through Aries. Your passions are stoked, and it could be due to someone you meet through friends, your network of acquaintances or even online.

AT A GLANCE
April 6—Saturn turns retro in Sagittarius
April 9—Mercury retrograde in Taurus
April 11—Full moon in Libra
April 15—Venus turns direct in Pisces
April 21—Mars enters into Gemini
April 26—New moon in Taurus
April 28—Venus enters Aries

May 2017
A beautiful month

Compared to last month, May could feel like a walk in the proverbial park. Not only does Mercury turn direct, but there's a new moon in your sign, always a welcome gift from the universe.

May 3 is a day to savor: Mercury turns direct in Aries and joins Venus in that sign. With your sign's ruler and the planet that governs love and romance forming beneficial angles to your sun until May 16, the next two weeks are fun, romantic, adventurous and socially busy. Your mental energy is remarkable, and the only possible drawback is that you don't finish what you start. Once Mercury enters grounded, stable Taurus on the 16th, however, you have greater patience and staying power.

May 10 features a full moon in Scorpio that sheds light on something in your daily work routine. You might complete a project, be applauded by the higher-ups or find yourself at the center of attention for something you did in the past. There's an emotional intensity to this moon and greater psychic awareness. It forms a beneficial angle with powerful Pluto in Capricorn, so regardless of how the specifics unfold, you're in control.

With the new moon in your sign on May 25, you're filled with enthusiasm and feel positive, self-assured and pleased with the direction in which your life is headed. This new moon happens just once a year, and it's a good idea to prepare for it several days before it arrives. Make a wish list. Back those desires with strong emotion, act as if the things on your list are already a part of your life, and then let the universe get busy creating what you want.

AT A GLANCE

May 3—Mercury turns direct in Aries
May 10—Full moon in Scorpio
May 16—Mercury enters Taurus
May 25—New moon in Gemini

June 2017
Time to create!

June holds seven astrological events that add up to another crowded month. But since you usually move and think at the speed of light, it shouldn't be a problem for you! You would rather have too much to do than too little.

On June 4, Mars enters Cancer and your financial area. This transit, which lasts until July 20, gives you an opportunity to find new sources of income. You might be freelancing in some capacity or someone you know needs your particular expertise and pays you as a consultant. Cancer is an intuitive sign and you'll get inklings and nudges about what to do and when to do it.

Circle June 6 and 9. Three astrological events happen. On the 6th, Mercury enters Gemini, and Venus moves into Taurus. On the 9th, Jupiter turns direct in Libra. Whew! Let's start with the Mercury transit, which lasts until the 21st.

You're happiest when Mercury is in your sign, and when you're happy, it's easier to achieve what you desire. Your thoughts zip along, exploring whatever grabs your interest. Your writing and verbal skills are stellar, and you can talk to anyone about almost anything. Because Jupiter turns direct in fellow air sign Libra, your creativity expands. You might decide to start writing that book you've thought about. Or you may pour your creative energy into a blog or website, music or art. There's no telling, and the sky is pretty much the limit when you feel this good.

The Venus transit through Taurus suggests a more grounded approach to love and romance and how you manage your money. If a romance begins during this transit, which ends on July 4, there may be a component of secrecy about it. You might not "go public" until Venus enters your sign.

The full moon on June 9, in Sagittarius, highlights elements of a personal or business partnership. It may be something as simple as you and your partner throwing a party at your place. Sagittarius is such a gregarious sign that the day is apt to be a bit wild and crazy! Enjoy it.

On the 21st, Mercury joins Mars in Cancer, in your financial area. Now you've got the ideas and the energy to increase your income. Friends and/or siblings may be helpful in this regard. Again, because there's such an intuitive component to Cancer, you'll get hints and clues about the direction in which you should move. Be alert for synchronicities, too, which may occur in clusters.

The new moon in Cancer on the 23rd could bring the big payoff you've been working toward. New financial opportunities and perhaps a new opportunity of some kind for your family.

AT A GLANCE
June 4—Mars enters Cancer
June 6—Mercury enters Gemini, Venus enters Taurus
June 9—Full moon in Sagittarius, Jupiter turns direct in Libra
June 21—Mercury moves into Cancer
June 23—New moon in Cancer

July 2017
Romantic

July won't be any calmer or more evenly paced than June. In fact, it's just as busy, with seven astrological events.

Between July 4 and 31, Venus transits your sign, always a welcome event! You feel more self-confident, may decide to change your appearance in some way—new clothes, new hairstyle—and may meet a romantic interest. A Venus transit through your sign marks one of the most romantic and artistic periods this year. In addition, Jupiter is now moving in direct motion in fellow air sign Libra, through the romance/creativity area of your chart. It doesn't get much better than this!

The next day, July 5, Mercury enters Leo, a fire sign harmonious with your sign, and stokes your communication skills. You are *on* now, Gemini, and between the 5th and the 25th, you are able to dazzle with the written or spoken word. Socially, you're very much in demand, and there may be a certain charisma about you that attracts others quickly.

The full moon on July 8 joins Pluto in Capricorn, a powerful combination that sheds light on resources you share with others—money, energy or goods. If there's a challenge, Pluto enables you to spot it quickly and solve it. It's also easier now for you to compartmentalize your emotions.

On July 20, Mars joins Mercury in Leo until the 25th, when Mercury enters Virgo. For these five days, you're a powerhouse of ideas and communication and may have more contact with neighbors and siblings than you normally do. Mars will be in Leo until September 5.

The new moon in Leo on July 23 brings in new opportunities related to communication. If you have writing aspirations, then you may have a chance to write a novel or book. Or perhaps your boss taps you to start the company newsletter or to come up with a marketing strategy. However these opportunities unfold, both Mercury and Mars are riding tandem with this new moon, fueling the energy.

Between July 25 and September 29, Mercury transits Virgo and your home becomes the hub for gatherings, discussions and a lot of activity. This transit is long for Mercury because on August 12, it turns retrograde. More on that in the August roundup.

Venus transits Cancer and your financial area from July 31 to August 26. During this transit, you may be spending more money, but could also be earning more. You're in the right place at the right time when it comes to money.

AT A GLANCE

July 4—Venus enters Gemini
July 5—Mercury goes into Leo
July 8—Full moon in Capricorn
July 20—Mars enters Leo
July 23—New Moon in Leo
July 25—Mercury goes into Virgo
July 31—Venus enters Cancer

August 2017
Bumpy

Eclipses are always big events astrologically. Lunar eclipses tend to bring up inner needs and concerns and often shake us up emotionally. Solar eclipses trigger external events and bring in opportunities. Often with solar eclipses, we must sacrifice or give up something to make room for the new opportunity.

In addition to the eclipses, there's a Mercury retrograde this month. But let's start with the eclipses.

The lunar eclipse in Aquarius on August 7 falls in that area of your chart that governs your beliefs and worldview. In some way, your beliefs may be challenged—by a friend, partner, relative or someone within your environment. It pushes your buttons, and you feel you must defend what you believe. You have an ally during this eclipse—Jupiter in Libra—which helps you to balance your emotions and to effectively deal with the challenge.

The solar eclipse on August 21 in Leo should be exciting and may present you with some very interesting new opportunities with communication and in your public life. Both Mars and Venus are close to the eclipse degree, and Jupiter forms a wide but beneficial angle to it. Uranus, the planet of the unexpected, makes an exact and beneficial angle to it. All of this adds up to the new opportunities coming at you out of the blue and catching you by surprise. Read more about this eclipse on page 22 in the introduction.

Between August 12 and September 5, Mercury is retrograde in Virgo, in the home/family area of your chart. Since misunderstandings are common during these periods, make a special effort to communicate clearly and succinctly. Pay close attention to details in your home life—know where your kids are and what they're doing! And always follow the rule of the three Rs: revise, review and re-think.

Saturn turns direct in Sagittarius on August 25, after a lengthy period of dormancy. This movement is great for your partnerships, both business and personal, and it's easier to make decisions and move ahead in this area now.

On August 26, Venus enters compatible fire sign Leo, where it will be until September 19, and a new romance may be in the offing, perhaps with someone in your neighborhood or who is a part of your work environment.

AT A GLANCE
August 7—Lunar eclipse in Aquarius
August 12—Mercury turns retro in Virgo
August 21—Solar eclipse in Leo
August 25—Saturn turns direct in Sagittarius
August 26—Venus enters Leo

September 2017
Enjoy the journey

This month is far more relaxing than the summer has been. You might want to consider taking a trip at some point after Mercury turns direct in Leo on September 5. You've earned some fun, Gemini! With Mars entering Virgo on the day that Mercury turns direct, you may want to include the entire family on this little getaway. Mars stays in Virgo until October 22, and during this period, you may move forward with home renovation projects that have been on your to-do list. If your home is on the market, it could sell during this transit.

The 6th brings a beautiful full moon in Pisces, in your career area. You complete a project or something at work is winding down. Because the Pisces moon is so imaginative, you may be casting around for your next idea. Don't rush into anything. Allow yourself time to sift through and absorb experiences.

Between September 19 and October 14, lovely Venus transits Virgo. This means that Venus and Mars are now traveling together, a sure combo for romance and sexual chemistry. It also indicates there even if there are flare-ups and disagreements at home, things are quickly resolved because your excellent grasp of details reveals exactly how to mitigate the situation.

September 20 features a new moon in Virgo. What a nice lineup now, with the new moon, Mars, Venus and Mercury all in Virgo, in the home/family area. You may get an offer on your home or find the perfect house for you and your family. Or, you may have an opportunity for freelance work that you can do from home.

Mercury enters fellow air sign Libra on the 29th, and you're now on a creative roll, Gemini.

September 5—Mercury turns direct in Leo, Mars enters Virgo
September 6—Full moon in Pisces
September 9—Mercury enters Virgo
September 19—Venus goes into Virgo
September 20—New moon in Virgo
September 29—Mercury moves into Libra

October 2017
Five-star month

October is one of the two most romantic and creative times for you all year. So be prepared to have some up close and personal hours with your muse. She's at your beck and call for much of this month.

The full moon in Aries on October 5 lights up your social calendar in a major way. Friends seem to be coming out of the proverbial woodwork, vying for your time and company. Since Uranus is also in Aries, there's an air of unpredictability to events that unfold.

Your ruler, Mercury, entered Libra on the 29th of last month and will be there until the 17th, spurring you to get moving with your creative projects. If you're involved in a relationship, this transit opens up channels of communication. You and your partner may take in a concert, an art show or a book festival. With Saturn now moving direct through your partnership area, you two may decide to take the relationship to the next level of commitment.

Jupiter makes a major transition on October 10, when it enters Scorpio, where it will be until November 9, 2018. During this period, your daily work routine will expand in some way. You could be promoted and assume more responsibility, or you might find a new job that is more satisfying personally and pays you more. Or, it's also possible that you have a chance to strike out on your own. Be alert for synchronicities that offer insight and guidance about the direction you should take. Mercury joins Jupiter in Scorpio on the 17th and your mind and your consciousness are able to dig deeply into any area that interests you. Until November 5, when Mercury enters Sagittarius, your research skills are extraordinary.

On the 14th, Venus enters Libra, joining Mercury there for several days before that planet enters Scorpio. You're much more self-confident during this Venus transit, and other people find you charismatic and irresistible. Your love life picks up—someone new?—and your muse is ready to advise and serve! Don't fritter away this alignment of the stars.

The new moon on the 19th also falls in Libra, so here come all the new opportunities related to romance, creativity, pleasure and fun and children. One distinct possibility with this new moon is that you and your partner discover you're going to be parents.

As though this isn't enough positive energy, the universe tosses one more planet into the Libra pot on the 22nd, when Mars enters that sign. Whenever Mars and Venus travel together through the romance area of your chart—and there's a new moon to boot—it's likely that you'll meet someone special. If you're already involved in a relationship, then you and your partner enjoy an absolutely beautiful time together.

AT A GLANCE
October 5—Full moon in Aries
October 10—Jupiter moves into Scorpio
October 14—Venus enters Libra
October 17—Mercury enters Scorpio
October 19—New moon in Libra
October 22—Mars enters Libra

November 2017
Insights

Compared to the last several months, November probably feels laid back and chill. Your life isn't quite as hectic, except around Thanksgiving in the U.S., when visitors may be coming into town.

The full moon in Taurus on November 4 lights up the personal unconscious area of your chart. The stuff that comes to light is about power you may have disowned over the years. Or perhaps memories from a previous life surface in dreams or visions or when you're relaxing. You may be more stubborn with the moon in Taurus but also more persistent.

On the 5th, Mercury enters Sagittarius, joining Saturn in that sign, in your partnership area. You're better able to see the larger picture now of the various relationships in your life. Sagittarius is typically a gregarious sign (although the planet Saturn is not!), but you may go with the gregarious part of the equation and get into a party mode. At your place? Well, sure, why not? Sign contracts and make your travel plans this month; on December 3, Mercury turns retro in Sagittarius.

Venus enters Scorpio on the 7th, a transit that heightens your sexuality, helps smooth things over in your daily work routine and may prompt you to get serious about an exercise routine. An office flirtation could turn into something more. Be careful, Gemini. Remember the adage about not mixing work and pleasure? The Venus transits last until December 1.

The new moon in Scorpio on the 18th could usher in a job promotion and/or raise for you. Or, also likely, you're offered a job that pays more and has flexible hours.

AT A GLANCE
November 4—Full moon in Taurus
November 5—Mercury enters Sagittarius
November 7—Venus goes into Scorpio
November 18—New moon in Scorpio

December 2017
Shop early

This month is crammed with events, and the action gets off to a running start with Venus entering Sagittarius on December 1, before the Mercury retrograde begins. So for two days, mind and heart are on the same page, and your focus is on a personal or business partnership. Or, you're putting together an office holiday party. This transit lasts until December 25.

December 3 marks the beginning of the last Mercury retrograde of the year, which lasts until December 22. It's smart to do your holiday shopping on either side of these dates, unless you don't mind being in the return line on December 26. Since the retro occurs in your partnership area, you and a partner may not see eye to eye consistently during this period. Misunderstandings are common. By now, you know the rule of the three Rs for Mercury retro: revise, review and reconsider. Also on the 3rd, there's a full moon in your sign. You're trying to complete something, perhaps for a deadline, and are distracted by flights of imagination or someone in your environment who is demanding a lot of your attention. You may also find that your social calendar is so full that you have to be discriminating about which events or festivities you attend!

Mars enters Scorpio on December 9, a transit that takes you into the new year. This one should give you the physical energy you need to push through deadlines and obligations at work before the holidays arrive. Don't let your physical exercise routine slide just because you're busy. You need it now more than ever. Your sexuality is heightened by this transit.

The new moon in gregarious Sagittarius on December 18 is the last time for 29 to 30 years that the moon will be traveling with Saturn in Sadge. Rather than letting the somberness of Saturn drag you down, go with the fun-loving aspect of Sadge. You and your partner should head out for a night on the town! The new moon ushers in new opportunities in partnerships and possibly for international travel and higher education as well.

On the 20th, Saturn enters Capricorn, the sign it rules, and for the next two and a half years, you may be exploring the paranormal in depth—reincarnation, life after death or communication with the dead. Other people's resources may not be as accessible to you as they once were, and you'll have to earn more money to take up the slack. Your profession/career may take a much more serious and committed turn.

December 22 is a day for celebration. Mercury turns direct in Sadge!

Finally, on Christmas day, Venus joins Saturn in Capricorn. One possible ramification of these two planets traveling together is a serious, committed relationship. You and a partner move in together, get engaged or tie the knot.

December 1—Venus enters Sagittarius
December 3—Mercury turns retro in Sagittarius, full moon in Gemini
December 9—Mars enters Scorpio
December 18—New moon in Sagittarius
December 20—Saturn enters Capricorn
December 22—Mercury turns direct in Sagittarius
December 25—Venus enters Capricorn

Reflection

How has 2017 measured up for you? Did you meet your creative goals? Professional goals? What new structures did you build in your life this year? A new relationship or career? Note the highlights below.

_____

_____

_____

_____

_____

Happy New Year!

Cancer 2017

Since your sign is ruled by the moon, pay close attention to the lunations each month—the new and full moons—and to the four eclipses in 2017. If you know your natal rising sign, it's a good idea to keep track of that sign's ruling planet, too. Let's say your rising or ascendant is Taurus. If you look in the introduction (on page 14), you'll find that Taurus is ruled by Venus, so its various transits and the angles it makes to other planets will be significant for you.

The monthly roundups also include information on the various transits each month, retrogrades, the angles the transiting planets make to your sign and what it all means for you.

This year promises to be enormously creative for you. It's possible that you will be more insistent on your personal freedom, on the right to call your own shots at every level of your life. If you've considered starting your own business, this could be the year to do it.

January 2017
New love, new venues

The year begins with Mercury in retrograde, a hangover from 2016, but on the 8th it turns direct again in Sagittarius, and four days later it enters Capricorn. There are ways to navigate Mercury retro so it isn't quite as painful as it often is. Follow the rule of the three Rs: review, revise and reconsider. Don't launch new projects during this retro or sign contracts, and don't make travel plans. If you have to travel during the retro, then be as flexible as possible because your itinerary is sure to change unexpectedly! Also, re-read the Mercury retrograde section in the introduction for a reminder of how these retrogrades impact our lives.

Once Mercury turns direct, things at work smooth out and when it enters Capricorn, your conscious focus is on partnerships and on your career. You're resolute, determined and goal-oriented. Mercury remains in Capricorn until February 7.

Between January 3 and February 3, lovely Venus joins Neptune and Mars as it transits fellow water sign Pisces, and forms a beautiful angle to your sun. This could be quite a romantic and creative time for you. You may meet someone special from another country, and the attraction could be powerful, visceral. If you're already in a committed relationship, then things for you and your partner should unfold smoothly during this transit. It's also possible that you receive money from an unexpected source.

On the 12th, the full moon in your sign sheds light on a personal issue or concern. Uranus forms a difficult angle to this moon, so there may be jarring news, perhaps about your career or an unexpected event of some sort that throws you off. But with both Mars and Neptune in supportive water sign Pisces, you have the intuitive knowledge to deal with whatever this is. Also on the 12th, Mercury joins Pluto in Capricorn, a powerful combination that brings clarity and focus to your conscious mind.

January 28 features a new moon in visionary Aquarius in that area of your chart that governs shared resources. Your partner's income may increase thanks to a raise. A mortgage or loan is approved, you get a break on your insurance or you earn additional money through a new source.

Also on the 28th, Mars enters Aries, where it will be until March 9. Since it rules this sign, it functions well here, and your career benefits. It energizes everything about your professional life. You may put together a new strategy that the higher-ups love or launch a new product of some kind. However this transit unfolds, you're fired up, ready for action and movement.

AT A GLANCE
January 3—Venus enters Pisces
January 8—Mercury retrograde ends
January 12—Full moon in Cancer, Mercury joins Pluto in Capricorn
January 28—New moon in Aquarius, Mars enters Aries

February 2017
Erratic

Thanks to a pair of eclipses and some other transits, February is a wild, unpredictable month. Your best bet for navigating it smoothly is to take a few minutes after you wake up each morning to set your intentions. Visualize your day in the most positive light possible. Place yourself in an optimistic frame of mind.

On February 3, Venus enters Aries and the career area of your chart, joining Mars there until March 9. This combination indicates that you have the physical energy to get things done, and there's an entrepreneurial flavor to your work. You're quite passionate about what you're doing, and this passion infuses what you do. There could also be a romance brewing with a co-worker or someone you have met through your job.

On the 6th, Jupiter turns retrograde in Libra and turns direct on June 9. During this retro period, things in your family/domestic life may move more slowly than usual. Expansion is still occurring, but in a more internal sense. Your worldview and political and spiritual beliefs are broadening, perhaps through books, lively discussions with other seekers or through social media.

February 7 features Mercury's transit into Aquarius, where it remains until February 25. During this period, you may hear that a mortgage or loan has been approved or that your partner's income has changed. It's also possible that you'll be delving into esoteric topics—reincarnation, life after death, communication with the dead, telepathy and other paranormal phenomena.

Once Mercury enters fellow water sign Pisces on the 25th, you feel comfortable in your head, your own skin. Your imagination soars, and your intuitive ability deepens. You might be considering a return to college or grad school or, at the least, taking a few courses in something that intrigues you.

Now let's talk about this month's two eclipses. These events always help us to clarify things in our lives. They may not do so gently, but they do it in a way that seizes our attention. The lunar eclipse in Leo on February 10 occurs in your financial area. Emotions are stirred about money—perhaps the lack of it—and you realize you must act quickly to rectify the situation. With Mars in Aries forming a beneficial angle to this eclipse degree, you're able to do so. Jupiter also forms a beneficial angle to the eclipse degree, but may not be as much help as usual because it's retrograde. Breathe, Cancer. Breathe through it.

Two weeks later, on the 26th, the solar eclipse in fellow water sign Pisces should usher in new opportunities in higher education, international travel and your spirituality.

AT A GLANCE
February 3—Venus enters Aries
February 6—Jupiter turns retrograde in Libra
February 7—Mercury enters Aquarius
February 10—Lunar eclipse in Leo
February 25—Mercury enters Pisces
February 26—Solar eclipse in Pisces

March 2017

Career

This month's planetary lineup places the focus squarely on your career. Think about what you would like to achieve professionally—a new job, a raise, a promotion, a new career path— then visualize it as though it has happened already. You're aiming for the new opportunities of the new moon in Aries and your career area on March 27! You've got plenty of supportive planets to help you achieve what you want.

On March 4, Venus turns retrograde in Aries and remains that way until April 15. It means that things in your professional life may not move quite as smoothly or as quickly as you would like, and money may be slow in getting to you. That said, you'll enjoy Venus in direct motion in your career area between April 28 and June 6, so think of this retrograde period as a time to reassess.

Mars enters compatible earth sign Taurus on March 9. Between then and April 21, you'll be networking and building alliances for something you're trying to implement or achieve. Mars in Taurus gives you plenty of physical energy to do whatever needs to be done. If you don't have a regular physical routine, now is the time to start one.

You'll enjoy the full moon in compatible earth sign Virgo on March 12. Culmination and completion are indicated for a communication project. You're able to see all the connecting dots on this project and meet your deadline. If you and your family are researching neighborhoods where you might like to live, you may find the perfect spot. A brother or sister may need your emotional support now.

Mercury enters Aries and your career area on March 13 and remains there until the 31st. During this period, you're brimming with ideas, and your challenge is to choose exactly the right one to implement. You may be brainstorming with co-workers, and your mind will be busy 24/7. This could create disrupted sleep cycles, so be sure to get plenty of rest and allow yourself to kick back and chill for a while each day.

While Mercury is in Aries, the new moon in that sign occurs on the 27th. This one should bring in new professional opportunities—a raise or promotion, a new career track or new connections and networks. Be careful with this transit, however, that you finish what you start!

On the 31st, Mercury enters Taurus, then it turns retro on April 9. We'll discuss that under the April roundup. But get ready for it now, by completing projects, finalizing travel plans and signing contracts.

AT A GLANCE
March 4— Venus turns retrograde in Aries
March 9—Mars enters Taurus
March 12—Full moon in Virgo
March 13—Mercury enters Aries
March 27—New moon in Aries
March 31—Mercury enters Taurus

April 2017
Merc retro alert

The Mercury retrograde that begins on April 9 lasts nearly a month, until May 3. Because it begins in the early degrees of Taurus, the planet slips back into Aries, where it eventually turns direct. By now, you know to follow the three Rs for a Mercury retro: revise, review and reconsider. Once Mercury turns direct in Aries and moves through your career area until May 16, you should be able to develop the promises of last month's new moon!

From April 6 to August 25, Saturn moves retrograde through Sagittarius and the daily work/health area of your chart. This retrograde unfolds more slowly than a Mercury retro, so the impact isn't felt quite as strongly. That said, you'll find that your usual rate of activity is slowed down during this period. Others may try to impose responsibilities on you that you would reject when Saturn is in direct motion. You say *yes* when you should say *no*. Since Saturn rules the structures in our lives, you may be reassessing commitments you have made in the past.

The full moon in Libra on April 11 lights up your home/domestic area and marks the completion of some sort of creative project—home renovations, an addition to your house or a photographic or musical project. Since Jupiter retrograde forms a beneficial angle to this full moon, the luck and expansion quality of Jupiter won't be operating at full force. Just the same, you'll feel magnanimous.

On April 15, Venus turns direct in fellow water sign Pisces. Your love life picks up once again, your imagination soars, and your muse is fully present! Use the period between April 15 and 28, when Venus enters Aries again, to prepare yourself mentally and psychically for the realization of your professional goals. Venus will be in Aries until June 6, a lengthy period of career activity and forward movement.

Mars transits Gemini from April 21 to June 4. Your communication skills are sharp and direct, and you have an opportunity to dive deeply within yourself to resolve issues or concerns that have been brewing for years.

The new moon in Taurus on April 26 should bring in new friends, acquaintances and networks of individuals who are beneficial to you in some way. There could be a new financial opportunity of some kind, too, so remain alert!

AT A GLANCE
April 6—Saturn turns retro in Sagittarius
April 9—Mercury retrograde in Taurus
April 11—Full moon in Libra
April 15—Venus turns direct in Pisces
April 21—Mars enters into Gemini
April 26—New moon in Taurus
April 28—Venus enters Aries

May 2017
Calm & beneficial

Compared to the last couple of months, May is a relatively calm month astrologically. The best news is that on May 3, Mercury turns direct in Aries, in your career area. Between now and May 16, when Mercury moves into Taurus, things in your career should move forward again. Projects that seemed stalled suddenly pick up steam, and communication is flying back and forth between you and co-workers.

The full moon in fellow water sign Scorpio on May 10 forms a beneficial angle to your sun sign and to Pluto in Capricorn, lighting up the creativity and romance area of your chart. You're in the power seat, Cancer, and as long as you heed your considerable intuition, you won't make a faulty move. Since Scorpio is such an emotionally intense sign, you're likely to feel things deeply today and for several days on either side of this moon. Use those strong emotions in a positive way to eradicate internal barriers—in beliefs or attitudes—that may be blocking your progress.

Between May 16 and June 6, Mercury transits compatible earth sign Taurus. Your conscious mind is grounded and practical, and you have more patience. Your social calendar probably fills up quickly during this three-week period. Just be sure not to overload yourself. Get plenty of sleep and carve out daily time for yourself.

The new moon in Gemini on May 25 may bring in an opportunity to work behind the scenes in some capacity on a project that involves some form of communication and/or travel or both. There may be an element of surprise about this opportunity—a positive surprise!

AT A GLANCE
May 3—Mercury turns direct in Aries
May 10—Full moon in Scorpio
May 16—Mercury enters Taurus
May 25—New moon in Gemini

June 2017
A five-star month

This month may prove to be one of your favorites this year. There's a new moon in your sign and a number of planets that line up in Cancer.

On June 4, energetic Mars enters Cancer and will be there until July 20. During this period, your physical energy is heightened, you're able to accomplish more in less time, and you have great drive and ambition. Consider joining a gym or signing up for Pilates or yoga classes because it's important that you burn off excess energy during this transit. Also, if you don't have a regular exercise routine, this is the ideal time to start one.

Combined, June 6 and 9 feature three astrological events, so be ready to rock and roll with the changing energies. On the 6th, Mercury enters Gemini, and Venus enters Taurus. On the 9th, Jupiter turns direct in Libra. The first transit lasts until June 21, and during this period, you're networking behind the scenes and building alliances. Your communication skills are sharpened, and you could be putting together a website or blog for personal and/or professional use. You're also planting seeds for when Mercury enters your sign on the 21st. More on that in a moment.

The Venus transit lasts until July 4, and it's possible you meet a special romantic interest through friends or through some group to which you belong. It's also possible that you meet someone online. Venus in compatible earth sign Taurus is a sensual transit, and you may feel like surrounding yourself with beauty of various kinds—art, a garden, a fountain or carefully prepared foods. You may be spending a lot of time with friends during this transit.

Jupiter turning direct in Libra should bring greater balance and expansion of some sort in your life. Home renovation projects that have been on the back burner can now move forward. Someone may be moving into your home—a relative, a parent or even a friend. Or it's possible that you and your family move to a larger home. Or, if your home has been for sale, it sells, and you get your asking price.

The full moon on June 9 is in Sagittarius and joins Saturn retrograde in the area of your chart that rules daily work and health. Since full moons are about completion and harvest, you may finish up a project at work and be casting around for your next assignment. If you've got a regular exercise routine, then it's likely you're starting to see the physical results. Pretty cool, right? You enjoy setting a goal and reaching it.

On the 21st, Mercury joins Mars in your sign, a transit that lasts until July 5. During this period, your mind moves at lightning speeds, and you're able to think on your feet and make decisions on the fly. Your intuition is exceptionally powerful now, too. Emotionally, you feel good, as though you're in the flow of life, and that feeling certainly increases with the new moon in your sign on June 23.

This new moon happens just once a year and sets the tone for the rest of the year, birthday to birthday. Take a few minutes several days before this date to focus on what you would like to see happen in the next twelve months. Make a list. Post it where you'll see it often. Back each desire with emotion. With both Mercury and Mars in your sign on the same day of the new moon, you've got considerable power within to make things happen, Cancer.

AT A GLANCE
June 4—Mars enters Cancer
June 6—Mercury enters Gemini, Venus enters Taurus
June 9—Full moon in Sagittarius, Jupiter turns direct in Libra
June 21—Mercury moves into Cancer
June 23—New moon in Cancer

July 2017
Frenzied but powerful

July's transits are apt to keep you moving at full tilt from sunrise to sunset. It's important you don't run yourself ragged! Let's take a closer look.

On July 4, Venus enters Gemini, where it will be until the end of the month. During this period, you have greater access to your own unconscious. It's smart to keep a journal next to your bed because your dreams provide insight and information. A secret romance is possible, but once Venus enters your sign on the 31st, you may be telling friends and family about the relationship. There's strong communication between you and your new romantic interest.

The following day, the 5th, Mercury enters Leo and your financial area, a transit that lasts until July 25. Your conscious thoughts turn to money—how much you earn and spend, how you can earn more, save more, invest more…. You get the idea. With Saturn and Uranus both in fire signs as well, there's an unpredictable quality to all these thoughts about finances, and some of your ideas are actually quite solid.

The full moon in Capricorn on July 8 highlights your partnership area—business and personal. It's conjunct potent Pluto, so there could be power struggles of some kind with a partner, or you're in the driver's seat in a dispute. Either/or, that's how Pluto works. Equally possible is that a deal that has been in negotiation reaches completion. The loose ends are tied up.

Mars leaves your sign on the 20th and enters Leo and your financial area, where it will be until September 5. This transit should energize your finances in some way. You're working hard to attain or achieve a particular financial baseline, and you're the powerhouse that makes it all happen and come together. In fact, you see evidence of this with the new moon in Leo on the 23rd, when a new financial opportunity of some kind comes your way. A new job? A second job? A freelance gig? A new client?

On the 25th, Mercury moves into compatible earth sign Virgo, the communication area of your chart. This should be a dynamite transit for you, with your writing and verbal skills in perfect synch and your eye for details, for the minutia, second to none. You may have more contact than usual with siblings and neighbors and may be doing a lot of running around and doing errands. This transit lasts for a while; Mercury turns retro next month. More on that in the August roundup.

And finally, on the 31st, Venus enters your sign, marking one of the most romantic and creative periods for you all year. It lasts until August 26 and may prove to be financially prosperous as well. Your muse is eager to help in any way!

AT A GLANCE
July 4—Venus enters Gemini
July 5—Mercury goes into Leo
July 8—Full moon in Capricorn
July 20—Mars enters Leo
July 23—New Moon in Leo
July 25—Mercury goes into Virgo
July 31—Venus enters Cancer

August 2017
Backtracking again

Months in which eclipses occur are often emotional and tense because they urge us to evolve and move ahead in some way. They may involve some sort of lack that we suddenly recognize. Sometimes, a crisis of some kind is the only way we do that. Lunar eclipses trigger dramas—we have to confront our emotions about something and deal with them. Solar eclipses trigger external events and can usher in twice as many opportunities as an ordinary new moon. So get ready, Cancer. August could be a wild month!

The lunar eclipse in Aquarius on August 7 occurs in that area of your chart that governs other people's resources. There may be some drama surrounding your partner's income. Emotions are heightened. Jupiter forms a beneficial angle to the eclipse degree, which helps you to deal with this drama in a more balanced way and suggests that things shake out fine in the end. Keep that in mind when you're in the midst of all this.

The solar eclipse in Leo on August 21 occurs in the financial area of your chart. New financial opportunities are ushered into your life, almost as if to compensate for the issue with your partner's income that the lunar eclipse brought to light. Uranus forms an exact and beneficial angle to the eclipse degree, indicating a sudden, unexpected facet to the events.

On the 12th, Mercury turns retrograde in Virgo, the communication area of your chart. This retro lasts until September 5, when Mercury turns direct in Leo, your financial area. Reread the roundup for April, when Mercury was last retrograde and follow the general guidelines.

Since this retro occurs in your financial area, be sure to watch your money transactions—check statements, pay cash for purchases when you can and don't buy or sell stocks or make new investments. If you do have to travel, your destination may be one to which you return at a later date.

Saturn turns direct in Sagittarius on the 25th, a nice bonus for any month. You'll find that things at work will now unfold more smoothly, and you'll have a better idea about how to proceed with projects and deal with co-workers. Saturn is moving toward its appointment with Capricorn at the end of the year, a cycle that will last two and a half years and impact your partnership area. More on that in December's roundup. For now, enjoy what Saturn reveals about your daily work and health.

Venus enters Leo and your financial area on August 26 and will be there until September 19. Once Mercury turns direct on September 5, the Venus transit should help to increase your income. You may be spending more, but you'll also be earning more. It's also possible that you meet a romantic interest who shares your values.

AT A GLANCE
August 7—Lunar eclipse in Aquarius
August 12—Mercury turns retro in Virgo
August 21—Solar eclipse in Leo
August 25—Saturn turns direct in Sagittarius
August 26—Venus enters Leo

September 2017
Discernment

There's a lot going on astrologically this month, so if you were hoping for a respite from last month's eclipses, September won't be it!

On the 5th, Mercury turns direct in Leo, so get busy doing everything you postponed doing during the retrograde. Mercury will be in your financial area until September 9, when it moves into compatible earth sign Virgo once again and lights up the communication area of your chart. Your mind zips along at the speed of light during this transit, which lasts until September 29, and you're able to connect the dots so well that little escapes your attention.

Also on the 5th, Mars enters Virgo, where it will be until October 22. While Mars and Mercury travel together in this sign, you're one busy bee, writing and answering email, perhaps doing some public speaking or organizing something in your neighborhood or community.

The full moon in fellow water sign Pisces on the 6th is closely conjunct Neptune. This combination makes you sort of dreamy and imaginative. Something reaches a culmination or completion. It could be that your overseas travel plans are finalized or that you attend a workshop or seminar in an esoteric topic that interests you.

On the 19th, Venus joins Mars and Mercury in Virgo, your communication area. You may meet a romantic interest through a sibling or friend and the person may live in your neighborhood or community. With these three planets in discerning Virgo, your writing skills are top notch. This transit lasts until October 14 and should be quite pleasant for you.

On the 20th, the new moon in Virgo joins the lineup of planets in this sign! This moon should usher in new communication opportunities and perhaps a new friendship with a neighbor. You may be spending more time with your siblings or with friends who are like siblings.

Mercury enters Libra on the 29th, so between that date and October 17, there's plenty going on in your family and home life. If you have kids, your house is going to be the hotspot for other kids. Be sure to have plenty of goodies on hand and stuff to keep them occupied!

AT A GLANCE
September 5—Mercury turns direct in Leo, Mars enters Virgo
September 6—Full moon in Pisces
September 9—Mercury enters Virgo
September 19—Venus goes into Virgo
September 20—New moon in Virgo
September 29—Mercury moves into Libra

October 2017
Expansive

Another super busy month and it kicks off with a full moon in fire sign Aries on October 5. This one lights up your career area and marks the completion or culmination of a professional concern, project or goal. Pluto forms a challenging angle to this full moon, suggesting tension or a disagreement with a boss or other authority figure. Let your intuition guide you on how to handle whoever this person is.

On the 10th, Jupiter makes a significant move. It enters fellow water sign Scorpio. For the next year or so—until November 2018—you'll enjoy an expansion of your creative skills. Your muse will be up close and personal, and your creative endeavors and output may surprise you! If you and your partner have considered starting a family, it may happen during this transit. Jupiter also expands your love life and whatever you do for fun and pleasure. You might take up a new hobby or sport or enjoy some other physical outlet you haven't tried before.

On the 14th, Venus joins Mercury in Libra, and you may feel the need to beautify your home in some way—new furniture, colorful art, fresh flowers, new quilts or a whole new look. Love and romance are heightened, and it's easier to find the right balance in your relationships. This transit lasts until November 7.

Mercury enters Scorpio on the 17th, joining Jupiter in the creativity and romance section of your chart. Nice combo! Your conscious mind is focused on creative endeavors, your kids and on fun and pleasure. You may also be doing research of some sort, digging deeply into a topic that relates to a project you're working on. The intuitive component of Mercury in Scorpio is strong. Heed that inner voice. This transit ends on November 5.

The new moon in Libra on the 19th brings new opportunities related to home, family and relationships. If your house is on the market, you could get an offer. Or you find a neighborhood that would be better suited for you and your family. Someone could move in or out of your place. However this unfolds, you'll enjoy it.

On the 22nd, Mars joins Venus in Libra. This powerhouse combo indicates that a home renovation project is resumed or begun with enthusiasm and vigor. You may be updating appliances, repainting rooms or replacing furniture items. The Mars transit ends on December 9.

AT A GLANCE
October 5—Full moon in Aries
October 10—Jupiter moves into Scorpio
October 14—Venus enters Libra
October 17—Mercury enters Scorpio
October 19—New moon in Libra
October 22—Mars enters Libra

November 2017
Fun & pleasurable

Finally! You get to enjoy a month when life moves a bit more slowly and smoothly, and there aren't any precipitous ups and downs. In fact, you'll enjoy the full moon in compatible earth sign Taurus on the 4th. Your social life will start perking nonstop, and you'll see signs of it a few days on either side of the full moon. It's a great time to network and to solidify friendships.

The next day, on the 5th, Mercury enters Sagittarius, where it will be until the end of the year. Be forewarned: the last retrograde of 2017 begins next month, on December 3, and runs until December 22. So finalize travel plans now, sign contracts, keep moving ahead on whatever you're doing and be prepared to slow down on December 3.

Venus transits Scorpio from November 7 to December 1. While it's traveling with expansive Jupiter, your love life and sex life are on a definite upswing. If you meet someone during this transit, the relationship is apt to be intense and visceral. If you're already involved with someone, you and your partner rediscover why you're together. This period is one of the most romantic and creative for you all year.

On November 18, along comes the new moon in Scorpio, ushering in new creative and romantic opportunities. With this lineup in the most intuitive sign in the zodiac, your psychic antenna twitches constantly, guiding and directing you in your choices and decisions.

AT A GLANCE
November 4—Full moon in Taurus
November 5—Mercury enters Sagittarius
November 7—Venus goes into Scorpio
November 18—New moon in Scorpio

December 2017
Big Saturn shift

Wow! After a relatively restful November, December is anything but that. Take a few minutes at the beginning of the month to brainstorm with yourself about what you would like to experience and achieve in 2018. Think of this list as desires, not resolutions!

On December 1, Venus moves into fire sign Sagittarius, and things at work zip along at a frantic pace as you try to wind up projects before the year's end. A flirtation or romance with a co-worker is possible, but your intuition will guide you in this regard. If you feel emotional resistance within yourself, back off.

On the 3rd, there are two events: Mercury turns retrograde in Sagittarius and a full moon in Gemini. By now, you know the guidelines for these retros! But since this is the holiday shopping season, you might consider getting the shopping done before December 3 or after the 22nd, when Mercury turns direct again. Otherwise, you may be in the return line on December 26.

The full moon in Gemini brings something to light in your personal unconscious. Perhaps you complete a series of sessions with a therapist or finish up a communication project. Your dreams may provide insight and information, so keep paper and pen on your nightstand.

On the 9th, Mars enters Scorpio, a transit that takes you to January 26, 2018. During this period your sexuality is heightened, and you're after the absolute bottom line in everything. Your physical energy is especially good, and you should consider starting a regular exercise routine if you don't have one already.

The new moon in Sagittarius on the 18th should bring an opportunity at work, with foreign travel, publishing or higher education. Whatever it is, you'll recognize it when it lands on your doorstep!

Saturn makes a significant move on December 20. It enters Capricorn, where it will be for the next two and a half years. During this transit through your partnership area, you may encounter restrictions or limitations of some kind in both business and personal partnerships. Your partner may need more emotional support during this period. That said, Saturn's opposition to your sun teaches you discipline and responsibility and how to bolster the structures in your life. Strides that you make in your partnerships tend to have a long-lasting effect.

Mercury turns direct in Sagittarius on December 22 and on the 25th Venus joins Saturn in Capricorn. With Mercury direct, you're in good shape for the holidays and for moving into the new year. Venus in Capricorn should actually be beneficial in any partnership, but particularly in your profession. You're in the right place at the right time!

AT A GLANCE
December 1—Venus enters Sagittarius
December 3—Mercury turns retro in Sagittarius, full moon in Gemini
December 9—Mars enters Scorpio
December 18—New moon in Sagittarius
December 20—Saturn enters Capricorn
December 22—Mercury turns direct in Sagittarius
December 25—Venus enters Capricorn

Reflection

Before the new year rolls in, take some time to reflect on where you've been in 2017, what you've learned and the changes that have come about in your life. Did the year meet your expectations? Jot your notes below.

_____

_____

_____

_____

_____

Happy New Year!

Leo 2017

Your sign is ruled by the sun, so pay close attention to angles that transiting planets make to your sun sign, whether they're beneficial or challenging. All retrogrades are noted with advice about how to navigate the retrograde periods successfully.

In the monthly roundups, you'll also find all the information you need on the new and full moons for each month, the transits of other planets and the angles they make to your sun and what it could all mean for you.

For you, Leo, 2017 is about your daily work and the maintenance of your daily health, about cooperating with employees and co-workers and about the service you do for others without thought of compensation. Good deeds, in other words. You may discover new ways of doing a routine job—or find a new job or profession altogether.

January 2017
A mixed bag

Welcome to 2017! It may get off to a slow start with Mercury retrograde in Sagittarius until January 8. This Mercury retro is a hangover from 2016 and may be causing miscommunication with a romantic partner or with children. Once it's over, you can get on with the stuff you have postponed—traveling, signing contracts or moving forward with projects.

Before the retro ends, though, Venus enters Pisces, where it remains until February 3. This transit is excellent for obtaining a mortgage or loan, a break on your insurance rates or even for inheriting money—excellent, that is, after Mercury turns direct. It's also possible that you meet a romantic interest who is rather dreamy and imaginative.

January 12 features two events—a full moon in Cancer and Mercury joining Pluto in Capricorn. The full moon lights up your personal unconscious, so inner stuff may surface— issues from the past that concern your parents and family or issues you haven't resolved. Now you have the opportunity to put them to rest once and for all. Mercury linking up with Pluto is a powerful combination that keeps your conscious mind focused on work, your career and the daily maintenance of your health.

The new moon on the 28th falls in Aquarius, your partnership area. A new business opportunity may come your way—or you and a partner decide to take your relationship to the next level. On the same day, Mars enters fellow fire sign Aries. This transit, which lasts until March 9, should be a good one for you. You're physically energetic, more charismatic, and may be planning some sort of quest or adventure that excites you.

AT A GLANCE
January 3—Venus enters Pisces
January 8—Mercury retrograde ends
January 12—Full moon in Cancer, Mercury joins Pluto in Capricorn
January 28—New moon in Aquarius, Mars enters Aries

February 2017
Drama!

Months that feature eclipses are sometimes frantic, tense and emotional, particularly if the eclipse falls on or close to your sun, moon or rising. The lunar eclipse on February 10 falls at 21 degrees, Leo. This means that if you were born in mid-August, you're going to feel this eclipse quite strongly. There may be some drama that surfaces concerning a personal issue or relationship that you have to deal with quickly. This is what eclipses do—prompt us to act rapidly so that we clear out the old and make way for the new. The best way to navigate this eclipse is to take it a moment at a time!

The solar eclipse on February 26 falls in Pisces, in that section of your chart that rules shared resources. This eclipse should bring in new opportunities to delve into the esoteric, perhaps through a workshop or book that you write, and you may get a break with a mortgage or loan or on insurance. Another possibility is that your partner lands a raise.

On February 3, Venus enters fellow fire sign Aries, a major plus for you because it forms a beautiful angle to your sun. Romance may find you through an unusual venue—while you're traveling or having some sort of adventure, in a college or grad school class you're taking or even through a church or spiritual organization. Your sense of beauty is enhanced during this transit, and it's possible that a new source of income comes your way.

In March, Venus turns retro, slides back into Pisces, then returns to Aries on April 28 and remains there until June 6. So you'll get a taste of what it's all about during the first run this month. Stay tuned, Leo!

Jupiter moves retrograde in Libra from February 6 to June 9. During this period, publishing ventures may slow down and communication may be bumpier than usual. But you have an opportunity to reassess what you're doing. If you and your family have been considering a move, you may be looking at various neighborhoods to find the one that speaks to you. During a retrograde, the expansion associated with Jupiter happens mostly in an internal sense. You could be exploring various spiritual belief systems, may join online groups that stimulate this inner growth or attend workshops about the nature of consciousness. In other words, heady stuff interests you!

Mercury enters Aquarius, your opposite sign, on February 7, and you and your professional and personal partners enjoy clear communication and exchanges of ideas. Your conscious attention is focused on finding cutting edge ideas and implementing them. On February 25, Mercury moves into dreamy Pisces, and your focus shifts to your creative endeavors. You may feel torn in two directions about a project. Go with your gut, Leo. A day later, the solar eclipse discussed earlier occurs in the same sign where Mercury is.

February 3—Venus enters Aries
February 6—Jupiter turns retrograde in Libra
February 7—Mercury enters Aquarius
February 10—Lunar eclipse in Leo
February 25—Mercury enters Pisces
February 26—Solar eclipse in Pisces

March 2017
Finances & career

This month may prove to be as wild and unpredictable as February simply because there's a lot going on. It all gets off to a bumpy start on March 4, when Venus turns retrograde in Aries until April 15. Yes, this retrograde can mess up your love life, but not irreparably. Just keep disputes with your partner to a minimum. Choose your battles carefully. Some things aren't worth arguing about. Watch your spending, too. Try to pay cash for everything.

Sometimes, Venus retros involve physical discomforts and inconveniences—the heat at home or at work goes out, for instance, or the CD player or radio in your car doesn't work right. Minor stuff, but irritating.

Between March 9 and April 21, Mars transits earth sign Taurus and your career area. During this period, you're able to move steadily and inexorably toward a professional goal. You are careful in how you proceed, are mindful of presenting material in a practical, efficient manner and have the physical energy to get things done. You would benefit from a regular exercise program, too, particularly during this time when your inclination is to work twelve-hour days.

With the full moon in earth sign Virgo on March 12, your financial area is highlighted. You may have to delve into the details about your bank balance or your stock portfolio, but you're equipped to do this well with the moon in Virgo. This moon forms a beneficial angle with Pluto, so even though tensions may be high, it looks as if you come out ahead of the game.

From March 13–31, Mercury transits fellow fire sign Aries. Your conscious attention turns to a trip overseas that you may be planning or to a book you're writing or revising. You may be visiting graduate schools or submitting applications to your selected schools. You also could sign up for a workshop or seminar.

On the 27th, the new moon is in Aries, so now you've got this very nice lineup in another fire sign, all of which benefit you by forming powerful angles to your sun sign. This new moon could usher in new opportunities in publishing, overseas travel and the exploration of your spiritual beliefs. There are any number of ways these opportunities could come about—and social media may be one of the most promising.

On the 31st, Mercury enters Taurus and your career area, and for the next nine days, you make great progress professionally. Then Mercury turns retrograde. More on that in next month's roundup. But remember that you'll have another shot at Mercury's movement through Taurus after it turns direct again and enters Taurus once more.

AT A GLANCE
March 4— Venus turns retrograde in Aries
March 9—Mars enters Taurus
March 12—Full moon in Virgo
March 13—Mercury enters Aries
March 27—New moon in Aries
March 31—Mercury enters Taurus

April 2017
Dos & don'ts

April is filled with astrological events, including the second Mercury retrograde of the year. It runs from April 9 to May 3, when it turns direct in Aries and then moves into Taurus again in mid-May. Reread the section on Mercury retros in the introduction and keep those three Rs in mind: revise, review and reconsider. In addition, don't start anything new, sign any contracts, make travel plans or buy any high-end appliances or electronics. Sounds like a lot of DO NOTS, right? So what kinds of things *can* you do during a retro?

Look up old friends. Revive a project you put on a back burner. Take out an old book manuscript, go through it and see if it can be improved. Laugh frequently. Look at everything as an adventure. If, for instance, you get held up in an airport for eight hours, head out to the nearest town for a look around.

The full moon in Libra on April 11 lights up your communication sector and is closely conjunct retrograde Jupiter in Libra. You won't get as much bang for your buck as you might if Jupiter were in direct motion, but there will be expansion of some kind in your communication options.

On the 15th, Venus turns direct in Pisces, and you may hear that a mortgage or loan has been approved. Or that you're receiving a royalty check or an insurance reimbursement. Whatever the venue, unexpected money comes your way. Also, your love life should straighten out now!

Between April 21 and June 4, Mars transits air sign Gemini, a sign compatible with your own. This transit should kick start your social life in a major way. You may be spending a lot of your free time with friends and your network of acquaintances and building new alliances. Gemini is a social, communicative sign and also one that enables you to multitask. Make good use of this transit!

This month's new moon falls on the 26th, in Taurus, in your career area. New moons always mean new opportunities that often surprise you, and with this one, your professional life benefits. The opportunity could be anything—a promotion, a new job and career path, a move to a different building or a chance to become self-employed. However the opportunities unfold, Taurus confers resilience, patience, fortitude and pragmatism.

From April 28 to June 6, Venus transits Aries. You may find romance in some far-flung corner of the world, in a college or graduate school class, in a workshop or seminar or through a spiritual group. Venus forms a beneficial angle to your sun, so regardless of where and when you meet this special person, you ooze charisma and magnetism.

AT A GLANCE
April 6—Saturn turns retro in Sagittarius
April 9—Mercury retrograde in Taurus
April 11—Full moon in Libra
April 15—Venus turns direct in Pisces
April 21—Mars enters into Gemini
April 26—New moon in Taurus
April 28—Venus enters Aries

May 2017
Relaxed pace

All things considered, May is a rather calm month astrologically. Good thing, too, because the summer months are going to be incredibly busy. The best news is that early in May—on the 3rd—Mercury turns direct and joins Venus in Aries. Mercury will be in Aries until May 16. This beautiful combination indicates that your conscious mind will be focused on love, romance, the arts, your creativity or other cultures and countries. If you're a writer or in the public relations field, the ideas and words flow out of you.

May 10 features a full moon in Scorpio, the area of your chart that governs home and family. Scorpio is such an emotionally intense sign that there could be a flare-up of drama with someone at home—a teen, your partner or a parent. You should be winding up home renovation projects, and you and your family may head out for a long weekend.

Between May 16 and June 6, Mercury in Taurus transits your career area again and now professional concerns move forward at a swift clip. Here's your second chance get things done in your career.

The month nears an end with a new moon in Gemini on May 25. Look for opportunities to surface with friends—a new friend, perhaps—and for a chance to set a dream you have into motion.

May 3—Mercury turns direct in Aries
May 10—Full moon in Scorpio
May 16—Mercury enters Taurus
May 25—New moon in Gemini

June 2017
Social

In June, it may feel as if life is moving at the speed of light. But there are ways to make the most of the transits you'll experience, beginning with Mars entering Cancer on June 4. This aspect ends on July 20, when it goes into your sign, so think of its movement through Cancer as a time to plant seeds for what you would like to reap in your life next month.

While Mars is in Cancer, create space for yourself and your family. Allow your intuition to guide you toward the right people and opportunities that enable you to work behind the scenes in some capacity. Perhaps what you're looking for is a flexible schedule that allows you to work part-time from your home. It's important that you deal with anger as it surfaces rather than bottling it up. Keep to the speed limit when driving!

Circle June 6 and 9 on your calendar. On the 6th, Mercury enters Gemini, a sign it rules, and Venus enters Taurus, which it rules. On the 9th, Jupiter turns direct in Libra. The first transit forms a beneficial angle to your sun and indicates your social life picks up substantially. You'll have so many opportunities to hang out with friends, go to dinner, movies or the theater and to network that you'll have to pick and choose. You and a friend may decide to join forces and work on a communication project together. Or you may start carpooling to work or taking the kids to and from school. This transit ends on June 21.

The second transit, where Venus enters Taurus, should facilitate all career matters. You're the right person at the right time and place. You might be tapped to head up a particular project at work, your manuscript could sell or you could land a raise or promotion. Or, you might fall in love with a co-worker.

When Jupiter turns direct in Libra, life feels less dense, events flow more smoothly and relationships are easier to navigate. Since Jupiter rules publishing, this motion could bode well for you if you've submitted a manuscript for a book.

On the 18th, the full moon in fellow fire sign Sagittarius highlights one of your children, a romance or a creative project, and does so in a positive way. In one or all of these areas, events culminate and reach completion. The final plans for an international trip could fall into place.

On the summer solstice, June 21, Mercury joins Mars in Cancer. Pay closer attention to your dreams during this transit. They may hold information and insight about relationships and concerns in your life. Your conscious focus is on your family and home life and on what's happening inside of you—the emotions you feel, the thoughts you think and how your thoughts and beliefs create what you experience.

On the 23rd, the new moon in Gemini should bring in new opportunities where you can work simultaneously on different projects or with a team of like-minded individuals. As a Leo you rarely lack for things to say, but with this new moon, your verbal skills are heightened.

AT A GLANCE
June 4—Mars enters Cancer
June 6—Mercury enters Gemini, Venus enters Taurus
June 9—Full moon in Sagittarius, Jupiter turns direct in Libra
June 21—Mercury moves into Cancer
June 23—New moon in Cancer

July 2017
Bonus month

If you live in the U.S. and you've got something special planned for July 4 festivities, then Venus entering Gemini on that date will add to the fun. Between July 4 and 31, your social life may unfold like a novel filled with romance, adventure and synchronous encounters. Your networking—virtual and otherwise—could pay off in unexpected ways. If a new romantic interest enters your life, it may be someone you meet through friends or through one of your networks of acquaintances.

Mercury transits Leo from July 5 to 25, another bonus for you this month. Your self-confidence is boosted by both the Mercury and Venus transits, and your gift of gab ensures that you'll be able to converse with anyone about virtually anything. If you're involved in a committed relationship, then you and your partner should enjoy a period in which you're socializing frequently and enjoying it.

The full moon in Capricorn on July 8 is closely conjunct Pluto and highlights a work issue or concern. If you're on deadline for a project, you make the deadline and reap the applause of bosses and co-workers. Pluto in Capricorn is a lengthy transit and is transforming your daily work routine from the bottom up. The transformation has its challenges, but by the time this planet enters Aquarius in 2024, your daily work routine will look entirely different than it does now.

Mars enters your sign on July 20, joining Mercury there, and forms a beneficial angle to Venus. Wow. You are now a powerhouse of energy and drive, Leo. No goal is too lofty to reach, no horizon is too distant to travel toward. Infused with clarity about what you want, you move forward with confidence and resolve.

Then on the 23rd, along comes the new moon in your sign. This moon happens just once a year and sets the tone for the next twelve months. Several days before, focus on what you would like to achieve and experience during the next twelve months. Make a list. Post it where you'll see it often. Back each desire with emotion and visualization. Then let the universe do its job in granting your desires.

On July 25, Mercury enters Virgo and your financial area, where it will be for a quite a while because of next month's retrograde, which begins on August 12. While Mercury is in direct motion, your conscious focus is on what you earn and spend. If you need to set up a budget, then this period is the perfect time to do it. Between July 31 and August 26, Venus transits Cancer. Any relationship that begins during this transit may be kept under wraps for some reason, but only until Venus enters your sign next month. Things with your family and in your home life unfold smoothly.

AT A GLANCE
July 4—Venus enters Gemini
July 5—Mercury goes into Leo
July 8—Full moon in Capricorn
July 20—Mars enters Leo
July 23—New moon in Leo
July 25—Mercury goes into Virgo
July 31—Venus enters Cancer

August 2017
Exciting

Think back to the February eclipses. How did they impact your life? What specific events occurred? Did you evolve in some way? August may be similar in texture and tone because there's a lunar eclipse in Aquarius, your opposite sign, on August 7 and a solar eclipse in your sign on August 21.

Let's look first at the lunar eclipse. Drama may surface that involves a partnership—business or professional. Thanks to warrior Mars in your sign, you may feel the need to defend yourself or your beliefs or behavior. The best way to navigate the drama is to say your piece and be done with it. Don't dwell on how right you may be and how wrong the other person is. Fortunately, Jupiter in Libra forms a beneficial angle to the eclipse degree, so it looks as if things shake out fine in the end.

The solar eclipse in Leo on the 21st is a powerhouse lineup—sun, moon and Mars in your sign—and Uranus forming a beneficial angle to the eclipse degree. There will be elements of surprise in this eclipse—the job offer that comes out of the blue, a marriage proposal, an unexpected move or an opportunity for travel. No telling how the specifics will pan out. However, new opportunities land on your doorstep, and your challenge is to pick and choose the opportunity that suits you best.

On the 12th, Mercury turns retrograde in Virgo, your financial area. The retro lasts until September 5. During this period, be sure to keep a close eye on your finances. Check and re-check bank balances. Watch your spending and pay cash when you can. And, of course, follow the three Rs—revise, review and reconsider—and only sign contracts before and after the retrograde dates.

Saturn turns direct in fellow fire sign Sagittarius on August 25, and that will be cause for celebration. Things on the creative front finally start moving forward again. Your love life finds a more solid structure—you and your romantic interest may decide to become exclusive or to move in together. Between August 26 and September 19, Venus transits your sign and you're now in one of the most romantic and creative periods all year. Everything hums along at a perfect pitch—your love life, your creative drive, your relationship with your children. You're imbued with self-confidence and charisma, and other people are attracted to your energy and presence.

AT A GLANCE
August 7—Lunar eclipse in Aquarius
August 12—Mercury turns retro in Virgo
August 21—Solar eclipse in Leo
August 25—Saturn turns direct in Sagittarius
August 26—Venus enters Leo

September 2017
$, $, $

It's another crowded month astrologically and things get off to a fine start when Mercury turns direct in the final degrees of your sign, on September 5. Between September 9 and 29, Mercury transits Virgo, then slips into Libra. During the transit through Virgo, your finances will once again be your focus. But this time, with Mercury in direct motion, your mind will be clearer, and you'll know how to proceed to increase your income. You'll be able to connect all the dots.

Also on the 5th, Mars joins Mercury in Virgo, endowing you with all the physical energy and forward movement you need to achieve your financial goals. This transit lasts until October 22. During this time, pay close attention to your exercise routine and nutrition. You may experiment with various diets or nutritional programs, could sign up for yoga or Pilates classes and may do research on vitamins and minerals.

The full moon in Pisces on the 6th is conjunct Neptune, so there may be some confusion about finances you share with someone else—a spouse, parent or child. For creative work, this combination is great and enables you to intuitively find what you need. You may be nearing completion of a project.

Between September 19 and October 4, Venus transits Virgo and your financial sector. This transit should boost your income, but you may be spending more as well. If a romance begins during this transit, you'll connect the dots on this individual quickly. Follow your intuition. If the relationship doesn't feel right, back out.

The new moon in Virgo on the 20th should usher in new financial opportunities. With Venus and Mars also in this sign now, you'll be in good shape to make things happen, to seize the opportunity and run with it.

Mercury enters Libra on the 29th and your communication skills are highlighted. You can negotiate just about anything during this transit—which lasts until October 17—a truce, a peace agreement or a deal!

AT A GLANCE
September 5—Mercury turns direct in Leo, Mars enters Virgo
September 6—Full moon in Pisces
September 9—Mercury enters Virgo
September 19—Venus goes into Virgo
September 20—New moon in Virgo
September 29—Mercury moves into Libra

October 2017
Opportunities abound

October is another crowded month astrologically and the action begins with the full moon in Aries on the 5th. This moon lights up the long distance travel sector of your chart and may have you hungering for a trip to some distant spot. It also spotlights higher education, publishing, foreign cultures and people and your worldview. Since the moon forms a beneficial angle to your sun, the events that unfold on October 5, and for several days on either side of that day, should be positive.

Jupiter makes a major shift on the 10th, moving from Libra into Scorpio until November 2018. During this thirteen-month transit, you may move to a larger home or property or may expand your existing home. Your family may grow. There could be a birth or perhaps an adult child, relative or parent moves in. Jupiter is now forming a challenging angle to your sun, and its expansion could mean more work and responsibility for you in some area of your life. But this won't be a problem for you, Leo. You would rather have too much to do than too little.

Between October 14 and November 7, Venus moves through compatible air sign Libra and facilitates all your communication, eases any trouble you've had with siblings and neighbors, and generally makes life more pleasant. Your aesthetic sense increases during this transit, and you may buy art or a musical instrument and take music lessons of some type. Romance could be kindled with someone in your neighborhood.

Mercury joins Jupiter in Scorpio on the 17th, a transit that lasts until November 5 and urges you to find the absolute bottom line in everything you experience. This transit favors research, particularly into esoteric topics. In fact, you may launch some sort of spiritual quest during this transit that endures long after Mercury has moved on.

The new moon in Libra on October 19 and Mars joining Venus in the sign on October 22 practically guarantees a romantic liaison of some kind. You may find, too, that money arrives from unexpected sources. If you have a book manuscript out with an agent or publisher, the new moon could bring the sale you've been waiting for. Since Leo is the sign of the actor, this new moon and the other lineup of planets in Libra could usher in acting gigs that thrill you.

AT A GLANCE
October 5—Full moon in Aries
October 10—Jupiter moves into Scorpio
October 14—Venus enters Libra
October 17—Mercury enters Scorpio
October 19—New moon in Libra
October 22—Mars enters Libra

November 2017
Harvest

Compared to the last several months, November is a breeze. Good thing, too, because December may make you feel like you're living your life in fast forward.

The full moon in Taurus on November 4 should bring a professional project to completion. This moon forms a wide, beneficial angle to Pluto in Capricorn, suggesting that you've done the hard work and now reap the rewards.

On November 5, Mercury enters fellow fire sign, Sagittarius, a terrific transit for you–until next month, when the trickster planet turns retrograde, for the last time this year. The dates: December 3–22. Be sure to do your holiday shopping on either side of those dates! While Mercury is moving in direct motion through Sadge, your muse is whispering in your ear, feeding you all kinds of creative ideas. You brainstorm with friends and family and may travel to find information that you need.

On the 7th, Venus joins Jupiter in Scorpio, a very nice partnership that turns up the heat in your love life and may prompt you to change your appearance in some way—new clothes, a new hairstyle or a new look! You may also beautify your home in some way or spend more money than unusual on your house. If your home is for sale, you could get an offer during this transit, which ends December 1.

The new moon in Scorpio on the 18th joins Venus and Jupiter in that sign and ushers in new opportunities in romance, in finances and in your home/family. November 18 would be an ideal day to close a deal on your new home.

November 4—Full moon in Taurus
November 5—Mercury enters Sagittarius
November 7—Venus goes into Scorpio
November 18—New moon in Scorpio

December 2017
Creative frenzy

You may feel like you're running an endless marathon for much of December. Even during the Mercury retro period from December 3 to 22, there's a lot of excess energy around you. Mercury's retro through Sadge slows down your creative production, but you can still follow the three Rs—revise, review and reconsider—and get a lot done. On the same day that Mercury turns retro, there's a full moon in Gemini that pushes your social life into a distinct uptick.

Venus transits Sagittarius from December 1 to 25, marking one of the most romantic and creative periods for you all year. In spite of the Mercury retro, your love life feels wonderful, and your muse is at your beck and call. It would be wise to keep a notepad or your tablet at your fingertips to jot down ideas.

On the 9th, Mars joins Jupiter in Scorpio, and the energy at home intensifies. Mars is a butt-kicker and you swing into action—completing projects before the holidays, meeting deadlines and getting stuff done. Then, on the 18th, the new moon in Sagittarius comes along, joining Mercury retro in the romance and creativity section of your chart. New opportunities should surface in this area. Just don't sign any contracts until after Mercury turns direct on December 22.

Saturn enters Capricorn on the 20th, where it will be for the next two and a half years. Saturn governs structures, limitations and responsibilities and discipline. During its transit, the responsibilities in your daily work life will multiply, and you'll learn how to navigate your work more successfully. Saturn rules Capricorn, so it functions well here and shores up the existing structures and foundations in your life.

Venus joins Saturn in Capricorn on the 25th, a transit that takes you into the new year. This combination could signal that you and a partner take your relationship to the next level.

AT A GLANCE
December 1—Venus enters Sagittarius
December 3—Mercury turns retro in Sagittarius, full moon in Gemini
December 9—Mars enters Scorpio
December 18—New moon in Sagittarius
December 20—Saturn enters Capricorn
December 22—Mercury turns direct in Sagittarius
December 25—Venus enters Capricorn

Reflection

As 2017 winds down, take a few minutes to think about what you did, achieved and felt. Were your expectations met? Did your life change in a major way? What would you change or do differently?

_____

_____

_____

_____

_____

Happy New Year!

Virgo 2017

Your sign, like Gemini, is ruled by Mercury. Pay close attention to what that planet is doing each month—whether it's retrograde, the angle it's making to your sun sign and when it changes signs.

In the monthly roundups, you'll also find information on the transits of other planets, the new and full moons, eclipses and everything else you need to know to navigate each month successfully.

For you, 2017 is about delving into realms that others aren't even aware exist. You investigate the unknown, the hidden, become a seeker of truth—your own truth, discovered through your own efforts and not because someone else has defined it. Your powers of observation and discernment increase this year, and your spirituality deepens.

January 2017
Adjustment

Welcome to 2017! January has a lot of astrological activity going on, and that means you're going to be busy. But first, let's talk about the Mercury retrograde in Sagittarius, a hangover from 2016 that may slow things down a bit until January 8, when it turns direct again.

Reread the Mercury retrograde section in the introduction (page 20) for guidelines on how to deal with it. Since this retro occurs in the family/home sector of your chart, be sure you communicate clearly with everyone in your personal environment because the potential for misunderstandings is greater during this period. If your home is on the market, don't finalize any deals until after January 8 when Mercury turns direct. If you have to travel during the first eight days of the month, try to be as flexible as possible; your itinerary probably will change without warning.

Between January 3 and February 3, Venus moves through Pisces and the partnership sector of your chart. You and your partner may decide to move in together, get engaged or married or perhaps start a family. You strike a nice balance now and enjoy a beautiful intuitive connection. In business, you meet the ideal business partner, the person whose support and insight enable you to strike out on your own.

January 12 features two astrological events—a full moon in compatible water sign Cancer and Mercury joining Pluto in fellow earth sign Capricorn, forming beneficial angles to your sun sign. The full moon highlights your network of friends and acquaintances and indicates that your social life picks up significantly. Because Cancer is involved, there may be news about a family member or a home renovation project may be completed.

Mercury and Pluto travel together until February 7. During this period, your conscious mind is crystal clear, focused and grounded, and you know exactly how to tackle a creative project. In romance, you know precisely what you're looking for and won't settle for less.

The 28th also features two events—a new moon in Aquarius, and Mars enters Aries. The new moon brings in opportunities in your daily work life and in the way you maintain your daily health. You may land a promotion and a raise, move to a new, larger office or head up a team of your co-workers. It's an ideal time to start a diet, a new nutritional program or to join a gym. Mars in Aries is so energetic and triggers such forward momentum that you'll need a way to burn off excess energy. If a gym isn't your thing, then find some other physical outlet that suits you.

During the Mars transit, which lasts until March 9, you may apply for and get a mortgage or loan, or your partner may be working longer hours for extra cash. You may feel restless during this transit and could be looking for ways to change certain facets of your life.

AT A GLANCE
January 3—Venus enters Pisces
January 8—Mercury retrograde ends
January 12—Full moon in Cancer, Mercury joins Pluto in Capricorn
January 28—New moon in Aquarius, Mars enters Aries

February 2017
Brainstorm

Months that feature eclipses can be wildly emotional and tense. Quite often, something comes to a head that has to be dealt with immediately.

February 10 features a lunar eclipse in Leo, in that area of your chart that concerns institutions and the personal unconscious. Issues you haven't resolved may surface today or for several days on either side of the eclipse. It's likely that some sort of drama ensues and you have to act quickly to deal with whatever this is. Uranus forms a beneficial angle to the eclipse degree, suggesting that whatever is triggered seems to come out of the blue but is ultimately positive for you.

The solar eclipse in Pisces on February 26 ushers in new partnerships—personal or business. Neptune forms a close, beneficial angle to the eclipse degree, so the opportunities could deal with some facet of the arts, music, acting or writing. Heightened creativity is a given.

Now that we've talked about the eclipse, what else is happening in February? Good things, actually. On February 3, Venus enters Aries, joining both Uranus and Mars in that sign. The energy of Venus and Mars traveling together in the area of shared resources could indicate a romance that is adventurous and passionate, where things unfold quickly. Before this transit is done, the two of you may be living together. That kind of speed! Next month, however, Venus turns retrograde, so things could slow down. Venus enters Taurus on June 6. More on that transit in the June roundup.

Between February 6 and June 9, Jupiter is retrograde in Libra, the financial area of your chart. If you're self-employed, this retro may slow down your earnings somewhat. But you now have the opportunity to think about how you earn your daily bread. Do you enjoy your work? Your profession? If not, what would you enjoy doing? What steps can you take to start doing what you enjoy and earning money at it?

Between February 7 and 25, Mercury moves through Aquarius and your daily work area. You've got plenty of cutting edge ideas during this transit, so be sure to record them and brainstorm with co-workers about which ones might be useful. You may be socializing more with co-workers now or with people you meet through a group to which you belong. You might experiment with various nutritional and exercise programs until you find one that suits you.

From February 25 to March 13, Mercury transits Pisces, and your focus turns to partnerships, perhaps a partnership that is inherently creative. You and this partner may team up for a particular project—a book, a screenplay, an art exhibit or a documentary.

February 3—Venus enters Aries
February 6—Jupiter turns retrograde in Libra
February 7—Mercury enters Aquarius
February 10—Lunar eclipse in Leo
February 25—Mercury enters Pisces
February 26—Solar eclipse in Pisces

March 2017
Getting stuff done

The transits in March will be more to your liking, Virgo, as planets enter signs that are compatible with yours. But first, let's take a look at the Venus retrograde in Aries that begins on March 4 and ends on April 15. A romance may slow down somewhat, or you may be reconsidering the relationship. Don't make hasty decisions, however. Wait until after Venus turns direct. There are other possible repercussions of this retro: a mortgage or loan doesn't come through, errors in your bank statements or your insurance gets messed up. Double check everything concerning finances.

Between March 9 and April 21, Mars moves through fellow earth sign Taurus and forms a beneficial angle to your sun. You'll enjoy this transit. You've got plenty of physical energy, and you are able to move forward with publishing projects or plans for an overseas trip, or you may sign up for a workshop or conference that features forward-thinking presenters. Mars in Taurus is an excellent transit for joining a gym—and actually using it!

On the 12th, the full moon in your sign forms a beneficial angle to powerful Pluto. You're completing projects and tying up loose ends, and Pluto has your back. You're in the power seat. There could be news of a personal nature that delights you.

Between March 13 and 31, Mercury joins retrograde Venus in Aries. This transit is like an idea generator for you. Your conscious focus flits from one topic to another, searching for this bit of information or that bit. Then you're able to connect these disparate dots and create a coherent picture. You're better able to figure out if your current relationship is the one for you.

The 27th brings a new moon in Aries and new financial opportunities. Your partner could get a raise, your insurance rates drop or your mortgage is approved. You could also inherit money or receive a rebate you hadn't expected. You feel more adventurous, with a deep need for freedom right now.

Finally, on March 31, Mercury joins Mars in Taurus. Until June 6, your conscious mind is grounded and focused on tasks, and you move steadily forward in all your endeavors.

March 4— Venus turns retrograde in Aries
March 9—Mars enters Taurus
March 12—Full moon in Virgo
March 13—Mercury enters Aries
March 27—New moon in Aries
March 31—Mercury enters Taurus

April 2017
Reconsidering

If it's spring where you live, you'll want to spend time outside this month and the various transits give you plenty of opportunities to do just that.

Between April 6 and August 25, Saturn moves retrograde in the home/family section of your chart. Some of your home improvement projects may slow down or stall and that gives you the perfect excuse to work outside, preparing soil for a garden and selecting what you would like to grow. This retrograde makes it easier for you to take a deeper look at your family structure. If you're estranged from a family member, how can you mend the rift?

April 9 to May 3 marks the second Mercury retro of 2015. Mercury turns retro in Taurus, so it's time to reconsider, revise and review. One area you may be reviewing is your spirituality. Are you on a path that feels right for you in terms of your spiritual beliefs? You may explore various belief systems during this retro period—through books, online groups or even by taking classes or workshops.

The full moon in Libra on April 11 highlights your finances—what you earn and spend, how to increase your income and whether you should establish a budget, ask for a raise or look for other ways to earn money. Thanks to a beneficial angle from Jupiter retrograde, it looks as though you find the answers you need. Any news you hear should be positive.

Venus turns direct in Pisces and your partnership area on April 15, and on the 28th, it enters Aries again. Look back at the January roundup, when Venus was last in Pisces, to see what you can expect. You may find the ideal business partner who understands your vision for what you'd like to do and helps you to launch your own business. Once Venus enters Aries again, you may experience some of the same things you did back in February and early March, when Venus was last in Aries.

Mars enters Gemini and your career area on April 21. Between then and June 4, you pour your energy into professional matters. You network, may do some pubic speaking and also may be doing a lot of writing related to your career. In fact, if you're a professional writer or speaker, this transit is perfect!

The new moon in Taurus on the 26th should be very much to your liking. It ushers in opportunities in the areas of publishing, higher education, foreign travel and your worldview. In other words, Virgo, whole new vistas open up with this new moon. All that's required of you is to seize the opportunities as they surface.

AT A GLANCE
April 6—Saturn turns retro in Sagittarius
April 9—Mercury retrograde in Taurus
April 11—Full moon in Libra
April 15—Venus turns direct in Pisces
April 21—Mars enters into Gemini
April 26—New moon in Taurus
April 28—Venus enters Aries

May 2017
Career surprises

May is calmer than April, and there could be some significant career surprises surfacing!

Mercury turns direct in Aries on May 3, always a cause for celebration. Pack your bags and hit the road, Virgo. But before you leave town, be sure to sign contracts and finish up whatever you put on the back burner during the retrograde. Your mortgage or loan should be approved now, so be sure to take care of that before you leave, too. With Mars still in your career area, it would be wise to combine business with pleasure on your trip.

The full moon on May 10 is in compatible water sign Scorpio and forms a beneficial angle to Pluto. This moon highlights your neighborhood and community, siblings and communication. Whatever form your communication takes today, it's powerful and transformative. You may be completing a book or other project and are pleased with the results. There's a bottom line quality to the Scorpio moon that enables you to see through masks and camouflage in the people around you.

Between May 16 and June 6, Mercury transits fellow earth sign Taurus. This transit is ideal for engaging in an activity that requires grounding, steady work, reliability and tenacity. If you're a healer, for instance, then the transit strengthens your ability to transmute and transmit energy and to effectively communicate what you're doing and why.

The new moon in Gemini on May 25 brings a new opportunity in your career—or several!— or in the way you communicate and network. You might be promoted, get a raise or even be offered a new job with better pay and benefits. Mars is still in your career area, too, so there's a lot of forward motion and energy being poured into professional matters now.

May 3—Mercury turns direct in Aries
May 10—Full moon in Scorpio
May 16—Mercury enters Taurus
May 25—New moon in Gemini

June 2017
Busy & positive

This month is fast-paced, so you may want to slip on your magical running shoes, Virgo, in order to keep up!

Mars enters Cancer on June 4, forming a beneficial angle to your sun. Watch what happens to your social life between now and July 20. You'll have your choice of things to do, people to hang with, places to go. You'll have opportunities to achieve your wishes and dreams, perhaps through helpful friends and acquaintances and/or supportive family members.

June 6 and 9 feature three astrological events. On the 6th, Mercury enters Gemini, a sign it rules, and Venus enters Taurus, which it rules. On the 9th, Jupiter turns direct in Libra. The Mercury transit lasts until June 21 and focuses your attention on your career. You've got the gift of gab now, Virgo, and may be doing a lot of talking at meetings and gatherings with co-workers. You may be asked to blog about your company's products or services. If you're self-employed, then you'll be doing more self-promotion.

The Venus transit through Taurus lasts until July 4 and should be very much to your liking. Romance may find you while you're traveling overseas or taking a workshop or class. Synchronicity may bring about the encounter. Before this transit begins, get into the habit of waking each morning and saying, "Something amazingly awesome is going to happen to me today." This proclamation is how author Pam Grout, *E-Cubed*, starts her morning and she says it has "revolutionized" her life. You may also earn money through publishing—magazine articles, a book or travel pieces.

Jupiter turning direct in Libra—in your financial area—suggests that your earnings could expand now that Jupiter's energy is functioning at full tilt. You may take a second job or sell something you've written or created. One way or another, expansion is the name of this game.

The full moon in Sagittarius on June 9 joins Saturn in the home/domestic area of your chart. If your house has been on the market, then this full moon could bring in a serious offer. Or, you find a house that would suit your family better than your current home. It's possible that you've been shouldering more than your share of responsibility lately, but have kept silent about it. The Sagittarius full moon now makes the situation impossible to ignore. You feel a powerful need for freedom.

Between June 21 and July 5, Mercury joins Mars in Cancer. This duo traveling together indicates you're particularly good at investigating and researching now, and may be interviewing people about a specific topic. You act on your decisions and won't make a wrong move unless you ignore your intuition, which is especially strong with two planets in water sign Cancer.

The 23rd features a new moon in Cancer, another indicator of your deepening intuition. You have opportunities to meet new people and make new friends with this moon, and in some way, shape or form, you're able to move closer to achieving a dream or desire. Pretty cool way to end the month, right?

AT A GLANCE
June 4—Mars enters Cancer
June 6—Mercury enters Gemini, Venus enters Taurus
June 9—Full moon in Sagittarius, Jupiter turns direct in Libra
June 21—Mercury moves into Cancer
June 23—New moon in Cancer

July 2017
Creative & optimistic

If you think May and June were busy, then July may bowl you over!

Between July 4 and 31, Venus transits Gemini and your career area. Sweet! Now you can see how your hard work these past few months pays off. You make a sale, get a promotion or raise, sell your novel or screenplay…. You get the idea. Venus facilitates your professional life. You're in the right place at the right time.

If you're single, this transit could signal a flirtation or romance with someone you meet through your profession or through your network of friends and acquaintances.

On July 5, Mercury enters Leo, where it will be until the 25th. Think of this transit as the time to resolve inner issues that surface so that when Mercury enters your sign, your mind isn't cluttered with fear-based thinking, doubts or resistance.

The full moon in Capricorn on July 8 is closely conjunct Pluto in the creativity and romance section of your chart. This powerful combination highlights a creative project you're close to completing, and you're pleased with it and can readily defend any critiques that other people provide. If you have kids, you're completely in the flow with them. There's a strong give-and-take in your relationships with them.

From July 20 to September 5, Mars moves through fire sign Leo, and for the five days it's traveling with Mercury, you're able to delve deeply into your own psyche, clearing out the old to make way for the new. The process is important because when Mars transits your sign from September 5 to October 22, it will be a powerful, active time, and you'll be able to move forward with all your endeavors.

The new moon in Leo on July 23 indicates that you may have an opportunity to work behind the scenes in some capacity and to shine at what you do. With next month's new moon in your sign, Virgo, you're going to be primed and ready for the big time!

From July 25 to September 29, Mercury transits your sign. The transit is lengthy because for part of that time, Mercury will be retrograde in your sign—August 12 to September 5. We'll talk more about this in the August roundup.

On the 31st, Venus enters Cancer and now your social life is about as good as it gets. Love and romance are possible with someone you meet through friends and acquaintances. Even if you experience a moodiness at times, you generally are happier and more optimistic.

AT A GLANCE
July 4—Venus enters Gemini
July 5—Mercury goes into Leo
July 8—Full moon in Capricorn
July 20—Mars enters Leo
July 23—New moon in Leo
July 25—Mercury goes into Virgo
July 31—Venus enters Cancer

August 2017
Strut your stuff

By now, you understand the nature of eclipses, that they often make a month feel frenzied, tense and infused with a sense of urgency. This emotional texture is because eclipses highlight a relationship, situation or an issue that demands immediate attention. So let's take a look at this month's eclipses.

Lunar eclipses deal with internal events. Usually, one of our buttons is pushed. The lunar eclipse on August 7 occurs in Aquarius, in the daily work routine area of your chart. It's possible that a remark or action by an employee or co-worker sets you off. Or a sudden, unexpected change in your work schedule could do it. Fortunately, Jupiter in Libra forms a beneficial angle to the eclipse degree, so things aren't as dire as they initially seem.

The solar eclipse in Leo on August 21 should be a humdinger. It ushers in new opportunities for you to strut your stuff, Virgo. You may have an opportunity to work behind the scenes in some way, doing something you enjoy. Mars is within four degrees of the eclipse degree, indicating that an enormous amount of energy and drive lies behind these opportunities. In addition, Uranus forms an exact and beneficial angle to the eclipse degree, suggesting that the opportunities are sudden and unexpected.

On August 12, Mercury turns retrograde in your sign. Yes, it's a big ouch that doesn't end until September 5. Reread the roundup for April about the general guidelines to follow during a Mercury retrograde. The rule of the three Rs is especially important—revise, review and reconsider. This retro actually gives you time to think about your various projects, relationships and goals and to readjust as needed. People you haven't seen in a long time may resurface in your life.

Saturn turns direct in Sagittarius on August 25, a major plus for your home and family life. It will be much easier now to move forward with home improvements and international travel plans. Any limitations and restrictions you've experienced these past months should ease up considerably.

On the 26th, Venus enters Leo, where it will be until September 19. This transit is beneficial for any work you're doing behind the scenes or that involve institutions like hospitals, prisons, nursing homes or hospice work. Because Leo is such a gregarious sign, you may be out and about a lot, socializing with friends. If a romance is kindled during this transit, there's apt to be an element of secrecy about it. You're seeding things during this transit, getting ready for when Venus enters your sign next month, one of the most romantic and creative times for you all year.

AT A GLANCE
August 7—Lunar eclipse in Aquarius
August 12—Mercury turns retro in Virgo
August 21—Solar eclipse in Leo
August 25—Saturn turns direct in Sagittarius
August 26—Venus enters Leo

September 2017
5-star month

It's another busy month, and September may be one of the best times for you all year. Your ruler, Mercury, turns direct in Leo on September 5 and four days later enters your sign, where it will be until September 29. Perfect. During this period, you feel very much in tune with yourself, your verbal skills are in top shape and your mind hums along at a perfect pitch. However, also on the 5th, Mars enters your sign, and now you're a powerhouse of mental and physical energy. Consider dusting off that book or screenplay you started and dive back into it. Tackle any creative project that interests you and move forward with it.

All this action is followed on the 6th by a full moon in Pisces, in your partnership area. You and your partner may want to spend this evening having a romantic dinner, or even get away for a couple of days to explore an area you haven't visited before. Because Neptune is conjunct this full moon, there's a dreamy, almost surreal quality to it that not only heightens romance and love, but is excellent for creative work.

Circle the 19th. Venus enters your sign and will be there until October 14. These weeks will be among the most romantic and creative for you all year. The only competitor for that slot is when Venus enters the romance and creativity section of your chart on December 25 and takes you into the new year. In other words, Virgo, from now into January 2018, you should be in an excellent position in your life to do just about anything you desire.

As if this isn't enough, the new moon in your sign is on the 20th. This one sets the tone for the next year, so prepare for it several days ahead of time. Make a wish list of what you would like to experience and achieve over the course of the next twelve months. Post it where you'll see it often. On the day of the new moon, perform some small ritual—it can be anything— that illustrates your openness to the universe's abundance.

Mercury enters Libra and your financial area on the 29th, and your conscious focus turns to money—what you earn, what you spend and how to earn more. You may take a more balanced approach to your finances.

AT A GLANCE
September 5—Mercury turns direct in Leo, Mars enters Virgo
September 6—Full moon in Pisces
September 9—Mercury enters Virgo
September 19—Venus goes into Virgo
September 20—New moon in Virgo
September 29—Mercury moves into Libra

October 2017
Your $ month

It looks as if October could be your money month, particularly from mid-month forward, with two planets and a new moon in your financial area. But don't go on a shopping spree until the money is in your hands!

The full moon in Aries on October 5 highlights resources you share with others—parents, a spouse, a child or even a roommate. Although the moon isn't conjunct Uranus, the planet of sudden surprises is also in Aries, so something unforeseen may come your way. If you're refinancing your home, for instance, then a deal could be finalized today or at some point during the days on either side of the full moon.

October 10 features a biggie—Jupiter enters Scorpio, forming a beneficial angle to your sun sign, and will be there until November of next year. During this transit, your knowledge is expanded in some way, and you learn new skills more easily. If you're in business, your sales increase, and you may hire more employees. Expansion is the name of Jupiter's game. Your communication skills are sharp, your ideas are well-received and neighbors are friendlier and more helpful than they have been in the past. If you're a writer, this transit should help your book, stories, articles or novel find a publisher.

On the 14th, Venus enters Libra, where it will be until November 7. You may be spending more on luxury items, but you're also earning more. The additional income could come from a raise, a second job or from a painting you've done or a book you've written. Whatever the source, the additional income is welcome!

Mercury joins Jupiter in Scorpio on the 17th. With these two planets traveling together, your conscious mind is deeply intuitive. This partnership is excellent for research, particularly into esoteric topics, and confers insight into the nature of reality and consciousness. This transit lasts until November 5.

The new moon in Libra on October 19 occurs in your financial area. This should bring in a new source of income and opportunities to express yourself creatively through art, music or the written word. Three days later, on the 22nd, Mars joins Venus in Libra. With these two planets traveling together so soon after a new moon, romance and love are knocking softly at your door. The Mars transit, which lasts until December 9, moves you steadily forward in your new income-earning opportunity.

AT A GLANCE
October 5—Full moon in Aries
October 10—Jupiter moves into Scorpio
October 14—Venus enters Libra
October 17—Mercury enters Scorpio
October 19—New moon in Libra
October 22—Mars enters Libra

November 2017
Plan ahead

This month is relatively calm even with the Thanksgiving holidays coming up in the U.S. Be forewarned, though, that the last Mercury retro of the year runs from December 3 to 22, which may put a major crimp in your holiday shopping. Try to get your shopping done early this year so you don't end up standing in the return line on December 26!

The full moon in Taurus on November 4 highlights international travel, foreign cultures and people, higher education and spirituality. You might attend a workshop or seminar, sign up for a graduate school or an adult education course, or you may be traveling to some far-flung port! If so, there may be an element of a quest in this trip, where you're seeking specific information or experiences.

From November 5 to January 11, 2018, Mercury transits Sagittarius and the domestic area of your chart. The transit is long because of the Mercury retro. If you're planning on going away for the holidays, make your plans now. If visitors are coming to your place for the holidays, make sure your preparations are done before December 3. In other words, Virgo, hustle now. If you and your family are traveling, choose a FUN spot that everyone will enjoy.

On the 7th, Venus joins Jupiter in Scorpio. Your sexuality is heightened, love and romance are in the air and you're feeling exceptionally good about yourself and where you are in your life. If you're in a relationship when this transit begins, you and your partner rediscover all the reasons you're together. If you're not in a relationship when this transit begins, you may well be by the time it ends! This combination of planets also favors any kind of creative work.

With the new moon in Scorpio on the 18th, you may find the perfect neighborhood in which to live—even if you aren't actually looking! A new writing or speaking gig is also a possibility. With the various combinations of planets in Scorpio now—a water sign that's compatible with your sun sign—you're in a comfortable spot in life. Enjoy it!

AT A GLANCE
November 4—Full moon in Taurus
November 5—Mercury enters Sagittarius
November 7—Venus goes into Scorpio
November 18—New moon in Scorpio

December 2017
Preparations

As you enter the last month of the year, things are lined up nicely for you. Hopefully, your holiday shopping is completed, and you're prepared for the Mercury retrograde that begins on December 3. But before that arrives, Venus switches signs on December 1 and enters Sagittarius. It will be there until December 25. During this period, things at home should be quite pleasant and pleasing. You and your partner may be involved in a publishing venture that you're doing from your home or are immersing yourselves in some type of social media, perhaps for a publicity campaign.

Okay, then along comes the Mercury retro on the 3rd, in Sagittarius, right where Venus is, and a full moon in Gemini, too. Follow the usual rules and DO NOTS during this retro period, and you'll get through it fine. If you have appointments to keep, be sure to give yourself extra time just in case... well, in case Mercury the trickster tosses a curve ball your way!

The full moon in Gemini in your career area signals the completion or culmination of something you've been working on, and what perfect timing! Once the project is done, you won't have to take work home with you over the holidays. You may be socializing more on and around this full moon—office parties, dinners with friends, the theater or movies.

On the 9th, Mars joins Jupiter in Scorpio, and now you're a powerhouse whose goal is *to get things done!* Mars co-rules Scorpio and functions well in this sign. You have a kind of bottom line attitude during this transit, which lasts until January 26, 2018, and are able to delve deeply into anything you research or undertake.

The new moon in Sagittarius on the 18th ushers in new opportunities in publishing, foreign travel and on the domestic front. If you and your partner don't have kids yet, but have been considering it, then there could be some wonderful news. It's also possible that someone moves into or out of your home.

Saturn makes a major move on the 20th and enters fellow earth sign Capricorn forming a powerful angle to your sun sign. During this two-and-a-half-year transit, your creative endeavors are right on target. You have a solid foundation on which to build and the universe has your back, Virgo! Does it get any better than this? Two days later, Mercury turns direct and suddenly, the entire world seems brighter, lovelier and more fun!

On Christmas day, Venus joins Saturn in Capricorn. During this transit, which ends January 17, 2018, you may become involved with someone older than you or an existing romance becomes more serious and committed. This duo also favors creative work. It looks as if you're going to enter 2018 on a very high note!

AT A GLANCE
December 1—Venus enters Sagittarius
December 3—Mercury turns retro in Sagittarius, full moon in Gemini
December 9—Mars enters Scorpio
December 18—New moon in Sagittarius
December 20—Saturn enters Capricorn
December 22—Mercury turns direct in Sagittarius
December 25—Venus enters Capricorn

Reflection
It's beneficial to reflect on where you have traveled this year. Have you achieved your goals? Made significant strides in relationships? In your career? Jot your notes below.

_____
_____
_____
_____
_____

Happy New Year!

Libra 2017

Your sign is ruled by Venus, so pay particular attention to that planet's transits each month. It will be noted when Venus makes angle to other planets and if it's retrograde or changing signs. If you know your natal rising sign, it's a good idea to keep track of that sign's ruling planet, too. Let's say your rising or ascendant is Virgo. If you look in the introduction, you'll find that Virgo is ruled by Mercury, so its various transits and angles it makes to other planets will be significant for you.

The monthly roundups also include information about the new and full moons, eclipses, the transits of the other planets and how it all impacts you.

This year, Venus turns retrograde in Scorpio on October 5, slips back into your sign on October 31, and turns direct in Libra on November 16. Read the October roundup for the possible repercussions for you.

The year should be strong financially. You'll have ample opportunities to make more money, perhaps through various venues. As your sense of abundance grows and expands, you attract the people and situations that help you to continue in this vein.

January 2017
Getting ready

Welcome to 2017! It promises to be an interesting year for you, Libra, with expansive Jupiter in your sign until October 10. But before you dive into this new year with all the energy at your disposal, there's a little hangover from 2016 to deal with—Mercury is retrograde in Capricorn and then in Sagittarius until January 8.

The best way to navigate a Mercury retro is by following a few simple guidelines. Read about them in the introduction under the Mercury retrograde section. The most important rule is to revise, review and reconsider rather than launching anything new. Since this retro affects the home/family area of your chart, be sure to double check appointment dates and times and to pay off holidays bills as soon as they come in. If you have to travel during the first eight days of January, be flexible and go with the flow. Your itinerary may change suddenly. Since Sagittarius is also involved in the retrograde, hold off on submitting manuscripts and other forms of communication until after the 8th.

On the 3rd, your ruler, Venus, enters Pisces, and your daily work area. This transit should ease any tensions with co-workers or employees and could indicate a bonus or increased pay for something related to work. A flirtation with a co-worker or someone you meet through work may heat up. The transit lasts until February 3.

Circle January 8. Mercury turns direct in Sagittarius and won't act up again until April. On the 12th, there are two astrological events: a full moon in Cancer and Mercury joins Pluto in Capricorn. The full moon occurs in your career area and should mark the completion or culmination of a project that you've been working on for some time. With Cancer, there's usually an intuitive component, so be aware of synchronicities that may provide insight and guidance and for any unusual interactions with animals. They often act as messengers.

Mercury and Pluto joining up in your domestic area could indicate that your house becomes a hub of activity—perhaps kids bring their friends over or visitors drop by unexpectedly. Power plays are possible with teenagers. Keep your cool, Libra.

The 28th features two astrological events—a new moon in fellow air sign Aquarius and Mars entering Aries and your partnership area. The new moon in your creativity and romance area suggests that new opportunities arrive that enable you to show off your creative gifts in some way. Many Libras are gifted musically, artistically or verbally, so be prepared to seize the opportunity and run with it. In terms of romance, it's possible that a new love interest enters your life. Since this area of your chart is also about fun and pleasure, you may take up a new hobby or have an opportunity to do something you really enjoy.

Mars in Aries fires up your partnerships—business and personal. You're now a whirlwind who pursues what—and who—you want. If you're already in a relationship, then you and your partner may embark on some oddball adventures together. Anyone up to climbing Kilimanjaro? The transit ends on March 9.

AT A GLANCE
January 3—Venus enters Pisces
January 8—Mercury retrograde ends
January 12—Full moon in Cancer, Mercury joins Pluto in Capricorn
January 28—New moon in Aquarius, Mars enters Aries

February 2017
New opportunities

Okay, let's get the challenging stuff out of the way first. Months in which eclipses occur can be fraught with tension and a sense of urgency because eclipses tend to bring issues and situations to our attention that have to be dealt with quickly. Lunar eclipses concern internal feelings; solar eclipses are about external events. Both types of eclipses usually address relationships.

The lunar eclipse is first this month, and it occurs in Leo on February 10. This eclipse triggers emotions concerning friends, some facet of the dreams and wishes you hold for yourself or perhaps your public persona. There's an element of surprise to whatever sets you off emotionally because Uranus forms a close and beneficial angle to the eclipse degree and so do Saturn and Jupiter, which is transiting your sign. For you, this lunar eclipse should be positive.

The solar eclipse in Pisces on February 26 ushers in new opportunities in your daily work environment, in the way you maintain your health and in any type of creative work that deals with imagination and intuition. Neptune forms a close conjunction to the eclipse degree, indicating that your ideals are highlighted and that your spiritual beliefs may somehow play into the larger picture.

Now, on to the rest of the month's transits! On February 3, Venus joins Mars in Aries in your partnership area. When Venus and Mars travel together in passionate Aries, your love life and your sex life heat up substantially. It's a good time for you and your partner to take a long, romantic weekend and rediscover each other. Another possibility with this duo is that you find exactly the right partner to help you launch your business. Next month, on March 4, Venus turns retrograde in Aries, so make headway before that happens.

Jupiter turns retrograde in your sign on February 6 and doesn't turn direct again until June 6. When Jupiter isn't functioning at its full capacity, things occur more slowly than they might otherwise. The planet's expansive nature occurs inwardly during the retro period and gives you an opportunity to reassess where you are in your life and if the direction in which you're headed is the right one for you.

On February 7, Mercury enters fellow air sign Aquarius and the creativity and romance sector of your chart. Your conscious focus turns to those areas now and your vision is far-reaching. You're able to spot cutting edge trends and may hang out with individuals who are idiosyncratic and geniuses at what they do. On the 25th, Mercury enters Pisces and your daily work area, and now you can apply what you've learned these past few weeks into your daily work life.

AT A GLANCE
February 3—Venus enters Aries
February 6—Jupiter turns retrograde in Libra
February 7—Mercury enters Aquarius
February 10—Lunar eclipse in Leo
February 25—Mercury enters Pisces
February 26—Solar eclipse in Pisces

March 2017
Bumpy

It's a busy month astrologically, and some of the events may be upsetting for you, like the Venus retrograde in Aries that begins March 4 and ends April 15, when Venus turns direct in Pisces. Since Venus rules your sign, you'll be sensitive to this retro. This period could be one in which the road in romance and love, with creative projects and in a business partnership could be bumpy. You may be reassessing a relationship, taking a deeper look at whether it's what you actually want. Just don't make any irrevocable decisions until after Venus turns direct.

Between March 9 and April 21, Mars transits Taurus and the shared resources sector of your chart. You won't be easily thwarted in your pursuit of a mortgage, loan or a break on your insurance rates. In fact, you may be relentless! This transit can also awaken your sensuality as well as your animal passions. You have a lot of physical energy, and it would be smart to join a gym, take up running or sign up for yoga classes. If you're researching esoteric topics, this transit should give you the patience to find what you need.

The full moon in Virgo on March 12 falls in the most private sector of your chart. A long-buried issue or memory could surface on or around the time of this full moon. It might even be a past-life memory. Maybe it's time to treat yourself to a past-life regression from a qualified therapist.

On the 13th, Mercury joins retrograde Venus in Aries, in your partnership area. It will be there until the 31st. During this transit, you may be more daring, more willing to explore ideas that are edgy, different or unusual. Your thinking is more adventurous.

On the 27th, along comes the new moon in Aries, so perhaps all these ideas you've been exploring now pay off in a new opportunity of some kind or a new partnership. You might get an offer to work with a partner in some exciting capacity. Just be sure you don't obsess about your personal relationships!

On the 31st, Mercury enters Taurus, and your mind becomes more realistic, grounded and stable. Good thing, since the transit occurs in the shared resources area—other people's money. Your partner's income figures into this equation.

AT A GLANCE
March 4— Venus turns retrograde in Aries
March 9—Mars enters Taurus
March 12—Full moon in Virgo
March 13—Mercury enters Aries
March 27—New moon in Aries
March 31—Mercury enters Taurus

April 2017
Promising

April hums with astrological activity. It features a full moon in your sign, two planets turning retrograde and another planet turning direct. In other words, a mix of influences and energies.

Between April 6 and August 25, Saturn will be moving retrograde through Sagittarius. This period gives you the opportunity to reassess your responsibilities in certain areas of your life. Since it falls in that sector of your chart that deals with siblings and your neighborhood/ neighbors, these relationships may play into the retrograde. Your communication skills are also involved. You may lack confidence in speaking before groups. To navigate this retro successfully, try writing affirmations that you post where you'll see them often. *Life loves me and provides for me.* Or: *I'm a marvelous writer and speaker. Abundance flows into my life.* All of these are powerful. Or, create your own.

Mercury turns retrograde in Taurus on April 9, slips back into Aries and your partnership area, then turns direct in that sign on May 3. By now, you know the drill for navigating these periods. Reread the January entry to refresh your memory. In addition to the three Rs, travel cautions and not signing contracts, use this period to complete stuff you started before Mercury turned retro rather than beginning anything new. While Mercury is retro in Taurus, don't apply for mortgages or loans. While it's retro in Aries, be sure you and your partner communicate clearly with each other because misunderstandings are part and parcel of this period.

The full moon in your sign on the 11th is conjunct Jupiter. Even with Jupiter retrograde now, you benefit from its largesse. If you and your partner have hit some bumps in your relationship during the Venus retro—which ends when Venus turns direct in Pisces on the 15th—then plan a romantic night out. If you're not involved with anyone right now, then throw a party, Libra, and hang out with friends. The point is to feel as good and happy as possible.

Mars enters fellow air sign Gemini on the 21st and may stir your nomadic urges. You may also decide to go to graduate school, work or study abroad or sign up for some sort of spiritual retreat and blog about your experience. Mars in Gemini can result in your spreading yourself too thinly, taking on too many projects and scattering your energy. But Gemini is a versatile, multi-task sign, and with Mars forming a beneficial angle to your sun, this transit may be just what you need to get started on a writing project.

The new moon in Taurus on the 26th should usher in opportunities to explore the hidden side of life—the paranormal, life after death, reincarnation and other esoteric subjects. It helps to ground you emotionally. You may be more stubborn during the several days on either side of this moon.

From April 28 to June 6, Venus transits Aries and your partnership area. A lot of passion is surfacing in a partnership and perhaps some restlessness as well. It's a good time for you and your partner to take off for a long weekend and become re-attuned to each other.

AT A GLANCE
April 6—Saturn turns retro in Sagittarius
April 9—Mercury retrograde in Taurus
April 11—Full moon in Libra
April 15—Venus turns direct in Pisces
April 21—Mars enters into Gemini
April 26—New moon in Taurus
April 28—Venus enters Aries

May 2017
Take a break

Compared to last month, May is relatively quiet, and it might be a great time to get away for few days before the busier summer arrives. In fact, anytime after May 3, when Mercury turns direct in Aries, would be excellent. Once Mercury turns direct, your partnerships straighten out, communication straightens out and your life in general straightens out. You and your partner may enter a particularly adventurous period together, where your ideas pour out fast and furiously, and your biggest challenge is who is going to record them first!

The 10th features a full moon in Scorpio, in your financial area. Neptune forms a wide, beneficial angle to this full moon, suggesting an inspired approach to completing some sort of financial deal or project. Mercury will be direct by the full moon, so it's safe to sign contracts and seal the deal.

Between May 16 and June 6, Mercury moves through earth sign Taurus and the shared resources sector of your chart. You may be figuring out how to stretch your budget, and you and your partner discover ways to cut your insurance premiums or to pay off an outstanding credit card bill. You may also come up with a way to earn some additional cash, perhaps by selling something you've created.

The new moon in fellow air sign Gemini joins Mars in this same sign and should bring in new opportunities in communication, travel, higher education and in exploring your spirituality. With Jupiter still in your sign, expansion in some phase of your life continues, even though Jupiter is retro until June 9.

AT A GLANCE
May 3—Mercury turns direct in Aries
May 10—Full moon in Scorpio
May 16—Mercury enters Taurus
May 25—New moon in Gemini

June 2017
Expansive

Your career/professional life will take a major upward swing between June 4 and July 20 when Mars moves through Cancer. This period is when forward momentum is strong and you can achieve a lot of what you want and need to do professionally. Mars is your booster rocket, and when it's in Cancer, there's a strong intuitive component that enables you to make the right decisions when you don't have a lot of time to mull things over.

June 6 through the 9th will make your head spin. On the 6th, Mercury enters Gemini and Venus enters Taurus, and on the 9th, Jupiter turns direct in your sign. The first transit, which lasts until June 21, indicates that you may be doing a lot of writing and/or public speaking, and you may be doing it overseas or in front of a classroom. If you're planning to attend an educational function in another country, this period is the perfect time to do it.

From June 6 to July 4, Venus transits Taurus. Your partner or a parent or someone else with whom you share resources may get a raise or a break on insurance or mortgage rates. You're lucky now when it comes to other people's money and attract the right people at the right time.

Then there's Jupiter. Ah. This one will feel deliciously good, Libra. From June 9 to October 10, when Jupiter enters Scorpio, the planet of expansion is functioning the way it should. Your life expands in some significant way. Look back to January of this year and last fall, when Libra was moving through the same degrees as it will do now. What was going on in your life then? What kinds of opportunities appeared? Some of these same types of things should occur now.

The full moon in Sagittarius on June 9 signals the culmination or completion of travel plans, a move to a different neighborhood or even something to do with a sibling or neighbor. Saturn retrograde is also in Sagittarius at this time. Even though Saturn isn't conjunct this full moon, there could be an element of permanence to events today.

On June 21, Mercury joins Mars in Cancer and your career area. With these two planets traveling together, you're able to express your ideas clearly and with conviction and to implement whatever action is needed to move a project or relationship forward. The Mercury transit ends on July 5.

The new moon in Cancer on June 23 should be a beauty for you, with a new professional opportunity surfacing. A promotion? A new career path? A job offer you simply can't refuse?

AT A GLANCE
June 4—Mars enters Cancer
June 6—Mercury enters Gemini, Venus enters Taurus
June 9—Full moon in Sagittarius, Jupiter turns direct in Libra
June 21—Mercury moves into Cancer
June 23—New moon in Cancer

July 2013
Social & creative

July is a wild month, with five planets entering new signs and, of course, the usual new and full moons. It might be wise to make sure that each day this month you carve out time for yourself separate from work and family. That means you should steal away!

The action begins on July 4 when Venus, your ruler, enters fellow air sign Gemini. During this transit, which ends on the 31st, your literary interests may attract you to publishing or writing, if you aren't in either of those fields yet. Music and art also figure prominently. You and a partner or romantic interest may take in the opening of a museum exhibit, a concert and maybe even a fireworks show!

The next day, the 5th, Mercury enters fire sign Leo, a sign compatible with your air-sign sun, and your social life suddenly picks up considerable steam. You and a friend may brainstorm about a joint creative project. Don't finalize that deal until the new moon in Leo on July 23. You have great willpower during this transit and won't take no for an answer if you believe you're right. Your intellect shines. This transit ends on the 25th.

The full moon on July 9 joins Pluto in Capricorn, in the family/home area of your chart. Power plays may be part of what this full moon reveals, perhaps between you and one of your children or someone else in your household. Your emotions are pretty intense on and around this full moon, and yet, your charisma is unmistakable. This combination has a strong psychic component.

On the 20th, Mars joins Mercury in Leo, a dynamic combination. Your mind moves fast, figuring all the angles. In social situations, you work the room like a politician, and your magnetism attracts exactly the people and circumstances that can help you in some way.

The new moon in Leo on July 23 brings in opportunities to make new friends and connections that help you in some way to move toward achieving your wishes and dreams. It's a perfect day for getting together with acquaintances and friends. You may be asked to speak at a workshop or seminar. This moon gives you the confidence to do so.

Mercury enters Virgo on the 25th and, thanks to a retrograde next month, won't be moving into your sign until September 29. Prepare for the retro now by launching new projects, finalizing travel plans and submitting manuscripts and other documents. You're able to connect all the fine details and approach everything you do in a methodical, efficient way.

On the 31st, Venus enters Cancer and your career area, a great bonus that will facilitate your professional endeavors. This transit, which lasts until August 26, may also bring a new romantic interest into your life, perhaps someone you meet through work. Co-workers and bosses are helpful during this transit.

AT A GLANCE
July 4—Venus enters Gemini
July 5—Mercury goes into Leo
July 8—Full moon in Capricorn
July 20—Mars enters Leo
July 23—New moon in Leo
July 25—Mercury goes into Virgo
July 31—Venus enters Cancer

August 2017
Sense of urgency

Okay, let's get the rough news out of the way first. Not only is there a Mercury retro this month, but two eclipses that may trigger a sense of urgency. Eclipses help us to clear out the old so we can make room for the new, and they often do this in abrupt ways.

On August 7, the lunar eclipse in fellow air sign Aquarius falls in the romance/creativity sector of your chart. Something in this area or with your kids is triggered by this eclipse, and your emotional reaction is to act quickly and decisively. But Jupiter in your sign has your back, so whatever unfolds looks as if it ends well.

The solar eclipse in Leo on August 21 should bring in new opportunities to exhibit your talents and strut your stuff! An opportunity to work with a group or a team of like-minded individuals may surface. You may have to end or release something in your life to make way for these new opportunities, but whatever it is has outlived its purpose.

Mercury turns retrograde on August 12, in Virgo, will slide back into Leo and turn direct in that sign on September 5. Once again, follow the three Rs for these periods: revise, review and reconsider. Reread the Mercury retrograde section in the introduction. Since this retro occurs in the area of your chart that rules the personal unconscious, issues you haven't resolved or that you thought you resolved may surface again. Your dreams are likely to provide insight and information, so make a conscious effort to recall them. People you haven't seen in a long time could show up in your life again—if not in person, then through social media. Synchronicity could be vibrant and helpful during this transit.

On the 25th, Saturn turns direct in Sagittarius, a welcome change. Now you can structure your life so that every piece is more judiciously balanced. Your verbal and written communication may have a more serious undertone, and your relationships with siblings and neighbors unfold with greater ease.

Between August 26 and September 19, Venus transits Leo and forms a beneficial angle to your sun. Romance may be on the horizon, perhaps with someone you meet through friends or online, or even through work you do before the public. One thing you might enjoy doing during this transit is having an end of summer party! Invite your friends, neighbors, family. Everyone! Even a Mercury retro can't put a damper on festivities like that—but in honor of the retro, be flexible about the time it starts.

AT A GLANCE
August 7—Lunar eclipse in Aquarius
August 12—Mercury turns retro in Virgo
August 21—Solar eclipse in Leo
August 25—Saturn turns direct in Sagittarius
August 26—Venus enters Leo

September 2017
Moving forward

This month features six astrological events that are sure to keep you moving! But there are two events you're going to love: Mercury turning direct in Leo on September 5 and then moving into your sign on the 29th, which sets you up nicely for October.

With Mercury moving direct in Leo, your social life picks up momentum once again, and any new contacts you make are helpful in some way in the achievement of your wishes and dreams. Your communication skills shine. Mercury joins Venus in this sign until the 19th. The combination could kindle a romance with someone you now know as just a friend.

On the same day, Mars enters Virgo, where it will be until October 22. During this period, you may visit a therapist. It won't be a traditional therapist. You may seek out a Jungian with whom you can discuss the archetypal nature of your dreams or perhaps of visions that come to you during meditation. Or you may seek out a past-life therapist. By the time Mars enters your sign in late October, you're revved up and ready to move forward with everything in your life.

The full moon on September 6 joins Neptune in Pisces, in the daily work area of your chart. This combination inspires you creatively. Your compassion and intuitive ability deepen. It also signals the completion of something at work or the culmination of a project that is near and dear to your heart.

Between September 19 and October 14, Venus transits Virgo. There could be a romance happening behind the scenes, perhaps with a co-worker or employee (be careful, Libra!), or you're doing intense creative work and need more solitude than usual. One way or another, you're preparing for Venus entering your sign in mid-October, which will be one of the most romantic and creative times for you all year.

The 20th features a new moon in Virgo. This one should attract an opportunity for service of some kind, a volunteer type of service or something you do for others without any expectations of compensation. Perhaps you volunteer at an animal rescue organization or at a food kitchen or for a children's literacy organization.

Once Mercury enters your sign on the 29th, you're in your element. You're oozing with self-confidence and ready to tackle whatever life brings your way.

AT A GLANCE
September 5—Mercury turns direct in Leo, Mars enters Virgo
September 6—Full moon in Pisces
September 9—Mercury enters Virgo
September 19—Venus goes into Virgo
September 20—New moon in Virgo
September 29—Mercury moves into Libra

October 2017
Romantic

The month gets off to an adventurous start with the full moon in Aries on October 5. This one highlights your business and personal partnerships. You may feel restless as this moon approaches, as if you need to be doing something different with your life, perhaps something more adventurous. Your passions are stoked, too, and you should carve out time for you and your spouse or partner today.

On the 10th, Jupiter enters Scorpio for a run of about thirteen months—until the first week of November 2018. During this transit, your earning capacity expands. Your expenses may, too, but that's fine because you'll have the money to meet them. There's an intensity about Scorpio that will be evident during this transit, but in a good way. You'll be able to dig deeply into anything you research and find exactly what you need, when you need it. If you travel internationally during this transit, you may actually be on a quest of some kind—for a certain type of spiritual experience.

And on the 14th—drum roll, please—Venus enters your sign. The period between now and November 7 is filled with romance, creative adrenaline and a general feel-good mood. You brim with self-confidence, your love life hums along at a perfect pitch, as do most of your relationships now, and you're so filled with creative ideas that your challenge is which idea to play with first.

On the 17th, Mercury joins Jupiter in Scorpio in your financial area. Now your intellect is so expansive and intuitive that you know which ideas will work for a creative project and dive into it. This transit lasts until November 5. Keep in mind that the last Mercury retro this year falls in December. More on that in next month's roundup.

It's wise to prepare for the new moon in your sign on the 19th by making a list of what you would like to achieve and experience in the next year. This moon comes around only once a year and sets the tone for the next twelve months, so give the list some thought, and then let the universe bring it all your way.

On the 22nd, Mars joins Venus in your sign. Wow! This combination ensures that you get things done and run into few, if any, obstacles. Forget the little engine that said, *I think I can, I think I can,* as it chugged up the mountain. The mantra for your forward momentum is a resounding, *Done!* The Mars transit lasts until December 9.

AT A GLANCE
October 5—Full moon in Aries
October 10—Jupiter moves into Scorpio
October 14—Venus enters Libra
October 17—Mercury enters Scorpio
October 19—New moon in Libra
October 22—Mars enters Libra

November 2017
Looking ahead

Compared to last month, November is relatively calm. It's a good time to prepare yourself for next month's Mercury retrograde by launching projects now, signing contracts, finalizing travel plans for the holidays and, yes, getting the jump on holiday shopping.

November 4 brings a full moon in Taurus in the shared resources sector of your chart. A partner's income—business or personal—is highlighted in some way. You are not as quick to bend to other people's wishes or demands now; there's a strong element of stubbornness in the Taurus moon. Stand your ground for what you think is right. Your mother or another nurturing female in your life may also play into the day's events. Be alert, too, for any synchronicities that occur. They may provide guidance, warnings and insight.

Mercury enters fire sign Sagittarius on the 5th, a sign that's compatible with your sun, and suddenly, you're raring to get stared on a writing project. Your mind travels to the farthest reaches of the globe and the solar system. You may plan an overseas trip, and you'll have a specific location in mind. The one challenge with this transit, which doesn't end until January 11, 2018, is that you may not be able to shut off your thoughts when you go to bed. Meditating beforehand will be helpful.

On the 7th, Venus enters Scorpio and your financial area. You may be tempted to buy some high ticket items—art, electronics or an HDTV. Just be sure you've got the cash in your account before you do so. Your income may spike this month; Venus in this position can increase your earnings. If your expenses also rise, you should have the cash to meet your bills. This transit lasts until December 1.

In fact, with the new moon in Scorpio on the 18th, you can expect a new money opportunity. A job that pays more? A second job? An unexpected royalty check?

AT A GLANCE
November 4—Full moon in Taurus
November 5—Mercury enters Sagittarius
November 7—Venus goes into Scorpio
November 18—New moon in Scorpio

December 2017
Mixed energies

This month is one of the busiest all year. It also may be a confusing month, thanks to the Mercury retrograde in Sagittarius that runs from December 3–22. In addition to following the rules of the three Rs and the various DO NOTS, try to do your holiday shopping on either side of these dates so you aren't in the return line on December 26. This Mercury retro could slow down any publishing projects in which you're involved and may also mess up your travel plans. But if you do travel during the retrograde period, look at it as an adventure!

Also on the 3rd, the full moon in fellow air sign Gemini lights up your communication skills, may bring in social invitations and could make you feel energized and somewhat restless. You may be longing to get away to some sun-soaked beach.

On the 1st, Venus joins Mercury in Sagittarius, where it will be until December 25. If romance finds you during this period, it may be with an individual from another country or culture or with someone who has strong spiritual beliefs. Your creative drive, particularly as it pertains to self-expression, will be especially strong.

Mars joins Jupiter in Scorpio on the 9th, where it will be until January 26, 2018. This dynamic duo gets stuff done. Whether it's research, earning more money or tying up loose ends at work, you're on the case, a powerhouse.

The 18th features a new moon in Sagittarius and since Venus is still in that sign, one of the new opportunities could be a romantic interest. Or perhaps your novel or an article you've written sells. With Saturn also still in Sadge, the opportunity is solid.

Saturn enters Capricorn on the 20th, and it will be there for the next two and a half years. Its transit through the domestic/family area of your chart indicates that a parent may need more help and assistance, or that your kids need more structure and rules in their lives. It's also possible that you have a chance to work out of your home now and need to set up a structure for doing so.

Circle the 22nd on your calendar. Mercury turns direct! Celebrate!

On December 25, Venus joins Saturn in Capricorn, making the holidays a pleasant time all the way around. Between now and January 17, 2018, you may be beautifying your home in some way.

AT A GLANCE
December 1—Venus enters Sagittarius
December 3—Mercury turns retro in Sagittarius, full moon in Gemini
December 9—Mars enters Scorpio
December 18—New moon in Sagittarius
December 20—Saturn enters Capricorn
December 22—Mercury turns direct in Sagittarius
December 25—Venus enters Capricorn

Reflection

Are you satisfied with the way 2017 turned out? If not, why not? What were the high points? The low points? How did your experiences in 2017 play into your expectations and desires for 2018?

_____

_____

_____

_____

_____

Happy New Year!

Scorpio 2017

Since your sign is co-ruled by Mars, pay particular attention to that planet's transits each month. Mars doesn't turn retrograde this year, so it moves through eight signs. It will be noted when Mars makes angle to other planets and changes signs. If you know your natal rising sign, it's a good idea to keep track of that sign's ruling planet, too. Let's say your rising or ascendant is Virgo. If you look in the introduction, you'll find that Virgo is ruled by Mercury, so its various transits and angles it makes to other planets will be significant for you. Your ruler, Pluto, stays in Capricorn all year, and it will be noted when other planets form angles to it.

The monthly roundups also include information on the new and full moons, eclipses and the transits of other planets and what it all means for you!

2017 is about beginnings and endings for you. Some relationships and situations will fall out of your life, and new people and situations will enter. You'll feel compelled to look beyond the obvious, to find new ways of doings things. Once Jupiter enters your sign in October, you'll really be in your element for the next thirteen months.

January 2017
Slow start, then romantic

Welcome to 2017! The year gets off to a slow start because Mercury is retrograde in Sagittarius until January 8, a hangover from 2016. Reread the Mercury retrograde section in the introduction and follow the general guidelines. Since this retro occurs in your financial area, keep close tabs on your bank statements, credit card bills, spending and ATM withdrawals. If you spot discrepancies, take care of them immediately.

Between January 3 and February 3, Venus moves through fellow water sign Pisces, joining Mars in that sign. This period is one of the most romantic and creative for you all year. Your muse is at your beck and call, whispering in your ear. Your self-confidence is excellent and others are attracted by your charisma and magnetism. Your imagination during this transit is expansive, practically infinite, and whatever you can imagine, you can create. Whenever Venus and Mars travel together, as they will until the 28th, and when Mars enters Aries, your love life and sex life should be quite satisfying.

The full moon in fellow water sign Cancer on January 12 illuminates your spirituality and your family and home life and forms a beneficial angle not only to your sun sign, but to transiting Mars in Pisces as well. This powerhouse combination deepens your intuition and enables you to dig deeply into whatever you tackle.

On the same day, Mercury reenters Capricorn, where it turned retro in December, and joins Pluto in that sign. This combination gives you tremendous focus and determination. You're able to set goals and lay down strategies for achieving them.

The new moon in Aquarius on January 28 should usher in new opportunities in your domestic/family life. You might close on your new home, someone may move in or out of your house or you may begin renovations on your place. You might have an opportunity to work out of your home. However this lunation unfolds, you may be more stubborn now about doing things your way.

On the same day, Mars enters Aries and the daily work section of your chart. During this transit, which lasts until March 9, you're a whirlwind of activity at work. You initiate new projects and may head up a team of co-workers for a particular project. The wind is at your back now, Scorpio. Take advantage of it.

AT A GLANCE
January 3—Venus enters Pisces
January 8—Mercury retrograde ends
January 12—Full moon in Cancer, Mercury joins Pluto in Capricorn
January 28—New moon in Aquarius, Mars enters Aries

February 2017
Drama

Months in which eclipses occur can be tense, emotional and infused with a sense of urgency. This happens because eclipses bring issues and situations to our attention that usually have to be dealt with quickly. Lunar eclipses concern our inner worlds—emotions and intuitions— and can reveal what Carl Jung called our "shadow" selves. Solar eclipses are about external events. Both types of eclipses usually address relationships. So before we talk about this month's transits, let's take a look at the two eclipses.

February 10 features a lunar eclipse in Leo, in the career area of your chart. This one may trigger emotional drama concerning your professional life. It could be that a co-worker or boss sets you off, and you feel the need to defend yourself or your actions. Or perhaps you hear a rumor of some kind that troubles you. However the actual events unfold, there's a sudden, unexpected quality to it all because Uranus and Saturn form close angles to the eclipse degree. Jupiter also forms a close angle to the eclipse degree, suggesting that once the emotional drama is out in the open, things should work out in your favor.

The solar eclipse on February 26 is in fellow water sign Pisces and occurs in the creativity/romance section of your chart. This one should bring new opportunities for self-expression, in romance and love, and in everything you do for fun and pleasure. You might land a project that will enable you to really exhibit your creative abilities or meet a new romantic interest, or you and your partner may discover you're going to be parents. Neptune is closely conjunct the eclipse degree, indicating a deeply intuitive/spiritual element to events.

On February 3, Venus enters fire sign Aries. Your passions ramp up now, Scorpio, and so does your capacity for jealousy. That said, this transit should facilitate activities in your daily work routine. It's a good time to launch projects and make new connections with people, particularly around the time of the solar eclipse. It's possible that an office flirtation turns into a full-blown romance, but be careful about mixing business with pleasure. This transit is lengthy because on March 4 Venus turns retrograde, slips back into Pisces and turns direct in that sign on April 15.

Jupiter turns retrograde in Libra on February 6. Between then and June 9, when it turns direct again, you may be reevaluating certain areas of your life. You may be asking yourself if you really want to go to graduate school or take that trip overseas that will entail sitting on a plane for fifteen hours!

On the 10th, the same day as the lunar eclipse, Mercury enters Aquarius, and it looks as if your home becomes a hub of activity and discussions. You and friends or family members may be brainstorming about a possible move, a project or some cutting edge trend. This transit lasts until the 25th, when Mercury enters Pisces. That transit will be more to your liking. Your intuition deepens, your muse is up close and personal and there's a clear channel of communication between you and your children. This transit lasts until March 13.

AT A GLANCE
February 3—Venus enters Aries
February 6—Jupiter turns retrograde in Libra
February 7—Mercury enters Aquarius
February 10—Lunar eclipse in Leo
February 25—Mercury enters Pisces
February 26—Solar eclipse in Pisces

March 2017
Changeable

This month promises to be somewhat wild and unpredictable with several planets changing signs and one planet turning retrograde. Buckle up!

Between March 4 and April 15, Venus moves retrograde through Aries, then Pisces. Your love life may encounter some bumps and bruises and miscommunications. Checks you're expecting could be delayed. But don't panic, Scorpio. The retrograde gives you a chance to reevaluate a romantic relationship and to take a closer look at the way you handle your money. For the first nine days of the month, Mars is traveling in Aries, too, urging you to get moving on projects at work and to get to the gym or to that pilates or yoga class to work off excess energy.

On the 9th, Mars enters Taurus and your partnership area. Your animal passions surge to life, a bonus for you and your spouse or partner as the transit ramps up your sex life. This transit may cause you to be more stubborn than usual, but it also deepens your patience and persistence. The transit ends April 21.

The full moon in compatible earth sign Virgo on March 12 highlights friendships and your network of acquaintances. Thanks to a beneficial angle from Pluto, which rules your sign, you're in the driver's seat. Just be sure to wield your power carefully. A wish or dream that you have may culminate with this full moon.

Between March 13 and 31, Mercury joins Uranus in Aries. All sorts of ideas pour through you during this transit, and your challenge is to select the best ones and use them in your daily work. The combination of these two planets may cause mental restlessness, particularly if you're doing research. You may be too impatient to dig and dig for answers. If that's the case take the easier route—Google it!

The new moon in Aries on March 27 brings new opportunities in your daily work—a promotion? A new job? Greater responsibilities? If you're hungry for travel, then the opportunities that surface could enable you to travel more for your job.

Mercury enters Taurus on March 31, and your mental focus turns to partnerships. We'll talk more about this transit in next month's roundup because Mercury will turn retro in Taurus on April 9.

AT A GLANCE
March 4— Venus turns retrograde in Aries
March 9—Mars enters Taurus
March 12—Full moon in Virgo
March 13—Mercury enters Aries
March 27—New moon in Aries
March 31—Mercury enters Taurus

April 2017
Your muse is back!

It's another busy month astrologically. Two planets turn retrograde, another planet turns direct, and yet another planet enters a new sign. This mix of energies is best navigated the way you navigate most things in your life—intuitively.

Between April 6 and August 25, Saturn moves retrograde in Sagittarius in your financial area. During this lengthy period, you may be reevaluating the financial structures in your life—how you earn and spend your money, invest it and save it. You may be shuffling your budget around, trying to figure out how to save more so you can do the things you really enjoy. Another facet to this retrograde is that you may realize you're shouldering more than your share of responsibility and may have to take steps to remedy it.

On April 9, Mercury moves retrograde through Taurus, slips back into Aries and turns direct in that sign on May 3. During this period, miscommunication can occur much too easily between you and your partners—both personal and professional. It's important to communicate clearly with these individuals to mitigate any misunderstandings. Be sure to follow the rule of three Rs: revise, review and reconsider. Recheck any appointments you have scheduled. Read over the Mercury retro section in the introduction for general guidelines.

The full moon in Libra on April 11 is conjunct Jupiter retrograde in the area of your chart that rules the personal unconscious. You may feel a greater need for balance in your life. Your dreams could provide insight and information on how to achieve that. With Uranus in Aries opposed to this full moon, you feel a powerful need for more personal freedom, and events that occur today could drive home that point.

You'll love April 15, when Venus turns direct in Pisces, in the creativity and romance sector of your chart. Suddenly, your muse is back, whispering the plot and characters of a bestseller in your ear. For the next thirteen days, until April 28, you brim with self-confidence and charisma and attract just the right circumstances and people to nudge you along a more creative and fulfilling path. This period is also one of the most romantic for you all year. If you're already in a relationship, then things unfold smoothly between you and your partner. If you're single, then you may meet someone special.

Between April 21 and June 4, Mars transits Gemini. This transit accentuates your sexuality and need/capacity for intimacy. You and your partner or you and a parent or child—anyone with whom you share resources—may butt heads over finances. During this period, you express energy mentally and intellectually and may take on too many projects at once. It's a good transit for writing and researching esoteric topics.

The new moon in Taurus on April 26 should bring new opportunities in partnerships. You and your romantic interest may decide to move in together or get married. You could meet exactly the right business partner to help you launch a new endeavor. You feel particularly stubborn and resolute now and can see a clear path forward to achieving whatever you desire.

April 6—Saturn turns retro in Sagittarius
April 9—Mercury retrograde in Taurus
April 11—Full moon in Libra
April 15—Venus turns direct in Pisces
April 21—Mars enters into Gemini
April 26—New moon in Taurus
April 28—Venus enters Aries

May 2017
Energy shifts

On May 3, when Mercury turns direct in Aries, you feel the shift in energy. Ideas now flow more smoothly, without the twists and turns that have marked the retrograde period. You move forward now with projects at work and may plan a little adventure—a road trip, perhaps—to some spot you've never visited. It could be a quest of some sort for you—the hunt for an artifact or a particular out-of-print book or even a quest for a specific type of experience.

The full moon in your sign on the 10th illuminates something in your personal life. Neptune forms a wide but beneficial angle to this moon, suggesting a spiritual or artistic component to the day's events and your realizations. Your emotions are likely to be more intense than usual today and for several days on either side of this full moon, and your insight and intuition are broad and deep.

On the 16th, Mercury enters Taurus, your opposite sign. Your conscious focus is on partnerships, contracts and, yes, your expectations in these areas. Are your business and personal partnerships evolving the way you hoped? If not, what changes can be made? You have clear goals in mind, and if you're flexible, you'll see that there isn't just one path forward. This transit ends on June 6.

The new moon on May 26 joins Mars in Gemini. The two aren't conjunct, but Mars is the energy that makes things happen. New opportunities surface in joint finances. This means you could get a break on your mortgage, insurance or a loan. Your partner or someone else with whom you share financial resources may get a raise. An unexpected royalty check or reimbursement could arrive. New friends and connections are possible and so is a writing or communication project that brings in additional funds.

AT A GLANCE
May 3—Mercury turns direct in Aries
May 10—Full moon in Scorpio
May 16—Mercury enters Taurus
May 25—New moon in Gemini

June 2017
Mixed energies

There's a lot going on this month, so as you try to keep pace with the shifting energies, be sure to carve out time each day for yourself. If you don't have a regular meditation practice, then June is the ideal time to start one.

Between June 4 and July 20, energetic Mars transits fellow water sign Cancer and forms a beneficial angle with your sun sign. Now is a great time to move ahead with your plans for graduate school or for signing up for a workshop or seminar. It's also an excellent time for overseas travel. If you haven't made your plans yet, by all means, do so, and be sure you don't travel during the next Mercury retro, which occurs between August 12 and September 5. If you're a writer with a completed book, start your submissions to agents/publishers during this period.

June 6 through June 9 may be a wild, unpredictable period. Three astrological events occur: Mercury enters Gemini, a sign it rules; Venus moves into Taurus, which it rules; and Jupiter turns direct in Libra. Mercury will transit Gemini from June 6–21, and during this period, your mental focus is on communication and networking and on resources you share with others. You may be researching and writing about metaphysical topics—reincarnation, ghosts or the afterlife. Or you could be doing something as mundane as searching for the best possible mortgage interest rate. You also may be spending more time with friends.

Venus enters Taurus, your opposite sign, on this same day and doesn't move on until July 4. During this period, your love life with your partner certainly picks up. The two of you may take in concerts or art exhibits or get involved on a joint creative project of some kind. If you have a business partner, the two of you are probably on the same page in terms of your company's goals and vision.

On the 9th expansive Jupiter turns direct in Libra. This shift is always welcome. Now Jupiter will be functioning at optimum levels, working to expand various areas of your life. You'll feel luckier, as though you're in the right place at the right time. You're planting seeds for Jupiter's transit through your sign, which happens once every twelve years. This change occurs on October 10, and we'll talk more about it in the October roundup.

On the 9th, the full moon in Sagittarius lights up the financial area of your chart. Saturn retrograde is also in Sadge, but not conjunct the moon. Pluto forms a challenge to it. You may come into conflict with an authority figure about money and finances and may have to take a closer look at your earnings and monthly bills. Although Scorpios are generally adept with their money and know how to save and invest, you may have had some heavy expenses lately. This full moon may also fire you up about travel—a trip you will be taking or one you're already on!

Between June 21 and July 5, Mercury transits fellow water sign Cancer, and you feel right at home within yourself. You're able to absorb information more readily, your conscious awareness of your surroundings is enhanced, and your memory is excellent. A single scent can transport you years into the past, with full blown accompanying memories. Mars is also in Cancer until July 20, and when these two planets travel together, Mars pushes your mind and intellect forward, into unexplored terrain.

The new moon in Cancer on June 23 should bring in new opportunities for foreign travel, higher education and spiritual pursuits. And because the moon is in the sign that rules home and hearth, there could be some new opportunity concerning your family. Your capacity to nurture and be nurtured may also be part of whatever unfolds.

AT A GLANCE
June 4—Mars enters Cancer
June 6—Mercury enters Gemini, Venus enters Taurus
June 9—Full moon in Sagittarius, Jupiter turns direct in Libra
June 21—Mercury moves into Cancer
June 23—New moon in Cancer

July 2017
Financial gains

If you were hoping for a month in which you could kick back and chill, July probably won't be it! The action begins on July 4, when Venus enters Gemini. This transits lasts until July 31 and brings luck with other people's money and resources. You gain financially through partnerships now. An unexpected royalty check or insurance reimbursement could arrive. You also attract the right people at the right time.

On the 5th, Mercury enters Leo and your career area and will be there until the 25th. During this period, there's a certain flamboyance and flair about the way you communicate that keeps others riveted. It's especially beneficial when you're talking with peers and bosses about projects in which you're involved. You're able to converse with anyone and communicate your ideas clearly.

The full moon in compatible earth sign Capricorn on July 8 highlights your writing and communication ability and enables you to clearly see your goals and lay down a strategy for achieving them. You're more resolute than you usually are about what you want to do professionally and personally. You may have more contact now with siblings, neighbors and people in authority. Pluto is conjunct this full moon, so wield your power carefully!

Between July 20 and September 5, Mars transits Leo and your career area. Wow! Think of this transit as a booster rocket that propels you professionally. You're a whirlwind of energy, the one who not only gets stuff done, but seems to be able to do it all. Your focus and resilience impress everyone around you. Because Mars now forms a challenging angle to your sun sign, it's important that you steer clear of confrontations in your environment. It's fine to hold your own, but don't do it just to prove you're right!

The new moon in Leo on the 23rd could bring professional accolades and recognition for your work. New opportunities surface in your career. A promotion? Raise? Perhaps a new career path altogether? A new boss? Remain alert and aware.

Venus enters fellow water sign Cancer on July 31, a transit that lasts until August 26 and should be quite pleasant for you all the way around. Things with your family unfold with greater ease, and if you're traveling internationally, the trip should come off without a hitch. It's also possible that a romance is sparked with someone from a different culture while you're traveling, or even in a class or seminar.

This transit will prove to be a real bonus in August, when there are two eclipses that are sure to stir up emotions and high drama.

AT A GLANCE
July 4—Venus enters Gemini
July 5—Mercury goes into Leo
July 8—Full moon in Capricorn
July 20—Mars enters Leo
July 23—New moon in Leo
July 25—Mercury goes into Virgo
July 31—Venus enters Cancer

August 2017
High drama & possible pay raise

Months that feature eclipses can be frantic and imbued with a sense of urgency. It's because eclipses tend to bring issues and relationships right into the forefront of our awareness and we often have to act quickly and decisively.

The lunar eclipse on August 7 is in Aquarius, in the domestic/family area of your chart. Both Mars and Jupiter form beneficial angles to the eclipse degree but difficult angles to your sun sign. An upset of some kind at home—perhaps with a parent—may trigger an emotional reaction that cascades. So keep your annoyance to yourself and avoid a confrontation. That said, learn from whatever it is that upset you.

The solar eclipse in Leo on August 21 falls in your career area. Several professional opportunities may surface—a raise or promotion, recognition by bosses and peers for work well done or perhaps a new job offer. This eclipse is followed on the 26th by Venus entering Leo and the same area of your chart, so a raise certainly looks likely! The Venus transit ends on September 19.

Between August 12 and September 5, Mercury moves retrograde in Virgo, slides back into Leo, and turns direct in that sign. Read over the Mercury retrograde section in the introduction for general guidelines about navigating it more successfully. During this period, when misunderstandings happen way too easily, be sure to communicate clearly. There could be mix-ups with friends about social events and confusion about appointments and schedule changes. Follow the rule of the three Rs to mitigate the effects of the retrograde: review, revise and reconsider. Dust off projects you put aside and take a second look.

On the 25th, Saturn turns direct in Sagittarius, in your financial area. Money matters that seemed to have been stalled or lingering in limbo the last several months now move ahead. You might, for instance, find a better investment strategy for your savings or seek out a financial advisor.

AT A GLANCE
August 7—Lunar eclipse in Aquarius
August 12—Mercury turns retro in Virgo
August 21—Solar eclipse in Leo
August 25—Saturn turns direct in Sagittarius
August 26—Venus enters Leo

September 2017
Culmination & manifestation

The good news is that Mercury turns direct on September 5, in Leo, in your career area, and will be there for the next four days, until Mercury enters Virgo again on September 9. During these four days, you're focused on your career and professional matters. You may be brainstorming with co-workers, even socializing with them once Mercury enters Virgo, and could be blogging or writing about your company and its services. Mars also enters Virgo on the 5th, so this will be a busy day.

On the 6th, the full moon in fellow water sign Pisces brings culmination to a creative endeavor, romance or to some situation/issue with a child. Thanks to the imaginative nature of Pisces, this is an excellent time to practice visualization of your wishes and desires. What kind of life would you like to be living? While doing this, be sure to appreciate everything around you.

On the 19th, Venus joins Mercury and Mars in Virgo, and your social calendar fills up quickly. It's possible that you meet a romantic interest through friends or through a social event or club to which you belong. These three planets travel together until the 29th, when Mercury moves into Libra, and during this time your focus is romance, creativity, money and achieving your desires.

The new moon in Virgo on the 20th has excellent company with Mercury, Venus and Mars. It should bring new opportunities for networking and making friends and in communication.

Between September 29 and October 17, Mercury moves through Libra and the quiet part of your chart. This is a great time to seed ideas and desires for when Mercury enters your sign on October 17.

AT A GLANCE
September 5—Mercury turns direct in Leo, Mars enters Virgo
September 6—Full moon in Pisces
September 9—Mercury enters Virgo
September 19—Venus goes into Virgo
September 20—New moon in Virgo
September 29—Mercury moves into Libra

October 2017
Luck abounds

Another busy month! And you, Scorpio, are about to enter one of the luckiest periods this year. On October 10, Jupiter, the planet of expansion, luck and serendipity, will enter your sign and remain there until November 2018. This transit through your sign occurs every twelve years and is like a reboot of optimism and positive experiences in your life. During the next thirteen months, it will be easier for you to achieve your desires and to expand any area of your life where you place your intent, focus and emotion.

Before this transit begins, there's a full moon in Aries on the 5th. Something in your daily work routine culminates or is completed. This moon may not be your favorite, but it certainly sets your emotions on fire and enables you to see your way toward your next project or endeavor. Don't start it just yet; let the idea bubble around inside you for awhile.

Between October 14 and November 7, Venus transits Libra and the quiet area of your chart. "Quiet" in that the twelfth house is everything behind the scenes, your personal unconscious and the place where you seed your desires. Venus in Libra brings a need for greater balance and equanimity. You may be working on a creative endeavor and need solitude to complete it. If a romantic relationship begins during this transit, it may be kept under wraps for some reason. But once Venus enters your sign on November 7, it's no longer a secret!

When Mercury enters your sign on the 17th, you're primed for research and for drilling down into any topic that seizes your interest. Your conscious mind is exceptionally intuitive and perceptive. You have a need now to perceive the hidden order of things, to pierce that order and find the truth. This transit lasts until November 5.

The new moon on October 19 joins Venus in Libra and should usher in new opportunities to delve into your own unconscious for answers. Consider treating yourself to a past-life regression or to a workshop on lucid dreaming. Mars joins Venus in Libra on the 22nd, adding energy and forward momentum. Remember: you're seeding your desires during this period so that when Venus and Mars enters your sign, you reap the benefits. Venus enters your sign on November 7, and Mars follows suit on December 9.

AT A GLANCE
October 5—Full moon in Aries
October 10—Jupiter moves into Scorpio
October 14—Venus enters Libra
October 17—Mercury enters Scorpio
October 19—New moon in Libra
October 22—Mars enters Libra

November 2017
Romantic, creative & fun!

Kick back this month and take time for yourself. Astrologically, November is relatively slow compared to last month. However, there are two events that will thrill you: Venus enters your sign, and there's a new moon in Scorpio. But let's begin with the full moon in Taurus on November 4.

This one occurs in your partnership area and should bring a culmination to a business deal or to some issue in a personal partnership. Neptune retrograde forms a conjunction with this full moon, suggesting that a partner's idealism may be involved in whatever transpires. Pluto also forms a wide beneficial angle to this full moon, indicating that something transformative is afoot. On top of all this, Jupiter in your sign has your back, Scorpio, so move forward without fear or regret.

Mercury enters Sagittarius and your financial area on the 5th. This means your conscious focus between November 5 and December 22 is on money—what you earn and spend, what you save and how you budget and invest. The final Mercury retro for the year begins on December 3 and ends on December 22, so it's wise to start your holiday shopping this month and to prepare for the retro by beginning new projects and signing contracts now.

Between November 7 and December 1, you enjoy one of the most romantic and creative times all year. Venus transits your sign. Your charisma, magnetism and sexuality are at an all time high, and any relationship that begins during this period will be emotionally intense and passionate. During this transit, you may earn money from creative endeavors and will be spending money doing what you enjoy.

The 18th features a new moon in your sign. This new moon comes along just once a year and sets the tone for the next twelve months. It's important that you prepare for it by making a list of what you hope to achieve and experience in the next year, back it with emotion, visualize it happening and post the list where you'll see it often. It should bring new opportunities in any area of your life where your focus and intent are placed.

November 4—Full moon in Taurus
November 5—Mercury enters Sagittarius
November 7—Venus goes into Scorpio
November 18—New moon in Scorpio

December 2017
Looking ahead

As the last month of the year begins, it's a good idea to go holiday shopping before Mercury turns retrograde in Sagittarius on the 3rd. Otherwise, you may be standing in the return line on December 26. Also make your travel plans, if possible, before the 3rd and after the 22nd. And, of course, follow the rules of the three Rs: revise, review and reconsider.

The full moon in Gemini on December 3 should bring some sort of financial deal to a closure. However, since Mercury turns retro on the same day, it would be best to a sign a contract on the 1st or 2nd! Otherwise, you may be revisiting the details in the contract after Mercury turns direct.

Back to December 1! Venus enters Sagittarius today and will be there until the 25th. Usually this transit would bring greater ease and flow to your finances, but because Mercury is retro for most of this transit, there may be delays in receiving money you're owed. On the romantic and creative front, however, there's improvement. If you and a partner are rehashing issues from the past, you should be able to resolve them. Once Mars enters your sign on the 9th, you become a whirlwind of psychic energy and nothing stands in your way of attaining what you desire—not even a Mercury retrograde! The Mars transit lasts until January 26, 2018.

On the 20th, Saturn enters Capricorn, where it will be for the next two and a half years. Saturn governs structures, limitations, discipline and responsibility and rules Capricorn, so it's at home here and functions at optimum capacity. It's now forming a beneficial angle to your sun and helps you to create better structures in relationships, finances, family and career. During this transit, you achieve through your own efforts, you plan carefully and structure your life so that everything is judiciously balanced.

Finally, on the 22nd, Mercury turns direct in Sagittarius. Now you can shop till you drop, make your travel plans, launch new projects and get ready for the holidays without worrying about plans changing at the last second! This transit ends on January 11, 2018.

On the 25th, Venus joins Saturn in Capricorn. Any romance that begins between now and January 17, when this transit ends, may become something serious. The other positive benefit of this transit is that a creative project in which you're involved finds the proper structure.

AT A GLANCE

December 1—Venus enters Sagittarius
December 3—Mercury turns retro in Sagittarius, full moon in Gemini
December 9—Mars enters Scorpio
December 18—New moon in Sagittarius
December 20—Saturn enters Capricorn
December 22—Mercury turns direct in Sagittarius
December 25—Venus enters Capricorn

Reflection

How has your life changed this year? Are you happy with the changes? What, if anything, would you do differently? How can you use what you learned and achieved in 2017 to attain what you desire in 2018? Jot your thoughts below.

_____
_____
_____
_____
_____

Happy New Year!

Sagittarius 2017

Since your sign is ruled by Jupiter, pay particular attention to that planet's transits and the angles other planets make to it. Until October 10 of this year, Jupiter will be in air sign Libra, forming a beautiful angle to your sun sign. It will be in retrograde motion between February 6 and June 9, so its usual expansive energy will be turned inward. Once it enters Scorpio and the quieter area of your chart, you have a chance to seed your unconscious with desires and what you would like to achieve when Jupiter enters your sign in November 2018.

If you know your natal rising sign, it's a good idea to keep track of that sign's ruling planet, too. Let's say your rising or ascendant is Virgo. If you look in the introduction, you'll find that Virgo is ruled by Mercury, so its various transits and angles it makes to other planets will be significant for you.

In the monthly roundups, you'll also find information on the new and full moons, the transits of the other planets, retrogrades and what it all means for you!

In 2017, your originality roars to the forefront of your life. You're not afraid to veer off the beaten path and discover new paths, new friends and new connections that others overlook. You're inventive and more intuitive and insist on your personal freedom.

January 2017
A potpourri of energies

Welcome to 2017! Have you put together your New Year's resolutions? Are you ready to achieve your desires and goals?

The year gets off to a slow start with a hangover from 2016—a Mercury retrograde in Capricorn, in your financial sector. Mercury turns direct again on the 8th, in your sign, then reenters Capricorn on the 12th. The best way to successfully navigate a Mercury retro is to follow a few guidelines. First, reread the section on Mercury retrograde in the introduction to 2017 and follow the suggestions, in particular the rule of the three Rs: revise, review and reconsider, rather than beginning anything new.

Once Mercury is in Capricorn again, your conscious focus turns to money—bills from the holidays that are coming due, your earnings, your expenses and your budget. Because Sagittarians are usually passionate about travel, you may be saving for an overseas trip. Don't schedule travel for any period when Mercury is retrograde!

Between January 3 and February 3, Venus transits Pisces and the family/domestic area of your chart. During this period, your imagination soars and that favors any kind of creative endeavor. Try an ocean theme in one of your rooms. That would satisfy Venus in water sign Pisces. Things at home should unfold smoothly, but you may feel the need to beautify your environment in some way.

On January 12, there are two astrological events: a full moon in Cancer and Mercury joins Pluto in Capricorn. The combination of transits means that the money axis in your chart is activated. The full moon highlights your partner's income and resources you share with others—parents, a child or a roommate. There could be news in any of these areas—your partner gets a raise, your roommate is moving out or your child needs a loan. The Mercury/Pluto placement brings your focus to *your* earnings. A financial deal or concern is completed.

The 28th features two astrological events as well: a new moon in compatible air sign Aquarius and Mars entering fellow fire sign Aries. The new moon should bring in new opportunities in communication—a writing or speaking project, perhaps, or you have an opportunity to build a website or start a blog. If you've been looking at neighborhoods in order to relocate, you may find the ideal spot.

With Mars entering Aries and the romance/creativity section of your chart, your animal passions are awakened. You may feel driven to dive into a creative endeavor or to embark on a quest to some exotic locale. Once Venus joins Mars in Aries on February 3, romance, love and sex, pleasure and your creative endeavors are all part of the picture. The Mars transit lasts until March 9.

AT A GLANCE
January 3—Venus enters Pisces
January 8—Mercury retrograde ends
January 12—Full moon in Cancer, Mercury joins Pluto in Capricorn
January 28—New moon in Aquarius, Mars enters Aries

February 2017
A crazy mix

Months in which eclipses occur can be tense, emotional and imbued with a sense of urgency. This happens because eclipses tend to bring situations and relationships right up close, in your face, and you have to deal with whatever it is quickly and decisively. The first eclipse—lunar—occurs in Leo on February 10. This one may trigger an emotional reaction concerning your career and professional life, your spiritual beliefs or something connected to higher education or international travel. The news that precipitates these emotions seems to come out the blue and, thanks to a challenging angle from Pluto, may involve power issues of some sort. This one may be uncomfortable for you, so just deal with the situation, be done with it and move on.

On the 26th, the solar eclipse in Pisces falls in the domestic/family area of your chart. This eclipse should result in new opportunities to express yourself creatively, positive opportunities for your family and perhaps the sale of your existing home and the purchase of a new home. It's also possible that you and your partner discover you're going to be parents!

What about the rest of the month? On February 3, Venus joins Mars in Aries, beginning what will be one of the most romantic and creative periods for you all year. This dynamic duo indicates that if a romantic relationship begins during this period, passions will run high! Your muse is in attendance 24/7, so don't fritter away this period! Ideas will be pouring through you. Since this area of your chart also deals with children, there may be stuff going on with your kids, too, but it's positive!

Between February 6 and June 9, Jupiter moves retrograde through Libra. The expansiveness of Jupiter now turns inward. Your spiritual beliefs are broadening, you may feel a deep need to travel and explore how people in other cultures live, and you could be reassessing where you are in your life and where you would like to be in the near future.

Mercury enters Aquarius on the 7th, sharpening your communication skills considerably. Your focus may turn toward future trends, politics, the family of man or who we human beings are as a collective. You may be writing or speaking about these topics, too. The transit lasts until the 25th, then Mercury enters Pisces, and your domestic life and family snap into greater focus. If you have teenage children, your home may become the hub where everyone meets.

AT A GLANCE
February 3—Venus enters Aries
February 6—Jupiter turns retrograde in Libra
February 7—Mercury enters Aquarius
February 10—Lunar eclipse in Leo
February 25—Mercury enters Pisces
February 26—Solar eclipse in Pisces

March 2017
Erratic

There's a lot going on this month. Three planets change signs, one planet turns retrograde and there are new and full moons, of course. Let's take a closer look.

On March 4, Venus turns retrograde in Aries and between then and April 15, when it turns direct in Pisces, your love life may undergo some bumps and bruises. You and your partner may not agree on certain elements of your relationship. You may be rethinking what you want from this relationship. However, as long as you keep the channels of communication open, this retro isn't an insurmountable problem. In terms of your creativity, you may be reviewing a project, moving pieces around and refiguring.

On the 9th, Mars enters Taurus and suddenly your nose hits the grindstone. You may be up against a deadline at work, selecting team members for a new project or doing something in your daily work routine that requires steady, consistent effort. Between now and April 21, when Mars moves on, you may be working with a trainer at your gym or taking yoga or pilates classes, or you're engaged in some sort of physical exercise routine.

The full moon in Virgo on the 12th highlights your profession and career, co-workers and your public persona. Something in your career reaches a culmination, or you complete a project. With powerful Pluto forming a beneficial angle to this full moon, any news you receive should be positive. Where you often can see the big picture, Sagittarius, the moon in Virgo enables you to connect the minutia and details.

Between March 13 and 31, Mercury transits Aries and the romance/creativity sector of your chart. Venus retrograde is also there, so you may be giving a lot of thought to a personal relationship and to a creative endeavor. If you and your partner are both involved in this endeavor, be sure to talk things through every step of the way.

On the 27th, the new moon in Aries brings in a new opportunity in romance or in your creative endeavors. Or both! You may have a chance to embark on some sort of adventure that appeals to your nomadic soul, and it's possible that romance finds you while you're on the road!

Mercury enters Taurus on March 31, and since this is going to involve a retrograde in April, we'll discuss it in the April roundup.

AT A GLANCE
March 4—Venus turns retrograde in Aries
March 9—Mars enters Taurus
March 12—Full moon in Virgo
March 13—Mercury enters Aries
March 27—New Moon in Aries
March 31—Mercury enters Taurus

April 2017
Go with the flow

This month could feel somewhat confusing at times. In addition to the lunations, two planets turn retrograde, another planet turns direct and Mars enters a new sign. The best way to navigate all this is to remain as flexible as possible, Sagittarius, and go with the flow.

On the 6th, Saturn turns retro in your sign and doesn't turn direct again until August 25. During this period, you may be identifying sources of irritation in your life and restructuring the situations and relationships that cause it. Whether the source is your job or a boss, a partner or a child, lack of money or too much responsibility, identifying the source is the first step in solving the situation.

Mercury turns retrograde in Taurus on the 9th, slips back into Aries and turns direct in that sign on May 3. It's important that you follow the three Rs: revise, review and reconsider. Since this retrograde begins in the daily work area of your chart, don't start new projects, hire new employees or make any major decisions concerning your work—like quitting your job! Once Mercury slips back into Aries on the 20th, you may be revising a creative endeavor. A former lover or romantic interest could resurface in your life.

A few days before the full moon in Libra on April 11, your social calendar should begin to fill quite quickly. Friends and acquaintances seem to pop out of the proverbial woodwork, and your main challenge will be balancing your social life with the rest of your life. This moon is conjunct Jupiter, so it's likely that your network will expand in some way. An artistic endeavor reaches completion.

On the 15th, Venus turns direct in Pisces. Things in your family now unfold with greater smoothness. If a home renovation project has been put on hold, you can now move forward with it again and are clearer about what you're doing. It may not be renovation so much as beautification.

Between April 21 and June 4, Mars transits Gemini, your opposite sign, and you and your business partner are brainstorming about your vision for your company or joint endeavor. You and your romantic partner may be discussing the nuances of your relationship and could decide to take your commitment to the next level. This period is active and restless, and it's important that you get sufficient sleep. Between April 28 and June 6, Venus transits Aries once again, meaning that you enjoy this transit twice this year. Your magnetism and self-confidence soar, and your creativity is like a force of nature.

The new moon in Taurus on the 26th could bring a new job offer, a promotion or a raise. If you're the boss of a company, you may be hiring new employees. If you're assigned a new project at work, it should be something you enjoy.

Between April 28 and June 6, Venus transits Aries and the romance/creativity section of your chart, just as it did earlier this month. So, lucky you, Sadge. You get two periods of the most romantic and creative times all year.

AT A GLANCE
April 6—Saturn turns retro in Sagittarius
April 9—Mercury retrograde in Taurus
April 11—Full moon in Libra
April 15—Venus turns direct in Pisces
April 21—Mars enters into Gemini
April 26—New moon in Taurus
April 28—Venus enters Aries

May 2017
Beneath the surface

May is somewhat tamer than April was, particularly after Mercury turns direct in Aries on May 3. For several days, Mercury and Venus travel together, and your conscious mind is focused on enjoyment, romance and creativity. You think about these things, mull them over and leap into them. If a romance begins after the 3rd, you dive in with all the passion of a fire sign, and your conscious focus doesn't shift until the 16th, when Mercury enters Taurus and the daily work routine area of your chart. Then you're very much in the work groove, tackling everything you have to do with uncharacteristic patience!

The full moon in Scorpio on May 10 may bring completion to a project you've been working on behind the scenes. Issues that surface can now be dealt with quickly and effectively, and intuitively, you'll know exactly what to do.

On May 25, the new moon in Gemini brings a new business partner, or you and a romantic partner take your relationship to the next level. If you're married or in a committed relationship already, then this new moon could bring renewed commitment. And since the moon is in sociable Gemini, you may make new friends or be offered some sort of communication project.

May 3—Mercury turns direct in Aries
May 10—Full moon in Scorpio
May 16—Mercury enters Taurus
May 25—New moon in Gemini

June 2017
Keeping up

There's a lot going on this month, and you may be challenged to keep up with the shifting energies!

On the 4th, Mars enters water sign Cancer and the shared resources area of your chart. During this transit, which lasts until July 20, forward momentum is a given, specifically with obtaining mortgages and loans and finding the best insurance rates. It's possible that your parents or others in your environment need help with drawing up a will or living wills. Home improvement projects may move along at a manageable pace during this period.

June 6 to 9 could drive you batty. On the 6th, Mercury enters Gemini and Taurus enters Venus, and on the 9th, Jupiter turns direct in Libra. Let's take these one at a time. Mercury rules Gemini and functions well here. During this transit—which ends on the summer solstice—you and your partner are communicating well. You may be discussing the summer ahead, planning a vacation or strategizing about business deals. However the specifics unfold, communication and networking are hallmarks of this transit.

Between June 6 and July 4, Venus moves through Taurus, a sign it rules. You feel more sensuous and attuned to nature. You may spiff up your work area in some way—new, colorful paint, freshly cut flowers or blooming plants. It's also possible that a flirtation at work may be kindled into a full-blown romance!

Jupiter turning direct in Libra is excellent news. It means the planet of expansion and luck will now function at full tilt, expanding your life in significant ways. Jupiter is in that area of your chart that governs your social life and network of acquaintances and your wishes and dreams. It's possible you meet someone—or a group of people—who help you to move closer to what you would like to achieve or what you dream of doing.

On the 9th, the gorgeous full moon in your sign could bring a personal matter to a conclusion or culmination. Neptune forms a challenging angle to this moon, however, so there could be some confusion at home or with a family member. You may not have the full information.

Mercury joins Mars in Cancer from June 21 to July 5. During this period, you may be researching or writing about metaphysical topics—life after death, reincarnation or communication with the dead. Your mind is particularly intuitive now, so heed that inner voice.

Two days later, on the 23rd, the new moon in Cancer ushers in new opportunities for your family and domestic life, but also with resources you share with others. Your partner or spouse, for instance, could get a raise. If he or she is self-employed, then earnings around this time may spike upward significantly.

AT A GLANCE
June 4—Mars enters Cancer
June 6—Mercury enters Gemini, Venus enters Taurus
June 9—Full moon in Sagittarius, Jupiter turns direct in Libra
June 21—Mercury moves into Cancer
June 23—New moon in Cancer

July 2017
Nomadic

July isn't a month for a respite from the shifting astrological energies! In fact, July may be more challenging than June. That said, there's plenty in July to boost your self-confidence and happiness.

Venus transits Gemini from July 4 to 31, and you and your partner enjoy a pleasant period together where you seem to be on the same page about the most important stuff. The channels of communication are open. You may be socializing a lot as a couple and could be traveling—something that always feeds your soul, Sadge.

When Mercury enters fellow fire sign Leo on July 5, you're very much in your element. Now you're primed and ready for travel, sampling other cultures and wandering through ancient ruins that stoke the fires of your imagination. You may be delving into some facet of higher education or expanding your spirituality through workshops or seminars. This transit lasts until July 25, then Mercury enters Virgo, where it will be for quite a while because of a Mercury retro next month. We'll discuss this in the August roundup.

The full moon on July 8 falls in Capricorn, in your financial area, within a degree of where Pluto is now situated. A money matter reaches a culmination or completion, or there is news about your financial situation. It looks as if you're in control of the situation, however. Pluto has your back.

Once Mars enters Leo on July 20, it will spend five days traveling with Mercury. This combination should spell adventure and enjoyment, perhaps while traveling and exploring some foreign locale. Then Mercury moves on, and Mars is flying solo in Leo until September 5. You've got the wind at your back during this transit, Sadge, and may feel invincible. Just don't take unnecessary risks and exercise caution while driving—i.e., abide by the speed limits!

The 23rd features a new moon in Leo. You may have new opportunities for travel, be preparing for graduate school in the fall or could be out and about much more in a public sense. If you've auditioned for a part in a play or movie, then you may land the part. If you're a writer on a book tour, your material is well-received. If you're in sales, then you're in the groove and can sell virtually anything to anyone.

Mercury enters Virgo on July 25, turns retro on August 12, slips back into Leo, and turns direct in that sign on September 5. Until the retro begins, your focus is squarely on your career and profession. You may be doing more writing or public speaking than you usually do or communicating more with co-workers and bosses. Mercury rules Virgo and functions well here.

Between July 31 and August 26, Venus moves through water sign Cancer. This transit facilitates financial dealing with banks and mortgage and insurance companies. Your intuition is especially sharp and your BS radar is humming at a perfect pitch when it comes to any romantic interests you meet during this period!

AT A GLANCE
July 4—Venus enters Gemini
July 5—Mercury goes into Leo
July 8—Full moon in Capricorn
July 20—Mars enters Leo
July 23—New moon in Leo
July 25—Mercury goes into Virgo
July 31—Venus enters Cancer

August 2017
New romance

Here we are, at the second series of eclipses for 2017. The first one is a lunar eclipse in Aquarius on August 7. Fortunately for you, Sadge, Aquarius is compatible with your fire sign sun. Both Mars in Leo and Jupiter in Libra are signs that are compatible with yours, forming beneficial angles to the eclipse degree. It's likely that the feelings triggered for you on or around the date of the eclipse will be positive. It may involve writing/communication or your neighborhood/neighbors.

On the 12th, Mercury turns retrograde in Virgo, slides back into Leo on the 31st and turns direct in that sign on September 5. Reread the roundup for April (page 132), when Mercury was also retrograde, and take a look at the Mercury retro section in the introduction (page 20) for the general guidelines to follow. This retro impacts your profession and career area. You may be reviewing and revising projects you thought were finished or going over the details of an existing project to determine whether it's still viable. Be sure to follow the rules of the three Rs and don't launch anything new.

The solar eclipse in Leo on August 21 is like a double new moon—double the new opportunities. Since it's in a fellow fire sign, it should be positive for you. You may have new opportunities for foreign travel or a chance to attend a workshop, seminar or college/graduate school classes. You may also have a chance to be out in front of the public more than usual. Public speaking? A book tour? An exhibit?

On the 25th, Saturn finally turns direct in your sign, a major plus for all areas of your life. Structures you have put in place are now strengthened, and it's much easier to achieve your goals. Once Venus enters fellow fire sign Leo on the 26th, it's possible that a new romantic interest enters your life. And, thanks to Saturn now being direct in your sign, it could be a serious relationship.

AT A GLANCE
August 7—Lunar eclipse in Aquarius
August 12—Mercury turns retro in Virgo
August 21—Solar eclipse in Leo
August 25—Saturn turns direct in Sagittarius
August 26—Venus enters Leo

September 2017
Career focus

It's another busy month, but at least the eclipses are over, and Mercury turns direct in Leo on September 5. On the 9th, it enters Virgo and your career area, and then you're able to finish projects that may have gotten stalled when Mercury turned retro last month. Between the 9th and the 29th, when it enters Libra, you may be doing more writing and public speaking. If you attend any conferences related to work, expect to be networking.

Also on the 5th, Mars enters Virgo, a transit that lasts until October 22. Think of this transit as your career's booster rocket, particularly after Mercury, and then Venus, join Mars in your career sector. This period is when you get things done. There's a lot of forward momentum, doors open and the right people show up at the right time.

The full moon on September 6 falls in water sign Pisces. There could be news related to your home/family or to a creative endeavor—or both! Neptune forms a close conjunction to this moon, suggesting some confusion around the news. You may not have all the information you need.

On the 19th, Venus joins Mercury in Virgo and your career area. This transit should be quite beneficial for your career. A raise or promotion could be in the offing, your co-workers and bosses are impressed by your work and your relationships with people in your professional environment unfold with greater smoothness. If you're self-employed, then you land a plump assignment or a well-heeled client. This transit lasts until October 14.

The 20th features a new moon in Virgo, in your career area. This should usher in new professional opportunities, and you may get an inkling of whatever it is several days before this new moon occurs. Possibilities? A raise/promotion or perhaps even a new career path.

Mercury enters Libra on the 29th, and between then and October 17, your social calendar fills up quickly. It's the kind of thing you love, Sadge—hanging out with friends, partying, exchanging ideas and traveling on the spur of the moment.

AT A GLANCE
September 5—Mercury turns direct in Leo, Mars enters Virgo
September 6—Full moon in Pisces
September 9—Mercury enters Virgo
September 19—Venus goes into Virgo
September 20—New moon in Virgo
September 29—Mercury moves into Libra

October 2017
Preparation

It's another busy month astrologically and will be particularly significant for you because your ruler, Jupiter, moves into Scorpio. More on that in a moment.

October kicks off with a full moon in fire sign Aries, in the romance and creativity section of your chart. Wow! Your passions, restlessness and creative drive ramp up big time. There may be news about a creative endeavor or relationship, or something in these areas culminates or reaches completion. You and your romantic interest may take off on the spur of the moment for a romantic interlude in some spot you haven't visited before.

When Jupiter moves into Scorpio on the 10th, it's entering the quiet part of your chart and will be there until November 2018. During this period, your personal unconscious is expanding, you have greater access to your dreams and your psychic awareness increases. You're planting seeds for when Jupiter enters your sign in November 2018, something that happens once every twelve years.

Between October 14 and November 7, Venus transits Libra, a sign it rules. During this period, you may be spending more time with friends and acquaintances, could be working on some sort of creative team endeavor and are networking more than usual. You may meet a romantic interest through friends or through some club or organization to which you belong.

On the 17th, Mercury joins Jupiter in Scorpio. Your conscious mind turns toward research, delving into the unseen and the mysterious, and you may be involved in a writing project that requires solitude. This time, you're planting seeds for when Mercury enters your sign on November 5.

The new moon in Libra on the 23rd has great company with Venus also in this area. It looks as if that person you meet through friends may become more than just a romantic interest. You two may discover that you have a lot in common, and things between you evolve fairly quickly. If you're not involved with anyone right now, then it may be that you make new friends who help you in some way to move closer to achieving your wishes and dreams.

Once Mars joins Venus in Libra on the 22nd, you're primed and ready to take on a creative endeavor that may be near and dear to your heart. It could be a collaboration with the new love interest in your life.

AT A GLANCE
October 5—Full moon in Aries
October 10—Jupiter moves into Scorpio
October 14—Venus enters Libra
October 17—Mercury enters Scorpio
October 19—New moon in Libra
October 22—Mars enters Libra

November 2017
Relax!

Finally! November is a month where, for the most part, you can kick back and chill.

The full moon in Taurus on November 4 signals the completion or culmination of a work project or perhaps a health or nutritional program you've been following. You see the results you had hoped for and are ready for the next phase. It's also possible that you'll receive work-related news or news about your finances. Taurus is a practical, grounded sign and may prompt you to take a closer look at what you're spending.

On November 5, Mercury enters your sign, and you're primed for action, travel and fun! You're able to grasp the larger picture of a creative endeavor or relationship and understand how to proceed. This transit lasts through the end of the year because next month Mercury turns retrograde on December 3. One thing you should do to prepare for this retro is to get your holiday shopping out of the way before the 3rd or after December 22nd, when the retro ends.

Venus transits Scorpio between November 7 and December 1. During this period, your sexuality is heightened, and if a relationship begins during this transit, you're apt to keep things quiet. That lasts only until Venus enters your sign on December 1. You may be working against a deadline on a creative endeavor that requires solitude and focus.

The 18th features a new moon in Scorpio. Since Venus is in the same sign, this pair could signal a new romantic interest or a chance to work behind the scenes in some capacity on a research project or creative endeavor.

AT A GLANCE
November 4—Full moon in Taurus
November 5—Mercury enters Sagittarius
November 7—Venus goes into Scorpio
November 18—New moon in Scorpio

December 2017
Excellent

As you enter the last month of 2017, the stars are lining up in your favor. Between December 1 and 25, Venus transits your sign. This is one of the most romantic and creative times for you all year. The only other period that equaled this was Venus's transit through Aries between February 3 and June 6. Even when Venus was retro during that first period, things weren't all that bad! During this transit, your charisma and vivaciousness attract many different kinds of people and opportunities. Romance may be high on your list and you'll find that your muse is up close and personal, at your beck and call 24/7. Take advantage of this period, Sadge, and don't fritter it away with socializing!

On the 3rd, there are two events: Mercury turns retrograde in your sign and a full moon in Gemini. By now, you're well versed in the DOS and DON'TS of a Mercury retro. In addition to what has been discussed during other retrogrades, there are a couple of other things you can do to mitigate the effects. Since the retro is in your sign, it's imperative that you communicate clearly with people in your environment. Rather than rushing forward into relationships, situations and projects, take your time and slow down. Carve out ten or fifteen minutes a day when you can sit quietly and meditate or just daydream. Be sure to do something you enjoy each day of this retro, which lasts until December 22.

The full moon in Gemini brings news about a partnership—personal or business—and about some sort of communication project. You and your romantic partner may decide to deepen your commitment to each other—you move in together, get engaged or married or decide to start a family.

Between December 9 and January 26, 2018, Mars transits Scorpio. You may be deep into a research project or preparing for a presentation of some kind. Since this transit occurs in that part of chart that governs institutions, you could be spending more time than usual visiting hospitals, nursing homes or even prisons. This doesn't mean that *you* will be confined in any of these places. You may be volunteering time and energy that involves these institutions or perhaps visiting a friend or relative. You're seeding your wishes and desires for the new year, specifically for when Mars enters your sign in late January.

The 18th is a day to anticipate! The new moon in your sign ushers in all sorts of fresh energy and opportunities for self-expression and travel and for being involved in some facet of publishing or higher education. This new moon happens just once a year and sets the tone for the next six months, so make a list of what you would like to achieve in the next twelve months. Post it where you'll see it often!

On December 20, Saturn enters Capricorn, where it will be for the next two and a half years. During this lengthy transit, you get more serious about your finances. You may start saving more of what you earn or investing in areas or in ways that are more in line with your beliefs. The structures in your life that work are now strengthened. You become more disciplined in your approach to just about everything.

On the 22nd, Mercury turns direct in your sign and now, Sadge, it's time to throw a party to celebrate! Pack your bags, move forward with everything that went on hold during the retrograde. Finish up your holiday shopping. Take your sweetheart out for a romantic dinner or a long weekend.

Venus enters Capricorn on December 25 and will be there until January 17, 2018. During this period, your earnings should increase. You might find a second job or even a new job that pays you more. You also could meet someone special who shares your values.

AT A GLANCE
December 1—Venus enters Sagittarius
December 3—Mercury turns retro in Sagittarius, full moon in Gemini
December 9—Mars enters Scorpio
December 18—New moon in Sagittarius
December 20—Saturn enters Capricorn
December 22—Mercury turns direct in Sagittarius
December 25—Venus enters Capricorn

Reflection
You tend to look forward rather than back, but spend a few minutes writing your observations about 2017. Are you generally pleased with what the year delivered? What would you change and why? How can you use what you learned this year to achieve your dreams in 2018?

_____
_____
_____
_____
_____

Happy New Year!

Capricorn 2017

Your sign is ruled by Saturn. It's one of the slower-moving planets and takes two and a half years to transit a single sign. For most of this year, it's in Sagittarius. Then on December 20, it enters your sign, Capricorn, and that can be a bonus for you. You will be shouldering more responsibility and will be working toward the realization of dreams/goals you've had for some time. Even if you're putting in longer hours, the path ahead feels good to you. Whatever you're after can be realized because Saturn helps us to attain our desires, to make them tangible.

Noted in the monthly roundups are when Saturn is retrograde, when it turns direct and the angles the other planets make to it. In the monthly roundups, you'll also find information about the new and full moons, eclipses, the transits and retrogrades of other planets and what it all may mean for you!

2017 is a year in which cooperation, friendships and partnerships are important. Don't be in a rush to get things done or show resentment when something doesn't come out the way you hoped. Simply do what you do best—keep moving ahead, adjusting your strategy to fit the changing landscape.

January 2017
Slow beginning builds to powerhouse

Welcome to the new year! This one begins a bit slowly, with Mercury retrograde in your sign, a hangover from 2016.

Read through the Mercury retrograde section in the introduction (page 20) for general guidelines on how to successfully navigate any Mercury retrograde. Since this one occurs in your sign, it's vital that you communicate clearly with everyone in your environment; the potential for misunderstandings is great. Double check all dates and times for appointments. Leave a little earlier for work every morning. This is a time to slow down, mull over and work on projects and creative endeavors you've already started. The retrograde ends on January 8, when Mercury turns direct in Sagittarius, then returns to your sign on the 12th, joining powerful Pluto. It remains there until February 7, and during that period, you're a powerhouse of focused activity.

Between January 3 and February 3, Venus transits Pisces and that area of your chart that rules communication. This transit forms a beneficial angle to your sun and indicates that your communication abilities flow smoothly, a welcome relief after the Mercury retro! It's also possible that you meet someone in your neighborhood or community, perhaps through a sibling, who interests you romantically. You may also be trolling bookstores or art exhibits and may attend a concert or musical festival.

The full moon in Cancer on January 12 brings a relationship issue to a culmination or completion. Your intuition is deepened during this full moon, and you're more nurturing and attentive to your partner.

January 28 features a new moon in Aquarius, in your financial area. This one should bring in new sources of income. It could be through a second job, a raise or some other unexpected venue. Also on that day, Mars enters Aries, where it will be until March 9. This transit could bring disagreement or dissent at home, particularly if you are put in a position where you must stand up for yourself. You may be making some renovations to your home or completing a project you began and put aside.

AT A GLANCE
January 3—Venus enters Pisces
January 8—Mercury retrograde ends
January 12—Full moon in Cancer, Mercury joins Pluto in Capricorn
January 28—New moon in Aquarius, Mars enters Aries

February 2017
Mixed energies

Months in which eclipses occur tend to be tense and riddled with a sense of urgency. This happens because eclipses bring situations and relationships right to the forefront of your awareness, and you may have to act quickly and decisively.

The lunar eclipse in Leo on February 10 may trigger an emotional reaction concerning resources you share with others. Perhaps one of your adult children has gotten into a financial bind, and you have to bail her out, which strains your bank account. Or perhaps your mortgage application is rejected, and you aren't able to close the deal. However the specifics unfold, it comes at you out of the blue, and you must act quickly to rectify the situation.

The solar eclipse in Pisces on February 26 should usher in new opportunities in communication and your creative endeavors. With Neptune also in Pisces, your imagination is in full swing during this eclipse. You're able to use your innate organizational skills to translate the abstract into something concrete.

Now, what about the rest of the month? Venus enters Aries on the 3rd, joining Mars in the family area of your chart. When Venus and Mars travel together, particularly in passionate Aries, your love life ramps up. Because both planets now form a challenging angle to your sun sign, though, there could be some dissension or heated discussions at home, perhaps with your children. Next month, Venus turns retrograde, but we'll talk more about that in the March roundup.

Between February 6 and June 9, Jupiter moves retro through Libra and your career area. This retrograde isn't like that of Mercury, but it does put expansive Jupiter into a dormant state. Things in your career may go a bit more slowly than you would like, but it gives you a chance to re-evaluate your professional life. Jupiter's expansion becomes more of an inner process where you broaden your spiritual beliefs and take a deeper look at who you are as an individual, separate from your roles as parent, spouse, child, employee or CEO.

On the 7th, Mercury enters Aquarius and will be there until the 25th. Your conscious focus turns to money—what you earn and spend, what you save and whether or not you need a budget! Capricorns are usually pretty conscientious about saving money, but in the event you feel like splurging—and can afford it—do it now, while Mercury is in direct motion. In April it turns retrograde again.

Between February 25 and March 13, Mercury transits compatible water sign Pisces and your communication ability has a deeper psychic component to it. Your imagination is especially strong during this transit, which makes it a terrific time to visualize what you desire. If you can imagine it, you can bring it into your life.

AT A GLANCE
February 3—Venus enters Aries
February 6—Jupiter turns retrograde in Libra
February 7—Mercury enters Aquarius
February 10—Lunar eclipse in Leo
February 25—Mercury enters Pisces
February 26—Solar eclipse in Pisces

March 2017
Heightened creativity

It's a busy month, but should be less stressful than February was. That said, there's one potential rough spot—Venus turns retro in Aries on March 4, slides back into Pisces and turns direct again in that sign on April 15. This retro impacts the family/domestic area of your chart, so there could be some disagreements between you and your partner or between you and your kids. Money may be a bone of contention. Perhaps you're facing a hefty expense this month and money you're owed doesn't arrive promptly. Or perhaps your kids want a raise in their allowance. However the specifics unfold for you, just keep in mind that this, too, shall pass!

Between March 9 and April 21, Mars moves through fellow earth sign Taurus and the romance/creativity section of your chart. This transit is your muse's booster rocket and facilitates all your creative endeavors. Your sexuality is heightened, your physical energy is remarkable and your hunger for experience and enjoyment may prompt you to try new physical activities—rock climbing, for instance, or mountain biking.

The full moon in Virgo, also an earth sign, on March 12 should be quite nice for you. A project or activity is completed, and you're better able to connect the dots on something you're researching or studying. This full moon forms a beneficial angle to your sun and to Pluto, so if any challenges surface, they're resolved in your favor.

Mercury enters Aries on the 13th and remains there until the 31st. During this transit, your home is likely to be the hub of gatherings, particularly if you have teenagers. You may be planning adventures of one kind or another—topics you would like to research or countries you would like to explore. A mental restlessness is inherent in this transit. Once Mercury enters Taurus on the 31st, you're in more familiar territory, and your mind is grounded and focused.

The 27th brings a new moon in Aries. New opportunities surface with your family and in your domestic environment. You might, for instance, put your home on the market or receive an offer if your home is for sale. Someone may move in or out of your place—a parent, a child, even a boarder. You may have an opportunity to travel or to explore something that interests you.

AT A GLANCE
March 4— Venus turns retrograde in Aries
March 9—Mars enters Taurus
March 12—Full moon in Virgo
March 13—Mercury enters Aries
March 27—New moon in Aries
March 31—Mercury enters Taurus

April 2017
Keep moving

There's a lot going on this month, and you'll have to pace yourself to keep up with the shifting energies. Between April 6 and August 25, your ruler, Saturn, moves retrograde. During this period, you may be scrutinizing the larger picture of your life—where you are, where you're headed and where you would like to be in a year or two or five. You may be looking more closely at the structures in your life and considering what you would like to change.

On the 9th, Mercury turns retrograde in Taurus, slips back into Aries on the 20th and turns direct in that sign on May 3. First, look through the Mercury retrograde section in the introduction for general guidelines to follow. Since this retro hits two areas of your chart— home/family and creativity/romance—all those aspects of your life are affected in some way. While Mercury is retro in Aries, for example, you may have trouble with appliances and electronics. Relationships with family members may go awry. While it's retro in Taurus, there can be problems with creative endeavors—a need for revisions or rejections—and with your love life. Try not to make any irreversible decisions during this retrograde. You may regret it after Mercury turns direct!

The full moon in Libra on April 11 should bring a professional matter to a conclusion. Something that has concerned you is resolved in your favor. You're quite the diplomat now, and that skill serves you well with peers and bosses. A new project may get a green light, but don't sign anything until after Mercury turns direct on May 3. Jupiter is conjunct this moon, and even though it's retrograde, it confers protection and expansion. Between now and the new moon in Taurus on the 26th, think about the opportunities you would like to experience in romance and creativity. Make a wish list!

On the 15th, Venus turns direct in Pisces, and now your love life gets back on track. If a neighbor or sibling needs additional help and support, you're the one to provide it. On the 28th, Venus enters Aries again, where it will be until June 6, and it's time to tackle your home improvement or renovation projects. You may be working from home on a creative endeavor and will need space and time to get things exactly as you want them.

Between April 21 and June 4, energetic Mars transits Gemini and the daily work area of your chart. Think of Mars as your energy bar, Capricorn. It enables you to dive into whatever you're doing and get stuff done! You may be networking more with co-workers and employees and bolstering your company's website or blog. Communication is key.

The 26th features a beautiful new moon in fellow earth sign Taurus. New opportunities surface in romance, in creative endeavors and with your children. You could meet your soul mate or land a fantastic project that enables you to work on what you love, or you and your partner may discover that you're going to be parents. However the specifics unfold for you, this new moon is one to savor.

From April 28 to June 6, Venus transits Aries and your love life certainly heats up. Regardless of how chaotic and hectic things are at home, you feel equipped to deal with any obstacle or challenge that surfaces. Then again, that's your nature. When you come up against an obstacle, you either find a way around it or barrel through it.

AT A GLANCE
April 6—Saturn turns retro in Sagittarius
April 9—Mercury retrograde in Taurus
April 11—Full moon in Libra
April 15—Venus turns direct in Pisces
April 21—Mars enters into Gemini
April 26—New moon in Taurus
April 28—Venus enters Aries

May 2017
Take your time

May should be a slower-paced month than April was. Good thing, too, because the summer ahead promises to be astrologically hectic!

On the 3rd, Mercury turns direct in Aries, and you're aware that your thoughts are lighter and less scattered and that your goals are clearer. Your ideas have a free flow that they may have lacked during the retrograde. Go with them, Capricorn, and see where they lead you. Mercury stays in Aries until May 16. Once it transits Taurus, between May 16 and June 6, you're really in your element. You and your romantic partner communicate well, your muse shadows you and you and your kids have an excellent rapport. Mentally, you're more grounded and pragmatic. Any creative endeavors you undertake during this transit are tackled with utter efficiency.

The new moon in Gemini on May 25 should usher in new opportunities in your daily work. You might hire new employees, be tapped to head up a research or brainstorming team or land a terrific freelance project. New opportunities for networking and in communication could also surface.

AT A GLANCE
May 3—Mercury turns direct in Aries
May 10—Full moon in Scorpio
May 16—Mercury enters Taurus
May 25—New moon in Gemini

June 2017
Unpredictable but intuitive

Buckle up, Capricorn. June is a wild month! The action begins with Mars entering Cancer on the 4th, a transit that lasts until July 20. During this period, your partnerships, both personal and business, are on a definite roll. Thanks to the strong intuitive component of Cancer, you and your partner have the same vision for your company/services. If you do encounter a disagreement, talk it out.

In a committed relationship, your sexuality is heightened during this transit. You and your partner should carve out time daily for yourselves.

On June 6, Mercury enters Gemini, and Venus enters Taurus. On the 9th, Jupiter turns direct in Libra. Let's take these one at a time. The Mercury transit lasts until June 21 and brings your conscious focus squarely to your daily work routine. How can you be more efficient in your working environment? How can you improve conditions for your employees? What types of new products/services can you offer? How can you use technology more efficiently in marketing your products?

Once Mercury joins Mars in Cancer on the 21st, you're a powerhouse of forward thrust and momentum. Any differences you run into with a business or personal partner can be resolved through honest communication. Your conscious mind is more intuitive during this transit, which lasts until July 5.

Between June 6 and July 4, Venus transits Taurus, and it's one of the most romantic and creative for you all the year. The only other period like it is when Venus transits your sign between December 25 and January 17, 2018. Your self-confidence soars, and you're on a roll creatively that can be used in any way you want. Feel like booking a trip to some far-flung corner of the globe? Make it so. Would you like to try writing a screenplay? Get busy. You get the idea. During this period, the sky is the limit, Capricorn, particularly for someone with your resolve.

With Jupiter turning direct in Libra, in your career area, it's a major plus for your professional life. Whatever has been stalled now moves forward in a grand, expansive manner. Jupiter is like the jovial uncle who rushes toward the family with his arms thrown out and gives bear hugs to everyone.

On the 9th, the full moon in Sagittarius may stir up a restlessness to travel, and you may be researching possible locales. You should have greater access now to your own unconscious, and if old issues surface, just deal with them and resolve them once and for all.

On the 23rd, the new moon in Cancer ushers in new partnership opportunities—in business and in your personal life. You and your romantic partner may decide to deepen your commitment to each other by moving in together or getting married. There could also be new opportunities with your home and domestic environment—you receive an offer for your house, someone moves in or out or you find the perfect spot for yourself and your family.

AT A GLANCE
June 4—Mars enters Cancer
June 6—Mercury enters Gemini, Venus enters Taurus
June 9—Full moon in Sagittarius, Jupiter turns direct in Libra
June 21—Mercury moves into Cancer
June 23—New moon in Cancer

July 2017
Ah, those moons

The shifting energies this month may be challenging to keep pace with, so be sure that you get plenty of exercise and sleep! Four planets change signs, and there's a full moon in your sign.

On the 4th, Venus enters Gemini, where it will be until the 31st. If you live in the U.S., then the 4th is a holiday, and you may be socializing with family or neighbors, taking in a fireworks display and generally enjoying yourself. Once you get back to work, your relationship with employees and co-workers should unfold with greater ease. There's a possibility that an office flirtation turns into a something more, but be careful, Capricorn, about mixing business and pleasure!

Between July 31 and August 26, Venus moves through Cancer and the partnership area of your chart. You and your partner should make a point of getting away for a romantic interlude during this transit. Chill out, be lazy together and rediscover all the reasons the two of you are together!

On the 5th, Mercury enters Leo, where it will be until the 25th. During this transit, your mental focus is on resources you share with others—a partner, parent, child or even a roommate. If money is tight right now, you and/or your partner may be exploring ways to earn some extra income. Between July 25 and August 12, Mercury moves through fellow earth sign Virgo. This transit is comfortable for you. Your mind clicks along at a steady pace, and it's an ideal time for research, planning a long a trip and exploring your spiritual beliefs. You might attend a writers' conference or workshop.

The full moon in your sign on the 8th is conjunct powerful Pluto. A project, situation or relationship issue is resolved or culminates in a way that benefits you. You feel self-assured and confident about the direction of your life.

The new moon in Leo on the 23rd should usher in new financial opportunities. You may get a break in your insurance premiums or a refund, and if you applied for a mortgage or loan, it should come through. It's also possible that your partner gets a raise or that an unexpected royalty check arrives. With Mars also in Leo at this time, you experience plenty of forward momentum in whatever you're working on, and your creative drive is strong.

AT A GLANCE
July 4—Venus enters Gemini
July 5—Mercury goes into Leo
July 8—Full moon in Capricorn
July 20—Mars enters Leo
July 23—New moon in Leo
July 25—Mercury goes into Virgo
July 31—Venus enters Cancer

August 2017
Roller coaster

The month could be somewhat bumpy. There are two eclipses, and Mercury turns retrograde in Virgo. Let's first take a look at the eclipses.

The lunar eclipse in Aquarius on the 7th occurs in the financial area of your chart. Lunar eclipses tend to push our buttons, particularly about how we find security and safety in our lives, how we are nurtured and how we nurture others. Inner issues that surface have to be dealt with swiftly. There's often a sense of urgency. So this eclipse may trigger such feelings about your finances.

The solar eclipse in Leo on the 21st is like a double new moon, and the opportunities that flow your way concern money. You could sell your novel or screenplay, receive an unexpected check or even inherit money. It's a good day to buy a lottery ticket! Sometimes with solar eclipses, we have to relinquish something in order to embrace the new.

On the 12th, Mercury turns retrograde in Virgo, slides back into Leo and turns direct in that sign on September 5. By now, you know the drill with these Mercury retrogrades. But just in case you've forgotten, take a look at the Mercury retrograde section in the introduction and follow the general guidelines, this retro impacts two areas of your chart: foreign travel/worldview and resources you share with others.

On the 25th, Saturn turns direct in Sagittarius and now moves steadily forward toward its appointment with Capricorn on December 20. During its final months in Sadge, you're bolstering your inner structures, exploring your motives, needs and desires.

Venus enters Leo on the 26th, and between then and September 19, you could be earning money from a creative endeavor. Your love life may take a surprising turn. Jupiter forms a beneficial angle to Venus now, and that could be helpful for your professional life.

AT A GLANCE
August 7—Lunar eclipse in Aquarius
August 12—Mercury turns retro in Virgo
August 21—Solar eclipse in Leo
August 25—Saturn turns direct in Sagittarius
August 26—Venus enters Leo

September 2017
Mostly five stars

Now that the eclipses are behind you, September should be an easier month, particularly once Mercury turns direct in Leo on the 5th. On September 9, it enters Virgo once more, and now you're in your element again, moving forward with projects or activities that were put on hold during the retrograde. You have an excellent grasp of details during this transit and may be refining some aspect of yourself—your wardrobe or hairstyle, for instance. This transit ends on September 29, when Mercury enters Libra and the career area of your chart. During Mercury's run through Libra, which lasts until October 17, diplomacy, tact and courtesy are your tickets to getting along with bosses and peers. You may be part of a team endeavor and discover you're an excellent mediator!

On the same day that Mercury turns direct, Mars enters Virgo, so for a while the two planets are traveling together in that sign. Until October 22, Mars is forming a beneficial angle to your sun, and you're able to accomplish a great deal. Mars is the wind at your back, Capricorn, so raise your sails and get moving!

The full moon in Pisces on the 6th illuminates something about your neighborhood or neighbors or about your relationship with your siblings. Perhaps a neighborhood project in which you're involved is nearing completion or an issue with a brother or sister now culminates. Your imagination is especially strong during this full moon, so get out your watercolors and brushes and paint how you're feeling. Or dust off that manuscript you put away, and get to work! Neptune is conjunct this full moon, and that means you can tap into collective reservoirs of ideas.

Between September 19 and October 14, Venus transits earth sign Virgo and forms a beautiful angle to your sun sign. This period is ideal for international travel, taking courses or attending seminars and for delving into your spirituality. It also favors romance, of course, and if you meet someone special during this transit, the relationship will unfold smoothly. You'll know rather quickly whether the romance is going somewhere or is just a fling.

The 20th brings a new moon in Virgo—great timing, with Venus also there!—and should usher in new opportunities for travel and higher education and for romance and creative endeavors. Next month's new moon occurs in your career area, so give some thought about what you would like to develop in that area and how this new moon might help you to do that.

Mercury enters Libra and your career area on the 29th. Between then and October 17, your conscious focus is on professional matters. You may be socializing with bosses and peers more than usual, networking with other companies in allied fields and could be leading a team of some kind at work.

AT A GLANCE
September 5—Mercury turns direct in Leo, Mars enters Virgo
September 6—Full moon in Pisces
September 9—Mercury enters Virgo
September 19—Venus goes into Virgo
September 20—New moon in Virgo
September 29—Mercury moves into Libra

October 2017
Exciting

October is one of those months in which movers and shakers—that's you, Capricorn!—should do just fine in spite of how hectic things may be. Things get off to a running start on the 5th, with a full moon in fire sign Aries. Something culminates within your family or in your domestic environment. There may be news about a parent or other family member who needs your support or help. You experience some restlessness with this full moon, which forms a challenging angle to your sun, so burn it off through physical exercise. Hit the gym, take a Pilates class or go rock climbing.

On the 10th, Jupiter enters Scorpio, a major transit that lasts until November 2018. For hints about what this may mean for you, look back about twelve years to late October 2005. What was going on in your life during the fall of that year? Jupiter will now be forming a beautiful angle to your sun, and it will be possible for you to achieve your wishes and dreams during the next thirteen months. Expansion is the key word with this transit.

Venus enters Libra and your career area on the 14th. Between then and November 7, your professional life moves at a pleasing pace. Your hard work is recognized by the folks in charge, and a promotion or award could be in the offing. Women are especially helpful now in career matters, and you attract people and circumstances that facilitate what you do. You may become involved in an artistic or a musical project.

Between October 17 and November 5, Mercury joins Jupiter in Scorpio. This transit is ideal for any kind of research. You're able to delve deeply into whatever you tackle and find the answers you need. Jupiter expands your conscious awareness of your environment and urges you to get out and network with friends and acquaintances. You and a friend may join forces on a project of some kind.

On or around the new moon in Libra on the 19th, new opportunities surface in your career. It could be anything from a promotion to a new career path. You may have a chance to strike out on your own in some capacity, perhaps through a creative venue. Whatever the specifics are of these new opportunities, they get a substantial boost when Mars enters Libra on the 22nd. It will be in your career area until December 9 and should provide forward momentum for everything you undertake. So now you have Venus and Mars traveling together in your career area, and one thing that can mean is that a flirtation with someone in your work environment could turn into a romance.

AT A GLANCE
October 5—Full moon in Aries
October 10—Jupiter moves into Scorpio
October 14—Venus enters Libra
October 17—Mercury enters Scorpio
October 19—New moon in Libra
October 22—Mars enters Libra

November 2017
Life is good!

This month should be less frenzied than October. However, since the last Mercury retro of the year occurs between December 3 and 22, you may want to start your holiday shopping before December 3 so you aren't standing in the return line on the 26th! We'll talk more about this retro in December's roundup.

The full moon in Taurus on the 4th falls in the romance and creativity section of your chart and should be quite pleasant for you! Good news may arrive concerning a creative endeavor you have submitted for consideration. Even if you're asked to tweak the project in some way, you're glad to do it. You want the best possible product. You and your partner may plan a romantic getaway on or around the time of this moon. Since Taurus is a sensuous sign, take advantage of the energies!

On the 5th, Mercury enters Sagittarius and will be there until December 22 because of the retro. While it's moving in direct motion through the quiet part of your chart, you may be working on something that requires solitude. But even solitude should be broken up with free time to spend with friends, to travel, to exercise and to do the other things you enjoy. Your mind is restless during this transit, but you're able to envision the larger picture of whatever you're involved in.

Venus joins Jupiter in Scorpio on the 7th. When these two planets travel together and form a beneficial angle to your sun sign, life is good! You feel more optimistic, your magnetism and self-confidence soar and you attract new and interesting people who help you in some way in achieving your wishes and dreams. Your sexuality is also heightened during this transit, which ends on December 1.

As if that isn't enough, there's a new moon in Scorpio on the 18th that should bring new opportunities in research, exploration, friends and networks. You may be building a website, starting a blog or expanding your Facebook community in some way. Because the moon represents the mother and women generally, you may have interactions with your mother or other women in your life that are apt to be emotionally intense.

AT A GLANCE
November 4—Full moon in Taurus
November 5—Mercury enters Sagittarius
November 7—Venus goes into Scorpio
November 18—New moon in Scorpio

December 2017
Whirlwind

Are you ready? December may feel like a relay race! Not only does Mercury turn retro for the last time this year, but four planets change signs, and one of those changes is major.

Between December 1 and 25, Venus transits Sagittarius. Even though it's in the quiet part of your chart, Sadge is a gregarious sign, and you may be socializing quite a bit. But the socializing will be broken up with periods where you and your partner spend time alone together, working on a joint creative endeavor or simply enjoying each other!

On the 3rd, Mercury turns retrograde in Sadge and by now, you know how to mitigate the effects of these retrogrades. Here's the list of DO NOTS: Don't sign contracts, make travel plans, buy appliances or costly electronics, start a company or launch a project. Instead, follow the three Rs: revise, review and reconsider.

On the same day that Mercury misbehaves, the full moon in Gemini lights up the daily work area of your chart. There's work-related news or a project is completed. But because Mercury turns retro on the same day, you may have to go back and tweak some aspects of the project—i.e., revise!

On the 9th, Mars joins Jupiter in Scorpio and will be there until January 26, 2018. This powerhouse combination promises to be a whirlwind of activity. You may be trying to finish everything before the end of the year, for example, and find that your physical energy is exceptional. During this period, physical exercise is important, so don't cheat!

The new moon in Sagittarius on the 18th may bring new opportunities for travel, in publishing and higher education and for working behind the scenes in some capacity. This new moon is just two days away from Saturn entering your sign, so enjoy the energy it brings!

Saturn, your ruler, takes two and a half years to move through a sign. On the 20th, it enters Capricorn, where it will be until March 22, 2020. During this period, the structures in your life will be tested in some way. You may find that certain relationships no longer serve your best interest, and these individuals will fall away from your life. Any romantic relationships that begin during this transit may get serious quickly. You may come up against difficult bosses or others in authority, but because you're such a hard, dependable worker, they won't be a problem for you. Saturn tests you, yes, but its rewards can be fantastic!

On the 22nd, you should throw a party! Mercury turns direct again and won't turn retro until late March 2018.

Between December 25 and January 17, 2018, Venus transits your sign, marking a highly romantic and creative time for you. You're in the flow of life now, in synch with the people you care about, and it's easier to bring about your wishes and desires. Your self-confidence is rock solid, and you attract exactly the right people, at the right time. Not a bad way to end 2017, Capricorn!

AT A GLANCE

December 1—Venus enters Sagittarius
December 3—Mercury turns retro in Sagittarius, full moon in Gemini
December 9—Mars enters Scorpio
December 18—New moon in Sagittarius
December 20—Saturn enters Capricorn
December 22—Mercury turns direct in Sagittarius
December 25—Venus enters Capricorn

Reflection

It's been a significant year. But in what ways? Are your relationships unfolding the way you would like? What about your career, family life and finances? How can you use what you've learned this year, the strides you've made, to make 2018 an even more powerful year? Jot your thoughts below.

_____
_____
_____
_____
_____

Happy New Year!

Aquarius 2017

Your sign is ruled by Uranus, which is continuing its seven-year journey through fire sign Aries. It will be in this sign until mid-May 2018. In the monthly roundups, you'll find references to when Uranus turns retrograde and direct and when other planets form angles to it. Since Aries is compatible with your sign and forms a beneficial angle to it, life should be exciting and unpredictable for you now.

The monthly roundups also include information about the new and full moons, eclipses, the transits of the other planets and what all of it means for you!

This year, your creativity and innovative thinking are on the rise. You communicate well and others are drawn to your ideas. The routines of daily life will bore you, so it's smart to find new methods and venues that engage your adventurous spirit. In business, diversify as much as possible.

January 2017
New opportunities

The year gets off to a slow start with a hangover from 2016—Mercury retrograde in Capricorn. It slides back into Sagittarius and then turns direct in that sign on January 8. These retrograde periods are usually marked by miscommunication, mix-ups in travel plans, appliances breaking down and things not quite working the way you expect and hope. The point is that we're supposed to slow down and reevaluate what we're doing.

By following some simple suggestions, you can mitigate some of the fallout. Read over the Mercury retrograde section in the introduction for general guidelines to follow. This retrograde could result in snafus and misunderstandings with friends.

On the 3rd, Venus enters Pisces and your financial area, where it will be until February 3. You may be spending more, but your income should also increase. You may earn money through a creative endeavor of some kind—photography, dance, art, writing, interior design or, perhaps, through an app you created. Until the 28th, Mars is traveling with Venus through Pisces, and the combination deepens your imagination and makes it easier to realize your desires. If you're single, it's possible that a romance begins with someone who shares your values.

Once Mars joins Uranus in Aries on the 28th, you become a spinning dervish of energy and activity. You attract eccentric individuals who may be geniuses in their respective fields, and life has an exciting and unpredictable edge to it. This transit lasts until March 9.

On January 12, the full moon in Cancer highlights issues in your family/domestic environment, perhaps with your mother or other females. A work project may culminate, or there could be news of some kind related to your daily work routine. Perhaps your boss has decided that employees can now work from home several days a week!

The 28th is a day to relish. The new moon in your sign happens just once a year and sets the tone for the next twelve months. Prepare for this one by making a list of what you would like to experience and achieve in the next year and post it where you'll see it often. You may want to include some affirmations to post with it. *Life loves me and provides for me; abundance flows into my life in surprising ways every day.* Start with those two and add your own!

AT A GLANCE
January 3—Venus enters Pisces
January 8—Mercury retrograde ends
January 12—Full moon in Cancer, Mercury joins Pluto in Capricorn
January 28—New moon in Aquarius, Mars enters Aries

February 2017
Networking

Months that feature eclipses can be challenging, stressful and imbued with a sense of urgency. This is due to the nature of eclipses. They tend to bring relationship issues right into the forefront of our awareness so that we have to deal with whatever it is quickly. The lunar eclipse in Leo on February 10 occurs in your partnership area. An issue with a personal or business partner comes roaring to the surface of your awareness on or around the date of the eclipse. A power struggle of some sort may ensue. However, with Jupiter forming a beneficial angle to the eclipse degree, things should turn out in your favor.

The solar eclipse in Pisces two weeks later, on February 26, should bring new money opportunities. If you've been job hunting, for example, then you may find a job that pays well. Or you could get a raise, land a terrific freelance project or sell a creative endeavor. With Neptune closely conjunct the eclipse degree, these financial opportunities, whatever they are, seem to be in line with your ideals and perhaps even with your spiritual beliefs.

On the 3rd, Venus enters Aries, a transit you'll enjoy. A romance with someone in your neighborhood or community could be one of the bonuses of this transit, and it's possible you meet the person through a sibling or neighbor. Your emotions run pretty high during this transit—passion, jealousy and love. You may feel restless at times. The good part of this transit lasts until March 4, when Venus turns retrograde.

On the 6th, expansive Jupiter turns retrograde in fellow air sign Libra and turns direct again on June 9. During this period, Jupiter enters a kind of dormancy and its expansive nature turns inward. You have a chance to review your beliefs. Are they still serving you well or are they cutting you off from other opportunities? Given your druthers, what would you like most to do with your life? How can you realistically implement this desire into your experience?

On the 7th, Mercury enters your sign, and now you're at the top of your game! Your communication skills are sharp, your conscious mind is beautifully focused and ideas are flowing through you quickly. This transit lasts until the 25th. Combined with the energy of that new moon in your sign last month, start creating, Aquarius!

From February 25 to April 13, Mercury transits Pisces. Your conscious focus now turns to creativity, finances and perhaps how you can combine the two to make a living.

AT A GLANCE
February 3—Venus enters Aries
February 6—Jupiter turns retrograde in Libra
February 7—Mercury enters Aquarius
February 10—Lunar eclipse in Leo
February 25—Mercury enters Pisces
February 26—Solar eclipse in Pisces

March 2017
Greater clarity

The shifting energies this month may be challenging to keep pace with, so make sure you carve out time daily just for yourself! On March 4, Venus turns retrograde in Aries, slips back into Pisces on April 2 and turns direct in that sign on April 15. During this retrograde, you are mulling over your emotional needs and expectations in a romantic relationship. You may have doubts. Don't make any hard and fast decisions about things until Venus turns direct. You may feel that money is tight now.

Between March 9 and April 21, Mars transits Taurus and the home/family section of your chart. It's a great time for home improvement projects or to house hunt. Your physical energy is excellent and anything you tackle—from the personal to the professional—is done so with a steady patience and resilience that gets the job done.

The full moon in Virgo on March 12 brings news about a financial matter. A loan or mortgage is approved, a royalty check or insurance refund arrives or a student loan is paid off. If you're doing research, you find what you need and are able to connect all the dots so that the full picture emerges.

Between March 13 and 31, Mercury transits Aries, and you're really fired up about something—a communication project, an upcoming trip or adventure or perhaps a neighborhood celebration. Your mind is quick, decisive and able to make snap judgments. You're intuitive about the dynamics in relationships. On March 31, Mercury enters Taurus, where it will be moving direct until April 9, when it will turn retrograde. Get prepared for this retro now by launching new projects, signing contracts and making travel plans for after May 3, when Mercury turns direct.

The new moon in Aries on March 27 should be a good one for you. New opportunities surface to do some of the things you enjoy. You aren't hesitant about forging a path toward what you desire, and your desires gain greater clarity.

AT A GLANCE
March 4—Venus turns retrograde in Aries
March 9—Mars enters Taurus
March 12—Full moon in Virgo
March 13—Mercury enters Aries
March 27—New moon in Aries
March 31—Mercury enters Taurus

April 2017
Romance, creativity & fun

Seven astrological events this month may cause you to feel as if you're living on a constantly shifting sand dune! But you're a master at navigating difficult terrain. You're a visionary person and have probably already foreseen some of these challenges and have taken steps to mitigate whatever unfolds.

Between April 6 and August 25, Saturn moves retrograde through Sagittarius. This period provides ample time for you to take a closer look at the structures in your life. Have you outgrown some of your friendships and/or beliefs? Which beliefs are holding you back from achieving what you desire? How can you solidify the relationships that work well? How would you live your life differently in order to achieve your goals?

On the 9th, Mercury turns retro in Taurus, slips back into Aries and turns direct in that sign on May 3. Read over the Mercury retrograde section in the introduction for general guidelines. The retro begins in the home/family section of your chart, then moves into the communication area. It's especially important to communicate clearly with everyone in your environment. Try not to buy appliances or electronics during this period, unless you absolutely have to.

A full moon in Libra on April 11 should be very much to your liking. You receive news that's in your favor—about a legal or educational matter or about an international trip you're taking. A relationship is highlighted in some way, and you realize greater balance is needed.

Venus finally turns direct again on April 15, in Pisces. Your love life and finances should straighten out now. During the next thirteen days, Venus and Neptune travel together in Pisces, creating an environment rich with creativity. Your imagination soars, and you can easily tap into a well of inspiration and idealism in your creative endeavors. Between April 28 and June 6, Venus transits Aries. Your passions ramp up. Your self-confidence is excellent and attracts the right people at the right time. Enjoy the ride, Aquarius!

Between April 21 and June 4, Mars moves through Gemini and the creativity and romance section of your chart. This transit is your booster rocket, the additional fuel you need to dive into a creative endeavor and carry it through to completion. Your love life heats up, and you're adamant about doing whatever it is that brings you joy and pleasure. Your mind is particularly versatile now.

The 26th features a new moon in Taurus. This one should bring opportunities related to your home/family life. If you and your family have been house hunting, then you find the ideal place. If your home is on the market, you could get an offer. You may discover that you and your partner are going to become parents, or someone moves into or out of your home.

April 6—Saturn turns retro in Sagittarius
April 9—Mercury retrograde in Taurus
April 11—Full moon in Libra
April 15—Venus turns direct in Pisces
April 21—Mars enters into Gemini
April 26—New moon in Taurus
April 28—Venus enters Aries

May 2017
Enjoyable

Compared to last month, May should be the proverbial walk in the park. Good thing, because the summer ahead will be busy and active.

On the 3rd, Mercury turns direct in Aries. Celebrate! Book a trip somewhere. Move forward now with projects that you put on hold during the retrograde. Set a launch date for your new business or website. From May 3 to 16, your focus is on action—doing and getting stuff done. You may be spending more time than usual with siblings or people in your neighborhood. Between May 16 and June 6, Mercury transits Taurus, and you have the patience and resilience to implement ideas and projects that were begun when Mercury was in Aries. Your home and family are your primary focus.

The full moon in Scorpio on May 10 occurs in your career area. This moon is emotionally intense and can trigger psychic experiences. Your professional life is highlighted in some way—a project reaches completion, you may hear news about your company or a colleague that's important for you to know or perhaps you're recognized for the work you've done. Pluto forms a beneficial angle to this moon, indicating that you're in a powerful position for bringing about the change you desire.

May 25 features a new moon in fellow air sign Gemini. You'll enjoy this one, Aquarius. New opportunities surface in romance, creativity, communication and with your kids. You may start writing that novel or screenplay you've been mulling over. You also may be socializing and networking more than usual and doing more of whatever it is that you enjoy.

Overall, May is an enjoyable month!

AT A GLANCE
May 3—Mercury turns direct in Aries
May 10—Full moon in Scorpio
May 16—Mercury enters Taurus
May 25—New moon in Gemini

June 2017
Hectic in a good way!

Ready to rock 'n' roll, Aquarius? June may feel like an endless dance marathon, and it's important that you get plenty of rest and carve out time for yourself every day. You would benefit from both a meditation practice and a regular exercise routine.

On June 4, Mars enters Cancer and that area of your chart that represents your daily work routine and the maintenance of your health. It will be in that position until July 20. During this period, you're able to navigate your various projects and responsibilities in an intuitive way. The challenge with this transit is to not take everything personally! If you can do that, the transit will unfold with greater smoothness. Mars in Cancer forms a harmonious angle to your career area, so you'll have ample opportunities to advance professionally. You may be working out of your home more frequently.

On the 6th, Mercury enters Gemini, and Venus enters Taurus. On the 9th, Jupiter turns direct in Libra. Let's take Mercury first.

This planet rules Gemini and functions well in this sign. Your focus between June 6 and June 21 is on romance, creativity, your kids and everything you do for fun and pleasure. If you're involved right now, then you and your partner should be getting along well during this period. Conversation flows easily, you agree on most things and the two of you may be socializing quite a bit. If you're not involved right now, then that may change during July's transits, when Venus will be in Gemini. Creatively, you're on a roll, so make good use of this transit, and don't just fritter your time away!

Between June 6 and July 4, Venus moves through Taurus. This transit triggers your sensuality—and not just in terms of sex. Life itself feels more sensual now. The caress of the wind transports you, and a vista of emerald green thrills you. You have more patience, resilience and appreciation for the beauty in life. You may feel compelled to beautify your surroundings in some way.

On the 9th when Jupiter turns direct in air sign Libra, you sense the shift in energy. You suddenly feel luckier, happier and more optimistic. Jupiter now moves on through Libra until October 10, when it enters Scorpio and your career area. That transit will last until November 2018 and will be big for your career, so plant the seeds now for the changes you would like to experience professionally.

The full moon in Sagittarius on June 9 should ramp up your social life. You may have so many invitations that you'll be able to pick and choose. Saturn is also in Sadge, indicating that any new friendships that begin on or around the time of this moon will endure.

Between June 21 and July 5, Mercury transits water sign Cancer. You may have to make some adjustments to your daily work routine and the way you maintain your health. You might try, for instance, a new diet or nutritional program or sign up for classes at the gym that you haven't sampled before. At work, an adjustment of your hours or the way you interact with co-workers/employees could be in order. Intuitively, you'll know how to proceed. Mercury is traveling with Mars now, and when these two join forces, your intellect and communication skills are sharper.

The 23rd features a new moon in Cancer, so there's a lot of emotional energy to deal with now. New opportunities come your way now in daily work—new responsibilities perhaps and a promotion or a new project of some kind. If you're self-employed, the new project that comes your way thrills you.

AT A GLANCE
June 4—Mars enters Cancer
June 6—Mercury enters Gemini, Venus enters Taurus
June 9—Full moon in Sagittarius, Jupiter turns direct in Libra
June 21—Mercury moves into Cancer
June 23—New moon in Cancer

July 2017
Hang loose

There's a lot going on astrologically, but in some ways July will be an easier month for you than August, which features two eclipses, one of which will be in your sign. In a sense, July is your month to hang loose, go with the flow of the shifting energies and bolster your reserves for next month.

Venus enters Gemini on July 4, marking the beginning of one of the most romantic and creative times for you all year. If a romance begins between now and July 31, when the transit ends, it's sure to unfold smoothly, and you and your partner will enjoy great communication and joy in each other's company. During this period, your creative adrenaline is pumping fast and furiously, so make good use of the time and energy. Dive into your creative endeavors.

Between July 5 and 25, Mercury moves through Leo. During this transit, your communication with other people is quite strong, with an excellent exchange of ideas. If you and a business or personal partner disagree on something, compromise may be necessary.

The full moon in Capricorn on July 8 highlights issues you may have pushed aside that now have to be resolved. It may also bring news about career matters—a project reaches completion or you realize the steps you have to take to achieve something. Pluto is closely conjunct this moon, suggesting that you're in control of any situation that surfaces.

From July 20 to September 5, Mars transits Leo and your partnership area. Like the Mercury transit, this one is opposed to your sun. The opposition can result in conflict with other people because you're both certain you're right. Compromise solves the dilemma. This transit confers a lot of physical energy, so it's a good idea to keep physically active.

The new moon in Leo on the 23ʳᵈ should bring in new opportunities to strut your stuff and gain recognition for something you're doing or have done. You may meet the ideal partner for a business you're launching. Or, you and your partner decide to deepen your level of commitment to each other.

Mercury enters Virgo on the 25ᵗʰ. It will turn retrograde next month, on August 12, so prepare for that now by signing contracts, making travel plans that fall on either side of the retro dates—it ends September 5—and implementing new endeavors. Connect all the dots!

On the 31ˢᵗ, Venus enters Cancer and your daily work area. During this transit, which ends August 26, your daily work routine should unfold with greater ease. Women play prominent roles and prove helpful. Heed your intuition.

AT A GLANCE
July 4—Venus enters Gemini
July 5—Mercury goes into Leo
July 8—Full moon in Capricorn
July 20—Mars enters Leo
July 23—New moon in Leo
July 25—Mercury goes into Virgo
July 31—Venus enters Cancer

August 2017
Feels like a roller coaster

Months in which eclipses occur are often tense and imbued with a sense of urgency. However, this month's eclipses fall on the axis of Aquarius/Leo, so you may feel as if you're on a roller coaster that's nearly careening out of control. You're not, of course, and once you step back a little in order to see the larger picture, it's easier to gain perspective on what's happening.

The lunar eclipse on August 7 falls in your sign. You may have an emotional reaction to an issue that surfaces or to someone in your personal life. Rather than stewing over whatever it is, say your piece and be done with it. The quicker you act, the more quickly it all blows over. Jupiter forms a close angle to the eclipse degree, suggesting that you may blow things out of proportion, but it all shakes out in your favor in the end.

The solar eclipse in Leo on August 21 should be a powerhouse of new opportunities for you. New partnerships, new venues for self-expression and greater expansion in some area of your life. You and a professional partner create the overall strategy for your company and agree on a vision for the products or services you provide. You and your personal partner may decide to move in together or get married.

On August 12, Mercury turns retrograde in Virgo, slides back into Leo and turns direct in that sign on September 5. Once again, look over the Mercury retrograde section in the introduction for general guidelines. This retro hits two areas of your chart—shared resources and partnerships. Scrutinize all financial statements. If a check you're expecting is delayed, keep after the person/company who owes the money. With a partner, be open to compromise.

Saturn turns direct in Sagittarius on August 25 after a lengthy period of dormancy. You now have a clearer idea of your responsibilities and are more disciplined in the way you approach work, your obligations to your family and to yourself. Friendships and your various networks of contacts are strengthened.

Venus enters Leo on August 26, and you feel the shift in energy. You and your partner are more loving toward each other and applaud each other's achievements. This transit, which lasts until September 19, also facilitates your relationship with co-workers and friends. During this period you can make friends with virtually anyone.

AT A GLANCE
August 7—Lunar eclipse in Aquarius
August 12—Mercury turns retro in Virgo
August 21—Solar eclipse in Leo
August 25—Saturn turns direct in Sagittarius
August 26—Venus enters Leo

September 2017
Yin/yang energies

Once Mercury turns direct in Leo on the 5th, you're feeling quite upbeat about life. On the 9th, Mercury enters Virgo again, where it will be until September 29. During this transit, you may be pickier than usual, more self-critical and perhaps even more critical of others. If you can set aside the tendency to criticize, this transit can help you connect the dots with your investments and with insurance matters. Interest may be kindled in the paranormal.

Also on the 5th, Mars enters Virgo and will be there until October 22. Since it will be traveling with Mercury for some of the transit, you'll work more efficiently and may feel compelled to do some writing or speaking. You might start a blog or a newsletter for your company.

On the 6th, the full moon in Pisces brings a financial matter to your attention. News about your finances is possible, or a financial transaction—like obtaining a mortgage, for instance—is completed. This moon has strong imaginative and psychic components, so be sure to take time to explore your inner world.

Between September 19 and October 14, Venus transits Virgo and travels for a time with Mars in that sign. When these two planets join forces, the yin/yang energies are present and often find expression in a romantic relationship or creative endeavor. It's now easier for you to obtain a mortgage, loan and breaks in insurance premiums.

On the 20th, the new moon in Virgo brings new opportunities to delve into the esoteric. Your sexuality may be heightened during this new moon, particularly with Mars and Venus also in the same area of your chart. You may have a new opportunity for self-expression through writing and speaking.

When Mercury enters fellow air sign Libra on the 29th, the shift in energy suits you. Your conscious mind is more balanced, and you're able to see things from another person's point of view. You're also more social and eager to get out into the larger world and exchange ideas and experiences with others. This transit ends on October 17.

AT A GLANCE
September 5—Mercury turns direct in Leo, Mars enters Virgo
September 6—Full moon in Pisces
September 9—Mercury enters Virgo
September 19—Venus goes into Virgo
September 20—New moon in Virgo
September 29—Mercury moves into Libra

October 2017
Five stars

It's a busy month in the heavens, but most of what's going on should please you, and it all begins on the 5th with a full moon in compatible fire sign Aries. This one highlights your relationship with a sibling or neighbor and may signal the completion of a writing or communication project. There could also be news related to either area mentioned above. You may be spending more time traveling today than you usually do—carpooling or running errands. Be sure you have some inspiring CDs to listen to!

On the 10th, Jupiter enters Scorpio and the career area of your chart. Aren't you lucky! During the next thirteen months, your professional life will expand tremendously. You may land a significant promotion and raise; could change careers paths altogether; or find a job that pays better and is more personally rewarding. Or, you might launch your own business. You feel deeply certain that you can achieve whatever you desire now. Go for it, Aquarius! As Captain Picard of *Star Trek* used to say, *Make it so!*

Between October 14 and November 7, Venus moves through fellow air sign Libra. You may take a trip abroad, meet someone from a different country or culture for whom you have strong romantic feelings or you may decide to go to graduate school or law school. Venus forms a beneficial angle to your sun sign during this transit, so your self-confidence should be soaring, and your self-expression and creativity are excellent.

On the 17th, Mercury joins Jupiter in Scorpio and until November 5, your mind seems to be exploding with all sorts of ideas about the nature of reality and the cosmos. You may delve into the paranormal and have psychic experiences. In whatever you take on, you're after the bottom line.

The new moon in Libra on the 19th brings opportunities for foreign travel, higher education, the law or spirituality and the arts. Your novel could sell, you might land an audition for a part you subsequently get or you have your first art exhibit. Since Venus is still in Libra, you could fall head over heels for someone you meet.

On the 22nd, Mars joins Venus in Libra, and the two travel together until November 7. Any relationship that begins now should be pleasurable, sensual and, well, fun! Mars remains in Libra until December 9.

AT A GLANCE
October 5—Full moon in Aries
October 10—Jupiter moves into Scorpio
October 14—Venus enters Libra
October 17—Mercury enters Scorpio
October 19—New moon in Libra
October 22—Mars enters Libra

November 2017
Career opportunities

November is a slower-moving month, giving you a breather before December's accelerated pace. It begins with a full moon in Taurus on the 4th, and what a beauty this one is. Neptune is closely conjunct, suggesting a rather dreamy day filled with idealism and ideas and great creativity. Something in your family or domestic situation is highlighted. A home improvement project is completed, or perhaps you find the perfect roommate. You're more stubborn than usual, so be careful that you're stubborn for a good reason rather than just being contrary.

On the 5th, Mercury enters compatible fire sign Sagittarius, and your social calendar gets crowded very quickly. You're in the mood for fun and hanging out with friends. You and a group of friends may do something really wild and adventurous—like ghost hunting or looking for Big Foot. This transit lasts until early 2018 because on December 3, Mercury turns retro. By now, you know the drill for these retrograde periods. But to prepare, get your holiday shopping done before the retro begins or after Mercury turns direct again on December 22.

On the 7th, Venus joins Jupiter in Scorpio, in your career area. This transit, which lasts until December 1, should facilitate all your professional endeavors. You're the talk of the town, Aquarius, and attract the right people and circumstances at exactly the right time. A promotion and raise may be in order. If you're not involved when this transit begins, you may be before it ends. Your romantic interest could be someone with whom you work or whom you meet through work.

The 18th features a new moon in Scorpio, in your career area. This is a fabulous follow-up to Venus and Jupiter in the same sign and indicates new career opportunities that could be all over the map. The possibilities? A promotion, raise, new career path or new responsibilities. This new moon happens just once a year and sets the tone for your professional life for the next year. Prepare for it. Make a wish list. Back it with emotion. Post the list where you'll see it often.

AT A GLANCE
November 4—Full moon in Taurus
November 5—Mercury enters Sagittarius
November 7—Venus goes into Scorpio
November 18—New moon in Scorpio

December 2017
Unpredictable

Bottom line? December is a wild month, with frequent shifts in energy. Also, Mercury will be moving retrograde between December 3 and 22, so let's start there. The first step in navigating this retrograde in Sagittarius is to revise, review and reconsider. Don't sign contracts or launch new endeavors. If you have to travel, be as flexible as possible because your itinerary may change suddenly and without warning. Double check all appointments, and do your holiday shopping on either side of the retrograde.

Before the retro begins, Venus enters Sagittarius on December 1, a beautiful transit for you that ends December 25. During this period, you're socializing more and, thanks to the approach of the holidays, doing a lot of partying! Romance is possible with someone you meet through friends or through a club to which you belong. If you're already involved with someone, then you and your partner may get away for a romantic weekend. Just remember that your plans may change suddenly. But that can be part of the adventure!

On the 3rd, in addition to Mercury turning retro, there's a full moon in Gemini that highlights a romance, creative endeavor, your kids or a communication project. Neptune forms a challenging angle to this full moon, suggesting that any confusion you experience today may be due to a lack of information. You don't have the full story. The fact that Mercury turns retro on the same day doesn't help the confusion factor!

On the 9th, Mars joins Jupiter in Scorpio in your career area. Wow! This powerhouse enables you to move full steam ahead in your professional life and even with Mercury retrograde, you're able to achieve whatever you tackle. Mars will be in this position until January 26, 2018, so make the most of it! This duo creates a perfect climate for research, particularly medical and/or esoteric research.

The 18th features a new moon in Sagittarius. This one could be cause for celebration. New opportunities for foreign travel emerge, new friends enter your life and perhaps new publishing opportunities appear as well because Sadge rules that industry.

Circle the 20th on your calendar. Saturn enters Capricorn, a major transit, and it will be there for the next two and a half years. Saturn rules Capricorn and functions well in this sign. During this period, you will become much more conscious of the structures in your life—which ones benefit you, which ones don't. You may become more disciplined in your approach to career matters and may start laying out strategies for achieving your goals. If you encounter restrictions or limitations in certain areas of your life, you'll barrel through them in typical Aquarian fashion—through your intellect and by tapping the resources of your vast network of contacts.

Mercury turns direct on the 22nd, so now you can plan your holiday parties and New Year's festivities without running into a hundred snafus. On the 25th, Venus joins Saturn in Capricorn and will be there until January 17, 2018. A romance that begins during this period could be with an older individual or with someone who's a workaholic. For an existing relationship, there could be a strengthening of your commitment to each other, or you may decide that the rules in the relationship don't suit you.

AT A GLANCE
December 1—Venus enters Sagittarius
December 3—Mercury turns retro in Sagittarius, full moon in Gemini
December 9—Mars enters Scorpio
December 18—New moon in Sagittarius
December 20—Saturn enters Capricorn
December 22—Mercury turns direct in Sagittarius
December 25—Venus enters Capricorn

Reflection

You're such a forward-thinking person that reflection is at the bottom of your list of things to do. But if you take 30 to 60 seconds to look back at this year, it may provide perspective on how to make the most of 2018. Did you meet your goals in 2017? How has your life changed? Are you happy with where you are now? Note your thoughts below.

_____

_____

_____

_____

_____

Happy New Year!

Pisces 2017

Your sign is ruled by Neptune, which is continuing its fourteen-year transit through Pisces. That transit began in early April 2011 and ends in January 2026. Neptune in Pisces provides ample opportunities for self-expression, to delve into your creativity and spirituality and to integrate your ideals into your life. Jupiter co-rules your sign, and until October 10, it's in Libra, expanding the shared resources part of your chart. Once it moves into water sign Scorpio, you will be enjoying an absolutely beautiful thirteen-month period.

In the monthly roundups, you'll find references to when other planets form angles to Neptune as well as information on new and full moons, eclipses, the transits and retrogrades of the other planets and what it could all mean for you!

Overall, 2017 should please you. You're going to be building new foundations in your life, making new contacts and forging ahead in your creative endeavors. Thanks to Neptune's continued transit of your sign, your imagination will continue to take you to new worlds to explore.

January 2017
Slow start

The year gets off to a slow start because of a hangover from 2016—a Mercury retrograde that began in Capricorn. Mercury slipped back into Sagittarius, where it turns direct on January 8. During the first week of the year, things may feel off professionally. Plans and projects may go awry and appointments may be rearranged or cancelled at the last moment. Once Mercury turns direct, why not celebrate with a post-New Year's party and bring 2017 in the right way? On the 12th, Mercury re-enters Capricorn, joining Pluto there, and you're in your element once again until February 7. During this transit, you're networking more with friends and acquaintances and may be socializing frequently. Your career goals for this year are becoming much clearer, and you may be able to visualize how you can integrate your ideals into your daily work life.

Between January 3 and February 3, you're in one of the most romantic and creative periods for you all year. Venus moves through your sign, attracting the right people at the right time. A romance could begin during this transit that brings you great joy, and perhaps you and your romantic interest have so much in common that you also become business partners.

The 12th features a full moon in fellow water sign Cancer, in the romance/creativity sector of your chart. A creative endeavor is completed, or you gain insight about something in the endeavor that has to be tweaked. With this moon, your intuition is heightened, so use that instead of logic to tweak whatever it is. Your intuition also offers perfect insight into a romantic relationship.

On the 28th, there are two astrological events: a new moon in Aquarius and Mars enters Aries. With the first event, you may have an opportunity to work behind the scenes in some capacity, perhaps on a cutting edge project that excites you. You're seeding your desires for actualization at the next new moon, which will be in your sign.

Mars will be in Aries until March 9, and during this time, you make a lot of progress financially. You may be working longer hours, so you're being paid for overtime, or you could take a second job. Perhaps you go the freelance route or have a chance to do some consulting. However the specifics unfold, you feel as if you're moving toward greater financial freedom.

AT A GLANCE
January 3—Venus enters Pisces
January 8—Mercury retrograde ends
January 12—Full moon in Cancer, Mercury joins Pluto in Capricorn
January 28—New moon in Aquarius, Mars enters Aries

February 2017
New opportunities

February features two events that can be troublesome—a pair of eclipses. The lunar eclipse on February 10 falls in Leo. You may feel a sense of lack concerning your daily work. This feeling could be brought on by something a co-worker or employee says, and it triggers a cascade of associated emotions. Perhaps you feel you aren't getting the attention or accolades that you deserve. The best way to deal with your emotions it to acknowledge them—and then release them.

The solar eclipse in your sign on the 26th packs the whammy of a double new moon. New opportunities surface in your personal life and may entail your creative and artistic endeavors, your love life, your career, your family or any area that's important to you. Neptune is closely conjunct the eclipse degree, so there could be an element of spirituality to any opportunity that unfolds.

On February 3, Venus enters Aries and your financial area. It will be there for a while because next month Venus turns retro in Aries, slides back into Pisces and turns direct in your sign on April 15. While Venus is in direct motion in Aries, it's traveling with Mars, a terrific combo for making more money. You have the self-directed momentum now to implement new ideas concerning what you earn. Luck is also on your side. A romance could be kindled, too, with someone who shares your values, and it's likely to be passionate and sensual.

Jupiter has been in Libra since the fall of last year and will continue its passage through that sign until October 10. It has led to expansion in some area of your life—possibly in your partner's income, in resources you share with others or in the ease with which you can obtain mortgages, loans and reasonable insurance rates. All of this will slow down between February 6 and June 9, when Jupiter is moving retro. It will be a time when you scrutinize your spiritual beliefs, educational goals and general direction in life.

On the 7th, Mercury enters Aquarius and moves through it until the 25th, when it slips into your sign. While it's in Aquarius, you may be up against a deadline that demands solitude to complete a project. You have greater access to your own unconscious during this transit, and your dreams are apt to provide insights and answers. Once it enters your sign, where it will be until March 13, you feel more comfortable in your own skin, your imagination soars and your considerable intuition deepens.

AT A GLANCE
February 3—Venus enters Aries
February 6—Jupiter turns retrograde in Libra
February 7—Mercury enters Aquarius
February 10—Lunar eclipse in Leo
February 25—Mercury enters Pisces
February 26—Solar eclipse in Pisces

March 2017
Ideas pour in

If you thought that March would be a month to kick back, think again! There's plenty going on, and it begins with Venus turning retro in Aries on March 4. It doesn't turn direct again until April 15, in Pisces. Then on the 28th it enters Aries again. During this period, money you're owed may be delayed, so watch your expenses this month. Be sure to check bank statements carefully. If you do your banking online, change your password.

This retrograde can also impact your creative endeavors and your love life. With the first, you may have to tweak a project to someone else's satisfaction. In romance, you and your partner may hit some bumps in your relationship. Just don't make any irreversible decisions!

Between March 9 and April 21, Mars transits Taurus, an earth sign compatible with your sun. This period favors all forms of communication and should propel you into new venues for self-expression. Your physical vitality is also excellent, and it would be a great time to join a gym or take up running or some other form of regular exercise.

The full moon in Virgo on March 12 occurs in your partnership area. You gain insights into a business or personal partnership, or there may be news in this area. Virgo is a discerning sign, excellent with details, but also prone to criticism of self and others, so refrain from critiques of others! You may feel creatively inspired, too, perhaps to complete an endeavor you've been working on.

On the 13th, Mercury enters Aries and will be there until the 31st. During this transit, with Venus still retro in this sign, your focus is on finances—how to earn more or how to budget your money more effectively. Where can you cut your expenses? You may be flooded with good ideas during this transit, so be sure to record them as they come to you. They will prove useful in days to come.

The 27th features a new moon in Aries. With the fire sign energy now quite concentrated, you may be feeling there's nothing you can't achieve. And you're right! This new moon should usher in new financial opportunities.

On the 31st, Mercury joins Mars in Taurus, where it will be for quite a while because next month—on the 9th—Mercury turns retro. Until then, though, you are grounded, practical, resilient and more stubborn than usual!

AT A GLANCE
March 4—Venus turns retrograde in Aries
March 9—Mars enters Taurus
March 12—Full moon in Virgo
March 13—Mercury enters Aries
March 27—New Moon in Aries
March 31—Mercury enters Taurus

April 2017
Bumpy

April is a month that will make your head spin. Promise yourself a few things: to get enough sleep, carve out time for yourself daily and to associate only with positive, upbeat people. Because you're the psychic sponge of the zodiac, soaking up the moods of the people around you, it's important that the people you spend the most time with are happy!

Between April 6 and August 25, Saturn moves retro through Sagittarius and your career area. During this period, you may be reevaluating your professional goals and looking back over where you have been and forward to where you would like to be in the near future. Are the structures in your professional life serving you well? If not, how can you change them?

On April 9, Mercury turns retrograde in Taurus, slips back into Aries on the 20th and then turns direct in that sign on May 3. Look over the Mercury retrograde section in the introduction for general guidelines. This retrograde impacts your financial and communication areas. Pay special attention to your finances—what you spend, ATM withdrawals, credit card bills and bank statements. And say what you mean rather than beating around the bush.

The full moon in Libra on April 11 illuminates a financial matter—specifically your partner's income or issues connected to mortgages, loans, insurance premiums or royalties. You may also become more aware of a need for greater balance in some area of your life and are able to see an issue from the other person's point of view.

The 15th is a great day for a celebration—Venus turns direct again in your sign. Finally! Your romantic and creative travails are now history. In fact, between April 15 and 28, you're in one of the most creative and romantic times for you all year. Your muse is at your beck and call, your self-confidence and magnetism are at their peaks and you're feeling as good as you did in January, when Venus was in your sign. Your love life is now just about perfect.

Between April 21 and June 4, Mars moves through Gemini, a transit that's sure to stir up activity in your home environment. If you have kids, then your place becomes the gathering hub. Family dinners feature lively conversations and exchanges of ideas. During this transit, you may be building a website or blogging or communicating with the larger world in some way. The challenge with this transit is to not take on so many projects that your energy is scattered.

On April 26, the new moon in compatible earth sign Taurus ushers in new opportunities in communication. You might be hired, for example, to develop and write a community newspaper or e-zine that focuses on your company's services or products. However the specifics unfold, this new moon should be pleasant for you.

Between April 28 and June 6, Venus transits Aries and your financial area. You may be spending more during this period, but you are also earning more. In a relationship, your passions are fired up, and you may be more impulsive than usual in romance. Guard against bouts of jealousy or envy.

April 6—Saturn turns retro in Sagittarius
April 9—Mercury retrograde in Taurus
April 11—Full moon in Libra
April 15—Venus turns direct in Pisces
April 21—Mars enters into Gemini
April 26—New moon in Taurus
April 28—Venus enters Aries

May 2017
Relaxing

If it's now spring where you live, then May is a month to indulge your love of the outdoors—start a garden, take long walks through nature and appreciate the natural world. Circle May 3 as a day to celebrate: Mercury turns direct in Aries. Now you can plan your trip, sign contracts and move forward with your various projects and endeavors. Mercury will be in Aries until May 16, when it enters Taurus. While it's in Taurus, your focus is on practicality and efficiency, and you make steady progress on whatever you're doing. This transit lasts until June 6.

The full moon in fellow water sign Scorpio on May 10 highlights an issue dealing with spirituality, research, higher education, international travel or the paranormal. Scorpio is an emotionally intense sign, so in the days leading up to this full moon and on the day of, you may be more emotionally charged up than usual. But your imagination and intuitive ability are stellar.

The new moon on May 25 joins Mars in Gemini. New opportunities surface in terms of your domestic life, communication and networking. You and your family may find the perfect home and/or neighborhood, or if your home is on the market, you receive an offer. The combination indicates that the momentum Mars in Gemini has built up now pays off.

AT A GLANCE
May 3—Mercury turns direct in Aries
May 10—Full moon in Scorpio
May 16—Mercury enters Taurus
May 25—New moon in Gemini

June 2017
Energetic

June is a wildly shifting month astrologically. Pace yourself, and don't take on so much that you feel burdened.

Mars transits fellow water sign Cancer between June 4 and July 20, and you are ramped up creatively and on a roll. Whether you're preparing paintings or photos for an exhibit or website, writing the great American novel or redecorating your home or office, you have the physical energy to get the job done. Your sexuality is also heightened during this transit, and you may have a romantic fling. If you're involved with someone, then you and your partner may want to get away for a romantic weekend at some point during this transit.

June 6 to 9 is a period that could leave you overwhelmed. On the 6th, Mercury enters Gemini and Venus enters Taurus. On the 9th, Jupiter turns direct in Libra. Let's look at each of these events.

Mercury transits Gemini from June 6 to 21. Whether you're in school or not, study, research and learning are part of this transit. You're reading more books, surfing more websites and may be searching for some particular nugget of information. You're also more communicative and could be in a more social frame of mind. Once Mercury joins Mars in Cancer on the 21st, you're back in the intuitive flow. Your focus is on enjoyment, romance, your children and creative endeavors. In whatever you do, Mars acts as your booster rocket. This transit ends on July 5.

Between June 6 and July 4, Venus moves through Taurus, a sign that it rules, so it functions well here. You feel more sensual, your self-confidence increases and you may feel compelled to beautify your surroundings in some way. As a Pisces, you enjoy being around water, so adding a fountain to your yard, patio or meditation area would be an ideal touch to soothe your soul.

When Jupiter, the planet of luck and expansion, turns direct in Libra on the 9th, it's now functioning at full capacity. Jupiter rules your career area, so you should see significant progress professionally. You might, for instance, land a promotion or a raise or find a new job that is more personally satisfying. The planet now moves toward its rendezvous with Scorpio on October 10, a 13-month transit that will be beneficial for you.

The 9th features a full moon in Sagittarius that highlights your profession/career. A project reaches completion, there's news about a professional matter or the dynamics of your relationship with a peer or boss comes to light. Or all of the above! Saturn is also in Sagittarius, but isn't anywhere close to this full moon. If Saturn has been restricting you professionally in some way, you now understand the reasons why.

On June 21, the summer solstice, Mercury enters Cancer. You've had a lot of Cancer energy recently, and this transit, which lasts until July 5, makes you feel as though you are in your element. Your mental focus is on home, family, romance, creativity and the sheer enjoyment of being alive!

The new moon on June 23 is also in Cancer, a fabulous way to wind up the month. This one brings new opportunities for creative self-expression, in romance, and in whatever you enjoy doing. If travel is your passion, then this new moon hands you a new opportunity to indulge yourself. If you enjoy decorating your house, then the new moon brings in the money that allows you to go hog wild.

AT A GLANCE
June 4—Mars enters Cancer
June 6—Mercury enters Gemini, Venus enters Taurus
June 9—Full moon in Sagittarius, Jupiter turns direct in Libra
June 21—Mercury moves into Cancer
June 23—New moon in Cancer

July 2017
Forward momentum

If you were hoping that July would be a month for relaxation, think again! On July 4, Venus enters Gemini, and this transit, which lasts until the 31st, should facilitate communication between you and a partner. If you're not involved with anyone, then the transit creates greater harmony at home—with parents, your children or female friends. The transit to really anticipate, though, begins on the 31st and lasts until August 26. Venus will be in fellow water sign Cancer then, and this period promises to be the most romantic and creative time for you all year. This would be an excellent time to take a vacation with the one you love. The only other period that came close to this was when Venus was in your sign from January 3 to February 3.

Between July 5 and 25, Mercury moves through Leo and the daily work area of your chart. This transit can lend itself to drama in the workplace, with employees or co-workers, and unless you're in need of drama, it's best to avoid conflict of any sort. However, during this transit you have tremendous willpower, and ideas that come to you will carry your unique style.

The full moon on July 8 joins Pluto in Capricorn, an earth sign compatible with your sun. There could be news concerning a friend, a professional issue or colleague or a project reaches completion. Or all of the above. With Pluto in your court, however, you're in the driver's seat.

On the 20th, Mars joins Mercury in Leo, and for the next five days, these two planets combine energies to move things forward in your daily work routine. Mars provides the momentum, and Mercury provides the ideas and communication. Then on the 25th, Mercury enters Virgo, your opposite sign, and your focus is a partnership, either business or personal. You're better equipped to delve into details that have eluded you and come away with a better understanding of the dynamics of the relationship. This transit lasts until August 12, when Mercury turns retro.

And then there's the marvelous 31ˢᵗ, when Venus enters Cancer, and you begin to live what feels like a blissful life!

AT A GLANCE

July 4—Venus enters Gemini
July 5—Mercury goes into Leo
July 8—Full moon in Capricorn
July 20—Mars enters Leo
July 23—New moon in Leo
July 25—Mercury goes into Virgo
July 31—Venus enters Cancer

August 2017
Bumpy & then blissful

Months that feature eclipses are often laced with tension and a sense of urgency. This is due to the nature of eclipses, which highlight issues and relationships that usually need immediate attention. The lunar eclipse on August 7 is in Aquarius, in that part of your chart that rules the personal unconscious. On or around the date of this eclipse, you may have to address something within yourself—a resistance, attitude or feeling that surfaces. Your mother or another woman could be the trigger for whatever unfolds.

The solar eclipse in Leo on August 21 is like a double new moon—double the new opportunities that surface for you in your daily work routine. Possibilities? You're promoted and now have a chance to really shine in your workplace; you hire a new employee who has all the qualities you're seeking; or your company moves into a new building. If you're self-employed, you land a new project or job that thrills you. Pretty cool, right?

On the 12ᵗʰ, Mercury turns retro in Virgo, slips back into Leo and turns direct in that sign on September 5. By now, you know the drill about how to best navigate a Mercury retro. But let's reiterate. Don't sign contracts; you may have to revisit the terms at a later date. If you have to travel, be flexible and look at it all as an adventure because your itinerary may change without warning. Avoid purchasing large ticket items—a car, electronics or appliances. However, if your washing machine dies during the retro, by all means buy a new one, but check the delivery and other details carefully. Follow the rule of three Rs: revise, review and reconsider.

On the 25ᵗʰ, Saturn turns direct in Sagittarius and whatever delays you've encountered professionally in the past few months should now move forward again. On December 20, Saturn will enter Capricorn, a position more compatible with your sun sign.

Between August 26 and September 19, Venus transits Leo and the daily work area of your chart. During this period, there could be some drama in the workplace—with co-workers and/or employees. But otherwise, Venus facilitates your daily work life.

August 7—Lunar eclipse in Aquarius
August 12—Mercury turns retro in Virgo
August 21—Solar eclipse in Leo
August 25—Saturn turns direct in Sagittarius
August 26—Venus enters Leo

September 2017
Nearly perfect

On the 5th, you have reason to celebrate! Mercury turns direct in Leo and, on the 9th, returns to Virgo, where it was when it went retro last month. Things at work lighten up and whatever was delayed during the retro can now move forward. Also on the 5th, Mars enters Virgo, where it will be until October 22. This means that once Mercury transits Virgo between September 9 and 29, the two planets are traveling together, and the energy of Mars propels you forward in all your partnership endeavors.

Your communication skills are excellent during this period. While your Pisces sun envisions the large picture, Mercury and Mars connect all the myriad dots, and you have a firmer grasp on the dynamics of your personal and business partnerships.

The full moon in your sign on September 7 is conjunct Neptune, your ruler, and should be a beauty! Your imagination is deepened, and whatever you can imagine, Pisces, you can do. If there's any confusion on or around the date of this moon, you're able to sort things out.

On the 19th, Venus joins Mercury and Mars in Virgo. Wow! Venus will be in this position until October 14, and during this period, you and your romantic partner should try to get away for a long weekend. It's the ideal time to reconnect in a meaningful way and remind yourselves why you're together.

The new moon in Virgo on the 20th just sweetens the whole package! You and your partner may deepen your commitment to each other by taking the relationship to the next level. You move in together, get engaged or set a wedding date. In business, the ideal partner comes your way.

Between September 29 and October 17, Mercury transits Libra and the shared resources area of your chart. It's a good time to apply for a mortgage or loan, to prepare your will or hunt for a better car or health insurance rates. This transit also favors delving into the paranormal.

September 5—Mercury turns direct in Leo, Mars enters Virgo
September 6—Full moon in Pisces
September 9—Mercury enters Virgo
September 19—Venus goes into Virgo
September 20—New moon in Virgo
September 29—Mercury moves into Libra

October 2017
Five stars

October is another month of rapidly shifting energies, with four planets changing signs. Let's talk first about the major shift: Jupiter enters Scorpio on October 10 and for the next thirteen months will form a fabulous angle to your sun. You may travel abroad several times, could study abroad or may even travel in pursuit of a particular quest. You might decide to return to college or go to grad school. However the particulars of this transit unfold, your worldview and spirituality expand quickly and in often surprising ways. So start thinking about what you will do with this enormously positive energy.

On the 5th, the full moon in Aries lights up your financial area. You may realize that it's time to create a budget for yourself. Or, you may start looking for a second job to increase your earnings or for a different job that will pay you more and bring you greater personal satisfaction.

Between October 14 and November 7, Venus moves through Libra and the shared resources area of your chart. This transit makes it easier to obtain mortgages and loans and breaks on your insurance premiums. You may receive an unexpected royalty check or an insurance refund, or you might even inherit money. You're in a position to help a female friend, sister or another woman who may require additional support right now. In romance, a relationship should feel more balanced, more equal. And if it doesn't, you and your partner strive to make it so.

On the 17th, Mercury joins Jupiter in Scorpio, and what fun this will be! Even though you may feel and think more intensely than usual, your mind is sharp, penetrating and deeply intuitive. This combination favors research of any kind, but particularly research into the paranormal or the esoteric.

The new moon in Libra on the 19th ushers in new financial opportunities. Your partner or spouse may land a nice raise, someone could repay a loan, or you could sell an artistic product—a novel, screenplay, painting or photograph. If you're involved in any kind of legal issue, you get a break.

Mars enters Libra on the 22nd and will be there until December 9. Now you've got quite a powerful lineup of Libra energy in your court. Any relationship that begins during this period should be nicely balanced, aesthetic, artistic, communicative and sensual. Any time Mars and Venus travel together, romance is key, and your sexuality is heightened.

October 5—Full moon in Aries
October 10—Jupiter moves into Scorpio
October 14—Venus enters Libra
October 17—Mercury enters Scorpio
October 19—New moon in Libra
October 22—Mars enters Libra

November 2017
Enjoyable

November gives you a breather from the rapidly shifting energies of the past several months. Things get off to a beautiful start with the full moon in compatible earth sign Taurus on November 4. A communication project reaches completion or culminates in some way. You hear news that you have sold an article or book or something else you have produced. This full moon has allies—Jupiter in Scorpio, Neptune in Pisces and, until the 5th, Mercury in Scorpio. Plan something special. You've earned it!

On the 5th, Mercury enters Sagittarius and your career area, where it will be through the end of the year because on December 3, it turns retrograde. Until then, this transit enables you to see the bigger picture and to plan and strategize with that broader view in mind. You may travel for work, socialize with peers and bosses and do a lot of networking. Since Mercury is retro for so much of December, it's wise to do your holiday shopping this month, before the retro begins. Otherwise, you may be standing in the return line on December 26.

Between November 7 and December 1, Venus joins Jupiter in Scorpio. The two most benevolent planets in the zodiac are now forming a beneficial angle to your sun. Does it get any better than this? Your finances and romantic options expand, your artistic aspirations come into play, and you and your partner should enjoy a period of intense, positive emotion toward each other.

Then, on the 18th, along comes a new moon in Scorpio and new opportunities for foreign travel, increased understanding and greater insight into your closest relationships. You may have a chance to explore your spiritual beliefs in much greater depth.

AT A GLANCE
November 4—Full moon in Taurus
November 5—Mercury enters Sagittarius
November 7—Venus goes into Scorpio
November 18—New moon in Scorpio

December 2017
Hectic

As you enter the last month of 2017, start thinking about your expectations for the rest of the month and for the new year. What would you like to achieve and experience in 2018? Make a wish list. Back it with vivid images and powerful emotions.

The month actually gets off to a great start, with Venus entering Sagittarius and your career area. Perfect. Now is the time to get things done professionally. Other people are attracted to your energy and ideas, and it's easier to get along with co-workers, bosses and people you meet through your work. This transit continues until December 25 and should work its magic in spite of Mercury's mischievousness.

Okay, on the 3rd, Mercury turns retro in Sagittarius, and there's a full moon in Gemini. This retro is the last one of the year and ends on December 22. This one impacts your career area, so be sure to revise and review projects carefully, tie up loose ends so you don't have to carry anything into the new year and, as always, communicate clearly with bosses, co-workers and employees.

The full moon in Gemini on the 3rd could cause some tension at home, perhaps with children or even with parents. The key here is communication, even though Mercury is retro!

Between December 9 and January 26, 2018, Mars transits Scorpio, a sign it co-rules, so it functions well here. So now, Mars and Jupiter are traveling together. Events may move more quickly, particularly after the 22nd when Mercury turns direct. Your sexuality is heightened and your intuition is deepened.

December 18 features a new moon in Sagittarius, in your career area. New opportunities surface in your career—a raise, promotion or perhaps even a new career path. It depends, as so many things do, on where you have been placing your attention.

On the 20th, Saturn makes a major shift and moves into Capricorn, where it will be for the next two and a half years. During this period, Saturn forms a beneficial and supportive angle to your sun. The structures that exist in your life are strengthened and throughout the next several years you find the support you need wherever you turn.

On the 22nd, Mercury turns direct in Sagittarius. Yay! You know what to do now, right? Venus joins Saturn in Capricorn on the 25th until January 17, 2018. This is an ideal spot for Venus during the holidays. Let loose. Have fun. Hang out with friends and loved ones. Enjoy yourself!

AT A GLANCE
December 1—Venus enters Sagittarius
December 3—Mercury turns retro in Sagittarius, full moon in Gemini
December 9—Mars enters Scorpio
December 18—New moon in Sagittarius
December 20—Saturn enters Capricorn
December 22—Mercury turns direct in Sagittarius
December 25—Venus enters Capricorn

Reflection
You started the month by looking ahead, so what better way to end the last month of the year than by looking back? Was it a good year for you? Did you experience and achieve what you had hoped? Jot your thoughts below.

_____
_____
_____
_____
_____

Happy New Year!

2018

Introduction to 2018

Welcome to 2018!

Be sure to read over the introduction to the book (pages 8–22), which discusses some of the astrological basics you should keep in mind as you read through the monthly predictions for each sign.

In each monthly roundup, you'll find information about astrological activity pertinent to each month and what it may mean for you—when planets change signs, turn retrograde or make challenging or beneficial angles to other planets and eclipses, new and full moons and retrogrades. All of this information is intended to help you successfully navigate each month.

For a handy reference, I've included lists on the new and full moon dates and the dates of the Mercury retrogrades this year. The eclipses are also noted.

For most of this year, until November 8, expansive Jupiter is in Scorpio. Everyone benefits from a Jupiter transit, but for water and earth signs, this transit is especially powerful. Some of the luckiest times this year are when Venus and Jupiter travel together through Scorpio. This happens between September 9 and October 30.

Saturn went into Capricorn late last year and continues to transit that sign until late March 2020. This means that all earth and water signs will be impacted most strongly. Since Pluto is also in Capricorn this year—and for many years to come!—power issues surface for these signs as well.

In May, Uranus enters Taurus, turns retrograde in August and slides back into Aries where it remains until 2019. Hold on, earth and water signs, the ride will be wild!

Neptune continues its leisurely and dreamy transit of Pisces for many years, so once again, earth and water signs are impacted most strongly.

New and Full Moons for 2018

For a description of new and full moons, refer back to page 21 in the introduction to 2017. Turn to the next page for a list of all the new and full moons in 2018.

These moons are calculated for Eastern time.

NEW MOONS 2018

January 16—Capricorn
February 15—Aquarius: solar eclipse
March 17—Pisces
April 15—Aries
May 15—Taurus
June 13—Gemini
July 12—Cancer: solar eclipse
August 11—Leo
September 9—Virgo
October 8—Libra
November 7—Scorpio
December 7—Sagittarius

FULL MOONS 2018

January 1—Cancer
January 31—Leo: lunar eclipse
March 1—Virgo
March 31—Libra
April 29—Scorpio
May 29—Sagittarius
June 28—Capricorn
July 27—Aquarius: lunar eclipse
August 26—Pisces
September 24—Aries
October 24—Taurus
November 23—Gemini
December 22—Cancer

Eclipses have a specific function in astrology. Read about them in the introduction to 2017, on page 22.

Mercury Retrograde

Mercury turns retrograde—that is, it appears to move backward relative to the earth—three times a year, and the retro period lasts for about three weeks.

During this time, miscommunication is often rampant and appliances and electronics break down. It's wise not to launch any new projects or to sign contracts, since Mercury rules contracts. Mercury also rules moving parts, so it's smart not to buy a car or electronics during these periods. Travel can be iffy—plans go south quickly and itineraries change without warning. Everything moves more slowly. By following the guidelines above, you can mitigate some of the effects of these retrogrades. Also, it's best to revise, review and reconsider, what I call the rule of the three Rs, rather than start anything new. If you're a writer, don't submit manuscripts during the retro.

The Mercury retrograde periods are noted in the monthly predictions, but here's a quick reference.

MERCURY RETROGRADES IN 2018

March 22–April 15, Aries
July 26–August 19, Leo
November 16–December 6, Sagittarius

The only planets that don't turn retrograde are the sun and the moon. In the monthly roundups, you'll find references to when the other planets turn retro and what it may mean for you.

A Mercury Retrograde Story

Read through the Mercury retrograde story in the introduction for 2017 (page 9). That story illustrates how the trickster planet can create utter chaos on a national scale. On a personal level, it can create confusion and occasional bedlam.

Between May 18, 2015 and June 11, 2015, Mercury was retrograde in Gemini, my sign. On the 19th, the day after the retrograde started, I noticed that our washing machine wasn't working correctly. Although it filled with water, it didn't swish the clothes around and wouldn't go into the spin cycle. So, we called an appliance repair shop and a guy showed up that afternoon. The verdict? The machine's motherboard was shot. "Replacing the motherboard is going to cost you as much as a new machine."

Uh-oh, I thought. Did I really want to order an appliance during a Mercury retrograde? The bottom line was that we needed a washer, so, yes. My husband and I went online, found the store that had the best prices, and we ordered a new washing machine. But when the confirmation email came through, we saw we had ordered a dryer, not a washing machine! I got on the phone with customer service, explained the confusion and changed the order. On the day before the machine was supposed to be delivered, the delivery service called and left an automated message on the answering machine.

"Your dryer will be delivered tomorrow between noon and 4:00 p.m."

I called them and explained it was supposed to be a washing machine and was told that it would be another week before it could be delivered. It was eventually delivered and works fine, but it drove home the point that if you buy a large ticket item during a retrograde, it's important to double check the details!

Two days after this experience, my sister, Mary, texted me. *Mercury must be retrograde; you won't believe what just happened to me.* She was taking care of her son's dogs while he and his wife were in Europe and had locked herself out of the house. She ended up having to call a locksmith to get into the house, and it cost her nearly 300 bucks.

So in the monthly roundups when you see that a Mercury retro is coming up, prepare for it by scheduling travel and important events on either side of the dates. Be ready to pay closer attention to details.

Aries 2018

Since Mars rules your sign, pay close attention to what it's doing each month, which angles it makes to other planets and vice-versa. This year, Mars turns retrograde on June 26 in Aquarius, slips back into Capricorn and turns direct in that sign on August 27. In the June roundup, you'll find out how this retrograde may affect you. As a result of the retrograde, Mars transits only three other signs this year—Sagittarius, Capricorn and Pisces.

The monthly roundups also include information on the retrogrades of other planets, aspects transiting planes make your sun sign, eclipses and the new and full moon activity.

With Uranus continuing its movement through your sign, Aries, life is still unpredictable! 2018 is a year for playing your hunches and going with the flow.

January 2018
Career & a bit of drama

Welcome to 2018! The best news is that the year doesn't begin with Mercury retrograde, as 2017 did. For the first eleven days of the month, Mercury is in fellow fire sign Sagittarius, a great spot for you. In fact, you may be on the road, embroiled in an adventure or conducting some sort of research related to your work or to a particular passion you have.

You'll want to be back in town by the 11th, though, when Mercury enters Capricorn and the career area of your chart, where it will be until the 31st. During this period, you're all about setting professional goals and laying down a strategy for achieving them. You're ambitious and focused.

Between January 31 and February 18, Mercury moves through Aquarius, an air sign compatible with your sun sign. The 31st could be somewhat tense due to a lunar eclipse in Leo, which may trigger some intense feelings about a romantic relationship or a creative endeavor. While Mercury is in Aquarius you may be spending more time socializing and hanging out with friends. You're brimming with ideas, so be sure to jot them down. They'll come in handy later.

Your ruler, Mars, starts the year in Scorpio, and that means you may be more secretive than usual about something you're doing or involved in. Your resolve is impressive, and your uncharacteristic patience during this transit enables you to stick with anything you start. On the 26th, Mars enters Sagittarius, and you become the forward thinker, the one who sees the bigger picture. Leave it to someone else to connect the dots!

January 16 features a new moon in Capricorn. This one should usher in new career opportunities—a promotion, raise, new responsibilities or perhaps even a career change.

On the 17th, lovely Venus enters Aquarius, where it will be until February 10, and suddenly, your social life ramps up big time. Balance is the key here, Aries. Pick and choose your social invitations carefully. You may meet a romantic interest through friends or through an organization to which you belong. Mercury joins Venus on the 31st, and as long as these two travel together—until February 10—your conscious thoughts are very much on romance, creativity and money.

Also on the 31st, as mentioned earlier, there's a lunar eclipse in Leo. There could be some drama with this one!

AT A GLANCE
January 1—Full moon in Cancer
January 11—Mercury enters Capricorn
January 16—New moon in Capricorn
January 17—Venus enters Aquarius
January 26—Mars enters Sagittarius
January 31—Mercury enters Aquarius, lunar eclipse in Leo

February 2018
Ride the tide

February is actually a laid back month astrologically—except for the solar eclipse in Aquarius on February 15. These eclipses are like double new moons and bring double the new opportunities. But often, with a solar eclipse, you also have to give up something. Uranus forms a fairly close conjunction to the eclipse degree, suggesting that new opportunities surface suddenly and unexpectedly. You may have an opportunity, for instance, to work with a terrific team of bright individuals on a particular project or endeavor. Or maybe you're hired by a startup social media company. However the specifics unfold, there's a dynamic quality on the day of, and the days before and after, this eclipse.

On the 10th, Venus enters Pisces, and the area of your chart that rules the personal unconscious. Until March 6, you have greater access to your own psyche. Your dreams may provide insights and information, and you might even experience out of body travel. Your imagination and intuition are particularly strong. If a romantic relationship begins during this transit, you may keep it under wraps for some reason. But once Venus enters your sign in March, it will all be out in the open.

On the 18th, Mercury joins Venus in Pisces and will be there until March 6. This transit favors any kind of imaginative writing—science fiction, fantasy or the paranormal. Your interest in this area may deepen, and you could sign up for a workshop or seminar that delves into esoteric topics. Or you might decide to attend a writers' workshop.

March 2018
5 stars until Mercury turns retro!

March is a busy month astrologically, with a lot of shifting energies. Be sure to get sufficient rest, and don't run yourself ragged! It's okay if some things don't get done until tomorrow or next week.

March 1 features a full moon in Virgo, and Neptune forms an almost exact opposition to it. This can lead to some confusion in your work environment due to lack of information. You don't have the full story. So before you make any decisions, dig around for the facts.

On the 6th, you have two terrific transits going on. Mercury and Venus both enter your sign, marking the beginning of one of the most romantic and creative periods for you all year. Mercury remains until May 13 because of a retro next month, and Venus remains in Aries until March 31. The only other period in 2018 that equals this is between June 13 and July 9, when Venus transits Leo and the romance/creativity sector of your chart.

While Mercury is moving direct through your sign, your mind zips along fast and furiously, leaping from one thing to another, sifting through information and ideas at the speed of light. When you're struck by a particular idea, you play with it until you understand how it can be implemented.

During Venus's transit through Aries, your romantic passions may leap from one extreme to another. Jealousy to ecstasy, despair to jubilation. You get the idea. Try to pace yourself in a romantic relationship. Also, during this transit be careful about how you spend money. You may spend it faster than it's coming in!

Between March 8 and July 10, Jupiter is retrograde in Scorpio. This retro isn't as immediate and in-your-face as Mercury retros often are. The planet's expansion now takes an inward turn, and you're more focused on your spiritual and emotional growth. Philosophy and spiritual traditions interest you. You might decide to return to college or grad school or may reconnect with old friends.

March 17 features two events: Mars enters Capricorn and your career area, and there's a new moon in Pisces. Mars will be in Capricorn until May 16, and during this period, you're focused on your career and professional matters. You make things *happen* and do so in a way that is efficient, organized and structured. You've also got Saturn in this area, adding backbone and spine to whatever you undertake.

The new moon in Pisces brings new opportunities to flex your imagination and intuition. You may have a chance to work behind the scenes in some capacity or to work on an artistic project or in something where your intuition comes into play.

Between March 22 and April 15, Mercury is moving retrograde in Aries. Ouch. During these periods, life often seems to stumble along from one snafu to the next. To mitigate the effects, it's best to revise, review and reconsider rather than initiate anything new. If you have to travel, particularly by air, be flexible. Your itinerary could change without warning. Look at it as an adventure! People you haven't seen in a long time may resurface in your life. Look over the Mercury retrograde section in the introduction and follow the suggested guidelines in order to navigate this period more successfully.

The 31st also features two events: Venus enters Taurus, a sign it rules, and there's a full moon in Libra. Venus transits your financial area until April 24 and brings a quiet efficiency to the way you handle your money. You may be spending more, but you could also be earning more. It's possible, too, that you meet a romantic interest who shares your values. Stay alert, Aries!

The full moon in Libra highlights a personal or business partnership. There may be news about one of these partnerships or about a legal matter. You and a romantic partner may decide to get engaged. Some tension may ensue because both Neptune and Mars form challenging angles to this moon. But don't worry about it. You shake off tension the way a dog shakes off water!

AT A GLANCE
March 1—Full moon in Virgo
March 6—Mercury enters Aries, Venus enters Aries
March 8—Jupiter turns retro in Scorpio
March 17—Mars enters Capricorn, new moon in Pisces
March 22—Mercury turns retro in Aries
March 31—Venus enters Taurus, full moon in Libra

April 2018
New opportunities

The best news this month? Mercury turns direct on April 15, in your sign. Finally, your life can move forward again, at the pace that suits you. And if you live in the U.S., it's just in time for tax day!

But the 15th has another beautiful surprise—a new moon in Aries! This happens just once a year and sets the tone for the next twelve months. Take some time at the beginning of April to jot down what you would like to achieve and experience in the next twelve months. Back each item with emotion, vividly imagine it and then step out of the way and let the universe actualize these things for you.

On April 17, Saturn turns retrograde in Capricorn and doesn't straighten out again until September 6. This retro gives you the opportunity to review the structures in your life—what works and what doesn't—and to figure out how to change the structures that don't function the way you would like or whether it's time to release the old structures altogether. Since this retro occurs in your career area, you may be looking closely at your profession. Is your job satisfying? Are you working in a career that suits you? If not, what would you rather be doing?

Between April 24 and May 19, Venus transits Gemini. During this period, it's possible that you earn additional income through writing, public speaking or through some type of social media. If you're single, romance may be as close as your own neighborhood, and the special person could be someone you meet through siblings or a neighbor.

The 29th features a full moon in Scorpio, so prepare yourself for an emotional or psychic roller coaster. It's not necessarily bad, just intense. You may hear news about a mortgage, loan or insurance quote for which you've applied. Your mother or other women could play into the events on or around this full moon.

AT A GLANCE
April 15—New moon in Aries, Mercury turns direct in Aries
April 17—Saturn turns retrograde in Capricorn
April 24—Venus enters Gemini
April 29—Full moon in Scorpio

May 2018
Big energy shift

If it's spring where you are, that in itself is cause for celebration. But there's also a major shift in planetary energies this month that should be good. Uranus leaves your sign, Aries, and enters Taurus. We'll talk about that more in a bit.

On May 13, Mercury enters Taurus and your financial area. Between then and the 29th, your conscious focus is on money—what you earn and spend, how you budget and how you can increase your income. You have the patience and fortitude now to tackle a communication project that can bring in additional income. It could involve writing a book or article, building a website or starting a blog.

Between May 29 and June 12, Mercury moves through Gemini, a sign it rules, so the planet's energies function well here. You may be spending more time than usual with siblings and neighbors and could be networking a lot in your free time. Your mind is quick and inventive now, and you're filled with ideas.

On the 15th, the new moon in Taurus should deliver new moneymaking opportunities that may come out of the blue. You'll have to act quickly in order to seize whatever this is, so be alert! The suddenness of the opportunity is due to another event that occurs today: Uranus enters Taurus.

During the seven years Uranus was in your sign, it undoubtedly brought many changes into your life. At the time, the changes may have seemed abrupt and jarring, but you can now look back and see that Uranus was just doing its job—clearing away old patterns and relationships that no longer served you well. You might have changed jobs or careers, gotten divorced or married or had a child. Maybe you moved. Perhaps all these things happened. In retrospect, though, you can see that you're in a much better place now in your life. So what can you expect with Uranus transiting Taurus until October?

Your finances may change abruptly, and hopefully the change is positive! You win the lottery, inherit money, your business takes off beyond your wildest dreams or your novel hits the bestseller list. Regardless of the specifics, you find innovative and unusual ways to earn money. Also, your values may change in some way. Uranus turns retrograde in August, then slides back into your sign and enters Taurus again in March 2019. It will be in this sign until early July 2025.

On the 16th, Mars enters Aquarius, where it will be until late August, thanks to a retrograde that begins on June 26. But while it's moving in direct motion, your social life is greatly energized. You make new contacts and new friends, and in some way, these individuals are helpful to you for achieving your dreams.

Between May 19 and June 13, Venus moves through Cancer and the domestic area of your chart. Your home life should be pleasant during this period, with a nice flow of emotions and intuition. Then, to top off the month, there's a full moon in fellow fire sign Sagittarius on May 29. This one ignites your nomadic lust and hunger for adventure. Indulge it! Also on the 29th, Mercury enters Gemini and the communication area of your chart. This transit ends June 13 and favors all kinds of communication. Be adventurous in your writing and speaking. If you're a blogger, write about your passions and take risks.

AT A GLANCE
May 13—Mercury enters Taurus
May 15—New moon in Taurus, Uranus enters Taurus
May 16—Mars enters Aquarius
May 19—Venus enters Cancer
May 29—Full moon in Sagittarius, Mercury enters Gemini

June 2018
Spiritual warrior

June is one of those months when the shifting astrological energies are a mixed bag for you, Aries. The most irritating shift will occur toward the end of the month, on the 26th, when your ruler, Mars, turns retrograde in Aquarius. Things slow down to the point where you may feel frustrated at the maddening snail pace with which your life is moving.

The retro extends from June 26 to August 27. In mid-August, Mars slips back into Capricorn, so two areas of your chart are affected—your social life and your career. You have an opportunity to figure out your hot buttons about these two areas and the flash points and to transform them in some way. There's a spiritual warrior quality about this retrograde.

On June 12, Mercury enters Cancer, and your intuition is deepened. When it comes to your family and domestic life, there's a strong emotional flow to how you think and perceive your relationships with your partner, children and parents. On the 29th, Mercury enters fellow fire sign Leo, and your focus is on a romantic relationships and your creative endeavors. Your muse is at your beck and call between then and July 26, when Mercury turns retro. We'll talk more about the retrograde in next month's roundup.

The 13th features two events: a new moon in Gemini and Venus joining Mercury in Leo. The new moon brings an opportunity to show off your writing and public speaking skills and to network with new acquaintances and friends. With Venus in Leo until July 9, you're now in one of the most romantic and creative periods of the year. You and your romantic partner could team up on a creative endeavor and discover new passions you have in common. You may be spending more money than usual on enjoyable activities, but it all feels good. Your self-confidence soars, and you attract the right people at the right time.

On or around the full moon in Capricorn on the 28th, there's news about a professional matter or project. Since Saturn is closely conjunct this moon, the news is important.

AT A GLANCE
June 12—Mercury enters Cancer
June 13—New moon in Gemini, Venus enters Leo
June 26—Mars turns retrograde in Aquarius
June 28—Full moon in Capricorn
June 29—Mercury enters Leo

July 2018
The nature of your reality

As the second Mercury retro of the year approaches on July 26, there are some things you can do to prepare for it. If you have been considering the purchase of a computer, car or other high ticket item, buy before July 26 or after August 19, when Mercury turns direct. Are you in contractual discussions? Wind them up before or after the retro period. The same goes for travel plans. If you're going to be submitting anything or launching a business, do it before or after those dates. And then figure out what you're going to be revising, reconsidering and reviewing during the retrograde.

Since it occurs in the romance and creativity area of your chart, you and your partner should be in agreement about the ways in which you communicate. Text messaging won't work for a disagreement! Face to face is preferred.

On the 9th, Venus enters Virgo and will be there until August 6. During this period, your relationship with co-workers and employees should unfold with greater ease, but you may be more prone to self-criticism and being judgmental. On the romantic front, an office flirtation could heat up. If you're involved in a relationship, you may have to adjust your attitude in some way for things to work more smoothly.

Jupiter finally turns direct again in Scorpio on July 10. Your spiritual beliefs expand as you seek to understand the nature of reality. Are the quantum physicists correct? Are we all connected at some level? Your willpower and determination are your greatest assets now.

On July 12, the solar eclipse in Cancer brings new opportunities concerning your home and family life. You could move or find the ideal neighborhood for yourself and your family, or you and your partner may discover you're going to be parents. Eclipses often thrust change upon us, and solar eclipses do so by temporarily sweeping the familiar away from us so we have to consider other options.

This eclipse is followed by a lunar eclipse in Aquarius on July 27. A remark from a friend or family member may punch one of your buttons. Instead of blowing up, just let it roll away from you, and then later, when you're calmer, ask yourself why you reacted the way you did. Lunar eclipses often reveal something about our inner selves.

AT A GLANCE
July 9—Venus enters Virgo
July 10—Jupiter turns direct in Scorpio
July 12—Solar eclipse in Cancer
July 26—Mercury turns retrograde in Leo
July 27—Lunar eclipse in Aquarius

August 2018
Strut your stuff

Just when you thought the eclipses were over for the year, August features a solar eclipse in Leo on the 11th. This one should usher in new opportunities in your creative endeavors that enable you to strut your stuff, Aries, and to exhibit your considerable talents. If you're single, a new romantic interest is also a possibility. Solar eclipses sometimes demand that we give up something before these new opportunities can enter our lives, so if there's a habit you would like to break, now is the time to get serious about it.

On the 6th, Venus enters Libra, a sign it rules, and you and your partner should enjoy a smooth period between then and September 9. You're more aware now of how necessary balance is to your relationship and strive to bring more of it into your dealings with each other.

Mercury turns direct in Leo on the 19th, a welcome development for your love life and your creative endeavors. Treat yourself to something special—a massage, a shopping spree or a workshop.

The full moon in Pisces on the 26th could bring surprising news of some kind and the completion of a creative endeavor you've worked on for some time. Since this full moon has a dreamy quality to it, you and your partner should carve out time for yourselves at some point during the day.

On the 27th, Mars turns direct in Capricorn, and you become a whirling dervish of activity in your professional life. You're now able to create effective strategies, set realistic goals and set your sights on progress.

AT A GLANCE
August 6—Venus enters Libra
August 11—Solar eclipse in Leo
August 19—Mercury turns direct in Leo
August 26—Full moon in Pisces
August 27—Mars turns direct in Capricorn

September 2018
Good news

September is a month of shifting energies, and the action begins on the 5th, when Mercury enters Virgo, a sign that it rules. Mercury is a happy camper in both Virgo and Gemini, so it is functioning at full capacity, enabling you to connect all the various details at work. You're able to sort through vast amounts of information to find exactly what you need. Your communication skills are excellent during this transit, which lasts until the 21st. Between then and October 9, it transits Libra, and your conscious focus is on your business and personal partnerships. Don't take on so many projects that you scatter your focus!

On the 6th, Saturn turns direct in Capricorn. This change in motion benefits all your professional endeavors. You've been reevaluating the various structures in your career and now have a clearer idea about which structures work and which ones need to be rebuilt.

The 9th features two events: Venus enters Scorpio, and there's a new moon in Virgo. The first transit lasts awhile because on October 5 Venus will turn retrograde. While it's moving direct, however, your passions are deepened, and you may feel more emotional than usual. Your sexuality is also heightened, and you may be looking for the truth about a relationship.

The new moon in Virgo on the same day should bring new communication opportunities. You might be tapped, for instance, to write your company's weekly newsletter or you may decide to start a blog or build a website to promote something you or your company are doing. The new moon occurs in the same area of your chart where Mercury is right now, so you're going to be feeling very chatty!

Between September 10 and November 15, Mars moves through compatible air sign Aquarius. Your social life picks up big time, and Mars enables you to make great strides in achieving any goals that you set. Think of Mars as your booster rocket, the wind at your back.

Mercury enters Libra on September 21, and now your conscious focus turns to business and personal partnerships. Your artistic sense is greatly sharpened, and you may be admiring art, reading more literature and generally feeling a greater appreciation for the beauty in the world.

On the 24th, the full moon in your sign should bring news that is personally satisfying. This is the harvest time of the month, Aries, and if you have laid the groundwork throughout the rest of the month, the payoff should occur on or around the time of this full moon. Today, you are more of who you really are—a restless adventurer whose middle name is action!

AT A GLANCE
September 5—Mercury enters Virgo
September 6—Saturn turns direct in Capricorn
September 9—Venus enters Scorpio, new moon in Virgo
September 10—Mars enters Aquarius
September 21—Mercury enters Libra
September 24—Full moon in Aries

October 2018
Bumpy road with romance

Your love life may take a couple of hits this month after Venus turns retrograde in Scorpio on October 5. Disagreements between you and your partner may center on fundamental issues in the relationship. It's best not to make major decisions about the relationship until after the retro ends on November 16, when Venus turns direct in Libra. If you're not involved with anyone, then the retro may impact your creative endeavors or your finances in some way. An example of a financial snafu would be that a check or refund you or your partner have been expecting doesn't arrive on time.

October 8 features a beautiful new moon in Libra, in your partnership area. You might find the ideal partner to help you launch a business or creative endeavor or the right agent or editor for your book or novel. If you're involved with someone, then the two of you may decide to deepen your commitment and move in together or get engaged or married. If you're single, then this new moon could bring a new romantic interest.

On the 9th, Mercury enters Scorpio again, joining Jupiter in that area of your chart that rules the paranormal—life after death, communication with the dead, telepathy or precognition. The combination of Mercury and Jupiter is ideal for any kind of medical or paranormal research. Mercury will be in Scorpio until October 31. Next month, it will be retrograde from November 16 to December 6.

The full moon on October 24 occurs very close to Uranus in Taurus. Both planets are in your financial area, so any news you hear about money will come out of the blue. A raise? Money from a freelance project or some other source?

On the 31st, Mercury enters Sagittarius, and until it turns retro on November 16, your focus is on a trip you're taking or planning, your spiritual beliefs or your educational goals and plans.

AT A GLANCE
October 5—Venus turns retrograde in Scorpio
October 8—New moon in Libra
October 9—Mercury enters Scorpio
October 24—Full moon in Taurus
October 31—Mercury enters Sagittarius

November 2018
Mercury retro alert

With the year winding down, November should be calmer, right? Well, no. Let's start with the Mercury retrograde on November 16 that begins in Sagittarius and ends with Mercury turning direct in Scorpio on December 6. It's wise to do your holiday shopping on either side of the retrograde, but not during it, particularly if you're buying electronics, appliances, a car or other high ticket items. Since the Thanksgiving holidays tend to be one of the busiest air travel times all year, be sure to make your plans and buy your tickets when Mercury is direct. And of course, follow the three Rs: revise, review and reconsider, rather than launching anything new. As with any Mercury retro, old friends may resurface, perhaps reconnecting with you through Facebook or other social media.

Look over the Mercury retrograde sections in the introduction to the book. The suggested guidelines will help you navigate this period more successfully.

On the 7th, the new moon in Scorpio should open opportunities for research and investigation, perhaps into the paranormal, and for opportunities in more mundane areas—mortgages, loans or breaks in your insurance premiums. Any planet in Scorpio tends to be emotionally intense, but especially the moon, which rules our capacity to nurture self and others and also rules our inner worlds and our intuitive selves.

On the 8th, Jupiter enters Sagittarius and forms a beautiful angle to your sun. It will be in this position until December 3, 2019. During this journey, you may be traveling overseas, pursuing an educational goal or spiritual quest, exploring your belief system in some way or getting involved in some facet of publishing. Jupiter is happy in Sadge and functions well here. Your life expands significantly during this transit, and luck shadows you like a loyal puppy. Make the most of this!

On the 15th, Mars enters Pisces, where it will be through the end of the year. During this period, your sexuality is deeply connected to your emotions, and you go out of your way to avoid conflict and confrontations. If you're working behind the scenes in some capacity—detective, investigator, writer, researcher, costume designer or artist—you're able to pull together various facets of a project and make things work!

Mercury retrograde begins on the 16th, but there is compensation—Venus turns direct in Libra. Now your business and personal partnerships feel more comfortable and familiar, and any disagreements you've had with a partner should smooth out. Or, if you've decided a relationship no longer works for you, the change in motion makes it easier to part ways amicably.

The full moon in Gemini on the 23rd brings a communication project to completion. You may be spending time with siblings and neighbors and connect with people through social media in a more meaningful way.

AT A GLANCE
November 7—New moon in Scorpio
November 8—Jupiter enters Sagittarius
November 15—Mars enters Pisces
November 16—Mercury turns retrograde in Sagittarius, Venus turns direct in Libra
November 23—Full moon in Gemini

December 2018
Onward!

All things considered, December is a fairly tranquil month astrologically, which is exactly what you need, Aries, before you leap into 2019!

Between December 2 and January 7, 2019, Venus moves through Scorpio once again. It's like a second chance to do what didn't get done when Venus was in this sign in September. Expect to feel things intensely, and, yes, your sexuality will be greatly heightened. Once Mercury turns direct in Scorpio on December 6, things between you and a romantic partner improve in the communication department. And when your communication improves, so does everything else. Part of what your holidays should include is a romantic weekend away, just the two of you, perhaps after the 12th, when Mercury enters Sagittarius, where it will be until January 4, 2019.

If you're not involved in a relationship now, then the combination of Venus in Scorpio and Mercury direct in that sign brings the kind of emotional and psychic momentum that can be used in just about any area of your life where you place your attention—earning more money or developing greater spiritual awareness or within your career or family.

The new moon in Sagittarius on December 7 should bring new opportunities in anything that Sadge represents—foreign travel, higher education, your spiritual beliefs and worldview or publishing. And with Jupiter also in this house and sign, how can you lose?

On December 22, the full moon in Cancer caps off the year. Something culminates within your family life. News of a pregnancy? A pending move? A parent who moves in with you? However the specifics unfold for you, this moon is a powerhouse at zero degrees of a cardinal sign that stimulates the other four points in your chart as well. Great energy to propel you into the new year.

AT A GLANCE
December 2—Venus enters Scorpio
December 6—Mercury turns direct in Scorpio
December 7—New moon in Sagittarius
December 12—Mercury enters Sagittarius
December 22—Full moon in Cancer

Reflection

Take some time to reflect on 2018. What kind of year was it for you? Was there enough adventure and fun to keep you immersed? Did your life change in a significant way? If so, how? Jot your thoughts below.

_____

_____

_____

_____

_____

Happy New Year!

Taurus 2018

Venus rules your sign, so pay attention to what it's doing each month. This year, it will be retrograde between October 5 and November 16. The retro begins in Scorpio, then Venus slides back into Libra before it turns direct. In 2018, Venus transits every sign except Sagittarius and Capricorn.

The monthly roundups note when Venus makes angles to other planets, or vice-versa, and what it means for you. You'll also find information on the new and full moons each month, the transits of other planets and on eclipses.

In May, Uranus enters your sign, a major shift of energy that will impact your life in surprising ways before it turns retrograde in August, slips back into Aries in November and then finally enters Taurus again in 2019. You may want to flip forward to the March roundup in 2019 to read about the possible impact of this shift.

2018 will be an interesting year for you, Taurus, particularly after Uranus enters your sign in May. It's likely that innovation and creativity will be your closest allies and that synchronicity will occur frequently for guidance, insight and confirmation. Consider keeping a journal this year if you don't already.

January 2018
Variety

Welcome to 2018! Unlike 2017, the year doesn't begin with a Mercury retrograde. Instead, it kicks off with a beautiful full moon in Cancer on January 1, which could bring news about your family. Venus is in Capricorn now, opposite this moon, so be careful that you don't erect walls around yourself when dealing with others.

Between January 11 and 31, Mercury transits fellow earth sign Capricorn and forms a favorable angle to your sun. During this period, your conscious focus is on your career and your worldview and beliefs, and you may be trying to figure out how your beliefs shape the reality you experience.

On the 16th, the new moon in Capricorn should be very much to your liking. You may have an opportunity to travel overseas either for work or pleasure or perhaps a combination of both. There could be a professional opportunity coming up as well, and you're in the power seat, Taurus. Seize it!

Between January 17 and February 20, Venus transits Aquarius and your career area. This should sweeten the professional pot considerably. You're the one with the ideas, with your finger on the pulse of cutting edge trends and the visionary who can now take the company—or your own business—into the next successful phase. A flirtation with someone you meet through work may blossom into romance.

Mars enters Sagittarius on the 26th, a transit that lasts until March 17. During this period, you have the courage of your convictions and act on them. As a Taurus, you tend to be stubborn and slow to act at times. However, when it comes to your beliefs, you don't hesitate at all. You may be involved in competitive sports during this transit and have terrific speaking skills. Your sexuality is heightened, too, but you're non-committal about a relationship. Foreign travel could be part of this transit, and if so, then you're on a quest of some kind—for information, insight or understanding.

Two events occur on the 31st: Mercury joins Mars in Sagittarius, and there's a lunar eclipse in Leo. With Mercury and Mars traveling together until February 18, when Mercury moves into Pisces, you are more idealistic and versatile and not quite as stubborn as usual. You can grasp the larger picture of whatever you're involved in. You also may be restless and eager for an adventure or a trip to some exotic port.

The lunar eclipse in Leo on this same day may trigger some drama in your home life. Someone—a parent, child or partner—is acting out, and you may become the brunt of it. Or, also possible, you're the one who acts out, and your family takes the brunt!

January 1—Full moon in Cancer
January 11—Mercury enters Capricorn
January 16—New moon in Capricorn
January 17—Venus enters Aquarius
January 26—Mars enters Sagittarius
January 31—Mercury enters Aquarius, lunar eclipse in Leo

February 2018
Career opportunities

Months in which eclipses occur can be riddled with tension and a sense of urgency. This is due to the nature of eclipses—to bring things to our immediate attention that need to be dealt with quickly. This month's solar eclipse, though, should be a beauty for you. It occurs in Aquarius, in your career area, and should result in new professional opportunities. You may find that you're the one people turn to for ideas, answers and insights into what works in your company and what doesn't. A promotion and raise could be part of the surprises!

Between February 10 and March 6, Venus moves through compatible water sign Pisces. Your social calendar gets crowded quickly, and you discover that you enjoy hanging out with artistic types whose imaginations are as active and vital as yours is during this transit. You may take a romantic interest in someone you meet through friends or through a club to which you belong. Pisces is such a compassionate sign that you may find other people confiding in you and coming to you for advice.

On February 19, Mercury joins Venus in Pisces and will be there until March 6. During this period, your imagination is exceptionally fertile and intuitive. You're very much in the flow, and the universe will respond through synchronicities that act as guidance and provide insight.

AT A GLANCE
February 10—Venus enters Pisces
February 15—Solar eclipse in Aquarius
February 18—Mercury enters Pisces

March 2018
A tad chaotic

There's a lot going on astrologically this month, including a Mercury retrograde in Aries that runs from March 22 to April 15. Be sure to read the Mercury retrograde overview in the introduction to the book (page 9) and follow the general guidelines suggested. If you're going to be launching a business, signing contracts or planning a trip, be sure to do all these things on either side of the retrograde. Otherwise, you may be revisiting the contract or could experience sudden unforeseen changes to your travel itinerary. The best time to launch a new endeavor of any kind is during a new moon and when Mercury is moving in direct motion.

Even though the new moon in Pisces on the 17th is a bit close to the beginning of the Mercury retro, it might be a good day to launch a business or creative endeavor. Once the retro begins, however, it's best to revise, review and reconsider.

The new moon in Pisces is a great time to get out and about with friends, to socialize and have fun. It could bring new friends into your life, new contacts and perhaps an opportunity to become involved in a creative project with a group of like-minded individuals.

The full moon in Virgo on March 1 brings news or insights about a romantic relationship, a creative endeavor or your kids. You may complete a project you've been working on or are able to connect details in a way that has eluded you before. Your mother or other women in your life may play a part in today's full moon picture.

Both Mercury and Venus enter Aries on March 6. Until Mercury turns retro on the 22nd, this duo traveling together enables you to work behind the scenes in some capacity. Your passions are likely to be more volatile, but you'll also have a better grasp of who and what push your buttons. You're seeding your unconscious during this period for when Venus transits your sign between March 31 and April 24.

Jupiter turns retrograde in Scorpio on March 8 and remains that way until July 10. During these four months, you're reevaluating a personal or business partnership. Does it suit your needs? Is the other person dependable? Do you have the same vision for your company or relationship? Your spiritual beliefs are expanding in some way, and you may be actively pursuing an exploration of various belief systems.

On the 17th, the same day as that new moon in Pisces, Mars enters Capricorn. During this transit, which lasts until May 16, you're pursuing your goals with admirable tenacity and patience. Neither Taurus nor Capricorn are quitters, and even if you're assigned to a project you aren't particularly excited about, you do the work without complaint.

Two events occur on March 31: Venus enters your sign, and there's a full moon in Libra. We'll talk more about the Venus transit in April, so for right now, let's look at this full moon in Libra. Your daily work routine and the maintenance of your health are highlighted. With work, a project or issue culminates. In terms of your health, you may realize you need greater balance in your life and start carving out time each day just for yourself.

AT A GLANCE
March 1—Full moon in Virgo
March 6—Mercury enters Aries, Venus enters Aries
March 8—Jupiter turns retro in Scorpio
March 17—Mars enters Capricorn, new moon in Pisces
March 22—Mercury turns retro in Aries
March 31—Venus enters Taurus, full moon in Libra

April 2018
Romantic & creative

April isn't quite as fast-paced as March was and should be pleasant all the way around—in spite of the Mercury retrograde. Your ruler, Venus, is transiting your sign until April 24, a period in which things come your way with little or no effort on your part. This is one of the most creative and romantic times for you all year, when life flows your way. You feel self-confident and powerful. Your muse is at your beck and call 24/7, so use this time for your creative endeavors. If you're in a relationship, you and your partner may be spending more time together and perhaps get away for a long, romantic weekend somewhere. The only other period that will match this falls between July 9 and August 6.

Once Venus enters Gemini on the 24th, your financial star begins to rise. Even if you're spending more, you're earning more. You attract the right investors for your business or service, and your communication skills are stellar. You're able to network with ease. This transit lasts until May 19.

On the 15th, there are two astrological events: Mercury turns direct, and there is a new moon in Aries. You'll feel the shift in energy when Mercury turns direct because things will generally move along with greater ease. Sign your contracts, pack your bags and plan your launch dates for new endeavors. An ideal time would be at next month's new moon in your sign!

The new moon in Aries is closely conjunct Uranus, the planet of surprises, so news you hear on or around this new moon will come out of the blue. You may be tapped to head up a team at work for some type of creative endeavor or to do something that draws on your leadership abilities.

Between April 17 and September 6, Saturn is retrograde in Capricorn. During this period, you may be examining the philosophical and spiritual structures in your life, your career goals and plans and your relationship with authority figures—your parents, boss or the government generally.

The full moon in Scorpio on the 29th highlights a business or personal partnership. You're able to perceive the bottom line in this relationship, and because Scorpio is such an emotionally intense sign, your insights may feel raw and unfiltered.

AT A GLANCE
April 15—New moon in Aries, Mercury turns direct in Aries
April 17—Saturn turns retrograde in Capricorn
April 24—Venus enters Gemini
April 29—Full moon in Scorpio

May 2018
Hectic & exciting

Mercury enters your sign on May 13, and between now and May 29, your head and your heart are in complete agreement. You're better able to plan, to strategize and to take the abstract and make it tangible. You'll have time this month to brainstorm about what you would like to achieve and experience for the next twelve months because there's a new moon in your sign. This moon only comes along once a year and sets the tone for the next year. Seed and achieve your dreams, Taurus, that's the name of the game.

On May 15, there are two astrological events: Uranus enters your sign, and there's a new moon in Taurus. Uranus—the planet that represents sudden, unforeseen events, individuality, breaks with convention, revolution, genius and eccentricity—will be in Taurus until November, but because it's retrograde for part of this time, it returns to Aries and then reenters your sign next year.

During this transit, your urge for freedom will be powerful, and you will buck convention and insist on pursuing your own path—spiritually, emotionally and creatively. You may suddenly change jobs or careers, get married or divorced, start a family, move or travel on the spur of the moment. The purpose of Uranus transits is to clear away the stuff in your life that no longer works in order to make way for the new.

The new moon in your sign on May 15 ushers in new opportunities in any area of your life where you have seeded an intense desire. You might meet your soul mate, land the ideal job, get a raise or be promoted. And with Uranus now in your sign, these opportunities will occur suddenly and without warning.

On May 16, Mars enters Aquarius and your career area. Between then and June 26, when Mars turns retrograde, this planet is your professional booster rocket. You're a whirlwind of ideas, intellectual stimulation and action, and your focus is to achieve and do. We'll talk more about the retro in next month's roundup.

Between May 19 and June 13, Venus transits compatible water sign Cancer and the communication sector of your chart. During this pleasant transit, you're very much in the flow of life, in touch with your emotions and your intuition and radiate a kind of magnetism that others find appealing. If you're single, you may meet a romantic interest through your siblings, neighbors or friends. This transit favors communication through the written word.

The full moon in Sagittarius on May 29 highlights shared finances, usually your partner's income, but it could be a financial dealing with a parent, child, friend or even a bank. There could be news about a raise, a mortgage or loan for which you've applied or a break in your insurance premiums, or perhaps an unexpected royalty check arrives. On the same day, Mercury enters Gemini and your financial area. Your conscious focus turns to money—what you earn, save and spend. You may be talking and writing about finances, too. Just be sure you do so in a positive sense! Mercury remains in Gemini until June 12.

AT A GLANCE
May 13—Mercury enters Taurus
May 15—New moon in Taurus, Uranus enters Taurus
May 16—Mars enters Aquarius
May 19—Venus enters Cancer
May 29—Full moon in Sagittarius, Mercury enters Gemini

June 2018
New financial opportunities

It's another busy month in the stars, and the first transit kicks off on June 12, when Mercury enters Cancer. This transit, which lasts until the 29th, brings an intuitive flow to your intellect. You're able to make snap decisions based on nothing more than a hunch. Your capacity for nurturing is deepened, particularly with loved ones.

The 13th features two events: a new moon in Gemini and Venus entering Leo. The first indicates that new financial opportunities may surface as well as new opportunities in communication. You might, for instance, start a blog or build a website for your company or for your own business. You could be doing some public relations work, too, tapping your large network of acquaintances and friends.

When Venus transits Leo between June 13 and July 9, it moves through your domestic/family environment. You may be spending money on your home to beautify it in some way. If you're considering selling your house, you may decide to spiff it up first—for example, new furniture, fresh paint on the walls or a new bathroom. In other words, you spend money. The irony, though, is that once you beautify the place, you may decide to stay! If you aren't involved in a relationship right now, that may change between July 9 and August 6, when Venus moves through the romance and creativity sector of your chart.

On June 26, Mars turns retrograde in Aquarius. Even if you didn't know the exact date, you probably would feel the shift in energy or see signs of it in your professional life. A project or professional relationship that has been humming along well suddenly slows down or develops problems. This retro lasts until August 27, when Mars turns direct in Capricorn. During this two-month period, you're reevaluating your career and professional goals.

The full moon in fellow earth sign Capricorn on the 28th should be a beauty for you. It illuminates a spiritual belief that you hold or your relationship with authority or both. If you're planning a trip overseas, this full moon may prompt you to change some of the details. Best to solidify your plans before Mercury turns retro next month.

On the 29th, Mercury joins Venus in Leo. This duo prompts you to exhibit your talents and creative ability in some way.

AT A GLANCE
June 12—Mercury enters Cancer
June 13—New moon in Gemini, Venus enters Leo
June 26—Mars turns retrograde in Aquarius
June 28—Full moon in Capricorn
June 29—Mercury enters Leo

July 2018
A crazy mix

Months in which eclipses occur are often tense, emotional and imbued with a sense of urgency. The function of eclipses is to highlight relationships and issues in an immediate, personal way, and usually we must act quickly. There are two eclipses this month—a solar eclipse in Cancer on July 12 and a lunar eclipse in Aquarius on July 27.

The solar eclipse should usher in new opportunities in communication and networking. You might land a writing, speaking or research gig or have a chance to become involved in some aspect of public relations. Since the eclipse is in Cancer, it's possible that an opportunity surfaces concerning your family or home. You might have a chance to sell your current place and move elsewhere, for instance. Or you find the ideal neighborhood for yourself and your family.

The lunar eclipse in Aquarius on the 27th highlights a professional issue or relationship, and you must act quickly to deal with whatever surfaces. If your career has been your primary focus for a long time, then you could gain or be denied recognition for what you've done.

Between July 9 and August 6, Venus transits Virgo and the romance/creativity area of your chart. You're particularly fortunate this year because you get to enjoy the two best Venus transits—the one through your sun sign between March 31 and April 24 and now this one! Dive into your creative endeavors during this period. Your muse is ready to rock and roll with you into any project you select. If you're not involved in a relationship when this transit starts, don't be surprised if you've met someone special by the time it ends. Your self-confidence acts as a powerful attractor.

On the 10th, Jupiter turns direct, always a bonus! It occurs in Scorpio, in your partnership area. You will now feel the full benefits of this planet's expansive nature—new partnership opportunities arrive in either your professional or personal life or in both! You're able to discern the bottom line in just about any situation or relationship without too much conscious effort on your part.

Between July 26 and August 19, Mercury moves retrograde through Leo and that area of your chart that rules home, family and your domestic life. Sometimes during retrograde periods, appliances break down. If that happens, don't hesitate to replace what you need, but double check delivery times and make sure the store has the right appliance in their computer records! Be sure to follow the usual guidelines for a Mercury retro. If you can't recall them, look back at the entry for March (page 202).

AT A GLANCE
July 9—Venus enters Virgo
July 10—Jupiter turns direct in Scorpio
July 12—Solar eclipse in Cancer
July 26—Mercury turns retrograde in Leo
July 27—Lunar eclipse in Aquarius

August 2018
Social

There's another eclipse this month—a solar eclipse in Leo on August 11 that should bring about new opportunities to exhibit your talents and impacts your home life in some way. Perhaps you and your partner have a chance to exchange houses with someone in another country, or you get a great deal on a home you're buying or obtain your asking price on the house you're selling. Sometimes, the opportunities presented by a solar eclipse appear a month later.

Between August 6 and September 9, Venus moves through Libra. It rules this sign, so it's happy here and functions at full capacity, creating a more satisfying work environment for you. You're more aware of the balance of power in your relationships with co-workers and employees and strive to see things through other people's eyes. An office flirtation could turn into a romance, but be careful, Taurus, about mixing business with pleasure!

On the 19th, Mercury turns direct again in Leo. Hit the road, Taurus, and treat yourself and your partner/family to an adventure—the sort that creates such vivid memories that you'll remember it years from now.

The full moon in compatible water sign Pisces should be very much to your liking. Your social life ramps up, and you have your choice of invitations! There could also be news about a creative endeavor in which you're involved, and the news looks positive.

On the 27th, Mars turns direct in Capricorn. Now you've got the wind at your back, Taurus, and because your professional goals are much clearer now, you're able to make great headway in your career. On September 10, Mars enters Aquarius and your career area, where it originally turned retrograde, so get ready for a lot of forward momentum in your professional life.

AT A GLANCE
August 6—Venus enters Libra
August 11—Solar eclipse in Leo
August 19—Mercury turns direct in Leo
August 26—Full moon in Pisces
August 27—Mars turns direct in Capricorn

September 2018
Five stars

This month should be great for you, Taurus, but particularly on the romance and creativity front. On September 5, Mercury enters Virgo and that sector of your chart, and you and a romantic partner enjoy a beautiful flow of communication. Your intellect is clearly focused on goals related to a creative endeavor, and you and your partner may be brainstorming about how to market the product or service.

On the 6th, Saturn turns direct in Capricorn and for the next four days travels with Mars, enabling you to tackle difficult projects, relationships and situations in a focused, practical way.

There are two astrological events on September 9th: a new moon in Virgo, and Venus enters Scorpio. The new moon indicates that if you're not involved with anyone, your situation may change. If you are in a relationship, then you and your partner rediscover why you're attracted to each other and may uncover exactly what you have in common. It's also possible that you have an opportunity to try another type of creative endeavor that interests you. If you've always wanted to write, for example, then you may be approached to write an article, book or even a screenplay. If photography is one of your passions, then you may have a chance to exhibit your work.

With Venus moving through Scorpio, your focus turns to business and personal partners. You and your romantic partner may decide to deepen your level of commitment and move in together or set a date for a wedding. There may be some emotional intensity during this transit, which is lengthy, thanks to a Venus retrograde that begins on October 5. More on that in next month's roundup.

On the 10th, Mars enters Aquarius and your career area once again, and it will be there until November 15. Make this transit count, Taurus. Maintain your focus on your career, don't hesitate to put in the time needed to achieve what you want and watch what happens!

Mercury enters Libra on the 21st. Your conscious focus turns to your daily work routine. You may recognize a need for greater balance in your life between work and home/family. Now it's also important to compromise when you need to instead of digging in your heels!

The full moon in Aries on the 24th illuminates an issue or belief that you should deal with so that you can move forward in your various endeavors. It may be that you have disowned your personal power over the years, that you hold a grudge against someone about something done years ago or that you have never forgiven your mom, dad or ex about something. Pay close attention to your dreams around the time of this full moon. It's where your healing may start.

AT A GLANCE
September 5—Mercury enters Virgo
September 6—Saturn turns direct in Capricorn
September 9—Venus enters Scorpio, new moon in Virgo
September 10—Mars enters Aquarius
September 21—Mercury enters Libra
September 24—Full moon in Aries

October 2018
Surprises

Overall, October should be a good month for you, Taurus, with just one small glitch: your ruler, Venus, turns retrograde in Scorpio on the 5th and remains that way until November 16, when it turns direct in Libra. During this period, communication often goes awry, with mixed up signals and misunderstandings. Since the retrograde occurs in your partnership area, take extra care in communications with personal and professional partners.

Venus retrogrades give you a chance to take a deeper look at your relationships and determine if they meet your needs. It's also an excellent time to look honestly at your beliefs about money. Is there a belief you have that may be holding you back from earning more?

On the 8th, the new moon in Libra should attract new opportunities in your daily work routine. A promotion? Increased responsibility? Hiring new employees? There may also be new opportunities in the way you maintain your health. It would be the ideal day to start a new exercise routine or nutritional program. With this new moon, you're more aware of the importance of balance in all areas of your life.

Between October 9 and 31, Mercury joins Venus retro in Scorpio. Fortunately, both planets aren't retrograde! With this duo, you may be researching the paranormal, life after death, spirit communication, some facet of medicine or the ancient past. You go where your interests take you.

On the 31st, Mercury enters Sagittarius. Your conscious focus turns to joint resources. How can you and your partner pool your resources more effectively? Is one of you shouldering a greater financial responsibility than the other? How can that be rectified?

The 24th features a beautiful full moon in your sign, and because Uranus retrograde is closely conjunct this moon, any news you hear will be sudden and unexpected, perhaps even jarring, but not necessarily in a negative way. A project also reaches completion, but perhaps not in the way you thought it would! In other words, Taurus, it's a day of surprises.

AT A GLANCE
October 5—Venus turns retrograde in Scorpio
October 8—New moon in Libra
October 9—Mercury enters Scorpio
October 24—Full moon in Taurus
October 31—Mercury enters Sagittarius

November 2018
Planetary shift

The new moon in Scorpio on November 7 forms a beneficial angle with Neptune in Pisces, so today's energy is a curious mix of idealism, emotional intensity and imagination. You and your romantic partner may deepen your commitment to each other and move in together or set a date to get married. In business, you may find the ideal partner for a team project. You may have an opportunity to dive into a creative project that reflects your ideals.

On the 8th, there's a major shift—Jupiter enters Sagittarius, where it will be for the next thirteen months. The expansion that occurs during this transit could include international travel that enables you to explore the philosophy and spiritual traditions of other countries and cultures. Higher education and publishing are also part of Jupiter's expansive agenda for you. So before this transit begins, make a wish list of what you would like to experience and achieve during the next thirteen months.

Between November 15 and December 31, Mars moves through compatible water sign Pisces. Now it's possible to make tremendous strides in achieving your wishes and dreams. Your intuition deepens, and you attract the right people at the right time. Synchronicity becomes your middle name.

Be sure that before Mercury turns retrograde in Sagittarius on the 16th that you make your holiday travel plans, sign contracts, submit manuscripts, schedule appointments and get projects underway. In other words, do all the things that you should avoid during the retro period, which lasts until December 6. Once it begins, remember to follow the three Rs: revise, review and reconsider. This is the last Mercury retro of 2018.

In addition to the Mercury retro on the 16th, Venus turns direct in Libra. Since Venus rules your sign, you probably feel the subtle shift in energy. Suddenly, your daily work routine eases up, any disagreements you've had with employees or co-workers clear up and that office flirtation becomes something deeper.

With the full moon in Gemini on the 23rd, you hear news about your finances. A raise, perhaps? An opportunity to earn additional income? It could be that something you have written sells and provides a new creative outlet for you.

AT A GLANCE
November 7—New moon in Scorpio
November 8—Jupiter enters Sagittarius
November 15—Mars enters Pisces
November 16—Mercury turns retrograde in Sagittarius, Venus turns direct in Libra
November 23—Full moon in Gemini

December 2018
Moving forward

As you enter the last month of the year, take a few minutes to think about what you would like to achieve and experience in 2019. Make a list. Post it where you'll see it often. Then start thinking about the actions you can take to make these things happen!

On December 2, Venus enters Scorpio again, where it was in September before it turned retrograde. Think of it as a second chance to do what you didn't do in September in the areas of partnerships. This transit carries you into 2019, when Venus enters Sagittarius on January 7.

Circle the 6th on your calendar: Mercury turns direct in Scorpio. With the planet of communication and the planet of love and money traveling together in intense Scorpio, you and your business and personal partners should be talking up a storm, fine-tuning your agenda for the rest of this year and into 2019. It would be an ideal time for you and your romantic partner to take off for an exotic romantic spot.

Mercury joins Jupiter in Sagittarius on the 12th, and they travel together until January 4 of next year. During this time, Jupiter expands your intellectual interests and communication endeavors. This duo spells FUN.

The new moon in Sagittarius on the 7th should bring in new financial opportunities for your spouse or partner. If you've applied for a mortgage or loan, it comes through. You may have an opportunity to head overseas, perhaps in search of spiritual insights.

The full moon in Cancer on the 22nd may bring news about a writing or speaking project in which you're involved. Your home and family life are highlighted. You may be juggling details for the holidays, particularly if family members are coming into town. Your intuition is powerful and spot on today, so listen to that inner voice and save yourself time!

AT A GLANCE
December 2—Venus enters Scorpio
December 6—Mercury turns direct in Scorpio
December 7—New moon in Sagittarius
December 12—Mercury enters Sagittarius
December 22—Full moon in Cancer

Reflection
You began the month by thinking ahead to your goals for 2019, and now you can end the month and the year by reflecting on where you have been this year. Did you achieve everything you had hoped? Are you happier? More financially secure? Take stock, Taurus, and jot your thoughts below.

_____
_____
_____
_____
_____

Happy New Year!

Gemini 2018

Mercury rules your sign—and Virgo—so note what the planet of communication is doing each month. The retrograde period that is likely to impact you the most is when it occurs in your own sign. But this year you lucked out. Mercury is retro in fire signs Aries, Leo and Sagittarius. That said, every Mercury retro will play tricks on you in some way. You just have to be ready to navigate whatever it is.

In these monthly roundups, you'll also find information on the transits of other planets, which ones are making angles to your sun sign and the full and new moons and eclipses. The retrogrades of other planets are also noted.

It's a year to think outside of the box, Gemini. You generally do that, anyway, but in 2018 the more innovative you can be, the happier you'll be. Let your curiosity guide you, be adventurous and find your niche.

January 2018
Make a deal

Welcome to 2018! January promises to be a month of shifting energies. But that shouldn't be a challenge for you. As a mutable air sign, you're more capable than most signs in going where the tides carry you. However, even for you, months in which eclipses occur can be challenging, so let's start there.

The lunar eclipse in Leo on the 31st may stir up some drama with a sibling or neighbor. Mars forms a close, beneficial angle to the eclipse degree, suggesting that you're ready to defend your position and may win the dispute! Just be aware that the point isn't to win, but to understand why the dispute occurs.

Now that we have that out of the way, let's take a look at the rest of the month. On January 1, the full moon in Cancer may bring financial news or news that concerns your home/family life. It's also possible that some financial dealing you had toward the end of last year now culminates in a contract and a deal.

On the 11th, Mercury enters Capricorn and the same area of your chart, and between now and the 31st, you're focused on your financial goals. You may be looking at how much you earn versus your expenses. If there's an imbalance, don't despair! If you react by saying *I never have enough money,* you'll just attract more of the same. Instead, ask this: *Why am I so rich?* Doesn't that feel better? Repeat it often, and pretty soon, the circumstances for making more money will become apparent.

The new moon in Capricorn on the 16th brings new financial and career opportunities. Even if something seems insignificant at first, don't dismiss it. Explore whatever the opportunity is, play with it, see how it feels. If it feels good, then seize and run with it.

Between January 17 and February 10, Venus transits Aquarius and travels with Mercury for almost the entire time. These two are chatting about everything as they brainstorm—spiritual beliefs, international travel and cultures and higher education. And they also may be talking about romance—what you're seeking in a partner. The more positive you are, the greater the chance that you meet someone with whom the chemistry is just about perfect.

From January 26 to March 17, energetic Mars transits Sagittarius, your opposite sign and suddenly, you're a spinning dervish who gets things done. If you're starting your own company, this transit helps you to attract the right partner and support. If you're involved in a committed romantic relationship, then the two of you may decide to deepen your commitment to each other, or if you're in a negative place, try to work out your differences.

January 1—Full moon in Cancer
January 11—Mercury enters Capricorn
January 16—New moon in Capricorn
January 17—Venus enters Aquarius
January 26—Mars enters Sagittarius
January 31—Mercury enters Aquarius, lunar eclipse in Leo

February 2018
Expect the Unexpected

This month's solar eclipse in Aquarius falls on February 15. Any new opportunities that surface on or around the eclipse date are likely to concern your spirituality, worldview or international travel and are a chance to use your vast database of information in a creative way. Even if there's a crisis of some sort on or around the eclipse date, it's a chance to reboot a particular area of your life and to make necessary changes. Uranus forms a beneficial angle to the eclipse degree, indicating that the opportunities surface suddenly and unexpectedly.

Between February 10 and March 6, Venus moves through Pisces and the career area of your chart. This beautiful transit should facilitate all your professional and creative endeavors. Your imagination is particularly rich now, and your intuition is deepened considerably. If you're not involved in a relationship right now, then you may meet a romantic interest through a colleague or through work. There's a quiet softness to Venus in Pisces that others find immensely attractive.

On the 18th, Mercury joins Venus in Pisces in your career area. These two planets have fun together, brainstorming at an intuitive level and imagining everything that is possible. Until March 6, when Mercury moves into Aries, you can accomplish just about anything you desire. But be careful what you ask for!

AT A GLANCE
February 10—Venus enters Pisces
February 15—Solar eclipse in Aquarius
February 18—Mercury enters Pisces

March 2018
Busy

March is fast-paced, with a lot of shifting energy, and it's important that you try to pace yourself. It all starts on March 1, with a full moon in earth sign Virgo. This moon lights up the domestic/family area of your chart and could bring news related to your family. Saturn forms a wide but beneficial angle to this full moon, suggesting that the news is of a serious nature. The full moon may highlight the structure within your family. Is it stable? Strong? Resilient?

March 6 features two astrological events: both Mercury and Venus enter compatible fire sign Aries. Until Mercury turns retro on March 22, your social calendar fills up quickly. You may be spending more time than usual with friends, some of whom may help you to move closer to your wishes and dreams. The retrograde lasts until April 15, and during this period, friends you haven't seen for a while may resurface in your life.

The usual advice applies to this retrograde—rather than launching anything new, it's best to revise, review and reconsider. Avoid signing contracts, making travel plans, buying electronics, appliances or a car. If you do have to travel, be flexible because your itinerary may change suddenly and unexpectedly. Since Mercury is your ruler, you tend to feel these retros more intensely.

Venus will be in Aries until March 31, and during this period, your passions are running fast and furiously, and your self-confidence is high. You attract the right people at the right time and could meet a romantic interest through a club or group to which you belong. If you're already in a relationship, then you and your partner may be entertaining or may be out and about more than usual, taking in museum exhibits and concerts.

On the 31st, Venus enters Taurus until April 24, a period in which you may be internalizing and processing recent experiences. Your dreams are more vivid, easier to recall and reveal insights that are helpful.

Jupiter turns retrograde in Scorpio on March 8 and doesn't turn direct again until July 10. During these four months, Jupiter's expansive energy is turned inward, toward spiritual growth. You may be more interested in the exploration of your spirituality than in the trappings of the material world. However, because the retro occurs in that area of your chart that rules your daily work routine and the maintenance of your daily health, you may uncover ways to improve both areas. With your work, for instance, you may decide to change your approach to what you do. With your health, you may change the way you eat or how you think about food.

On the 17th, two astrological events occur. Mars enters Capricorn, where it will be until May 16, and there's a new moon in Pisces, in your career area. The first transit enables you to vigorously pursue your goals, to lay down professional strategies and to do whatever is necessary to get to where you want to be. With the new moon in Pisces forming such a beneficial angle to Mars, new career opportunities are bound to surface. It could be anything from a promotion to a new job or even a change in careers. Your imagination is particularly strong with this new moon. Envision what you desire, back it with emotion and allow the universe to deliver it!

March 31 also features two astrological events: Venus enters Taurus and will be there until April 24, and there's a full moon in Libra. During the Venus transit, you may be more secretive than usual about romantic matters and are likely to be more sensual, as well. If you become involved in a relationship during this transit, you may keep it under wraps. But by the time Venus enters your sign, you'll be announcing it to the world. The full moon in fellow air sign Libra highlights your creative endeavors and relationships—with your kids or a romantic partner. Any news you hear could be related to any of these areas.

March 1—Full moon in Virgo
March 6—Mercury enters Aries, Venus enters Aries
March 8—Jupiter turns retro in Scorpio
March 17—Mars enters Capricorn, new moon in Pisces
March 22—Mercury turns retro in Aries
March 31—Venus enters Taurus, full moon in Libra

April 2018
Pace yourself

April will unfold at a more even pace than last month. So if March left you feeling a big ragged around the edges, April will give you a chance to recover. The last half of the month will be very much to your liking because on the 15th, Mercury turns direct in Aries. And since Mercury rules your sign, you'll probably feel this almost immediately. Suddenly, everything feels lighter, happier and brighter. Do something special for yourself to celebrate, Gemini.

Between April 17 and September 6, Saturn moves retrograde through Capricorn. During this period, you may be taking a closer look at the various structures in your life—work, home/family, finances and relationships of every type—and deciding which ones need to be strengthened, reshaped or even released because they no longer fit who you are.

Between April 24 and May 19, Venus moves through your sign, and you enjoy one of the most creative and romantic periods all year. The only other period that matches it is when Venus moves through Libra, between August 6 and September 9. Your muse is at your beck and call, your love life hums along at a perfect pitch, people are attracted to the energy you radiate, and you're the right person in the right place at the right time. Enjoy it!

The full moon in Scorpio on April 29 highlights your daily work area and the way you maintain your health. You're able to see the bottom line of just about anything you tackle today. This full moon favors research and psychic work.

AT A GLANCE
April 15—New moon in Aries, Mercury turns direct in Aries
April 17—Saturn turns retrograde in Capricorn
April 24—Venus enters Gemini
April 29—Full moon in Scorpio

May 2018
Movers & shakers

May could be a month of surprises. A major planetary shift occurs when Uranus, which has been in Aries for the last seven years, enters Taurus. It will be there until November when, thanks to a retrograde, it slips back into Aries. Next year, it reenters Taurus and will be there until 2025.

Uranus's job is to shake up the status quo suddenly and without warning in order to get rid of what no longer works in your life and to make space for the new. This transit occurs in that area of your chart that rules the personal unconscious. So for you, Gemini, the seven-year journey of Uranus through Taurus may shake up stuff you've buried inside yourself, issues you haven't resolved or power you have disowned over the years. You'll notice this more in the beginning of the transit. Just try to go with the flow.

Between May 13 and 29, Mercury transits Taurus and the same area of your chart where Uranus will be moving in just two days. Use this period to empower yourself from the inside out. Rather than dwelling on the past, immerse yourself in the present. It's your point of power. Your intellect is rock solid now, efficient and practical. You are also more stubborn than usual.

The new moon in Taurus on the 15th, the same day that Uranus enters this sign, brings in new opportunities to work on a project behind the scenes that requires steadfastness and pragmatism. The opportunity is likely to surface suddenly and unexpectedly, so be ready to seize it, Gemini!

Between May 16 and June 26, Mars transits fellow air sign Aquarius and forms a beneficial angle to your sun. On June 26, Mars turns retro, and we'll talk about that in June's roundup. While it's moving direct in Aquarius, Mars propels your forward in all your endeavors. Your intellect is sharpened, you seem to have an endless reserve of energy and your decisiveness prompts a boss or peer to put you in charge of a team endeavor.

On the 19th, Venus enters Cancer and your financial area, where it will be until June 13. During these three weeks, your income may increase—and so may your expenses. It's also possible that you meet a romantic interest who shares your values. If you're already involved in a relationship, then you and your partner should enjoy a tranquil period in which you're both in the flow. You finish each other's sentences and you know what the other is thinking and feeling.

The 29th brings a full moon in Sagittarius, your opposite sign, and highlights a business or personal partnership, a contract negotiation, travel plans and/or an education matter. You could hear news concerning any of these areas. There's a certain gregariousness to Sagittarius, so perhaps it's time to throw a party! With Mercury entering your sign on this same day, you're now primed for networking, talking and writing and clarifying your goals. Mercury remains in your sign until June 12.

May 13—Mercury enters Taurus
May 15—New moon in Taurus, Uranus enters Taurus
May 16—Mars enters Aquarius
May 19—Venus enters Cancer
May 29—Full moon in Sagittarius, Mercury enters Gemini

June 2018
New opportunities

June is one of those months when the changing energies may make you feel like you're trying to walk across beach dunes where the sands shift constantly. But if any sign is equipped for adapting to circumstances, it's you, Gemini.

Mercury enters Cancer on the 12th, joining Venus in your financial area for just a day, before Venus moves into Leo. This transit, which lasts until the 29th, brings an intuitive fluidity to your intellect. You may experience intuitive nudges concerning money, your family and home life and your values.

The 13th features two astrological events: a new moon in Gemini and Venus entering Leo. This new moon comes along just once a year and sets the tone for the next twelve months. Plan for it ahead of time by creating a wish list of what you would like to experience and achieve in the next year, birthday to birthday. Post it where you'll see it often. Back the desire with emotion. This new moon should usher in plenty of new opportunities to do all the things you enjoy and at which you shine: writing and public speaking, networking and digging for information. It could bring a new romantic interest into your life, new professional opportunities or even a move.

Venus moves through Leo from June 13 to July 9, and chances are good that you will enjoy this transit. You'll feel more self-confident, and your charisma and magnetism will attract interesting people. If you're not involved in a relationship, you may meet someone special through a sibling or neighbor.

Between June 26 and August 12, Mars moves retrograde through Aquarius. During this period, you may be taking a deeper look at your spiritual beliefs and may be researching foreign countries you would like to visit, perhaps in pursuit of particular knowledge or insight. Generally, a Mars retro shouldn't impact travel the way a Mercury retro does. But because this retro falls in that area of your chart that rules foreign travel, it's best to travel on either side of the retrograde.

The 28th features a full moon in Capricorn, which falls close to Saturn in the same sign. You may be more serious than usual on or around this date or any news you have may have serious overtones. Serious doesn't necessarily imply negative; you could get a job offer, for instance. That's serious! Other people's resources and money may figure into this day's energy.

Between June 29 and September 5, Mercury transits compatible fire sign Leo, so you are very much in your element. You're able to move full steam ahead on your various projects and tend to be in a gregarious mood. Your intellect is sharp and often dramatic. However, Mercury will be retrograde between July 26 and August 19, and we'll talk about that in next month's roundup.

AT A GLANCE
June 12—Mercury enters Cancer
June 13—New moon in Gemini, Venus enters Leo
June 26—Mars turns retrograde in Aquarius
June 28—Full moon in Capricorn
June 29—Mercury enters Leo

July 2018
Unpredictable

Buckle up! July is an eclipse month, and that means that a sense of urgency could infuse everything! July 12 features a solar eclipse in Cancer, and the 27th features a lunar eclipse in Aquarius. Let's look at the solar eclipse first.

It occurs in your financial area and should bring double the usual opportunities of a new moon. This could mean a new source of income, and because Jupiter in Scorpio forms a wide but beneficial angle to the eclipse degree, it might be a substantial boost in your income. It's a perfect time to bring about what you desire, Gemini, so get busy visualizing and fiddling around with your wish list.

The lunar eclipse on the 27th could be a bit dicey. Mars retrograde is conjunct the eclipse degree so it's possible that someone in your environment pushes one of your buttons. Your initial reaction is anger. But rather than explode at the person, bite your tongue, mull things over and say your piece when you're calmer.

Before either of the eclipses, Venus enters Virgo on July 9. This transit through your family/domestic area lasts until August 6 and should result in smoother sailing at home—with parents, kids or your partner. You may feel the urge to beautify your home in some way—fresh paint, new furniture or new flooring or rugs. Your love life should benefit from this transit as long as you avoid criticism of others.

On the 10th, Jupiter turns direct in Scorpio, always a welcome change. Your daily work routine may expand now in beneficial ways, and if you play your cards right, the boss takes notice, and you could receive a bonus or raise.

And on the 26th, here comes the Mercury retrograde in Leo. With this second Mercury retro of the year, you should know by now what steps to take to mitigate the effects. Take a look back at the March roundup (page 214) about the general rules to follow and look over the Mercury retrograde section in the introduction to the book (pages 9 and 20). Since this retro occurs in the third house of communication, Gemini's natural home in the zodiac, it's important that all of your communication, written and verbal, be succinct and clear. The tendency for misunderstanding—and for drama because of it—will be particularly strong. The retrograde lasts until August 19.

AT A GLANCE
July 9—Venus enters Virgo
July 10—Jupiter turns direct in Scorpio
July 12—Solar eclipse in Cancer
July 26—Mercury turns retrograde in Leo
July 27—Lunar eclipse in Aquarius

August 2018
Nearly 5 stars

This month features a solar eclipse in Leo on August 11. Pluto and Neptune form challenging angles—squares—to the eclipse degree. Squares usually create tension, and with both Neptune and Pluto in the mix, there could be a disagreement with an authority figure and some confusion to the day's events, possibly because you don't have all the information you need. Even so, this eclipse should bring new opportunities in communication. It could be almost anything—a writing or speaking opportunity, a chance to build a website or start a blog for your neighborhood or community or a ghostwriting project. However the specifics unfold, remember that eclipses often infuse the air with a sense of urgency.

Between August 6 and September 9, Venus moves through fellow air sign Libra and the romance and creativity section of your chart. Wow, lucky you, Gemini! The only other period that is as favorable as this one occurred when Venus transited your sign between April 24 and May 19.

Your romantic relationships and creative endeavors flow so smoothly that you may feel as if you awakened in an alternative universe. Your muse is eager to help in any way possible, so be sure to set aside time each day for your creative work. If you're not involved when this transit begins, chances are excellent that you will have met someone special when the transit ends. If you have children, your relationship with them improves and deepens. Your artistic perceptions are especially strong.

On the 19th, Mercury turns direct in Leo. Celebrate! Take a few days off and hit the road with a partner or friend. Then get back to work and dive into your creative endeavors. Mercury in Leo brings fire and passion to your mentality, and that will show up in every facet of your life between now and September 5, when Mercury enters Virgo.

The full moon in Pisces on August 26 may bring career news or closure to a professional project. This full moon stimulates your imagination, compassion and intuition. Heed that inner voice to avoid conflict.

Mars finally turns direct again in Capricorn on August 27 and heads toward its appointment with Aquarius on September 10. Now that its movement has straightened out, matters involving other people's money should unfold more smoothly. This includes things like mortgages, loans, insurance premiums and your spouse's income.

AT A GLANCE
August 6—Venus enters Libra
August 11—Solar eclipse in Leo
August 19—Mercury turns direct in Leo
August 26—Full moon in Pisces
August 27—Mars turns direct in Capricorn

September 2018
Momentum

It's another one of those months of quickly shifting energies. Other signs might have to scramble to keep pace with it all, but you shouldn't have any trouble doing so. Gemini enjoys perpetual speed!

Mercury enters Virgo on September 5 and remains there until the 21st. This transit may produce a lot of lively conversation at the dinner table, and if you have teenage kids, your home may be the hub for gatherings. Mercury in this sign brings great discernment to your intellect and an attention to details. It may also make you more critical of yourself and others, a behavior to avoid!

Saturn turns direct in Capricorn on the 6th, so now it and Mars are traveling together through the shared resources area of your chart. Mars is the energy that propels things forward, and Saturn confers the structure. To take advantage of these two energies, tackle any project that requires persistence and focus.

On the 9th, there are two astrological events: a new moon in Virgo and Venus enters Scorpio. Jupiter and Pluto form close, beneficial angles to this moon, so any new opportunities that surface will be expansive and transformative and may be connected to your family and domestic life. The transit of Venus through Scorpio lasts until the end of the year because in October, Venus turns retro. We'll talk more about it in October's roundup. But until it turns retrograde, your daily work life should benefit in that things unfold with greater ease and employees and co-workers are helpful. There's a powerful emotional component to Venus in Scorpio, and your sexuality is heightened. Be careful about getting involved with a co-worker.

Between September 10 and November 15, Mars transits Aquarius and forms a great angle to your sun. You may be traveling internationally during this period or could be involved in higher education, publishing or some sort of spiritual pursuit. Regardless of the specifics, this transit brings forward momentum to all of your various endeavors.

Mercury enters fellow air sign Libra on the 21st, and now you're really in your element, Gemini. Your focus is on romance, fun and creativity!

The full moon in Aries on September 24 ramps up your social life. You and a group of friends may do some brainstorming about a novel or script you would like to write. Or perhaps you make plans to do something really adventurous—hike a mountain, swim with dolphins or join an Amazon expedition. Your passions run fast and furiously during this full moon.

AT A GLANCE
September 5—Mercury enters Virgo
September 6—Saturn turns direct in Capricorn
September 9—Venus enters Scorpio, new moon in Virgo
September 10—Mars enters Aquarius
September 21—Mercury enters Libra
September 24—Full moon in Aries

October 2018
The good with the not-so-good

October is a mix of astrological energies, some good and some not so good. The latter begins on October 5, when Venus turns retrograde in Scorpio. It will slip back into Libra and the romance/creativity part of your chart and turn direct there on November 16. During this retro, you may feel you're taking two steps forward and one step back, particularly when it comes to your creative endeavors, money and your love life.

Initially, this retro impacts your daily work routine. Relationships with employees and co-workers may feel a bit off, and it's best to avoid conflict even if you're right about something and the other person is wrong. On the 31st, when Venus slips back into Libra, you may be scrutinizing a creative endeavor and restructuring it in some way.

The 8th features a beautiful new moon in Libra that should lift your spirits considerably. A new romance may be in the offing and so may a new creative endeavor. If you and your partner have been thinking about starting a family, this new moon would be a perfect day to make it happen!

From October 9 to 31, Mercury moves through Scorpio. This transit deepens your intuition considerably and brings a kind of bottom line mentality that favors any kind of research. Your perceptions about other people and situations are particularly sharp. The last Mercury retrograde of 2018 begins November 16, in Sagittarius, so sign contracts and make travel plans before that date.

The full moon in Taurus on October 24 lights up the most private area of your chart. You now have a chance to resolve issues you've ignored or buried. There could be news, too, and because Uranus is so close to this full moon, the news arrives suddenly and unexpectedly and takes you by surprise. Saturn forms a close and beneficial angle to this moon, indicating that the news is of a serious nature. Job offer, perhaps? A chance to work behind the scenes on something?

On October 31, Mercury enters Sagittarius, and your mental focus turns to partnerships until November 16, when Mercury turns retro. We'll talk more about this in November's roundup.

AT A GLANCE
October 5—Venus turns retrograde in Scorpio
October 8—New moon in Libra
October 9—Mercury enters Scorpio
October 24—Full moon in Taurus
October 31—Mercury enters Sagittarius

November 2018
Mercury retro alert

Let's talk first about the Mercury retrograde from November 16 to December 6. It begins in Sagittarius, then slides back into Scorpio where it turns direct. In addition to following the usual guidelines for this retro period (read July's roundup on page 219) take special care during this period to communicate clearly with your professional and personal partners. Since the retro begins in your partnership area, this is where the potential for miscommunication is greatest. Once Mercury slips back into Scorpio on December 1, that same care should be taken with employees and co-workers.

The 7th features a new moon in Scorpio. Pluto, Neptune and Saturn form beneficial angles to this new moon, suggesting that new opportunities may appeal to your idealism and your artistic sense. They may also offer a new structure of some sort in your daily work life. A larger office? Faster computer? A promotion?

On the 8th, Jupiter begins a brand new cycle. It enters Sagittarius, your opposite sign, and it will be there until December 2019. Jupiter rules Sadge, so it's happy here. The expansion it brings to your life during the next thirteen months is in the partnership area, publishing, higher education or international travel. If you're already involved in a relationship, then you and your partner may decide to tie the knot. Or, if one of you feels a need for greater personal freedom, you may end the relationship. You might have an opportunity to live and work abroad, to take graduate level classes or to attend or teach a series of workshops.

Between November 15 and December 31, Mars transits Pisces and your career area. What a fabulous year-end boost for all professional matters! You've now got the energy of Mars at your back, and because it's in imaginative Pisces, your creative drive is especially strong. After December 6, when Mercury turns direct, use Mars to launch new projects.

Two astrological events mark November 16: Mercury turning retrograde in Sagittarius, which we've talked about, and Venus turning direct in Libra. Now your love life straightens out again, and your muse isn't playing the trickster! This transit lasts until December 2.

The full moon in your sign on November 23 brings news! You might land a new writing assignment, be asked to speak at a conference or workshop or be asked to a party or celebration with friends.

AT A GLANCE
November 7—New moon in Scorpio
November 8—Jupiter enters Sagittarius
November 15—Mars enters Pisces
November 16—Mercury turns retrograde in Sagittarius, Venus turns direct in Libra
November 23—Full moon in Gemini

December 2018
Onward

As you enter the last month of 2018, give some thought to what you would like to achieve and experience in 2019. Make a wish list. Don't worry about how these things will come about; simply trust that they will.

On the 6th, Mercury turns direct again so hit the mall and get busy with your holiday shopping! Six days later on the 12th, it enters Sagittarius again and remains there until January 4, 2019. Since this period favors travel, choose a destination and make your plans.

Before any of the above happens, Venus enters Scorpio on December 2 and remains there until January 4, 2019. This transit favors your daily work, and because the holidays are close, employees and co-workers are probably in celebratory moods. An office romance may heat up and so does your sexuality.

The new moon in Sagittarius on the 7th bodes well for new opportunities with both professional and personal partners. You might for instance, find the perfect person to team up with for a creative endeavor, a trip and/or an adventure or some sort of publishing endeavor.

The full moon in Cancer on 22nd brings financial news. It should be a particularly powerful full moon because it falls at 0 degrees and 49 minutes, or a cardinal sign. So be prepared, Gemini, for an end of the year bonus or nice money surprise!

AT A GLANCE
December 2—Venus enters Scorpio
December 6—Mercury turns direct in Scorpio
December 7—New moon in Sagittarius
December 12—Mercury enters Sagittarius
December 22—Full moon in Cancer

Reflection

Slow down enough to take stock of how this year went for you. Did you experience and achieve what you wanted? Are you happier? More productive? Is your bank account fatter? What significant events occurred? Jot your notes below.

_____

_____

_____

_____

_____

Happy New Year!

Cancer 2018

Your sign is ruled by the moon. The lunar daily movements are beyond the scope of this book, but pay special attention to the months in which there are eclipses and take note of the new and full moons each month.

The monthly roundups include information on the transits, the planets that are forming angles to your sun sign and the various retrogrades.

For most of this year, until November 8, Jupiter transits fellow water sign Scorpio and forms a beneficial angle to your sun sign. This transit facilitates many aspects of your life—love and romance, creativity, what you do for fun and pleasure and your relationship with your kids. You may be traveling internationally with the one you love or even on your own, in pursuit of a particular experience or type of knowledge. When Uranus enters Taurus in May, it will form a terrific angle to your sun sign. Expect surprises!

January 2018
Mixed

Welcome to 2018! Fortunately, the year doesn't start out with a Mercury retro like 2017 did, so you can get off on the right foot immediately, with a full moon in your sign on January 1. There could be news on or around this date that concerns something that's personally important to you. It may concern your family.

On the 11th, Mercury enters Capricorn, and you and your business partner may be laying out your strategy for the year ahead. During this transit, which lasts until the 31st, you and your romantic partner may team up for a creative endeavor. This possibility becomes even greater with the new moon in Capricorn on the 16th. Venus is closely conjunct this new moon, suggesting that you and your partner may deepen your commitment to each other. You might move in together, get engaged or start a family.

On the 17th, Venus enters Aquarius and will be there until February 10. During this period, your partner or someone else with whom you share financial resources may get a raise or a bonus. You might receive royalties, an insurance payment or an inheritance. It will be easier to obtain a mortgage or loan.

Between January 26 and March 17, energetic Mars moves through Sagittarius and forms a beneficial angle to your career area. Now you've got the wind at your back, Cancer, and can zip through your daily work in half the time it usually takes you. You also are better able to see the larger picture of your career, and everything you do day by day at work feeds into this bigger picture. You may travel overseas at some point during this transit and have business dealings with people from other countries.

On the 31st, Mercury joins Venus in Aquarius. It will be in that sign until February 18. During the ten days that Mercury and Venus travel together, your intellect is forward-thinking, ideas come to you easily, and with your powerful intuition, you're able to recognize which ideas might work and run with them.

The 31st also features a lunar eclipse in Leo, in your financial area. Neptune forms a challenging angle to the eclipse degree that suggests you may have to make some quick adjustments concerning money. You might discover a mistake in your checking account, for instance, or in your paycheck and will need to take care of it immediately. Urgency is often a component of any eclipse.

AT A GLANCE
January 1—Full moon in Cancer
January 11—Mercury enters Capricorn
January 16—New moon in Capricorn
January 17—Venus enters Aquarius
January 26—Mars enters Sagittarius
January 31—Mercury enters Aquarius, lunar eclipse in Leo

February 2018
Creative

There's a solar eclipse this month, in Aquarius, so this could add to tensions and trigger a sense of urgency. But solar eclipses generally aren't as emotional as lunar eclipses and tend to concern outer rather than inner events. New opportunities ushered in with this eclipse could include: a raise for your partner, a mortgage at a low interest rate or low cost insurance. You may also have a chance to delve into the paranormal.

Before the eclipse, on the 10th, Venus enters Pisces. This transit, which lasts until March 6, should be beautiful for you. Your self-confidence attracts the right people at the right time, and if you're traveling overseas, it's possible that you meet a romantic interest, perhaps a fellow traveler. Your compassion and intuition are deepened.

On the 18th, Mercury joins Venus. When this duo travels together in imaginative Pisces, there's no limit to your creativity. You might even team up with a partner or friend for some type of creative endeavor that thrills both of you. Mercury and Venus stay in Pisces until March 6.

AT A GLANCE
February 10—Venus enters Pisces
February 15—Solar eclipse in Aquarius
February 18—Mercury enters Pisces

March 2018
Team work

March is a full month with shifting astrological energies that may leave you breathless, so don't scrimp on sleep and be sure to take time daily for yourself. Things get off to a running start on March 1, with a full moon in compatible earth sign Virgo. This moon highlights communication and daily travel—a commute versus international travel. You're able to see the details in a project that may have eluded you before and are able to make course corrections easily. There could be news about a neighbor or sibling.

March 6 features two astrological events. Both Mercury and Venus enter Aries and your career area. Your mental focus is on professional matters, and you take a leadership role, perhaps by heading up a team for a particular project. With Venus here as well, you attract the right people at the right time, and co-workers see you as the person with foresight and answers.

Mercury turns retrograde on the 22nd and doesn't turn direct again until April 15. During the retro period, you may feel like you're taking two steps forward and a step back. But don't despair! The best way to navigate a Mercury retro is by following the rule of the three Rs: revise, review and reconsider. Don't launch new projects, and don't sign contracts. Since the retro occurs in your career area, take extra care to communicate clearly with co-workers and bosses.

On the 31st, Venus enters earth sign Taurus, where it will be until April 24. This placement is much more comfortable for you and indicates that you'll be spending more time socializing and hanging out with friends. If a romance begins during this transit, it may be with someone you meet through friends or through an organization to which you belong.

Jupiter turns retrograde in Scorpio on March 8, in the romance/creativity section of your chart. Up until now, Jupiter has been expanding your options in this area. During the retrograde period, which lasts until July 10, the expansion occurs inwardly. You may be more concerned with your spiritual awareness and how, or if, it is part of your creative endeavors and your romantic relationships.

The 17th also features two astrological events: Mars enters Capricorn, and there is a new moon in Pisces. With Mars in your partnership area until May 16, you and a business partner aggressively pursue your strategy and goals. *You make things happen.* You and your romantic partner could possibly team up in a business venture.

The new moon in Pisces may bring an opportunity in publishing, higher education or overseas travel. Your imagination is particularly strong and intuitive now. It's a perfect day to write a fantasy short story or to start a fantasy novel. Plant seeds for next month's new moon in your career area!

On the 31st, Venus enters Taurus, which we have talked about already, and there's a full moon in Libra. There could be news concerning your mother or another female in your life. Initially, the news could be confusing. You may not have the full story, so don't jump to conclusions. You may decide to beautify your home in some way. Have the entire family pitch in!

AT A GLANCE
March 1—Full moon in Virgo
March 6—Mercury enters Aries, Venus enters Aries
March 8—Jupiter turns retro in Scorpio
March 17—Mars enters Capricorn, new moon in Pisces
March 22—Mercury turns retro in Aries
March 31—Venus enters Taurus, full moon in Libra

April 2018
Career bonus

April is considerably calmer than last month. The latter half of the month will be a vast improvement over the first two weeks because on April 15 Mercury turns direct, and there's a new moon in Aries. This new moon, in fact, should be a major bonus for your career. A promotion or raise or both are possibilities. If you're self-employed, you could land the perfect project, find the ideal client or make a substantial sale. There's a fearlessness about you now that's enhanced by Mercury's placement in Aries, where it will be until May 13.

On May 17, Saturn turns retrograde in Capricorn, in your partnership area, and will remain that way until September 6. While it's in a dormant state, you may be reevaluating the structures of your business and personal partnerships. Do they serve your best interest? Are you comfortable with the relationships as they exist now? How would you change them if you could?

Between April 24 and May 19, Venus transits Gemini and the most private area of your chart. There's a certain irony with this transit. Gemini is a sociable sign and isn't crazy about being cooped up in solitude. So during this transit, get out and about, network and have fun.

Don't become a hermit. If you need to work in solitude, perhaps to meet a deadline, by all means do so. But indulge Gemini's social nature. If you're not involved in a relationship right now, a romance is possible with someone special you meet when you're out and about! If you're involved, then you and your partner are communicating well.

On the 29th, the full moon in Scorpio highlights a romantic relationship or a creative endeavor. There could be news related to either or both of these areas. Children, if you have them, also feature into any news you hear.

AT A GLANCE
April 15—New moon in Aries, Mercury turns direct in Aries
April 17—Saturn turns retrograde in Capricorn
April 24—Venus enters Gemini
April 29—Full moon in Scorpio

May 2018
Big shift

One of the outer planets changes signs this month, and that is going to prove beneficial to you, Cancer. But before Uranus enters Taurus, Mercury begins its transit through that sign on the 13th, and until May 29, you are doing quite a bit of socializing. Your intellect is grounded and stable, and you have the patience to see projects through to the end. You may be taking a closer look at your financial situation, too—a wise thing to do when Mercury is in even-tempered Taurus.

The 15th features two events: a new moon in Taurus and Uranus entering that sign after seven years in Aries. Let's take a look first at the new moon. With Mercury and Uranus also in earth sign Taurus, both planets and this new moon form beneficial angles to your sun sign that facilitate the flow of energies. New people who enter your life now are likely to be extremely helpful in achieving your dreams and goals. If you're self-employed, you may land projects with some of these individuals. Mercury will be in Taurus until May 29.

The Uranus transit through Taurus will last until November of this year, and then because of a retrograde, it slips back into Aries until 2019. On a personal level, you may develop innovative ways to make money and will get plenty of guidance from your intuition. Your attitude toward money and possessions could change radically for the better! You'll attract plenty of idiosyncratic individuals into your life during this time and some of them may be geniuses at what they do. Uranus transits are intended to shake us out of our routines and ruts so that the things that no longer work in our lives fall away from our experience, making room for the new. Take note of what happens during the first week of the transit. It will give you an idea of the kinds of events you'll experience.

Between May 16 and June 26, Mars moves through Aquarius. Then on June 26, it turns retrograde, slips back into Capricorn on August 12 and turns direct in that sign on August 27. While it's in direct motion in Aquarius, you're able to draw on other people's resources—money, energy or time. You may sell a new project, launch a new product or receive royalties and insurance payments. Remember, Mars is the planet that makes stuff happen. So whenever you see an opening, seize it and run with it.

From May 19 to June 13, Venus transits your sign and makes this one of the best periods for you all year. Things flow your way. Romance, creativity and success are heightened. You feel self-confident and optimistic, and other people sense this and flock to you. The only other period that is equal to this is when Venus transits Scorpio and the romance and creativity area of your chart later this year. Enjoy it! And since your muse is at your service, take advantage of it!

The full moon in Sagittarius on May 29 brings news about your daily work, a co-worker or an employee. You may be recognized in some way for your work. Mercury enters Gemini on this same day, and while it tours the most private area of your chart, you're better able to recognize issues you have buried and even dreams you have misplaced. It's an excellent time for keeping a journal and focusing on the positive aspects of your life. This transit lasts until June 12.

AT A GLANCE
May 13—Mercury enters Taurus
May 15—New moon in Taurus, Uranus enters Taurus
May 16—Mars enters Aquarius
May 19—Venus enters Cancer
May 29—Full moon in Sagittarius, Mercury enters Gemini

June 2018
Relax

Consider June a month for kicking back and taking it easy. Do what you enjoy. You're shoring up your energy for a flurry of activity in July.

Between June 12 and 29, Mercury transits your sign, and now you're really in your element. Your emotions and your reactions may be heightened, but you're immersed in an intuitive flow that is familiar and comforting.

On the 13th, two astrological events occur: there's a new moon in Gemini, and Venus enters Leo and your financial area. The new moon brings new communication opportunities, perhaps something behind the scenes where you work with a team or a group of like-minded individuals. As Venus transits Leo and your financial area until July 9, you may be spending more, but you may also be earning more. Don't try to figure out how this increased income will happen; trust that it will. If a romantic relationship begins during this transit, you and the other person may share some of the same values, and there could be some drama connected to how you meet.

On the 26th, Mars turns retrograde in Aquarius and turns direct again on August 27. While Mars is in this dormant state, certain financial matters may slow down. Perhaps the raise your partner was supposed to get is delayed for some reason, or a royalty check you were expecting is held up. Use this retrograde to find new ways to empower yourself and to deal with conflict in your life.

The full moon in Capricorn on June 28 highlights your ambition, professional matters and partnerships. There could be news in any or all of these areas. A project or creative endeavor is completed.

The next day, on the 29th, Mercury joins Venus in Leo. The planet of communication will turn retrograde next month, on July 26. Before that happens, get your contracts signed, make your travel plans and launch your new ideas.

AT A GLANCE
June 12—Mercury enters Cancer
June 13—New moon in Gemini, Venus enters Leo
June 26—Mars turns retrograde in Aquarius
June 28—Full moon in Capricorn
June 29—Mercury enters Leo

July 2018
Varied

The two eclipses this month, one of them in your sign, may infuse July with a sense of urgency and tension. Just remember that the purpose of eclipses is to bring issues, relationships and situations to our immediate attention so that we must deal with them quickly. They help us to make significant changes in our lives that we might not make otherwise.

The solar eclipse in your sign on July 12 should usher in new personal opportunities that allow you to use your considerable intuition and imagination in a positive, creative way. But because Pluto is opposed to the eclipse degree, there could be a confrontation with an authority figure—a parent, boss or the larger authority of government—that precipitates a crisis of some kind. Once you have dealt with whatever it is, you recognize the opportunity that is being presented.

With the lunar eclipse in Aquarius on July 27, there may be some drama related to your partner's income—or the income of anyone with whom you share financial obligations, like a child, parent or roommate. Taxes, investments and debt may also be involved. You have to take quick action to resolve whatever it is. It may be emotionally draining, but you're now able to see what changes must be made.

Before either of these eclipses occurs, Venus enters compatible earth sign Virgo on July 9, a transit that lasts until August 6 and should be terrific for you. If you're not involved, a romance could start with someone you meet through neighbors or siblings or during your daily travels. This transit also favors communication of all kinds. It's a perfect time to start a blog or build a website, at least until July 26, when Mercury turns retrograde. Expand your social media presence, too, Cancer.

On the 10th, Jupiter turns direct in Scorpio, and from now until November 8, when it moves into Sagittarius, your romantic and creative options expand like crazy. Any creative endeavors in which you're involved are successful, and you're able to draw on resources you may not have known you have.

Mercury's retrograde in Leo begins on July 26 and lasts until August 19. It occurs in your financial area, which means you'll have to pay close attention to your accounts. Check and double check the figures. Keep close tabs on your ATM usage. And, of course, follow the usual guidelines for navigating this period successfully: revise, review and reconsider. Don't start anything new, and don't sign contracts.

AT A GLANCE
July 9—Venus enters Virgo
July 10—Jupiter turns direct in Scorpio
July 12—Solar eclipse in Cancer
July 26—Mercury turns retrograde in Leo
July 27—Lunar eclipse in Aquarius

August 2018
Solar eclipse

This month features a solar eclipse in Leo on August 11. Since it occurs in your financial area, this is where you can expect new opportunities to surface. A new source of income is possible that could come to you through a creative endeavor (the Leo component). Pluto forms a difficult angle to the eclipse degree, so there could be tension or problems with an authority figure. But you persevere, and in the end, you're the winner!

Venus enters Libra on the 6th, and from then until September 9, things at home should flow smoothly. Venus rules Libra, so it functions well in this sign. You may be spending money on a home beautification project—perhaps buying art, new furniture or adding onto your home. If you and your partner live together, this transit could spark the kind of romance that brought you together in the first place.

On the 19th, Mercury turns direct in Leo, so those financial opportunities promised by the solar eclipse should start showing up now. It's now safe to pack your bags and hit the road, sign contracts and launch new projects and ideas.

The full moon in Pisces on the 26th should be a beauty. Both Uranus and Saturn form favorable angles to it, suggesting that any news you hear is unexpected, could involve a creative endeavor and have a lasting impact. Publishing or long-distance travel could be involved, too.

Mars turns direct in Capricorn on the 27th, so don't hesitate to move ahead with all your business dealings.

AT A GLANCE

August 6—Venus enters Libra
August 11—Solar eclipse in Leo
August 19—Mercury turns direct in Leo
August 26—Full moon in Pisces
August 27—Mars turns direct in Capricorn

September 2018
Five stars

September is another busy month astrologically, with several planets changing signs, another planet turning direct and the usual full and new moons. Let's take a closer look.

Between September 5 and 21, Mercury transits Virgo, an earth sign compatible with your sun sign. Your mind is busy during this transit, sifting through details to find the way ideas connect. It favors research, communication and networking, and because Mercury rules Virgo, it functions well in this sign. Once Mercury enters Libra, where it will be until October 9, your conscious focus turns to home and family, or if you work out of your home, you may be trying to balance work and family.

Saturn turns direct in Capricorn on the 6th, a bonus for your partnerships. Now you have a clearer idea about the structures of these relationships and whether they serve your best interest.

The 9th features two events: Venus entering Scorpio and a new moon in Virgo. The Venus transit lasts through the end of the year because in October Venus turns retrograde. We'll talk more about that in October's roundup. While it's in direct motion, however, you'll be enjoying one of your best periods in 2018. Your sexuality is greatly heightened, your love life is intense and you feel more attractive and self-confident. Your creative drive is at an all time high, and with your muse in attendance 24/7, any creative endeavor you tackle will succeed.

The new moon in Virgo should bring new communication opportunities. You might, for instance, land a great freelance project, and with Mercury now in direct motion until November 16, you can negotiate a contract that suits you.

Between September 10 and November 15, Mars transits Aquarius and the shared resources area of your chart. You and/or your partner will be aggressively pursuing new sources of income. You have great ideas and simply need a strategy for implementing them.

The full moon in Aries lights up your career area. There could be career news or news about someone with whom you work. A project you've been working on is completed, and you may be asked to head up a team or other endeavor.

September 5—Mercury enters Virgo
September 6—Saturn turns direct in Capricorn
September 9—Venus enters Scorpio, new moon in Virgo
September 10—Mars enters Aquarius
September 21—Mercury enters Libra
September 24—Full moon in Aries

October 2018
Bumpy road with love & money

It's a relatively tranquil month, and the only glitch is Venus turning retrograde in Scorpio on October 5. On the 31st, it slides back into Libra and turns direct in that sign on November 16. A Venus retrograde messes with your love life, your creativity and sometimes with your finances. Think of this period as favorable for evaluation rather than action. You may be taking a deeper look at what you value about the people you love, about your creative endeavors and about your relationship with or beliefs about money. Once Venus slips back into Libra, you may be taking a deeper look at what you value in your family and home life.

The 8th brings a new moon in Libra, in your family/home area. Someone may move into your place—or out of it. Either way, it spells opportunity for you. If your home has been on the market, then this new moon could bring a viable offer. If you've been looking for a home, you may find the ideal place.

Mercury joins Venus retrograde in Scorpio on the 9th and will be there until the 31st. You may be thinking about romance, your creative endeavors and your kids (if you have any) during this transit. It's an excellent time for any kind of research because your intellect is focused on that bottom line. If your research involves travel, use your considerable intuition to find what you're looking for. Pay attention to synchronicities; they may offer guidance and insight.

The full moon in Taurus on the 24th should suit you. Taurus is an earth sign compatible with your water sign sun and should bring an inner stability and greater patience. Your social calendar may fill up around the time of this full moon, so be sure to make room in your schedule for fun and friends!

On the 31st, Mercury enters Sagittarius, where it will be moving direct until November 16. During this period, your conscious focus is on your daily work and how you maintain your health. You may start a new exercise routine or nutritional program. You may have a better grasp of the larger picture of whatever your work entails.

October 5—Venus turns retrograde in Scorpio
October 8—New moon in Libra
October 9—Mercury enters Scorpio
October 24—Full moon in Taurus
October 31—Mercury enters Sagittarius

November 2018
Planetary shift

Let's get the bad news out of the way first. Mercury turns retro in Sagittarius on November 16, slips back into Scorpio on December 1 and turns direct in that sign on December 6. During this retrograde, two areas of your chart are impacted—your daily work and health and romance and creativity. The first area indicates that you may be returning to a project that was delayed or postponed and putting a different spin on it. You may also be revisiting a health concern or a diet or nutritional program.

Once Mercury moves back into Scorpio in December, your love life and creative endeavors are impacted. Rather than diving into a new creativity project, dust off something you stuck in a drawer months ago. Instead of dumping your current partner, wade through the miscommunication until Mercury turns direct, and then decide what you want to do about the relationship.

The new moon in Scorpio on November 7 should be a beauty for you. Not only does it occur before Mercury's retrograde begins, but it promises new opportunities in your love life, in creative endeavors, with your kids and with anything you do for fun and pleasure. Both Neptune and Pluto form beautiful angles to this new moon, suggesting that your ideals are involved somehow in the opportunities and that you're the one calling the shots.

On the 8th, Jupiter makes a major shift. It leaves Scorpio and enters Sagittarius, where it will be for the next thirteen months. During this time, your daily work expands, perhaps with more responsibilities, a promotion or even a new job. It all depends on where you place your intention and focus. Another component of this transit is international travel. Perhaps you land a job that enables you to travel to countries you've always wanted to see—and now someone else is footing the bill. Jupiter in fire sign Sagittarius forms a powerful and favorable angle to your financial area, so almost anything is possible.

Between November 15 and December 31, Mars transits fellow water sign Pisces. That means it's forming a beneficial angle to your sun sign, and you've got a lot of momentum behind you, maybe enough momentum to blast through any obstacles that Mercury retrograde tosses in your path. Just don't get too cocky, Cancer! But use this energy to move closer to the achievement of your goals. During this transit, your spiritual beliefs, imagination and intuition will play major roles in your decisions.

Okay, November 16. Mercury turns retrograde in Sagittarius. Look back to the Mercury retro advice for July (page 231) and for March (page 227). The good news is that it's the last retro of 2018! Also on the 16th, Venus turns direct in Libra, and between now and December 2, when it moves into Scorpio, your home life should unfold with greater ease. You may go to concerts and art exhibits, beautify your home in some way or spend time with women who are important in your life. You may be spending more money on your home, but hey, it's worth it to be surrounded by beauty!

The full moon in Gemini on the 23rd occurs in the most private area of your chart. Gemini is a sociable sign, though, so get out and about, Cancer. Don't become a hermit. Don't get bogged down in the issues you've buried. Your point of power lies in the present. Take advantage of that!

AT A GLANCE
November 7—New moon in Scorpio
November 8—Jupiter enters Sagittarius
November 15—Mars enters Pisces
November 16—Mercury turns retrograde in Sagittarius, Venus turns direct in Libra
November 23—Full moon in Gemini

December 2018
Romantic & creative

Let's start with the good stuff! Well, actually, most of the astrological news this month is good stuff. But the best? Mercury turns direct in Scorpio on December 6.

Between then and December 12, when it moves into Sagittarius, you have a chance to straighten out whatever went haywire in your love life and creative endeavors during the retrograde. Your sexuality is greatly heightened, and you have a tremendous capacity for tackling any subject in great depth. Your intuition is practically infallible; listen to it. Once Mercury moves into Sagittarius on the 12th, your focus is on clearing everything off your desk before the new year. Tie up loose ends, launch your new projects and brainstorm with your team. The energy with this transit probably feels inexhaustible. Mercury in Sagittarius will carry you into the new year to January 4, 2019.

On the 2nd, Venus enters Scorpio, and from then to January 7, 2019, you will be enjoying one of the most romantic and creative periods all year. The only other period in 2018 that equals this was when Venus was in your sign, between May 19 and June 13. You feel self-confident, attractive, desirable, sexual and sensual. Since you radiate this vibrant energy, others pick up on it and are drawn into your life. You're the magnet!

The new moon in Sagittarius on December 7 should bring new opportunities in your work, with the way you maintain your daily health, with international travel, higher education, spiritual pursuits, publishing and everything else that Sagittarius governs. It may not bring opportunities in all those areas—but it could! One thing is sure with the Sadge new moon; you're in a gregarious mood and should indulge it!

Then on the 22nd, there's a full moon in your sign, Cancer. And because you're a cardinal sign and this moon falls at the most potent of degrees for a cardinal sign—0 degrees and 49 minutes—this is a beautiful way to end 2018 and move into the new year. This full moon galvanizes you, energizes you and fills you with optimism and hope about 2019.

As Captain Picard of *Star Trek* used to say, *Make it so!*

AT A GLANCE
December 2—Venus enters Scorpio
December 6—Mercury turns direct in Scorpio
December 7—New moon in Sagittarius
December 12—Mercury enters Sagittarius
December 22—Full moon in Cancer

Reflection
Reflection is as natural to you as breathing. Looking back on 2018, did you achieve and experience what you had hoped? Are you happier? More prosperous? How will what you learned benefit you in the new year?

_____

_____

_____

_____

_____

Happy New Year!

Leo 2018

Your sign is ruled by the sun, so pay close attention to angles that transiting planets make to your sun sign, whether they're beneficial or challenging. All retrogrades are noted, with advice about how to navigate the retrograde period successfully. In each of the monthly roundups, you'll find information about the new and full moons, when planets change signs and the impact it may have on you.

Overall, 2018 is an interesting year for you, with many changes, surprises and pivots. You're seeking, analyzing, investigating and observing everything around you. It would be a good year to keep a journal of your unusual experiences, synchronicities you experience and vivid dreams that you have.

January 2018
Great start

Welcome to 2018! Fortunately, the year doesn't begin with Mercury retrograde, as 2017 did. However, January and February both feature an eclipse, which we'll discuss shortly.

On January 1, the full moon in Cancer occurs in the most private area of your chart and signals the completion of something you've been involved in. If you've been in therapy, for example, then you may decide you've gotten all you need from it. If you've been working on a particular creative endeavor, then you finish it on or around the time of this full moon. There could be news about your mother or another nurturing female in your life.

On the 11th, Mercury enters Capricorn, and your conscious focus turns to your daily work. Between then and the 31st, when Mercury moves into Aquarius, you may be strategizing with a team, setting personal and professional goals and putting in longer hours. Once Mercury enters Aquarius, where it will be until February 18, your mind is flooded with ideas, and you're more forward-thinking about everything. You and your partner may be redefining your relationship so that it's more satisfying for both of you.

With the new moon in Capricorn on the 16th, new opportunities surface in your daily work. You might be promoted, get a raise or bonus or be picked to head up a team. If you're self-employed, a lucrative project could land at your doorstep. You might decide to start a new physical exercise routine or nutritional program.

Between January 17 and February 10, Venus transits Aquarius and the partnership area of your chart. If you're involved in a relationship, then you and your significant other may deepen your commitment to each other by moving in together, getting engaged or starting a family. If you're not involved with anyone now, then you may be before this transit ends. Venus in Aquarius is also beneficial for your business partnerships.

You'll enjoy the period from January 26 to March 17, when Mars transits Sagittarius and the romance/creativity sector of your chart. Your sexuality will be heightened, and if you meet someone in whom you're romantically interested, you will pursue the person without holding back! On the creativity front, you've got the wind at your back now, Leo, so make the most of this transit. The sky really is the limit!

The 31st features two astrological events: Mercury enters Aquarius, joining Venus in your partnership area, and there's a lunar eclipse in your sign. We've talked about Mercury's transit, so let's take a look at the lunar eclipse. Neptune forms a challenging angle to the eclipse degree, suggesting that you may have to make a rapid adjustment to a fluid personal situation. You may not have all the information you need, however, so things may be confusing and tainted with high drama.

AT A GLANCE
January 1—Full moon in Cancer
January 11—Mercury enters Capricorn
January 16—New moon in Capricorn
January 17—Venus enters Aquarius
January 26—Mars enters Sagittarius
January 31—Mercury enters Aquarius, lunar eclipse in Leo

February 2018
Intuitive month

Compared to last month, February is relatively calm except—and it's a biggie—for a solar eclipse in Aquarius on February 15. Uranus forms a close and beneficial angle to the eclipse degree, suggesting that new partnership opportunities come out of the blue. You will have to make quick decisions about whether they're legitimate and serious enough to be considered. Hint: let your intuition figure this out!

Between February 10 and March 6, Venus transits Pisces and the shared resources area of your chart. If you have been thinking about applying for a mortgage to buy a home or for refinancing an existing home, this transit makes the process much easier, and it's unlikely that you'll run into any hurdles. It's also possible that your partner lands a raise or bonus.

On the 18th, Mercury joins Venus in Pisces, and they travel together until March 6 when they both change signs. Your mind is more intuitive during this transit, and you feel more compassionate toward others. Your imagination is also especially powerful now, and whatever you can imagine, Leo, you can create. So get busy with your wish list, back those desires with emotion, then get out of the way and allow the universe to do its job.

AT A GLANCE
February 10—Venus enters Pisces
February 15—Solar eclipse in Aquarius
February 18—Mercury enters Pisces

March 2018
New ideas

The first Mercury retrograde of the year starts on March 22 in Aries and ends April 15. If you've got international travel plans during that period, then travel with a sense of adventure because your itinerary will probably change suddenly and unexpectedly. Rather than starting new endeavors, it's smart to follow the three Rs: revise, review and reconsider. Also, don't sign contracts unless you don't mind revisiting the details of the contract at a later date. Communicate clearly with everyone because during a Mercury retro miscommunication and misunderstandings often develop.

If you have trouble with appliances or electronics, by all means call the experts. If you have to replace an appliance or a piece of electronic equipment—like a computer—buy what you need, but double check delivery times. Look over the Mercury retrograde section in the introduction (pages 9 and 20) and follow the suggested guidelines so the retro is less stressful for you!

On March 1, the full moon in Virgo highlights a financial issue. You're able to see your way clearly to earning more money and budgeting your present income in a more realistic way. You might apply for a part-time job that will help you supplement your income or may land a freelance gig of some kind. Whatever the specifics, this full moon helps you connect the dots.

On the 6th, both Mercury and Venus enter Aries and form beneficial angles to your sun. While Mercury is direct and traveling with Venus, your heart and your head are on the same page. You're eager, impatient and passionate about the ones you love and what you're doing. You think and act like an entrepreneur, a trailblazer. Then on the 22nd, Mercury turns retrograde, and Venus continues on her merry way through Aries until March 31, lighting up your love life, your creativity and your income. There could be some involvement in publishing or higher education.

Once Venus enters Taurus and your career area, where it will be from March 31 to April 24, your professional life is going to ramp up in a positive way! We'll discuss the possibilities in the April roundup.

Jupiter turns retrograde in Scorpio on March 8 and doesn't straighten out again until July 10. While Jupiter is in this dormant state, its expansion takes place internally, as you reevaluate your spiritual beliefs and how, or if, you are integrating those beliefs into your family life.

The 17th features two astrological events: Mars enters Capricorn, and a new moon in Pisces. Mars stays in Capricorn until May 16 and brings a whirlwind of energy to your daily work. Remember the old Mr. Clean ads? That's you during this transit, Leo. The new moon in Pisces could bring opportunities to earn money through some sort of creative endeavor that involves imagination. Or your partner or someone else with whom you share financial resources gets a raise or a bonus.

Circle the 22nd on your calendar for the day Mercury turns retrograde, which we've discussed already.

The 31st features two events: Venus enters Taurus, and there is a full moon in Libra. This moon lights up the communication segment of your chart. You and your siblings may have a get-together and invite the neighbors, or you may get a group together and attend a concert or art exhibit.

AT A GLANCE

March 1—Full moon in Virgo
March 6—Mercury enters Aries, Venus enters Aries
March 8—Jupiter turns retro in Scorpio
March 17—Mars enters Capricorn, new moon in Pisces
March 22—Mercury turns retro in Aries
March 31—Venus enters Taurus, full moon in Libra

April 2018
Career opportunities

A lot less is going on astrologically in April than there was last month. In fact, with Venus moving through your career area between March 31 and April 24, you're in the perfect position for a raise, promotion or even a new job/career. You're the apple of the boss's eye during this transit and are looked upon as the one with the answers. You have greater patience and resoluteness now. If you're self-employed, then this transit may bring new clients and projects and new sources of income.

If you're not involved with anyone right now, then you may meet someone through a co-worker or through your profession. Venus in Taurus deepens your sensuality, and one possible repercussion is that you eat more rich foods than usual and gain a few pounds!

On the 15th, Mercury turns direct in Aries, and there's a new moon in that sign. Mercury turning direct is always a cause for celebration. Pack your bags and hit the road, Leo. Sign your contracts, submit your ideas and manuscripts and launch your new projects. But wait for a few days so that Mercury stabilizes.

The new moon in Aries may bring an opportunity to travel overseas, a publishing contract or early acceptance to the graduate school of your choice. You may also have a chance to explore spiritual beliefs of different countries and cultures. On or around the time of this moon, you may be feeling restless and impatient.

Saturn turns retrograde in Capricorn on April 17 and remains in this dormant state until September 6. During these months, you will be evaluating structures in your daily work life—relationships with employees and/or co-workers, the way you carry out your responsibilities and what you're trying to build or achieve. Once Saturn turns direct again, you'll be able to implement what you've learned.

Between April 24 and May 19, Venus transits compatible air sign Gemini. During these several weeks, your social life takes center stage. You're out networking, meeting and greeting or perhaps attending professional conferences for recruiting purposes or to publicize your company's product or your own. A romantic interest may be sparked during this transit.

The full moon in Scorpio on April 29 triggers a lot of emotional intensity at home or within your family. It could involve your mother or another female in your life, and your best course is to temper the drama through calm, decisive action.

AT A GLANCE
April 15—New moon in Aries, Mercury turns direct in Aries
April 17—Saturn turns retrograde in Capricorn
April 24—Venus enters Gemini
April 29—Full moon in Scorpio

May 2018
Erratic

The rapidly shifting energies this month may leave you breathless! Be sure to carve out time each day for yourself—for meditating, daydreaming or physical exercise.

One of the outer planets is changing signs on May 15. Uranus, after seven years in Aries, is moving into Taurus, where it will be until November. Then, because of a retrograde, it slips back into Aries and remains there until 2019. Uranus's job is to shake up the status quo, and it's going to do that with your career. You may change jobs several times during these years or could change your career path entirely. You will find new, innovative ways to earn a living and will attract idiosyncratic people who may be geniuses in their professions or have unusual talents.

On the same day that Uranus enters Taurus, there's a new moon in that sign. Pay close attention to any new career opportunities that surface on or around the date of this new moon. They may provide clues about what kinds of changes Uranus in Taurus holds for your professional life. Possibilities with this new moon: a promotion, a raise, a move to a different office or more responsibility.

Between May 13 and 29, Mercury moves through Taurus and your career area. There's so much focus on professional matters now that it may be a challenge to find a balance between your personal and your professional responsibilities. This transit makes you more stubborn than usual, but also more resilient and patient. On the 29th, Mercury enters Gemini where it will be until June 12. During this period, you may be working with groups—a professional team, for instance, or a publicity firm. You're networking more frequently.

Between May 16 and June 26, Mars is moving direct in Aquarius, your opposite sign. You are aggressively pursuing your goals in a partnership—with an agent, manager, supplier or some other person with whom you do business. You and your personal partner may be sparring over details in your relationship. You may feel, for example, that your partner doesn't express his or her appreciation for you often enough. Adjustments may need to be made in the relationship so that it's more satisfying to both of you.

Between May 19 and June 13, Venus moves through Cancer. This transit favors inner reflection. Your dreams may be more vivid and lucid during this period and may hold insights and information that can be helpful. If you get involved in a romantic relationship during this time frame, you may keep it to yourself, a trend that will last until Venus enters your sign, Leo, on June 13.

The 29th features two events: there is a full moon in fellow fire sign Sagittarius, and Mercury enters Gemini. We've talked about Mercury in Gemini, but what may the full moon in Sadge hold? Quite a bit, actually. It lights up the creativity and romance sector of your chart as well as everything you do for fun and pleasure. There could be news about a creative endeavor— you land an audition, get the part or sell your novel. A romance takes off. You hit the road with a friend or lover. You get the idea.

AT A GLANCE
May 13—Mercury enters Taurus
May 15—New moon in Taurus, Uranus enters Taurus
May 16—Mars enters Aquarius
May 19—Venus enters Cancer
May 29—Full moon in Sagittarius, Mercury enters Gemini

June 2018
Five star

It's another busy month, but one you're going to love because Venus transits your sign from June 13 to July 9. The only other period that is as romantic and creative as this one won't happen until early in 2019, so enjoy these three weeks to their fullest! Your self-confidence will soar, Leo, and the people around you will feel it. You're the magnet toward which others are drawn. If you're not involved in a relationship when this transit begins, you probably will be by the time it ends. Even if the relationship doesn't turn into something serious, which it could, it will be fun and pleasurable. On the creativity front, you're on a roll. Take advantage of it!

On the same day Venus enters Leo, there's a new moon in Gemini that will double your fun and bring new opportunities for networking and new communication projects. This new moon should also bring about plenty of social invitations, and you won't lack for fun stuff to do and interesting people to meet.

Backtracking a day, to the 12th, Mercury enters Cancer, where it will be until June 29. During this period, it's smart to plant seeds for what you would like to do and experience when Mercury enters your sign on the 29th. Your conscious mind will be more intuitive during the Cancer transit, and you should have greater recall of your dreams. Keep a journal and pen at your bedside; the dreams may contain insights and information that will prove useful. If you need information about a future event, then request a precognitive dream before you go to sleep.

The Mars retrograde in Aquarius runs from June 26 to August 27, when it will turn direct in Capricorn. While it's retro in your partnership area, you may feel at times that you and your personal partner are dancing on eggshells, that the relationship is fragile in some way. Issues you thought you both understood may seem murky or confused now. One step forward, two steps back: that's how Mars retro can make you feel. One of the best ways to deal with the retro is to engage in physical activity daily—the gym, a run, yoga or even a long walk in a natural setting. And remember, this too shall pass!

The full moon in Capricorn on June 28 may bring news about work. A project you've pitched gets a green light, you find the ideal employee for an opening in the company or you reach a goal.

From June 29 to July 26, Mercury is moving direct through your sign, and you're definitely in your element. Your mind is sharp, dramatic and rich with ideas. Any creative endeavor you tackle should go extremely well. Then you hit the Mercury retrograde, which we will talk about in next month's roundup.

AT A GLANCE
June 12—Mercury enters Cancer
June 13—New moon in Gemini, Venus enters Leo
June 26—Mars turns retrograde in Aquarius
June 28—Full moon in Capricorn
June 29—Mercury enters Leo

July 2018
Challenges

Two eclipses this month could trigger angst and a sense of urgency that often accompanies these events. The first, a solar eclipse in Cancer, occurs on July 12. Opportunities that surface are connected to your family and roots and to your own spiritual growth. Pluto is opposed to the eclipse degree, and Neptune forms a beneficial angle to it. Since the eclipse occurs in the most private sector of your chart, there may be a tendency for secrecy.

The lunar eclipse in Aquarius on July 27 indicates that you and a romantic interest may decide to deepen your commitment to each other through engagement or marriage, but there could be some sort of internal crisis concerning individual identities. You or your partner may be unsettled about becoming *us*. Retrograde Mars in Aquarius is close to the eclipse degree, so don't make any definitive decisions until after it turns direct on August 26.

On the 9th, Venus enters Virgo and your financial area, where it will be until August 6. This transit should benefit your income—an unexpected check arrives or you get a raise or refund. Your expenses could increase during this transit, but you'll have the money to cover them.

Jupiter turns direct in Scorpio on the 10th. Between now and November 8, when Jupiter moves into Sagittarius, the planet's expansive nature will impact your home/family life. Perhaps someone moves into your place—a roommate, a lover or one of your grown kids. Or you add on to your existing home or even look for a larger place, possibly with some land.

On July 26, Mercury turns retro in Leo and turns direct again on August 19. Whenever Mercury turns retro in your own sign, you experience odd snafus—you lock yourself out of your own home, for instance, and have to call a locksmith. Or you're at the grocery store with a full cart and realize you've forgotten your wallet. So check and double check details like this during the retrograde. Also, follow the usual guidelines given in the March roundup.

AT A GLANCE
July 9—Venus enters Virgo
July 10—Jupiter turns direct in Scorpio
July 12—Solar eclipse in Cancer
July 26—Mercury turns retrograde in Leo
July 27—Lunar eclipse in Aquarius

August 2018
Solar eclipse in your sign

The solar eclipse in your sign on August 11 is important. It signals the beginning of something new—a relationship, job, career, creative endeavor or even a new source of income. You may have to give up something in order for the new opportunities to flow into your life, but whatever you're giving up is probably something you have outgrown. Greet the day with excitement.

On the 6th, Venus enters Libra, and between then and September 9, your aesthetic sense is heightened. You may be writing or blogging about art, music, photography, literature or dance. You and a friend, neighbor or sibling could attend a concert or art exhibit or some other kind of performance. If romance is sparked during this transit, it could be with someone you meet in your neighborhood or through a sibling or friend. Your self-confidence is excellent, and you're in a sociable mood.

The 19th is a day to celebrate: Mercury turns direct in Leo, and now you can really enjoy this transit and Venus's movement through Libra. You recognize the importance of balance in your life, that it's essential to your happiness and well-being.

The full moon in Pisces on November 26 receives a favorable beam from Uranus, so any news you hear today is sudden, unexpected and probably good! It may concern your partner's income, a loan, mortgage or insurance issue. The news could also be about a creative endeavor.

The month winds up with Mars turning direct in Capricorn on August 27. Now you can move forward confidently with your various work projects and can lay out new strategies for achieving your goals.

AT A GLANCE
August 6—Venus enters Libra
August 11—Solar eclipse in Leo
August 19—Mercury turns direct in Leo
August 26—Full moon in Pisces
August 27—Mars turns direct in Capricorn

September 2018
Fluctuating energies

It's another month of shifting energies, and there's plenty for you to love and enjoy.

On September 5, Mercury enters Virgo, where it will be until the 21st, and your conscious focus turns to finances. If you're wishing for a new source of income, the new moon in Virgo on the 9th could bring it to you. It might be a lucrative part-time job or a freelance project you can do from home. Or, if you have an employer, you might land a raise.

Saturn turns direct in Capricorn on the 6th, so now Mercury and Saturn are moving on parallel tracks in earth signs, excellent for bringing stability to your daily work and your finances.

On the 9th, there's a new moon in Virgo, and Venus enters Scorpio and the family/home sector of your chart, where it will be, off and on, through the rest of the year. On October 5, Venus turns retrograde, and we'll talk about it in next month's roundup. The placement is emotionally intense, psychic and sexual. Avoid family dramas and confrontations during this transit. Even though your perceptions about people in your immediate environment will be astute, it's best to keep these insights to yourself unless they are positive. If a romance is kindled during this transit, it will be a whirlwind of passion.

Between September 10 and November 15, Mars transits Aquarius once again. In a sense, you now have a chance to revisit issues and concerns you had in May and June, before Mars turned retrograde. Now you can make course corrections and rectify whatever may have gone wrong.

Mercury moves through Libra from September 21 to October 9. Your mood is lighter, your mind more artistic and creative, and you're more outgoing and eager to socialize. This period is perfect for negotiating and signing contracts.

The full moon in Aries on the 24ᵗʰ should be terrific for you. Aries is also a fire sign and endows you with plenty of physical vitality, independence and passion. Don't be surprised if you suddenly decide to take a trip on or around this full moon, which falls in that area of your chart that rules foreign travel. There could also be news about a publishing project or something connected to higher education.

AT A GLANCE
September 5—Mercury enters Virgo
September 6—Saturn turns direct in Capricorn
September 9—Venus enters Scorpio, new moon in Virgo
September 10—Mars enters Aquarius
September 21—Mercury enters Libra
September 24—Full moon in Aries

October 2018
Self-expression

On October 5, your love life may take a hit when Venus turns retrograde in Scorpio, slips back into Libra and turns direct in that sign on December 2. This retro impacts two houses—your home/family life and the communication areas of your chart. While it's retro in Scorpio, you may have less disposable income to spend on your home. A refurbishing project may be delayed. You will be mulling over your closest relationships—with your kids, parents, a partner and siblings. If you find them lacking in some way, keep it to yourself. Once Mercury reenters Libra, strive for balance in love, finances and your creative endeavors.

The new moon in Libra on the 8ᵗʰ may be tainted somewhat by Venus's retrograde, but you'll still enjoy the new opportunities that surface for self-expression in your daily life. Siblings, neighbors and friends will figure prominently. An example of some things that may come your way: free tickets to a concert and a chance to go backstage; a move to a different neighborhood or home; or an opportunity to travel somewhere close to home that you've never been before. However the specifics unfold, you should enjoy this one.

From October 9 to 31, Mercury enters Scorpio and travels with Venus retrograde. Mercury is chatty and may encourage you to talk about your problems with your love life, your finances or your creative endeavors. But Scorpio is inherently private and secretive, and you would be better off keeping your thoughts to yourself. Talking about them and hashing them over repeatedly with friends only empowers whatever is wrong. Use this transit for research. Write a short story or a novel. Use your emotions creatively.

The full moon in Taurus on October 24 brings something in your career to culmination or completion. You hear news about your profession or career, and because Uranus is closely conjunct to this moon, the news is sudden and unexpected. Saturn is also forming a beneficial angle to this full moon, indicating that the news is rock solid and has a long-term impact.

Mercury moves through fellow fire sign Sagittarius from October 31 to the end of the year, with a retrograde in between. The retrograde occurs on November 16, so until then, your conscious focus is on travel, fun, romance and your various creative endeavors.

AT A GLANCE
October 5—Venus turns retrograde in Scorpio
October 8—New moon in Libra
October 9—Mercury enters Scorpio
October 24—Full moon in Taurus
October 31—Mercury enters Sagittarius

November 2018
Big Jupiter shift

Jupiter, the planet of abundance, luck and expansion, is going to make a shift this month that should delight you, Leo. On the 8th, it enters fellow fire sign Sagittarius and the area of your chart that governs romance, creativity, children and everything you do for fun and pleasure. Jupiter rules Sagittarius, so it functions well in this sign. During the thirteen months that Jupiter will transit Sadge, your love life and creative endeavors and options in both areas will expand. You and your partner might have a child. You could easily turn a hobby into a business. International travel is a distinct possibility during this transit and so is anything connected to publishing.

On the 7th, the new moon in Scorpio brings a breath of fresh air to your home/family life. The possibilities? You get your asking price for your home; someone moves in or out of your house; or you and your partner discover you're going to become parents. However the specifics unfold, the beneficial angles that three other planets make to this new moon promise that the events on or around this new moon will please you.

From November 15 to December 31, Mars moves through Pisces. This transit galvanizes the shared resources area of your chart. Your partner may be aggressively pursuing avenues that will bring in a bonus or raise. Your sexuality is intimately linked with your emotions during this transit, and your intuition is deepened. You may be delving into esoteric areas or perhaps researching the paranormal.

On the 16th, Mercury turns retrograde in Sagittarius—the last time this year—and turns direct again on December 6, in Scorpio. By now, you probably know the drill on these retro periods, but reread the July roundup and the section in the introduction on Mercury retrogrades. Since this one begins in the romance/creativity area of your chart, where beautiful Jupiter is currently transiting, pay special attention to your creative endeavors and, of course, to your love relationships. And remember: revise, review and reconsider. Also on the 16th, Venus turns direct in Libra, a beautiful irony since Venus rules love and romance, the very area where the Mercury retrograde begins. Dive into any artistic/creative area during this transit, which lasts until December 2, and just watch what unfolds!

The full moon in Gemini on November 23 brings lots of holiday social invitations. Get out there and network, schmooze and enjoy yourself, Leo.

AT A GLANCE
November 7—New moon in Scorpio
November 8—Jupiter enters Sagittarius
November 15—Mars enters Pisces
November 16—Mercury turns retrograde in Sagittarius, Venus turns direct in Libra
November 23—Full moon in Gemini

December 2018
Moving forward

As you enter the last month of 2018, take time to think about what you would like to experience and achieve in the next year. Make a wish list. Set goals. Keep the list handy so that you can refer to it often.

On December 2, Venus enters Scorpio again, and it will be there until January 17, 2019. Think back to September when Venus transited this sign. What kinds of things happened? What types of emotions did you experience? Was there a lot of drama at home? During this transit, you have an opportunity to set right whatever went wrong.

Mercury turns direct in Scorpio on the 6th, a big hurrah! It moves into Sagittarius six days later and will be there until January 4, 2019. During the Sadge part of this transit, your conscious focus is on a love relationship or a creative endeavor. You grasp the larger picture now and are able to make course corrections so that you and a partner are more in synch. With your creative work, you're in a state of near bliss.

Then on December 7 a beautiful new moon in Sagittarius joins Jupiter, and all sorts of options and opportunities open up with romance and creativity, with your children and with whatever you do for fun and pleasure. This feel-good time may tempt you to overindulge, so be careful!

The full moon in Cancer on the 22nd is ideal for taking an honest, penetrating look at how 2018 has unfolded and what you would like to embrace in the new year.

AT A GLANCE
December 2—Venus enters Scorpio
December 6—Mercury turns direct in Scorpio
December 7—New moon in Sagittarius
December 12—Mercury enters Sagittarius
December 22—Full moon in Cancer

Reflection

Take a look back at this year. How did it go in the areas that you value most? Are you happier? Healthier? More in tune with who you are? Jot your thoughts below.

_____

_____

_____

_____

Happy New Year!

Virgo 2018

Your sign is ruled by Mercury. It governs communication, travel, the intellect, the conscious mind and anything that deals with writing, teaching, speaking or learning. Three times a year it turns retrograde, and the areas Mercury rules go haywire. Pay close attention to what Mercury is doing each month, the angles other planets make to it and when it's retrograde.

In the monthly roundups, you'll also find information on the new and full moons, eclipses, when the transiting planets enter new signs and the angles they make to your sun sign.

2018 could very well turn out to be your power year, Virgo. You'll have ample opportunities to expand your business dealings and to gain recognition, fame and big bucks. If you don't feel successful yet, believe that you are. The bigger you think, the greater self-confidence you radiate, and other people pick up on this. Doors open. Think outside the box, and use your analytical mind to connects the dots.

January 2018
Terrific start to new year

Welcome to 2018! Fortunately, the year doesn't begin with Mercury retrograde, as 2017 did. In fact, things get off to a positive start with a full moon in compatible water sign Cancer on January 1. In a sense, it's a fitting completion to the holidays. There may be news about a family member or a friend or about a project you started last year. This full moon highlights that area of your chart that governs your network of friends, the people you hang with and your wishes and dreams.

Venus has been in Capricorn since Christmas Day 2017 and will be there until January 17, making this period one of the most romantic and creative for you all year. The only other period that comes close to this occurs when Venus is in your sign, between July 9 and August 6. On the 11th, Mercury joins Venus, and while they're traveling together, your head and your heart are in complete agreement. Mercury remains in Capricorn until the 31st, and you're intensely focused on your creative endeavors. Whether you're writing a book or preparing for an exhibit or engaged in some other activity, you have your goals clearly in mind and know exactly how to proceed. If you recently met someone special, you may be thinking a lot about the relationship. Just take things a day at a time and let the relationship unfold.

The new moon in Capricorn on the 16th could usher in a new romantic interest and a chance to exhibit your creative talents. With so much emphasis on Capricorn and that area of your chart that rules romance, creativity and what you do for enjoyment, you're in high spirits. You exude self-confidence and feel you can achieve practically anything.

Between January 17 and February 10, Venus moves through Aquarius. This transit affects your daily work in a positive way. Co-workers and bosses are more amenable to your ideas, and you're recognized in some way for the high quality of your work. An office flirtation may turn into a romantic interlude.

From January 26 to March 17, energetic Mars moves through Aquarius. It will be traveling for a time with Venus, a recipe for romance and sex. You may attract some rather unusual people during the Mars transit, idiosyncratic individuals who think outside the box. Learn what you can from them.

On the 31st, Mercury joins Mars in Aquarius, and there's a lunar eclipse in Leo. The Mercury transit lasts until February 18 and adds to the already edgy energy of Mars in this sign. Ideas now come to you fast and furiously, and as a Virgo, you're able to sift quickly through them and decide which ones to keep and which ones to discard.

Now, about that eclipse. This lunar eclipse in Leo occurs in the most private part of your chart. But because Leo is an exuberant sign, you may feel that your self-expression is being stifled somehow. Eclipses are usually accompanied by a sense of urgency—*OMG, the sky is falling!*—and with this one, you may feel frustrated that you aren't moving quickly enough to resolve whatever is going on. Neptune forms a close and challenging angle to the eclipse degree, suggesting that you don't have the full story.

AT A GLANCE
January 1—Full moon in Cancer
January 11—Mercury enters Capricorn
January 16—New moon in Capricorn
January 17—Venus enters Aquarius
January 26—Mars enters Sagittarius
January 31—Mercury enters Aquarius, lunar eclipse in Leo

February 2018
Unexpected opportunities

This month is relatively quiet—except for a solar eclipse in Aquarius on February 15. Uranus forms a beneficial angle to the eclipse degree, so opportunities that come your way on or around the time of this eclipse are sudden and unexpected. You'll have to decide quickly whether the opportunities are worth your time and effort. With Mars in this sign and your ruler, Mercury, close to the eclipse degree, you'll be in a forward-thinking frame of mind and won't have any hesitation about knowing what to do.

On the 10th, before the eclipse occurs, Venus enters Pisces, your opposite sign. This placement for Venus is romantic, dreamy, compassionate and imaginative. You and a romantic partner may deepen your commitment to each other during this transit. You could move in together, get engaged or married or start a family. With business partners, things unfold with greater ease.

Between February 18 and March 6, Mercury transits Pisces, too. While the planet of communication travels with the planet of love and romance, these two are chatting up a storm. You're figuring things out about a romantic relationship and chances are that you like what you see.

AT A GLANCE
February 10—Venus enters Pisces
February 15—Solar eclipse in Aquarius
February 18—Mercury enters Pisces

March 2018
Taking risks

This month's rapidly shifting energies could be challenging. But Virgo adapts well to just about any situation, and the trick in March is to go with the flow as best you can.

The full moon in your sign on March 1 brings news that is personally satisfying. It could concern a work project or creative endeavor. Your head and your heart are in agreement today. You can feel change in the air.

On the 6th, both Mercury and Venus enter Aries and will travel together until the 31st, when Venus moves into Taurus. Mercury turns retrograde on the 22nd and stays that way until April 15. Since Mercury is your ruler, let's talk about it first. While it's in direct motion, moving along with Venus, your passions may run to extremes. One moment you're fired up about something or someone, and the next moment you're having second thoughts. Aries is very much a trailblazer, however, and you may take risks you wouldn't ordinarily take—risks with your approach to work, relationships or implementation of ideas.

Before the retrograde begins, read over the Mercury retrograde sections in the introduction to the book and follow the suggestions for getting through this period more successfully. Since this one occurs in that area of your chart covering shared resources (and joint finances), be sure to keep close tabs on your bank accounts, ATM withdrawals, investments and mortgage payments.

During this retrograde, you may be reconsidering a romantic relationship, but wait until after the retro is finished before you make any hard and fast decisions.

Jupiter turns retrograde in Scorpio on March 8 and stays that way until July 10. During this period, the planet's expansion takes place inwardly. You're more focused on your spiritual development and on how your beliefs are woven through your worldview. Since Jupiter is retrograde in the communication area of your chart, you'll have a lot of ideas that you may be able to use down the road, so write them down.

March 17 features two astrological events: Mars enters Capricorn, and there is a new moon in Pisces. The new moon brings opportunities in business and personal partnerships. If you're involved in a relationship already, then you and your partner may decide to deepen your commitment to each other. You could move in together, get engaged or married or start a family. If you're single, then this new moon may bring a new romantic interest into your life. In business, you may find the ideal agent, manager or partner.

Mars transits Capricorn until May 16, a major plus for you because it it's in the romance/creativity section of your chart. Your sexuality is heightened and so is the adrenaline that fuels your creativity. You're able to set realistic goals about your creativity and your romantic relationships.

Circle March 22 on your calendar, when Mercury turns retrograde.

Venus enters Taurus on the 31st, and there's a full moon in Libra. Thanks to challenging angles from a couple of other planets, this full moon could be difficult. News that you hear may be troubling, but don't jump to conclusions. You don't have the full story. Seek balance and get out and about with upbeat friends.

Venus transits Taurus, a sign it rules, from March 31 to April 24 and forms a beautiful angle to your sun sign. During this transit, you may have dealings with publishers, could travel internationally and may meet a romantic interest who is from a foreign culture or country. Your sensuality is deepened.

AT A GLANCE
March 1—Full moon in Virgo
March 6—Mercury enters Aries, Venus enters Aries
March 8—Jupiter turns retro in Scorpio
March 17—Mars enters Capricorn, new moon in Pisces
March 22—Mercury turns retro in Aries
March 31—Venus enters Taurus, full moon in Libra

April 2018
New business opportunities

April is a relatively quiet month. So rest up because May will be another month of rapidly shifting energies.

On April 15, there are two astrological events: a new moon in Aries, and Mercury turns direct in Aries. The new moon may bring an opportunity to launch a new product or business. However, since Mercury is turning direct today, wait a couple of days until Mercury has stabilized. For all other Mercury endeavors, get busy making travel plans, submitting manuscripts and proposals and moving forward with communication projects.

On the 17th, Saturn turns retrograde in Capricorn and remains that way until September 6. During these months, you may be reevaluating the foundation of a romantic relationship or of a creative endeavor. Are the structures sound? What changes could you make to strengthen them? You may discover that your children would benefit from tighter controls and rules.

From April 24 to May 19, Venus transits Gemini and the career area of your chart. Your career should benefit from this transit. You could get a promotion or a raise, and co-workers and bosses regard you in a favorable light. Since your gift of gab is highlighted now, you may be doing a lot of networking and building public relationships for the company or for your own business. If a romance starts during this transit, it could be with someone you meet through work or your profession.

The full moon in Scorpio on April 29 brings an emotional intensity to your personality that can be best used in a creative way. It favors in-depth research, writing and all forms of communication. Saturn retrograde forms a beneficial angle to this full moon, suggesting that insights you have or news that you hear is of a serious nature.

AT A GLANCE
April 15—New moon in Aries, Mercury turns direct in Aries
April 17—Saturn turns retrograde in Capricorn
April 24—Venus enters Gemini
April 29—Full moon in Scorpio

May 2018
Rockin' and rollin'

May is one of those months that rocks, Virgo, and you'll need to stay alert and in the flow to make the most of the shifting energies.

On May 13, Mercury enters Taurus and stays there until May 29. During this transit your focus is on making the abstract practical, tangible and understandable to others. You may find that you're more stubborn, particularly about things that are important to you, and that you have more patience than usual. Use this time to tackle any project that requires time, solitude or resoluteness. You may be planning a trip overseas, could take a workshop or seminar or may enroll in graduate courses.

The 15th features two events: a new moon in Taurus and Uranus moving into that sign after seven years in Aries. Let's talk first about the Uranus transit. It will last until November, and then because of a retrograde, Uranus slips back into Aries until 2019. While it's in Taurus, it will form a terrific angle to your sun sign and impact your life in a positive way. Uranus's job is to shake up the status quo, to get us out of our ruts and routines so that we create space in our lives for the new. This transit is exciting as long as you embrace the changes that occur. It's likely that your deepest beliefs, your worldview and spirituality, are likely to change in some way during the next seven years. You could decide to return to college or go to graduate school or law school. You might even move overseas.

The new moon in Taurus on the 15th may give you some inkling of what the Uranus transit holds. Pay attention to the new opportunities that surface with this new moon. Higher education, publishing, foreign cultures and travel can all figure into the opportunities that unfold.

Between May 16 and June 26, Mars moves in direct motion through Aquarius and the daily work area of your chart. On June 26, it turns retrograde, which we'll talk about in June's roundup. Until then, this transit enables you to make tremendous progress in your daily work. You're the one with the cutting edge ideas, the workaholic who stays until the job is done.

Venus enters compatible water sign Cancer on May 19 and until August 6 your social life is a whirlwind. Other people are attracted to your self-confidence, wit, efficiency and intuition, which deepens during this transit. If a romance develops during this transit, it may be with someone you meet through friends, a group to which you belong or even through a family member. There's a pleasantness to this transit that makes you feel good not only about yourself, but about life in general.

On May 29, there's a full moon in Sagittarius and Mercury enters Gemini, where it will be until June 12. The full moon brings news about your home/family. If, for instance, your home is on the market, you could get an offer that satisfies you. Or you hear from a realtor who claims that he or she has found the ideal new place for you. This moon enables you to grasp the larger picture of whatever concerns you.

While Mercury is in Gemini transiting your career area, you're networking and connecting with professional peers and bosses. You may be involved in a publicity campaign for your company and its products or services, or you may be working on publicity for your own company. Mercury rules Gemini, so it functions well here.

May 13—Mercury enters Taurus
May 15—New moon in Taurus, Uranus enters Taurus
May 16—Mars enters Aquarius
May 19—Venus enters Cancer
May 29—Full moon in Sagittarius, Mercury enters Gemini

June 2018
Busy & positive

It's going to be an interesting month, Virgo, and it begins with Mercury entering Cancer on June 12. For just a day, it travels with Venus and ramps up the communication in your social life. In other words, you're not just partying; there's purpose and design to your contact with the people you're hanging out with. Once Venus moves on the 13th, Mercury is perfectly happy traveling solo through intuitive, nurturing Cancer, connecting people and communicating with strangers in a way that draws them into the fold. It forms a beneficial angle to your sun sign, so this transit should feel very good to you. You may be engaged in publicity for your services/products or those of your company. The Mercury transit lasts until June 29, when Mercury enters Leo. We'll talk about this in the July roundup, which will feature the second Mercury retrograde of the year.

On the 13th, Venus enters Leo, and there's a new moon in Gemini. The Venus transit, which lasts until July 9, could have you working behind the scenes on a creative endeavor that demands your full attention. If you're on a deadline, this transit helps you to meet it. The challenge with this placement is that Leo is a sociable sign, eager to get out and be seen, to hobnob, to network and to connect with others. But this transit takes place in the most private and quiet part of your chart. If a romance begins during this transit, you may keep it under wraps until you're sure it's going somewhere.

The new moon in Gemini ushers in new professional opportunities. The possibilities range from a promotion and raise, a new office or a change in schedule to a new career path altogether. There will be synchronicities to guide you toward the opportunities best suited for you and the place where you are in life.

On June 26, Mars turns retrograde in Aquarius. Between now and August 27, things in your daily work life may slow down or not pan out as you would like. You will be reevaluating your work routine, your relationships with co-workers and your work goals. These retrograde periods are intended to give you time to reconsider the directions in which you're headed.

The full moon in Capricorn on June 28 may bring news about a romantic relationship, a creative endeavor, your children or even about a professional matter. It highlights that area of your chart that governs enjoyment and pleasure and enables you to see facets of a romantic relationship that you may not have noticed before.

On June 29, Mercury enters Leo and will be direct in that sign until July 26. While it's direct, you've got the gift of gab coupled with a flourish for the dramatic. Use that energy to write the great American novel!

AT A GLANCE
June 12—Mercury enters Cancer
June 13—New moon in Gemini, Venus enters Leo
June 26—Mars turns retrograde in Aquarius
June 28—Full moon in Capricorn
June 29—Mercury enters Leo

July 2018
Mostly good

In spite of two eclipses and the beginning of a Mercury retrograde, there's a lot to like about July. From the 9th until August 6, Venus transits your sign, making this period one of the most romantic and creative all year. The only other period that will match this is when Venus moves through Capricorn and the romance/creativity area of your chart in early 2019. During both transits your self-confidence soars, your muse is at your beck and call and others are attracted to your charisma and magnetism. If a relationship begins during this transit, it will be a delight. Whether it develops into a serious relationship is really beside the point because you are enjoying yourself. Be sure to delve into your creative endeavors during this transit. You have an infallible sense of what works and what doesn't.

On the 10th, Jupiter turns direct in Scorpio, a bonus. Your communication skills and projects expand now, and your conscious mind is hungry to explore new vistas in spirituality, higher education and international travel. This trend continues until November 8, when Jupiter enters Sagittarius.

On the 12th, there's a solar eclipse in Cancer. Eclipses are often accompanied by a sense of urgency and tension because they tend to bring issues and relationships into our awareness, and we have to deal with things quickly. This eclipse should bring in new friendships, new opportunities for your family and home life and new opportunities that will enable you to achieve your wishes and dreams. Neptune forms a beneficial angle to the eclipse degree, suggesting that your ideals and artistic skills are a part of the opportunities that unfold. Pluto is opposed to the eclipse degree, an indication that power plays could be a part of the day's events.

Between July 26 and August 19, Mercury moves retrograde through Leo. This is the second Mercury retro of the year. Look back to the guidelines in March for the best way to navigate this period, and look over the Mercury retro sections in the introduction. Since this retro occurs in Leo, your creative talents may feel stymied in some way; however, you have greater access to dream recall, and your dreams may provide insights and information that prove helpful. Remember to follow the three Rs: revise, review and reconsider.

On the 27th, the lunar eclipse in Aquarius may trigger emotional reactions to people in your work environment. A comment made by a co-worker could push one of your buttons. Rather than taking it personally, just shrug it off. In fact, any emotional reactions you have around the time of this eclipse should be acknowledged—then released.

AT A GLANCE
July 9—Venus enters Virgo
July 10—Jupiter turns direct in Scorpio
July 12—Solar eclipse in Cancer
July 26—Mercury turns retrograde in Leo
July 27—Lunar eclipse in Aquarius

August 2018
Intriguing

The solar eclipse in Leo on August 11 may bring in opportunities for self-expression, perhaps in some new venue. If you're a novelist, for example, then you may have a chance to try your hand at non-fiction. If you're an actor, you could land a part unlike anything you've played before. If you're a parent, you have a chance to engage with your child in a new, creative way. Sometimes with a solar eclipse, you have to give up or surrender something before the new opportunities surface.

Before the eclipse occurs, Venus enters Libra on August 6 and remains there until September 9. During this transit, your expenses may increase, but your income should too. You realize the importance of balance in financial matters, and rather than spending frivolously, you spend on items that are personally important. You and your romantic partner are on the same page in terms of your values and what's important to you. If you're not involved with anyone right now, use this transit's energy in a creative way. Venus rules Libra and functions well in this sign.

On the 19th, Mercury turns direct in Leo. Now it's time to decide what you would most like to do and do it! Travel? Do it. It doesn't matter where you go; the journey really is the point. Record everything you see and experience. The material may prove useful to you in the future.

The full moon in Pisces on the 26th highlights your personal and business partnerships. If there's news in this area, it will arrive out of the blue. Uranus forms a beneficial angle to this full moon, so the news—though sudden—should be positive.

Mars turns direct in Capricorn on the 27th, and now your love life and your creative endeavors leap into forward motion once again. Your energy is focused, and your goals are clear.

August 6—Venus enters Libra
August 11—Solar eclipse in Leo
August 19—Mercury turns direct in Leo
August 26—Full moon in Pisces
August 27—Mars turns direct in Capricorn

September 2018
Setting the tone

Thanks to the emphasis on Virgo this month, you'll enjoy most of September. And it all begins on September 5, when Mercury enters your sign, where it will be until the 21st. During this transit, your mind is focused, efficient and detailed. This transit favors any sort of research, writing or public speaking. It's also a good time to get rid of stuff you don't need. Tackle your closet, garage, attic or office.

Between September 21 and October 9, Mercury transits Libra and your financial area. You may be spending more on the improvement of your home, office or property, but it's important to your peace of mind to surround yourself with beauty. You have a keener sense about balancing the various facets of your life and may be taking a closer look at your finances—what you earn and what you spend. Is it time to set up a budget?

On the 6th, Saturn turns direct in Capricorn. One possible repercussion of this movement is that the structure of a romantic relationship is strengthened. You and your partner may decide to become exclusive. On the creativity front, you find your stride with a particular endeavor. You *plug in* and step into the flow.

The 9th features two astrological events: a new moon in your sign, and Venus enters compatible water sign Scorpio. This new moon occurs just once a year and sets the tone for the next twelve months. Take some time before the 9th to figure out what you would like to experience and achieve in the next twelve months. Create your bucket list. Post it where you'll see it often. This new moon should bring in a number of opportunities that are personally satisfying and could range from a new relationship or creative endeavor to a new job, project or even career.

Venus transits Scorpio from September 9 to October 5, when it turns retrograde. Due to the retrograde, it won't move into a new sign until early 2019. While it's direct in Scorpio, your communication skills are particularly sharp, your perceptions are deeply insightful and your sexuality and psychic ability are heightened. If a relationship begins during this transit, it's going to be passionate and intensely emotional, and there may be an element of secrecy to it. We'll talk about the retrograde in next month's roundup.

Between September 10 and November 15, Mars transits Aquarius and the daily work area of your chart. You now become a spinning dervish of activity and are able to accomplish more than you have in the previous six weeks. Your ideas are prolific, forward-thinking and cutting edge.

The full moon in Aries highlights your finances, especially those that you share with others—parent, child or partner. You may be trying to figure out how to make your money go farther, and the news you hear may help that to happen.

AT A GLANCE

September 5—Mercury enters Virgo
September 6—Saturn turns direct in Capricorn
September 9—Venus enters Scorpio, new moon in Virgo
September 10—Mars enters Aquarius
September 21—Mercury enters Libra
September 24—Full moon in Aries

October 2018
Emotions run deep

There's lots going on this month, and it all starts on October 5, when Venus turns retrograde in Scorpio. Yes, this retrograde may play havoc with your love life, finances, sex life, creativity and… well, you get the idea. But it also gives you the opportunity to take an honest look at your closest relationships, your creative endeavors and your financial picture and to evaluate what works—or doesn't—in each of these areas.

On October 31, Venus slips back into Libra—your financial area—where it turns direct on November 16. While it's in Libra, it's a good idea to pay cash for your major purchases so that you don't overspend!

A new moon in Libra on October 8 should bring in new financial opportunities. You might, for instance, land a freelance job or get a part-time job that you enjoy and that pays well. You may also be hired for a creative project of some kind.

Between October 9 and 31, Mercury moves through Scorpio and will travel for a while with Venus retrograde. During this period, your conscious focus is on the absolute bottom line—about romantic relationships, money, creativity and even the nature of reality! Scorpio is an emotionally intense and often secretive sign, and with these two planets plus Jupiter in that sign, the depth of what you feel may surprise you.

The full moon in Taurus on October 24 should bring surprising and unexpected news. It could concern your worldview, spirituality, higher education, international travel or anything governed by the ninth house. Saturn forms a favorable angle to this full moon, indicating that the news you hear is firmly grounded in reality.

On October 31, Mercury enters fire sign Sagittarius and the family/domestic area of your chart. It's moving in direct motion until November 16, and during this period, your home is the hub for parties and good times and for lively discussions. We'll talk more about this transit in the November roundup; it's the last Mercury retro of the year.

October 5—Venus turns retrograde in Scorpio
October 8—New moon in Libra
October 9—Mercury enters Scorpio
October 24—Full moon in Taurus
October 31—Mercury enters Sagittarius

November 2018
Jupiter moves on

Mercury will be retrograde in Sagittarius from November 16 to December 6, when it turns direct in Scorpio. The Thanksgiving holidays fall during this retrograde, so be sure to have your plans—travel and otherwise—in place before the retro starts. The home/family area of your chart is impacted by this retrograde, and in December, when Mercury slips back into Scorpio, the communication area of your chart is affected.

Since Mercury rules moving parts, appliances sometimes break down during retrogrades. If that happens, and the appliance is essential and you have to replace it, by all means do so. But double check your order and the delivery date. Rather than launching new projects/products, follow the rule of the three Rs: revise, review and reconsider. Reread the March and July roundups for other tips on how to navigate the retrograde period.

On the 7th, before the retrograde begins, there's a new moon in Scorpio. If you've been scouting new neighborhoods for a possible move, then on or around this new moon you may find the ideal spot for you and your family. You may have an opportunity to spend more time with a sibling, could land a writing or speaking gig that pays well or may find a neighbor with whom you can carpool to and from work.

On the 8th, Jupiter makes a big shift. After more than a year in Scorpio, it enters Sagittarius, and now its largesse extends to your family and home life. It will be in Sadge until early December 2019, and during this period, you may move, buy a home or property, go back to school, travel internationally or embark on a spiritual quest of some sort. You could add on to your existing home, or your family expands in some way—a birth or marriage, or a parent or adult child moves in.

On the same day that Mercury turns retrograde, Venus turns direct in Libra, and until December 2, when it moves back into Scorpio, you enjoy some of the same benefits you did between August 6 and September 9. You may be feeling quite sociable during this transit. People are attracted to your charisma and gift of gab, and someone you encounter may have a freelance job for you.

The full moon in Gemini on November 23 brings career news. The possibilities? You hear that you've been tapped for a promotion and raise; you hear you've been hired for the job you want; your novel or screenplay sells; or you're recognized for a professional endeavor.

November 7—New moon in Scorpio
November 8—Jupiter enters Sagittarius
November 15—Mars enters Pisces
November 16—Mercury turns retrograde in Sagittarius, Venus turns direct in Libra
November 23—Full moon in Gemini

December 2018
Taking you into the new year

As you enter the last month of 2018, take some time to think about what you would like to achieve and experience in the new year. Make a list. Post it where you'll see it often. Visualize and back the visualization with emotion. Think of it as a list of desires rather than resolutions.

On December 2, Venus enters Scorpio. On the 6th, Mercury turns direct in that sign, and for the next six days, these two planets travel together. During this period, your conscious focus is on your love life and sexuality and how you feel about the most intimate relationships in your life. Your emotions run deep during these two transits, and you may find that your intuition and insights are enhanced.

Between December 12 and January 4, 2019, Mercury transits Sagittarius again. This means that during the holidays, your home probably becomes the hub for parties and festivities and all the good stuff that accompanies Christmas and the New Year. You can sense the bigger picture in whatever you tackle—whether it's at work, with your creative endeavors or in love and romance.

The new moon in Sagittarius on the 7th ushers in new opportunities for travel and for your home and family life. With expansive Jupiter also in this sign, the opportunities should be satisfying and beneficial and may involve publishing, higher education and your spiritual beliefs.

The full moon in Cancer on the 22nd is perfect for the holidays. Your social calendar fills rapidly, and wherever you go, people are in celebratory moods. You may hear good news about something you've got in the works and are now one step closer to achieving a wish or dream.

AT A GLANCE
December 2—Venus enters Scorpio
December 6—Mercury turns direct in Scorpio
December 7—New moon in Sagittarius
December 12—Mercury enters Sagittarius
December 22—Full moon in Cancer

Reflection

You began the month looking forward into 2019, and now you can end the month by looking back at 2018. Did the year meet your expectations? Did you experience and achieve what you had hoped? What, if anything, would you have done differently? Jot your thoughts below.

_____

_____

_____

_____

_____

Happy New Year!

Libra 2018

Your ruler is Venus, so pay particular attention to what the planet of love, romance and money is doing each month. Take note of the angles that other planets make to it and when it changes signs. In 2018, Venus moves through ten of the twelve signs and is retrograde in Scorpio between October 5 and November 16.

In the monthly roundups, you'll find information on the transits of other planets, the new and full moons, eclipses and what it all means for you.

2018 is a good year for you, Libra. Jupiter in Scorpio is transiting your financial area until November, and this means your income should be increasing and will be coming from various sources. It's a year in which an old cycle is ending and a new one is beginning, so be clear about your goals and be flexible in how you can attain them. Look for cues in your environment through synchronicities.

January 2018
Varied & exciting

Welcome to 2018! Fortunately, this year doesn't begin with a Mercury retrograde, as 2017 did. On January 1, the full moon in Cancer lights up the career area of your chart, and you're able to see what you like and dislike about your professional life and which relationships work—or don't work. You're able to discern where and how to make course corrections. There's a nurturing, intuitive element to this full moon, and you may feel more emotional than usual about your family.

Mercury, the planet of communication, enters Capricorn on the 11th and will be there until the 31st. While it's in this sign, you may be mulling over your professional goals—that's the Capricorn part of it. But because it's in that sector of your chart that rules home/family, you may also be mulling over goals concerning your home life. Do you and your family yearn to move to a different neighborhood? City? Some other part of the country? Do you and your partner want to start a family?

If your answer to any of the above questions is yes, then the new moon in Capricorn may usher in opportunities to do what you've been contemplating. It could also bring a professional opportunity—perhaps a chance to work from home?

Between January 17 and February 10, Venus transits Aquarius and that area of your chart that rules romance and creativity. This period should be one of the best for you all year—the most romantic and creative. If you're involved, then you and your partner may decide to commit to each other more deeply. In terms of creativity, you're on a roll, so run with it, Libra! Your muse is at your beck and call. It's even possible that you and your romantic interest embark on a creative endeavor together. The other period that will match this one occurs when Venus is in your sign, between August 6 and September 9.

Mars, the planet that governs sexuality, physical energy and aggression, moves through Sagittarius from January 26 to March 17. This transit occurs in that area of your chart that rules communication, short-distance travel, siblings, your neighbors, neighborhood, community and friends. You may be doing more writing than usual—blogging for a website or perhaps writing a book or novel. With Mars making a friendly angle to your sun, the wind is at your back now. Take advantage of it.

On the 31st, Mercury enters Aquarius, where it will be until February 18. You've just enjoyed Venus's transit through the romance and creativity area of your chart, and now you get to mull over everything you experienced. Your ideas during this transit are edgy, trendy and idiosyncratic, so keep track of them. They'll prove useful down the road.

The other event that occurs on the 31st is a lunar eclipse in Leo. Months that feature eclipses are sometimes fraught with tension and a sense of urgency. Part of the reason for this is that eclipses tend to bring issues right into the forefront of our awareness so that we must deal with whatever it is immediately. With this eclipse, news you hear may trouble you, but you don't have all the details, so don't rush to judgment! You may feel that your creative talents are eclipsed in some way. They aren't—but it's how you feel.

AT A GLANCE
January 1—Full moon in Cancer
January 11—Mercury enters Capricorn
January 16—New moon in Capricorn
January 17—Venus enters Aquarius
January 26—Mars enters Sagittarius
January 31—Mercury enters Aquarius, lunar eclipse in Leo

February 2018
New opportunities

On February 15, there's a solar eclipse in fellow air sign Aquarius, in that area of your chart that governs romance, creativity and your kids. This eclipse should bring new opportunities in any of these areas. If you and your partner would like to start a family, this eclipse could be the trigger for it. Other possibilities? You sell a creative endeavor, meet a new romantic interest or have a chance to work on some cutting edge trend. Uranus is friendly to the eclipse degree, suggesting that these opportunities surface suddenly and unexpectedly.

On the 10th, before the eclipse occurs, Venus enters Pisces, where it will be until March 6. During this transit, your compassion deepens, and there's a softness to your personality that appeals to others. In your daily work life, your relationship with co-workers and employees improves. If a romance begins during this transit, it will have a beautiful intuitive flow to it.

Between February 18 and March 6, Mercury transits Pisces and travels for a time with Venus. When these two pair up in this intuitive sign, your conscious mind and your heart seem to merge and simply flow over any obstacles. Your imagination is greatly enhanced, and you're able to bring wonderful ideas to the table.

If you're wondering what happened to February's full moon, it occurred on January 31!

AT A GLANCE
February 10—Venus enters Pisces
February 15—Solar eclipse in Aquarius
February 18—Mercury enters Pisces

March 2018
Hectic

It's a busy month astrologically, and your biggest challenge will be to balance your personal and professional life. If you assume too many obligations, you could crash and burn rather quickly.

The full moon in Virgo on March 1 lights up the most private sector of your chart—the twelfth house. You're able to make internal connections that may have eluded you before—like why certain patterns in your life seem to repeat themselves. There could be news about a work-related project in which you're involved, or a project may be completed or culminates in some way.

On the 6th, Mercury and Venus both enter Aries and the partnership area of your chart. Mercury will turn retrograde in that sign on the 22nd and will turn direct again on April 15. Venus will be in Aries until March 31. While these two are traveling together in direct motion, your heart and mind will be focused on your spouse or partner or on a business partnership. A business partner is anyone with whom you interact professionally—

a manager, agent, peer, editor or accountant. These two transits facilitate your dealings with all partners, personal and professional, and because there's a trailblazing aspect to Aries, don't be surprised if you and your partner come up with new ideas that excite you both.

During Mercury's retro in Aries, don't launch any new businesses or products or hire new employees. Instead, follow the rule of the three Rs: revise, reconsider and review. Don't make travel plans, either, unless you don't mind revisiting them once Mercury turns direct! And don't sign contracts. Yes, there are a lot of DO NOTS. But Mercury retro enables you to reconsider your partnerships, how they work—or don't—and to pinpoint what you would change if you could. People you haven't seen in a while may surface. Be sure to look over the Mercury retrograde section in the introduction for the suggested guidelines on how to navigate this period more successfully.

On the 8th, Jupiter turns retrograde in Scorpio, in your financial area. It lasts until July 10. During this period, Jupiter's expansive nature turns inward. You may be scrutinizing your beliefs about money, how or if your spirituality is integrated into the way you earn your living and whether your values are really your own or were adapted from parents and family.

On the 17th, Mars enters Capricorn, and there's a new moon in Pisces. Mars will be in Capricorn until May 16, stirring up stuff at home and with your family. You may decide to renovate your home by adding onto it. Or you may decide to replace the roof, get new flooring or knock down walls. Since Capricorn is involved, it's possible that you may be working hard to achieve your professional goals.

The new moon in Pisces should bring in new opportunities in your daily work life and with your creative endeavors. You might, for instance, land an assignment that enables you to use your prodigious imagination and people skills. If you're self-employed, clients and projects fall in your lap.

March has two full moons—the Virgo full moon on the 1st and a full moon in in your sign on March 31. The Libra full moon brings news of a personal nature that could be troubling. But you don't have the full story, so don't freak out. Simply gather all the facts. And because your sign is one of the most romantically-oriented, plan something special for you and your partner.

Also on the 31st, Venus enters Taurus and will be there until April 24. This transit favors other people's resources. Your partner, for example, could get a raise. If you've applied for a mortgage or loan, you get it. A royalty check or insurance reimbursement could arrive, or a loan is repaid. Venus rules Taurus and functions well in this sign.

AT A GLANCE
March 1—Full moon in Virgo
March 6—Mercury enters Aries, Venus enters Aries
March 8—Jupiter turns retro in Scorpio
March 17—Mars enters Capricorn, new moon in Pisces
March 22—Mercury turns retro in Aries
March 31—Venus enters Taurus, full moon in Libra

April 2018
New partnership opportunities

April won't be as frenetic as March was, but there's plenty going on, and you'll have to be ready to seize opportunities as they present themselves.

On the 15th, Mercury turns direct, and there's a new moon in Aries. Now you can travel without worry that your flight will be cancelled or that your cruise will pull out of port without you. Sign your contracts, launch your new projects and move forward. The new moon in Aries helps you do that. New opportunities surface in partnerships—in business and in your personal life. If you're already involved with someone, you and your partner may decide to get married, move in together or start a family. In business, you may be tapped to head a team researching a potentially new product or service. Or you and a friend or colleague may launch your new business.

On the 17th, Saturn turns retrograde in Capricorn, in the home/family area of your chart and turns direct again on September 6. During these months, you may be reevaluating the structures in your family life. Are your relationships with your parents, partner and children solid? If not, what can you do to strengthen them? If you're single and live alone, would getting a roommate help you out financially? Is it time to start looking for a new place to live?

Between April 24 and May 19, Venus transits fellow air sign Gemini and your solar ninth house. This area of your chart governs publishing, foreign travel, higher education and the higher mind, spirituality and philosophy. Whether you're self-employed or work for someone else, overseas travel may be part of what you experience during this transit. If you've written a book, then it could sell. You might take graduate level classes or attend a workshop or seminar or get the opportunity to teach. You're a connector now, a networker, someone who brings various types of people together for a common purpose or cause. This week should be pleasant, fun, entertaining, creative and romantic.

The full moon in Scorpio on the 29th highlights your finances. You're able to see the absolute bottom line of whatever you are dealing with in the money department. There could be news, too, about money—an unexpected check might arrive.

AT A GLANCE
April 15—New moon in Aries, Mercury turns direct in Aries
April 17—Saturn turns retrograde in Capricorn
April 24—Venus enters Gemini
April 29—Full moon in Scorpio

May 2018
Planetary shift

It may be another frenetic month. One of the outer, slower-moving planets—Uranus—changes signs. On May 15, Uranus enters Taurus after spending seven years in Aries. It will be in Taurus until November, and then, because of a retrograde, it slips back into Aries until 2018. This planet's job is to shake up the status quo in our lives and to move us out of our ruts and routines so that beliefs and habits that no longer serve us fall out of our experience, making room for the new.

Uranus will be transiting the shared resources area of your chart, so you may encounter sudden changes concerning your partner's income, alimony or child support, bank loans, mortgages, taxes or inheritances. This area is also about the paranormal—life after death, reincarnation, communication with the dead, ghosts—and about sexuality and death. It's possible that a loved one passes on during this period and that you inherit money. It's also possible that your intuitive ability is deepened considerably, and you begin to have psychic experiences. You may not be able to rely on your usual sources of income and will need to be innovative about how you earn your living.

But Uranus and the new moon in Taurus on the same day will help in that regard. The new moon will bring new financial opportunities.

Before either of the above events occur, Mercury enters Taurus on the 13th and will be there until the 29th, endowing you with patience and resilience. You won't take *no* for an answer during this transit and will simply move forward with your own agenda. Your communications during this period won't be ambiguous or vague. Between May 29 and June 12, Mercury moves through Gemini, a sign that it rules, and now you become a multitasker capable of juggling many projects and issues simultaneously.

When Mars enters Aquarius on May 16, you suddenly become a spinning dervish of activity with an abundance of energy and resolve. Until June 26, when Mars turns retrograde, your love life zips along at a pace that suits you, and your sexuality is heightened.

Venus enters Cancer and your career area on May 19, and between then and June 13, professional matters unfold with greater ease. Peers and bosses look to you as the person with the answers. You could get a raise or promotion, and your professional relationships prove to be more beneficial than they usually are.

May 29 features two events: there's a full moon in compatible fire sign Sagittarius, and Mercury enters Gemini. This full moon enables you to see the full picture concerning a communication project and/or a relationship with a sibling. You're after the whole truth, and Sagittarius delivers it. There could be news about a neighbor or a sibling.

Mercury will be in Gemini from May 29 to June 12 and forms a beneficial angle to Mars in Aquarius and to your sun. The combination makes you a force to be reckoned with.

AT A GLANCE
May 13—Mercury enters Taurus
May 15—New moon in Taurus, Uranus enters Taurus
May 16—Mars enters Aquarius
May 19—Venus enters Cancer
May 29—Full moon in Sagittarius, Mercury enters Gemini

June 2018
Momentum

June is another one of those months of shifting astrological energies that may leave you spinning in circles. Until the 12th, when Mercury enters Cancer, it's wise to lay the foundation for professional matters you'll tackle once the planet of communication moves into your career area. Network, schedule meetings and appointments with clients and do whatever you need to do so that from June 12 to June 29, you can simply dive right in. In other words, build the momentum!

On June 13, there's a new moon in Gemini, and Venus enters Leo, where it will be until July 9. The new moon will bring opportunities in communication—writing, speaking or blogging. You may have a chance to contribute articles to a particular website—and get paid for it! Or you could sell a novel or screenplay, teach a seminar or workshop or travel overseas. Because Gemini is a fellow air sign, you'll benefit tremendously from this new moon.

With Venus transiting Leo for about three weeks, your social life will pick up considerably. Friends will be a source of pleasure and fun. If you're not involved right now, you may meet a romantic interest through friends or through a club or organization to which you belong. It's also possible that you and a friend embark on some sort of creative endeavor together.

The end of the month has three events bunched together. On the 26th, Mars turns retrograde in Aquarius; on the 28th, there's a full moon in Capricorn; and on the 29th, Mercury enters Leo. The Mars retro lasts until August 27, when Mars turns direct in Capricorn. During this period, your love life and creative endeavors may feel somewhat off. Your physical energy may not be up to par. But keep up your daily exercise routine and stay focused on whatever you're doing. Pay special attention to your romantic partner and make time to have fun with them, to laugh and to do things you both enjoy.

The full moon in Capricorn helps you to clarify your professional goals and those concerning your family and home life. There could be news about a home improvement project (a cost estimate?) or about a family member, perhaps your mom.

Between June 29 and July 26, Mercury moves in direct motion through Leo. For part of this time, it travels with Venus, and these two enjoy each other's company. Leo has a flair for the dramatic and flamboyant, and those qualities emerge in your communication and in your love life. On July 26, Mercury turns retrograde, which will be covered in July's roundup.

June 12—Mercury enters Cancer
June 13—New moon in Gemini, Venus enters Leo
June 26—Mars turns retrograde in Aquarius
June 28—Full moon in Capricorn
June 29—Mercury enters Leo

July 2018
Financial headway

Let's start with Mercury's turn in direction on July 26, a retrograde that will last until August 19. Reread the March roundup about the retro, and follow the suggested guidelines in the Mercury retro section in the introduction of the book to help mitigate the effects.

In addition, since this retro impacts your friends and networks, be sure to communicate clearly with everyone in your various circles of acquaintances. The possibility of misunderstandings is always more pronounced during a Mercury retro, and it's easy for people to come away from these experiences with their feelings hurt. Leo is all about creativity, so with Mercury retro in that sign, you may feel your creativity is being stifled in some way or that it's not being recognized in the way you would like.

On July 9, before the retro starts, Venus enters Virgo and remains there until August 6. For this period of time, you may be working on a creative endeavor that demands solitude and focus or on a creative project that takes place behind the scenes, out of the limelight. If a romantic relationship begins during this transit, it may be kept under wraps—at least until Venus enters your sign on August 6.

Jupiter turns direct in Scorpio on July 10, a bonus for you, Libra, since this occurs in your financial area. You now have a much clearer idea of how to integrate your spiritual beliefs into how you earn your living. Your financial picture should enjoy Jupiter's largesse once again as it continues its journey in direct motion through Scorpio to keep its appointment with Sagittarius on November 8.

On the 12th, there's a solar eclipse in Cancer, in your career area. This is like a double new moon, so double the new opportunities! You could end up in a new career, new job or new location. You might be promoted or land a plump raise. Pluto forms a challenging angle to the eclipse degree, however, so there could be some tensions/disagreements with people in authority. Neptune, however, is friendly to the eclipse degree, suggesting that you take the high road. There's a strong intuitive element to the Neptune placement. Regardless of the specifics, this eclipse is about beginnings.

On the 27th, the lunar eclipse in Aquarius could trigger a disagreement with a romantic partner or one of your children or about one of your creative endeavors. Maybe it's not even a disagreement, but just a random comment someone makes, and you take it the wrong way. Rather than reacting with anger or sarcasm, set the whole thing aside, and find a more productive frame of mind!

AT A GLANCE
July 9—Venus enters Virgo
July 10—Jupiter turns direct in Scorpio
July 12—Solar eclipse in Cancer
July 26—Mercury turns retrograde in Leo
July 27—Lunar eclipse in Aquarius

August 2018
Romantic & creative

It may be another busy month, Libra. On the 11th the solar eclipse in Leo should bring ample opportunities for you to achieve your wishes and dreams. The opportunities may come through a friend or through a group or organization to which you belong. Pluto in Capricorn forms a challenging angle to the eclipse degree, indicative of a confrontation or dealings with authority figures.

However, because Venus will be in your sign at the time of the eclipse (it enters Libra on the 6th), you should come out just fine. In fact, this Venus transit, which lasts until September 9, should be as romantic and creative for you as the earlier Venus transit through Aquarius— January 17 to February 10. Take advantage of your muse clinging to you like Velcro during this transit. Dive into your creative endeavors, and until the 19th, when Mercury turns direct, revise and fine tune your projects.

If you're not involved with anyone at the beginning of this transit, you probably will be by the end. If you are in a relationship, then you and your partner should enjoy several weeks of fun and pleasure.

On the 19th, Mercury turns direct in Leo, and now your social life takes off again. You're in a creative frame of mind and may feel—rightfully so!—that the world is your oyster.

The full moon in Pisces on August 26 brings news about your work, a co-worker or an employee. If you've been submitting resumes and applying for jobs, then the news could be that you have gotten one of the jobs. Uranus is friendly to this full moon, suggesting that the news catches you by surprise. Perhaps the job you get is one you haven't even applied for; it simply lands on your doorstep.

On the 27th, Mars turns direct in Capricorn, and things now settle down somewhat at home, with your family. Everyone is less contentious, and it's easier to get stuff done—like cleaning your closets, the attic and the garage!

August 6—Venus enters Libra
August 11—Solar eclipse in Leo
August 19—Mercury turns direct in Leo
August 26—Full moon in Pisces
August 27—Mars turns direct in Capricorn

September 2018
Self-expression

September is packed with astrological events, and the action begins on the 5th, when Mercury enters Virgo, a sign it rules. It will be there until the 21st, and during this time, you're seeding ideas and desires so that when Mercury enters your sign on the 21st, you can take full advantage of its energy. You may be working on a public relations campaign or a writing project while Mercury is in Virgo. You also have greater access to your own unconscious and can recall your dreams with greater clarity and detail.

Mercury will be in your sign from September 21 to October 9, and during this time, communication and travel opportunities should open up. You're exceptionally communicative and able to express yourself well. You recognize the need for greater balance in your life. Even though you're known as someone who can compromise, this trait increases during Mercury's transit. Just be careful that you don't bend like a tree in the wind to accommodate the people around you.

On the 6th, Saturn turns direct in Capricorn, so for several days it and Mars travel together through the home/family sector of your chart. The energies of these two planets is vastly different—Saturn restricts, and Mars moves ahead, so there may be some tug of war within your family life. But on 10th, things ease up when Mars enters Aquarius. Suddenly, your sexuality is heightened, and you are focused primarily on enjoyment and pleasure, your creative endeavors and your love life. Mars stays in Aquarius until November 15.

The 9th features two events—Venus enters Scorpio and your financial area, and there's a new moon in Virgo. Until October 5, when Venus turns retrograde in Scorpio, you enjoy greater ease financially. New sources of income may surface so that even if your expenses spike this month, you'll have the money to cover them.

The new moon in Virgo on the 9th brings new opportunities to explore your own unconscious. You may do this through dreams, therapy or even a past-life regression. It's all part of the preparation for the new moon in your sign next month.

On the 24th, the full moon in Aries brings culmination to a business or personal partnership. You and your romantic partner may decide to end things or deepen your commitment.

September 5—Mercury enters Virgo
September 6—Saturn turns direct in Capricorn
September 9—Venus enters Scorpio, new moon in Virgo
September 10—Mars enters Aquarius
September 21—Mercury enters Libra
September 24—Full moon in Aries

October 2018
Bumpy road with love

Let's take a look at the Venus retrograde that begins on October 5. These retros generally affect your love life, finances and to some extent, your creativity. Think of it as bumps and bruises, not as major catastrophes! The more challenging time for you with this retro occurs from October 31, when Venus slides back into your sign, to November 16 when it turns direct. You may be taking a deeper look at your most intimate relationships and also scrutinizing your relationship with money and your beliefs about it. If at any point you feel overwhelmed by your insights, take a long walk through nature, visit an art gallery or go to a concert. In other words, do something that soothes your soul!

Despite the Venus retro, you'll enjoy the new moon in your sign on the 8th. As noted before, a new moon in your sign happens just once a year and sets the tone for the next twelve months. It's to your advantage to prepare for it by creating a list of what you would like to experience and achieve in the next year. New moons are about beginnings and new prospects that are personally satisfying.

Between October 9 and 31, Mercury transits Scorpio and travels with Venus retrograde. The combined energy of this duo enables you to delve deeply into financial matters, your core values, your sexuality or a love relationship, and to arrive at the bottom line—the essential truth of whatever you're exploring.

The full moon in Taurus on the 24th brings completion to a shared financial matter. If you and your partner have applied for a mortgage or loan, then it comes through. There could be news that comes out of the blue that your partner or someone else with whom you share financial resources is getting a raise and/or promotion.

Between October 31 and November 16, Mercury is moving direct through Sagittarius, a beautiful transit that enables you to grasp the larger picture of your daily life—relationships with siblings, neighbors, friends and the other people with whom you have frequent contact. On the 16th, Mercury turns retrograde for the last time this year. We'll discuss this in next month's roundup.

October 5—Venus turns retrograde in Scorpio
October 8—New moon in Libra
October 9—Mercury enters Scorpio
October 24—Full moon in Taurus
October 31—Mercury enters Sagittarius

November 2018
Mercury retro alert

It's another busy month with the planets. You'll have to stay focused on the task at hand in order to get stuff done because there will be plenty of distractions!

The new moon in Scorpio on November 7 should bring new opportunities financially. It could be that you take a part-time job, get a freelance gig or a raise, sell a project or receive a royalty check. The opportunity can come through any of a number of venues.

On the 8th, Jupiter makes a major shift. After more than a year in Scorpio, it enters Sagittarius, where it will be until December 2, 2019. Jupiter rules Sagittarius, so it functions well here. During the next thirteen months, international travel and publishing may figure prominently in your life. You could return to college or go to grad school or law school. A move into a larger, more comfortable neighborhood is a possibility. Jupiter now forms a beneficial angle to your sun and life in general becomes easier, fuller and more joyful.

Between November 15 and December 31, Mars transits Pisces. Your daily work life suddenly becomes a whirlwind of activity and momentum. There's a nice intuitive flow to this transit, so listen to your inner voice, be vigilant for synchronicities and trust that all is unfolding the way it should. The one drawback to Mars in Pisces is that the sign can sometimes be ambivalent when it comes to making decisions. So once you decide something, carry through with it.

All right, the Mercury retrograde. It begins on November 16 in Sagittarius, slips back into Scorpio and turns direct in that sign on December 6. Look over the Mercury retro section in the introduction, and reread the roundups for March and July for guidelines on how to successfully navigate the retrograde. In addition, keep in mind that the retro hits you in two areas of your chart: communication and finances. Pay close attention to all your written communications, think before you blurt and check and recheck scheduled appointments. Keep tabs on what you spend and earn. Yes, these periods can be irritating. But they also urge us to slow down and live more mindfully.

Also on the 16th, Venus turns direct in your sign, a major bonus! Until December 2, you get to enjoy that heightened romance and creative drive that you experienced between August 6 and September 9, before Venus turned retro. Take advantage of it!

The full moon in fellow air sign Gemini on November 23 may bring news about an international trip, a publishing endeavor or a communication project. Something culminates in one of these areas. There's a lot of conversation and discourse in your environment and at the end of the day, you may feel like turning off all your devices, disconnecting from the virtual world and settling on the couch with a great book.

AT A GLANCE
November 7—New moon in Scorpio
November 8—Jupiter enters Sagittarius
November 15—Mars enters Pisces
November 16—Mercury turns retrograde in Sagittarius, Venus turns direct in Libra
November 23—Full moon in Gemini

December 2018
Enjoyment

As you enter the last month of the year, take some time to think about what you would like to experience and achieve in 2019. List your desires and dreams. Keep the list where you'll see it often.

Between December 2 and January 7, 2019, Venus transits emotionally intense Scorpio and your financial area again, as it did between September 9 and October 5, before it turned retro. If there's anything you didn't get right the first time around, Libra, you now have a second chance. And, once again, new financial opportunities will present themselves, and you'll know intuitively which ones are viable.

On the 6th, much to your relief, Mercury turns direct in Scorpio. For the next six days, it travels with Venus, and these two have a lot to say to each other about money, romance and creativity. So listen closely! On the 12th, Mercury enters freedom-loving Sagittarius again, and your conscious focus is likely to be on the holidays and enjoying yourself.

The 7th features a new moon in Sagittarius, which only adds to your enjoyment. With Mercury and Jupiter also in this sign, there's a festive mood about everything you do and feel. This moon should result in ample opportunities for travel, self-expression and creativity.

The full moon in Cancer on December 22 highlights your career area, and you enjoy a completion of whatever professional endeavor you're involved in. There could be news about your career that delights you.

AT A GLANCE
December 2—Venus enters Scorpio
December 6—Mercury turns direct in Scorpio
December 7—New moon in Sagittarius
December 12—Mercury enters Sagittarius
December 22—Full moon in Cancer

Reflection

How did 2018 turn out for you? Did you achieve what you had hoped? Experience what you wanted? What, if anything, would you change? How can you use what you learn this year to achieve what you want next year? Jot your thoughts here.

_____

_____

_____

_____

_____

Happy New Year!

Scorpio 2018

Your ruler is Pluto, and your co-ruler is Mars. Pluto has been in Capricorn since late November 2008 and will be there until 2025. It moves just a few degrees a year. But take note of when it's retrograde and when other planets make angles to it. Mars moves more quickly, but because of a retrograde, it only transits four signs this year. Pay attention to when it makes angles to other planets—or vice-versa—and when it's retrograde.

The monthly roundups include information on the new and full moons, eclipses, when planets enter signs and the angles they make to your sun sign.

2018 should be a great year for you. Expansive Jupiter continues to transit your sign until November, expanding your life in exciting, unprecedented ways. New people will enter your life, and you'll experience positive, pivotal events—a marriage, a career change, the birth of a child or a significant move.

January 2018
New opportunities

Welcome to 2018! This year gets off to a much more positive start than 2017 did. It doesn't begin with a Mercury retrograde. The full moon in fellow water sign Cancer on January 1 could bring news about an overseas trip you have planned or about a workshop or class you have signed up for. It highlights your spiritual beliefs and worldview and your family. Full moons often signify completions and culmination, so perhaps this full moon symbolizes the real end of 2017 for you.

Between January 11 and 31, Mercury moves through compatible earth sign Capricorn and enables you to focus on your goals concerning writing and other forms of communication. It's easier to strategize about how you can use your enhanced skills more effectively in your career. Mercury forms a beneficial angle to your sun during this transit and facilitates your natural ability for in-depth research.

The 16th features a new moon in Capricorn, which really ramps up the earth energy. In addition to the new moon and Mercury, Pluto is also in the sign of the goat. This lineup indicates that new opportunities put you in the driver's seat, just where you like to be, Scorpio! You might have a chance for a writing project or speaking/teaching gig, may find a neighborhood that would be ideal for you and your family and you may have a chance to do something unique and different with a sibling, neighbor or friend. There could also be opportunities for short distance travel.

Between January 17 and February 10, Venus transits Aquarius and the family/domestic area of your chart. This transit should smooth out any disagreements at home, and although there's an edginess to the energy, it's the sort of edginess you understand. You may be more stubborn during this period, particularly when it comes to your independence and personal freedom.

On the 26th, Mars enters Sagittarius and your financial area. Between now and March 17, a lot of your energy is poured into work—i.e., how you make your living. You aggressively pursue your financial goals, and it may entail international travel, taking classes to hone your skills and enlisting the help of an expert.

The 31st features two events: a lunar eclipse in Leo and Mercury entering Aquarius, where it will be until February 10. Let's talk about the eclipse first, which occurs in your career area.

Months in which eclipses occur are often fraught with tension and a sense of urgency. This is because eclipses bring issues to our immediate attention so that we have to deal with them quickly. With lunar eclipses, the issues are internal and emotional. You may feel, for example, that your creativity is being stifled in some way in your professional life or perhaps your boss says or does something that pushes one of your buttons. Rather than blowing up, take a few deep breaths and back off.

The Mercury transit should bring a lot of dinner time conversation with family and friends, an exploration of cutting edge trends and continual brainstorming for ideas. Keep a computer file or notebook handy to jot down the ideas as they come to you. They may prove valuable down the road.

AT A GLANCE
January 1—Full moon in Cancer
January 11—Mercury enters Capricorn
January 16—New moon in Capricorn
January 17—Venus enters Aquarius
January 26—Mars enters Sagittarius
January 31—Mercury enters Aquarius, lunar eclipse in Leo

February 2018
5 stars

On the 15th, the solar eclipse in Aquarius falls in the home/family area of your chart. New opportunities should surface in that area. You and your partner, for instance, may discover you're going to be parents. Or perhaps someone moves into or out of your home. Or, you get an offer on your home that meets your asking price. You move. Any news you hear today or during the several days on either side of the eclipse takes you by surprise.

Before the eclipse occurs, on February 10, Venus enters fellow water sign Pisces, where it will be until March 6. This period will not only be fun, but is one of the most creative and romantic periods for you all year. Your muse whispers constantly in your ear—*write this, photograph that, compose this, solve it this way*—and your most loyal sidekicks are your intuition and imagination. In the romance department, your love life flows at a pace that suits you. If you aren't involved with anyone when this transit starts, you probably will be by the time it ends. The only other periods that equal this transit for its sheer pleasure is when Venus moves through your sign. That happens in the fall, from September 9 to October 31, then again from December 2 to January 7, 2019.

Between February 18 and March 6, Mercury joins Venus in Pisces in the romance/creativity sector of your chart. Your communication and intuitive skills are greatly heightened, and the flow between you and your romantic partner should be excellent.

AT A GLANCE
February 10—Venus enters Pisces
February 15—Solar eclipse in Aquarius
February 18—Mercury enters Pisces

March 2018
Hectic & passionate

March is jammed, and you will need to be vigilant to take advantage of the shifting energies. It all starts on March 1, with a full moon in compatible earth sign Virgo that brings news, possibly about a health issue or some concern you have about work. With expansive Jupiter in your sign for most of this year, the news is likely to be positive. This full moon should also keep you busy socially and enhance your communication skills.

On the 6th, both Mercury and Venus enter Aries, a combination that's sure to propel you forward in your daily work life. You have numerous ideas about a project or service that your company offers, and your co-workers and/or employees are fully supportive of whatever you come up with. These two planets travel together in direct motion until March 22, when Mercury turns retrograde, which lasts until April 15. Venus moves through Aries until March 31, and during these weeks, your passions are running fast and furiously, and you may be more impatient than usual, particularly in a romantic relationship or when working on a creative endeavor. If a relationship begins during this transit, you may feel that you've been swept up in a tornado!

Once Venus moves into Taurus on March 31, partnerships are highlighted—personal and professional. On the personal front, you and a romantic partner may deepen your commitment to each other by moving in together, tying the knot or starting a family. Or, if one of you wants to deepen the commitment and the other doesn't, then you may part ways.

Mercury's retrograde in Aries begins on March 22. Before it starts, it's best to sign contracts, make travel plans, launch new projects or businesses, make submissions and buy high ticket items like computers and other electronics if you need them. In other words, do all the things you should avoid doing during the retro period. If you follow the three Rs—revise, review and reconsider—you will navigate this retrograde more successfully than you might otherwise. When you're making your travel plans—especially air travel—schedule dates on either side of the retrograde. And read over the Mercury retrograde section in the introduction.

Jupiter turns retrograde in your sign on March 8 and remains that way until July 10. During this retrograde period, the planet's expansive nature becomes more internal. You may experience a broadening of your spiritual beliefs, a deepening of your considerable intuition and your perceptions about people's motives will be crystal clear. No other sign has the kind of B.S. detector that Scorpio does, and this skill only grows sharper with the retrograde.

The 17th has two astrological events: Mars enters compatible earth sign Capricorn, and there's a new moon in Pisces. The Mars transit through the communication sector of your chart lasts until May 16. During this time, you're so singularly focused on your goals that you pursue them relentlessly. You put in the effort and hours you feel you should to get the job done.

Now, the new moon in Pisces. You'll love this one, Scorpio. The new opportunities that surface range from a new romantic interest to a new creative endeavor and, perhaps, a new hobby or passion. Your focus will be on enjoyment, fun and pleasure. This new moon has a strong intuitive component as well, so listen to that inner voice!

On the 31st, Venus enters Taurus, which we talked about earlier in the roundup, and there's a full moon in Libra. There could be some challenges on or around the time of this full moon, thanks to difficult angles from Mars and Neptune. It highlights the most private part of your chart, the personal unconscious. It enhances your dream recall and past-life memories.

AT A GLANCE
March 1—Full moon in Virgo
March 6—Mercury enters Aries, Venus enters Aries
March 8—Jupiter turns retro in Scorpio
March 17—Mars enters Capricorn, new moon in Pisces
March 22—Mercury turns retro in Aries
March 31—Venus enters Taurus, full moon in Libra

April 2018
Unexpected news

April won't be quite as frantic as last month. But there's enough going on to keep you on your toes! On April 15, there are two events: there's a new moon in Aries, and Mercury turns direct in the same sign. The new moon should bring in new opportunities in your daily work life—a promotion, a new employee, a move to a larger, more comfortable office or a new project that delights you. If you're self-employed, then you might get new clients and/or projects or sell a manuscript or other product/service. Uranus is closely conjunct this new moon, so any opportunities that surface will do so suddenly and unexpectedly.

On the 17th, Saturn turns retrograde in Capricorn and will turn direct again on September 6. During this lengthy retro, you will be looking more closely at the structures in your life—the relationships that work or don't, the neighborhood in which you live, your home and family or your work and career. You may be revamping your professional goals and the ways in which you communicate with the people to whom you are closest.

Between April 24 and May 19, Venus moves through air sign Gemini and the shared resources area of your chart. This transit should facilitate any interaction with banks, insurance companies or loan officers. Your partner or spouse or anyone else with whom you share financial resources—a parent, child or roommate—may get a substantial raise. You may be socializing more than usual, too, working your network of friends and acquaintances and may be involved in some sort of publicity campaign. A royalty check or insurance reimbursement could arrive.

The full moon in your sign on the 29th brings news of a personal nature—you get the job you applied for, make a sale, land a new account or win a contract. Saturn forms a beneficial angle to this full moon, indicating that the news is solid, serious and *real*.

AT A GLANCE
April 15—New moon in Aries, Mercury turns direct in Aries
April 17—Saturn turns retrograde in Capricorn
April 24—Venus enters Gemini
April 29—Full moon in Scorpio

May 2018
Tumultuous

May could be a tumultuous month, filled with more plot twists than a Dan Brown novel. The energy emphasis is on Taurus, your opposite sign, and because Taurus and your sign share an axis, you will be strongly impacted by these transits, too.

On May 13, Mercury enters Taurus, where it will be until the 29th. During this transit, your conscious mind is focused and resilient. You're more stubborn than usual, too, and while that's fine for pushing through challenges and solving problems, guard against being stubborn just because you're certain you're right and the other guy is wrong.

Two events occur on May 15: there's a new moon in Taurus and Uranus enters the same sign. You and your romantic partner may deepen your commitment to each other by moving in together, getting married or starting a family. Or you may call it quits. Black or white, either/or. You don't experience many nuances in your relationships, Scorpio, and that's because your perceptions about people and their motives are so clear. On the business front, this new moon could bring in the ideal agent, editor, accountant, manager or client.

Uranus also moves into Taurus today, until November when, due to a retrograde, it slips back into Aries until 2019. There may be an abrupt, unforeseen quality to these new opportunities. Uranus has spent the last seven years in Aries, in the daily work area of your chart. During that time, it swept away people and situations in your work that no longer served your best interest. It shook up your work routine. Uranus in Taurus will do the same kind of thing, but in your partnerships. You could get married or divorced, move or embark on a new career. But one thing is certain: between now and July 7, 2026, when the transit ends, a certain part of your life will be disrupted and turned inside out, so that the new can flow in.

Mars enters Aquarius on May 16, and until June 26, when it turns retrograde, your home is a humming hub of activity. If you have kids, they're coming and going with their friends and the scene could get a bit chaotic. But it's a positive kind of chaos, filled with lively conversations. Your home improvement projects move full steam ahead. You may get involved with a group of like-minded, idealistic individuals.

Between May 19 and June 13, Venus transits fellow water sign Cancer and forms a beautiful angle to your sun. Whenever Venus is in another water sign, you're in for a treat, Scorpio. Your love life, finances, intuition and creative endeavors unfold with greater ease and smoothness. You may be traveling overseas for business or pleasure, could enroll in graduate level courses or take workshops or seminars in topics that interest you. Or, equally possible, you could be teaching workshops. Your self-confidence shines and attracts people who are helpful.

On the 29th, two astrological events are worth noting: a full moon in fire sign Sagittarius and Mercury entering Gemini. This full moon brings financial news or news from a publisher or someone in higher education. A project in which you're involved culminates. Your financial picture is much clearer to you during this full moon, and you understand exactly what you have to do to increase your net worth.

Between May 29 and June 12, Mercury transits Gemini. It rules this sign and functions well here, stirring up conversations about things that go bump in the night, reincarnation, alternate realities, UFOs, Big Foot and other facets of the strange and weird. You might join a ghost hunting group or something similar. This area of your chart isn't just about mundane stuff like banks and loans and mortgages. Oddly enough, it's also about the paranormal!

May 13—Mercury enters Taurus
May 15—New moon in Taurus, Uranus enters Taurus
May 16—Mars enters Aquarius
May 19—Venus enters Cancer
May 29—Full moon in Sagittarius, Mercury enters Gemini

June 2018
Erratic

June's energies are all over the place. It's like a meal whipped together by an eccentric relative—a pinch of this, a dash of that and, oh yes, let's toss this into the mix, too. It starts well for you, with Mercury entering Cancer on the 13th, where it will travel for a single day with Venus. This transit lasts until June 29 and brings a strong intuitive component and a nurturing quality to your conscious mind. You're able to find whatever you're looking for with greater ease simply by following your intuition. You may be researching or writing about various spiritual traditions or could be researching foreign countries for a planned trip abroad.

The 13th brings a new moon in Gemini, and Venus enters Leo and your career area. This interesting combination of energies brings new professional opportunities—a new job, new clients, a new office, a new boss or a promotion—and/or new financial opportunities for you and your partner. Venus in Leo can be flamboyant, dramatic and gregarious, and as it transits your career area, it brings these qualities with it. A work flirtation could evolve into a romance. You may be strongly attracted to this person but you exercise the same caution that you do in other areas of your life. This transit ends on July 9.

Mars turns retrograde in Aquarius on the 26th, slips back into Capricorn and turns direct in that sign on August 27. During this retrograde, your intuitive, right-brain grasp of people and situations is even stronger than usual. Mars's energy turns inward and enables you to make significant internal strides with an issue or relationship so that by the end of the retrograde, you're clear about how to proceed.

The full moon in Capricorn on the 28th brings news about a professional matter—a communication project gets the green light, a manuscript sells or a publicity campaign takes off. Your life goals are clear.

On June 29, Mercury joins Venus in Leo, in your career area. While these two travel together (until July 9, when Venus moves on), you shine! Your communication skills and presence are magnetic, and you attract the right people at the right time. Mercury turns retro on July 27, which we'll talk about in the July roundup.

AT A GLANCE
June 12—Mercury enters Cancer
June 13—New moon in Gemini, Venus enters Leo
June 26—Mars turns retrograde in Aquarius
June 28—Full moon in Capricorn
June 29—Mercury enters Leo

July 2018
Challenging

July may be challenging. Mercury turns retrograde, and there are two eclipses. Let's start with them. The solar eclipse on July 12 is in Cancer, a fellow water sign.

Solar eclipses usually concern external events and are like double new moons in terms of opportunities. This one could bring opportunities connected to publishing, overseas travel, higher education or your spiritual beliefs and, because it's in Cancer, your family. You might, for instance, sell a book or novel, get into the grad school of your choice or travel overseas on some sort of spiritual quest. You and your partner may discover you're going to be parents!

Pluto is opposed to the degree of this eclipse, which indicates trouble with an authority figure. By holding firm to your core ideals, though, you overcome the challenge. Neptune is friendly to the eclipse degree, suggesting that you or the authority figure lack the full story.

The lunar eclipse in Aquarius on July 27 occurs in your home/family area. Lunar eclipses often impact us emotionally and intuitively. Someone in your family may make an offhanded remark that sets you off. Rather than reacting with anger, it's best to just let the comment slide away from you, and later, when you're calmer, explore why you reacted the way you did.

With expansive Jupiter still in your sign, Scorpio, your insights and perceptions are spot on.

Before either of these eclipses occur, Venus enters Virgo on the 9th. This transit, lasting until August 6, should rev up your social life if that's what you're after. If you're in a more solitary place, then use this transit to shore up your network of acquaintances and friends in both virtual reality and in physical reality. You might launch a publicity campaign for your company's products or services, or if you're self-employed, for your own products or services.

On the romantic front, you may meet someone special through friends or through a group or club to which you belong. Thanks to Virgo, your discernment will tip you off quickly about whether this individual is worth your time. It's also possible that you and several friends brainstorm for a joint creative endeavor.

On the 10th, Jupiter turns direct in your sign, certainly cause for celebration. Between now and November 8, when Jupiter enters Sagittarius, you once again get to enjoy this planet's expansiveness in your outer life, as you did earlier this year.

Mercury turns retro in Leo on July 26. This lasts until August 19. Look back at the roundup for March, and follow the guidelines there for successfully navigating this period. Also, read over the Mercury retro section in the introduction. Since this retro occurs in your career area, take special care to communicate clearly with everyone in your professional arena. Double check times and dates for all appointments and meetings. You may feel that your artistic and creative talents aren't being appreciated, and whether it's actually true is beside the point. Don't pout and go all moody, as you are sometimes prone to do. Keep that smile on your face and optimism in your heart, and follow the rule of the three Rs: revise, review and reconsider!

AT A GLANCE
July 9—Venus enters Virgo
July 10—Jupiter turns direct in Scorpio
July 12—Solar eclipse in Cancer
July 26—Mercury turns retrograde in Leo
July 27—Lunar eclipse in Aquarius

August 2018
Wild ride

There's another eclipse this month, so buckle up! August may be a wild ride. The solar eclipse in Leo on August 11 should usher in new professional opportunities—a promotion, raise, new office, new boss, new responsibilities or perhaps even a new career path.

However, both Pluto and Neptune form challenging angles to the eclipse degree, suggesting that an authority figure may toss a few hurdles in your way. Neptune, though, is in perfect synch with your sun sign, so you come out ahead in the end. Whether the authority figure is a boss, parent, partner or someone else, that person doesn't have the full details. You may want to enlighten the person—nicely, of course!

On the 6th, Venus enters Libra, where it will be until September 9. Venus rules this sign, so it functions well here. This transit through the most private part of your chart indicates that you may be spending time behind the scenes, perhaps working to complete a creative endeavor. If you have a partner for this project, you become aware of the need for balance. In other words, Scorpio, don't boss the person around! Be open to his or her ideas.

If a romance begins during this transit, it's likely to be kept under wraps for a while. You and the other person enjoy your solitude together, getting to know each other. But once Venus enters your sign on September 9, you two are ready to explore the outer world together.

On the 19th, Mercury turns direct in Leo. Finally! Celebrate in some way. Take a trip, pack up the family and head to the beach. Do something fun!

The full moon in Pisces on the 26th should be a beauty for you. Not only is it in a fellow water sign, but it occurs in the romance/creativity sector of your chart. A romantic relationship culminates. You and your partner may decide to move in together, get married or start a family. Any news in these areas surfaces suddenly and unexpectedly, thanks to a beneficial angle from Uranus.

On the 27th, Mars finally turns direct in Capricorn, and your communication endeavors take off! Your professional goals are much clearer now, and you're ready to tackle whatever comes your way.

AT A GLANCE

August 6—Venus enters Libra
August 11—Solar eclipse in Leo
August 19—Mercury turns direct in Leo
August 26—Full moon in Pisces
August 27—Mars turns direct in Capricorn

September 2018
Busy

September is jammed with astrological events—seven of them. Things get off to a start on the 5th, when Mercury enters compatible earth sign Virgo. Between now and September 21, you may be doing more networking and partying with friends than usual. You could be involved in a publicity campaign for a product or service offered by you or your company. Mercury rules Virgo, and because it functions so well here, your communication skills during this transit are sharp and right on target.

On the 6th, Saturn turns direct in Capricorn, and this movement makes Mercury in Virgo quite happy because these two planets are both in earth signs and form beneficial angles to each other and to your sun sign. Your conscious mind is grounded and focused, and you're able to connect all the necessary dots when it comes to your relationships with your siblings and neighbors and the other people in your daily life.

From September 9 through January 7, 2019, Venus will be in and out of your sign because of a retrograde that begins on October 5. While it's moving direct in your sign, you experience one of the best times for you all year—in romance, creativity, with children and in everything you do for pleasure and fun. The only other period that equaled this was when Venus was in Pisces between February 10 and March 6 and possibly when Venus was in Cancer, between May 19 and June 13. Your self-confidence soars, your intuition deepens and your magnetism increases. People are attracted to you in droves. In fact, it could get overwhelming, and you may have to take a breather from all the adulation!

As if this isn't enough, there's also a new moon in Virgo today. This moon brings new friends and acquaintances who prove helpful in your achieving your wishes and dreams. You could land a writing or speaking gig or may be asked to teach a course, workshop or seminar.

If you're not involved with anyone right now, then the combo of Venus in Scorpio and this new moon could result in a new romantic interest whom you meet through friends.

Between September 10 and November 15, Mars transits Aquarius again. Look back to the May roundup, before Mars went retrograde. You may experience a repeat of some of those experiences and events. This transit occurs in the home/family sector of your chart. It favors any kind of home improvement projects and forward momentum with family matters.

From September 21 to October 9, Mercury transits Libra. During this time, you're more consciously aware of relationship dynamics in your life—not just with lovers and partners, but with children, co-workers, friends, parents and siblings. Your mind is also finely tuned to aesthetics—art, music and literature—and you could be blogging or writing about your artistic interests.

The full moon in Aries on September 24 may bring news about a work-related project or about a job. You could be called back for a second interview, or you learn that you've gotten the job. Since Saturn forms a challenging angle to this full moon, it's wise to carefully consider what the job entails before you start!

AT A GLANCE
September 5—Mercury enters Virgo
September 6—Saturn turns direct in Capricorn
September 9—Venus enters Scorpio, new moon in Virgo
September 10—Mars enters Aquarius
September 21—Mercury enters Libra
September 24—Full moon in Aries

October 2018
Bumpy road

October is a less frenzied month, but has some bumps you should be aware of. The first bump begins on October 5. Venus turns retrograde in your sign, slips back into Libra and turns direct in that sign on November 16. This retro can have repercussions for your love life and finances—things that go awry for no particular reason. But even more pertinent is that your physical comfort is affected.

You might be driving along in your car, for instance, and your AC or heat suddenly goes on the fritz. Or it happens in your home. Or you decide to have your hair colored, and the beautician messes up, and your hair turns pink! Or you might decide to take your dog to the dog park, which is ten miles from your home, and when you arrive there, you discover it's closed. Discomforts and inconveniences. It's best to take these things in stride, do whatever needs to be done and let your annoyance roll away from you.

The new moon in Libra on the 8th brings opportunities in relationships and with all your creative endeavors. Regardless of how the specifics unfold, the opportunities are preparing you for the new moon in your sign next month, which comes along just once a year and sets the tone for the next twelve months. With that in mind, be diligent about where you place your attention and how you use your energies.

From October 9 to 31, Mercury moves through your sign and travels with Venus. Even though Venus is retro, these two have a lot to chat about! Your conscious focus is on your usual Scorpio stuff. What's the true nature of reality? Can the dead communicate with the living? What were your past lives? You are also after the absolute bottom line in everything you do—from romantic encounters and creative endeavors to your daily work, career and research into whatever fascinates and intrigues you.

The full moon in Taurus on October 24 reveals the inner dynamics of a partnership, business or personal. There may also be news about a partner, or because this moon is in Taurus, about finances. Whatever the news, it will catch you off guard because it's conjunct Uranus, the planet of surprises!

Between October 31 and November 16, Mercury moves in direct motion through Sagittarius—and your financial area. Now your attention turns fully to money—what you earn, spend and save and what you would like to earn, spend and save! In next month's roundup, we'll talk about the Mercury retro that begins on November 16.

AT A GLANCE
October 5—Venus turns retrograde in Scorpio
October 8—New moon in Libra
October 9—Mercury enters Scorpio
October 24—Full moon in Taurus
October 31—Mercury enters Sagittarius

November 2018
New moon opportunities

In spite of Mercury's retrograde, November looks like a good month for you, Scorpio. As it begins, take a few minutes to brainstorm about what you would like to achieve and experience in the next twelve months. Make a list. Keep it realistic, but don't hesitate to dream. If you want to earn a million bucks over the course of the next year but feel an emotional resistance to the idea—i.e., don't really believe its possible—then make the sum whatever you feel comfortable with. And that's really the key to this wish list. If you believe it, if you can imagine it, if you *feel* it, then it's certainly possible. Post the list where you'll see it often. The list is your preparation for the new moon in your sign on November 7.

Both Pluto—your ruler—and Neptune are friendly to this new moon, indicating that the opportunities that surface are powerful, may be transformative and coincide with your ideals and spiritual beliefs. And what's particularly wonderful about this new moon is that Mercury isn't retrograde, so the opportunities are likely to pan out.

Jupiter makes a major shift on the 8th. After being in your sign for more than a year, it enters Sagittarius and the financial area of your chart. It will be there until December 3, 2019, and during this period, your earnings should spike significantly. Your expenses may rise, too, but you'll have the money to cover them. So, if making a million bucks is on your wish list, you've chosen the ideal time to make it happen! Jupiter rules Sagittarius and functions well in this sign. It's entirely possible that the bulk of your earnings could come through publishing, higher education or from a foreign country.

Mars transits Pisces from November 15 to December 31, and what an interesting ride this will be. Your sexuality is greatly heightened, and your intuition is deepened. Your enthusiasm for your various creative endeavors prompts you to dive into whatever you're passionate about—a particular creative path, a romantic relationship, travel, research or just enjoying yourself.

On the 16th, two events occur: Mercury turns retrograde in Sagittarius, and Venus turns direct in Libra. Read over the March and July roundups for the last two Mercury retrogrades and the Mercury retro section in the introduction. Follow the suggested guidelines. Since this one occurs in your financial area, be sure to check and recheck your accounts, stock portfolio, 401K and the payment of your bills. With Jupiter also in this sign, anything that goes awry will do so in a big way.

Venus will be in Libra until December 2, when it enters your sign once again. While in Libra, you'll have a chance to experience some of the things you did between August 6 and November 9, so read over the August roundup.

The full moon in Gemini on the 23rd occurs in the shared resources area of your chart. You could be working alongside your partner, a parent, child or roommate or with anyone else with whom you share finances. The project could be a publicity campaign, writing a newsletter, blogging or networking for business. A project is completed, or there's news about it. Or both!

AT A GLANCE
November 7—New moon in Scorpio
November 8—Jupiter enters Sagittarius
November 15—Mars enters Pisces
November 16—Mercury turns retrograde in Sagittarius, Venus turns direct in Libra
November 23—Full moon in Gemini

December 2018
Romantic & creative

Take a few minutes at the beginning of the month to think about what you would like to experience and achieve next year. If you did this for the new moon in your sign, then look over that list and add to it if needed.

December is a fairly quiet month. On the 2nd, Venus enters Scorpio once again and will be there until January 4, 2019. Lucky you! This is another fabulous period, when your love life and your creativity are heightened, and life generally unfolds with greater smoothness. It will be even better once Mercury turns direct in your sign on December 1. Look back to the September and October roundups for the specifics on Venus and Mercury in your sign.

Mercury enters Sagittarius on December 12 and will be there until January 4, 2019. During this transit, you're caught up in the holiday spirit, and the free-wheeling energy of Sagittarius makes this transit fun and joyful. Just be careful that you don't overspend and wake up to a financial nightmare in the new year!

The new moon in Sagittarius on December 7 heightens Mercury's transit through this sign. New financial opportunities should surface—perhaps through publishing, international travel or a workshop or course that you teach. This new moon is followed on the 22nd by a full moon in fellow water sign Cancer that highlights your spirituality, family and travel plans you may have for the holidays or the New Year. It's a great moon for the year's end and is perfect for coming up with your New Year's resolutions!

AT A GLANCE
December 2—Venus enters Scorpio
December 6—Mercury turns direct in Scorpio
December 7—New moon in Sagittarius
December 12—Mercury enters Sagittarius
December 22—Full moon in Cancer

Reflection
You probably don't need to reflect much on this past year. You do this naturally. But jot a few thoughts below on how this year went for you. Did it meet your expectations?

_____
_____
_____
_____
_____

Happy New Year!

Sagittarius 2018

Welcome to 2018! In these monthly roundups, you'll find information about the new and full moons, when planets are turning retrograde or direct and what angles the transiting planets form to your sun sign. Since Sagittarius is ruled by Jupiter, pay close attention to what it's doing. Jupiter is in Scorpio for most of the year, in the quietest part of your chart, so its expansiveness takes place primarily within your unconscious. It means your dreams and imagination are particularly vivid and may hold insights that are helpful.

On November 8, Jupiter enters your sign, where it will be until December 3, 2019. During this thirteen-month period, your life will expand in unimagined ways! This happens every twelve years, so look back to 2006 for some hints about what this transit may mean for you.

Lucky you, Sadge! 2018 should be a good year for you. New doors open, new opportunities surface and the only thing you have to do is decide which opportunity to seize, which path to take. The period from January 26 to March 17, when Mars transits your sign, will be especially productive.

January 2018
Shifting energies

January is crowded with astrological events, and the energies will be shifting rapidly enough to challenge even you. Let's start with the lunar eclipse in fellow fire sign Leo, on January 31.

Eclipses often infuse a month with a sense of urgency and a certain anxiety level. They tend to bring issues right into our faces so that we often have to move quickly and make immediate decisions. Lunar eclipses usually impact our inner lives and our emotions, and this one in Leo may make you feel that your creativity or freedom is stifled in some way. This feeling could surface because someone in your work or home environment makes a remark that pushes one of your buttons. As a result, you may dive into a creative endeavor as soon as you can or buy a plane ticket to some remote spot in the world! Either of those choices is preferable to anger.

Long before the eclipse rolls around, there's a full moon in Cancer on January 1. This moon brings family news or news about your partner's income. If you're in the midst of a divorce, for instance, then you may hear about what the settlement will be. Or you could inherit money or find out that you're getting an insurance refund.

On the 11th, Mercury enters Capricorn and joins Venus in your financial area. They travel together until the 17th, when Venus changes signs. These two have quite a bit to chat about concerning your thoughts and beliefs about money—how you earn it, spend it and save it (or not). You may be mulling over ideas about how to increase your income and may even lay out a plan that will help you to attain greater earnings. Venus has been in your financial area since December 25, 2017 and may have helped to increase your earnings.

Between January 17 and February 10, Venus transits compatible air sign Aquarius, and romance may be as close as your neighborhood or even your backyard. If you do meet someone special during this transit, the introduction could come through a sibling or someone you see frequently in your daily life. It's also possible that a lead on earning additional income—perhaps for a long trip you're saving for—comes through a neighbor.

On the 16th, the new moon in Capricorn may be just what you need for an income boost. This one should bring in new financial and career opportunities. And because Saturn is also in Capricorn now, the opportunities that surface have a long-term impact.

You'll love the period from January 26 to March 17, when energetic Mars is in your sign. Mars is like the Energizer Bunny and keeps you revved up and in forward motion. You're able to accomplish a great deal now in any area where you place your attention and focus. Your physical energy and sexuality are also heightened. If you don't already have a regular exercise routine, then start one during this transit. You may find you'll need to burn off some of your physical energy.

Mercury enters Aquarius on the 31st, the same day as the lunar eclipse, and travels with Venus until February 10, when the planet of romance enters Pisces. Mercury will be in Aquarius until the 18th and will be feeding you an abundance of cutting edge ideas that you'll want to discuss with friends, neighbors or anyone who listens. Jot the ideas down. You may be able to use them later on.

AT A GLANCE
January 1—Full moon in Cancer
January 11—Mercury enters Capricorn
January 16—New moon in Capricorn
January 17—Venus enters Aquarius
January 26—Mars enters Sagittarius
January 31—Mercury enters Aquarius, lunar eclipse in Leo

February 2018
Heightened intuition

February isn't as frenetic as last month was. But as February 15 approaches, you may start feeling a certain tension or anticipation because of the solar eclipse in Aquarius on that day. Uranus forms a beneficial angle to the eclipse degree, suggesting that any news you hear or any opportunities that surface will occur suddenly and without warning. The opportunities could include a new communication project, a chance to work with like-minded individuals, travel or even a search for a neighborhood that would suit you and your family better than where you live now. Be vigilant for synchronicities that act as guidance.

Between February 10 and March 6, Venus transits Pisces and the home/family sector of your chart. During this period, your intuitive ability and compassion deepen. Things in your family life hum along at a pace that may not be exciting enough for you, but the slower pace actually gives you a chance to indulge your creativity. Your relationships have a dreamy, romantic quality to them.

On the 18th, Mercury joins Venus in Pisces, and these two planets will travel together until March 6. Your mind and your heart are in synch during these few weeks, and you may find yourself feeling nostalgic or more wrapped up in your emotions than usual. As a Sagittarius, you're an action-oriented individual, but try to enjoy your heightened intuition and imagination.

AT A GLANCE
February 10—Venus enters Pisces
February 15—Solar eclipse in Aquarius
February 18—Mercury enters Pisces

March 2018
Wild & unpredictable

It may be a wild, unpredictable month, but the roller coaster ride will thrill you.

The month begins with a full moon in Virgo and news about your profession or career. If you've been sending out resumes and interviewing for jobs, then you could hear that you have landed the job you want. Or there could be several offers, and you'll have a choice. With Saturn forming a beneficial angle to this moon, the offer is solid.

On the 6th, both Mercury and Venus enter fellow fire sign Aries, transits that really suit your energy and temperament. Until the 22nd, when Mercury turns retrograde for the first time this year, you enjoy one of the most romantic and creative periods all year. If you're in a relationship, your love life is stellar and filled with passion, joy and adventure. If you're not involved with anyone, you may well be by the time this transit ends on March 31. With Mercury also in Aries, your head and your heart are on the same page.

Regardless of your creative interests and skills, your muse is at your beck and call during this transit, so don't squander the energy by partying 24/7! You may have many unusual ideas and strategies, and it's wise to jot them down.

Between March 31 and April 24, Venus transits Taurus, a sign that it rules, and brings a smooth flow to your daily work life. You're able to work longer hours with greater focus and patience in order to complete a project or to achieve a goal.

Now, about that Mercury retrograde in Aries. It begins on March 22 and ends on April 15. Read over the section on Mercury retrograde in the introduction, and follow the rules of the three Rs—revise, review and reconsider. In addition, since this retro occurs in the romance/creativity area of your chart, be sure to express yourself clearly to your partner and your kids. A lot of miscommunication occurs during a Mercury retrograde. If you're going to launch a business or creative endeavor, wait until the retro is over and do it on the day of a new moon.

Jupiter turns retrograde in Scorpio on March 8 and doesn't turn direct again until July 10. During these four months, Jupiter's expansion turns inward. You may be taking a deeper look at your spiritual beliefs, could decide to go to graduate school or law school or could even embark on some sort of spiritual quest that takes you overseas.

The 17th has two events: Mars enters Capricorn and there's a new moon in Pisces. The Mars transit, which lasts until May 16, galvanizes you to earn more money and to pursue your professional goals more diligently. Even if your expenses spike during this transit, so does your income.

The new moon in Pisces brings new opportunities connected to your home/family and your creative endeavors. It's possible that you land a freelance gig that enables you to work from home, or perhaps you take time off from work to start a project that's important to you. You could find the ideal roommate or take in a boarder to increase your income.

We talked about the Venus transit through Taurus which begins on March 31. Also on that day, there's a full moon in compatible air sign Libra. This one should kick your social life into high gear and could bring news about a friend or acquaintance. You're more aware now of the importance of balance in your relationships with others.

AT A GLANCE
March 1—Full moon in Virgo
March 6—Mercury enters Aries, Venus enters Aries
March 8—Jupiter turns retro in Scorpio
March 17—Mars enters Capricorn, new moon in Pisces
March 22—Mercury turns retro in Aries
March 31—Venus enters Taurus, full moon in Libra

April 2018
5 stars

April should be a great month for you, Sagittarius! And things get off to a start on April 15, with a new moon in fellow fire sign Aries and Mercury turning direct in Aries. The new moon in the creativity and romance sector of your chart should bring in a new romantic interest and new creative endeavors that will thrill you. If you're already involved in a relationship, then this new moon could result in a deepening commitment.

If you're self-employed, then you may land a project or win over a client that makes a significant difference in your business. Your muse will be ready to dive into any creative endeavor, so don't fritter the energy away!

Now that Mercury turned direct, it will be in Aries until May 13. Your conscious focus will be on romance, creativity, your kids and enjoyment. You may discover a new hobby or passion that consumes you! Oh and, Sadge, it's safe to pack your bags and treat yourself to a travel adventure. If you do, be sure to take along a copy of Jack Kerouac's *On the Road*.

On the 17th, Saturn turns retrograde in Capricorn, in the financial area of your chart. It lasts until September 6. During this period you may be mulling over your attitudes and beliefs about money. If you feel you don't earn enough, then what belief is holding you back?

Between April 24 and May 19, Venus transits Gemini and the partnership area of your chart. If you're involved in a relationship, then you and your partner may deepen your commitment to each other by moving in together, getting engaged or married or starting a family. Your business partnerships during this period flourish. Your social and communication skills are heightened during this period.

The full moon in Scorpio on the 29th favors research and shines a very bright light on your own unconscious—your deeper motives and your core beliefs about life and who you are. Retrograde Saturn forms a beneficial angle to this full moon, indicating that you're serious about your process of self-discovery.

AT A GLANCE
April 15—New moon in Aries, Mercury turns direct in Aries
April 17—Saturn turns retrograde in Capricorn
April 24—Venus enters Gemini
April 29—Full moon in Scorpio

May 2018
Planetary shift

There's a major shift this month that should impact your daily work life and the way you maintain your health. On May 15, the planet Uranus changes signs. Uranus's job is to disrupt the status quo and kick you out of ruts and routines so that the things that no longer work in your life fall away from it, making room for the new. For the last seven years, Uranus has been in Aries, in the romance and creativity section of your chart, and has formed a beneficial angle to your sun sign. This period was probably exciting and unpredictable for you, just the way you like things to be. You may have gotten married—or divorced—moved, fallen in love, traveled, discovered new depths to your creativity and found new and wonderful ways to enjoy yourself.

Uranus transits Taurus until November, and then because of a retrograde, it slips back into Aries until 2019. While it transits Taurus, you may change jobs, land a promotion, change your exercise routine or nutritional program or experience abrupt ups and downs in your finances, career or family life. In any area of your life where you have settled into a rut, Uranus is going to turn it inside out and shake it free of debris!

The emphasis this month is definitely on Taurus, starting with Mercury entering the sign on May 13, then the Uranus transit on the 15th, as well as a new moon in that sign. Mercury's transit through Taurus lasts until May 29, and during these weeks, you may be more stubborn, patient and resilient. You're focused on a particular project or client, and if it requires overtime, you're fine with it.

The new moon on the 15th should bring new opportunities with your work and your health. If you want to lose weight or start a new nutritional or weight loss program, today is the day to do it. If you're self-employed and ready to begin interviewing prospective employees, start today.

Mars enters Aquarius on May 16 and will be moving direct through that sign until June 26, when it turns retrograde. While it's in direct motion, you are fired up about your various endeavors. You could be working on a publicity campaign of some kind for your company or business that involves blogging, building a website and using social media. We'll talk about the retrograde in next month's roundup.

From May 19 to June 13, Venus transits Cancer. There's a strong intuitive and family component to any transit involving this water sign. It will be moving through the shared resources area of your chart, facilitating your ability to obtain a mortgage or loan or to obtain a good insurance rate. Your partner's income may increase, and it's possible that you could inherit money. Women play an important role during this transit—friends, siblings or a partner.

On the 29th, it's time to party! There's a full moon in your sign, and Mars in Aquarius forms a beneficial angle to it. That means that if you throw a party, your eccentric and fascinating friends will certainly put in an appearance! Also on the 29th, Mercury enters Gemini and your partnership area. Mercury rules this sign, so it functions well here and should stir up a lot of conversation between you and your romantic partner and you and your business partners. You may be brainstorming with a friend or partner about a communication project—a book, a publicity campaign or the development of an app.

May 13—Mercury enters Taurus
May 15—New moon in Taurus, Uranus enters Taurus
May 16—Mars enters Aquarius
May 19—Venus enters Cancer
May 29—Full moon in Sagittarius, Mercury enters Gemini

June 2018
Financial stuff

It's another busy month astrologically, and you'll especially enjoy what the Venus transit does for your love life! But first, on the 12th, Mercury enters Cancer, where it travels for just a day with Venus, because on the 13th, the planet of love and romance enters fellow fire sign Leo. Mercury remains in Cancer until June 29, and during these weeks, your conscious thoughts are on resources you share with others—a personal or business partner, child, parent or roommate. You may be worrying about joint finances and juggling your bills. It's best not to fret about money. Instead, come up with a plan that will enable you to pay off your bills/credit cards. Perhaps a part-time job would help!

On June 29, Mercury enters fire sign Leo and turns retrograde in that sign on July 26. We'll talk about that in the July roundup. While Mercury is in Leo, your communication skills have a particular flare and drama that favors writing—a novel, screenplay or publicity materials. For nine days, Mercury travels with Venus in this sign, and you are really on target with everything you tackle. Your love life is filled with passion and pizazz, your creative drive is powerful and you're so self-confident that people flock to you. Venus remains in Leo until July 9.

The same day that Venus enters Leo, there's a new moon in Gemini. This one brings new partnership opportunities. On a personal level, you and a partner may deepen your commitment to each other by getting married, moving in together or starting a family. On a professional level, the ideal business partner may show up at exactly the right time.

Mars turns retrograde in Aquarius on June 26, will slide back into Capricorn and then turn direct in that sign on August 27. During this retro period, you may feel less confident about the direction your life is taking. Rather than making drastic changes, take a deeper look at your goals and speak up for yourself when you need to. Don't be argumentative or insist that your way is the only way. Physical activity helps keep you grounded during these months.

The full moon in Capricorn on the 28th highlights your finances—what you earn and spend, how or if you budget and what your financial goals are. There may be news about your finances—a loan is repaid or an unexpected check arrives, or you land a freelance gig of some kind. There could also be news about your profession or career that figures into the financial aspect of this lunar energy.

June 12—Mercury enters Cancer
June 13—New moon in Gemini, Venus enters Leo
June 26—Mars turns retrograde in Aquarius
June 28—Full moon in Capricorn
June 29—Mercury enters Leo

July 2018
Mixed

Months in which eclipses occur can be imbued with tension and a sense of urgency. This is due to the nature of eclipses, which tend to bring relationship issues and situations into our immediate awareness so that we must act quickly. In other words, eclipses are sometimes synonymous with crisis. This month, there are two eclipses.

The first, on July 12, is a solar eclipse in Cancer. This one should bring new opportunities related to your family and resources you share with others—a spouse or partner, parents, children, a roommate or even a bank or mortgage company. Powerful Pluto forms a challenging angle to the eclipse degree, so you may be up against an authoritarian figure— a parent or boss, for instance, or a law enforcement officer, judge or an institution. Just keep your wits about you, and allow your intuition to guide you.

While solar eclipses generally concern external events, lunar eclipses concern our inner worlds of emotion and intuition. The lunar eclipse in Aquarius on July 27 may trigger emotions about your siblings or neighbors or something in your daily world. Mars retrograde is conjunct the eclipse degree, suggesting short tempers and impatience.

But before the eclipses occur, Venus enters Virgo and your career area on July 9. Between then and August 6, when the transit ends, you should be able to make great professional strides. Peers and bosses are in your court, and it will be much easier for you to garner support for your pet projects. If you're self-employed, this period should be stellar for you— a spike in sales, the ideal clients and your income rising!

On the 10th, Jupiter turns direct in Scorpio and heads toward its appointment with your sign on November 8. Your willpower and determination enjoy renewed strength and focus, and you may embark on a spiritual quest of some kind that takes you overseas.

On the 26th, Mercury turns retrograde in fellow fire sign Leo and turns direct again on August 19. Look back at the March roundup for the guidelines to follow to make the retrograde period easier to navigate. Since this one occurs in that area of your chart that governs international travel, you may want to postpone any overseas travel plans you've been considering. And as always, follow the rules of the three Rs: revise, review and reconsider.

AT A GLANCE
July 9—Venus enters Virgo
July 10—Jupiter turns direct in Scorpio
July 12—Solar eclipse in Cancer
July 26—Mercury turns retrograde in Leo
July 27—Lunar eclipse in Aquarius

August 2018
Imaginative

There's another eclipse this month—a solar eclipse in fellow fire sign Leo on August 11. This one should usher in new opportunities related to higher education, international travel, your creative endeavors and your spiritual beliefs. You might, for instance, have an opportunity to travel overseas with a church group or religious organization. Or you may have a chance to teach a seminar or workshop or to take graduate level courses in something that interests you.

Both Pluto and Neptune form challenging angles to the eclipse degree, suggesting that the opportunities appeal to your idealism but may involve trouble with an authority figure.

From August 6 to September 9, Venus transits Libra, a sign it rules. This transit should ramp up your social life, but also favors any sort of publicity you might be doing for your company's services/products. Venus functions well in Libra and infuses you with a pleasant romanticism and an artistic sense. If you're musically or artistically inclined, then this transit certainly encourages your muse to feed you whatever you need. If you meet anyone special during this transit, the introduction may come through friends.

On the 19th, Mercury turns direct again in Leo. For you, the nomad of the zodiac, Mercury turning direct is usually a reason to celebrate. It means you can hop a plane or boat and head into parts unknown without worrying about sudden changes in your plans. Now you can sign contracts without having to revisit the details at a later date and submit your manuscripts, screenplays and other creative endeavors. This transit lasts until September 5.

On the 26th, the full moon in Pisces brings sudden, unexpected and positive news concerning your home, family or a creative endeavor. It's also possible that something in one of these areas reaches completion—a home improvement project, for example. Or a pregnancy ends with the successful birth of a baby!

AT A GLANCE
August 6—Venus enters Libra
August 11—Solar eclipse in Leo
August 19—Mercury turns direct in Leo
August 26—Full moon in Pisces
August 27—Mars turns direct in Capricorn

September 2018
Artistic & intuitive

September is crowded with astrological events, and things get off to a start on the 5th, when Mercury enters Virgo, a sign it rules, and the career area of your chart. During this transit, which lasts until the 21st, your focus is on professional matters. You excel at details now, so tackle projects that require you to connect the dots. You get additional help on the 6th, when Saturn turns direct in Capricorn—an earth sign compatible with Virgo—and bolsters your efforts. The change in Saturn's movement is excellent news for your finances. Whatever was delayed during the retro should pick up speed and forward momentum again. Perhaps a check that was delayed now arrives.

Two events occur on the 9th: Venus enters secretive Scorpio, and there's a new moon in Virgo. Until Venus turns retrograde on October 5, your sexuality and intuition are deepened, and your need for bottom line answers is a propelling factor in everything you do. The answers you crave are probably in the area of romance, your own motivations and in your creative endeavors.

The new moon in Virgo should bring about new professional opportunities—a promotion, a larger office or a raise. Or if you're just embarking on your career, you land the dream job.

From September 10 to November 15, Mars moves through compatible air sign Aquarius and the communication area of your chart. It forms a beneficial angle to your sun during this transit and brings wind to your sails! Everything you tackle or become involved in now seems to move at a greater speed. Many ideas that come to you now are cutting edge, so be sure to jot them down. They may come into play at some point. You and a sibling or neighbor may team up for something—for a neighborhood beautification project, to write a book or to start a blog or website.

From September 21 to October 9, Mercury transits Libra and forms a beneficial angle to your sun sign. Your conscious mind has a more artistic bent, you find it easier to appreciate the beauty around you and you're more social. You're also aware of the importance of balance in your relationships.

The full moon in fellow fire sign Aries on September 24 shines a light on your love life, creative endeavors and your kids. There could be news related to one or all of these areas. You may complete a creative endeavor on or around the date of this full moon. One thing is fairly certain: your passions are heightened, and you're in the mood for love!

AT A GLANCE
September 5—Mercury enters Virgo
September 6—Saturn turns direct in Capricorn
September 9—Venus enters Scorpio, new moon in Virgo
September 10—Mars enters Aquarius
September 21—Mercury enters Libra
September 24—Full moon in Aries

October 2018
Hectic

October is a busy month astrologically and may require vigilance on your part to take advantage of the opportunities that come your way.

On October 5, Venus turns retrograde in Scorpio, slips back into Libra and turns direct in that sign on November 16. While Venus is retro in Scorpio, you have an opportunity to take a closer look at your most intimate relationships. Are they working out the way you want? If not, what adjustments can be made? Do you want to make the adjustments or do you want the other person to do it? If your answer is the latter, then it might be best to end the relationship because your happiness or contentment shouldn't depend on what someone else does or doesn't do. Once Venus slides back into Libra on October 31, you may be scrutinizing some of your friendships in the same way.

Sometimes, Venus retrogrades entail physical discomforts. It might be cold outside, and the heat in your car or home goes on the fritz. Or because Venus is associated with money and creativity, a check is delayed or a creative endeavor hits a few bumps. The good news is that these retros don't last forever!

The new moon in Libra on October 8 should be a beauty for you. New opportunities emerge in friendships and contacts that enable you to move closer to achieving your wishes and dreams. You may work on a creative endeavor with a team or group of like-minded individuals. A new romantic interest could enter your life. Sometimes new moons deliver fortune cookie types of events and opportunities!

From October 9 to 31, Mercury transits Scorpio, and your conscious mind is focused on deeper issues and psychological motives—the core of who you are and what makes you who you are. This transit favors any kind of paranormal or psychological research and any creative endeavor that requires looking deep within for inspiration.

The full moon in Taurus on October 24 is a whopper! Uranus is conjunct this full moon, and Saturn forms a beneficial angle to it. Any news you hear is likely to be sudden and unexpected. With Saturn in the mix, the news is sobering. That doesn't necessarily mean the news is negative. If you've been applying for jobs, for instance, and hear that you're being called back for a second interview, the call back isn't frivolous!

Mercury enters your sign on October 31. Since there is a retrograde involved with this planet next month, we'll discuss it in November's roundup!

AT A GLANCE
October 5—Venus turns retrograde in Scorpio
October 8—New moon in Libra
October 9—Mercury enters Scorpio
October 24—Full moon in Taurus
October 31—Mercury enters Sagittarius

November 2018
Exploration

November is a mixed bag of astrological events. Some of them will feel good to you and others, not so much. While Mercury is moving direct in your sign—until November 16—you're on a definite roll. You're connecting with people—in person or virtually—whose philosophical and spiritual beliefs interest you. If you're traveling, then you're really in your element, and the more exotic the setting, the happier you are. Your mental focus is on the bigger picture of whatever you're doing in work, play, love and creativity.

Then between November 16 and December 6, Mercury is retrograde, and life slows down. Reread the roundup for March and July, when Mercury was retrograde, and follow the suggestions in order to mitigate some of the effects. Also, look over the Mercury retro section in the introduction to the book. Since it's retro in your sign, the travel guidelines are particularly important. It's also important not to submit manuscripts during this retrograde; Sagittarius rules publishing.

On the same day, Venus turns direct in Libra, and for a couple of weeks you enjoy the same types of experience you did between August 6 and September 9, so look back at the August roundup.

The new moon in Scorpio on the 7th should bring in new opportunities for the exploration of consciousness, the paranormal and everything that goes bump in the night. You may have a chance to conduct research in these areas or to write about them. If a relationship begins during this new moon, it will be passionate and sexual.

On the 8th, expansive Jupiter finally enters your sign, and this really is a reason to celebrate. It will be in Sagittarius until December 2019, and during this thirteen-month period, your life will expand in unimagined ways. You may have an opportunity to travel more frequently to those far-flung corners of the world that interest you. You may go to graduate or law school, get married or divorced, start a family or become an empty nester. The type of expansion you experience depends on where you are in your life and where you place your energies.

From November 15 to December 31, Mars transits Pisces. This transit charges up your imagination and your creative drive and brings a soft compassion and caring to your home life. You may decide to spruce up your house in some way, to beautify it with festive colors or add gorgeous potted plants, or you may decide to buy some new furniture items.

The full moon in Gemini on November 23 brings a communication project to completion. There may be news about a writing/communication project, or you might be invited to teach a workshop or seminar. There's also a possibility that you're able to more fully grasp the inner dynamics of a your relationship with your partner.

November 7—New moon in Scorpio
November 8—Jupiter enters Sagittarius
November 15—Mars enters Pisces
November 16—Mercury turns retrograde in Sagittarius, Venus turns direct in Libra
November 23—Full moon in Gemini

December 2018
Onward

As the last month of the year begins, take a few minutes to think about what you would like to achieve and experience next year. Make a list. Don't worry about how these things will come about; simply trust that they will. Post your list where you'll see it often.

December is actually a calmer month than the previous two. On December 2, Venus reenters Scorpio, where it will be until January 7, 2019. This second time around enables you to complete whatever you didn't have a chance to finish in September and early October, before Venus turned retrograde. You may want to reread the September roundup for hints about what you may experience during this second transit.

On the 6th, Mercury turns direct in Scorpio and for six days travels with Venus. Then on the 12th, Mercury moves into your sign for the second time this year and remains there until January 4, 2019. Reread the November roundup for clues about what you can expect when Mercury is in your sign again. This time, though, your vigor and enthusiasm for life are even more powerful.

On the 7th, there's a new moon in your sign. This one comes around just once a year, and you should try to prepare for it in advance. What types of opportunities would you like to surface? With Jupiter also in your sign now, don't hesitate to think big or to let your imagination run wild. Jupiter is your ally and will work on your behalf to deliver! Some possibilities with this new moon: a chance to travel, which is usually high on your list of desires; an opportunity to study something new and exciting; a quest of some kind; or an opportunity that is deeply satisfying.

The full moon in Cancer on December 22 brings news about a mortgage or loan, an inheritance, an insurance premium or resources you share with others—a partner, spouse, roommate, child or sibling. Your spouse, for instance, could hear that he or she has gotten a raise. A royalty check could arrive. It's a nice surprise, whatever it is.

AT A GLANCE
December 2—Venus enters Scorpio
December 6—Mercury turns direct in Scorpio
December 7—New moon in Sagittarius
December 12—Mercury enters Sagittarius
December 22—Full moon in Cancer

Reflection

Was it a good year overall? Which areas of your life improved? Are you happier? More prosperous? Did you get to visit the countries you wanted to? Take a few minutes to jot down your thoughts about 2018.

_____

_____

_____

_____

_____

Happy New Year!

Capricorn 2018

Your sign is ruled by Saturn, the planet that governs physical reality, discipline, responsibility limitations and restrictions and structure. In December 2017, Saturn entered your sign for the first time in 29 years. It will be there until March of 2020. During this two-and-a-half-year transit, the structures in your life will change. You may assume more responsibility in some area of your life, but the potential for great achievements is also good.

During this transit, self-reflection is necessary in order for you to better understand who you are, what you desire from your life and how you can best achieve those desires. Powerful Pluto has been transiting your sign since late November 2008 and will continue to do so until late November 2024. The combination of these two planets indicates long-range, irrevocable change and powerful transformation in your life. You may get married or divorced or meet your soul mate. You may start a family or become an empty nester. Your finances or career may undergo abrupt change. However the specifics unfold for you, you usually have a strategy for dealing with whatever comes your way.

2018 puts you in a much stronger position in just about every area of your life. Jupiter in Scorpio forms a beneficial angle to your sun sign and expands your network of acquaintances and friends, as well as your contacts through social networks. These contacts are helpful professionally and facilitate your goals.

January 2018
Mixed

Welcome to 2018! This year doesn't begin with a Mercury retrograde as 2017 did, but there's a lunar eclipse this month on the 31ˢᵗ which may create a degree of tension and a sense of urgency. The eclipse falls in Leo, in the shared resources area of your chart. A partner, parent, child or roommate—anyone with whom you share financial resources—may say or do something that necessitates a quick decision on your part. Lunar eclipses involve internal events, emotions and intuition, so you may have an emotional reaction to whatever is going on. Since the eclipse is in Leo, there may be some drama!

Before the eclipse comes around, there's a full moon in Cancer on January 1. There could be news about a family member or business partner. This full moon occurs in your partnership area and may shed light on your relationship with your partner or with a business partner. Full moons are about completion and culmination, so it's possible that a project that has been in the works since last year is nearly finished.

On the 11ᵗʰ, Mercury enters your sign. Your focus is powerful, and you're goal oriented. You're able to create excellent career strategies and make sound decisions in your professional life. This transit lasts until January 31, when Mercury enters Aquarius and your financial area. Your conscious attention turns to financial matters—what you earn, save and spend. If the bills for holiday expenditures are arriving, you may be fretting about it all. Don't waste your energy worrying. Do what you do best, and find a solution.

The new moon in your sign on the 16ᵗʰ brings opportunities that are personally satisfying and may offer up the financial solution you're looking for! And if that isn't enough, Venus enters Aquarius and your financial area the next day. So between January 17 and February 10, your income is likely to spike from unexpected sources of revenue. Your expenses may rise, too, but you'll have the money to meet them.

From January 26 to March 17, Mars transits Sagittarius and your solar twelfth house—the quiet part of your chart. But Sagittarius doesn't do well with *quiet*, so use this energy to dig around in your own unconscious, to remember your dreams or to figure out who you are. You might consider treating yourself to a past-life regression or to a trip to some foreign port.

AT A GLANCE
January 1—Full moon in Cancer
January 11—Mercury enters Capricorn
January 16—New moon in Capricorn
January 17—Venus enters Aquarius
January 26—Mars enters Sagittarius
January 31—Mercury enters Aquarius, lunar eclipse in Leo

February 2018
Financial bonus

Let's talk first about this month's solar eclipse. It occurs in Aquarius on February 15 in your financial area. Thanks to a friendly angle from Uranus to the eclipse degree, new financial opportunities will arrive suddenly and without warning. It could be a job offer, perhaps in the technology field; a freelance job that pays well; the repayment of a loan; or an unexpected payment for a service you rendered in the past. It could even be a raise, bonus or commission check. However the specifics unfold, you should be pleased and delighted.

Before the eclipse occurs, Venus enters Pisces on the 10th, and between then and March 6, your communication skills shine. There's a deeply imaginative and intuitive slant to this transit that will be evident in any type of creative endeavor you're involved in. If you're not involved in a relationship right now, then you may meet a romantic interest through a sibling or neighbor. The relationship is apt to be romantic and soulful.

From February 18 to March 6, Mercury travels with Venus, so your conscious focus is on romance and creativity, and there's a beautiful flow to your thoughts and desires. Since both planets form beneficial angles to your sun, you're very much in your element, and the people around you notice a certain gentle softness about you now. Your compassion deepens during this transit, and you may become involved with a charity of some kind or volunteer at an animal rescue facility.

AT A GLANCE
February 10—Venus enters Pisces
February 15—Solar eclipse in Aquarius
February 18—Mercury enters Pisces

March 2018
Family time & retrospection

March is a crowded month astrologically, with nine events that affect you in vastly different ways. It starts with a full moon in fellow earth sign Virgo on March 1. This day should be particularly nice for you because both Saturn and Neptune form beneficial angles to this full moon. Any news you hear will be positive and could involve publishing, higher education or international travel.

With a full moon in Virgo, you're able to grasp the smallest details of a particular philosophy or spiritual belief system.

Circle March 6 on your calendar. Both Mercury and Venus enter fire sign Aries and the home/family area of your chart. They travel together until the 22nd, when Mercury turns retrograde for the first time this year. While they're both in direct motion, however, you can expect lots of impatience and restlessness in your personal environment. It's as if everyone is suddenly fired up and ready to go, well, somewhere. It might be a perfect time for a family vacation to the beach or the mountains, a spot where physical activity is the norm. Your conscious focus is on your family during this transit.

During Mercury's retrograde in Aries from March 22 to April 15, it's best not to launch new projects or to make submissions. Follow the rule of the three Rs—review, revise and reconsider. If you're making travel plans this month or next, do so on either side of the retrograde dates. The same is true for signing contracts or buying large ticket items. You might want to reread the Mercury retrograde stories in the introductory material for 2017 and for 2018.

Jupiter turns retrograde in Scorpio on March 8 and remains that way until July 10. During these months, you may be taking a closer look at some of your friendships. Are your friends positive individuals? Are their spiritual beliefs similar to your own? Are they supportive? You may also be researching the paranormal and writing about it.

March 17 features two events also. Mars enters your sign, and there's a new moon in Pisces. Mars will be in your sign until May 16, and throughout this transit, you probably feel invincible and are convinced that nothing stands in your way. Mars endows you with a lot of physical energy, so it's smart to have a regular exercise program. You're able to accomplish a lot when Mars is in your sign, so set your agenda before the transit begins!

The new moon in Pisces on the same day should attract opportunities in communication. You might, for instance, be approached about ghostwriting a book. Or you might spearhead a publicity campaign for your or your company's product or services. If you've been thinking about moving and are scouting out neighborhoods, you could find the one that suits you and your family perfectly.

March seems to be the month when astrological events pair up, and there are two on the 31st: Venus enters Taurus, a sign it rules, and there's a full moon in Libra. The Venus transits lasts until April 24 and is especially important for you because it marks the most romantic and creative time for you all year. During this period, your love life should unfold with complete smoothness, and your muse is ready to help you in any way you want. The only other period that comes close falls between July 9 and August 6, when Venus transits earth sign Virgo.

The full moon in Libra brings news about your career. There could be a challenge with an authority figure—a boss, for instance. But with Mars still in your sign, you're able to do whatever is necessary to move ahead.

AT A GLANCE
March 1—Full moon in Virgo
March 6—Mercury enters Aries, Venus enters Aries
March 8—Jupiter turns retro in Scorpio
March 17—Mars enters Capricorn, new moon in Pisces
March 22—Mercury turns retro in Aries
March 31—Venus enters Taurus, full moon in Libra

April 2018
Mixed

You're dealing with a Mercury retrograde in Aries until April 15. Once it turns direct, everyone is in a better place. Anything you delayed doing during the retrograde can now be done easily and without running into one challenge after another. If you're contemplating a move, then the period from April 15 to May 13, when Mercury enters Taurus, is a good time to scout out neighborhoods and houses. There's also a new moon in Aries on the 15th, which suggests new opportunities related to your home/family. Perhaps one of those opportunities is that you find exactly the right house. Another possibility is that you and your partner find out you're going to become parents.

On the 17th, Saturn turns retrograde in your sign and remains that way until September 6. During this lengthy retrograde, you have an opportunity to take a look at the structures of your closest relationships. It's easier to establish parameters between yourself and others and to say no when you're asked to do something you don't want to do.

From April 24 to May 19 Venus transits Gemini and facilitates your daily work routine and your relationships with co-workers and employees. You might meet a romantic interest through your work or through a co-worker. Involvement in a publicity project that entails social media is also a possibility.

The full moon in Scorpio on April 29 should ramp up your social life. Your intuition and perceptions of others is especially strong on or around the time of this full moon. Be alert for synchronicities. They provide guidance and insight and signal that you're on the right path. There could be news concerning a friend. Whenever Scorpio is involved in a lunar event, the possibility of a psychic experience increases.

AT A GLANCE
April 15—New moon in Aries, Mercury turns direct in Aries
April 17—Saturn turns retrograde in Capricorn
April 24—Venus enters Gemini
April 29—Full moon in Scorpio

May 2018
Exciting & unpredictable

May features a major planetary shift with the planet Uranus. For the last seven years, it has been in fire sign Aries, and on May 15, it enters Taurus. It will be there until November, then slips back into Aries because of a retrograde and enters Taurus again in 2019.

Uranus is the planet of sudden, unexpected change. Its job is to sweep into any area of your life where you're mired in habit and routine, and it shakes things up and out so that new experiences, people and events can move into your life. This transit occurs in the romance, creativity and children section of your chart and forms a beneficial angle to your sun sign. So what can you expect?

First, look back at the last seven years. How has your life changed since 2011? Has one area experienced more change than other areas? Did you and your family move? Did you get married or divorced? Start a family? Change jobs/careers? With this transit, you may fall in love, get married, write the great American novel or sell your creative endeavors and actually make a living doing what you love. Or all of these things. You may have a child, adopt a child or start teaching children. Your creative endeavors are apt to be cutting edge, perhaps even visionary. Unusual people enter your life. You may discover a new hobby or activity that thrills you. In other words, change is in the air, and for you, it's positive.

Also, Saturn is in your sign now. So with both that planet and Uranus in earth signs, any new opportunities that surface are likely to have long-range effects.

On the 13th, Mercury enters earth sign Taurus, in the same area of your chart where Uranus will be on the 15th. When Mercury and Uranus travel together, as they do until May 29, your ideas are unique, insightful and so radically different that it's to your advantage to jot them down. You never know when an idea may prove useful later on.

In addition to Uranus's shift on the 15th, there's a new moon in Taurus. Talk about a profusion of earth energy! The new moon should bring opportunities in romance, creativity and with your kids—the same areas that are affected by the Uranus and Mercury transits. If you're in a relationship, for example, then you and your partner may decide to deepen your commitment to each other. If you're uninvolved, then this new moon could change that. The thing to remember with all this earth energy is that it works in your favor.

On May 16, Mars enters Aquarius and your financial area. Mars moves direct until June 26 (a retrograde we'll talk about in next month's roundup), and while it is, you're super motivated to make more money. Whether you're self-employed or work for someone else, this transit could bring about unusual ways to increase your income. Aquarius has a visionary quality that invariably peers into the future for what may be the next trend. So remain vigilant!

From May 19 to June 12, Venus moves through water sign Cancer, your opposite sign. This transit favors your personal and professional partnerships. On a personal level, you and your partner/spouse may deepen your commitment to each other in some way. If you're not married, then you may set a date. Or you could start a family or buy a home together. At the professional level, there's a greater ease in your relationships with people involved in the business side of your life. You're a team with a vision.

Two events occur on May 29: there's a full moon in Sagittarius, and Mercury enters Gemini. This one lights up the most private part of your chart. You have a better grasp of your own psyche—what makes you tick, your motives and who you are within yourself. It would be a great time to have a past-life regression or to attend a workshop about lucid dreaming or about the nature of consciousness. There could be news about a trip overseas or a publishing endeavor in which you're involved.

Between May 29 and June 12, Mercury transits Gemini. Since it rules this sign, Mercury functions well here and sharpens your communication skills. You may be heading up a team effort at work—working on publicity, networking with clients, updating the company's website or starting a blog. If you're self-employed, it's smart to socialize and make new contacts.

AT A GLANCE
May 13—Mercury enters Taurus
May 15—New moon in Taurus, Uranus enters Taurus
May 16—Mars enters Aquarius
May 19—Venus enters Cancer
May 29—Full moon in Sagittarius, Mercury enters Gemini

June 2018
Eclectic

June is a mix of energies, and in order to take full advantage of the various transits, try to go with the flow. If you encounter resistance from other people, find a diplomatic way around it.

Between June 12 and 29, Mercury moves through Cancer and brings a distinct intuitive flavor to your perceptions and thoughts. You and a partner—business or personal—strike a mutual chord in terms of what you envision for your relationship/business. With Cancer involved, your conscious focus also extends to home and family. It's possible, for example, that you take on a freelance project that you can do at home, and it may necessitate juggling schedules around so you have the time and space you need.

The 13th features two astrological events: a new moon in Gemini, and Venus enters Leo. The new moon should bring new opportunities in your daily work routine. You might be promoted, move to a larger office, land a great account/client, be tapped to head up a team or find the ideal employee. If you're self-employed, an opportunity for publicity and promotion could surface. You could be invited to speak at a conference or workshop where you have a chance to network.

This area of your chart also governs how you maintain your health on a daily basis, so an opportunity could arise to try a new diet or nutritional program, a new exercise routine or some sort of group activity like yoga or Pilates.

From June 13 to July 9, Venus transits Leo. During these several weeks, your creative drive is strong, and you have a flair for drama. If you're employed in the arts, you have a great sense of what works in a story, a photograph, a film, a piece of music or in any other creative endeavor. This transit also favors resources you share with others. You might find the ideal roommate, your partner could get a substantial raise, or your mortgage may be approved for a terrific interest rate.

And then there's romance. Venus in Leo is passionate, gregarious and dramatic, so all of those qualities are evident during this transit. One of the best way to use the energy is to plan a romantic getaway with your partner! The Venus transit lasts until July 9.

On the 26th, Mars turns retrograde in Aquarius, slips back into Capricorn and turns direct in your sign on August 27. During these two months, try not to overspend, particularly on frivolous stuff. Other expenses may come up that have to be paid promptly, so you won't want to deplete your resources. Once Mars turns direct in your sign again, your forward momentum on all fronts will be good again.

The full moon in your sign on the 28th should be very much to your liking. Uranus in Taurus and Saturn in sign are friendly to it, suggesting that any news you hear will be unexpected, with long-term affects.

Mercury enters Leo on June 29, joining Venus in that sign. These two will travel together until July 9, when Venus changes signs. These two have a lot to chat about, and you may discover that your head and your heart are on the same page where romance and money are concerned. As the saying goes, money can't buy you love. But when your finances are in good shape, it's less stressful on a romantic relationship. Mercury remains in Leo for a while because it turns retrograde next month.

AT A GLANCE
June 12—Mercury enters Cancer
June 13—New moon in Gemini, Venus enters Leo
June 26—Mars turns retrograde in Aquarius
June 28—Full moon in Capricorn
June 29—Mercury enters Leo

July 2018
Sense of urgency

Here comes the second round of eclipses for the year—two this month and another in August. Since these tend to have great impact, let's look at these first.

On July 12, the solar eclipse in Cancer should usher in new opportunities for your home/ family life and also for your business and personal partnerships. Whether the opportunities include a pregnancy/birth, a new job or career, a new romance or a business partnership, luck and abundance are part of the package. This is due to a wide but beneficial angle that expansive Jupiter makes to the eclipse degree. Neptune also forms a beneficial angle to the eclipse degree, suggesting an element of idealism or spirituality in these new opportunities. Pluto is opposed to the eclipse degree, indicating that feelings are intense and transformative.

On July 27, the lunar eclipse in Aquarius occurs in your financial area. Emotions swirl around the subject of money, and with retrograde Mars closely conjunct the eclipse degree, tempers may be short. You may have to act quickly and decisively.

Before the eclipses occur, Venus enters Virgo on July 9, a transit that should be just about perfect for you. Between July 9 and August 6, your social life picks up momentum, and you can afford to be choosy about what you do, where you go and whom you hang out with. If romance finds you during this transit, it could be with someone you meet in a workshop, seminar or class, or while traveling. You may dive into a creative endeavor that involves some aspect of your worldview or spiritual beliefs.

On the 10th, Jupiter finally turns direct again in Scorpio and moves on toward its appointment with Sagittarius on November 8. For the past several months, this planet's expansive energy has been in a kind of dormancy and internalized. Now its energy moves outward once again, expanding your network of friends and acquaintances. It also enhances your intuitive ability.

Between July 26 and August 19, Mercury is retrograde in Leo. Read the March roundup for general guidelines to follow during any retrograde that involves the planet of communication. Also look over the Mercury retrograde section in the introduction. Since this retro occurs in the shared resources area of your chart, be sure to keep a close eye on your financial statements—mortgage, credit cards and bank accounts. Your partner's income could be impacted as well during this period. Royalty payments could be delayed. And since dramatic Leo is involved, your creative endeavors may be slowed down in some way.

AT A GLANCE
July 9—Venus enters Virgo
July 10—Jupiter turns direct in Scorpio
July 12—Solar eclipse in Cancer
July 26—Mercury turns retrograde in Leo
July 27—Lunar eclipse in Aquarius

August 2018
Career opportunities

This month's solar eclipse, on August 11, falls in Leo and should bring new opportunities in your creative endeavors and also with shared resources. Your partner, for example, might get a raise or you could receive a royalty check, an insurance reimbursement or a refund. You could inherit money, too. It's also possible that you have a chance to delve into some facet of the paranormal—either with research or because of a personal experience of some kind.

Pluto and Neptune form challenging angles to the eclipse degree, suggesting an undercurrent of tension and/or confusion.

From August 6 to September 9, Venus moves through Libra. It rules this sign, so it functions at optimal capacity here. And, lucky you, it's transiting your career area. During this transit, your professional life unfolds with greater ease. Your relationships with peers and bosses are good. People are attracted to you and your ideas. If you're in sales, your numbers spike during this transit. If you're self-employed, you suddenly have multiple projects.

On the 19th, Mercury turns direct in Leo. Wait a few days to let Mercury stabilize, and then sign your contracts, plan your trips and do everything else that went on hold during the retrograde. Mercury will be in Leo until September 5.

The full moon in Pisces on the 26th brings sudden, unexpected news related to a creative endeavor, a sibling or a neighbor. If you've been considering a move, then you may find the ideal neighborhood. Be sure to follow your impulses and hunches.

Mars turns direct in your sign on August 27. Now you move forward with greater momentum on personal and professional endeavors. Look back to March for clues about how this transit may play out. It will be in your sign until September 10.

AT A GLANCE
August 6—Venus enters Libra
August 11—Solar eclipse in Leo
August 19—Mercury turns direct in Leo
August 26—Full moon in Pisces
August 27—Mars turns direct in Capricorn

September 2018
5 stars

September is jammed with astrological events and shifting energies. Fortunately, the majority of the transits and events occur in earth signs, so you'll do just fine.

It begins on the 5th, when Mercury enters fellow earth sign Virgo. This transit lasts until September 21, and during this time, your conscious mind is detail-oriented, precise and focused. Tackle anything that requires this kind of attention. Whether you're arranging your itinerary for a foreign trip or writing a book, Mercury in Virgo is helpful.

On the 6th, Saturn turns direct in Capricorn, another major plus for you. Look back to the first part of the year, before Saturn turned retro on April 17. What was going on in your life then? How was Saturn working in your favor, solidifying relationships and bolstering the structures in your life? That same type of energy will be functioning at optimal levels again.

Venus enters Scorpio, and there's a new moon in Virgo on September 9. Both of these events are in your favor. Let's take the new moon in Virgo first. The opportunities it brings expand your world in some significant way because Jupiter is friendly to this new moon. The possibilities range from a foreign trip to a publishing venture to something connected with higher education. Pluto also forms a beneficial angle to this new moon, suggesting that you're in control of the situation.

Venus travels direct in Scorpio until October 5, then it slips back into Libra on the 31st and turns direct again in that sign on November 16. While it's in direct motion, your sexuality is greatly heightened and so is your need to find the absolute bottom line truth of whatever you're doing. Your network of friends and acquaintances is expanding under Jupiter's influence, and as it travels with Venus, women play a more prominent role, particularly in your social life. Your creative drive is also stronger.

On the 10th Mars enters Aquarius and your financial area once again. Look back to the period from May 16 to June 26, when Mars turned retrograde. How was your financial situation? Were you more aggressive in pursuing financial goals? This same energy will be present again until November 15, when Mars enters Pisces.

From September 21 to October 9, Mercury transits Libra and your career area. This period should be one in which your artistic sensibilities blossom and spill over into your professional life. Your people skills are also enhanced. If you're self-employed, you land new clients and accounts, and your income should rise accordingly. If you work in a creative field, then you find exactly the right balance you need for a particular project or endeavor.

On the 24th, the full moon in Aries brings news about your family/home, or because Aries is involved, about some entrepreneurial venture in which you're involved. You may be more impatient or impulsive on or around this date. Don't speed while driving, but follow your impulses. They may lead you to something exciting and entirely new.

AT A GLANCE

September 5—Mercury enters Virgo
September 6—Saturn turns direct in Capricorn
September 9—Venus enters Scorpio, new moon in Virgo
September 10—Mars enters Aquarius
September 21—Mercury enters Libra
September 24—Full moon in Aries

October 2018
A bit bumpy in the romance department

For the most part, October will suit you. The one caveat to this is the Venus retrograde in Scorpio that begins on October 5 and ends on November 16. Since Venus rules love and romance, money and the arts, you could encounter some bumps in a romantic relationship. If so, you may take a second look at the relationship. Don't make any decisions, though, until after the planet turns direct. On the creative front, your endeavors could slow down or be delayed, and the same could be true with finances.

Sometimes during Venus retrogrades, we experience physical discomforts related to our environment. The AC or heat in our car, home or work place go haywire. If you're traveling, something about your accommodations gets messed up. These aren't earth-shattering events by any means, just minor irritations.

On the 8th, the new moon in Libra occurs in your career area and should bring new professional opportunities. If you've been job-hunting, then you may land the job you wanted. If you've been hoping to find a new career path, it may find you. You could get a raise and promotion, a new office or a new boss or have the chance to strike out on your own.

From October 9 to 31, Mercury transits Scorpio and travels with Venus retrograde. These two have plenty to chat about. If you're irritated by a relationship or situation related to Venus retrograde, Mercury encourages you to talk about it. That's probably the worst thing you can do; it only tends to perpetuate the irritation. Instead, get out and about with friends during this transit. Enjoy yourself. Research an area that interests you. Join a ghost hunting group. Have a séance. Fall in love.

The full moon in Taurus on October 24 could bring sudden news about a creative endeavor, a romantic relationship or one of your kids. The news is unexpected but positive. Plan a romantic getaway with the one you love.

On October 31, Halloween, Mercury enters Sagittarius and the quiet part of your chart. That's something of an oxymoron since Sagittarius is anything but quiet. But between now and November 16, when Mercury turns retrograde for the last time this year, you're able to understand the big picture of whatever you're involved in. You may also feel somewhat restless, nomadic and eager to get out into the world.

AT A GLANCE
October 5—Venus turns retrograde in Scorpio
October 8—New moon in Libra
October 9—Mercury enters Scorpio
October 24—Full moon in Taurus
October 31—Mercury enters Sagittarius

November 2018
Jupiter shifts signs

It's another astrologically crowded month, and it all begins with a new moon in Scorpio on November 7. You should enjoy this one. Not only is Scorpio a water sign that mixes well with your earth energy, but other planets are making beneficial aspects to this new moon. New opportunities may include new friends and social contacts, a chance to do "Scorpionic" things like ghost hunting, a past-life regression or research into the profound mysteries of life and the nature of reality.

On the 8th, Jupiter makes a major shift when it moves into Sagittarius. This transit lasts for about thirteen months and expands your opportunities for international travel, for higher education, for exploring your spirituality and worldview and for anything else that Jupiter governs. The transit occurs in the quiet part of your chart, the twelfth house, so it's excellent for expanding your own unconscious, for delving into who you are and what makes you tick.

From November 15 to December 31, Mars moves through compatible water sign Pisces. This transit galvanizes all forms of communication and short-distance travel. You may start a blog, build a website, start a book or do some public speaking. You also may find yourself making a lot of short trips—for errands, carpooling or general running around. Your siblings and neighbors also play into this transit in various ways, and you could be spending more time with them.

Now we come to the last Mercury retrograde of the year. It begins on November 16, with Mercury turning retrograde in Sagittarius, in the quiet area of your chart. It slides back into Scorpio on December 1 and finally turns direct in that sign on December 6. While it's retro in Sagittarius, old issues may surface, stuff you thought you had resolved. If you've been harboring a grudge against someone or holding onto anger, the retro prompts you to deal with it. Old friends and lovers you haven't seen in years could also resurface.

In order to navigate this retrograde more successfully, reread the March and July roundups for general guidelines, and look over the suggestions in the Mercury retro section in the introduction.

Also on the 16th, Venus turns direct in Libra, in your career area. Lucky you! From November 16 to December 2, you once again benefit professionally from this transit. Look back at the August roundup for how this transit impacts you.

The full moon in Gemini on November 23 should bring news about work. Your hours could change, you might be able to work periodically from home, you find the ideal employee, your project is green lighted by the powers that be or you're tapped to head a publicity campaign.

AT A GLANCE
November 7—New moon in Scorpio
November 8—Jupiter enters Sagittarius
November 15—Mars enters Pisces
November 16—Mercury turns retrograde in Sagittarius, Venus turns direct in Libra
November 23—Full moon in Gemini

December 2018
Looking forward

Take time early in December to evaluate your progress this year in all facets of your life. Then ask yourself what you would like to experience and achieve in 2019. Make a list. Post it where you'll see it often. This encourages you to create realistic goals for next year.

On December 2, Venus enters Scorpio once again, and, just in time for the holidays, your social life takes off. Friends are coming out of the proverbial woodwork. Romance is also in the air. If you're not involved right now, you may be before the year's end. If you're in a relationship, then things are undoubtedly going very well sexually, emotionally and creatively. This transit takes you into the new year and lasts until January 7.

On the 6th, Mercury turns direct in Scorpio, so now things improve immeasurably. Then on the 12th, Mercury enters Sagittarius and remains there until January 4, 2019. During this transit, you have an opportunity to tie up any loose ends from projects and endeavors that you began between October 31 and November 16, when Mercury turned retro in Sadge.

The new moon in Sagittarius on the 7th is an ideal time to have a holiday get-together. Sagittarius it a gregarious sign, and during the holidays, people tend to be in fun-loving moods. So indulge yourself!

The full moon in Cancer on the 22nd brings news about and insights into a business or personal partnership. The strong nurturing component of Cancer is evident, particularly in your relationship with loved ones.

AT A GLANCE
December 2—Venus enters Scorpio
December 6—Mercury turns direct in Scorpio
December 7—New moon in Sagittarius
December 12—Mercury enters Sagittarius
December 22—Full moon in Cancer

Reflection
Take a few minutes to jot down your thoughts about how this year went for you. Did you experience pivotal life events like a marriage or divorce? The birth of a child? A child leaving home? Did you make a career move? Are you happier now? How can what you learned this year benefit you in 2019?

_____

_____

_____

_____

_____

Happy New Year!

Aquarius 2018

Your sign is ruled by Uranus, the planet of sudden, unexpected change. Its job is to shake us out of our habits, routines and comfortable ruts so that new people and experiences can flow in. It usually does this by disrupting the routines and usually not in a gentle way! Uranus takes about seven years to transit a sign.

For the last seven years, it has been in fire sign Aries. During this transit, Uranus was friendly to your sun. It sharpened your communication skills, urged you to become more of an entrepreneur and to take risks and rearranged certain facets of your life. You may have moved, started a new job or career, gotten married or divorced or started a family.

On May 15, Uranus will move into Taurus and will be there until November, when it slips back into Aries due to a retrograde. In 2019, it enters Taurus again and will be there until July 2025. It would be to your advantage to have your natal chart in front of you so you can see where that sign actually is in your chart. For the purpose of this book, I use a solar chart—where your sign is placed on the ascendant. This means that in a solar chart, Taurus falls in your home and family area. Based on that, some of the possibilities of this transit might include: a move or a birth or someone moving into or out of your home. You may build a home, buy property, get married or divorced or launch a home-based business. In other words, pivotal life events are often part of a Uranus transit.

2018 should be a good year for you, Aquarius, as long you try to remain flexible and are alert for synchronistic cues from your environment.

January 2018
Mixed, then romantic

Welcome to 2018! The good news is that the year doesn't start with a Mercury retrograde, as 2017 did. In fact, the action begins on New Year's Day with a full moon in water sign Cancer, in the daily work area of your chart. There could be news about your job or a co-worker or, because Cancer is involved, news about a family member. If you've been working on a project since last year, you now complete it.

From January 11 to 31, Mercury moves through Capricorn and the quiet, contemplative area of your chart. This is something of an oxymoron since Capricorn is usually professionally ambitious and eager to be out and about in the larger world. That said, this transit brings your conscious attention to career matters and to your inner motivations. You may be working more behind the scenes during this period, perhaps because you're on deadline for a project or simply need more time alone to complete something.

On the 31st, there are two events: Mercury enters your sign, and there's a lunar eclipse in Leo. The Mercury transit lasts until February 18 and should be pleasant for you. Your mind works at lightning speed, unusual ideas come to you and you may be more stubborn than usual! You get together with like-minded friends during this transit. You love a lively discussion about ideas.

The lunar eclipse in Leo on January 31 falls in your partnership area. If something about a business or personal partnership has been brewing beneath the surface, then it probably emerges on or around the time of this eclipse. And because Leo loves drama, the scene that unfolds could be overly dramatic. It's best to just take a deep breath and disengage from any confrontation.

The 16th features a new moon in Capricorn. New professional opportunities that come your way could include a chance to work behind the scenes in some capacity—perhaps on a freelance project that boosts your monthly income.

Between January 17 and February 10, Venus moves through your sign, making this period one of the most romantic and creative for you all year. The only other period that's equal to it falls between April 24 and May 19, when Venus transits the romance and creativity sector of your chart. During this transit doors open, and people are attracted to you and your ideas. Life in general has a greater flow and smoothness to it. If you're not involved in a relationship, then you may be before this transit ends. It's a great time to dive into your creative endeavors. Your unusual ideas seek expression.

Between January 26 and March 17, Mars transits Sagittarius. You'll enjoy this period. You spend more time with friends and acquaintances and could head overseas with a group or with several friends on some sort of quest. Mars is the planet that makes stuff happen, and one way or another, you're moving toward the realization of a dream.

AT A GLANCE
January 1—Full moon in Cancer
January 11—Mercury enters Capricorn
January 16—New moon in Capricorn
January 17—Venus enters Aquarius
January 26—Mars enters Sagittarius
January 31—Mercury enters Aquarius, lunar eclipse in Leo

February 2018
New opportunities

The month isn't quite as crammed as January. But on February 15, there's a solar eclipse in your sign. These eclipses are about outer events (as opposed to the inner events of lunar eclipses), and this one should bring a new opportunity that is personally satisfying. Thanks to a beneficial angle from Uranus, the opportunity appears suddenly and unexpectedly, so be prepared to be surprised! It could impact any area of your life. It could be a birth, marriage, new job or career or a move. In other words, pivotal life events. With solar eclipses, something begins and something else ends.

Before the eclipse occurs, Venus enters Pisces on the 10th, where it will be until March 6. This transit should benefit you financially. You may sell a creative endeavor or land a freelance project that appeals to your artistic sensibilities. Whatever you can imagine during this transit, you can create. Venus in Pisces sometimes triggers a desire to change your appearance—a new hairstyle, new clothing and a new you! There's also a dreamy, romantic quality to this transit. If you're involved in a relationship, try to go with the flow. Plan a romantic getaway, a long weekend where the weather is warm and sunny and preferably near the ocean.

On the 18th, Mercury joins Venus in Pisces and the two travel together until March 6. They have plenty to chat about—love, money and creativity. You're more compassionate and loving during these two transits. Your imagination is ramped up, and your ideas are tinged with idealism. Your spirituality also deepens.

AT A GLANCE
February 10—Venus enters Pisces
February 15—Solar eclipse in Aquarius
February 18—Mercury enters Pisces

March 2018
Yikes!

March is one of the busiest months in 2018, with nine astrological events. This means rapidly shifting energy that you have to adapt to. Try to go with the flow, whatever it happens to be.

The full moon in Virgo on March 1 highlights resources you share with others—a parent, child, spouse or even a roommate. There may be positive news about a mortgage or loan for which you've applied. Both Saturn and Neptune form beneficial angles to this full moon, suggesting that there might be some confusion about money, but only because you don't have all the details. Once you have all the information you need, you can make an informed decision.

On March 6, Mercury and Venus enter Aries, transits you'll enjoy. Mercury's transit lasts until April 15 because it turns retrograde on March 22. We'll get to that in a moment. Venus's transit lasts until March 31. While both planets are in direct motion, your communication skills are stellar—energetic, vivacious and enthusiastic. You feel quite adventurous. If you've been thinking about opening your business and becoming self-employed in some way, do it before Mercury turns retro. The Venus transit amplifies all your emotions, particularly where romance and your creative endeavors are concerned. If a relationship begins during this transit, it's likely to be infused with passion.

Now, about that Mercury retrograde, the first one this year. Before we discuss it, reread the sections in the introductions to 2018 and 2017 about the kinds of things you may experience when the planet of communication is up to no good. This one occurs in the communication area of your chart, which enhances the possibility that you'll be misunderstood. If you have any appointments scheduled, double check the times and dates. Try not to get into squabbles with neighbors and siblings, also represented in this area of your chart, because you might end up saying something you can't take back.

The best guidelines for navigating any Mercury retrograde bear repeating: don't launch a new endeavor or business, get married or plan a trip. Follow the rule of the three Rs, if possible: revise, reconsider and review.

Jupiter turns retrograde in Scorpio on March 8, in your career area. Jupiter has been in this sign since mid-October 2017, and your career has undoubtedly benefited, expanding in new and exciting ways. Perhaps you started a new career or were promoted with a substantial raise. Maybe you've been traveling internationally for work or got a book published. Jupiter's expansion continues during the retrograde, which lasts until July 10, but now the expansion is more internal. Your spiritual beliefs and worldview expand in some way. You may embark on a spiritual quest that takes you overseas. However the specifics unfold, use this retrograde period to get to know yourself.

The 17th brings two astrological events: Mars enters Capricorn and the quiet part of your chart, and a new moon in Pisces occurs in your financial area. The Mars transit lasts until May 16, and if you're smart, you'll use its energy to plant seeds for what you would like to achieve and experience when Mars enters your sign in May. While the planet of action and sexuality is in Capricorn, you're working diligently behind the scenes on a project that may have a tight deadline. You could be delving into your own psyche, too, figuring out why you make certain decisions and move in particular directions. It would be a great time to get a past-life regression.

The new moon in Pisces should bring new money-making opportunities. They could come in the form of a part-time job, a freelance gig or the sale of a creative endeavor. A challenging angle from Saturn suggests that not all these possibilities pan out. But the one or two that do have staying power.

On March 31, Venus enters Taurus, where it will be until April 24, and there's a full moon in fellow air sign Libra. Since Venus rules Taurus, it functions well here. Your family life is pleasant during this transit. Everyone gets along, although you or someone around you may be more stubborn than usual. There may be a tendency to overindulge in rich foods, but you can easily balance that with moderation and regular exercise. Since Taurus is a sensual sign, your love life should hum along at a pace that suits you.

The full moon in Libra should bring something to a culmination point in a relationship. You're more aware of the need for balance in this relationship, but may be unsure about how to attain it. Talk it over with the other person. Several planets form difficult angles to this full moon, but now is the time to talk things over.

AT A GLANCE
March 1—Full moon in Virgo
March 6—Mercury enters Aries, Venus enters Aries
March 8—Jupiter turns retro in Scorpio
March 17—Mars enters Capricorn, new moon in Pisces
March 22—Mercury turns retro in Aries
March 31—Venus enters Taurus, full moon in Libra

April 2018
Relief

Fortunately, April's energies are much calmer than what you experienced in March. On the 15th, there's a new moon in Aries, and Mercury turns direct in that same sign. The change in Mercury's direction is a relief, and until May 13, you have the opportunity to revisit events and situations that occurred between March 6 and 22, when Mercury was last direct in Aries. Reread last month's roundup about Mercury.

The new moon in Aries is conjunct Uranus, so new opportunities that surface do so suddenly and without warning. You may land a writing project or a speaking gig or have an opportunity to teach. You and a sibling or neighbor may join forces on a project. Your trailblazing spirit takes you into a new adventure.

On the 17th, Saturn turns retrograde in Capricorn and remains that way until September 6. While Saturn has been in Capricorn—since mid-December of 2017—you have been shoring up the inner structures of your psyche and that, in turn, strengthens the structures in your external life. Now, as Saturn retrogrades, you dig deeper into yourself. You pay closer attention to your dreams, which may hold important insights and information. It would be to your benefit to read up on lucid dreaming, where you come awake inside your dreams and learn to manipulate and control them.

Between April 24 and May 19, Venus moves through Gemini. This is the other period mentioned in the March roundup—perfectly romantic, creative and joyful. You may discover a new hobby or passion during this transit and indulge yourself completely. It could be writing, mountain climbing, running a co-op or spearheading a publicity campaign. You've got the Midas touch during this transit, Aquarius. Don't squander it!

The full moon in Scorpio on the 29th highlights your career. There could be professional news (a promotion, a raise, a new boss or a new office), or something you've been working on reaches completion. Just remember that when Scorpio is involved, the bottom line is what you're after, and with a full moon in that sign, the bottom line is exposed.

AT A GLANCE
April 15—New moon in Aries, Mercury turns direct in Aries
April 17—Saturn turns retrograde in Capricorn
April 24—Venus enters Gemini
April 29—Full moon in Scorpio

May 2018
A Uranian shift

There's a major planetary shift this month that is part of May's concentration on Taurus's earth energy, and it occurs on the 15th. Uranus makes its transition into Taurus, where it will be until November. It then slips back into Aries because of a retrograde and remains there until 2019 when it reenters Taurus and stays for the next seven years, until July 2025. Since Uranus rules your sign, its movement is always important for you. Reread the introduction to your sign for 2018 about the Uranus transit and what it means for you.

Before Uranus moves into Taurus, Mercury does so on May 13 and remains there until May 29. During this time, your thought process will be unusually active, seeking out new ideas and new areas of research through books, the Internet and social media. You may be looking for ways to renovate your home as inexpensively as possible or could be getting rid of stuff in anticipation of a move. You're more stubborn than usual, too.

The 15th features Uranus's move into Taurus, but there's also a new moon in Taurus that should usher in some nice opportunities for your home and family life. You may have a chance to beautify your home in some way—new paint in brighter, bolder colors, new furniture or maybe even a new spring garden. Taurus often enjoys gardening, and even if it usually isn't an Aquarian thing, indulge the earth energy. Perhaps by summer you'll be eating vegetables and fruits from the garden!

From May 16 forward to mid-November, Mars will be in and out of your sign due to a retrograde. But while it's in direct motion until June 26, Aquarius, you've got the wind at your back and so much forward momentum that you can accomplish just about anything. Your sexuality and communication skills are also heightened. Pity the fool who starts an argument concerning something you feel passionate about!

From May 19 to June 13, Venus transits water sign Cancer. Your intuitive skills are enhanced during this period and serve you well in your daily work. If co-workers come to you with their concerns, you're an excellent listener and dispense good advice. The same is true if you're the boss and employees approach you about their concerns and problems.

Two events occur on the 29th: there's a full moon in Sagittarius, and Mercury enters Gemini. The full moon suits you—fire sign Sagittarius is compatible with your sun sign. And Mars is still in your sign, so there's plenty of energy to work with. Your social calendar is crowded, and you may be spending more time than usual with friends.

Mercury moves through Gemini until June 12. Your muse is relentlessly active during this transit. You may be writing, engaged in public speaking or teaching and mingling with people in new and exciting ways. You could be thinking a lot about romance—an existing relationship or one you would like to have.

May 13—Mercury enters Taurus
May 15—New moon in Taurus, Uranus enters Taurus
May 16—Mars enters Aquarius
May 19—Venus enters Cancer
May 29—Full moon in Sagittarius, Mercury enters Gemini

June 2018
Busy & romantic

It's a busy month with a wild mix of energies. To stay grounded, it's a good idea to start a regular exercise regime, if you don't have one already.

From June 12–29, Mercury transits Cancer. Your conscious focus is on your daily work routine and your family. You're able to tune in on other people's feelings and moods and, in some instances, absorb those moods. So, it's important that you associate with positive people. If someone in your environment is belligerent, simply disengage from the situation. Allow your intuition to guide you in decisions.

On the 13th, two events will thrill you: a new moon in Gemini and the beginning of Venus's transit through Leo. The new moon should bring in opportunities for you to delve into your creativity as only an Aquarian can by immersing yourself in the deeper part of your being that is wise beyond measure. Regardless of how this opportunity comes to you, it's likely that you recognize it the second it hits your doorstep.

The Venus transit occurs in your opposite sign and lasts until July 9. During this time, you and your partner could move in together, get engaged or married or deepen your commitment to each other in some way. If you're already married, then the two of you enjoy a romantic period in which you are reminded why you're together. On the creative front, you may find the ideal partner for a joint venture.

Mars turns retro in your sign on June 26, slides back into Capricorn and turns direct in that sign on August 27. Yes, this is a lengthy retrograde, but it enables you to take an honest look at the parameters you establish between yourself and others. With the Mars energy now directed inward, you may experience periods of frustration or anger about how slowly things are moving. Turn your focus elsewhere, like to the parts of your life that are working well!

The full moon in Capricorn on June 28 may bring sudden, unexpected news about your career. It should be positive. It's also possible that you complete sessions with a therapist or a series of health-related visits. Uranus forms a beneficial angle to this full moon, so events on or around this date occur quickly and catch you by surprise.

Mercury joins Venus in Leo on June 29. The two travel together until July 9, when Venus moves into Virgo. Until then, they are busy chatting it up about your romantic and business partnerships, and something may be brewing between them on the creative front. Mercury says,

Let's try this.... Venus briefly mulls it over and replies, *I'm on board!* Whether or not the idea goes somewhere depends on how quickly you can work before Mercury turns retro on July 26.

AT A GLANCE
June 12—Mercury enters Cancer
June 13—New moon in Gemini, Venus enters Leo
June 26—Mars turns retrograde in Aquarius
June 28—Full moon in Capricorn
June 29—Mercury enters Leo

July 2018
Frenzied but with perks

If you feel somewhat frenzied this month, blame the eclipses! The first one on July 12 is a solar eclipse in Cancer and should bring in new opportunities related to your family (the Cancer part of the equation) and your daily work. Possibilities? You and your partner could discover you're going to become parents, or your living situation changes in a positive way.

In terms of work, you could get a promotion or a new boss, hire a new employee, experience a spike in sales or be hired for a freelance job. Thanks to a beneficial angle from Neptune to the eclipse degree, whatever unfolds as a result of this event, your creativity and spiritual beliefs are involved. And thanks to expansive Jupiter's angle to this eclipse degree, your life is expanded in some way. Pluto forms a difficult angle, however, which could indicate that you run up against an authority figure. But with so many other beneficial aspects on your side, you come out ahead.

On the 27th, the lunar eclipse in your sign brings a personal issue or concern up front and center in your awareness. With Mars close to this eclipse degree, however, you're able to act quickly and decisively.

Before either of these eclipses occurs, Venus enters Virgo on July 9 and will be there until August 6. Your partner or someone else with whom you share resources may get a raise, a mortgage or loan for which you've applied is approved or a royalty check arrives. Avoid self-criticism and strive for perfection in everything you do during this transit.

Jupiter turns direct in Scorpio on the 10th, a nice bonus for your career. Jupiter's expansion now occurs in the outer world once again, and it moves on toward its appointment with Sagittarius on November 8.

From July 26 to August 19, Mercury is moving retrograde in Leo, your opposite sign. This retro occurs in your partnership area, so take extra care to communicate clearly with business partners and your spouse or romantic partner. You may feel somewhat stifled creatively. Rather than diving into a new project, follow the three Rs—revise, review and reconsider. Reread the section in the 2018 introduction on Mercury retrogrades, and follow those guidelines for a more successful navigation of this period.

July 9—Venus enters Virgo
July 10—Jupiter turns direct in Scorpio
July 12—Solar eclipse in Cancer
July 26—Mercury turns retrograde in Leo
July 27—Lunar eclipse in Aquarius

August 2018
Great energy

Before you kick back this month and enjoy the final days of summer, prepare yourself for the solar eclipse in your sign on August 11. Yes, it does seem that the cosmos has targeted the Aquarius/Leo axis unfairly this year, but take heart. In 2019, there's just one lunar eclipse that will hit the same axis—in Leo.

Yet, solar eclipses often portend a new chapter in our lives, new opportunities that enable us to move in unexplored directions. With this one, you may be tapped for a project that enables you to explore your creativity in new, exciting ways. Or you might team up with a friend or partner to launch or promote a business, website, book or some other product or service. It's also possible that you and a romantic partner may deepen your commitment to each other. You move in together, get engaged or married or start a family. Whatever the opportunities are, embrace them.

On the 6th, Venus enters fellow air sign Libra, and until September 9, you're in a wonderful place in life. Other people are attracted to you and your ideas, your self-esteem and self-confidence soar, and your creative adrenaline is flowing beautifully. If you're not involved with anyone when the transit begins, then before it ends you may meet someone special who is from a different culture or country. This is also a social transit, so don't be surprised if invitations roll in to attend concerts and art exhibits.

Mercury turns direct in Leo on August 19, and between then and September 5, your communication with a partner is dramatic and from the heart. You're able to straighten out anything that went awry when Mercury was retrograde.

The full moon in Pisces on the 26th brings sudden, unexpected news about a financial matter. It looks like good news, Aquarius, but don't go on a shopping spree until the money is in the bank!

AT A GLANCE
August 6—Venus enters Libra
August 11—Solar eclipse in Leo
August 19—Mercury turns direct in Leo
August 26—Full moon in Pisces
August 27—Mars turns direct in Capricorn

September 2018
Nearly 5 stars

Lots of astrological events crowd this month's calendar, and for the most part, you'll be happy about them.

On the 5th, Mercury enters earth sign Virgo, where it will be until September 21. This transit makes you more discerning, particularly about finances. You may be scrutinizing your budget and working on some way to increase your income and cut down your expenses. If you've applied for a mortgage, loan or new insurance, you won't gloss anything over. You pay attention to details now.

On September 6, Saturn turns direct in Capricorn and makes it easier for you to implement your particular strategies for achieving your goals. You may be more solitary during this transit, but it enables you to succeed at whatever you're doing. Before this transit is complete in April 2020, you will have much firmer structures in your life. Saturn rules Capricorn and functions well in this sign.

Venus enters Scorpio and your career area on the 9th, and there's a new moon in Virgo. The first transit lasts through the end of the year because of a retrograde. But until October 5, Venus is moving direct and brings a touch of magic to your career. People are more open and receptive to your ideas, doors open and there's a certain psychic intensity about you that other people sense. If a romantic relationship begins during this transit, it's likely to be emotionally powerful, sexually charged and transformative in some way.

The new moon in Virgo brings new financial opportunities for either you or your partner or for both of you. Your partner could get a raise, or you might be invited to teach a workshop or seminar on an esoteric topic or your particular area of expertise. You might also have the chance to lower the interest on your mortgage payment by refinancing or consolidating debt.

From September 10 to November 15, Mars transits your sign again. Look back to the May roundup, when Mars was also in your sign, to see what kinds of things you can expect. Your physical energy will be much stronger, and your resolve to pursue your interests and goals will be so powerful that you'll be moving full steam ahead on anything you tackle. Just be sure to have a regular physical exercise routine. You'll need to burn off some of that excess energy.

Mercury transits Libra from September 21 to October 9, and you'll be pleased with life during this time. Libra, a fellow air sign, is sociable and artistic, with a highly developed aesthetic sense. You may be taking in art exhibits and concerts and chatting up a storm with friends in your local environment and through social media. If you're a political activist, then transit enables you to get your point of view across with great force.

The full moon in Aries on September 24 brings news about a sibling, neighbor or communication endeavor, or a project you've been working on is completed. Aries infuses you with greater passion and enthusiasm, an entrepreneurial spirit and a kind of fearlessness.

AT A GLANCE

September 5—Mercury enters Virgo
September 6—Saturn turns direct in Capricorn
September 9—Venus enters Scorpio, new moon in Virgo
September 10—Mars enters Aquarius
September 21—Mercury enters Libra
September 24—Full moon in Aries

October 2018
Career focus

October is relatively calmer than last month, except that the planet of love and romance turns retrograde in Scorpio on October 5, slips back into Libra on the 31st and then turns direct in that sign on November 16. The thing to remember with a Venus retrograde is that even though it may affect your love life and finances, the impact is more internal. You may be taking a deeper look at your relationships with your spouse or partner, sister, daughter or other women in your life. Are these relationships meeting your needs?

There is sometimes a physical discomfort factor with Venus retro. The AC or heat in your home, car or office goes haywire, the hot water at home or the office stops working or you lock yourself out of your house. Since this retro occurs in your career area, projects that are important to you may be delayed. An office flirtation may end. Creatively, you may feel stifled. You really aren't, you just have to dig a bit deeper.

The 8th brings a beautiful new moon in fellow air sign Libra. You may have an opportunity to venture overseas with a group of like-minded people or to have your own art or photography exhibit. A publisher could bid on your book or novel. New opportunities also surface in friendships with creative, artistic people.

From October 9 to 31, Mercury transits Scorpio and your career area. Your focus is definitely on professional matters now. Even though Venus is retrograde in this same area, your communication skills remain sharp, and your intuition is spot on. If you launch any new products or projects, do so on the new moon in Libra or between then and the next full moon in Taurus on the 24th.

The full moon in Taurus should bring sudden, unexpected news related to your home, family or personal environment. Thanks to a beneficial angle to this moon from Saturn, the news will have long-term effects. Since Taurus often involves finances, the news could be in that area as well.

Mercury enters Sagittarius on October 21, turns retro on November 16, slides back into Scorpio on December 1 and turns direct in that sign December 6, carrying you into the new year. While it's moving direct in Sagittarius, you're hanging out more with friends, discussing politics, the nature of reality and your other passions. You're after the larger picture now.

October 5—Venus turns retrograde in Scorpio
October 8—New moon in Libra
October 9—Mercury enters Scorpio
October 24—Full moon in Taurus
October 31—Mercury enters Sagittarius

November 2018
Jupiter shift

It's a full month and most of it will suit you. On the 7th, the new moon in Scorpio should bring new professional opportunities—a promotion, a raise, the prosperous client who needs your services/product or a new job/career. If you have been hoping to become self-employed, then this new moon helps to bring about your dream. It's more powerful in the sense that it occurs before the Mercury retrograde on November 16.

On the 8th, Jupiter makes a major transition. After thirteen months in Scorpio, it moves into Sagittarius, a fire sign compatible with your sun sign. Between now and December 2019, your life expands in new and exciting ways. Jupiter rules Sagittarius and functions at optimal capacity in this sign. Here are some possibilities about what you can anticipate: new friends who share your interests and passions; foreign travel; publishing ventures; a deeper exploration of your spiritual beliefs and worldview; or involvement with some facet of higher education.

If you have your natal chart, find the house that Sagittarius rules. If it rules your second house, for example, then the expansion will be financial. If it rules the tenth house, then the expansion will occur professionally.

From November 15 to December 31, Mars transits Pisces and your financial area. You're deeply motivated now to earn more money, and your intuition can be helpful in this regard. Follow your hunches and impulses, ask for insights from your dreams, spend time meditating and follow up with action.

On the 16th, the universe seems to try to balance out the stars. Mercury turns retrograde in Sagittarius, but Venus turns direct in Libra! The retro lasts until December 6, and for clues about what it may entail and how to navigate it successfully, look back to the March and July roundups when Mercury was retrograde. Since this retro is in Sadge, the propensity is great for misunderstandings with friends. Communicate as precisely as possible—and not through 140 characters on Twitter! And as always, follow the three Rs: revise, review and reconsider rather than launching anything new.

With Venus turning direct in Libra, you have about two weeks to enjoy its bounties again. Look back to the August roundup, when Venus was last direct in this sign, to see how this energy may manifest itself. On December 2, Venus will move into Scorpio once again.

The full moon in fellow air sign Gemini on the 23ʳᵈ should be a beautiful day to spend with your partner or kids or simply doing whatever it is that you enjoy the most. There may be good news about a creative endeavor.

AT A GLANCE
November 7—New moon in Scorpio
November 8—Jupiter enters Sagittarius
November 15—Mars enters Pisces
November 16—Mercury turns retrograde in Sagittarius, Venus turns direct in Libra
November 23—Full moon in Gemini

December 2018
Anticipating 2019

As the final month of 2018 gets underway, take a few minutes to consider what you would like to experience and achieve in the year ahead. Make a list. Think of it as a list of desires rather than goals. Do you hope to meet your soul mate? Earn a six-figure income? Move? Buy your own home? Start a family? Whatever it is, vividly imagine yourself already living your desire. Back it with emotion. Post the list where you'll see it often.

On December 2, Venus enters Scorpio again and will be in that sign until January 7, 2019. Look back to the September roundup—when Venus was also in Scorpio in direct motion—for a hint about what you can expect. Since this transit occurs in your career area, professional matters should unfold smoothly and effortlessly, particularly after Mercury turns direct in Scorpio on December 6.

For six days, until the 12ᵗʰ, Mercury keeps you focused on your career and your professional relationships, and Venus makes it easy to hobnob and network. If you're self-employed, then you may be pushing against a self-imposed deadline to complete a project before the holidays. On the 12ᵗʰ, Mercury enters Sagittarius, where it remains until January 4, 2019, a perfect placement for enjoying yourself with friends and family over the holidays. Look back at the October roundup, when Mercury last entered Sadge, for what you can expect.

On the 7ᵗʰ, the new moon in Sagittarius brings a crowded social calendar. Invitations for the holidays start rolling in, and new opportunities surface for travel and fun. You're networking more than usual in anticipation of completing whatever you're working on so you can enter the new year with a clean slate.

The full moon in Cancer on December 22 brings news about your daily work or a completion. Perfect! Now you can head into the holidays with the knowledge that you won't be carrying baggage into 2019.

December 2—Venus enters Scorpio

December 6—Mercury turns direct in Scorpio

December 7—New moon in Sagittarius

December 12—Mercury enters Sagittarius

December 22—Full moon in Cancer

Reflection

Are you happy with the way 2018 turned out? What would you have done differently? How can you take the things you learned into the new year to achieve and experience what you want?

_____

_____

_____

_____

_____

Happy New Year!

Pisces 2018

Your sign is ruled by Neptune, which is continuing its fourteen-year transit through Pisces. That transit began in early April 2011, went retrograde for four months, slipped back into Aquarius, returned to Pisces in February 2012 and will stay there until January 2026. Neptune in your sign provides ample opportunities for self-expression, to delve into your creativity and spirituality and to integrate your ideals into your life.

Since Jupiter co-rules your sign, it's a good idea to check on Jupiter's status, too. Jupiter is in Scorpio for most of 2018, forming a beneficial angle to your sun sign. It will be retrograde from March 8 to July 10 and enters Sagittarius on November 8, where it will remain until December 2, 2019. Its transit through Sagittarius will benefit your professional life, and you can read all about it in the December roundup. The monthly predictions also include information on the new and full moons, eclipses, the transits and retrogrades of other planets and what it all may mean for you!

2018 is likely to be a positive year for you as long as you associate with positive, upbeat people. Your intuitive ability deepens, and your creativity expands. Between May and November, when Uranus transits compatible earth sign Taurus before it slips back into Aries again, exciting possibilities come your way!

January 2018
Great start

Welcome to 2018! This year, unlike 2017, does NOT start with Mercury retrograde. It begins with a beautiful full moon in fellow water sign Cancer and brings news about a romantic relationship, a creative endeavor or a member of your family. The intuitive and compassionate component to this moon deepens your own psychic ability and nurturing tendencies.

On the 11th, Mercury enters compatible earth sign Capricorn and remains there until January 31. This transit is ideal for the start of the new year. It keeps you focused and on a singular path toward the completion of a goal. It also prompts you to spend time with friends and any groups to which you belong. Through these social contacts, you're able to clarify a direction in a creative endeavor.

The new moon in Capricorn on the 16th should bring an opportunity that enables you to move closer to realizing a dream. New friends and acquaintances prove to be invaluable resources. Since Capricorn is involved in the lunar equation, the opportunities that surface could be related to your career and professional matters. Social media can prove beneficial. Don't have a Facebook page? Get moving. Are you on Twitter? Pinterest? Tumblr? Periscope? You don't have to go wild with these various venues, but at least have a Facebook page!

From January 17 to February 10, Venus moves through Aquarius and the quiet part of your chart. This period favors interactions with like-minded individuals, small groups that meet somewhere private. If a romance begins during this transit, you may choose to keep it private for a while. But once Venus enters your sign next month, all bets are off! You'll be announcing the news to family and friends.

Mars transits Sagittarius from January 26 to March 17, a major boost for professional matters. You're now able to accomplish a great deal in your career. Mars provides the forward momentum, and since it's in Sagittarius, your physical vitality is practically infinite. You grasp the big picture of whatever you're involved in professionally, and both international travel and publishing could be involved.

On the 31st, Mercury enters Aquarius, where it will be until February 18, and there's a lunar eclipse in Leo. The Mercury transit brings in edgy, idiosyncratic ideas, a penchant for visionary thinking and perhaps some needed solitude. You're planting seeds for when Mercury enters your sign next month.

The lunar eclipse in Leo may be accompanied by some tension, a sense of urgency and, yes, drama. It involves other people's resources—your partner's income and resources you share with a parent, child or roommate. You experience an emotional reaction to whatever the trigger is and must make a rapid decision. Since this eclipse is in Leo, a creative sign with a flair for drama, your own creative endeavors may come under fire.

January 1—Full moon in Cancer
January 11—Mercury enters Capricorn
January 16—New moon in Capricorn
January 17—Venus enters Aquarius
January 26—Mars enters Sagittarius
January 31—Mercury enters Aquarius, lunar eclipse in Leo

February 2018
Awesome

This month also features an eclipse—solar, in Aquarius. The opportunities that surface as a result of this eclipse will arrive suddenly and unexpectedly, and you'll have to act quickly to seize them. At least one opportunity could involve implementing a product or service that you believe can become a cutting edge trend. You're the power behind this idea and can easily persuade others to support it.

Before the eclipse arrives, Venus enters your sign on the 10th and stays there until March 6. These awesome weeks are so romantic and creative that you feel as though you have entered an alternative universe. If you have a regular 9-to-5 job but yearn to earn your living doing what you love, you might consider taking time off to dive into your creative endeavors. It's the ideal time for it, and the universe is now fully supportive. In romance, you and your partner are very much in tune with each other in all the areas that count. If you're not involved with anyone when this transit begins, you probably will be when the transit ends. The only other period that is like this one occurs between May 19 and June 13, when Venus transits Cancer and the romance/creativity area of your chart.

On the 18th, Mercury joins Venus in your sign. Does it get any better than this? Your heart, mind and soul are all on the same page. Your conscious awareness travels to the outer limits of the universe, seeking unusual ideas that you then use in some way. Your intuition and compassion are deepened.

AT A GLANCE
February 10—Venus enters Pisces
February 15—Solar eclipse in Aquarius
February 18—Mercury enters Pisces

March 2018
Hectic

March may have you running for the hills in search of a little peace and solitude. In addition to the new and full moon, two planets turn retrograde, and four planets enter new signs. Hectic is definitely the key word for this month.

The full moon in Virgo on March 1 illuminates your partnership area. There may be news about a romantic or business partner, or you find the ideal partner for your business. With Saturn friendly to this full moon, this partnership will be solid and long-standing. The same goes for any romantic partner you meet on or around this full moon.

On the 6th, both Mercury and Venus enter Aries and your financial area. If you're looking for ways to increase your income, Mercury in Aries helps you find what you need, and the venues may be unusual! Venus here should increase your earnings—but also your spending. Pay cash for your purchases.

On the 8th, Jupiter turns retrograde in Scorpio and doesn't turn direct again until July 10. The expansive nature of this planet now turns inward, and your spiritual beliefs begin to broaden and deepen. If you travel internationally, it's likely that you're on a quest of some kind.

Mars enters Capricorn on March 17, remaining there until May 16, and there's a new moon in your sign. Mars is now moving through that part of your chart that governs your wishes and dreams, the people you hang out with and clubs and organizations to which you belong. With Capricorn as part of the equation, you can make great strides professionally by networking. Other people may provide the means by which you attain some of your career goals. Even though Mercury is retrograde during part of this transit, Mars is the wind at your back and propels you forward.

The new moon in your sign happens just once a year and sets the tone for the next 12 months. Plan for it several days before by making a list of what you would like to experience or achieve in the next year. The items on your list should be regarded as desires rather than goals. Visualize and back these visualizations with emotion. Post the list where you'll see it often. This new moon brings in opportunities that are personally satisfying and can involve just about anything—a new romance, a new job, a new creative endeavor, a move or a spike in your income.

Mercury turns retrograde in Aries on March 22 and straightens out on April 15. Read through the Mercury retrograde section in the introduction for general guidelines that will help you navigate this period more successfully. Since this retro occurs in your financial area, be sure to double check bank statements, bills, ATM withdrawals and credit card purchases. Watch your spending, and pay cash when you can.

Two events occur on March 31: Venus enters Taurus, and there's a full moon in Libra. The Venus transit lasts until April 24 and brings greater ease to all of your communication. This transit enhances your sensuality, could result in stubbornness when it comes to romance and your creative endeavors and confers greater patience and resilience. Venus rules Taurus and functions well here.

The full moon in Libra brings news about a mortgage or loan for which you've applied, an insurance matter or a legal concern. A relationship may reach a culmination or completion.

March 1—Full moon in Virgo
March 6—Mercury enters Aries, Venus enters Aries
March 8—Jupiter turns retro in Scorpio
March 17—Mars enters Capricorn, new moon in Pisces
March 22—Mercury turns retro in Aries
March 31—Venus enters Taurus, full moon in Libra

April 2018
Family time

Compared to March, April is a lot calmer. The 15th features two events: there's a new moon in Aries, and Mercury turns direct in the same sign. The new moon in your financial area should stimulate money-making opportunities. Thanks to a conjunction of Uranus to this new moon, the opportunities come out of the blue and the only thing required of you is to seize them as they arrive. With Mercury now direct in your financial area, you're focused on financial matters and think more like an entrepreneur! Mercury remains direct in Aries until May 13.

On the 17th, Saturn turns retrograde in Capricorn and remains that way until September 6. During this retrograde, you may be scrutinizing the structures of your relationships with people, particularly with friends. Are these friends supportive? Do the friendships meet your needs?

From April 24 to May 19, Venus transits Gemini and the home/family area of your chart. This should be a pleasant period for you, with a lot of movement and activity around your place—people coming and going and plenty of lively conversations. You and your partner are communicating well, and everything in your domestic life should unfold with greater ease.

On the 29th, the full moon in Scorpio brings news that delights you and creates a significant and important change in your life. This moon falls in that area of your chart that governs higher education, spirituality, international travel, law, learning and any experience that expands your mind.

AT A GLANCE
April 15—New moon in Aries, Mercury turns direct in Aries
April 17—Saturn turns retrograde in Capricorn
April 24—Venus enters Gemini
April 29—Full moon in Scorpio

May 2018
Uranus shifts

This month there's a major shift for Uranus. This planet governs—among other things—sudden, unexpected events, and its job is to shake up the status quo and kick us out of our ruts and routines in order to create space for the new. For the last seven years, Uranus has been moving through Aries and your financial area and probably has created a bit of chaos. You may have changed or lost your job or some other source of income. Or perhaps you won the lottery and inherited a lot of money. However the specifics played out for you, the point is that you experienced *change* in your finances and how you earn your daily bread.

When Uranus enters compatible earth sign Taurus and that part of your chart that governs the conscious mind, it's likely that you will notice rather quickly the change in how you think and communicate and in your eagerness to learn new things. You might decide to write a book, have opportunities for public speaking or could start teaching in some capacity. If you have become rigid in your thinking over the years, then this transit may feel uncomfortable because it will shred that rigidity. Embrace the changes, whatever they are and whatever form they take. Reread the introduction to your sign for more details.

Before Uranus enters Taurus, Mercury enters that sign on the 13th and stays there until the 29th. You're more stubborn, patient and resilient and are determined to see projects through to completion. Any obstacles you encounter during this transit don't discourage you or stop you in your tracks. You simply find a way around them.

On the 15th, the same day that Uranus enters Taurus, there's a new moon in that sign. Talk about plenty of grounding energy! This new moon ushers in new opportunities for communication with your siblings and neighbors and in learning and teaching. The specifics of what that could mean range from a writing project, invitations to teach workshops or seminars or a move to another neighborhood.

From May 16 to November 15, Mars will be traveling through Aquarius, then back into Capricorn because of a retrograde next month. While it's transiting Aquarius in direct motion, there's a lot of activity going on behind the scenes. You could be working from home, might be involved in a creative endeavor that requires solitude or could decide to enter therapy. You're preparing yourself for when Mars enters your sign on November 15.

From May 19 to June 13, you enjoy one of the best times for you all year—Venus transits Cancer and the creativity/romance area of your chart. Your muse is attentive, and your lover and partner worship the ground you walk on. Wherever you are, whatever you're doing, people are attracted to you and your ideas. The only other period that matches this occurred between February 2 and March 6, when Venus transited your sun sign. So make the most of this period, Pisces!

On May 29, there's a full moon in Sagittarius, and Mercury enters Gemini. This full moon occurs in your career area and should bring professional news. Both Mars and Jupiter form beneficial angles to this full moon, so whatever the news is, it expands your professional options in some way and enables you to move forward with great momentum. Mercury's transit through Gemini, a sign it rules, should bring plenty of networking opportunities and open communication with family members and others in your personal environment. You may be conducting research of some kind and planning a trip, perhaps the family's summer vacation.

AT A GLANCE
May 13—Mercury enters Taurus
May 15—New moon in Taurus, Uranus enters Taurus
May 16—Mars enters Aquarius
May 19—Venus enters Cancer
May 29—Full moon in Sagittarius, Mercury enters Gemini

June 2018
Varied

On the 12th, Mercury joins Venus in Cancer, and for a single day these two travel together in the romance/creativity area of your chart. They have plenty to chat about. Plan something special for today. Whether it's spending time with your partner, taking a road trip or working on a creative endeavor, the energy favors enjoyment. Mercury remains here until June 29, and during this transit, your mind is exceptionally intuitive. Use that intuition to reach deep within yourself.

On the 13th, Venus enters Leo, and there's a new moon in Gemini. The Venus transit lasts until July 9 and should facilitate your daily work life. Your relationships with employees, co-workers and bosses should unfold more smoothly, and you're enjoying the projects you're involved in. But since Venus is in Leo, there may be more drama than usual. An office flirtation may turn into something more.

The new moon in Gemini brings new opportunities to your home and family life and offers opportunities for self-expression that should delight you. You and your partner may learn that you're going to be parents, you may decide to put your home on the market or you could be house hunting.

From June 26 to August 27, Mars is retrograde in Aquarius and slides back into Capricorn before it turns direct. While Mars is retrograde in Aquarius, you may be dealing with old issues that you've been pushing aside for a while, perhaps in the hopes that whatever it is would just go away. Now is the time to resolve the issues.

On June 28, the full moon in Capricorn should bring an influx of social invitations and news about a friend or, because Capricorn in involved, about a professional matter. Full moons are also about completion and culmination, so an event, situation or relationship may be ending or reaching a peak.

Mercury transits Leo from June 29 to September 5—long for Mercury, but it's due to a retrograde next month. While it's moving direct in Leo, it travels with Venus until July 9 and adds flair to your verbal and written communication. If you do any public speaking during this transit, you come across as an orator!

AT A GLANCE
June 12—Mercury enters Cancer
June 13—New moon in Gemini, Venus enters Leo
June 26—Mars turns retrograde in Aquarius
June 28—Full moon in Capricorn
June 29—Mercury enters Leo

July 2018
Good energy

This month's two eclipses may bring their share of tension and anxiety, but also usher in new insights, news and opportunities. The solar eclipse in Cancer on July 12 should bring new opportunities in romance and love, creativity and everything you do for enjoyment and pleasure. It may also bring new opportunities connected to home and family because it occurs in the sign of Cancer. Your ruler, Neptune, is friendly to the eclipse degree, and so is Jupiter, which turns direct five days before this eclipse. So the opportunities that surface will broaden your life significantly and may have a creative facet.

The lunar eclipse in Aquarius on the 27th may prompt you to look inward and take a closer look at why you react emotionally to certain issues.

Between July 9 and August 6, Venus transits Virgo, your opposite sign. As it moves through your partnership area, both personal and professional partnerships should benefit. You and your partner exercise more discernment about your relationship and shed unrealistic expectations of each other. A business partner—agent, manager, accountant or anyone involved in your professional life—makes suggestions that please you.

Once Jupiter turns direct in Scorpio on the 10th, its expansion turns toward the outer world once again. You may be traveling overseas before the end of the year or could land a nice publishing deal.

Mercury turns retro in Leo on the 26th and between then and August 19, when it turns direct again, irritating snafus may surface in your daily work life and with your creative endeavors. You may feel that your job stifles your creativity. There could be misunderstandings with bosses, employees and co-workers. Read over the Mercury retrograde section in the introduction for general guidelines to follow to navigate this period more successfully. Also, take a look at the March roundup, when Mercury was last retrograde.

July 9—Venus enters Virgo
July 10—Jupiter turns direct in Scorpio
July 12—Solar eclipse in Cancer
July 26—Mercury turns retrograde in Leo
July 27—Lunar eclipse in Aquarius

August 2018
Mostly sunny

There's another eclipse this month—solar, in Leo—that should bring in opportunities in your daily work routine. You might find a new job that pays more, hire new employees for your business (but don't do it until after Mercury turns direct on the 19th) or land a promotion or a new creative endeavor. Pluto forms a challenging angle to the eclipse degree, so there could be some sort of power struggle with a boss. However, with Jupiter still forming a powerful angle to your sun sign, the situation turns out fine. Neptune also forms a challenging angle to the eclipse degree, sometimes an indicator that you don't have the full story or all the details.

Before the eclipse, on the 6th, Venus enters Libra and the shared resources area of your chart. This transit should facilitate your closest relationships, but because Mercury is retrograde, you may not reap the benefits until after August 19. From the 19th forward, mortgages and loans are easier to obtain, your partner may see a spike in income or you could receive a royalty check or insurance refund.

On the 19th, Mercury turns direct in Leo and continues its journey through this fire sign until September 5. Now you can move forward with everything that went on hold during the retrograde—sign contracts, make your travel plans, hire employees or take the new job.

The full moon in your sign on August 26 brings sudden, unexpected news that should delight you. It can involve any area of your life and with Jupiter still forming a beautiful angle to your sun, it proves to be lucky, serendipitous and expansive.

Mars turns direct in Capricorn on August 27 and stays there until September 10. This transit should ramp up your social life once again and help move professional matters forward.

AT A GLANCE
August 6—Venus enters Libra
August 11—Solar eclipse in Leo
August 19—Mercury turns direct in Leo
August 26—Full moon in Pisces
August 27—Mars turns direct in Capricorn

September 2018
Pleasant

It's a busy month that will feature a pleasant, romantic and intuitive stretch from September 9 to October 5, when Venus is moving direct in fellow water sign Scorpio and traveling with Jupiter. On October 5, Venus turns retrograde, slips back into Libra on October 31 and turns direct in that sign on November 16. We'll talk more about the retrograde in next month's roundup. But while Venus is moving direct in Scorpio this month, your love life, sex life and creative life hum along at a perfect pitch. Your intuition during this transit is remarkably accurate, and it would be easy for you to set up a sideline business as a psychic! If you travel, you may have a romantic fling with someone you meet on the road.

On September 5, Mercury enters Virgo, a sign it rules, and your partnership area. This transit lasts until September 21 and facilitates communication with personal and business partners. You may be doing more writing or public speaking than usual and are able to connect the finer details on a project or business plan.

Once Mercury enters Libra on the 21st, your conscious focus turns to relationships and resources you share with others. Between September 21 and October 9, you may have dealings with attorneys, bankers or insurance people. If you're going through a divorce, this transit should help with a fair division of assets.

On the 6th, Saturn turns direct in Capricorn. Professional projects that have been stalled now gather momentum once again, and their structures and foundations are much stronger. You also have a better sense about friendships—which ones work and which ones don't.

On the 9th, Venus enters Scorpio, which we have talked about, and there's a new moon in Virgo. Thanks to beneficial angles from both Jupiter and Pluto, any opportunities that unfold as a result of this new moon expand your options significantly and create profound change. The new moon occurs in your partnership area, but because it's in Virgo, communication endeavors are also highlighted.

From September 10 to November 15, Mars transits Aquarius once again. Look back at the May roundup, when Mars was last in Aquarius, for how this transit affects you.

On the 24th, the full moon in Aries lights up your money area and could bring news about a financial matter. A project may reach completion, and you're paid the remainder of what you're owed.

AT A GLANCE
September 5—Mercury enters Virgo
September 6—Saturn turns direct in Capricorn
September 9—Venus enters Scorpio, new moon in Virgo
September 10—Mars enters Aquarius
September 21—Mercury enters Libra
September 24—Full moon in Aries

October 2018
Calmer

Astrologically, October is a much slower month and should be easy for you navigate. On the 5th, Venus turns retrograde in Scorpio, and there's potential for some hurdles and challenges in your love life, creative endeavors, sex life and perhaps with finances as well. Sometimes with Venus retrogrades, the challenges lie in physical discomforts. The heat or AC in your car, home or office burns out. Or at work, you're moved to a smaller office where you feel cramped. Or your seating on an international flight is changed, and you find yourself wedged into the middle seat for ten hours. Then the passenger directly in front of you lowers the back of his seat into your lap so he can take a snooze. Those kinds of discomforts.

The best way to navigate a Venus retro is to take things a step at a time. If you have a spat with your lover, don't obsess about it. Politely ask the passenger in front of you to please raise his seat a little. Call a repairman for the heat or AC.

The new moon in Libra on October 8 should bring new opportunities for relationships and for shared resources. This could mean that your partner gets a raise, you get a break on your homeowner's or health insurance or that the loan you've applied for comes through. Dealings with attorneys go well.

Between October 9 and 31, Mercury travels with both Scorpio and retrograde Venus. This trio of planets could take you overseas for business or pleasure or even a combination of both. You may also decide to take college or graduate level courses, a seminar or workshop or could be asked to teach a workshop. With Scorpio so prominent now, your conscious mind is particularly receptive to fluctuations in energy. You're able to accurately read other people's intentions and motives.

The full moon in Taurus on October 24 should bring news related to a communication project, siblings or your neighborhood and neighbors, and the news is sudden. Uranus is conjunct this full moon, and Saturn forms a beneficial angle to it. So even though the news is a curve ball, it has a long-range impact.

On the 31st, Mercury enters Sagittarius. In November, it turns retrograde, slips back into Scorpio and turns direct in that sign on December 6. Then on December 12, it enters Sadge again and remains there until January 4, 2019. This is an excellent transit for your career. It indicates you grasp the larger picture of whatever you're involved in and may be traveling internationally for professional reasons or communicating frequently with people from other countries.

AT A GLANCE
October 5—Venus turns retrograde in Scorpio
October 8—New moon in Libra
October 9—Mercury enters Scorpio
October 24—Full moon in Taurus
October 31—Mercury enters Sagittarius

November 2018
5 stars

It should be a delicious month for you on several levels, and it starts with the new moon in fellow water sign Scorpio on November 7. This one brings opportunities to stretch your imagination as far as it can possibly go—and for a Pisces, the distance is practically infinite. It may be a publishing contract, a chance to exhibit your creative endeavors or an invitation to write for a popular website. A trip overseas is also a possibility, perhaps for in-depth research. Both Pluto and Neptune form beautiful angles to this new moon, an indication that the opportunities, whatever they are, transform your life in some way and satisfy your ideals and spirituality.

The next day, November 8, Jupiter moves into Sagittarius and the career area of your chart. Buckle up for this one, Pisces. The transit lasts until December 3, 2019 and will expand your professional life in significant ways. You might change career tracks altogether, land a big promotion and pay raise, travel internationally for business or have a chance to work in the publishing industry in some capacity.

From November 15 to December 31, Mars transits your sign, the perfect energy to carry you through to the end of the year. Mars is the planet that makes things happen and even though Mercury will be retrograde for part of the Mars transit, you're able to make progress in all your endeavors—personal and professional. Mars is the wind in your sails!

On the 16th, Mercury turns retrograde in Sagittarius, slips back into Scorpio and turns direct in that sign on December 1. Since this retro begins in your career area, stick to projects that are already underway rather than starting anything new. Make sure the channels of communication with co-workers and bosses are clear and unobstructed. Read over the Mercury retrograde section in the introduction and follow the general guidelines so you can navigate this period more successfully.

Also on the 16th, Venus turns direct in Libra and stays there until December 2. Look back at the August roundup to see what this transit may bring. Your finances should straighten out now and so should your love life!

The full moon in Gemini on the 23rd lights up the family/home area of your chart. Your place now becomes the hub for parties and all sorts of social activities, ideal for the Thanksgiving holidays. There may also be news about a family member or about a communication project.

AT A GLANCE
November 7—New moon in Scorpio
November 8—Jupiter enters Sagittarius
November 15—Mars enters Pisces
November 16—Mercury turns retrograde in Sagittarius, Venus turns direct in Libra
November 23—Full moon in Gemini

December 2018
Taking stock

As the last month of 2018 begins, spend some time musing about what you would like to experience and achieve in 2019. Make a list. Think of this list as desires rather than goals, and post it where you'll see it frequently.

On December 2, Venus enters Scorpio again. Look back to the September roundup to see what may transpire for you into the new year, until January 7, 2019. This transit of Venus may not be quite as expansive now because Jupiter has moved into Sadge, but it should still hold great promise for your love life, finances and creativity.

On the 6th, Mercury turns direct in Scorpio and travels with Venus until the 12th, when Mercury enters Sagittarius and remains until January 4, 2019. During this period, thanks to Jupiter in Sadge, your conscious focus and communication abilities expand significantly. If you aren't traveling, then you're thinking about it, planning for it and day dreaming about it. And yes, you're in a partying mood, ideal for the approaching holidays!

The 7th features a new moon in Sagittarius. This one should bring new professional opportunities—a promotion, raise, travel or new contacts. If you're a writer with a manuscript, submit it between now and the next full moon on January 1, 2019.

The full moon in fellow water sign Cancer on the 22nd is the perfect moon for the holidays. There may be news about your family, or you're traveling to see them. Love and romance are highlighted.

AT A GLANCE
December 2—Venus enters Scorpio
December 6—Mercury turns direct in Scorpio
December 7—New moon in Sagittarius
December 12—Mercury enters Sagittarius
December 22—Full moon in Cancer

Reflection
What have you taken away from this year? What lessons or knowledge? Did you achieve your goals? Are you happier? Jot down your thoughts.

_____
_____
_____
_____
_____

Happy New Year!

2019

Introduction to 2019

Welcome to 2019!

Be sure to read over the general introduction at the beginning of the book (pages 8–22), which discusses some of the astrological basics you should keep in mind as you read through the monthly predictions for each sign.

In each monthly roundup, you'll find information about astrological activity pertinent to each month and what it may mean for you—when planets change signs, turn retrograde or make challenging or beneficial angles to other planets, as well as eclipses, new and full moons and retrogrades. All of this information is intended to help you successfully navigate each month.

For a handy reference, I've included lists on the new and full moon dates and the dates of the Mercury retrogrades this year. The eclipses are also noted.

Overall, 2019 features interesting changes in the slower moving planets. In December, expansive Jupiter enters earth sign Capricorn, sure to be positive for all earth and water signs. It joins Pluto in that sign. Uranus also enters earth sign Taurus for the second time and remains there for the next seven years. This transit should be exciting for all earth and water signs.

New and Full Moons for 2019

New moons, when the sun and moon are in the same sign, are all about new opportunities. They mark the beginning of a fresh cycle and favor setting goals, launching projects or starting anything. For maintaining something in your life, the new moon is the ideal time to set your intentions, visualize and believe that what you desire will come to you.

For more details on new and full moons, see the introduction to 2017 on page 21.

These moons are calculated for Eastern time.

NEW MOONS 2019

January 5—Capricorn: solar eclipse
February 4—Aquarius
March 6—Pisces
April 5—Aries
May 4—Taurus
June 3—Gemini
July 2—Cancer: solar eclipse
July 31—Leo
August 30—Virgo
September 29—Libra
October 27—Scorpio
November 26—Sagittarius
December 26—Capricorn: solar eclipse

FULL MOONS 2019

January 21—Leo: lunar eclipse
February 19—Virgo
March 20—Libra
April 19—Libra
May 18—Scorpio
June 17—Sagittarius
July 16—Capricorn: lunar eclipse
August 23—Aquarius
September 14—Pisces
October 13—Aries
November 12—Taurus
December 12—Gemini

Read about eclipses and their impact in the introduction to 2017 (page 22).

Mercury Retrograde

Mercury turns retrograde—that is, it appears to move backward relative to the earth—three times a year, and the retro period lasts for about three weeks. During this time, miscommunication is often rampant and appliances and electronics break down. It's wise not to launch any new projects or to sign contracts, since Mercury rules contracts. Mercury also rules moving parts, so it's smart not to buy a car or electronics during these periods. Travel can be iffy—plans go south quickly and itineraries change without warning. Everything moves more slowly. By following the guidelines above, you can mitigate some of the effects of these retrogrades. Also, it's best to revise, review and reconsider, what I call the rule of the three Rs.

The Mercury retrograde periods are noted in the monthly predictions, but here's a quick reference:

MERCURY RETROGRADES IN 2019

March 5–28: Pisces
July 7–31: Leo slips back into Cancer and turns direct in that sign
October 31–November 20: Scorpio

The only planets that don't turn retrograde are the sun and the moon. In the monthly roundups, you'll find references to when the other planets turn retro and what it may mean for you.

A Mercury Retrograde Story

Read through the other Mercury retrograde stories in the introductions (pages 9 and 185). They illustrate how the trickster planet can create utter chaos on a personal level and also on a national scale.

Some years ago, we foolishly set a closing date for the sale of our house, the move and the closing on our new house during a Mercury retrograde. Big mistake. It turned out to be a comedy of errors all the way around. The buyer of our home was doing the final walk through and found some details he wanted taken care of before we closed—i.e., screws were missing on several of the hurricane shutters. My husband had to run to the hardware store to buy some new screws, and meanwhile, the clock was ticking down to the closing time on the house. Since we were also closing on our new house that day, we had to call both title companies to let them know we were running late. We were afraid that we wouldn't make the closing on our new place by 5 p.m. and would be homeless for the night with our young daughter, two cats and all our belongings.

During the closing on the house we were selling, things got a bit heated when the buyer and the realtor (who supposedly represented us) tried to slip in some provision at the very end of the contract. We refused to sign. The title company intervened, and the deal was finally closed. By now, we had thirty-five minutes to make the closing on our new place. I called them and explained the situation, and they stayed open past their usual closing time to accommodate us.

We finally got into the house, but I wouldn't recommend selling your home or moving during a Mercury retrograde!

So in the monthly roundups when you see that a Mercury retro is coming up, prepare for it by scheduling travel and important events on either side of the dates. Be ready to pay closer attention to details.

Aries 2019

Mars rules your sign, so pay special attention to its movements each month—the angles it makes to your sun sign and to other transiting planets, whether it's involved in an eclipse or is traveling with Mercury when that planet is retrograde. This year, Mars moves through eight signs and won't be retrograde—good news for all of us, but especially for you! On December 31, 2018, it moved into your sign and will be there until February 14. Read all about what that means for you in the January roundup.

In the monthly roundups, you'll find information on the major transits each month, the new and full moons, eclipses, the motion of the planets and what it means for you.

January features a solar and lunar eclipse and that means you could experience some tension and anxiety.

Lucky you, Aries. You go into 2019 with your ruler, Mars, in your sign until February 14. It gives you a distinct edge on everyone else because Mars represents, among other things, your physical energy. You're able to get a lot done. In addition, you have the advantage of Jupiter in Sagittarius forming a powerful and beneficial angle to your sun sign until December 2. Expansion is the name of the game this year.

January 2019
Close to perfect

Mars begins the year in your sign, Aries, and what a wonderful way that is to start a new year! Anything that has been on hold—in your personal or professional life—now moves forward with great momentum and speed. You can accomplish a great deal between now and February 14, so don't fritter the energy away.

Between January 7 and February 3, Venus moves through fellow fire sign Sagittarius and is friendly to Mars and your sun sign. This trine between Venus and Mars is exact on January 19–20. During this entire period, your love life and sex life prove to be delightful! If you're not involved with anyone now, you may be before the transit is finished.

Venus in Sagittarius may take you on a trip overseas, and if it does, you may meet a special romantic interest while you're traveling. If you're a writer, your article or book could sell during this transit. This period should be quite creative for you, and extra income could arrive from unexpected sources.

Mercury, the planet of communication, begins the year in Sagittarius, so your conscious thoughts could be focused on international travel. From January 4–24, Mercury moves through Capricorn and the career area of your chart. You may be communicating more than usual with co-workers and bosses and laying out strategies for the year ahead. Once Mercury enters Aquarius, you're in more comfortable terrain. Unusual ideas come to you at all hours of the day, so keep a notepad handy. That transit lasts until February 10.

The solar eclipse in Capricorn on the 5th brings new professional opportunities. You may have an inkling about what these new opportunities are for several days on either side of the eclipse. You may have to let go of something before the new can rush in, but that's par for the nature of eclipses. Neptune forms a beneficial angle to the eclipse degree, suggesting that the new opportunity may involve your spiritual beliefs in some way and enable you to draw more fully on your creative abilities.

Uranus turns direct in your sign on January 6, a welcome change! The planet of surprises may have a few more in store for you before it reenters Taurus on March 6. The surprises are likely to be positive unless you have avoided the change that Uranus invariably brings. Then these last few months may be emotionally painful!

On the 21st, the lunar eclipse in fellow fire sign Leo occurs in the area of your chart that governs romance, creativity, children and everything you do for fun and pleasure. Something in one—or all—of these areas is brought to your attention, and you must act quickly and decisively to tend to it. But the end result is positive.

AT A GLANCE
January 4—Mercury enters into Capricorn
January 5—Solar eclipse in Capricorn
January 6—Uranus turns direct in Aries
January 7—Venus goes into Sagittarius
January 21—Lunar eclipse in Leo
January 24—Mercury goes into Aquarius

February 2019
Enjoyment

Since there are no eclipses this month and Mercury isn't retrograde, you'll find plenty to enjoy about February. And the good stuff begins on February 4, with a new moon in Aquarius, an air sign compatible with your sun sign. This one should bring new friendships and contacts, as well as a stream of excellent ideas that you should keep track of. They could come in handy. Mercury is closely conjunct this new moon, so the gift of gab is yours.

On February 3, Venus enters Capricorn, where it will be until March 1, and your professional life unfolds with greater ease. If you're a writer with a manuscript you hope to sell, the sale could happen during this transit. If you work for someone else, your boss and co-workers are attracted to your ideas and consider you the person with the answers.

From February 10 to March 5, Mercury is moving in direct motion through Pisces and the quiet part of your chart. This transit turns your mental focus to your own unconscious—issues you may have buried and your inner motives. With Mercury in Pisces, your creative drive is strong, and your imagination is enormously powerful.

Your ruler, Mars, enters Taurus on February 14 and transits your financial area until March 31. During this period, you're a moneymaker. Mars is the wind at your back and facilitates forward momentum in everything you tackle. You have more patience now than usual, too, so tackle projects that require steady, careful plodding.

The full moon in Virgo on February 19 lights up that part of your chart that deals with your daily work and the daily maintenance of your health. There could be news in either of these areas. You're able to connect the dots in a situation or project more readily now. Mars is closely conjunct to this full moon, suggesting plenty of action!

AT A GLANCE
February 3—Venus enters Capricorn
February 4—New moon in Aquarius
February 10—Mercury goes into Pisces
February 14—Mars enters into Taurus
February 19—Full moon in Virgo

March 2019
Interesting surprises

Except for the Mercury retrograde this month, March should be a good month with some interesting surprises.

On March 1, Venus enters compatible air sign Aquarius, and between now and March 26, your social life should hum with activity. If you're not involved in a committed relationship right now, you may meet a romantic interest through friends or a club to which you belong or even online. However, once Mercury turns retrograde in Pisces on the 5th, you may be reconsidering the situation. The retrograde lasts until March 28, and occurs in the quiet part of your chart—the twelfth house. So don't be surprised if buried issues surface and people you haven't seen in years resurface in your life.

Between March 26 and April 20, Venus transits Pisces and the area of your chart that governs your personal unconscious. This won't be your favorite time, but what you learn about yourself will prove valuable. Keep track of your dreams, they may contain insights and information that is helpful.

The 6th features two astrological events: a new moon in Pisces and a major shift for the planet Uranus, which moves into Taurus. It entered Taurus briefly in May 2018, slipped back into Aries and now enters Taurus again. Neptune is closely conjunct to this new moon, and both Jupiter and Saturn are friendly to it. New opportunities that surface—in the arts and creativity—are rock solid and expand your life in a significant way. If you're required to sign a contract, don't do so until after Mercury turns direct on March 28.

Uranus will be in Taurus until July 7, 2026, and during this period some aspect of your life will undergo abrupt and radical change. On a solar chart, where your sun sign is placed on the ascendant, Taurus is on the cusp of your second house and your financial area. So the change could occur with money—you win the lottery, lose a steady source of income or find a new source of income. It's to your advantage to have a copy of your natal chart in order to see where Taurus actually falls for you.

The full moon in Libra on the 20th occurs in your partnership area. This moon should bring news about a partnership—romantic or business—or a relationship reaches a culmination point. The moon is at 0 degrees, a powerful position for a cardinal sign. Be prepared to act quickly and think on your feet.

From March 31 to May 15, Mars transits compatible air sign Gemini and the communication area of your chart. This should be a favorable period for you. Mercury will be moving direct, and you're motivated to get things done. Networking proves beneficial and you come up with great ideas that you can easily implement into any area of your life.

AT A GLANCE
March 1—Venus enters into Aquarius
March 5—Mercury turns retrograde in Pisces
March 6—New moon in Pisces, Uranus enters Taurus
March 20—Full moon in Libra
March 26—Venus goes into Pisces
March 28—Mercury turns direct
March 31—Mars enters Gemini

April 2019
5 stars

It's a stellar month for you, Aries, and it begins on April 5 with a new moon in your sign. This moon occurs just once a year and sets the tone for the next twelve months. It's wise to prepare for it by making a list of what you would like to achieve and experience in the year ahead. Any new opportunities that surface are personally satisfying. Thanks to a beneficial angle from Mars to this moon, there's plenty of forward momentum in whatever you tackle, and your communication skills are especially sharp.

Jupiter turns retrograde in Sagittarius on the 10th and won't turn direct again until August 11. During this period, the planet's expansive energy turns inward. You may be reassessing your spiritual beliefs and worldview and could take courses or workshops that broaden your knowledge. Your interest in other countries and cultures has been heightened ever since Jupiter entered Sagittarius last year, and this trend continues.

From April 17 to May 6, Mercury moves through your sign, and you're now fully immersed in your element—fire! Passion infuses everything you do, and your ideas are plentiful, different and perhaps even unique. Your entrepreneurial spirit is greatly heightened.

The full moon in Libra on the 19th highlights your partnership area and brings news about a personal or business partnership or a legal matter—or both! If you're going through a divorce or involved in any legal proceedings, it should turn out in your favor because on the 20th, Venus enters your sign and brings an element of financial luck.

Venus will be in your sign until May 15, and this entire period should be one of the most romantic and creative for you all year. The only other period that equals it falls between July 27 and August 21, when Venus transits Leo. Your creative endeavors during this time flourish, and your love life is stellar. Life is good!

Pluto turns retrograde in Capricorn, in your career area, on March 25 and doesn't turn direct again until October 3. Pluto is the transformative planet and is all about power, revenge, purging and our shadow selves. While it's retro, you may notice that your shadow side is more apparent, particularly regarding your professional life. You have an opportunity to work on the shadow qualities in your personality and to dive into the depths of what motivates you.

On the 29th, Saturn also turns retro in Capricorn and remains that way until September 18. The combination of Saturn and Pluto retrograde in the same sign and area of your chart may feel like a double whammy of bad luck at times, and it may be challenging to maintain your optimism. However, Saturn's retro gives you the opportunity to examine the structures in your life—home and family, profession, friends and finances.

April 5—New moon in Aries
April 10—Jupiter turns retrograde in Sagittarius
April 17—Mercury enters Aries
April 19—Full moon in Libra
April 20—Venus enters Aries
April 25—Pluto turns retrograde in Capricorn
April 29—Saturn turns retrograde in Capricorn

May 2019
$

It looks as if the emphasis for this month is on your finances. So take a deep breath, Aries, and read it all with an open mind.

May 4 features a new moon in Taurus, in your financial area. This one should bring new income opportunities. You might sell a creative endeavor, land a great freelance gig, find a part-time job or even a new job that pays more. Neptune forms a beneficial angle to this new moon, suggesting that the opportunities that surface may involve your ideals, spirituality or creativity.

From May 6 to May 21, Mercury transits Taurus and your financial area, which brings your conscious awareness to money—how you earn it, spend it, save it and invest it. You may take an in-depth look at your financial picture and decide that a budget is in order. It's an excellent time to dive into a project that requires patience, persistence and resoluteness.

On the 15th, two astrological events occur: Venus enters Taurus and Mars enters Cancer. The Venus transit lasts until June 8 and should bring an element of luck to your finances. You might be at the right place at the right time to reap the benefits of an income-earning opportunity. Venus in Taurus also heightens your sensuality and your appreciation for beauty. It's possible that a new romance is kindled with someone who shares your values.

From May 15 to July 1, Mars transits Cancer and the home/family area of your chart. These six weeks should be productive. You might dive into home-improvement projects that have been simmering on a back burner for months and actually complete them. Because Cancer is such a nurturing sign, you may carve out more time for your family and the people who are like family. It's also likely that you set up an office at home and find a way to work from home a couple of days a week. However the specifics unfold for you, Mars in Cancer heightens your intuition and the nurturing aspects of your personality.

The full moon in Scorpio on May 18 brings a financial matter into focus—your partner's income, a mortgage or loan for which you've applied, an insurance settlement or refund or a tax issue. There may be news concerning any of these areas. Scorpio is an emotionally intense sign, so be prepared to be immersed in what you feel and intuit.

Mercury transits Gemini, a sign it rules, from May 21 to June 4. During this period, you may be socializing more frequently or networking for both business and pleasure, and your communication skills are enhanced. Now is the time to start or complete that novel or screenplay, Aries.

AT A GLANCE
May 4—New moon in Taurus
May 6—Mercury enters Taurus
May 15—Venus goes into Taurus, Mars enters Cancer
May 18—Full moon in Scorpio
May 21—Mercury goes into Gemini

June 2019
Great energy

It should be a great month for you, and it all begins on June 3, with a new moon in compatible air sign Gemini. You may have an opportunity to collaborate on a book with a friend or could be invited to teach a workshop or conduct a seminar. You may be networking and socializing more, and new and valuable contacts are made.

On June 4th, Mercury enters Cancer and the family/home area of your chart. This transit lasts until June 26 and brings an intuitive flow to your conscious mind. You're especially in tune with people in your immediate environment—family, co-workers and friends. Once Mercury enters fellow fire sign Leo on June 26, you're much more in your element and in the mood for romance and fun. It's easier to tap into your creativity, and ideas come to you at unexpected moments. Thanks to a retrograde next month, Mercury remains in Leo until July 31.

Between June 8 and July 3, Venus transits Gemini, and now some of that new moon energy may manifest itself. If a relationship begins during this transit, you could meet the person through a sibling or neighbor or in your daily travels. You might, for instance, be standing in line at your local coffee shop and strike up a conversation with the stranger in front of you, and the chemistry is immediate. Serendipity is your ally.

The full moon in Sagittarius on June 17 should be a beauty for you. You're filled with optimism about life in general, and there's a magnetism about you that other people simply can't resist. Retrograde Jupiter forms a wide conjunction with this full moon, so you're in an expansive mood.

From June 20 to November 27, Neptune is retrograde in Pisces. During the next five months, it won't be as easy for you to retreat into a fantasy world when you encounter something unpleasant. You won't be able to gloss over credit card debt, for instance, or red flags in a relationship. You will be reevaluating your dreams and delving into who you are in the core of your being.

AT A GLANCE
June 3—New moon in Gemini
June 4—Mercury enters into Cancer
June 8—Venus goes into Gemini
June 17—Full moon in Sagittarius
June 20—Neptune turns retrograde
June 26—Mercury enters Leo

July 2019
A challenge

July holds a few whoppers that could make the month challenging to navigate—a Mercury retrograde in Leo and a solar eclipse in Cancer. But before we arrive at either of those events, there's some good stuff in store for you.

On July 1, Mars enters Leo and the romance/creativity sector of your chart. Between now and August 18, you're really motivated in your various creative endeavors and are determined to *shine*. Your sexuality is heightened throughout this transit and so is your pursuit of enjoyment. You have so much physical energy that it would be smart to join a gym or take up a physical activity to do regularly. Even if you just get outside and take a brisk walk several times a week, you'll feel better.

The solar eclipse in Cancer on July 2 brings new opportunities to your family life. A door opens. You and your partner may decide to put your home on the market, or you start searching for a neighborhood that suits you better. Uranus forms a wide but beneficial angle to the eclipse degree, suggesting that opportunities come out of the blue, and you just have to be ready to seize them.

Between July 3 and July 27, Venus transits Cancer and brings a gentle softness to your home life. Your relationship with your partner and children is strengthened and deepened. You feel compelled to beautify your home and personal surroundings in some way—fresh paint on the walls, new furniture, plants or art.

On July 7, Mercury turn retrograde in Leo, slips back into Cancer on the 19th, then turns direct in that sign on the 31st. Reread the Mercury retrograde section in the introduction for tips on how to navigate this period successfully. Since the retro occurs in the romance/creativity section of your chart, things with a lover or partner may feel *off*. The potential for miscommunication is greater during the retrograde, so be sure to communicate clearly with everyone, but particularly with a partner, your children and anyone involved in your creative endeavors.

The lunar eclipse in Capricorn on July 16 may prompt you to take a deeper look at your profession and career. It may be prompted by a remark someone makes that rubs you the wrong way.

From July 27 to August 21, Venus moves through Leo, and you enjoy several weeks of bliss creatively and romantically. This period, like the one between April 20 and May 15, is when your muse is at your beck and call. The most challenging thing you could encounter is that your muse won't shut up! You and your partner should try to get away for a long romantic weekend and rediscover the reasons you're together.

Finally, on July 31, Mercury turns direct again in Cancer and, to sweeten the pot, there's a new moon in Leo today, too! This one brings new opportunities for self-expression and, if you're not involved, a new romantic interest. If you're in a relationship, then you and your partner may decide to start a family.

AT A GLANCE
July 1—Mars goes into Leo
July 2—Solar eclipse in Cancer
July 3—Venus enters Cancer
July 7—Mercury turns retrograde in Leo
July 16—Lunar eclipse in Capricorn
July 27—Venus enters Leo
July 31—Mercury turns direct, new moon in Leo

August 2019
Work & health

This month, the astrological energies come together in the area of your chart that governs your daily work routine and how you maintain your health on a daily basis. Let's take a closer look.

On August 11, Jupiter turns direct in Sagittarius, and you once again enjoy its expansiveness. If your publishing or educational endeavors have been sluggish or your travel plans have been delayed, that now changes. Also on the 11th, Mercury enters fellow fire sign Leo once more and remains there until August 29. Since it's traveling with Venus, your conscious mind is focused on romance and your creative endeavors. If you're not involved with anyone right now, that may change before Venus enters Virgo on August 21.

On the 12th, Uranus turns retrograde in Taurus, in your financial area. It remains that way until January 11, 2020. During this lengthy period, your urge for freedom—financial freedom?—becomes so powerful that you may take on a second job or freelance gig. It's a great time to delve into who you are and what makes you tick.

From August 18 to October 4, Mars transits Virgo and the daily work area of your chart. It travels with Venus from August 21 to September 14. The combination of these two planetary energies should create a smooth working environment. Your relationships with co-workers and employees improves, and your projects and ideas get the green light!

The full moon in Aquarius on the 15th ramps up your social life. You're in a festive mood and may be celebrating the completion of a project. Then, on the 29th, Mercury enters Virgo and brings order and efficiency into your life. Mercury will be in Virgo until September 14.

The 30th features a new moon in Virgo. Uranus retrograde forms a close and beneficial angle to this new moon, so you may suddenly change your work routine or the way you maintain your daily health. Your intuition is strong now. Listen to it!

AT A GLANCE
August 11—Jupiter turns direct, Mercury enters Leo
August 12—Uranus turns retrograde
August 15—Full moon in Aquarius
August 18—Mars enters Virgo
August 21—Venus goes into Virgo
August 29—Mercury enters Virgo
August 30—New moon in Virgo

September 2019
Relationships

From mid-month forward, the astrological energies fall primarily in your partnership area. Both Mercury and Venus enter Libra on September 14 and travel together until Mercury enters Scorpio on October 3. Your conscious thoughts are very much on relationship matters. You're more aware of the importance of balance in your partnerships and strive to treat others fairly. Your usual impatience and restlessness are tempered somewhat now, as a softer and gentler you emerges.

The full moon in Pisces also occurs on the 14th, and retrograde Neptune forms a close conjunction. The combination favors spiritual and creative pursuits that may require more solitude than usual, but that's fine with you. You're in the mood to immerse yourself completely in the flow.

On the 18th, Saturn turns direct in Capricorn—finally! Professional matters that have been slowed down or stalled out for the last several months now move forward again. You're able to implement what you learned during the retrograde and change the structures that no longer serve your best interests.

The new moon in Libra on the 29th may bring a new romantic interest or a new business partnership. If you're in a relationship, you and your partner may decide to deepen your commitment to each other by moving in together or getting married.

AT A GLANCE
September 14—Mercury and Venus enter Libra, full moon in Pisces
September 18—Saturn turns direct in Capricorn
September 29—New moon in Libra

October 2019
Mixed

It could be a hectic month for you, Aries, so be sure to get plenty of rest and to carve out time daily for exercise.

On the 3rd, Mercury enters Scorpio and the shared resources area of your chart. Your conscious focus is on financial matters—your partner's income, investments or a mortgage or loan for which you've applied. Scorpio is an emotionally intense sign that usually seeks the absolute bottom line in everything, so if you're conducting research, you do so thoroughly and completely. From October 31 to November 20, Mercury is retrograde. Reread the section in the introduction on Mercury retrograde for tips and guidelines on how to navigate these periods successfully. Since this one occurs in a financial area, it's wise to double-check all your transactions. When your buttons are pushed, think before you blurt out an emotional response that you may not be able to take back!

Pluto turns direct in Capricorn on the 3rd. Now that it and Saturn are both moving in direct motion in your career area, things should be coming together for you professionally. You're the right person in the right place at the right time.

From October 4 to November 19, Mars transits Libra and your partnership area. The planet of action provides forward momentum in all your endeavors, but particularly in your closest personal and business relationships. Take advantage of the energy. Have things lined up that you want to complete and achieve, then get to work.

Venus enters Scorpio on October 8, joining Mercury retrograde in the shared resources area of your chart. Venus will be in Scorpio until November 1, and during this period, your sexuality is heightened. You are also more sensitive to the unseen and the hidden.

The full moon in your sign on the 13th should be spectacular. Jupiter forms a beneficial angle to it and brings its expansiveness and good fortune to any news you hear. On the 27th, the new moon in Scorpio should usher in new financial opportunities. You might find a mortgage with a low interest rate, land a freelance job that pays well or receive a royalty check or an insurance refund.

Then, on October 31, just in time for Halloween, Mercury turns retro in Scorpio and stays that way until November 20,

AT A GLANCE
October 3—Mercury goes into Scorpio, Pluto turns direct
October 4—Mars enters Libra
October 8—Venus goes into Scorpio
October 13—Full moon in Aries
October 27—New moon in Scorpio
October 31—Mercury turns retrograde

November 2019
Nice!

The best news this month is that Mercury turns direct in Scorpio on November 20, right in time for the Thanksgiving holidays. You can now move forward again with everything that was delayed during the retrograde. Sign contracts, launch your new projects and consider planning a quick getaway out of town with the one you love!

Between November 1–25, Venus transits fellow fire sign Sagittarius, and in spite of Mercury's retrograde, this period should be quite enjoyable. It's a time that's nearly as creative and romantic as the period between July 27 and August 21, when Venus transited Leo. You may revise a novel or screenplay you've been working on, and now every little piece comes together. Your muse is feeding you the bigger picture and may be advising you to change the locale to a more vivid and exotic setting—that's the Sagittarian influence.

If you're not involved in a relationship when the transit starts, you may meet someone special before it ends. The person could work in higher education or publishing or be from another country/culture.

The full moon in Taurus on the 12th highlights your finances or brings a financial deal to a close. With both Saturn and Pluto forming beneficial angles to this full moon, any news you hear should have a solid footing in reality, putting you in the driver's seat. You might, for example, be offered a great job or freelance project that brings in a substantial paycheck. With retrograde Neptune also forming a beneficial angle to this moon, the news could help to fulfill a dream you have.

From November 19 to January 4, 2020, Mars transits Scorpio, a sign it co-rules. During this period, you're highly motivated to tackle difficult and esoteric topics and projects. You penetrate deeply into whatever you take on and dig and dig for the truth. Your sexuality is greatly heightened during this transit, and so is your intuition.

Once Venus enters Capricorn and your career area on the 25th, you're in an ideal position to forge ahead with all professional matters. You're in the right place at the right time, and you're the right person for the job. This transit lasts until December 20 and should enable you to tie up everything just in time for the holidays.

On the 26th, the new moon in Sagittarius should bring new opportunities for international travel or in publishing or higher education. Since the moon is in a fellow fire sign, you feel uplifted and optimistic. The only possible glitch is that Uranus in Taurus forms a challenging angle to this new moon that indicates you will have to make some sort of adjustment in your attitude before the new opportunities pan out.

Neptune turns direct in Pisces on the 27th. Now you can once again take full advantage of this planet's energy in terms of your imagination, spiritual pursuits and psychic ability.

November 1—Venus goes into Sagittarius
November 12—Full moon in Taurus
November 19—Mars enters Scorpio
November 20—Mercury turns direct
November 25—Venus enters Capricorn
November 26—New moon in Sagittarius
November 27—Neptune turns direct

December 2019
Jupiter's shift

As the month begins, take some time to think about what you would like to experience and achieve in the year ahead. Make a list. Don't think of these items as New Year's resolutions, but as *desires*. Post the list where you'll see it often.

On December 2, Jupiter makes a major transition. It moves from Sagittarius to Capricorn, where it will be until December 20, 2020. This should be a stellar period for your career. Professionally, everything expands for you. You could be promoted, switch career paths altogether, find a new job with higher pay or strike out on your own in some capacity. If you've been hoping to open your own business or to work full-time at something you love, then this could be the year that it happens.

Between December 9 and 29, Mercury transits Sagittarius, perfect for a fun-filled holiday. You're in your element now and may be traveling for business or pleasure or both. You could be asked to teach a class or conduct a workshop in your area of expertise. Your social life may be busy and joyful, too, so take advantage of that!

The full moon in Gemini on the 12th brings news about a communication project, a sibling or a neighbor. If you and your family have been looking for a new neighborhood that would suit your needs better, you may stumble across it around the time of this full moon.

Venus moves into Aquarius on December 20, a perfect spot for holiday festivities, and carries you into the new year. The transit ends on January 14, 2020. During these several weeks, you're surrounded by unusual, idiosyncratic people who may be geniuses in their respective fields. If you meet a romantic interest during this period, it may be through friends.

Now, about the solar eclipse in Capricorn on the 26th. This is the equivalent of a double new moon, so your opportunities will be double and will involve your professional life. You might be tapped to head a team on a particular project, sell a novel or screenplay or be promoted with a significant pay raise. The sky is the limit, Aries. Uranus forms a close, beneficial angle to this eclipse, suggesting that the opportunities seem to come out of the blue. Just be prepared to seize them!

On the 29th, Mercury enters Capricorn, and now all that career energy is bolstered. This transit carries you into the new year and ends on January 17, 2020. You're extremely focused and motivated.

AT A GLANCE
December 2—Jupiter enters Capricorn
December 9—Mercury enters Sagittarius
December 12—Full moon in Gemini
December 20—Venus goes into Aquarius
December 26—Solar eclipse in Capricorn
December 29—Mercury enters into Capricorn

Reflection
Take a few minutes before the new year arrives to think about how this year went for you. Has it unfolded the way you'd hoped? Are you happier? More prosperous? What pivotal life events happened in 2019? How can what you learned this year carry you forward into 2020 with greater conference?

_____
_____
_____
_____
_____

Happy New Year!

Taurus 2019

Pay special attention to what Venus, your ruler, is doing each month and the angles it's making to your sun sign and to other planets. In 2019, Venus won't have any retrograde periods, good news for your love life, finances and creative endeavors.

In the monthly roundups, you'll find information about the new and full moons, eclipses, retrogrades of Mercury and other planets, the transits the various planets are making and what it all means for you. For Mercury's retro periods, be sure to reread the section in the introduction about what happens when the planet of communication is retro and general guidelines you can follow.

2019 will be an intriguing year for you, Taurus. Once Uranus enters your sign in early March, you'll begin experiencing surprising twists in your life. Things will happen suddenly and without warning, and you'll have to go with the flow, whatever it is. Opportunities that unfold will enable you to shake off what no longer works in your life and to embrace the new and untried. Your sign is one of the most stubborn and not particularly fond of change, but with this transit, change will come regardless. By the time Uranus moves on in 2026, you'll look back with awe.

January 2019
Excellent start

Welcome to 2019! The year begins with Mars already in Aries, a holdover from last year, so you're fired up and ready to go. Mars is the planet that makes stuff happen and creates an undercurrent of forward momentum in everything you do. It's in that part of your chart that rules the personal unconscious, so you're psychologically ready!

On January 4, Mercury enters fellow earth sign Capricorn and remains there until the 24th. During this period, your focus is excellent, and you have the resoluteness and determination to complete whatever you start. A note of caution: If you're planning a trip overseas, make your plans this month or next because Mercury will be in retrograde from March 5 to 28.

On the 5th, the solar eclipse also falls in Capricorn. New opportunities should surface on or around the time of the eclipse in travel, higher education, publishing, spirituality or your profession. Neptune forms a beneficial angle to the eclipse degree, suggesting that the new opportunities could involve a creative endeavor and appeal to your idealism. Months in which eclipses occur are sometimes tense and infused with a sense of urgency because we're compelled to act quickly and decisively.

Uranus turns direct in Aries on January 6 and now moves toward its appointment with your sign in early March. You may be feeling the effects already—a suddenness to events that catches you off guard. Read more about it in the March roundup.

Your ruler, Venus, enters Sagittarius on January 7 and remains there until February 3. Any financial dealings with others—banks, mortgage or insurance companies—should go well. If you're in the midst of a divorce, the property settlement will be in your favor. Any creative endeavors may involve the strange and esoteric—past lives, ghosts or communication with the dead.

The lunar eclipse in Leo on January 21 falls in the family/home area of your chart. Since this type of eclipse impacts your emotions, your inner world, you may feel that your authority is challenged or that your creativity is being eclipsed by someone in your personal environment. You may need to deal quickly with the situation that has caused these feelings.

Between January 24 and February 10, Mercury transits Aquarius and your career area. Make good use of these few weeks. Implement your unusual ideas in projects, and use your enhanced communication skills to win over the competition.

AT A GLANCE

January 4—Mercury enters into Capricorn
January 5—Solar eclipse in Capricorn
January 6—Uranus turns direct in Aries
January 7—Venus goes into Sagittarius
January 21—Lunar eclipse in Leo
January 24—Mercury goes into Aquarius

February 2019
Nearly 5 stars

It should be an excellent month for you, particularly once Mars enters your sign on February 14, where it remains until March 31. Any time Mars transits your sign you experience forward momentum in every aspect of your life. You have an abundance of physical energy, can work long hours without tiring and possess the resoluteness and endurance necessary to get things done. Next month's Mercury retrograde may slow you down a little, so try to get as much done as possible in February.

On the 4th, the new moon in Aquarius should bring new professional opportunities. You could land a promotion or freelance gig, get a raise, be tapped to head up a research team or be recognized in some way by your boss and peers. Mercury is closely conjunct this new moon, and Jupiter forms a beneficial angle to it, suggesting a lot of discussion about these opportunities and an expansion in your career.

Venus transits fellow earth sign Capricorn between February 3 and March 1. Your love life hums along at a pleasing pace, and your creative drive is strong. With Venus in this position, you're in a great spot for any publishing endeavors, international travel or anything dealing with higher education. Just be sure you complete your travel by March 5, when Mercury turns retrograde.

Mercury enters Pisces on February 10 and moves direct through that sign until March 5. During this period, you may spend more time with friends and networking with people you meet. Your conscious mind is exceptionally intuitive, and your imagination is moving fast and furiously, dipping into the unknown and mapping it out. It's an excellent time for research.

The full moon in Virgo on the 19th highlights or brings news about a romantic relationship, creative endeavor or your children. Mars forms a great angle to this full moon, indicating that your sexuality is heightened and so is your capacity for sheer enjoyment.

February 3—Venus enters Capricorn
February 4—New moon in Aquarius
February 10—Mercury goes into Pisces
February 14—Mars enters into Taurus
February 19—Full moon in Virgo

March 2019
The Uranian shift

There's a lot going on this month, and it may be a wild ride! Let's take a look first at the planet Uranus. On the 6th, the planet of sudden, unexpected change, leaves Aries and enters Taurus. It did the same thing in 2018, but was in Taurus only for a few months before it turned retrograde. Now it will be in Taurus until July 7, 2025. Then in September of that year it will turn retrograde, slip back into Taurus in November and emerge finally into Gemini in April 2026.

During this transit, any area of your life where you are rigid and habitual will change. Relationships that no longer serve your best interest will fall out of your experience. If you've been working in a profession or at a job that you dislike, then you may lose that job, freeing you to do something you love. You get the idea. Uranus cleans out the dead wood, making room for the new and unknown.

On March 1, Venus enters Aquarius and your career area and leaves on March 26. This is a jump-up-and-down kind of transit because Venus brings greater ease to all your professional matters. Working relationships function more smoothly, your relationship with your boss is pain free and others see you as the person with answers. Between March 26 and April 20, Venus transits Pisces, and now you can sit back and chill with your friends, become reacquainted with your muse and generally enjoy yourself. If a romance starts during this transit, it may be with someone you meet through friends.

The one drawback is that Mercury turns retro in Pisces on the 5th and doesn't turn direct again until the 28th. Look over the guidelines in the introduction for navigating a retrograde more successfully and remember that by following the rule of the three Rs—revise, review and reconsider—you use the retrograde energy the way it's intended to be used. Since this one occurs in that area of your life that governs friends, publicity, wishes and dreams, people you haven't seen in a long time may resurface. Publicity campaigns may be delayed or encounter problems. You might have a falling out with a friend.

On the 6th, the same day that Uranus enters Taurus, there's a new moon in Pisces. In spite of Mercury's antics, this moon should bring in plenty of opportunities to forge new friendships. It's also likely that you'll have a chance to work on a new creative endeavor. Your intuition and imagination are hand-in-hand with this new moon.

March 20 brings a full moon in Libra that highlights your daily work routine and the way you maintain your health on a daily basis. There could be news concerning one or both of these areas. In your relationships with co-workers, you become more aware of a need for balance and harmony and realize it's just not worthwhile to argue with anyone.

Mercury turns direct on the 28th in Pisces, and now you can move forward with everything that was delayed and do so with confidence!

Between March 31 and May 15, Mars transits Gemini and your financial area, and the pursuit for higher income is on! You'll be making more contacts during this transit, and any of them could provide you with opportunities to increase your income.

AT A GLANCE
March 1—Venus enters into Aquarius
March 5—Mercury turns retrograde in Pisces
March 6—New moon in Pisces, Uranus enters Taurus
March 20—Full moon in Libra
March 26—Venus goes into Pisces
March 28—Mercury turns direct
March 31—Mars enters Gemini

April 2019
Backtracking

Three planets turn retrograde this month, so April may feel somewhat disjointed and slow-paced. On April 10, Jupiter turns retrograde in Sagittarius. On the 25th Pluto turns retro in Capricorn, and four days later Saturn turns retro in the same sign. Let's take a closer look.

The Jupiter retro lasts until August 11 and provides an ideal time for a spiritual or shamanic retreat. The expansive nature of this planet turns inward during this retrograde, and you delve more deeply into your spiritual beliefs. If you don't have a meditation practice, start one. Five or ten minutes a day is all you need. You may have flashes of a past life, see a ghost or communicate with the dead. You might want to find a reputable psychic or medium and have a reading.

Pluto's retrograde lasts until October 3. During these months, you may discover your darker side, what Carl Jung referred to as the "shadow." You may try to control the people in your personal environment—and the attempts will go haywire and blow up in your face. During this retro, it's best to work on your inner self rather than expect others to do what you want them to do.

Saturn's retro lasts until September 18. During these months, you'll be scrutinizing the structures and foundations of your various relationships—both personal and professional. Those that no longer serve your best interest may end. The relationships that work best will be apparent to you, and you'll build on them.

On April 5, the new moon in Aries lights up the quiet part of your chart, that of the personal unconscious. An opportunity to work behind the scenes in some capacity may surface. Or you may have a chance to experience a past-life regression or to go on a spiritual retreat.

Mercury enters this same area of your chart on the 17th and will be there until May 6. During these several weeks, you're fired up with ideas that you can implement once Mercury enters your sign. You're in a seeding phase now—the seeding of desires, wishes and dreams.

The full moon in Libra on the 19th brings news about work, a co-worker or an employee, or a project reaches completion. You become more aware of the need for harmony and balance in your closest relationships. Jupiter retrograde forms a wide but beneficial angle to this full moon, so what you learn or realize expands your inner world in some way.

Venus enters Aries on the 20th, joining Mercury. These two travel together until May 15, when Venus enters your sign. You may be working on a creative venture that requires more solitude than usual. You and your partner may be hunkered down together, working on this project.

AT A GLANCE
April 5—New moon in Aries
April 10—Jupiter turns retrograde in Sagittarius
April 17—Mercury enters Aries
April 19—Full moon in Libra
April 20—Venus enters Aries
April 25—Pluto turns retrograde in Capricorn
April 29—Saturn turns retrograde in Capricorn

May 2019
Awesome

May is definitely your month, Taurus, with some delicious surprises! It begins on May 4, with a new moon in your sign. As you know by now, this new moon comes along just once a year and sets the tone for the next twelve months. Take a few minutes at the beginning of the month to think about what you would like to experience and achieve in the next year, make a list and post the list where you'll see it often.

With this new moon comes opportunities that are personally satisfying. Neptune is friendly to this moon, indicating that the opportunities may involve the arts, a creative endeavor of some kind or your spiritual beliefs.

From May 6 to 21, Mercury transits Taurus, and now you're in familiar terrain. Your patience deepens but so does your stubbornness. Your conscious focus and resilience are fortified, and it's an excellent time to dust off a project that has been on hold and dive into it.

On the 15th, Venus joins Mercury in your sign, marking one of the most romantic and creative times for you all year. The only other period that's equal falls between August 21 and September 14, when Venus moves through the romance and creativity sector of your chart. Venus will be in your sign until June 8, and during this period, your muse shadows you 24/7. If you aren't involved with anyone when this transit starts, you probably will be by the time it ends. If you're in a relationship, then things between you and your partner unfold with greater ease. You rediscover why you are together.

Also on the 15th, Mars moves into compatible water sign Cancer, where it will be until July 1. This transit sharpens your communication skills and brings a beautiful intuitive edge to your personality that enables you to make decisions quickly and decisively based on your hunches. You may be making more short-distance trips, perhaps for your work.

The full moon in Scorpio on May 18 falls in your partnership area. Expect news about a personal or business partnership. Thanks to a close, beneficial angle from Pluto to this full moon, you're empowered by the news. The Scorpio moon is one of the most emotionally intense, so be prepared to for some deep feelings.

Mercury enters Gemini and your financial area on May 21, and between then and June 4, your conscious focus is on what you earn, spend and save. If you think you're living beyond your means, then set up a realistic budget and resolve to stick to it.

AT A GLANCE
May 4—New moon in Taurus
May 6—Mercury enters Taurus
May 15—Venus goes into Taurus, Mars enters Cancer
May 18—Full moon in Scorpio
May 21—Mercury goes into Gemini

June 2019
Money matters

With the new moon in Gemini on June 3, a new source of income should surface for you. It could be a freelance job, something that comes to you through your network of acquaintances, a writing or publicity gig or even a part-time job. All that's required of you, Taurus, is to be vigilant and recognize the opportunity as it surfaces.

On the 4th, Mercury enters Cancer, a water sign compatible with your sun sign. As the planet of communication transits intuitive Cancer until June 26, your conscious focus is on siblings, your daily life, your communications with people in your environment and your neighborhood. You're more psychic now, so don't ignore that inner voice that prompts you to follow an impulse.

Venus enters Gemini on the 8th, and this should be very good for your finances. Venus facilitates earning, but you may also be attracted to high ticket items—art, a new car, a rare book or a new computer. Just be sure that between June 8 and July 3, when this transit ends, that you pay cash.

The full moon in Sagittarius on June 17 highlights resources you share with others—a partner, child, parent, manager or agent—and areas ruled by Sagittarius—publishing, international travel or your worldview and spiritual beliefs. There may be news in any of these areas, and because Jupiter retrograde is widely conjunct this full moon, the news proves to be expansive in some way. Perhaps you can now go ahead with the purchase of a home or car. Or you may land a great publishing deal or win a scholarship to grad school.

Neptune turns retrograde in Pisces on June 20, where it will remain until January 11, 2020. During this extended period, your intuitive and psychic perceptions are much sharper, you have to deal with things as they are rather than as you wish they would be and your imagination may seize on ideas and flights of fancy from the past. If you have seen certain friends in a false light, you will now perceive them as they really are.

From June 26 to July 7, Mercury moves in direct motion through Leo and the home/family area of your chart. This transit brings your conscious focus to your creative endeavors (the Leo factor) and to your family and partner. You may be talking with a realtor or checking out online real estate sites for a possible move to another area.

AT A GLANCE
June 3—New moon in Gemini
June 4—Mercury enters into Cancer
June 8—Venus goes into Gemini
June 17—Full moon in Sagittarius
June 20—Neptune turns retrograde
June 26—Mercury enters Leo

July 2019
Hectic

This month's two eclipses may create some tension and a sense of urgency, but as with most things you experience, Taurus, your resilience and ability to think on your feet will get you through any hurdles successfully. The solar eclipse in Cancer on July 2 should bring in new opportunities connected to communication, your neighborhood, siblings and your daily life. Some possibilities: you secure a freelance writing project, find the ideal neighborhood in which to live or have the chance to spend quality time with a neighbor or sibling. You could head up a publicity team at work or launch your own side business in the communication field. Uranus forms a wide, beneficial angle to the eclipse degree, so any opportunities that surface do so suddenly and unexpectedly.

The lunar eclipse in Capricorn on July 16 challenges you to be more nurturing and less self-centered. Pluto forms a close conjunction with the eclipse degree, suggesting that powerful, hidden forces are at work.

Before the eclipses occur, Mars enters Leo on July 1 and joins Mercury in the home/family area of your chart. This transit may prompt you to get busy with home improvement projects that you have been postponing. Since Leo is part of the equation, there's a creativity component to this transit. Perhaps you're renovating a room for a home office, where you can do your creative endeavors.

From July 3–27, Venus moves through Cancer. This transit brings an intuitive flow to your conscious mind and facilitates your relationships with family members. If a romance begins during this period, it may with someone you meet through a sibling or with someone in your neighborhood whom you already know.

On July 6, Mercury turns retrograde in Leo and slips back into Cancer, where it turns direct on the 31st. Reread the Mercury retrograde section in this introduction for general guidelines on how to navigate this period. Since the retro impacts your home life and then the communication sector of your chart, be sure to double check all appointments or delivery dates, and with any creative enterprise, revise, review and reconsider rather than starting something new.

Venus enters Leo on the 27th and in spite of Mercury's movement, life at home and within your family unfolds with greater smoothness and warmth. You may really ramp up your beautification efforts at home now. But try not to buy any new furniture or other expensive gadgets until after Mercury has turned direct on July 31.

The 31st also brings a new moon in Leo. You and your partner may decide to move, to start a family or to increase your family!

AT A GLANCE
July 1—Mars goes into Leo
July 2—Solar eclipse in Cancer
July 3—Venus enters Cancer
July 7—Mercury turns retrograde in Leo
July 16—Lunar eclipse in Capricorn
July 27—Venus enters Leo
July 31—Mercury turns direct, new moon in Leo

August 2019
Busy & pleasurable

There's so much going on in August that you may have to take some periodic down time, Taurus, where it's just you and nature. On the other hand, with so much energy in the romance/creativity section of your chart, you may want to divide your time in nature between your muse and your romantic interest.

On August 11, Jupiter turns direct in Sagittarius and begins to move toward its appointment with Capricorn on December 2. Now you can once again enjoy Jupiter's expansive nature in the outer world and implement what you learned when it was retrograde.

Also on the 11th, Mercury enters Leo once more, where it was before the retro started on July 7. Between then and August 29, your home is the hub of activity for your kids and their friends, and you may find that all the youthful energy stimulates your creativity. Expect lively discussions at dinner!

Uranus turns retrograde in your sign on August 12 and won't turn direct again until January 6, 2020. For you, these months may be a period of intense personal analysis as you delve into your own psychology, trying to understand why you do what you do, make the decisions you make and feel as you do. At some point in this retrograde, your questions are answered in what Abraham Maslow called an *Aha*! moment.

The full moon in Aquarius on August 15 highlights your career area. Both Venus and Mars are opposite this full moon. So how does this translate for you? It means you may have trouble with the people in your work environment—both men and women—and that no one agrees about how to proceed on a project. If you're self-employed, things get a bit nuts, with your phone ringing constantly and emails and text messages pouring in. *What should I do about this? How should we handle that?* Just take a few deep breaths, try some yoga postures and focus on what IS working in your life.

From August 18 to October 4, Mars transits Virgo and the romance/creativity area of your chart. You aggressively pursue your creative projects, your romantic interest and everything that brings you pleasure. But you do so in your quiet, persistent way as a Taurus, using the discernment of Mars in Virgo. Your sexuality is heightened during this transit.

On the 21st, Venus joins Mars in Virgo and, get ready for this one, Taurus! It's a romantic, creative and enjoyable period and one of the best this year. You may be tempted to overindulge in everything you enjoy, but use the energy to delve into your creativity and give your imagination free reign. This transit lasts until September 14, and you'll have to become accustomed to your muse shadowing you constantly!

Mercury enters Virgo on the 29th, joining both Venus and Mars. This lineup means your conscious thoughts, your heart and your energy are all centered on romance, creativity and your children. It would be a terrific time to take a working vacation that stimulates your creativity, where romance is in the air and where you kids have so much to do that they are fully engaged. This transit ends on September 14.

The 30th brings a new moon in Virgo. This one means opportunities surface in all the areas we have just talked about. It forms a great angle with Uranus retrograde in your sign, suggesting that the opportunities are unexpected.

AT A GLANCE

August 11—Jupiter turns direct, Mercury enters Leo
August 12—Uranus turns retrograde
August 15—Full moon in Aquarius
August 18—Mars enters Virgo
August 21—Venus goes into Virgo
August 29—Mercury enters Virgo
August 30—New moon in Virgo

September 2019
Balancing act

Compared to last month, September isn't as frenzied. Most of September's astrological energy is in air sign Libra, so you are more aware of the need for balance in your relationships.

On September 14, both Mercury and Venus enter Libra, and there's a full moon in Pisces. With Mercury and Venus traveling together in the daily work area of your chart, your rapport with employees and co-workers should be excellent. Others support your ideas and projects. Venus rules both Taurus and Libra, so it functions well here. An office flirtation could become something more.

The full moon in Pisces should ramp up your social life and your creative drive. Both Neptune and Pluto retrograde form beneficial angles to this full moon, indicating that any news you hear is empowering and appeals to your idealism in some way.

Saturn turns direct in Capricorn on the 18th. Now you can implement what you learned during the retrograde about the various structures in your life. Any publishing ventures in which you're involved are on solid ground.

The new moon in Libra on the 29th brings new opportunities in your daily work and in the ways you maintain your daily health. You could be promoted, move to a larger more comfortable office, hire new employees or land a freelance job. On the health front, you may try a new diet or exercise routine and are more aware of maintaining a balance between your personal and professional life.

September 14—Mercury and Venus enter Libra, full moon in Pisces
September 18—Saturn turns direct in Capricorn
September 29—New moon in Libra

October 2019
Intuitive

This month's astrological energies shift to Scorpio, the partnership area of your chart. On October 3, Mercury enters Scorpio. Venus follows on the 8th, and on the 27th, there's a new moon in Scorpio. These transits suggest that personal and professional partnerships involve discussions in which nothing is overlooked or neglected, negotiations that go well and deeper connections that you eagerly explore.

Mercury is moving direct in Scorpio until the 31st, when it then turns retrograde and remains that way until November 20. Look over the section in the introduction on Mercury retrograde for general guidelines on how to navigate this period more successfully. Since it falls in your partnership area, be sure to sign contracts and finalize deals before the retro begins. On a personal level, strive to communicate clearly with your partner. The probability of miscommunication is much greater during a retrograde.

Venus remains in Scorpio until November 1 and enables you to delve deeply in any creative endeavor. You aren't satisfied with easy answers or fluff. You're after the bottom line truth. Your sexuality is heightened during this transit, and your aesthetic sense is deepened.

The new moon in Scorpio brings new opportunities in partnerships—a new business manager, editor or accountant. You and your partner may decide to take your relationship to a deeper level—you move in together, get married or start a family.

Also on October 3, Pluto turns direct in Capricorn, so now you can put your dark side behind you and move forward with a deeper understanding of the many facets of your personality!

From October 4 to November 19, Mars moves through Libra. Now is the time to get things done at work, Taurus. Projects have a forward momentum, your relationships with co-workers and employees are favorable, and it's an ideal time to start wrapping things up as the end of the year approaches.

The full moon in Aries on the 13th highlights your personal unconscious. Your own motives become clearer to you, and thanks to a beneficial angle from Jupiter, your insights expand your inner life in a significant way.

October 3—Mercury goes into Scorpio, Pluto turns direct
October 4—Mars enters Libra
October 8—Venus goes into Scorpio
October 13—Full moon in Aries
October 27—New moon in Scorpio
October 31—Mercury turns retrograde

November 2019
Shifting energies

There's a lot going on this month: two planets turn direct; Venus moves into two signs; Mars enters a new sign; and then there are new and full moons. The shifting energies may require rapid adjustment on your part.

On November 1, Venus enters Sagittarius and the shared resources of your chart. This transit, which lasts until November 25, should facilitate obtaining mortgages, loans and breaks on your insurance premiums. It's also possible that your partner lands a raise. On the creativity front, you've now got the big picture of any endeavor in which you're involved, and it will be much easier for you to finish this project.

The full moon in Taurus on the 12th should be very much to your liking. Pluto, Saturn and Neptune retrograde form beneficial angles to it, so that any news you hear is likely to be pleasing to you and will have long-term effects. The news also puts you in control of the situation.

Between November 19 and January 4, 2020, Mars transits Scorpio, a sign it co-rules. This transit occurs in your partnership area, which means that both personal and business partnerships come strongly into focus. Mars provides forward momentum in all business transactions, and in your personal life, you and your partner enjoy heightened sexuality in your relationship. This transit favors research into esoteric and medical topics.

On the 20th, Mercury turns direct in Scorpio. Now it's safe to hit the road, sign contracts, make your travel plans and get moving with everything that was put on a back burner during the retrograde.

Venus enters Capricorn on the 25th and remains there until December 20. It's now forming a beneficial angle to your sun sign, Taurus, and since Venus rules your sign, this transit is important. Your professional goals unfold with greater smoothness during this transit and may involve the arts. Now that Mercury is moving direct, it's a great time to travel overseas, and that travel may be a mix of business and pleasure. You may meet a romantic interest while traveling, and that relationship could blossom into an intriguing relationship.

On the 26th, the new moon in Sagittarius could bring a publishing contract or a chance to travel overseas or to teach a graduate level course or a seminar/workshop in your area of expertise. It may also usher in opportunities for just sheer good times and fun!

Neptune turns direct in Pisces on the 26th, and you are once again the recipient of this planet's stimulation of your imagination and psychic ability.

AT A GLANCE
November 1—Venus goes into Sagittarius
November 12—Full moon in Taurus
November 19—Mars enters Scorpio
November 20—Mercury turns direct
November 25—Venus enters Capricorn
November 26—New moon in Sagittarius
November 27—Neptune turns direct

December 2019
Jupiter shift

As the last month of the year begins, take a few minutes to think about what you would like to achieve/experience in the new year. Make a list. Think of these items as desires rather than resolutions. Post the list where you'll see it often.

On December 2, Jupiter makes a major shift by moving into Capricorn, where it forms a friendly angle with your sun. It will be in this position until December 20, 2020. During this period, you'll be traveling internationally and could be involved in some facet of publishing or higher education. Your worldview and spiritual beliefs will expand greatly. Your self-expression will also expand in a significant way. You might, for instance, find a hobby that becomes not only your passion, but a source of income. You're the right person in the right place at the right time.

From December 9–29, Mercury moves through Sagittarius, and now it's party time! Your social calendar is crowded with holiday invitations, and you have your choice of places to go and people to see. Just be sure that you clear your desk before the holidays so you can enter the new year with a clean slate! On the 29th, Mercury joins Jupiter in Capricorn, and this transit carries you into the new year. Until January 17, 2020, these two planets are traveling together, and Jupiter is expanding your communication skills in a major way. You may be writing or speaking about a foreign trip.

The full moon in Gemini on December 12 highlights your financial area. If news arrives about your finances, don't act hastily. Neptune forms a challenging angle to this full moon, suggesting confusion and lack of information.

Venus enters Aquarius and your career area on the 20th and will be there until January 14, 2020. Your career and professional life unfold with greater ease during this transit.

Co-workers and bosses are receptive to your ideas and suggestions, and you have a chance to really get creative. An office romance may be kindled.

The solar eclipse on December 26 should usher in new career opportunities. You might hear, for example, that you've been promoted, or that your bonus is larger than expected. Or you're asked to conduct a seminar or workshop in your area of expertise. With Jupiter closely conjunct the eclipse degree, the opportunities that surface are expansive.

AT A GLANCE
December 2—Jupiter enters Capricorn
December 9—Mercury enters Sagittarius
December 12—Full moon in Gemini
December 20—Venus goes into Aquarius
December 26—Solar eclipse in Capricorn
December 29—Mercury enters into Capricorn

Reflection
Take a few minutes before the new year to reflect on how this year went for you. What kind of changes did Uranus in your sign bring? Are you in a better place now? Are you happier? More prosperous? Healthier? Jot your thoughts below.

_____
_____
_____
_____
_____

Happy New Year!

Gemini 2019

Mercury, the planet of communication, rules your sign as well as Virgo. Pay close attention to what it's doing each month—whether it's retrograde, the angles it makes to other planets and the sign it's in. Mercury is retrograde three times a year, and for general guidelines on how to navigate it successfully, read that section in the introduction.

The monthly roundups also include information on the transits of the other planets, the new and full moons, eclipses and everything else that's relevant to the month.

For most of 2019, Jupiter is traveling through Sagittarius, your opposite sign, expanding your business and personal partnerships. If you're not involved with anyone at the beginning of the year, you probably will be by the end of the year. Or if you're in a committed relationship, you and your partner may decide to move in together or get engaged or married. In business, Jupiter expands your options. Even though you're a master of multi-tasking, be careful that you don't spread your energy too thinly!

January 2019
Edgy, but social & fun

The new year gets off to a strong start with Mars in Aries, which it entered on December 31. It will be there until February 14, and until then, your social life is fired up. Friends seem to be coming out of the woodwork, and some of these contacts could have tips and insights that help you move closer to the achievement of your wishes and dreams.

From January 4 to 24, Mercury transits Capricorn. Your conscious focus turns to resources you share with others—a partner, child or parent. It's a good time to apply for a mortgage or loan and to take a closer look at your finances. Is it time to set up a budget? Your attention is also brought to your career and to details you may need to tend to now that you're in a new year.

On the 5th, the solar eclipse in Capricorn ushers in new career opportunities—a new job, promotion, pay raise, a more spacious office or a new boss. Your partner may land a raise. New financial resources open up. A favorable angle from Pluto to the eclipse degree puts you in the driver's seat.

On the 6th, Uranus turns direct in Aries, and now, once again, you reap the benefits of this planet's unpredictable energies. Unusual and even idiosyncratic people enter your life. Uranus now continues its journey toward its appointment with Taurus in early March.

Between January 7 and February 3, Venus transits Sagittarius, your opposite sign. This transit highlights your partnership area. You and your romantic partner may spend more time together having fun. You may not feel like working as hard as you usually do, and it would be a great time to get away together for a long weekend. Do some creative brainstorming. You may stumble upon an idea that appeals to you both and embark on a joint creative endeavor.

With a lunar eclipse in Leo on the 21st, your buttons are pushed by someone in your daily life. Just ignore it. It's not worth brooding about. It could involve a creative endeavor, one of your kids or a neighbor.

Mercury transits Aquarius from January 24 to February 10 and forms a beneficial angle to your sun sign, always a plus. Your communication skills are heightened, and your ideas tend to be edgier than usual and more oriented toward the future. You may also be attracted to foreign-born people and other cultures and could be writing about your observations.

January 4—Mercury enters into Capricorn
January 5—Solar eclipse in Capricorn
January 6—Uranus turns direct in Aries
January 7—Venus goes into Sagittarius
January 21—Lunar eclipse in Leo
January 24—Mercury goes into Aquarius

February 2019
Rapidly shifting energy

February should be less tense than January, but the energies shift rapidly, so go with the flow, Gemini, and you'll be fine.

Venus enters Capricorn on the 3rd and facilitates any dealings you have with banks and insurance companies. Your partner may get a raise or one of you could receive a royalty check, repayment on a loan or an insurance refund. It's also possible that your career takes a new turn of some kind. Women prove helpful. This transit ends on March 1.

The new moon in Aquarius on the 4th should bring new opportunities in foreign travel, publishing, higher education and alternative thinking. If you're a writer whose manuscript has been making the rounds, then this new moon could bring an offer. If you're traveling now, then you may have an opportunity to visit a country that isn't in your itinerary. Thanks to a beneficial angle from Jupiter, these new opportunities, whatever they are, expand your options and prove to be fortuitous.

Between February 10 and March 5, Mercury is in direct motion in Pisces, in your career area. This transit facilitates professional matters because your intuition and imagination are enhanced, and you're able to peg other people's needs and motives quickly. You may be somewhat indecisive at times because Pisces is often torn between her head and her heart. On March 5, Mercury turns retrograde, and that will be covered in next month's roundup.

Mars transits Taurus from February 14 to March 31. Think of this period as one when you are sowing seeds of desire that will sprout when Mars enters your sign. You may be more solitary during this period, but it gives you the time and space you need to complete a creative endeavor or a work project or both! Your physical energy will be excellent, and it would be a good idea to start an exercise routine to burn off some of that energy. Make it something you know you'll do regularly.

The full moon in Virgo on the 19th brings news about a parent, child, partner or someone in your personal environment. Uranus forms a close angle to this full moon, indicating that the news is unexpected. It's a good time to complete a home renovation project.

February 3—Venus enters Capricorn
February 4—New moon in Aquarius
February 10—Mercury goes into Pisces
February 14—Mars enters into Taurus
February 19—Full moon in Virgo

March 2019
Uranus shifting

There's a major shift this month with one of the outer planets, Uranus, which enters Taurus on March 6 and begins a seven-year cycle in this sign. It will remain in this sign until July 7, 2025, when it enters Gemini. Due to a retrograde, it returns to Taurus in early November and finally enters Gemini again in April 2026.

While Uranus transits Taurus and that area of your chart that rules the personal unconscious, a lot of internal stuff will change for you, Gemini. Issues you pushed aside over the years will surface, and you'll have to resolve them. In doing so, you will be reclaiming power you have disowned. Uranus shakes out the dead wood in your life and makes room for the new. It doesn't do this in the gentlest way, but if you go with the flow (and a bit of chaos!), the end result for you is excellent.

Now, back to the beginning of the month. On March 1, Venus enters Aquarius and that part of your chart that rules your worldview and spiritual beliefs, publishing, international travel, higher education and philosophy. Until March 26, then, Venus facilitates your life in all of these areas. You might, for instance, head off for some exotic port of call with a friend or your partner, or you might conduct a workshop about an esoteric topic in which you're well-versed. If you're unattached when this transit begins, that may change before the transit is finished. After all, during this transit, Venus is friendly to your sun, and you're feeling more confident and attractive, and other people are attracted to you.

From March 26 to April 20, Venus transits Pisces and your career area. Fortunately, Mercury will only be retro for two days after this transit starts, and then you can take full advantage of everything Venus does for you professionally. People you work with support your ideas, and your boss is in your court. A promotion might be in the offing!

Between March 5 to 28, Mercury is retrograde in Pisces, your career area. Read over the Mercury retro section in the introductions to all three years. Follow the general guidelines that are provided, and then take specifics steps for this particular retrograde. Don't start anything new at work. If possible, go back to older projects that you put on hold, dust them off and revise them. Communicate clearly with all co-workers, employees and bosses. Take nothing for granted. Recheck all appointments and due dates, and remember to take a deep breath whenever you feel overwhelmed!

On the 6th, the same day that Uranus enters Taurus, there's a new moon in Pisces. In spite of the Mercury retrograde, new career opportunities surface: a promotion, a new job, a new career path altogether or new projects. If you're self-employed, a new client or freelance project lands in your lap. Just don't sign any contracts until after Mercury turns direct on March 28, otherwise you may be revisiting the terms.

The full moon in Libra on the 20th brings news about a creative endeavor, a romantic relationship or one of your kids. The news isn't expected and may require an adjustment in your attitude. In romance and love, Gemini, talk about your differences and don't make any hasty decisions.

Once Mercury turns direct again on the 28th, have a party! Go out with friends, and take in a concert or an art exhibit. Celebrate!

From March 31 to May 15, Mars transits your sign, and now you have all the forward thrust you need to get things done. You may be doing a lot of writing, traveling or networking during this period, but that's the sort of thing you love. Just remember to carve out a little time for yourself daily and to exercise regularly.

AT A GLANCE
March 1—Venus enters into Aquarius
March 5—Mercury turns retrograde in Pisces
March 6—New moon in Pisces, Uranus enters Taurus
March 20—Full moon in Libra
March 26—Venus goes into Pisces
March 28—Mercury turns direct
March 31—Mars enters Gemini

April 2019
Chaotic

It's going to be a strange and tumultuous month. Three planets are turning retrograde, and both Mercury and Venus are entering new signs. But first, on April 5, there's a new moon in compatible fire sign Aries. This one should stoke the fires in your social life, with so many invitations coming in that you have your choice of things to do. The Aries moon can prompt you to be impulsive and impatient and can trigger rash behavior. Exercise common sense. New friendships and contacts surface. Enjoy them.

On the 10th, Jupiter turns retrograde in Sagittarius, in your partnership area, and doesn't turn direct against until August 11. This planet's expansive nature now turns inward. For the next several months, you'll be scrutinizing how your spiritual beliefs, educational background, worldview and general outlook on life are reflected or integrated in both personal and professional partnerships. How do these partnerships measure up to your internal gauge? How do they *feel*?

Between April 17 and May 6, Mercury transits Aries, the same area where the new moon took place. These few weeks should be enjoyable for you, with unusual ideas flooding your conscious thoughts and a kind of entrepreneurial spirit moving you along.

On the 19th, there's another full moon in Libra because the one on March 20 was at 0 degrees, and this one falls at 29 degrees. Consider it a blessing. Mercury isn't retrograde, and now you have a chance to redo anything that got messed up during March's full moon!

Venus joins Mercury in Aries on the 20th, so now you're really on fire and may be spending a lot of time with friends or on social media or both! If you meet a romantic interest, it may be someone you meet through friends or through a dating website.

On the 25th and 29th respectively, Pluto and Saturn turn retrograde in Capricorn. Pluto's retro lasts until October 3, and during this lengthy period, you may become acquainted with your shadow self, as Carl Jung called it. You're capable of dealing with this darker side of your personality by reasoning your way to the root cause. Saturn's retrograde lasts until September 18 and enables you to reassess the structures in various areas of your life. You'll recognize the areas that need attention and will decide whether it's worth your time to bolster them.

AT A GLANCE
April 5—New moon in Aries
April 10—Jupiter turns retrograde in Sagittarius
April 17—Mercury enters Aries
April 19—Full moon in Libra
April 20—Venus enters Aries
April 25—Pluto turns retrograde in Capricorn
April 29—Saturn turns retrograde in Capricorn

May 2019
Calmer

It's a tamer month than April. One of the things you're doing is sowing seeds for what you want to experience and achieve in June, when an abundance of astrological energy shifts into your sign.

The new moon in Taurus on May 4 brings new opportunities to delve within yourself and to see your motives and psyche in a different way. It may occur through a creative endeavor, therapy or a past life regression or particularly vivid and insightful dreams. Once Mercury enters Taurus on the 6th, the opportunities, whatever they are, capture your full conscious attention. Remember, too, that Uranus is also in Taurus, so you're experiencing your own unconscious in a new and different way and could be writing or blogging about it. Mercury's transit lasts until May 21, when Mercury enters your sign—finally!—and remains until June 4.

During Mercury's transit through your sign, you're in fine shape. Your head and your heart are on the same page, and your communication skills are sharp and focused. Pity the fool who starts an argument with you.

From May 15 to June 8, Venus transits Taurus, a sign it rules, and suddenly, all this inner focus stuff evens out. You realize you have all the time you need to dig through your own psyche. If you become involved with someone during this transit, it may remain a very private relationship until next month. Your sensuality deepens with Venus in Taurus.

Also on the 15th, Mars enters Cancer and your financial area, where it will be until July 1. This transit may come at you like a rushing river of intuitive impressions. You could dream about a stock or company in which you should invest. A close friend or even a family member could be the source of new income.

The 18th brings a full moon in passionate Scorpio and highlights your daily work and the way you maintain your daily health. Deep emotions often accompany a moon in Scorpio, and the trick is to avoid getting sucked into the inner conflict. All too often, inner conflicts find their way into the external world, and the last thing you want is conflict at work with anyone.

On the 21st, Mercury enters your sign and now the fun begins, Gemini.

AT A GLANCE
May 4—New moon in Taurus
May 6—Mercury enters Taurus
May 15—Venus goes into Taurus, Mars enters Cancer
May 18—Full moon in Scorpio
May 21—Mercury goes into Gemini

June 2019
5 stars

It's a month made especially for you! Take a few minutes on June 1 to think about what you would like to experience or achieve in the next twelve months. Make a list, and post it where you'll see it often. On June 3, the day of the new moon in your sign, mull over each item on your list. Vividly imagine each thing happening. This new moon comes around just once a year and sets the tone for the next twelve months, so do something special for yourself on the 3rd. Do whatever makes you happy. Then step out of the way, and let the universe do its job.

On the 4th, Mercury enters Cancer and your financial area, where it will be until June 26. Your conscious focus is now on finances—what you earn, spend and save and how you can boost your income. The new opportunities that come in with the new moon may include writing or speaking gigs or a publicity campaign where you're hired to do publicity for a product, service or person. Mercury in Cancer also makes you more aware of your family ties and responsibilities—your roots.

From June 26 to July 7, Mercury is moving in direct motion in Leo, the communication and daily life section of your chart. If you're involved in a creative endeavor, get as much of it done as possible before Mercury turns retrograde in Leo on July 7. More about that in the July roundup. Mercury in Leo is comfortable for you, and you may discover you have a bit of a flair for drama during this transit. Pour it into your creativity.

Venus enters your sign on the 8th and remains for about three weeks, until July 3. This period is one of the most romantic, creative and pleasurable for you all year. It's equaled only by Venus in Libra from September 14 to October 8. You're at the peak of your game, and everyone wants to be your buddy, your lover or your confidante. You're self-confident, and every day is a new adventure! Your muse is eager to play, so leave some time for your creative endeavors.

The full moon in Sagittarius on June 17 highlights your partnership area. If there's news, it should be positive and uplifting. A joint project reaches completion. Jupiter retrograde is widely conjunct to this full moon, so you and your partner enjoy each other's company.

Neptune turns retrograde in Pisces on June 20, so from then until November 27, when it turns direct, facets of your professional life may feel surreal to you. Your intuition and imagination are heightened, and your spiritual insights are spot on. Neptune often has a dreamy quality to it, particularly in Pisces, a sign it rules, but when it's retrograde, it's time for a reality check. Things you might have ignored about your career are now faced head on.

AT A GLANCE
June 3—New moon in Gemini
June 4—Mercury enters into Cancer
June 8—Venus goes into Gemini
June 17—Full moon in Sagittarius
June 20—Neptune turns retrograde
June 26—Mercury enters Leo

July 2019
Busy

This month is jammed with astrological events—two eclipses, a Mercury retrograde, Venus entering two signs and Mars entering a new sign. And oh, the usual new and full moons.

On July 1, Mars enters Leo and your communication sector. Remember, Mars provides wind to your sails, and with it in Leo until August 18, adrenaline is pouring through you on the creative front. Whether this creativity takes form through some type of written or verbal communication or through some other venue, you're a veritable power house who makes things happen.

The solar eclipse in Cancer brings unexpected financial opportunities and perhaps an opportunity to the home/family area of your chart as well. Uranus forms a beneficial angle to the eclipse degree, so whatever surfaces will be sudden. You simply have to be ready to seize these opportunities when you recognize them.

Between July 3 and 27, Venus transits Cancer and your financial area, a benefit for your income. You may be spending more during this transit, but you'll earn more, too. In romance, you may meet someone special who shares your values. Venus in this sign also benefits your family—that's the Cancer component. You feel more nurturing toward loved ones and more nurturing toward yourself.

On July 7, Mercury turns retrograde in Leo, slips back into Cancer on the 19th and then direct in that sign on the 31st. Read over the Mercury retrograde section in the introductions and follow the general guidelines for navigating this period more easily. Since the retro occurs in Leo and that area of your chart that rules communication, your daily life, siblings and neighbors, be sure to communicate clearly with all of these individuals. If your daily schedule gets messed up in some way, don't freak out about it. Just make your corrections and move on. Since Leo is such an inherently creative sign, any artistic endeavors you're involved in should be revised, reviewed and reconsidered.

The lunar eclipse in Capricorn on July 16 occurs in the area of shared resources. Emotions may swirl during this eclipse, perhaps as a result of some remark a business or personal partner makes. But Jupiter retrograde is friendly to the eclipse degree, so things shake out better than you or anyone else expect.

From July 27 to August 21, Venus transits Leo. Mercury retrograde may put a damper on your love life and creative endeavors, but only until July 31st, when Mercury turns direct again. Once that happens, then you're filled with passion and creative drive that is practically unstoppable.

Along with Mercury turning direct on July 31st, there's a new moon in Leo. In some areas of the world, it occurs on August 1. This one should bring new creative and communication opportunities. If you and your family have been searching for a new neighborhood, you may find it on or around this new moon.

AT A GLANCE
July 1—Mars goes into Leo
July 2—Solar eclipse in Cancer
July 3—Venus enters Cancer
July 7—Mercury turns retrograde in Leo
July 16—Lunar eclipse in Capricorn
July 27—Venus enters Leo
July 31—Mercury turns direct, new moon in Leo

August 2019
A month of synchronicities

It's another month of rapidly shifting energies, but you and your mutable sign siblings won't have any problem keeping up with it all.

On August 11, two astrological events occur. Jupiter turns direct in Sagittarius and now moves toward its appointment with Capricorn on December 2. Once again, the expansive energies of this planet radiate into the external world. Your partnership options—business and personal—broaden. Mercury also enters Leo again today, the same spot it was in before the retrograde, between June 26 and July 7. You can move forward with confidence in your various projects. You may be spending more time with your siblings and neighbors, and if a move is on the horizon for you, it gets closer once Mercury and Venus enter Virgo, on August 29 and August 21 respectively. And once Mars enters Virgo later this month, you see the first major push toward this move.

On the 12th, Uranus turns retrograde in Taurus, and it carries you into the new year, to January 6, 2020. Uranus is always unpredictable, but when retrograde, that unpredictability turns inward. You may experience sudden startling insights into your own psyche. Synchronicities flourish. Signs are everywhere, and all you have to do is interpret them.

The full moon in Aquarius on August 15 interrupts the Virgo energy and draws your attention to the bottom line about your beliefs and worldview. News may be forthcoming about publishing projects or an international trip you're planning.

Between August 18 and October 4, Mars moves through Virgo and your family/home area. Here's your initial thrust toward a move. If it's just been a vague idea up to this point, it now begins to flesh out. Where would you and your partner like to live? What can you realistically afford? What type of neighborhood or city are you looking for? The Virgo element in this transit urges you to pay attention to these kinds of details.

On the 21st, Venus joins Mars in Virgo, and now your search becomes somewhat easier. You go with the flow, but still pay attention to details. Part of this transit also involves discernment in romance/love, creative endeavors and finances. Details, Gemini, details.

On the 29th, it's back to Virgo energy when Mercury enters that sign and remains until September 14. Your conscious mind is wrestling with so many details about home/family and a possible move that you may have trouble separating your desires from the reality.

As if that's not enough, the universe brings you a new moon in Virgo on August 30. Whew. Now what? It's to your advantage to find out exactly where Virgo lies in your chart. Maybe you have a Virgo moon, and this new moon is your lunar return. Fantastic! Whatever decisions you make will prove to be advantageous. But suppose this new moon falls elsewhere? Then take the meaning of the house and apply the new opportunities to that area.

AT A GLANCE

August 11—Jupiter turns direct, Mercury enters Leo
August 12—Uranus turns retrograde
August 15—Full moon in Aquarius
August 18—Mars enters Virgo
August 21—Venus goes into Virgo
August 29—Mercury enters Virgo
August 30—New moon in Virgo

September 2019
Romantic & creative

Compared to the last few months, September is quieter and more manageable—until the 14th, when three astrological events occur. Mercury and Venus both enter Libra, and there's a full moon in Pisces. As Mercury and Venus move through the romance and creativity section of your chart, you're in rare form, meeting each day with a renewed sense of optimism and self-confidence. Your muse is as loyal as a puppy now, tagging after you wherever you go and ready to assist in any creative endeavor you embark on. Your partner is attentive and romantic. Even your kids are behaving!

Mercury remains in Libra until October 3, and Venus remains there until October 8. While these two travel together, there's a lot of discussion about your various creative projects. You and your partner may brainstorm about a joint endeavor of some kind. You could also be involved in a creative project with kids.

The full moon in Pisces highlights your career area. Expect news about professional matters. Since Neptune is closely conjunct to this moon and Pluto forms a beneficial angle to it, the news puts you in the power seat. With Neptune there can often be some confusion or lack of full information. But once you get past that, things are fine. This full moon could bring a promotion.

Saturn turns direct in Capricorn on the 18th, a welcome reprieve. Now you can implement what you learned during the retrograde about the various structures in your life—family, career, finances, creativity and partnerships.

On the 29th, the new moon in Libra brings new creative and romantic opportunities. If you and your partner have talked about starting a family, this new moon could bring about that reality. If you aren't involved with anyone, this new moon may change that. Or it may act as an exclamation point to an existing relationship, where you and your partner decide to deepen your commitment to each other.

AT A GLANCE
September 14—Mercury and Venus enter Libra, full moon in Pisces
September 18—Saturn turns direct in Capricorn
September 29—New moon in Libra

October 2019
Self-discovery

It's another busy month astrologically. On October 3, Mercury enters Scorpio, and Pluto turns direct. Mercury will be moving direct until Halloween, and this period favors any sort of research that requires patience and deep probing. Your conscious mind is exceptionally intuitive now, and you're able to make quick decisions based on that inner voice. Your insights into other people are also powerful during this transit. In your daily work arena, you discover new ways of doing things and dealing with co-workers and employees.

When Pluto turns direct in Capricorn, you can leave your shadow self behind you and reap the benefits of what you've learned about yourself during the retrograde.

On the 4th, Mars joins Venus in Libra for several days. Your sexuality is greatly heightened, and so is your capacity for enjoyment. Between now and November 19, in fact, you and your partner should try to get away for a romantic weekend or a vacation and rediscover why you're together. There's a lot of forward momentum with this transit in terms of your creative endeavors, too, and you're able to advance your goals more easily.

Venus enters Scorpio on the 8th, joining Mercury in your daily work area, and helps to facilitate whatever you're doing. Scorpio is an emotionally intense sign, so you may be feeling things much more deeply than usual. Your capacity for intimacy increases.

The full moon in Aries on the 13th should be spectacular. Jupiter forms a favorable angle to this full moon, so any news you hear will be positive, and you'll feel enormously fortunate. Your social calendar is likely to get crowded on or around the time of this full moon.

The new moon in Scorpio on the 27th should bring new opportunities in your daily work life—a promotion, new responsibilities, a new boss or new employees. Uranus is opposed to this moon, so opportunities may surface without warning.

On the 31st, Mercury turns retrograde in Scorpio and will turn direct on November 20. By now, you know the drill for these retrogrades. But as a reminder, read through the Mercury retrograde section in the introduction, and follow the general guidelines. Since this one occurs in your daily work area, you may be revisiting projects and issues from the past.

AT A GLANCE
October 3—Mercury goes into Scorpio, Pluto turns direct
October 4—Mars enters Libra
October 8—Venus goes into Scorpio
October 13—Full moon in Aries
October 27—New moon in Scorpio
October 31—Mercury turns retrograde

November 2019
News

Buckle up! It's another busy month.

On November 1, Venus enters Sagittarius and the partnerships area of your chart, where it will be until the 25th. During these several weeks, you and a partner may be working on a joint creative project, and the chemistry between you should be good. You agree on the big picture, and only the execution of details may differ. Venus in Sadge enjoys a good time, and with the holidays approaching, there will be plenty of occasions to enjoy yourself—either with your partner or with others.

Venus enters Capricorn on November 25 and remains there until December 20. This transit facilitates all your dealings with banks and investment and insurance companies. Some of your professional goals become clearer to you and easier to achieve. Your partner could get a generous end of the year bonus or a raise.

The full moon in Taurus on the 12th brings news that has long-term effects and that should be quite beneficial to your career and even your finances. It's possible that some of your core beliefs have changed throughout this year and those changes are now reflected in your experiences.

From November 19 to January 4, 2020, Mars transits Scorpio. This transit enables you to clear your desk before the new year, so you can enter 2020 with a completely clean slate. With Mercury turning direct a day after Mars enters Scorpio, there won't be any significant slowdown at all.

Once Mercury turns direct, you can move full steam ahead again on everything you postponed during the retrograde.

On or around the new moon in Sagittarius on November 26, you and your partner may plan an overseas trip for the holidays. If you're a writer whose manuscript is making the rounds for submission, you could hear that you've made a sale!

And finally, on the 27th, Neptune turns direct again in Pisces and your career area. Now you can enjoy the full benefit of this planet's psychic insights and imagination once again.

AT A GLANCE
November 1—Venus goes into Sagittarius
November 12—Full moon in Taurus
November 19—Mars enters Scorpio
November 20—Mercury turns direct
November 25—Venus enters Capricorn
November 26—New moon in Sagittarius
November 27—Neptune turns direct

December 2019
Jupiter shift

As December gets underway, take a few minutes to think about what you would like to experience and achieve in the new year. Make a list. Think of this as a list of desires rather than resolutions. Post it where you'll see it frequently.

On the 2nd Jupiter makes a major transit from Sagittarius into Capricorn and will be there until December 20, 2020. Expansion and serendipity now occur in the shared resources area of your chart. Your partner's income increases. You may live or work overseas or have more contact than usual with individuals in other countries, or your company's services expand to foreign shores. A new spectrum of possibilities exists with this transit. Check your natal chart to find out where Capricorn is and what planets you may have in this cardinal earth sign. That area and planet will be the focus of Jupiter's expansion and luck.

From December 9 to 29, Mercury transits Sagittarius. Your conscious focus is squarely on partnerships. You and your partner/spouse may be swept up in the general good cheer that surrounds Christmas—office parties, house parties and celebrations with family and close friends. You may also be discussing the particulars of your relationship—what you envision for your life together and what you would like to do and experience as individuals and as a couple.

From December 29 to January 17, 2020, Mercury joins Jupiter in Capricorn. Your communication skills expand in some way when these two planets travel together. You're more goal-oriented, more focused and singular in your vision.

December 12 brings a full moon in your sign. A communication project is completed, and any news you hear may be confusing because Neptune forms a difficult angle to this full moon. But not to worry, Gemini. You're one of the most flexible signs and can roll with the punches any time.

From December 20 to January 14, 2020, Venus moves through fellow air sign Aquarius, and you're in for another terrific several weeks. If you're traveling, romance may find you at some point, and your creative drive will be particularly strong.

The solar eclipse in Capricorn on the 26th should be a treasure trove of new opportunities. Jupiter is closely conjunct the eclipse degree, and the opportunities that come your way will be lucky ones. Embrace them.

AT A GLANCE
December 2—Jupiter enters Capricorn
December 9—Mercury enters Sagittarius
December 12—Full moon in Gemini
December 20—Venus goes into Aquarius
December 26—Solar eclipse in Capricorn
December 29—Mercury enters into Capricorn

Reflection

Take a few minutes to look back over this year. Did it meet your expectations? Are you happier? More mindful? Do you feel more self-confident? What did you take away from this year? Jot your thoughts below.

_____

_____

_____

_____

_____

Happy New Year!

Cancer 2019

Since the moon rules your sign, pay close attention to this year's solar and lunar eclipses and to the new and full moons each month. In the roundups, you'll find information on retrogrades of the planets, on the angles that transiting planets are making to your sun sign and to each other and what it all means for you. As a lunar-ruled sign, it would be ideal if you had access to the daily motion of the moon, which changes signs every two and a half days.

2019 is an interesting year for you, Cancer. Both Saturn and Pluto are in Capricorn, your opposite sign, and are bringing about profound change in your business and personal partnerships. Also, with both planets in Capricorn, your career strategies and goals may be changing as well. On December 2, Jupiter will be joining these two planets, and the changes that have come about will now be easier to navigate as your options expand.

January 2019
Great start

Welcome to 2019! Your year gets off to a terrific start professionally because on December 31, 2018, Mars entered Aries and your career area. Mars is all about forward momentum, so now that the Christmas holidays are over, you're ready to leap into new projects and creative endeavors. Mars rules Aries, and that means it functions at optimum capacity here, helping to clear out the old and embrace the new. The transit lasts until February 14.

Between January 4 and 24, Mercury moves through Capricorn, your opposite sign, and brings your conscious focus to partnerships and to career matters (that's the Capricorn element). You're quite the organizer during this transit and strikingly disciplined in everything you undertake. You and a business partner may be brainstorming about your company's strategy for the new year and are able to accomplish a great deal. Once Mercury enters Aquarius on the 24th, your mind is freed from certain constraints, and you play around with unusual and idiosyncratic ideas. Test them against your considerable intuition.

A solar eclipse in Capricorn occurs on January 4, and you may feel the effects before it arrives. It should bring new opportunities in your partnership area and in your professional life. If you're considering starting your own business, then this eclipse could bring the opportunities that enable you to do so. And with Mars in your career area until mid-February, it's an ideal time to strike out on your own.

Uranus turns direct in Aries and your career area on January 6, and once again, this planet's electrical energy is at your disposal. Don't be surprised if unusual people enter your professional life now, people who may be experts, even geniuses, in their particular field. Take advantage of it.

Lovely Venus enters gregarious Sagittarius on January 7 and forms a beneficial angle to your career area. Sweet, Cancer! Love and romance may enter your life through your career doorway, and what fun this relationship will be. Another possibility is that you have an opportunity to dive into a new creative endeavor which you're passionate about. The other good thing about this transit is that it facilitates your daily work routine and relationships with co-workers and employees. The transit lasts until February 3.

The lunar eclipse in Leo on January 24 happens in your financial area. Your reaction to this eclipse depends on your beliefs about money, your earning capacity, your income and your creative abilities. If your alarm is triggered—by an unexpected bill, for example, or news about one of your creative endeavors—just deal with it as quickly as you can.

AT A GLANCE

January 4—Mercury enters into Capricorn
January 5—Solar eclipse in Capricorn
January 6—Uranus turns direct in Aries
January 7—Venus goes into Sagittarius
January 21—Lunar eclipse in Leo
January 24—Mercury goes into Aquarius

February 2019
Pleasant

February is somewhat tamer than January, with some pleasant transits that you'll enjoy.

On February 3, Venus enters Capricorn and sticks around until March 1. If you're involved in a relationship, then you and your partner may talk about deepening that commitment. It will be done, though, in an organized, practical way (Capricorn speaking here). Let's say you decide to live together. The Capricorn method of doing this is to have just a single residence, so one of you will have to sublease your apartment or rent/sell your home. If you decide to get married, it probably won't be done by a justice of the peace. A date will be set and a location will be chosen—everything proper.

On February 4, the new moon in Aquarius brings opportunities in the area of joint finances that will have long-term affects. Your partner, for instance, could get a raise that's substantial enough to change your lifestyle. Or perhaps your home sells above your asking price. If you're buying a home, you find a great interest rate and terms.

On the 10th, Mercury enters fellow water sign Pisces, and now your intuition deepens to the point where your insights about yourself and others may blow everyone out of the water. Your imagination also takes flight, soaring into the unknown and returning with fodder that you can use in a fantasy novel or some other artistic project. This transit lasts for a while because on March 5, Mercury turns retrograde. We'll discuss that in next month's roundup. But before it begins, be sure to read over the Mercury retrograde section in the introduction, and prepare for this by following the general guidelines.

Mars enters compatible earth sign Taurus on February 14 and stays until March 31. Your physical endurance and patience increase during this transit, so tackle things that require both characteristics. Your sensuality also deepens during this time. Everything and everyone take on a bright patina. Food tastes better, so there may be a tendency to overeat! Be sure to have a regular exercise routine. Your social calendar could get crowded, too. You're in demand, Cancer! Enjoy it.

On the 19th, the full moon in compatible earth sign Virgo highlights the communication area in your chart. Mars forms a beneficial angle to this full moon, so your verbal and written skills are sharp and penetrating. There could be news about a sibling or neighbor.

AT A GLANCE
February 3—Venus enters Capricorn
February 4—New moon in Aquarius
February 10—Mercury goes into Pisces
February 14—Mars enters into Taurus
February 19—Full moon in Virgo

March 2019
Mercury retro alert

March is jammed. Not only does it feature the first Mercury retrograde of the year, but Uranus makes a major shift, and both Venus and Mars enter new signs. But let's begin with March 1, when Venus enters Aquarius. Whatever new opportunities last month's new moon in Aquarius brought about, Venus now enhances. This transit ends on March 26 and during these several weeks, money arrives from other sources—a royalty check, an insurance rebate or credit from a bank error. And yes, your partner's raise is now in the bank!

Once Venus enters Pisces, a fellow water sign, things feel wonderful to you. You swim in the familiar waters of your intuition and imagination, and if you're traveling, it's even better. You can immerse yourself completely in whatever culture you're in. Your spiritual beliefs deepen. Fortunately, Mercury is retro only two days beyond when this transit begins.

Okay, now on to Mercury retrograde in Pisces that begins on March 5. It lasts until March 28, and during these several weeks, life may feel chaotic, particularly if you're traveling, are in college or grad school or are involved in creative work that requires an expansive imagination. By now, you have probably looked over the Mercury retro sections in the introductions to each of the three years, so you have an idea of the kind of snafus that can occur. Follow the general guidelines, and keep in mind that by listening to your intuition, you can avoid many of the retrograde pitfalls!

On the 6th, there are two events: there's a new moon in Pisces, and Uranus enters Taurus. The new moon may be dampened somewhat by Mercury's antics, but the moon itself is bolstered by Saturn. Any new opportunities that surface have long-term effects. Just don't sign any contracts until after Mercury turns direct on the 28th. Neptune is also closely conjunct this new moon, indicating that the opportunities may be artistic or spiritual in nature.

Also on March 6, Uranus enters Taurus. It did so briefly in 2018, then turned retro and slipped back into Aries. Now it will be in Taurus for the next seven years, until July 7, 2025. It will slip back into Taurus briefly and finally enter Gemini in April 2026. During Uranus's transit through Aries, some facet of your life underwent sudden, drastic change. This time around with Uranus, the changes will be somewhat kinder to you because the planet will be forming a beneficial angle to your sun sign. It's likely that unusual people will enter your circle of friends between now and 2026. You may get involved in political groups with a progressive message, may rebel against the status quo or may decide you don't have anything in common with some of your friends and end those relationships. You may also discover you have a talent for innovative thought and creative endeavors that impact the masses.

The full moon in Libra on March 20 is one of two full moons in that sign because this one falls at 0 degrees, and the next one, in April, is at 29 degrees. It highlights that area of your chart that rules home/family, and since it's in Libra, it also concerns relationships. How balanced are your relationships with your family? How would you change the dynamics if you could? There could be news about one of your parents.

Celebrate on the 28th, when Mercury turns direct in Pisces, and get busy doing all the things that were delayed during the retrograde.

Between March 31 and April 15, Mars transits Gemini. These weeks are about networking in any way you feel comfortable—through social media, in person or by email. You're seeding thoughts and desires that will blossom when Mars enters your sign on April 15. So be careful what you wish for!

AT A GLANCE
March 1—Venus enters into Aquarius
March 5—Mercury turns retrograde in Pisces
March 6—New moon in Pisces, Uranus enters Taurus
March 20—Full moon in Libra
March 26—Venus goes into Pisces
March 28—Mercury turns direct
March 31—Mars enters Gemini

April 2019
Career focus

It's another busy month of shifting energies. Three planets turn retrograde—Jupiter, Saturn and Pluto. Both Mercury and Venus enter Aries and your career area, and there's a new moon in Aries. The emphasis is on your career.

On April 5, the new moon in Aries should bring in new professional opportunities. It could be something as simple as a redefinition of your job responsibilities or something as complex and pleasing as a promotion. It depends on where you have placed your focus. If you have been seeking a different career path, then this new moon could bring it your way.

Jupiter turns retrograde in Sagittarius on April 10, and between then and August 11, when it turns direct again, its expansive nature turns inward. Your spirituality becomes more important to you, and you integrate it into your daily work life. You might start a meditation practice or join a vision quest. You might book an overseas trip to some remote corner of the world to explore ancient sites.

Between April 17 and May 6, Mercury transits Aries and your career area, and from April 20 to May 15, so does Venus. As this duo moves through Aries, your communication skills are sharper, your ideas are edgier and your passions are stoked. If a romance begins during this transit, it may be with someone you meet through your work, and it's likely to be a relationship that's passionate, sweeping and erratic.

The full moon in Libra on the 19th lights up the family/home area of your chart. There may be news about a family member or someone who is like family to you. Jupiter's retrograde in Sagittarius forms a beneficial angle to this moon, so the news is positive. If your home is for sale, this full moon could bring in an offer.

On the 25th, Pluto turns retrograde in Capricorn, and four days later, on the 29th, so does Saturn. During these retrogrades, which last until October 3 and September 18 respectively, you will be scrutinizing the various structures in your life (Saturn) and may become acquainted with your shadow side (Pluto).

AT A GLANCE

April 5—New moon in Aries
April 10—Jupiter turns retrograde in Sagittarius
April 17—Mercury enters Aries
April 19—Full moon in Libra
April 20—Venus enters Aries
April 25—Pluto turns retrograde in Capricorn
April 29—Saturn turns retrograde in Capricorn

May 2019
Networking

This month, the focus is on Taurus and your eleventh house of networking, publicity, your friends and the groups with whom you associate. On May 4, the new moon in Taurus brings in new opportunities in any or all of these areas. Taurus is grounded, patient, practical and usually finishes what he or she has started. These characteristics are inherent in this new moon and in Mercury's transit through the sign, which begins on May 6 and ends on May 21. There's a mystical side to Taurus that may surface during this transit and an awareness of other realms and dimensions that you may explore with friends.

Venus enters Taurus on the 15th, and Mars enters your sign. The first transit facilitates your networking and any publicity campaigns in which you're involved. Friends are supportive of all your endeavors. If a romance is kindled during this transit, it may be with someone you meet through friends or could be someone you already know as a friend.

This Mars transit through your sign lasts until July 1 and should be terrific for you, enabling you to get things done, to move forward in every area where you place your focus and energy. Your intuition is particularly strong, and your emotions are your truest gauge about the state of your life.

The full moon in fellow water sign Scorpio on the 18th brings news about a romantic relationship or a creative endeavor. Scorpio is an intense sign, and with the full moon bringing everything into sharp focus, you may feel more emotional than usual. Any news you hear, though, should work in your favor, thanks to a beneficial angle from powerful Pluto.

From May 21 to June 4, Mercury moves through Gemini, a sign it rules. This transit sharpens your communication skills and your people skills. Since it occurs in the area of the personal unconscious, you may be doing a lot of writing in solitude or may be contacted through social media.

May 4—New moon in Taurus
May 6—Mercury enters Taurus
May 15—Venus goes into Taurus, Mars enters Cancer
May 18—Full moon in Scorpio
May 21—Mercury goes into Gemini

June 2019
5 stars

June should be to your liking, and the good stuff begins on June 3, with a new moon in Gemini. Opportunities that surface may revolve around learning, research, communication—writing, speaking, teaching—and networking. You might have a chance to teach a course or workshop, could get a freelance writing project or could be hired for a behind-the-scenes project. Gemini is a sociable sign, so expect to be out and about more than usual.

On the 4th, Mercury moves into your sign and will be there until the 26th. What fun this transit should be! Head and heart are now on the same page. Your intuition runs deep and furiously and keeps you on track in your relationships. Once Mercury enters Leo on the 26th, your conscious focus turns to finances—what you earn, spend and save and how to earn more. You may become more budget conscious while Mercury is moving direct in Leo. Then on July 7, it turns retrograde in that sign. More about the retrograde in next month's roundup.

Venus enters Gemini on June 8, and until July 3, your creativity is animated. You're more eager to communicate what you know, feel and sense about the world. You may use blogging and social media as your platform, or if you're visually oriented, photography and art could be your vehicles for self-expression. You're sowing seeds of desire and intention with this transit so that when Venus enters your sign on July 3, you'll be primed and ready to reap the considerable benefits of that transit.

The full moon in Sagittarius on June 17 brings news about an overseas trip you're planning or about your daily work routine. You might hear, for example, that your boss is being transferred and that you're in line for a promotion. If you're self-employed, you might hear about a potential new client who is interested in your services or products.

Neptune turns retrograde in Pisces on the 20th and stays that way until November 27. During this lengthy retrograde, you may have to confront and deal with issues that you previously viewed through rose-tinted glasses. These issues may involve your beliefs—spiritual and political—and your general philosophical approach to life. It's a subtle process, though, and throughout your dreams may be especially vivid and insightful.

June 3—New moon in Gemini
June 4—Mercury enters into Cancer
June 8—Venus goes into Gemini
June 17—Full moon in Sagittarius
June 20—Neptune turns retrograde
June 26—Mercury enters Leo

July 2019
Stressful

Thanks to a pair of eclipses, July may be a stressful and filled at times with a sense of urgency. Eclipses tend to bring issues up front and center so that we have to deal with them quickly and decisively. On July 2, there's a solar eclipse in your sign, so on or around this date, expect new opportunities to crop up that are personally satisfying. Thanks to a beneficial angle from Uranus, the opportunities seem to come out of nowhere. You just have to be prepared to seize them!

The lunar eclipse in Capricorn on July 16 occurs in your partnership area but, because Capricorn is involved, may impact your career, too. There could be news in one or both of these areas that upsets or disturbs you. But thanks to a beneficial angle from Pluto, things shake out fine in the end, and you're in a more powerful position now.

Between July 1 and August 18, Mars moves through fire sign Leo and your financial area. This transit kicks you into high gear. You might take a part-time job to supplement your income or get a freelance job that helps pay the bills. You may be working longer hours and be paid for overtime.

On July 3, Venus enters your sign. Oh lucky you, Cancer! Until July 27, you enjoy an unprecedented period of romance, creativity and pleasure. Your muse is eager to help you write the great American novel or paint the next great masterpiece, and your partner is attentive and loving. If you have children, your relationship with them unfolds with greater ease. The only other period this year that matches this one occurs between October 8 and November 1, when Venus moves through fellow water sign Scorpio.

On July 7, Mercury turns retrograde in Leo, in your financial area. Ouch! First, read over the Mercury retrograde sections in each of the introductions, and follow the general guidelines to navigate this period more successfully. Since this occurs in your money house, be sure to double check all bank and investment statements, and don't buy or sell stocks until the retro ends. Also, because Leo is involved, you may be revisiting a creative endeavor. On the 19th, Mercury slips back into your sign, where it turns direct on July 31.

Venus enters Leo on July 27, and once the Mercury retrograde ends on the 31st, your finances should straighten out. Venus will be traveling with Mars until August 21, and with these two planets in your financial court, your income should increase. Your love life should pick up,

Cancer, and even if there are some minor dramas during this period, you come through it just fine.

On the same day that Mercury turns direct, July 31, there's a new moon in Leo, a cause for celebration. This moon brings in new financial and creative opportunities. Perhaps you sell a work of art, a novel, a screenplay or something else you've created.

AT A GLANCE
July 1—Mars goes into Leo
July 2—Solar eclipse in Cancer
July 3—Venus enters Cancer
July 7—Mercury turns retrograde in Leo
July 16—Lunar eclipse in Capricorn
July 27—Venus enters Leo
July 31—Mercury turns direct, new moon in Leo

August 2019
Financial affairs

It's another busy month astrologically, and the action really begins to heat up on August 11, when Jupiter turns direct in Sagittarius, and Mercury enters Leo once again. With Jupiter's motion, you can once more enjoy the outward expansion of this planet's energy, particularly in your daily work life.

With Mercury in Leo again until August 29, your conscious focus is on finances. Things are actually looking up now that Mercury is direct in this sign, and with Mars here, too, until August 18, you have the forward momentum you need to earn additional income. From August 29 to September 14, Mercury moves through compatible earth sign Virgo, and your communication skills are sharp, discerning and detail-oriented.

Uranus turns retrograde in Taurus on August 12 and stays that way into the new year, until January 6, 2020. This planet's energy often attracts unusual people into your life, but now they may seem to be coming out of the proverbial woodwork. You may be getting a bit eccentric yourself, Cancer! Your psychic insights throughout this retrograde are excellent.

The full moon in Aquarius on August 15 highlights resources you share with others—a partner, parent, child or roommate. There may be news in this area, but with Jupiter forming a beneficial angle to this full moon, the news should be positive.

From August 18 to October 4, Mars transits Virgo, and now your daily life seems to be slammed into fast forward. You may be commuting more for work, or if you're self-employed, you're on the road a lot. Your various communication projects are moving forward at a swift clip, and your work is more tightly focused on details.

Venus joins Mars on August 21, and these two will travel together until September 14, when Venus changes signs. You may meet a romantic interest through siblings or people in your neighborhood. If you're already in a relationship, then your love life and your sex life are great! Virgo can often be quite picky, though, so be sure to keep critiques and criticisms to yourself.

You can see the profusion of energy this month in Virgo, and it's all capped off with a new moon in that sign on the 30th. Any new opportunities that come your way will catch you by surprise. You may sell a book, be hired for a lucrative freelance project or, through a synchronicity, find the ideal neighborhood for you and your family.

AT A GLANCE
August 11—Jupiter turns direct, Mercury enters Leo
August 12—Uranus turns retrograde
August 15—Full moon in Aquarius
August 18—Mars enters Virgo
August 21—Venus goes into Virgo
August 29—Mercury enters Virgo
August 30—New moon in Virgo

September 2019
Mostly good

Compared to the last couple of months, September is a like a vacation. However, the 14th may be a challenge. There are three astrological events that day: both Mercury and Venus enter Libra, and there's a full moon in Pisces.

The transits for the first two planets end on October 3 and 8 respectively. While they're traveling together through the family/domestic area of your chart, life is less stressful. You may decide to spiff up your home in some way, beautifying the rooms with plants, fresh paint, new furniture or art. If you have young kids, encourage them to decorate the walls of their rooms. Get the entire family involved!

Discussions at home may revolve around art, literature, the beauty in nature and music. You're much more aware of the need for balance in all your relationships.

The full moon in Pisces should be romantic and creative for you. If you hear news about a creative endeavor, there may be cause for celebration. Neptune retrograde is conjunct this full moon, and Pluto retrograde is friendly to it. By adding these two into the mix, you should be pleased with today's events.

Saturn turns direct in Capricorn on September 18, good news for your partnerships. In both business and romance, you can now implement whatever you learned during the retrograde about the structures of the various relationships in your life.

The 29th features a new moon in Libra, where both Mercury and Venus are. This one brings new opportunities to your home life. Perhaps you and your partner discover you're going to be parents, or someone may move into or out of your house. You may decide to put your home up for sale.

AT A GLANCE
September 14—Mercury and Venus enter Libra, full moon in Pisces
September 18—Saturn turns direct in Capricorn
September 29—New moon in Libra

October 2019
Terrific!

Lucky you, Cancer! October promises to be one of your favorite months all year, particularly from October 8 to November 1, when Venus transits Scorpio and the romance/creativity sector of your chart. More on that in a moment.

Let's start with October 3, when Mercury enters Scorpio and that same area of your chart, and Pluto turns direct in Capricorn. Mercury turns retrograde on October 31, but while it's in direct motion, you're discussing and thinking about a creative endeavor and are moving ahead with it. If it involves research, there's no better sign than Scorpio to do the work. Mercury in this sign is like an archeologist, probing, digging and uncovering secrets. You're more intuitive and immersed in the creative flow.

The retrograde from October 31 to November 20 may cause upsets in a romantic relationship because of the potential for misunderstandings. So communicate clearly with your partner and kids, and follow the general guidelines in the Mercury retrograde section in the introduction. In addition, don't submit any creative endeavors during this period, and try not to make any rash decisions about a relationship.

Once Pluto turns direct in Capricorn, you can kiss your shadow side good-bye. Personal and business partnerships should straighten out now.

Between October 4 and November 19, Mars transits Libra. During these weeks, things at home unfold with speed. Any renovations or home improvement projects are probably completed before the transit ends, just in time for Thanksgiving! Your home becomes a hub of activity during this period, especially if you have kids. You strive for balance in all areas of your life.

October 8 is a day to relish and anticipate. Venus joins Mercury in Scorpio, and now your love life, creativity and capacity for enjoyment reach a sustained high note. This transit lasts until November 1, the day after the Mercury retro begins, so you get to enjoy all but a day of this transit with life moving in your favor.

The full moon in Aries on the 13th should bring positive news about your career. It could be anything—a promotion, raise, new clients or new projects. Jupiter forms a beneficial angle to this full moon, and it promises that the news, whatever it is, expands your options.

The new moon in Scorpio brings new opportunities in romance, in creativity and in whatever you do for pleasure. Your sexuality is heightened during Venus's transit of Scorpio, and this new moon is the exclamation point!

AT A GLANCE
October 3—Mercury goes into Scorpio, Pluto turns direct
October 4—Mars enters Libra
October 8—Venus goes into Scorpio
October 13—Full moon in Aries
October 27—New moon in Scorpio
October 31—Mercury turns retrograde

November 2019
Wild

November may feel like a wild and crazy month, and it starts off with Venus entering Sagittarius on November 1. This transit lasts until November 25 and facilitates everything in your daily work routine. Co-workers, employees and bosses are supportive of your ideas and various projects. You feel more appreciated. If you're self-employed, clients may be flocking to you, and projects land in your lap. An office romance could be kindled during this transit.

On November 25, Venus enters Capricorn and your partnership area, and oh, what fun this could be, Cancer! You and your partner enjoy a period of deepened interest in each other. A long romantic weekend getaway would be ideal for renewing your commitment to each other. On the business front, you find the ideal partner—a manager, agent, accountant or attorney—to keep your work focused and directed.

Mars enters Scorpio on November 19 and takes you into the new year, to January 4, 2020. Since Mars co-rules Scorpio, it functions well here. This transit certainly heightens your sexuality and intuition and your insights into others. You and a romantic partner feel intensely for each other, and passions run fast and furiously. Just be careful that those passions don't veer into the darker emotions like jealousy.

Mercury turns direct in Scorpio on the 20th, and it's time to celebrate. Now do everything that went on the back burner during the retrograde!

The new moon in fire sign Sagittarius on November 26 should bring new work opportunities. If you recently applied for a job, then you may hear that you got it. You could have an opportunity in publishing or in higher education, Sagittarius' domain, or may have a chance to travel overseas.

Neptune turns direct in Pisces on the 27th, a plus for everyone, but especially for water signs. You can now take advantage of Neptune's bolstering of your imagination and intuition.

AT A GLANCE
November 1—Venus goes into Sagittarius
November 12—Full moon in Taurus
November 19—Mars enters Scorpio
November 20—Mercury turns direct
November 25—Venus enters Capricorn
November 26—New moon in Sagittarius
November 27—Neptune turns direct

December 2019
Jupiter shift

As the last month of the year gets moving, take a few minutes to think about what you would like to experience and achieve next year. Make a list. Post it where you'll see it often. Think of these items as desires rather than resolutions.

On December 2, Jupiter makes a major shift. After thirteen months in Sagittarius, it enters Capricorn, and just wait and see what this does for you. Your partnerships in business and in your personal life expand. If you're in a relationship, then you and your partner may commit more deeply to each other. You might move in together, get married or start a family. If you want to start your own business, then Jupiter in Capricorn can help make it happen. Jupiter will now be traveling with Pluto in Capricorn for the next year, until December 20, 2020. This combination expands your personal power, Cancer, and puts you squarely in the driver's seat with career matters.

On December 9, Mercury enters Sagittarius, where it will be until December 29. Your conscious focus is on your daily work routine and how you maintain your daily health. Since the holiday season is so close, though, you're in a gregarious mood, and the high spirits of co-workers and employees are infectious!

The 12th features a full moon in Gemini. Any news you hear may be confusing. Neptune makes a challenging angle to this full moon, suggesting that you don't have all the information you need to make an informed decision.

Venus enters Aquarius on the 20th, and this transit takes you into the new year, until January 14, 2020. Money arrives from an unexpected source—a royalty check, an insurance rebate or a pay raise for your partner. With Venus in this sign, you need a lot of personal freedom in a romantic relationship.

Now we come to the solar eclipse in Capricorn on December 26, the second this year in that sign. This one should be very nice for you! Jupiter is closely conjunct the eclipse degree, and that means that any opportunities the eclipse brings your way will be positive and expansive and will cause you to feel optimism.

Mercury joins Jupiter and Pluto in Capricorn on the 29th and remains there until January 17, 2020. Your focus is laser-like now, and you're determined to make good use of all this earth energy. You're able to clear up any outstanding work projects so that you enter the new year with a clean slate, ready and excited for whatever the universe brings your way.

AT A GLANCE
December 2—Jupiter enters Capricorn
December 9—Mercury enters Sagittarius
December 12—Full moon in Gemini
December 20—Venus goes into Aquarius
December 26—Solar eclipse in Capricorn
December 29—Mercury enters into Capricorn

Reflection
You're one of the most introspective signs, so a few moments of reflection will be easy for you. What did you take away from 2019? Are you happy with the way the year unfolded? Are you pleased with where you are right this second? Record your thoughts below.

_____
_____
_____
_____
_____

Happy New Year!

Leo 2019

The sun rules your sign, and its daily motion is beyond the scope of this book. However, pay close attention to when transiting planets are aspecting—forming angles to—your sun sign. Included in the monthly roundups is information about what the inner, faster-moving planets are doing each month (Mercury, Venus, Mars), which planets are retrograde and when the slower-moving planets change signs or turn retrograde. You'll also find information about the solar and lunar eclipses this year.

Be sure to look over the Mercury retrograde sections in the introductions to the three years, and follow the general guidelines on how to navigate these periods more successfully.

For most of 2019, expansive Jupiter is transiting Sagittarius and forming a powerful and beneficial angle to your sun sign. It's a kind of Midas touch in that luck, abundance and prosperity follow you around like a faithful puppy. You're in the right place at the right time. You're the right person for the job, the raise or whatever it is. If you have aspirations to write a novel or book, by all means do so this year!

January 2019
Tense at times, but imaginative

Welcome to 2019! January holds some pleasant surprises, but first let's talk about the two eclipses this month that may cause you to feel unsettled.

The solar eclipse in Capricorn on January 5 should bring in new opportunities in your career and daily work area. But because the eclipse is in an earth sign—and Leo is a fire sign—you may not be comfortable with the energy. Also, Pluto is only five degrees away from the eclipse's degree, and that can create power issues between you and someone else. That said, though, the opportunities should please you. You might be promoted, change jobs, hire new employees or bring in new clients. If you're self-employed and work in the arts, your imagination will be stimulated by Neptune's favorable angle to this eclipse degree.

The lunar eclipse on the 21st is the one that may give you trouble. It's in your sign and may trigger emotional responses to criticism or remarks made by someone in your work environment. Just don't overreact. You sometimes take remarks too personally, and the remark probably wasn't intended that way! On or around the date of this eclipse, you may feel as if your creativity has been "eclipsed" in some way, and that could lead to your emotional turmoil. Your creativity hasn't actually been eclipsed, though, Leo. You're still the dynamo.

Now, on to the rest of the month. On the 4th, Mercury joins Jupiter and Pluto in Capricorn, and from then until January 24, you're focused on a particular project at work or on some facet of your career. With this much earth energy at your disposal, you're practical, efficient and organized and probably have a strategy laid out to achieve your goal in a particular time frame. The Capricorn element confers a singular, goal-directed vision.

On the 6th, Uranus turns direct in Aries. Now you can once again enjoy the edgy energy of this planet, which causes *stuff to happen.* Between now and March 6, when Uranus enters Taurus and your career area, you may travel overseas, be involved in publishing or higher education or even audition for a part in a movie or TV show. Whatever occurs during the rest of Uranus's journey through Aries will be sudden and unexpected.

On January 7, Venus enters Sagittarius, and until February 3, you enjoy one of the most romantic and creative periods for you all year. The only other time like this will happen between April 20 and May 15, when Venus transits Aries. During this period, life is exciting and enjoyable. Your creative adrenaline burns brightly, and your muse is in attendance 24/7. If your creative work is your passion, then you may be working longer hours and loving it. On the romantic front, you and your partner rediscover why you're together and may take off for a few days for an adventure. If you're not involved with anyone when this transit begins, you may be by the time it ends.

Mercury enters Aquarius on January 24, and between then and February 10, your attention is on partnerships. You and your personal partner may work together on a freelance project or, at the least, discuss how you might do this successfully. Aquarius is your opposite sign, and with Mercury here, your ideas are unique and unusual.

AT A GLANCE
January 4—Mercury enters into Capricorn
January 5—Solar eclipse in Capricorn
January 6—Uranus turns direct in Aries
January 7—Venus goes into Sagittarius
January 21—Lunar eclipse in Leo
January 24—Mercury goes into Aquarius

February 2019
Emphasis on pragmatism

It's a tamer month than January, with an emphasis on earth and water energy, so you're being asked to be practical and to pay attention to your emotions.

Venus enters Capricorn on February 3, joining Pluto in the daily work area of your chart until March 2. Any time Venus and Pluto travel together, powerful things happen. It's easier for you to enter and stay inside the flow of any situation, you find the support you need for your ideas and projects, and you have no shortage of admirers, friends and potential lovers.

If you didn't experience anything unusual around the time of the solar eclipse last month, then Venus may trigger opportunities. Sometimes the effects of an eclipse arrive a month later, and if this is the case, you'll be pleased by whatever unfolds.

The new moon in Aquarius on February 4 brings new partnership opportunities in business or in your personal life or both. You and a romantic partner may decide to deepen your commitment to each other or could embark on a business venture together. If you want to be self-employed, it could happen on or around the time of this new moon. What we gain from any new moon usually depends on where we have placed our attention, focus and desires.

Mercury enters water sign Pisces on February 10 and will be moving direct until March 5, when it turns retrograde. While it's direct, you're more intuitive and imaginative and find innovative solutions to any challenges with joint resources—i.e., banks, insurance companies or mortgages.

From February 14 to March 31, Mars transits Taurus and your career area. Mars is the planet that makes things happen, so you now have forward momentum professionally. Even though Mercury will be retrograde for about three weeks of the Mars transit, you should still be able to accomplish a lot. You may have to resuscitate older projects and implement them during the retrograde.

The full moon in Virgo on the 19th lights up your financial area. Mars in Taurus forms a close, beneficial angle to this new moon and may provide the thrust you need to bring a project to completion. Any news you hear concerning your finances should be good.

AT A GLANCE
February 3—Venus enters Capricorn
February 4—New moon in Aquarius
February 10—Mercury goes into Pisces
February 14—Mars enters into Taurus
February 19—Full moon in Virgo

March 2019
Uranus shift

March is jammed with astrological events, and one of them is major. Last year Uranus entered Taurus, then turned retrograde after several months and slipped back into Aries. On March 6, Uranus leaves Aries and enters Taurus again. Uranus is the planet that shakes things up, particularly in the areas where our lives are habitual and predictable. It's to your advantage to find out where Taurus falls in your natal chart. That house, that area of your life, will be where abrupt, unforeseen change occurs.

In a solar chart, where your sun sign is placed on the horizon, Taurus falls in your career area. Some possible ramifications of this seven-year transit: you change careers, are promoted and given a significant raise or launch your own business. If you're already self-employed, your business takes off. This transit ends on July 7, 2025, when Uranus enters Gemini. Due to a retrograde, it returns to Taurus in early November and finally enters Gemini again in April 2026.

From March 1 to 26, Venus transit Aquarius, your opposite sign. This period favors all kinds of partnerships. You discover, though, that during this transit you require a lot of freedom in any intimate relationship, time to do whatever you enjoy separate from your partner. In business you attract unusual individuals who may be geniuses in their field.

Okay, on to the Mercury retrograde, the first this year. It occurs in Pisces and lasts until March 28. As suggested earlier, look over the sections on Mercury retrograde in the introductions and follow the general guidelines. Since this retro occurs in the joint resources area of your chart, keep close tabs on your bank account, investment portfolio, ATM withdrawals and bills. The potential for snafus is increased during the retrograde. Also, since Pisces is involved, try to be decisive in your decisions.

On March 6, the same day that Uranus moves into Taurus, the new moon in Pisces may bring a new source of income—your partner might get a raise, a royalty check may arrive, you refinance your house for a lower interest rate or you sell a creative endeavor.

The full moon in Libra on March 20 falls at 0 degrees, which is why there will be another full moon in this sign on April 19, at 29 degrees. This moon highlights the communication sector of your chart, so there may be news about a writing or speaking project. You may be asked to start a blog or create a website for your company or may do that for yourself if you're self-employed. Since this area of your chart also governs siblings, neighbors and the neighborhood in which you live, don't be surprised if your brother or sister invites you over for dinner or a party.

From March 26 to April 20, Venus moves through Pisces and facilitates all your dealings with banks, insurance companies and the like. Your partner could get a raise during this period, and you may earn money through a creative endeavor. There's a nice, intuitive flow now in a romantic relationship. You may have experiences with ghosts and other things that go bump in the night. It would be a favorable time for a past-life regression.

Mercury turns direct on the 28th, always a relief. Now you can leap forward again with certainty that delays are history.

From March 31 to May 15, Mars transits Gemini and forms a beneficial angle to your sun sign. This one should be fun for you. Your social calendar fills up quickly, and any new contacts you make may bring you closer to achieving a wish or dream. Mars here also sharpens your communication skills.

AT A GLANCE
March 1—Venus enters into Aquarius
March 5—Mercury turns retrograde in Pisces
March 6—New moon in Pisces, Uranus enters Taurus
March 20—Full moon in Libra
March 26—Venus goes into Pisces
March 28—Mercury turns direct
March 31—Mars enters Gemini

April 2019
Fired up

It should be a good month for you, with plenty of fire-sign energy, like that of the new moon in Aries on April 5. This one should bring new opportunities to show off your entrepreneurial skills in publishing, higher education and international travel. Aries is an impatient, restless sign, and for a few days on either side of this new moon, you may be feeling a sense of urgency, as though you should be doing something new and different. This moon could provide the opportunity to do exactly that.

Jupiter is retrograde in Sagittarius from April 10 to August 11. During these months, Jupiter's expansive nature turns inward. You may embark on a spiritual quest of some kind—a shamanic retreat, a hike through the Andes or Europe to visit ancient sites. You might decide to return to college or go to law school.

On April 17, and then the 20th, Mercury and Venus enter Aries and travel together until May 6, when Mercury enters Taurus. The Venus transit lasts until May 15. While these two planets are traveling together, there's a lot of talk and thought about romance and the arts, your income and how you can combine these various things. Maybe a romance novel is in the offing? Both planets are forming beneficial angles to your sun sign, so creativity is definitely a factor.

The full moon in Libra on April 19 falls at 29 degrees, and it's the second full moon this year in Libra. Jupiter retrograde forms a beneficial angle to it, indicating that any news you hear expands your options. This full moon lights up the communication area of your chart and, because Libra is involved, may concern a relationship. Pluto forms a challenging angle to this full moon, suggesting that a boss or other authority figure is part of the picture. Just remember that balance is key in dealing with this individual.

On the 25th, Saturn turns retrograde in Capricorn, and on the 29th, Pluto follows suit. Both of these retros occur in that area of your chart that governs your daily work. Saturn's retro ends on September 18, and Pluto's ends on October 3. The first retrograde prompts you to take a deeper look at the structures in your daily work life and your relationships with co-workers, employees and bosses. How do these relationships measure up to your desires? The Pluto retro may bring out your dark side, Leo, a tendency called *me, me, me*.

April 5—New moon in Aries
April 10—Jupiter turns retrograde in Sagittarius
April 17—Mercury enters Aries
April 19—Full moon in Libra
April 20—Venus enters Aries
April 25—Pluto turns retrograde in Capricorn
April 29—Saturn turns retrograde in Capricorn

May 2019
Career focus

In May, it's all about your career and professional life, and it begins on May 4, with a new moon in Taurus in your career area. No telling what kinds of opportunities may surface on or around the date of this moon. Where have you been placing your intentions? How big are your desires? Have you been meditating and visualizing about what you desire? Some possibilities: a promotion/raise, a new job within your career field, a new career, a new boss or a new office.

On the 6th, Mercury enters Taurus, followed by Venus on the 15th. These two travel together until May 21, when Mercury enters Gemini. On June 8, Venus enters Gemini. While they're together, they help to bring the new moon opportunities into greater clarity. You have more patience to tackle and complete complicated tasks, and co-workers are supportive of your ideas and endeavors. If a romance is kindled during Venus's transit here, it may be with someone you meet through work or who is introduced to you by a co-worker. Taurus is a sensual sign ruled by Venus, so your enjoyment of beauty, good food, art and the finer things in life is deepened.

On the same day that Venus enters Taurus, May 15, Mars begins its transit of Cancer. Between now and July 1, you may be working behind the scenes on a creative endeavor that demands solitude, imagination and intuition. In a sense, you're seeding your personal unconscious in preparation for Mars's transit of your sign. This period is favorable for therapy, a past-life regression and dream recall.

The full moon in Scorpio on May 18 highlights your home life and family. Since Scorpio is an emotionally intense sign, your feelings may get hurt by something someone in your personal environment says or does. There could also be news about a parent or another family member. Since Pluto forms a beneficial angle to this full moon, your emotions at this time are powerful.

Between May 21 and June 4, Mercury transits Gemini, a sign it rules, and you're in a sociable and outgoing mood, eager to spend time with friends and brainstorm with other creative people. If you're self-employed, this transit helps you to make contact with new clients.

May 4—New moon in Taurus
May 6—Mercury enters Taurus
May 15—Venus goes into Taurus, Mars enters Cancer
May 18—Full moon in Scorpio
May 21—Mercury goes into Gemini

June 2019
Out & about

June should be fun! Summer has started, a new page has been turned and, on the 3rd, there's a new moon in Gemini, which should be very nice for your social life. As new friends enter your life, so do new opportunities for networking, publicity and communication projects. Today, you can talk to anyone about virtually anything. If you're in sales, you probably surpass your daily quota!

From June 4 to June 26, Mercury transits Cancer and joins Mars in the area of your chart that governs the personal unconscious. You're more intuitive during this transit and may experience frequent synchronicities that guide you, confirm decisions or offer insights. Mercury and Mars have a lot to chat about and may be stirring up issues you haven't resolved, and now you have a chance to deal with them.

Venus enters Gemini on June 8, and now your social calendar really gets crowded. This trend lasts until July 3, and you may have to balance work and play more judiciously. You could meet a romantic interest through friends, or perhaps you already know the person as a friend and discover the chemistry between you has been transformed into something else.

The full moon in gregarious Sagittarius on June 17 should be a beauty! This one occurs in the romance/creativity section of your chart, and because retrograde Jupiter is widely conjunct, you enjoy double the pleasure and double the fun. There could be news about a creative endeavor, and the news looks positive.

From June 20 to November 27, Neptune is retrograde in Pisces. Sometimes this period can be a reality check because it's more difficult to gloss over challenges. But it can also be a time when you're more in tune with your intuition, your own unconscious and your creativity.

Mercury moves into your sign on June 26, and until it turns retrograde on July 7, you're at the top of your game. More about the retro in July's roundup. While it's moving direct, though, plunge into your creative work, sign contracts, make your travel plans, go to auditions and submit projects. In other words, full steam ahead, Leo.

June 3—New moon in Gemini
June 4—Mercury enters into Cancer
June 8—Venus goes into Gemini
June 17—Full moon in Sagittarius
June 20—Neptune turns retrograde
June 26—Mercury enters Leo

July 2019
Erratic

Months that feature eclipses can sometimes be riddled with a sense of urgency. That may be how July feels to you, with the eclipses falling in Cancer and Capricorn, in your solar twelfth and sixth houses.

The solar eclipse on July 2 falls in Cancer, a water sign, in that area of your chart that rules the personal unconscious. Solar eclipses bring double the usual opportunities that new moons do, so you may have a chance to work behind the scenes in some capacity. You might, for example, be hired to ghostwrite a book, to work with a therapist who conducts past-life regressions or have an opportunity to attend a lucid dream workshop. These kinds of things are related to the twelfth house. Since Uranus forms a beneficial angle to the eclipse degree, you don't see the opportunities coming, and they take you by surprise.

The lunar eclipse on July 16 is in Capricorn and that area of your chart that rules your daily work. But because Capricorn is part of the equation, this eclipse could impact your career and professional goals, too. Something that occurs in your work environment prompts you to redefine your relationship with a person you work with—co-worker, boss or employee. You may also be reconsidering your career goals.

The good news about July is that Mars enters your sign, where it will be until August 18. This transit galvanizes you and propels you forward in all areas of your life. Despite any setbacks you may encounter, you just keep right on going, singular in your vision. It's a favorable time to get things done, Leo, so get moving!

On July 3, Venus enters Cancer, where yesterday's solar eclipse occurred. Venus will be in this sign until the 27th, and then it moves into Leo. Until then, you're seeding desires, working on yourself, perfecting your psyche and preparing it for when Venus transits your sign. Your dreams are especially vivid now and provide insights and information that are helpful. If a romance begins during this transit, you may keep it under wraps for a while, preferring to spend time alone with your new romantic interest.

Mercury turns retrograde on July 7 in your sign. It will slide back into Cancer and then turn direct in that sign on July 31. Read over the Mercury retrograde section in the introduction, and follow those general guidelines for navigating this retrograde more easily. This one impacts your personal life, so in whatever area you need to slow down and step back, you'll find things going haywire. Don't start new projects or try to force forward momentum in a relationship. Try to go with the flow, bumps, surprises and all.

On the 27th, four days before Mercury's retrograde ends, Venus enters your sign, and that's cause for celebration! From then to August 21, life unfolds with greater smoothness and excitement, particularly after the 31st. Your love life is satisfying, and your creativity reaches new heights. The only other period this year that matches this one occurs between November 1 and 25, when Venus transits Sagittarius and the romance/creative area of your chart.

On July 31, the same day that Mercury turns direct, there's a new moon in your sign! This moon happens only once a year, and it's smart to prepare for it because it sets the tone for the next twelve months. Think about what you would like to achieve and experience in the next year and focus on those desires. Then step out of the way, and let the universe shower you with new opportunities.

AT A GLANCE
July 1—Mars goes into Leo
July 2—Solar eclipse in Cancer
July 3—Venus enters Cancer
July 7—Mercury turns retrograde in Leo
July 16—Lunar eclipse in Capricorn
July 27—Venus enters Leo
July 31—Mercury turns direct, new moon in Leo

August 2019
Busy, but good

It's a busy month, but will be much better for you after Jupiter turns direct on August 11, in Sagittarius. From then until December 2, when Jupiter enters Capricorn, you get to enjoy this planet's expansiveness once again. It should be providing you with many opportunities to expand your creativity and increasing your capacity for enjoyment and living with an open heart.

Also on August 11, Mercury enters your sign again and will be there until August 29. Until the 21st, Mercury and Venus are traveling together, and what a wonderful journey it is. Your head and your heart are in agreement, and the angst you sometimes feel is blissfully absent.

Uranus turns retrograde in Taurus on August 12 and doesn't turn direct again until January 6, 2020. This impacts your professional life, but not like a Mercury retrograde does. It's subtler and triggers insights into your career and the people in your work environment. You may experience sudden emotional shifts and feel restless, with a need for greater independence.

The full moon in Aquarius on August 15 highlights your partnership area. Jupiter forms a wide but beneficial angle to this full moon, indicating that any news you hear will be positive and should expand your choices in some way. You might find the ideal business partner. You and your romantic partner could deepen your commitment to the relationship by getting married or starting a family.

The other transits this month focus on earth sign Virgo and your financial area. On the 18th, 21st and 29th, Mars, Venus and then Mercury enter Virgo. With these three planets in your financial area, you suddenly become much more grounded and realistic about money and pay closer attention to all the financial details. Whenever Mars and Venus travel together, these cosmic lovers bring about romantic happiness and a deeper understanding between you and your partner. The Mars transit ends on October 6, and the Venus and Mercury transits end on September 14.

Once you've got your finances in order, the universe brings you a new moon in Virgo on August 30, and that means new financial opportunities. Retrograde Uranus in Taurus forms a harmonious angle to this new moon, so you're surprised by these new opportunities. You don't see them coming!

AT A GLANCE
August 11—Jupiter turns direct, Mercury enters Leo
August 12—Uranus turns retrograde
August 15—Full moon in Aquarius
August 18—Mars enters Virgo
August 21—Venus goes into Virgo
August 29—Mercury enters Virgo
August 30—New moon in Virgo

September 2019
Self-expression

This year, Mercury and Venus are traveling together frequently, so the energy of the various signs they transit are bolstered.

This month, they both enter air sign Libra on September 14, and suddenly your conscious focus and your heart's focus are on relationships and communication. You may feel a shift within yourself that is gentler, kinder and more compassionate toward others. You feel more optimistic and upbeat, too, and this is reflected in the way you speak and write and the things you discuss. You may be spending more time with siblings and neighbors. If a romance is sparked during this transit, it may be with someone you already know, perhaps someone who lives in your neighborhood.

The full moon in Pisces also takes place on the 14th. This one highlights resources you share with others—a partner, child, parent or roommate. There could be news in this area. Since the moon is in imaginative Pisces, it's a favorable time to complete a creative endeavor.

Saturn turns direct in Capricorn on September 18. You probably feel the shift as soon as it happens. You have fewer oppressive thoughts, feel more confident about the relationships in your daily work life and know how to change the relationships that aren't as strong as you might like.

The new moon in Libra on the 29th brings new opportunities for creative self-expression. You and a friend may decide to embark on a joint effort of some kind. You might write a book together or start a blog or website. You may also have an opportunity to do something romantic with the one you love.

AT A GLANCE
September 14—Mercury and Venus enter Libra, full moon in Pisces
September 18—Saturn turns direct in Capricorn
September 29—New moon in Libra

October 2019
Communicator

The last Mercury retrograde of the year starts on Halloween in Scorpio and ends on November 20. You have the entire month to prepare for it, and that means that if you're going to be signing a contract for anything, do it before October 31. Also, make your travel plans now for travel after November 20. To prepare for the retrograde, look over the Mercury retrograde section in the introduction, and follow the general guidelines. Since this one occurs in the home/family area of your chart, be sure your appliances are functioning the way they should. Communicate clearly with everyone in your personal environment.

On October 3, Mercury enters Scorpio, and your home becomes the hub of activity and discussion. If you work out of your home, you could be doing research that involves heady issues—life after death, communication with the dead or the nature of reality. Your intuition and insights into people and situations are excellent during this transit.

Pluto also turns direct in Capricorn on the 3rd, and now you can draw on this powerful planet's energy in your daily work life and move ahead on your various endeavors. What you learned during this retrograde about your shadow side can now be put to good use in your relationships with co-workers, employees and bosses.

Between October 4 and November 19, Mars transits Libra and your solar third house. This area of your chart rules your daily life, communication and your conscious mind. Also included here are siblings, neighbors and short-distance travel. All of these areas are stimulated during this transit. If you've been working on a manuscript or screenplay or some other creative endeavor, this transit helps you speed to the finish line. You may be running around more than usual—errands, carpooling or commuting.

Venus enters Scorpio on October 8, and between then and November 1, your love life really starts humming along. Your partner is more attentive, you have in-depth talks about your relationship and your respective needs and expectations, and you feel everything more deeply.

The full moon in fire sign Aries on October 13 lights up your trailblazing spirit and stirs the adventurer in you. You and a friend or partner may hit the road on a whim and take off with little more than your ATM cards and big dreams. Jupiter forms a beautiful angle to this full moon, too, an added bonus that suggests this trip will expand your horizons.

The new moon in Scorpio on October 27 should bring new opportunities for your family and home life. If you've been thinking about putting your place on the market, this would be the day to do it. Otherwise, wait until after Mercury turns direct on November 20. Uranus is opposed to this new moon, suggesting that opportunities surface suddenly, and there could be some anxiety or worry about events.

AT A GLANCE
October 3—Mercury goes into Scorpio, Pluto turns direct
October 4—Mars enters Libra
October 8—Venus goes into Scorpio
October 13—Full moon in Aries
October 27—New moon in Scorpio
October 31—Mercury turns retrograde

November 2019
Fast forward

November is astrologically crowded, and in spite of Mercury's retrograde, you may feel like your life is jammed in fast forward.

On November 1, Venus moves into Sagittarius, and you enter one of the most pleasant periods all year. From now until the 25th, Venus acts as a facilitator in your creative endeavors, your love life, with your kids and with everything you do for fun and pleasure. You're a magnet that attracts what you need when you need it, and other people fall all over themselves just to spend time with you. If you're in sales, Leo, then this is the period when your numbers go through the roof. If you work in the arts, your muse has your back. If you aren't involved in a relationship when this transit starts, you probably will be when it ends. Enjoy this transit, and don't fritter away the great energy!

The full moon in Taurus on November 12 brings career news. If you've been job hunting, then you should get the call or e-mail that makes the difference. Or, you might hear that you're being promoted or tapped to lead a team. Both Saturn and Pluto in Capricorn form great angles to this full moon, indicating that the news makes a lasting difference and puts you leagues ahead of the competition.

From November 19 to January 4, 2020, Mars moves through Scorpio, a sign it co-rules. This transit heightens your sexuality and your need for bottom-line answers. It triggers a lot of activity in your home life, too, and with the holidays just around the corner, it looks as if your place is where the celebrations take place.

Mercury turns direct in Scorpio on the 20th, just in time for the Thanksgiving holidays. Now you can start your holiday shopping and make travel plans and do all the things you delayed doing while Mercury was retrograde.

From November 25 to December 20, Venus joins Saturn and Pluto in Capricorn. This trio of planets brings your focus to your daily work and professional matters, enabling you to clear your desk before the end of the year. Venus, like Jupiter, is a facilitator and usually brings an element of luck and serendipity.

The new moon in Sagittarius on November 26 ushers in new opportunities in romance and creativity, international travel, publishing and your spirituality. You and your partner may decide to start a family or to join forces in some creative endeavor.

Neptune turns direct in Pisces on the 27th, and now your creative drive really slams into high gear. You feel more inspired, and the ideas that flow through you seem to come from a higher source.

AT A GLANCE
November 1—Venus goes into Sagittarius
November 12—Full moon in Taurus
November 19—Mars enters Scorpio
November 20—Mercury turns direct
November 25—Venus enters Capricorn
November 26—New moon in Sagittarius
November 27—Neptune turns direct

December 2019
Solid opportunities

The final eclipse of the year happens on December 26 with a solar eclipse in Capricorn. This bolsters the considerable lineup of planets that are present in Capricorn and promises that new opportunities that surface on or around this eclipse date are solid, have long-term effects and will expand your life in some way because Jupiter is conjunct the eclipse degree.

Speaking of Jupiter, it enters Capricorn on December 2 and will be there until December 20, 2020. During this year-long transit, everything connected to your daily work life and career will expand. You'll feel as if some benevolent force is looking after you. Synchronicity will flourish, so be alert for those meaningful coincidences that seem to be guiding you.

From December 2 to 29, Mercury transits Sagittarius and enables you to see the larger picture for what you would like to achieve and experience in the next year. Make a list, and post it where you'll see it frequently. Romance and creativity are very much on your mind, and your capacity for enjoyment should reach new heights during this transit. Sagittarius always enjoys festivities and doesn't need much of an excuse for a party!

The full moon in Gemini on December 12 is perfectly timed for the holiday season. It lights up the friends area of your chart, and your social calendar fills quickly now. There could be news, too, about a friend, but because Neptune forms a challenging angle to this moon, you may not have the full story.

Venus moves through Aquarius and your partnership area from December 20 to January 14, 2020, a beautiful transit for the holidays and the start of the new year. Your relationships generally flow more smoothly during this transit, and your business and personal partnerships hit few if any challenges.

Mercury joins Jupiter, Saturn and Pluto in Capricorn on December 29 and stays there until January 17. Your desk is clear, and you can embrace 2020 with the certain knowledge that you are committed to living the best life that you can, with greater commitment to and enjoyment of whatever you hold near and dear. It's a perfect way to end one year and begin another.

AT A GLANCE
December 2—Jupiter enters Capricorn
December 9—Mercury enters Sagittarius
December 12—Full moon in Gemini
December 20—Venus goes into Aquarius
December 26—Solar eclipse in Capricorn
December 29—Mercury enters into Capricorn

Reflection
Yes, you're busy. But take a few minutes to reflect on what this year has been like for you. Are you happier? Do you feel good about where you are in life? What, if anything, would you change about the year?

_____
_____
_____
_____
_____

Happy New Year!

Virgo 2019

Your sign, like Gemini, is ruled by Mercury, the planet that governs communication, the conscious mind, travel, learning and a host of other areas. It spends about three weeks in a sign, and three times a year, it turns retrograde, where it appears to be moving backward through the zodiac. In the introduction, read over the Mercury retrograde section about the kinds of things that can occur during these retro periods and how to mitigate the impact. In the monthly roundups, pay close attention to where Mercury is each month and the angles that other planets make to it. You'll also find information on eclipses, the new and full moons and the transits of the other planets.

2019 should be an exciting year for you, Virgo, particularly from March 6 forward as Uranus transits fellow earth sign Taurus and forms a great angle to your sun. During the next seven years, many facets of your life will change, sometimes suddenly and without warning, but the changes will be for the better. Your relationships, career, finances, family life and creativity will all be in flux. Embrace it!

January 2019
Hectic but positive

Welcome to 2019! January is a packed month that includes two eclipses. The first one on January 5 falls in Capricorn, in the romance/creativity area of your chart. Solar eclipses are like double new moons and bring multiple new opportunities. Some possibilities with this one: a new romantic interest, creative endeavor or career change. Pluto in Capricorn forms a 5-degree conjunction to the eclipse degree, suggesting that you're calling the shots. Neptune is also friendly to the eclipse degree and brings a heightened spiritual awareness to everything that unfolds.

The day before the eclipse, on January 4, Mercury enters Capricorn, where it will be until the 24th. During this transit, your conscious focus is on your goals for the new year, romance and love, creativity and your kids. It's a favorable period to delve into your creative passions, whatever they are, and to spend quality time with your children.

On the 6th, Uranus turns direct in Aries and enjoys its last fling in this fire sign before entering Taurus on March 6. It entered Taurus briefly in 2018, then turned retro after several months. Read more about its transit in the March roundup. Expect a surprise related to shared resources—your partner may land a raise or an unexpected royalty check, insurance rebate or some other source of money arrives.

Between January 7 and February 3, Venus transits Sagittarius. You may feel motivated to beautify your home in some way, especially if it's winter where you live. You might paint rooms in brighter colors or buy potted plants or new furniture. Your relationship with family members is smoother. You and a friend or partner may take off for a long weekend, satisfying the nomadic itch that the Sagittarius element brings to Venus.

The lunar eclipse in Leo on January 21 triggers unresolved issues to surface, and you have to deal with them quickly and decisively. You may feel your creativity is being stifled in some way and take steps to rectify the situation.

Mercury enters Aquarius on January 24, and between then and February 10, you bring edgy and unusual ideas into your daily work life. Your intellect is sharpened and visionary. You can see how things should be done and set your vision in motion.

AT A GLANCE
January 4—Mercury enters into Capricorn
January 5—Solar eclipse in Capricorn
January 6—Uranus turns direct in Aries
January 7—Venus goes into Sagittarius
January 21—Lunar eclipse in Leo
January 24—Mercury goes into Aquarius

February 2019
Nearly perfect

February's astrological energy this month is mostly in fellow earth signs, and that suits you just fine. It's an excellent time to use that Virgo penchant for details to connect the dots in a personal or professional project.

Between February 3 and March 1, Venus transits Capricorn and the romance/creativity area of your chart. These weeks are among the best this year—the most romantic and creative, for sure. You and your romantic interest may spend a lot of time together, doing whatever you enjoy as individuals and as a couple. If the relationship is new, then these weeks are the first blissful rush. If the relationship is ongoing, then this transit helps to deepen the feelings between you. Creatively, you're on a roll, and regardless of what type of creative endeavor you're involved in, your muse bends over backward to help. The only other period this year that comes close to this is when Venus transits your sign between August 21 and September 14.

The new moon in Aquarius on February 4 brings new opportunities into your daily work and in the maintenance of your health. You might be promoted, hire new employees or even find a new job. Jupiter makes a harmonious angle to this new moon, and that means expansion!

Between February 10 and March 5, Mercury is moving direct through Pisces and your partnership area. You and your business partners—manager, accountant, agent or anyone involved in your professional life—may be in talks concerning new ventures. But because Mercury will be retrograde from March 5–28, sign contracts on either side of those dates.

Mars enters fellow earth sign Taurus on February 14 and will be there until March 31. During these weeks, you're motivated to get things done, and Mars helps you to do that in any area where you place your attention and intention. If you're traveling overseas, Mars in Taurus urges you to fully enjoy the sensuality of the places you're visiting.

The 19th features a full moon in your sign and highlights your personal life. Any news you hear should be positive because Mars in Taurus forms a strong angle to it. The news may serve as an impetus to *get moving!*

AT A GLANCE
February 3—Venus enters Capricorn
February 4—New moon in Aquarius
February 10—Mercury goes into Pisces
February 14—Mars enters into Taurus
February 19—Full moon in Virgo

March 2019
Exciting

The major transit this month occurs on March 6, when Uranus enters Taurus, where it will be until July 2026. It was in Taurus briefly in 2018, then turned retrograde and slipped back into Aries. But now it's in Taurus until July 2025. Due to a retrograde, it slips back into Taurus in November, then enters Gemini again in April 2026. Read the summary at the beginning of your sign.

If you have your natal chart, see where Taurus falls; that will be the area that undergoes radical, exciting change. In a solar chart, Taurus falls in your ninth house, which includes your worldview, spiritual beliefs, publishing, higher education and foreign travel and people. It's an excellent time to study anything that prompts your development and evolution. You might be a part of a foreign exchange program or have an opportunity to live in another country. You could decide to go to law school or graduate school, and your worldview and spiritual beliefs are likely to change in some way. You embrace change.

Before that transit begins, Venus enters Aquarius on March 1, and from then until March 26, your daily work life hums along on a more even keel. Co-workers and employees are supportive of your ideas, the boss is pleased with your efforts and you become the person everyone goes to for answers. In romance, you're attracted to someone with unusual ideas and decide to team up with this individual for a joint creative project. After Venus enters Pisces on March 26, your conscious focus turns to business and personal partnerships. From then until April 20, you and your romantic partner may have some unusual psychic experiences, and anything you do together on the creative front will be fun and go well.

Mercury turns retrograde in Pisces on March 5 and doesn't straighten out until March 28. Read over the Mercury retro section in the introduction for the general guidelines that make this period easier to navigate. Since it occurs in your partnership area, be sure to communicate clearly with the people in your immediate environment. Double check the times and dates for any appointments you have.

On the 6th, in addition to the Uranus transit, there's a new moon in Pisces. A new opportunity surfaces with a creative endeavor or in a partnership. But because of the retrograde, the opportunity may not surface as quickly as it would otherwise. If it involves a contract, don't sign until after the retrograde ends on March 28.

March 20 features a full moon in Libra, in your financial area. Since this full moon is at 0 degrees, there will be a second full moon in this sign, at 29 degrees, on April 19. This one brings financial news and draws your attention to your various relationships. Are they balanced? If not, what can you do to bring them more into balance?

Between March 26 and April 20, Venus move through Pisces, your opposite sign. You and your partner should enjoy a romantic and creative time together, and you're more in tune with each other. If you're not involved with anyone right now, then this transit should spur your creativity, particularly after Mercury turns direct on March 28. Once that happens, the planet of communication moves toward its appointment with Aries next month.

On March 31, Mars enters Gemini and your career area. From then until May 15, your professional life really picks up steam and forward thrust. This period is when you get things done and other people—friends, co-workers and your network—are instrumental in making it happen.

AT A GLANCE
March 1—Venus enters into Aquarius
March 5—Mercury turns retrograde in Pisces
March 6—New moon in Pisces, Uranus enters Taurus
March 20—Full moon in Libra
March 26—Venus goes into Pisces
March 28—Mercury turns direct
March 31—Mars enters Gemini

April 2019
Impatience

April is astrologically busy, and you may need to balance your energy with sufficient sleep! Three planets turn retrograde and two planets enter new signs. Let's start with the new moon in Aries on April 5. Unless you have your natal moon in a fire sign or other natal planets, this moon may feel uncomfortable, too restless and impatient. However, Aries is a trailblazer and an entrepreneur, so you can expect an opportunity to surface that will be something new, different and exciting!

Jupiter turns retrograde on April 10 and remains that way until August 11. During these months, Jupiter's expansive energy turns inward, and your spiritual beliefs broaden. You may embark on a quest of some kind that takes you overseas to ancient sites or into a new area of philosophical study and research.

Both Pluto and Saturn turn retrograde in Capricorn on the 25th and 29th respectively, in the area of your chart that governs romance, creativity and your children. The Pluto retro lasts until October 3, and during these months, your shadow side may show itself more frequently. You may become overly obsessive about details and more self-critical and analytical. Try not to think everything to death, Virgo! Saturn's retrograde lasts until September 18, and during these months you'll be scrutinizing the various structures in your life—those of your closest personal relationships and of your professional relationships.

On the 17th, Mercury enters Aries, and on the 20th, Venus follows. When these two planets travel together, they have a lot to chat about and this time the conversation focuses on love, money and art. Any dealings you have with banks and insurance companies should work in your favor. You might find a lower interest rate on your mortgage and decide to refinance your home. Your partner could get a significant raise, or a royalty check may arrive for something you've created. The Mercury transit ends on May 6, and the Venus transit ends on May 15.

Treat yourself to something special at the end of this extremely active month—a day at a spa, a hike into nature or a shopping spree.

AT A GLANCE
April 5—New moon in Aries
April 10—Jupiter turns retrograde in Sagittarius
April 17—Mercury enters Aries
April 19—Full moon in Libra
April 20—Venus enters Aries
April 25—Pluto turns retrograde in Capricorn
April 29—Saturn turns retrograde in Capricorn

May 2019
5 stars

Since the dominant astrological energy in May is in Taurus, a fellow earth sign, on May 4, you'll enjoy this month and will find plenty to enjoy! It starts with a new moon in Taurus. Even though Uranus doesn't conjunct this moon, they are sharing the same space and sign, an indication that new opportunities surface unexpectedly. All you have to do is recognize them and seize them. They may involve a new financial opportunity or something connected to publishing, higher education or international travel.

On May 6, Mercury enters Taurus and on the 15th, Venus follows. Once again, these two planets will be traveling together for a while, bolstering each other's energy and yours. The Mercury transit lasts until May 21 and brings a greater patience and resolve into your conscious awareness. Tackle any communication project that requires careful planning and execution. The Venus transit ends on June 8 and may prove to be one of the more romantic and sensuous times all year. If you're traveling, you may be sampling various types of food and wines, so be careful not to overdo it!

Mars enters Cancer on May 15, the same day that Venus enters Taurus. This transit lasts until July 1, ramps up your social life, deepens your intuition and brings your family life into sharper focus. Since it forms a beneficial angle to your sun sign, you're able to accomplish a great deal.

The 18th features a full moon in water sign Scorpio. This one receives a harmonious beam of energy from Pluto, and any news you hear is positive and powerful. Scorpio urges you to dig deeper for answers, and because you're a detail-oriented person, you accept the challenge. No telling what treasures you may find!

From May 21 to June 4, Mercury transits Gemini, a sign it rules, and your career area. Whether you're self-employed or work for someone else, this is the ideal time to network, communicate, write, blog and use all forms of social media to publicize your company's services or products. Mercury is happy in Gemini and facilitates multitasking. Just be careful that you don't take on too much!

AT A GLANCE
May 4—New moon in Taurus
May 6—Mercury enters Taurus
May 15—Venus goes into Taurus, Mars enters Cancer
May 18—Full moon in Scorpio
May 21—Mercury goes into Gemini

June 2019
Positive career stuff

There's a lot to like this month, and part of the focus will be on your career and professional life. The new moon in Gemini on June 3 brings new professional opportunities that could range from a promotion and raise to an entirely new career path. It depends on what you've been desiring and where you've been putting your attention. If you've been working toward starting your own business, then the energy of this new moon could make it happen.

On the 4th, Mercury enters Cancer and joins Mars in the same area of your chart. These two travel together until June 26, when Mercury changes signs again, and should result in new friendships and renewing older friendships. You may be involved in a publicity campaign of some kind and may discover that your dreams and ambitions are closer to achievement than you think!

Venus transits Gemini and your tenth house of career from June 8 to July 3. What fun this will be! Your professional life runs more smoothly, bosses and peers are drawn to your ideas and your personality is so magnetic that you don't lack for supporters. The Venus transit helps to magnify the energy of the new moon in Gemini five days ago.

The full moon in fire sign Sagittarius on June 17 highlights your home life. If there's news about home and family, then it's undoubtedly good because Jupiter retrograde is widely conjunct. Sagittarius is a gregarious sign, and you or someone you live with may throw a party or have a barbecue and invite the neighborhood!

Neptune in Pisces will be retrograde from June 20 to January 11, 2020. Neptune's retrograde sometimes acts as a reality check. In this case, the reality check may concern your partnerships, a creative endeavor or a decision that is difficult to make. Your imagination is still wildly active, but may be understood more readily in dreams. Be sure to keep a notepad and pen next to your bed. Train yourself to wake up after a dream and jot it down.

Mercury enters fire sign Leo on June 26, and until the 7th, is moving direct in that sign. Until the 7th, you may be working hard to complete something before a deadline—or before Mercury turns retrograde! Leo is ingenious and creative and helps you find the right solution!

AT A GLANCE
June 3—New moon in Gemini
June 4—Mercury enters into Cancer
June 8—Venus goes into Gemini
June 17—Full moon in Sagittarius
June 20—Neptune turns retrograde
June 26—Mercury enters Leo

July 2019
Mercury retro & eclipses

It's another busy month, with two eclipses and the start of a Mercury retrograde in Leo. Let's tackle the eclipses first. On July 2, the solar eclipse falls in compatible water sign Cancer, in that area of your chart that rules friends, the people you hang out with, your social life and your wishes and dreams. Uranus forms a close and beneficial angle to the eclipse degree, so any opportunities that surface on or around this date seem to come out of nowhere. You may have a chance to work on a publicity campaign, meet a circle of new friends and move closer to the achievement of a particular dream.

The lunar eclipse in Capricorn on July 16 may bring news about a romantic relationship, a creative endeavor or your children. With Pluto forming a harmonious angle to the eclipse degree, the new moon should put you in a more powerful position. But because eclipses bring issues up front and center in our awareness, even the ones that are beneficial can trigger anxiety and a sense of urgency.

On July 1, Mars enters Leo and for the next six weeks, until August 18, you may be working behind the scenes in some capacity. Whatever the work or project is, it stimulates your finances because Mars forms a strong angle to your financial area. The transit may also bring up issues you have buried that should now be resolved, if possible, so that you can take full advantage of Mars's transit through your sign!

From July 3 to 27, Venus moves through Cancer, transiting the same area that the solar eclipse triggered. One of the opportunities you may enjoy is a new romantic interest you met through friends or have known as a friend. The chemistry is right! This transit should also bring your muse along to clarify your creative goals. Once Venus moves into Leo on the 27th, where it will remain until August 21, you may feel driven to complete a particular creative endeavor.

Mercury is retrograde in Leo from July 7 to 31. Look over the Mercury retrograde section in the introduction for general guidelines about how to get through this retro with your sanity intact! Since it occurs in that area of your chart that governs the personal unconscious, this would be an excellent time to explore your past lives, your motives and your own psyche. With dramatic Leo as part of the equation, be sure to follow the three Rs: revise, review and reconsider all creative endeavors rather than begin something new.

On the 27th, Venus joins Mars in Leo, and whenever these two planets travel together, your love life picks up considerable steam. Mercury has slipped back into Cancer by now, but on August 11 it moves back into Leo again, and then you have a trio of planets traveling together. More on that in the August roundup.

On the 31st, Mercury turns direct, and there's a new moon in Leo! Okay, this is a lot of fire sign activity for you, Virgo, so put it to good use by diving into your creative projects, running wild with your lover and planting all the seeds of desire that will flourish for you in August, when the emphasis is on your sign!

AT A GLANCE
July 1—Mars goes into Leo
July 2—Solar eclipse in Cancer
July 3—Venus enters Cancer
July 7—Mercury turns retrograde in Leo
July 16—Lunar eclipse in Capricorn
July 27—Venus enters Leo
July 31—Mercury turns direct, new moon in Leo

August 2019
Perfect

You're going to love August, especially from mid-August onward. On August 11, Jupiter turns direct again in Sagittarius, and now you enjoy this planet's external expansion once again. Between now and when Jupiter enters Capricorn on December 2, your home life expands in some way—someone moves in or out, you build onto your house, there's a birth or you add an office.

On the same day, Mercury enters Leo once again, and you enjoy the same creative energy that you did before Mercury turned retrograde last month. Between August 29 and September 14, it transits your sign, and it won't be alone. Take a look at the lineup: on the 18th, Mars enters Virgo; on the 21st, Venus follows; on the 29th, Mercury enters Virgo; and on the 30th, there's a new moon in your sign. Let's take these one at a time.

Mars transits Virgo from August 18 to October 4, and during this period, you can accomplish just about anything. So take on your most challenging endeavor or relationship, and go to work! Once Venus joins Mars in your sign, where it will be until September 14, you've got the cosmic lovers journeying together once again, and you're on top of the world! You feel as if nothing can stop you from achieving whatever you desire. Other people find you to be magnetic and compelling and seek out your company. Your love life may hold some delicious surprises. Perhaps you and your partner decide to move in together or get married or, also possible, join forces on a creative endeavor. Regardless of how the specifics unfold, this period will be one of the most romantic and creative for you all year.

Since Venus isn't retrograde this year, you enjoyed another period like this between February 3 and March 1, when Venus was transiting Capricorn and the romance and creativity sector of your chart. You will experience yet another bonus period from November 25 to December 20, when Venus transits Capricorn once again.

Mercury, your ruler, moves through Virgo from August 29 to September 14, and now your head and your heart are on the same page. Your communication prowess comes roaring to the forefront, and you may be involved in so many projects that you'll need to use that discerning Virgo intellect to pick and choose.

The new moon in your sign on the 30th should attract new personal opportunities that thrill you. It could be anything from a new job to a communication project to new clients. Uranus in Taurus forms a beneficial angle to this new moon, suggesting that the opportunities surprise you; you don't see them coming.

This new moon comes around just once a year, and it's smart to prepare for it in advance because it sets the tone for the next twelve months. Make a wish list of what you would like to experience and achieve in the next year. Post it where you'll see it often. Visualize each item on your list happening, and imagine how excited you'll be. Then let the universe do its work and bring it all about! If you're an early Virgo, born between August 23–31, this new moon will be especially good for you.

Sprinkled throughout all this Virgo energy, there are some other events to note. Uranus turns retrograde in Taurus on August 12, and there's a full moon in Aquarius on August 15. The Uranus retrograde, which lasts until January 6, 2020, may trigger an inner restlessness and a need for more freedom and autonomy. You may have strange psychic experiences while traveling.

The full moon in Aquarius on August 15 falls in that area of your chart that governs your daily work routine and the way you maintain your daily health. Jupiter forms a harmonious angle to this full moon, suggesting that any news you hear should be positive and may prompt you to expand something in your work routine.

AT A GLANCE
August 11—Jupiter turns direct, Mercury enters Leo
August 12—Uranus turns retrograde
August 15—Full moon in Aquarius
August 18—Mars enters Virgo
August 21—Venus goes into Virgo
August 29—Mercury enters Virgo
August 30—New moon in Virgo

September 2019
Income spike

September is marginally less frantic than August, but still crowded with astrological events. On September 14, three events occur: Mercury and Venus enter Libra, and there's a full moon in Pisces. Mercury's transit lasts until October 3, and Venus's transit lasts until October 8. While the two are traveling together in your financial area, your income should spike, and even if your expenses rise during this period, you can cover the bills. Mercury can talk to virtually anyone about anything now and chats up a storm to increase your financial options.

The full moon in Pisces on September 14 occurs in your partnership area. Neptune retrograde is closely conjunct this full moon, and Pluto retrograde in Capricorn forms a beneficial angle to it. Any news you hear will empower you but only after a period of confusion. Once you get the full story, you know how to proceed.

On the 18th, Saturn turns direct in Capricorn. Now you can implement what you learned about the various structures in your life—which relationships work best and which ones need bolstering. With Saturn direct, you and a romantic partner may decide to deepen your commitment to each other. On the creative front, your endeavors are rock solid.

The new moon in Libra on the 29th brings in new sources of income, perhaps in the area of human relations, publicity or the law.

AT A GLANCE
September 14—Mercury and Venus enter Libra, full moon in Pisces
September 18—Saturn turns direct in Capricorn
September 29—New moon in Libra

October 2019
Mixed

Note to self: Mercury turns retrograde in Scorpio on October 31. That means that before that date, you should make your travel plans, complete negotiations and sign contracts, make submissions and start new projects. The retro lasts until November 20 and is the last one this year. It occurs in the communication area of your chart, and that means to watch your Ps and Qs, Virgo, when you talk or write to anyone. Check and double check what you say, particularly with siblings and neighbors, and with people with whom you come into contact in your daily life.

Since this retro begins on Halloween here in the U.S. and your kids are anticipating trick-or-treating, be aware that plans may shift suddenly.

Before the retro starts, Mercury enters Scorpio on October 3, and Pluto turns direct. While Mercury is behaving, you may be delving more deeply into esoteric topics—life after death, reincarnation or communication with the dead. The transit favors any kind of research where you have to dig deeply for answers and information. With Pluto turning direct in Capricorn, you're now more in control of romantic situations and your creative endeavors.

From October 4 to November 19, Mars transits Libra and your financial area. For four days, until Venus moves into Scorpio on October 8, Mars travels with Venus, a dynamite combination for your love life and your sex life. But more than that, this duo may help bring about the sale of an artistic endeavor (or several) that helps to increase your income. Once Venus moves into Scorpio on October 8, your muse brings you plenty of material for creative fodder. The nature of Scorpio is to dig deeply, like an archeologist, for hidden treasures. No telling what beauties may be uncovered during this transit, which ends on November 1.

The full moon in Aries on October 13 highlights resources you share with others. Jupiter forms a terrific angle to this full moon, so any news you hear should be positive and will expand your options in some way. Your partner may land a plump raise, or you might get an insurance refund or an unexpected royalty check. There's a trailblazing quality to Aries, and you may feel some of it during this full moon. Think of it as the wild child within!

The 27th features a new moon in Scorpio and should usher in new opportunities for writing/speaking, travel and research. You and your neighbors and/or siblings may have a block party, or you become more involved in your community in some way. Uranus is opposed to this new moon, which means the opportunities arrived suddenly and unexpectedly.

Then, on the 31st, Mercury turns retrograde in Scorpio.

October 3—Mercury goes into Scorpio, Pluto turns direct
October 4—Mars enters Libra
October 8—Venus goes into Scorpio
October 13—Full moon in Aries
October 27—New moon in Scorpio
October 31—Mercury turns retrograde

November 2019
Good news

November is busy! Venus transits two signs, both Mercury and Neptune turn direct, and that's in addition to the new and full moon. Let's start on November 1, when Venus enters Sagittarius, where it will be until the 25th.

This transit facilitates your home life, stimulates it and may turn your place into a hub of activity—i.e., parties! Sagittarius always enjoys a good time, and with Venus here, those good times may involve romance and ardent feelings. Also, don't be surprised if someone brings home a stray dog or cat. It might even be you, Virgo. Sagittarius has a fondness for animals, and your attitude now may be the more the merrier!

From November 25 to December 20, Venus moves through Capricorn and the romance/creativity section of your chart. Once again, you're treated to an almost idyllic period where your love life is blissful, your creativity soars and your magnetism draws people to you. You can make significant professional strides during this transit as well, thanks to the Capricorn part of this equation.

The full moon in Taurus on November 12 should be a good one for you! Not only is it in a fellow earth sign, but it receives a strong, supportive angle from Saturn, suggesting that any news you hear has long-term effects. Pluto forms the same kind of angle to it, as close as you come to a guarantee that the news puts you in control. The news could concern finances, a publishing project or something connected to higher education.

From November 19 to January 4, 2020, Mars transits Scorpio. It functions well here because it co-rules this sign. Mars now makes a beneficial angle to your sun sign, an indication that you enjoy an energetic period that enables you to clear off your desk before the holidays and to enter the new year revved up to go!

Mercury turns direct in Scorpio on November 20 and heads toward its appointment with Sagittarius on December 9. Until it gets there, you have another terrific period for research and delving into the esoteric side of life.

The new moon in Sagittarius on the 26th brings new opportunities for your domestic and family life. If your home has been on the market, you could get an offer for your asking price. Something in your living situation could change for the better. A roommate, adult child or an elderly parent might move in or out. Also, you might have a chance to head overseas.

On the 27th, Neptune turns direct in Pisces, and you and a creative partner can now move forward with confidence on your joint project.

AT A GLANCE

November 1—Venus goes into Sagittarius
November 12—Full moon in Taurus
November 19—Mars enters Scorpio
November 20—Mercury turns direct
November 25—Venus enters Capricorn
November 26—New moon in Sagittarius
November 27—Neptune turns direct

December 2019
Fun & pleasure

What would you like to experience and achieve in the year ahead? Make a list, post it where you'll see it often and back each desire with emotion. Then let the universe work its magic. Do this on December 2, when Jupiter enters Capricorn, where it will be until December 20, 2020. It's a perfect way to usher in this exciting transit that will expand your love life, creative endeavors and career. If you and your partner are considering starting a family, then it could happen during the next year. Your worldview and spiritual beliefs are likely to evolve in some way. Your capacity for enjoyment and pleasure will also expand.

Between December 9 and 29, Mercury moves through Sagittarius. It's an ideal spot for the holidays, with all the festivities and reunions. Your conscious focus is on home and family. You may decide to hit the road for a long weekend or do something else that everyone in the family enjoys. From December 29 to January 17, 2020, Mercury joins Jupiter in Capricorn, and you may delve into a creative endeavor, embark on a spiritual quest, build a website or start a blog.

The full moon in Gemini on December 12 highlights your career. You're able to tie up loose ends so that you can enter the new year with a clean slate. Any news you hear may be confusing, and it's wise not to make any decisions until you have all the details.

Venus transits Aquarius from December 20 to January 14, 2020 and facilitates everything you need to do at work to move with confidence into the new year. If a romance is sparked during this period, it may be with someone you meet through work. You feel a need for greater independence during this transit.

The solar eclipse in Capricorn on December 26 brings new opportunities in romance and creativity and in all endeavors with children. Jupiter is conjunct the eclipse degree, indicating good luck and serendipitous events. You're in the right place at the right time, Virgo.

AT A GLANCE

December 2—Jupiter enters Capricorn
December 9—Mercury enters Sagittarius
December 12—Full moon in Gemini
December 20—Venus goes into Aquarius
December 26—Solar eclipse in Capricorn
December 29—Mercury enters into Capricorn

Reflection

Since you began this monthlooking ahead, take a few minutes to end it by looking back. How did the year unfold for you? What did you learn that could benefit you in 2020? Are you happier? Record your thoughts below.

_____
_____
_____
_____
_____

Happy New Year!

Libra 2019

Your sign, like Taurus, is ruled by Venus. In the monthly roundups, pay close attention to its transits and the angles other planets are making to it and to your sun sign. Venus won't be retrograde this year, and that means it makes it through all twelve signs and visits three signs twice. You'll have three really stellar periods this year when Venus transits Aquarius and the romance/creativity section of your chart twice and again when it transits your sign. Those dates are: March 1 to 26; September 14 to October 8; and December 20 to January 14, 2020.

The monthly roundups also include information on retrogrades, eclipses, the transits of other planets and the new and full moons each month.

You'll enjoy 2019. For most of the year, expansive Jupiter transits fire sign Sagittarius and forms a beneficial angle to your sun sign. This angle, a sextile, is a facilitator that enables events, relationships, skills—and life!—to unfold effortlessly. Since the transit occurs in that part of your chart that governs communication, your neighborhood, your siblings and your conscious mind, all those areas will experience the Midas touch of Jupiter!

January 2019
A bit of anxiety

This month's energy is focused on earth sign Capricorn, the worker of the zodiac. It's probably not your favorite kind of energy, but you can start putting it to use on January 4, when Mercury enters Capricorn and the domestic area of your chart. From then until the 24th, you're determined to finish up any home improvement projects that lingered from last year. You may have to place tighter restrictions on your kids to get them back into the school mindset now that the holidays are over.

Before the solar eclipse in Capricorn on January 5, you may be feeling some anxiety and tension. This powerful eclipse brings new opportunities for your home life—the sale of your home, a move or a shift in living arrangements. But with Pluto conjunct within five degrees, there may be power plays involved with an authority figure. Neptune in Pisces forms a beneficial angle to the eclipse degree, so some type of spiritual or artistic endeavor may be part of the larger picture.

Uranus turns direct in Aries on January 6 and is sharing the partnership area of your chart with energetic Mars, which entered that sign on December 31, 2018. The two planets aren't conjunct, but they feed off of each other and attract unusual and idiosyncratic people. You and your partner may come up with some terrific ideas before Uranus moves into Taurus in March. Keep track of them. They may come in handy.

On the 7th, Venus enters compatible fire sign Sagittarius, and from then until February 3, your creativity is fueled by your passion for whatever you're doing. Communication is heightened, particularly with neighbors and siblings. In a romantic relationship, your need for independence and freedom is accentuated.

January 21 features a lunar eclipse in Leo. This type of eclipse concerns our inner worlds and our emotions, and you may react to something a friend says about a creative endeavor in which you're involved. Avoid drama. Let the remark roll away from you. That may not be easy to do, but if you pursue it, you may regret it later.

Mercury enters fellow air sign Aquarius on the 24th, and from then until February 10, your conscious focus in on romance and love. Aquarius is an idiosyncratic sign that can spot cutting edge trends before anyone else does, so jot down any unusual ideas that come to you. Be vigilant for synchronicities.

January 4—Mercury enters into Capricorn
January 5—Solar eclipse in Capricorn
January 6—Uranus turns direct in Aries
January 7—Venus goes into Sagittarius
January 21—Lunar eclipse in Leo
January 24—Mercury goes into Aquarius

February 2019
New opportunities

February is calmer than last month. No eclipses and no retrogrades!

On February 3, Venus enters Capricorn and from then until March 1, your home life should unfold with greater smoothness. Venus is a facilitator that enhances your sense of artistic beauty, so you may feel compelled to beautify your home and surroundings in some way. If it's winter where you live, fresh flowers and plants usually liven up rooms. If you're ambitious, repaint the rooms where you spend the most time. During this transit, Venus is square to your sun sign, usually a challenging aspect except that it's Venus we're talking about! You may be more interested in having fun and enjoying yourself and feel more sociable.

The new moon in Aquarius should be quite enjoyable for you. It ushers in new opportunities in love and romance and with your various creative activities. If you aren't involved with anyone right now, this moon may change that situation. Expansive Jupiter forms a beautiful angle to this new moon, and Mercury is conjunct within four degrees, indicating that your thoughts, intentions and expectations are a huge part of what you attract.

On February 10, Mercury enters intuitive and imaginative Pisces and the daily work area of your chart. Until March 5, when it turns retrograde, your awareness is in a soft, gentle place and enables you to ride the tide of imagination to wherever it may lead you. You're more compassionate toward employees and co-workers and your ideas are supported by the people around you.

Mars enters earth sign Taurus on February 14, and from then until March 31, you tackle projects and relationships that demand patience and a resolute determination. You and your partner may be pursuing other sources of income, perhaps through grants, loans or a second mortgage on your home. You're more grounded during this transit.

The full moon in Virgo on February 19 lights up the quiet part of your chart—your solar twelfth house, the personal unconscious. You're able to make connections now about issues you may have buried recently and can resolve them more easily. Mars forms a beneficial angle to this full moon and strengthens your resolve.

February 3—Venus enters Capricorn
February 4—New moon in Aquarius
February 10—Mercury goes into Pisces
February 14—Mars enters into Taurus
February 19—Full moon in Virgo

March 2019
Erratic

This month is a wild mix of energies, with one of the outer planets changing signs. Let's start there.

First, check your natal chart to find out where Taurus falls. That's the area that Uranus is going to enter on March 6. It entered Taurus briefly in 2018, then turned retrograde and slipped back into Aries. Now it will be in Taurus until July 2025, when it enters Gemini. Due to a retrograde, it slips back into Taurus, then enters Gemini again in April 2026. This planet's job is to shake up the status quo in any area where we have grown habitual and routine. It gets rid of the dead wood so the new can flow in.

When Uranus transited Aries, your opposite sign, it cleaned up your partnership area. Perhaps you got married or divorced, started your own business, changed careers or experienced a change in finances. Now, Uranus brings abrupt change to resources you share with others. You could inherit money, win the lottery or experience a downturn in income because a partner becomes unemployed. Again, the ramifications of the transit depend on where you have become rigid and habitual.

Before that transit begins, Venus enters Aquarius on March 1. Oh lucky you, Libra! Between now and March 26, you enjoy an immensely creative and romantic period. If you aren't involved when the transit starts, you may be by the time it ends. The only glitch is that Mercury will be retrograde for much of this transit, from March 5–28. But even with Mercury in retrograde, Venus still works its magic—just not as quickly.

Regarding Mercury, read over the Mercury retrograde section in the introduction, and follow the general guidelines on how to navigate these several weeks more successfully. Since this one occurs in Pisces, in your daily work area, be sure to communicate clearly with employees and co-workers, and encourage everyone in your work place to follow the rules of the three Rs—revise, review and reconsider, rather than starting new projects.

On the same day that Uranus enters Taurus, March 6, there's a new moon in Pisces. Neptune is conjunct this new moon, and Saturn is friendly to it. This means that the opportunities that surface creatively and in your daily work have a long-term impact. Just remember that if you hire new employees, land a nice freelance gig or take on new clients, don't sign any contracts until after the 28th, when Mercury is moving direct again.

The full moon in your sign on the 20th brings news of a personal nature that may require an adjustment of some kind, perhaps in attitude. This moon is at 0 degrees, Libra, so there will be another full moon in your sign at 29 degrees in April—and that one looks more positive. The emphasis during this full moon is on relationships.

Venus enters Pisces on March 26, and between then and April 20, your imagination is powerful enough to roam the universe and bring back ideas that you can use in your work, life and relationships. If a romance is kindled during this transit, it's likely to have a beautiful intuitive flow and gentleness to it.

On the 28th, Mercury turns direct. Now you can get moving with all the things that were put on a back burner during the retrograde!

Between March 31 and May 15, Mars transits your air sibling, Gemini, and now you really have the wind at your back. Get out there and network, socialize, blog, start your book or novel or apply to graduate school. This transit stimulates your intellect and your communication skills. Make it count!

AT A GLANCE
March 1—Venus enters into Aquarius
March 5—Mercury turns retrograde in Pisces
March 6—New moon in Pisces, Uranus enters Taurus
March 20—Full moon in Libra
March 26—Venus goes into Pisces
March 28—Mercury turns direct
March 31—Mars enters Gemini

April 2019
Backtracking

Three planets turn retrograde this month—Jupiter, Saturn and Pluto. Let's start there. On April 10, Jupiter turns retrograde in Sagittarius and stays that way until August 11. During these months, the expansive nature of the planet turns inward, and you may be fine-tuning your spiritual beliefs by reading about and sampling various philosophies. You may embark on a quest of some kind, like Indiana Jones in search of an elusive artifact. You may study the paranormal or have psychic experiences that spur a search.

Pluto turns retrograde in Capricorn on April 25, and Saturn in Capricorn follows four days later. The Pluto retrograde lasts until October 3, and during this time you may become more deeply acquainted with your shadow side. That's the part of you that bends like a branch in the wind to accommodate everyone else's needs and resents it. Power issues surface in your career and at home. Saturn's retrograde doesn't last quite as long—until September 18. It prompts you to scrutinize the various relationship structures in your life and to identify the ones that may need bolstering.

Before any of these retros begin, there's a new moon in Aries on April 5. Expect new opportunities to appear in partnerships—you find the ideal agent, manager or visionary that enables you to launch your own business or sell your novel or publicize your art or photography. Aries is a passionate, trailblazing sign, so don't be surprised if some wild and crazy idea occurs to you that you're able to implement.

On the 17th, Mercury enters Aries, and from then until May 6, your conscious awareness is focused on that wild, crazy idea. You talk about it with friends, blog about it and brainstorm with others about it. Gradually, it becomes crystal clear in your head. Two days later, on the 19th, there's a second full moon in your sign, and this one receives a friendly beam from Jupiter retrograde and a bit of a challenge from Pluto. But Jupiter, even in its weakened state, should prevail, and the news you hear ultimately puts you in a better place.

Venus enters Aries on April 20, and between then and May 15, you and your partner/spouse enjoy renewed passion in your relationship. You may even decide to team up on a creative endeavor or on some type of income-generating project.

AT A GLANCE
April 5—New moon in Aries
April 10—Jupiter turns retrograde in Sagittarius
April 17—Mercury enters Aries
April 19—Full moon in Libra
April 20—Venus enters Aries
April 25—Pluto turns retrograde in Capricorn
April 29—Saturn turns retrograde in Capricorn

May 2019
New financial opportunities

May features a lot of earth energy that helps you to ground yourself. Take on situations and work that require patience and resoluteness. You'll have plenty of both this month.

The new moon in Taurus on May 4 should trigger new financial opportunities for you. It may come through a client with whom you have worked in the past. Your partner may get a raise or promotion, or you land a bonus for work you've done. You'll have a clearer picture about this once Mercury, and then Venus, enter Taurus on May 6 and May 15 respectively. Also on the 15th, Mars enters Cancer and your career area.

Let's look at each of these transits separately. Mercury will be in Taurus until May 21 and brings a steadiness to your conscious thoughts. You're better able to control what you think and when you think it, thus avoiding negative streams of internal chatter that don't do you or anyone else any good. Your command of language is excellent now, and you're able to make the abstract practical.

Once Venus joins Mercury on May 15, your sensuality and appreciation for beauty peak. A royalty check or insurance refund may arrive, you may find a better mortgage rate or your loan could come through. If a romance begins during this transit, there may be mystical elements to the relationship. You might feel you have known the person in other lives. This transit ends on June 8.

Between May 15 and July 1, Mars moves through Cancer and your career area. Whenever Mars transits this area of your chart, you become a dervish of activity and can accomplish a great deal. Your intuition is sharpened considerably, and you're able to make quick decisions based on nothing more than a hunch or a feeling. Mars is the planet that makes stuff happen, Libra.

On the 18th, the full moon in Scorpio highlights your financial area. You're able to understand the beliefs and thoughts that may be preventing you from achieving the financial prosperity you desire and grasp how to adjust them. Since Pluto forms a friendly angle to this full moon, any news you hear about money puts you in a more powerful position.

Mercury enters Gemini on May 21, and between then and June 4, your communication skills are stellar. Mercury rules Gemini and functions well here. This transit favors all kind of writing, studying, research and learning. You may feel restless during this transit, an itch to be traveling and start planning a vacation for the summer. Just don't travel between July 7 and 31, when Mercury will be retrograde in Leo.

AT A GLANCE
May 4—New moon in Taurus
May 6—Mercury enters Taurus
May 15—Venus goes into Taurus, Mars enters Cancer
May 18—Full moon in Scorpio
May 21—Mercury goes into Gemini

June 2019
Career momentum

June is a mix of energy, and it all starts with a new moon in Gemini on the 4th. Be on the lookout for new opportunities to network. You may be asked to conduct a workshop or teach a class on a subject in which you're an expert. Or you may take a workshop or class. Gemini is perpetually curious, so on or around the time of this new moon, you may have a chance to research something that intrigues you.

Between June 4 and 26, Mercury joins Mars in Cancer and your career sector. Nice combination! Mars keeps you moving forward with your various professional projects, and Mercury keeps you in a communicative mindset, reaching out to co-workers and bosses with your ideas and suggestions.

On June 8, Venus enters Gemini and the same area of your chart where the new moon occurred four days earlier. This transit lasts until July 3 and should facilitate those new opportunities that the new moon brings. Your muse is feeding you all sorts of creative ideas, and you may be delving into a new endeavor of some kind. Writing, publishing, blogging and international travel may be part of what the new moon brings and that which Venus helps to bring about.

The full moon in Sagittarius on June 17 broadens your perceptions about what is possible. With Jupiter retrograde forming a wide conjunction to this full moon, you're ready to see your daily life in a new light. You may also look differently at your spiritual and political beliefs. Are those beliefs too constrictive? Any news you hear should be positive.

Neptune turns retrograde in Pisces on June 20 and remains that way until January 11, 2020. This lengthy retrograde allows you to look at your work and your creativity without illusions. It may not be the most pleasant introspection at times, but it's necessary.

From June 26 to July 7, Mercury moves in direct motion through Leo, and then it turns retrograde. We'll talk more about that in next month's roundup. While Mercury is behaving, you spend a lot of time with friends and acquaintances, may be working on a publicity campaign of some kind and have a distinct dramatic flair in your writing and speech.

AT A GLANCE
June 3—New moon in Gemini
June 4—Mercury enters into Cancer
June 8—Venus goes into Gemini
June 17—Full moon in Sagittarius
June 20—Neptune turns retrograde
June 26—Mercury enters Leo

July 2019
Unexpected opportunities

This month's two eclipses bring some surprising twists and turns and, perhaps, a bit of anxiety and urgency as well. The first one, on July 2, is a solar eclipse in Cancer. This one should bring new professional opportunities—perhaps a promotion that comes with a good raise or a chance for a new career path altogether. Uranus in Taurus is friendly to the eclipse degree, forming a 5-degree angle to it, indicating that the opportunities are sudden and unforeseen. Your task is to be alert for them and seize them!

The lunar eclipse in Capricorn on July 16 may not be particularly comfortable. Some inner quality emerges in you that you would rather not acknowledge—unbridled ambition, a coldness toward a family member or perhaps selfishness. It may all be brought on by a remark or a criticism made by someone in your personal environment. Learn from it. Lunar eclipses are often about self-discovery.

Before either of the eclipses occur, Mars enters Leo on July 1 and places you squarely in your creative element. During this transit, which lasts until August 18, your friendships and networks of acquaintances—your social circles—are your focus. It's through relationships that you learn to define yourself, and your best teachers are the people who enjoy your company.

Venus enters Cancer and your career area on July 3, a major bonus for your professional life. From then until July 27, career matters and relationships unfold with greater smoothness. Your peers are supportive of your ideas and suggestions, and your boss undoubtedly loves you. The one glitch in this beautiful picture is that Mercury turns retrograde in Leo on July 7, slips back into Cancer and turns direct in that sign on July 31. That may throw a wrench into the communication aspect of your life, but follow the general guidelines suggested in the Mercury retrograde section in the introduction to navigate this period more successfully. Also, since the retro is in Leo, don't let the retro stifle your creativity. It's a great time to review, revise and reconsider older projects.

From July 27 to August 21, Venus transits Leo. This transit should be really pleasant for you once Mercury turns direct on the 31st. Any romance that begins will be dramatic, flamboyant and fun! It could be with someone you meet through friends.

The same day Mercury turns direct, there's a new moon in Leo. And that means new opportunities to take your creativity in different directions and new friends!

AT A GLANCE
July 1—Mars goes into Leo
July 2—Solar eclipse in Cancer
July 3—Venus enters Cancer
July 7—Mercury turns retrograde in Leo
July 16—Lunar eclipse in Capricorn
July 27—Venus enters Leo
July 31—Mercury turns direct, new moon in Leo

August 2019
Dive within

This month features a lot of astrological events, and the emphasis is on earth signs.

Jupiter turns direct in Sagittarius on August 11, a bonus for all your communication and travel. You now have the opportunity once again to enjoy Jupiter's expansive nature in the external world. On the same day, Mercury enters Leo for the second time, and from August 11 to 29, you spend a lot of time with your network of friends and acquaintances.

Uranus turns retrograde in Taurus on August 12, and the retro takes you into the new year, until January 6. You have a greater need for freedom and independence during this lengthy period and may experience bouts of restlessness. Just take it all in, Libra, and don't worry about the small stuff.

August 15 features a full moon in Aquarius. There's news about a romance or a creative endeavor, and thanks to a beautiful beam from Jupiter, the news looks good. This one highlights your solar fifth house of romance, creativity, children and whatever you do for fun and pleasure. Take advantage of this energy by inviting friends over for a get-together.

From August 18 to the end of the month, the astrological events all fall in earth sign Virgo, in that part of your chart that governs the personal unconscious. On the 18th, Mars enters Virgo, followed by Venus on the 21st, Mercury on the 29th and a new moon in Virgo on the 30th. The Mars transit lasts until October 4 and makes it much easier for you to connect the dots within your own psyche. Issues you may have buried over the years could surface during this period, and it's best to resolve them now, in preparation for when Mars enters your sign in October.

The Venus transit lasts until September 14. You may be pickier now in romance and in how you communicate with others. If a romance begins during this transit, the two of you may be spending a lot of time alone together, getting to know each other. Once Venus enters your sign in September, you announce the news to everyone and then enjoy one of the most romantic times all year.

Mercury transits Virgo from August 29 to September 14. This period favors therapy, a past-life regression or workshops about consciousness and/or dreaming. You open up a dialogue with your inner self.

Then the new moon in Virgo on the 30th may bring an opportunity to work behind the scenes in some capacity. Thanks to a friendly beam from the Uranus retrograde in Taurus, these opportunities happen suddenly and unexpectedly. Be prepared!

AT A GLANCE
August 11—Jupiter turns direct, Mercury enters Leo
August 12—Uranus turns retrograde
August 15—Full moon in Aquarius
August 18—Mars enters Virgo
August 21—Venus goes into Virgo
August 29—Mercury enters Virgo
August 30—New moon in Virgo

September 2019
Beautiful

You're going to enjoy September! It's all about you, with Mercury and Venus entering your sign and a new moon in Libra. So before the month gets moving, resolve to treat yourself to something special.

On September 14, three astrological events occur: both Mercury and Venus enter Libra, and there's a full moon in Pisces. With the planet of communication traveling with the planet of love and romance until October 3, you're in a blissful place. Your love life hums along at an ideal pitch. Your muse is ready and eager to help, and your head and heart are in alignment. You're feeling social, too, and may be getting out and about more frequently with friends.

The full moon in Pisces on the 14th highlights your creativity and imagination and how you integrate those elements into your daily work. Neptune is conjunct to this moon within 4 degrees, and Pluto forms a harmonious angle to it. Even though both are retrograde, they bring an element of spiritual power.

On the 18th, Saturn turns direct in Capricorn, and you feel lighter and more buoyant. You now have a clearer idea about which relationships need to be bolstered and which ones you can release.

The new moon in your sign on the 29th comes along just once a year and sets the tone for the next twelve months. Plan for it a few days ahead of time by making a list of what you would like to experience and achieve in the next year, and post it where you'll see it often. Act as though these desires have already happened. This new moon should attract new opportunities that are personally satisfying and exciting.

AT A GLANCE
September 14—Mercury and Venus enter Libra, full moon in Pisces
September 18—Saturn turns direct in Capricorn
September 29—New moon in Libra

October 2019
Whirlwind

October is a busy month, and the best part of it is that Mars enters your sign on October 4 and remains there until November 19. Any time Mars transits your sun sign, your physical energy soars, and you're able to get more done. It's the planet that makes things happen. If you're self-employed, Mars brings in more clients, projects, contacts and money, and it does so without strenuous effort on your part. If you work for someone else, you're the whirlwind of activity in the office that leaves everyone else in the dust.

The one drawback to this transit is that on October 31, Mercury turns retrograde in Scorpio and doesn't turn direct again until November 20. So Mars's capacity for action is somewhat dampened in November, but you have most of October to enjoy it.

On the 3rd, Mercury enters Scorpio and your financial area. From then until the 31st, your conscious focus is on money—what you earn and spend, how you can save more and what you can afford to spend for the holidays. Your mind is particularly intuitive, and your insights into the motives and psyches of other people is exceptional.

Between October 8 and November 1, Venus transits Scorpio and travels with Mercury once again. Your bills may increase during this transit, but your income will, too. You'll have more than enough to cover expenses. Mercury and Venus may have a little chat about creating a realistic budget.

The full moon in Aries on October 13 highlights the partnership area of your chart. Any news you hear should be positive, thanks to the beautiful angle that Jupiter makes to this moon. Since Aries is a passionate and trailblazing sign, your emotions may be on fire on or around the time of this full moon.

The 27th features a new moon in Scorpio that should attract new financial opportunities. Uranus is opposed to this new moon, and that could create some anxiety, but things shake out fine.

Before Mercury turns retrograde on the 31st, be sure to read over the Mercury retrograde section in the introduction for general guidelines on how to navigate this period more successfully. Since the retro occurs in Scorpio and your financial area, double check bank and investment statements, and try to pay cash for purchases. Don't be surprised if issues from the past crop up. Deal with them, and move on. The retro lasts until November 20 and is the last one this year!

AT A GLANCE
October 3—Mercury goes into Scorpio, Pluto turns direct
October 4—Mars enters Libra
October 8—Venus goes into Scorpio
October 13—Full moon in Aries
October 27—New moon in Scorpio
October 31—Mercury turns retrograde

November 2019
Insightful

November is another busy month, with two planets turning direct and three planets changing signs. On November 1, Venus enters Sagittarius and forms a beautiful angle to your sun sign. Between then and November 25, your artistic sensibilities are heightened, and it comes through in all of your communications. This transit may trigger an itch for travel, and if possible, indulge it, but after Mercury turns direct on the 20th.

The full moon in Taurus on November 12 brings financial news—your mortgage application is approved, you get an insurance break or a royalty check arrives. It's also possible that your partner lands a raise.

Between November 19 and January 4, 2020, Mars transits Scorpio and your financial area. You're very motivated now to earn more income and come up with novel ways to do it. This transit deepens your intuitive and psychic ability and enables you to read people quickly and thoroughly—their motives and their secrets. You may have a few secrets of your own during this transit.

On the 20th, Mercury turns direct in Scorpio, a welcome change worth celebrating. Make your travel plans now, sign contracts and get moving with your new ideas and projects.

Venus transits Capricorn from November 25 to December 20, a perfect aspect for the Thanksgiving holidays. Both Saturn and Pluto are in Capricorn, too, and the combined energies of these three planets keep you focused on your home and family. However, since Capricorn is involved, you may be doing some work over the holidays so your desk can be cleared off before the new year.

The 26th features a new moon in Sagittarius, and what fun this will be! Sagittarius is a gregarious sign, and there will be plenty of opportunities to enjoy the holiday festivities. If you've been hoping to move to a different neighborhood, then you may find the ideal area on or around the time of this new moon.

Neptune turns direct in Pisces on the 27th, and now you can once again enjoy the heightened artistic sensibility and imagination that Neptune confers.

AT A GLANCE
November 1—Venus goes into Sagittarius
November 12—Full moon in Taurus
November 19—Mars enters Scorpio
November 20—Mercury turns direct
November 25—Venus enters Capricorn
November 26—New moon in Sagittarius
November 27—Neptune turns direct

December 2019
Jupiter shift

As the last month of the year gets off to a start, spend a few minutes thinking about what you would like to achieve and experience in the new year. Make a list. Post it where you'll see it often. Visualize the items on the list. Believe. Live as though the items on the list have already happened.

On December 2, Jupiter makes a major shift when it enters Capricorn, where it will be until December 20, 2020. During this year-long transit, everything about your home and domestic life will expand. Someone may move into your place, you could add on to your existing home or you might move into a larger home. You and your partner may discover you're going to become parents. Since Capricorn is involved, your career and professional life may also expand. If you have your natal chart, find out where Capricorn falls in your chart; that will be the area that expands.

On the 9th, Mercury enters Sagittarius and moves through it until December 29. This transit is perfect for the holiday spirit. It brings optimism, positive and uplifting feelings, and a kind of invincible feeling that you can do and be anything.

The full moon in Gemini on December 12 highlights that area of your chart that governs international travel, higher education, your worldview, philosophy and publishing. If there's news in any of these areas or about any communication endeavor in which you're involved, it may initially confuse you. It's only because you don't have all the details. Wait until you know the full story before making any decisions.

Between December 20 and January 14, 2020, Venus transits Aquarius and the creativity and romance area of your chart. This period is the last of three this year when your life hums along at a nearly perfect pitch. Others find you magnetic and attractive. Your muse is eager and ready to help, and your lover or spouse just can't get enough of you. What a perfect way to usher in the new year.

The solar eclipse in Capricorn on December 26 brings in new opportunities related to your home and family life and, because Capricorn is part of the equation, your career. Since Jupiter is closely conjunct, the opportunities expand your life significantly. You may feel as if you're in the right place at the right time, and that's because you actually are!

From December 29 to January 17, 2020, Mercury joins Jupiter, Saturn and Pluto in Capricorn. This lineup of planets brings significant focus to bear on the same area where the eclipse occurred. It enables you to tie up your various projects so that you begin the new year with a clean slate.

AT A GLANCE

December 2—Jupiter enters Capricorn
December 9—Mercury enters Sagittarius
December 12—Full moon in Gemini
December 20—Venus goes into Aquarius
December 26—Solar eclipse in Capricorn
December 29—Mercury enters into Capricorn

Reflection

What areas of your life expanded in 2019? Are you pleased with the way things have turned out? Are you happier? What did you learn about yourself this year? Spend a few minutes jotting down your thoughts about this year.

_____
_____
_____
_____
_____

Happy New Year!

Scorpio 2019

Pluto rules your sign, and Mars co-rules it. Since Pluto is the snail of the zodiac, there isn't much change in its movements from month to month. The planet has been in Capricorn since 2008, forming a beneficial angle to your sun sign, and that trend will continue until January 2025. However, it will enter Aquarius in March 2023, but then turns retrograde two months later and slips back into Capricorn. In the monthly roundups, note when Pluto is retrograde and when other transiting planets make angles to it.

Mars moves more quickly, and in 2019, it transits eight signs, including Scorpio, and won't be retrograde. Pay close attention to what it's doing each month and which planets are forming angles to it. You'll also find information on the other transiting planets and retrogrades, new and full moons and eclipses.

2019 is a year for you to strengthen the structures in your life, to set and achieve your goals and to reach out beyond your comfort zone. With both Saturn and Pluto in Capricorn, your communication skills are greatly heightened, and you're urged to use them to delve deeply into whatever interests you.

January 2019
Good start

Welcome to 2019! It gets off to a great start with Mercury entering Capricorn on January 4 and enhancing your communication skills. It's traveling with both Saturn and Pluto, so your intellect is focused, more serious and able to penetrate to the depths of whatever you're doing. This transit lasts until January 24, and then Mercury enters Aquarius. Between then and February 10, your mind is busy exploring unusual ideas and experimenting with how these ideas can be implemented. You may be looking for ways to refurbish your home so that it better reflects you and your family.

On the 5th, the solar eclipse in Capricorn should be quite positive for you. New opportunities surface in learning, studying, writing and speaking and, because Capricorn is involved, your career. Neptune in Pisces forms a beautiful angle to the eclipse degree, indicating that opportunities may involve the arts and your spirituality and imagination. Pluto is conjunct within 5 degrees of the eclipse degree, so the opportunities that surface put you in a more powerful place.

Uranus turns direct in Aries on January 6. You may feel a deeper need now for independence in your daily work, and it may urge you to strike out on your own or, at the very least, to make preparations to do so.

Between January 7 and February 3, Venus transits Sagittarius and your financial area. For the last year or so, you've been enjoying Jupiter's expansion in this area of your chart, and with Venus traveling with Jupiter, money flows in. Your expenses may spike, too, but you'll have the cash to cover any surprises that come up. In romance, you may meet someone whose beliefs and values are like yours.

The lunar eclipse in Leo on January 21 occurs in your career area. Since Leo is involved, your creativity is also impacted. You may feel that your professional autonomy or your creativity is eclipsed in some way, and it triggers a powerful emotional response. But because you're a Scorpio, you're able to restrain your response.

AT A GLANCE
January 4—Mercury enters into Capricorn
January 5—Solar eclipse in Capricorn
January 6—Uranus turns direct in Aries
January 7—Venus goes into Sagittarius
January 21—Lunar eclipse in Leo
January 24—Mercury goes into Aquarius

February 2019
Enjoyable

You should enjoy February. The astrological energies are mostly in water and compatible earth signs.

Venus enters Capricorn on February 3 and brings harmony to your daily life. Between now and March 1, any writing projects in which you're involved unfold effortlessly and with ease. People in your daily life are attracted to you and your ideas. If a romance begins during this transit, it may be with someone you meet through a sibling or neighbor.

The new moon in Aquarius on February 4 brings new opportunities to your family life. With Jupiter sending friendly beams to this new moon and Mercury closely conjunct, your home life expands in some way. Someone may move in—an adult child, a parent or perhaps a boarder. If your home is on the market, you get an offer. If you're buying a home, this new moon would be ideal for closing the deal. Just be sure to sign before Mercury turns retrograde on March 5.

Between February 10 and March 5, Mercury moves in direct motion through Pisces. Your conscious focus is on creativity, romance and whatever you do for pleasure and enjoyment. Your imagination is particularly expansive during this period, and whatever you can vividly imagine can develop in your life. If you don't have a meditation practice yet, now would be a great time to start. Five or ten minutes a day, Scorpio, is all you need to quiet your mind and soar into other realms.

Mars enters Taurus on February 14, and for the next six weeks, until March 31, your physical energy is excellent. You actively pursue both business and personal partnerships. You might, for example, launch your own business or land a freelance gig that brings in additional income. Your sensuality deepens during this transit—an appreciation for good food, sex and art.

The full moon in Virgo on February 19 highlights your social life. With Mars forming a beneficial angle to it, you're in the mood for spending time with friends. You're able to connect all the necessary details in a communication project.

AT A GLANCE
February 3—Venus enters Capricorn
February 4—New moon in Aquarius
February 10—Mercury goes into Pisces
February 14—Mars enters into Taurus
February 19—Full moon in Virgo

March 2019
Planetary shift

This month features a major shift for Uranus. For the last seven years, it has been in Aries, shaking things up in your daily work life. It entered Taurus briefly in 2018, then turned retro and slipped back into Aries again. But on March 6, it enters Taurus, where it will be for the next seven years, until 2025. During this transit, Uranus will sweep away the dead wood in any area of your life where you have become rigid or habitual. If you have your natal chart, look for where Taurus falls in your chart. That area will be the one that experiences the most change. During this transit, your need for independence and freedom may cause tension with partners and friends until you allow others the same freedom you insist upon.

On March 1, Venus enters Aquarius, and until the 26th, your home life should be pleasant and unhampered by problems. You may decide to revamp your home in some way, to spiff up the rooms with more colorful paint or different wall decorations. You and your partner may do some creative brainstorming about your future—where you would like to live and things you would like to experience or achieve.

Between March 26 and April 20, Venus transits Pisces and the creativity/romance area of your chart. The only other periods equal to this one fall between July 3–27 and October 8 to November 1, when Venus also transits fellow water signs. Your romantic partner is attentive and can't seem to get enough of you. The two of you may get away for a long romantic weekend or vacation to some locale that provides adventure and novelty. On the creative front, your muse is eager and ready to help. The temptation to fritter away this transit is strong. But try to spend at least a part of every day involved in your creative endeavors and doing what you enjoy.

Mercury turns retrograde in Pisces on March 5 and doesn't turn direct again until March 28. Be sure to look over the Mercury retrograde section in the introduction for general guidelines on how to navigate this period more successfully. Since it occurs in the creativity/romance area of your chart, be sure to communicate clearly with your partner and children. If you have to travel, double check your itinerary, and give yourself plenty of time to get to wherever you're headed.

On March 6, the same day that Uranus enters Taurus, there's a new moon in Pisces that brings new opportunities to flex your creativity and imagination. And, thanks to a beneficial angle from Saturn to this new moon, these opportunities have a long-range impact. Neptune is closely conjunct to this new moon, indicating that whatever surfaces has a strong artistic and spiritual component. Just don't sign any contracts until after the 28th, when Mercury will be direct.

The 20th features a full moon in Libra at 0 degrees. This one highlights the importance of balance in your closest relationships and your relationship with your own psyche. Your dreams could be especially vivid and filled with insights and information.

From March 31 to May 15, Mars transits Gemini. You may be spending a lot of time networking on social media, and it proves to be beneficial for something you may be researching or which you're involved in at work. It's an excellent time to refinance your home.

AT A GLANCE
March 1—Venus enters into Aquarius
March 5—Mercury turns retrograde in Pisces
March 6—New moon in Pisces, Uranus enters Taurus
March 20—Full moon in Libra
March 26—Venus goes into Pisces
March 28—Mercury turns direct
March 31—Mars enters Gemini

April 2019
Slowing down

Three planets turn retrograde this month (Jupiter, Saturn and Pluto), and that means a general slowing down in activities. But before any of it occurs, there's a new moon in Aries on April 5. It brings new opportunities in your daily work life and in the way you maintain your health. You might hear about a new diet or nutritional program and commit to it. Or you may have a chance to work more flexible hours which frees up valuable time you can use to explore other areas of interest. Aries is a trailblazing sign, so that will be a component of any opportunities that surface.

Jupiter turns retrograde in Sagittarius on April 10, and from then until August 11, its expansive energy turns inward. You explore your spiritual and religious beliefs or sample a variety of spiritual traditions. If you travel internationally, it may be part of a spiritual quest of some kind.

From April 17 to May 6, Mercury moves through Aries. Unusual ideas come your way, and it's to your benefit to record them and sift through them to see which ones can be implemented in your daily life or in your creative endeavors. It's easy to scatter your energy during this transit by spreading yourself too thinly.

The full moon in Libra on April 19 brings news about a relationship or highlights your psyche in some way. Or both! You're able to explore your own unconscious more deeply, something at which you excel, Scorpio, and do it in a more balanced way.

From April 20 to May 15, Venus transits Aries and travels with Mercury until April 6. Love, romance and your creative ventures are very much in your conscious awareness. Your passions may run from one extreme to another. Guard against the darker passions—envy and jealousy.

On April 25 and 29, Pluto and then Saturn turn retrograde in Capricorn. Since Pluto rules your sign, you may find that from April 25 to October 3, when the retro ends, your shadow side is more prevalent. But given the nature of Scorpio, you're probably well-acquainted with your shadow side and already know how to temper it. Use this transit to turn your shadow side inside out, and let it serve as fodder for your various creative interests.

Saturn's retrograde, which lasts until September 18, urges you to examine the various structures in your life—financial, familial, professional and personal—in order to decide which structures need bolstering. Since you may be more serious during this retro, find activities that help you to lighten up on yourself!

AT A GLANCE
April 5—New moon in Aries
April 10—Jupiter turns retrograde in Sagittarius
April 17—Mercury enters Aries
April 19—Full moon in Libra
April 20—Venus enters Aries
April 25—Pluto turns retrograde in Capricorn
April 29—Saturn turns retrograde in Capricorn

May 2019
New opportunities

This month's transits are more to your liking and include a full moon in your sign on May 18. This one lights up your personal life, allowing you to see deep within yourself more easily. Thanks to a harmonious beam from Pluto, any news you hear will put you in a more powerful position.

May 4 brings a new moon in Taurus, your opposite sign. Opportunities surface in both business and personal partnerships, but also in finances. Thanks to a friendly beam from Neptune in Pisces, the opportunities involve the arts or your spirituality and are satisfying.

On May 15, two events look promising for you: Venus enters Taurus, and Mars moves into fellow water sign Cancer. The Venus transit lasts until June 8, and during this period, your relationship with your spouse/partner hums along with greater ease and smoothness. You may decide to deepen your commitment to each other in some way. Mercury is traveling with Venus again, until May 21, and this grounds your conscious mind and enables you to make the abstract tangible.

The Mars transit lasts until July 1. During this period, Mars in Cancer makes a beautiful angle to your sun sign, bolstering your patience, resolve and determination. You're more intuitive now, and your insight into self and others is strong.

From May 21 to June 4, Mercury moves through Gemini, a sign it rules. This transit heightens your communication skills, and you may be networking and socializing more than usual. It will be easier to obtain better interest rates on your mortgage or on insurance. Do your research.

May 4—New moon in Taurus
May 6—Mercury enters Taurus
May 15—Venus goes into Taurus, Mars enters Cancer
May 18—Full moon in Scorpio
May 21—Mercury goes into Gemini

June 2019
Mixed

June is a mixed bag of shifting energies. To maintain your equilibrium, it's a good idea to get outdoors. Walk, garden, take a run or go hiking. If you don't already have a meditation practice, start one on June 4, when Mercury enters water sign Cancer. Your mind is more receptive to other realms and dimensions of existence, and it's easier to access the deeper parts of yourself for insight, answers and guidance.

Before that transit begins, there's a new moon in Gemini on June 3. Expect new opportunities for writing and speaking gigs, for networking with professional colleagues and for living more gregariously. It's a good time to enter the flow of events and situations and leave the worrying and fretting to someone else!

Between June 8 and July 3, Venus transits Gemini. You're quite the charmer now, and your wit and communication skills wow the people around you. You're also an excellent conversationalist during this transit. Any romance that begins during this period may be short-lived, but it will certainly be fun!

The full moon in Sagittarius on the 17th brings news about finances. You might hear, for instance, that you're getting a raise or perhaps a bonus or that a loan was approved. Sagittarius is a gregarious sign, so why not invite friends over for the evening?

Neptune turns retrograde in Pisces on June 20 and turns direct again in late November. During this lengthy retro, you may feel isolated or disconnected from a romantic partner. It's best to use this energy for creative endeavors.

AT A GLANCE
June 3—New moon in Gemini
June 4—Mercury enters into Cancer
June 8—Venus goes into Gemini
June 17—Full moon in Sagittarius
June 20—Neptune turns retrograde
June 26—Mercury enters Leo

July 2019
Spiritual growth & career focus

The nature of eclipses is to bring relationships and issues up close and personal so that we often have to act quickly and decisively. This month features a solar eclipse in Cancer on July 2 and a lunar eclipse in Capricorn on July 16.

The solar eclipse ushers in new opportunities for spiritual growth. Since it's in Cancer, your family and home life may also be the beneficiary of something new. Uranus forms a harmonious angle to the eclipse degree, so the opportunities surface suddenly and without warning. Possibilities? You have a chance to travel overseas on a spiritual quest of some kind, perhaps a shamanic journey. A writing project falls in your lap, or you're invited to teach a workshop or seminar. You and your partner discover you're going to be parents, or someone moves into or out of your home.

The lunar eclipse in Capricorn may bring something to completion, but with every ending, a new door opens. Pluto is friendly to the eclipse degree, and that means that whatever transpires puts you in a better position to call the shots. The area involved is your profession—the Capricorn part of the equation—and your solar third house, which rules communication and your conscious mind. Saturn is also in Capricorn, which brings a somewhat somber tone to this eclipse.

Before either of these eclipses occurs, Mars enters Leo and your career area on July 1, and for the next six weeks, until August 18, you are moving at full tilt to achieve or accomplish a professional goal. You've got a flair for the flamboyant and dramatic now, and it's smart to apply this energy to a creative endeavor.

On July 3, Venus enters fellow water sign Cancer and facilitates the opportunities that yesterday's solar eclipse promised. A new romance? A new research project? A new creative endeavor? Until July 27, you enjoy a romantic and creative period where life generally flows more smoothly, and your desires are granted with little or no effort on your part.

Mercury turns retrograde in Leo on July 7, slips back into Cancer and turns direct in that sign on July 31. The retro may slow things down professionally, but with Mars also in this sector of your chart, you continue to move forward. Look over the Mercury retrograde section in the introduction, and follow the general guidelines for navigating this period more successfully.

From July 27 to August 21, Venus joins Mars and Mercury in Leo, in your career area. Any time that Venus and Mars travel together, love is in the air. Sparks fly, and the chemistry is perfect. Your creative adrenaline is jammed in overdrive!

On the 31st, Mercury turns direct, and there's a new moon in Leo. Your career receives a significant boost through an opportunity of some kind. A promotion? A raise? You're tapped to head up a team? Whatever it is, with Mercury now direct, you can move forward with confidence.

July 1—Mars goes into Leo
July 2—Solar eclipse in Cancer
July 3—Venus enters Cancer
July 7—Mercury turns retrograde in Leo
July 16—Lunar eclipse in Capricorn
July 27—Venus enters Leo
July 31—Mercury turns direct, new moon in Leo

August 2019
Connecting the dots

This month's emphasis is on earth sign Virgo, which will enable you to be more efficient and detail-oriented. You'll be able to connect the dots in a relationship, project or situation. But before the Virgo transits occur, there are some other astrological events to consider.

On August 11, Jupiter turns direct in Sagittarius and Mercury enters Leo again, where it was before it turned retrograde last month. Now your career benefits from your communication skills. You can resume working on projects that you put aside during the retrograde. Jupiter's change in direction should be good for your finances. Between now and December 2, when Jupiter enters Capricorn, you'll have opportunities to increase your income. It may come through freelance projects, a raise, the sale of a creative endeavor or royalties.

On the 12th, Uranus turns retrograde in Taurus and remains that way until January 6, 2020. Loose ends may surface in a partnership, and you'll have to resolve them. You'll feel a greater need for freedom and independence in your closest relationships and may experience periods of restlessness about where your life is headed.

The full moon in Aquarius highlights your home and family life. Thanks to a friendly beam from Jupiter, any news you hear should be positive. If your home is on the market, you may get an offer or sell it for your asking price.

Mark August 18, 21 and 29 on your calendar, when Mars, then Venus and finally Mercury begin their transits of Virgo. Mars will be in Virgo until October 4, and during this transit, your social calendar lights up. You'll have your choice of places to go and friends to see and may be networking more than usual, too. Sometimes, Scorpio, you tend to be quite the loner, but that will look less appealing during this Mars transit. Once Venus joins Mars in Virgo, it's another enjoyable period when the chemistry is ideal in a romantic relationship. Any relationship that begins during this transit and any creative endeavor in which you get involved with will be unusual. Venus remains in Virgo until September 14.

When Mercury hooks up with Venus and Mars, your intellect becomes more discerning, and you're able to see the intricate details of a romantic relationship. This transit ends on September. Then along comes a new moon in Virgo on August 30, a kind of exclamation point to all this earth energy. New friends enter your life, and you may have an opportunity to do publicity work through social media.

AT A GLANCE
August 11—Jupiter turns direct, Mercury enters Leo
August 12—Uranus turns retrograde
August 15—Full moon in Aquarius
August 18—Mars enters Virgo
August 21—Venus goes into Virgo
August 29—Mercury enters Virgo
August 30—New moon in Virgo

September 2019
Take a breather

September is a bit quieter than August was, and you'll have time to pause and catch your breath—except on September 14, when there are three astrological events. Both Mercury and Venus enter Libra, and there's a new moon is in Pisces.

The Mercury transit lasts until October 3, and the Venus transit ends October 8. While these two travel together through the quiet part of your chart, the personal unconscious, you're able to delve deeply into your own psyche. As a Scorpio, you tend to do this anyway, but now you have a chance to converse with the hidden parts of yourself. You may become more aware of the need for balance in your life. If romance begins during this transit, it's going to be intriguing, and you may keep it a secret for awhile.

The new moon in Pisces occurs in the romance/creativity area of your chart. New opportunities surface in both of those areas, and this could be the new relationship that Venus in Libra promises.

On September 18, Saturn turns direct in Capricorn, and suddenly, life doesn't seem quite as somber as it has the past several months. You have a good idea which relationships need bolstering and are ready to do the work.

The new moon in Libra on September 29 brings new opportunities in relationships with friends and may result in a chance to work behind the scenes in some capacity—ghostwriting, editing or publicity. It's a romantic moon, so cuddle up with the one you love!

AT A GLANCE
September 14—Mercury and Venus enter Libra, full moon in Pisces
September 18—Saturn turns direct in Capricorn
September 29—New moon in Libra

October 2019
Powerful

The last Mercury retrograde of the year begins on October 31, in Scorpio, and ends on November 20. Since it's in your sign, you'll want to take steps to prepare for it. Sign any contracts and make travel plans before that date, and try to travel on either side of the retrograde. If you're going to have a dental or medical procedure, schedule it before or after the retrograde. Read over the Mercury retrograde section in the introduction, and follow the general guidelines for navigating this period more successfully.

Before it turns retro at the end of the month, Mercury enters your sign, on October 3rd. Your mind is particularly intuitive now and primed for investigation and research. Delve into any topic that fascinates you, and find the absolute bottom line. Once Venus enters Scorpio on October 8, your sexuality is heightened, and any romantic relationship unfolds smoothly and effortlessly—as long as you don't hold up any walls. A big plus for you is that your ruler, Pluto, also turns direct on the 3rd, and that means its power is once again working in your favor. When Mercury and Venus are traveling together through your sign—until Mercury turns retrograde—your creativity is also heightened, and you should try to spend time each day working on your various creative endeavors. Your muse is ready and eager to help. The Venus transit ends on November 1.

Mars enters Libra on the 4th, and between then and November 19, you're a whirlwind of activity behind the scenes. You might be up against a tight deadline or are trying to tie up various projects before year's end. If you've been looking for work, this is the time to continue sending out resumes and networking in person and through social media. Once Mars enters your sign, things will begin to zip along rapidly. Set the stage now for that transit.

The full moon in Aries on October 13 should be a beauty for you, firing up your passions and your entrepreneurial spirit. Since Jupiter is friendly to this full moon, any news you hear should be positive and may concern your daily work life or a health matter.

Before the new moon in your sign on October 27, take time to think about what you would like to experience or achieve in the next year. This new moon comes along just once every twelve months and is particularly potent in that it sets the tone for the next year, birthday to birthday. New opportunities that surface will be personally satisfying and may appear suddenly and unexpectedly, so be prepared to seize them, Scorpio.

On the 31st, Mercury turns retro in your sign. You'll feel things slowing down. If you have children, your Halloween plans may change.

AT A GLANCE

October 3—Mercury goes into Scorpio, Pluto turns direct
October 4—Mars enters Libra
October 8—Venus goes into Scorpio
October 13—Full moon in Aries
October 27—New moon in Scorpio
October 31—Mercury turns retrograde

November 2019
Bewildering

At times, November may feel like a confusing month. Blame it on Mercury's antics, which may be creating a bit of havoc in your life. But hang in there. The retro ends on November 20.

From November 1 to 25, Venus transits Sagittarius and your financial area. Even if your expenses spike during this period—holiday spending?—so does your income. The additional income could come through a part-time job, a freelance project, a raise that your partner lands or an insurance rebate. If a romantic relationship begins during this transit, it's likely to be free-wheeling.

On the 12th, the full moon in Taurus highlights your partnerships and finances. Fortunately, both Saturn and Pluto form beneficial angles to this moon, indicating that any news you hear will have long-term effects and put you in a more powerful position overall.

From November 19 to January 4, 2020, Mars transits your sign and sweeps you into the new year. Your physical energy is excellent, and you're able to accomplish and achieve more than usual. Since Mars co-rules your sign, you're certainly in your element now and possess a magnetism that draws other people to you. Your sexuality is greatly heightened, and your intuition is deepened. Fortunately, Mercury retrograde ends the day after Mars enters Scorpio, so you reap the full benefits from November 20 onward.

From November 25 to December 20, Venus moves through compatible earth sign Capricorn and travels with Saturn and Pluto. This period should be enjoyable for you, taking you through the Thanksgiving holidays and into December. You may be spending more time with siblings and neighbors and the people who populate your daily life. Your ambition is strong now, and if a romance begins during this transit, you may have to fit it in between your other responsibilities.

The new moon in Sagittarius on November 26 should bring in a new source of income, certainly a welcome opportunity. Now you'll have extra money for holiday shopping, a trip or whatever you heart desires. You may feel somewhat restless around the time of this full moon, with the open road whispering your name.

On the 27th, Neptune finally turns direct again in Pisces, and the conduit to your imagination and spirituality is wide open again.

November 1—Venus goes into Sagittarius
November 12—Full moon in Taurus
November 19—Mars enters Scorpio
November 20—Mercury turns direct
November 25—Venus enters Capricorn
November 26—New moon in Sagittarius
November 27—Neptune turns direct

December 2019
Excellent lineup

Take a few minutes at the beginning of the month to think about what you would like to experience and achieve in the new year. Make a list. Think of it as a list of desires rather than resolutions, and post it where you'll see if often. Imagine what it will feel like as each item on your list flows into your life.

On December 2, Jupiter enters Capricorn, joining both Saturn and Pluto there. Between now and December 20, 2020, your daily life and your career will expand significantly. If you have your natal chart, check to find out where Capricorn falls in your chart; that's the area where you'll experience the most expansion and luck. Saturn will help to build new structures and Pluto will make sure you stay on track!

From December 9 to 29, Mercury transits Sagittarius and your financial area. Your conscious thoughts turn to finances, travel or a search for truth about something that concerns you. On the 29th, Mercury enters Capricorn, and until January 17, 2020, it travels with Jupiter, Saturn and Pluto. That's quite a lineup of earth energy! You'll find that new structures are showing up in your life in the field of communication and in your career and that it may all be happening suddenly.

From December 20 to January 14, 2020, Venus moves through Aquarius and the family/domestic area of your chart. You may have a greater need for freedom and independence now and may spiff up your home in some way to reflect those feelings. You also may tackle esoteric topics through books and seminars.

AT A GLANCE
December 2—Jupiter enters Capricorn
December 9—Mercury enters Sagittarius
December 12—Full moon in Gemini
December 20—Venus goes into Aquarius
December 26—Solar eclipse in Capricorn
December 29—Mercury enters into Capricorn

Reflection

Your nature is to probe deeply into everything that interests you, so reflection is as natural to you as it is to fellow water sign Cancer. Looking back at this year, what are your feelings about it? What did you learn? How can you use what you learned to make 2020 an even better year? Jot your thoughts below.

_____

_____

_____

_____

_____

Happy New Year!

Sagittarius 2019

Your sign is ruled by Jupiter, considered to be the good guy in astrology because it's all about expansion, luck and serendipity. In actuality, no planet is bad, but some astrological energies—like Jupiter and Venus—are easier to deal with than say, Saturn. Yet, each planet has a necessary function. Where would we be without the structures that Saturn builds?

This year, Jupiter is in your sign until December 2. Its transit through Sagittarius began in November 2018, and between then and when it enters Capricorn, it has been and will continue to expand your life in some way. A new job, a new career path, a spike in income, a new love, a marriage, a birth or an international trip. You may be sampling various spiritual traditions, could teach workshops or seminars or may even go to graduate or law school. Pay close attention to the angles transiting planets make to Jupiter. It will be retrograde from April 10 to August 11.

The monthly roundups also include information on the transits, new and full moons, eclipses and retrogrades.

January 2019
Great start

On December 31, Mars entered Aries, and for the next six weeks, until February 14, it travels with Uranus through the creativity and romance area of your chart. Your passions are stoked, your drive and ambition are powerful, and you're able to accomplish quite a bit. With Mars in your court, you embrace the new year whole heartedly. Once Uranus turns direct on the 6th, your creativity may take off in a new direction.

Mercury enters Capricorn and your financial area on January 4, and between then and January 24, you're driven to earn, earn, earn. Your ability to strategize is heightened. If you're saving up for something special (an overseas trip?), you're able to set aside a percentage of your income to cover your expenses. Your intellect is particularly goal-oriented during this transit.

Between January 24 and February 10, Mercury transits compatible air sign Aquarius and the communication area of your chart. Your mind is sharp, and the ideas you have during this period are unusual. Keep track of them. They may come in handy later on. In your daily life, you engage with interesting people who are attracted by your ability to talk to anyone about virtually anything.

The solar eclipse in Capricorn on January 5 will be followed two weeks later, on January 21, by a lunar eclipse in Leo. The first eclipse concerns external events and may bring a new financial or career opportunity. With Pluto conjunct the eclipse degree and Neptune friendly to it, the opportunity appeals to your idealism and spiritual values.

The lunar eclipse in Leo may make you feel as if your creativity and freedom are eclipsed in some way, perhaps due to a criticism made by a boss or someone in your personal environment. But Mars in Aries and Jupiter in your sign are closely aligned during this eclipse, and it looks as if things shake out fine for you.

AT A GLANCE
January 4—Mercury enters into Capricorn
January 5—Solar eclipse in Capricorn
January 6—Uranus turns direct in Aries
January 7—Venus goes into Sagittarius
January 21—Lunar eclipse in Leo
January 24—Mercury goes into Aquarius

February 2019
Smooth sailing

February is an easier month—no eclipses and no Mercury retrograde yet! On February 3, Venus enters Capricorn, and between then and March 1, romance may find you through your professional life or even a freelance project that you take on. You may be tempted to spend on luxurious items, but if you do, pay cash. Your income should spike during this period. Venus is a facilitator, and as it transits your financial sector it attracts new money-making opportunities.

The new moon in Aquarius on February 4 could bring new communication projects or even involvement in a neighborhood project. Your need for freedom and independence is paramount.

Mercury enters Pisces on February 10, and between then and March 5, when it turns retrograde, your conscious focus is on home and family. Your intuition and imagination are especially powerful during this transit, and it would be wise to dive into any creative endeavor. It may be something as simple as spiffing up your living environment with fresh paint on the walls or new furniture or bedding.

Mars enters Taurus on February 14, and from then until March 31, you're tackling projects at work that demand patience, resilience and resolve. If you run up against challenges, Mars in Taurus helps you to move on through them.

The full moon in Virgo on February 19 highlights your career area. You're able to connect the dots now in any area that troubles you and are more detail-oriented than usual. Mars is friendly to this full moon and bolsters your insights. Any news you hear about your professional life should be positive.

AT A GLANCE
February 3—Venus enters Capricorn
February 4—New moon in Aquarius
February 10—Mercury goes into Pisces
February 14—Mars enters into Taurus
February 19—Full moon in Virgo

March 2019
Mercury retro alert

Astrologically, March is jammed with rapidly shifting energies. At some point during this month, you may feel a need to get away for a few days and indulge your Sagittarian nature—i.e., have fun!

First, there's a Mercury retrograde to contend with. It starts on March 5, in Pisces, and extends until March 28. Look over the Mercury retrograde section in the introduction, and follow the general guidelines for navigating this period more successfully. Since it occurs in your home and family sector, you may experience irritating delays or snafus with appliances and computers. During a Mercury retro it's best not to buy high-ticket items, but if your dishwasher breaks down or your computer crashes, by all means buy a new one. Just double check your order and the delivery date!

Before the retro begins, Venus enters Aquarius on March 1, and between then and March 26, life hums along at a nice pitch—except that Mercury is retro for much of this transit. It may, however, help mitigate some of the collateral damage of the retro! If a romance begins during this transit, be sure that you and your partner communicate easily and clearly with each other.

Two events occur on March 6: there's a new moon in Pisces, and Uranus enters Taurus. The new moon in a water sign may have you feeling somewhat dreamy and disconnected from the world of action and momentum in which you usually live. But it should bring in an opportunity to flex your imagination in new ways, in some type of creative endeavor. Your living circumstances may change—someone moves in or out, or you sell your home, buy a home and move.

For the last seven years, Uranus has been transiting your fire sign sibling, Aries, bringing abrupt and unforeseen change in self-expression, in romance and with your children. On March 6, it enters Taurus. It was there briefly in 2018, then turned retrograde and slipped back into Aries. But on March 6, it begins its journey through Taurus, where it will be until April 2026. During this lengthy transit, any number of things may happen, and it all depends on where you have become rigid and habitual. Uranus's job is to shake up the status quo and get rid of the dead wood in your life so that the new flows in. So what may happen? Marriage or divorce, loss of a job, a new career path, a change in your finances or the birth of a child. Pivotal life events, in other words.

The full moon in Libra on March 20 lights up your social life to the point where you have so many invitations to do stuff that you can pick and choose. Your friends are especially important to you now. There could be news about a legal matter.

Between March 26 and April 20, Venus moves through Pisces. You may be spending money on refurbishing your home or beautifying it in some way. You're feeling more romantic and creative, and you and your partner may team up on project. What you can imagine can now become real, so daydream away, Sadge!

Mercury turns direct on March 28, a welcome change! It now moves toward its appointment with Aries on April 17. Dive into everything you delayed during these past few weeks.

From March 31 to May 15, Mars transits Gemini, your opposite sign. Now your communication skills peak. You may be networking like crazy, or you could find the ideal partner to help you launch your own business. You and your romantic partner could take off at a moment's notice for some wild adventure.

AT A GLANCE
March 1—Venus enters into Aquarius
March 5—Mercury turns retrograde in Pisces
March 6—New moon in Pisces, Uranus enters Taurus
March 20—Full moon in Libra
March 26—Venus goes into Pisces
March 28—Mercury turns direct
March 31—Mars enters Gemini

April 2019
Challenging

April may be a somewhat dicey month, with three planets turning retrograde. Before you decide to go to bed and sleep for the entire month, let's take a closer look. On April 10, Jupiter turns retrograde in your sign and doesn't straighten out again until August 11. During these months, Jupiter's expansiveness turns inward. You may be studying and sampling various spiritual traditions or could embark on a spiritual quest that takes you overseas, to ancient sites. You might undertake a course of study in an esoteric topic that interests you.

On the 25th and 29th, Pluto and Saturn, respectively, turn retrograde in Capricorn, in your financial area. Pluto's retro lasts until October 3. The challenge during these months is to not allow your shadow side to rear its ugly head where money is concerned. If you feel yourself becoming greedy or envious of other people's prosperity, immediately turn your thoughts toward appreciation for what you have. We all have shadow sides, and they tend to surface when Pluto is retrograde. But we also have free will. Use it!

Saturn's retrograde ends on September 18. Use this time to examine the financial structures that are in place in your life. Do they serve you well? Do they feel restrictive? Don't make rash decisions about your money, but just take note of events that may be guidance in disguise. Since both Saturn and Pluto are retrograde in Capricorn, there may be restructuring and shadowy forces at work in your professional life.

Before these retros begin, there's a new moon in Aries on April 5. You'll enjoy this one. It occurs in the creativity/romance area of your chart and should bring in new opportunities in both areas. You might sell a novel or some other artistic endeavor you've created or could meet someone new with whom the chemistry is ideal, or you and your partner may discover you're going to be parents. This area of your chart also governs children. You may also uncover some new passion that makes your heart sing. Pursue it!

On the 17th, Mercury enters Aries, and on the 20th, Venus follows. The Mercury transits lasts until May 6 and the Venus transit until May 15. While these two planets travel together, your focus is on romance and creativity. Both areas will be heightened until May 15, and life generally will feel pleasurable, fun and exciting. The Venus transit marks one of the best times for you all year, and the only other times that equal it fall between July 27 and August 21, when Venus transits Leo, and between November 1 to 25, when it transits your sign. You're more optimistic, and other people are attracted to you and seek your company.

In between, on April 19, the full moon in Libra is a great time for a party with friends. You're in a gregarious mood, and if it's spring where you live, so is everyone else. There could be news about a friend or a publicity project of some kind, and thanks to a friendly angle from retrograde Jupiter, the news should be positive.

AT A GLANCE
April 5—New moon in Aries
April 10—Jupiter turns retrograde in Sagittarius
April 17—Mercury enters Aries
April 19—Full moon in Libra
April 20—Venus enters Aries
April 25—Pluto turns retrograde in Capricorn
April 29—Saturn turns retrograde in Capricorn

May 2019
Work & finances

May isn't quite as hectic as the past few months. The emphasis is on finances and your daily work. With a new moon in Taurus on May 4, followed by Mercury entering Taurus on the 6th and Venus entering it on the 15th, you've got plenty of patience and resilience to take on virtually anything.

The new moon could bring a new job, new employees, a new source of income, a new health routine or even a new nutritional program. Even though Uranus isn't conjunct this new moon, it's in the same sign and bolsters the Taurean energy. Neptune is friendly to this moon, an indication that any opportunities could involve creativity, the arts and your spirituality.

Mercury will transit Taurus until May 21. Use this period to complete projects and pitch new ideas. If you're self-employed, you may be working longer hours, perhaps to meet a deadline. Just be sure you allow yourself time for fun and pleasure, too.

The Venus transit lasts until June 8 and brings a strong sensuality with it. Taurus is such a sensual sign that food tastes better, sex is better and life is richer and brighter. Since Venus is forming a great angle to your financial area, your income may increase as well.

Also on the 15th, Mars enters Cancer and the shared resources section of your chart. This transit ends on July 1 and brings greater intuitive awareness to your financial resources. Your partner or spouse could land a raise, or you could receive a royalty check, insurance rebate or repayment on a loan.

The full moon in Scorpio on May 18 is ideal for delving into your own psyche. Your dreams will be more vivid and will contain information and insights that may prove valuable. Your sexuality is heightened during this full moon.

From May 21 to June 4, Mercury transits Gemini and travels for several days with Venus. You may be exploring new social media possibilities and studying or reading about esoteric areas—communication with the dead, reincarnation or psychic phenomena.

AT A GLANCE
May 4—New moon in Taurus
May 6—Mercury enters Taurus
May 15—Venus goes into Taurus, Mars enters Cancer
May 18—Full moon in Scorpio
May 21—Mercury goes into Gemini

June 2019
Partnership focus

The emphasis this month is on your opposite sign, Gemini. On June 3, the new moon in that sign brings in new opportunities in partnerships. You and your spouse may launch your own business or deepen your commitment to each other in some way. You have a chance to form new networks of friends and acquaintances or to work on a publicity campaign for a new client. With Mercury also in Gemini, your communication skills are sharp.

On June 4, Mercury moves into Cancer, and your conscious mind becomes more intuitive and receptive to signs and symbols that may hold valuable messages and insights. If you've been considering refinancing your home, do it between June 4–26, when this transit ends.

Venus joins Mercury in Gemini on June 8, and from then until July 3, it's a facilitator for your shared resources. Your partner or spouse could get a raise or an unexpected check arrives—repayment on a loan, an insurance rebate or a royalty payment—or both. If a romance begins during this transit, the flow of communication will be excellent.

The full moon in your sign on June 17 brings news that delights you. Retrograde Jupiter forms a favorable angle to this full moon, so the news expands your world in some way. News aside, it's a perfect day to spend with friends or to indulge your inner nomad and take off for parts unknown.

Neptune turns retrograde in Pisces on June 20. Between now and January 17, 2020, when it turns direct again, it's reality check time. You may not like everything you see, Sadge, but you have the resources to change things around. If you don't have a meditation practice yet, it's a great time to start and an ideal way to gain insight.

Mercury enters Leo on June 26, and from then until July 7, when Mercury turns retrograde, you have a flair for the dramatic and are on a roll with your creativity. You and your muse are best buddies now, so take advantage of Mercury's current direction. You'll have another shot at things in August, when Mercury is moving direct again in Leo.

AT A GLANCE
June 3—New moon in Gemini
June 4—Mercury enters into Cancer
June 8—Venus goes into Gemini
June 17—Full moon in Sagittarius
June 20—Neptune turns retrograde
June 26—Mercury enters Leo

July 2019
Eclectic

July is a mix of energies, and with two eclipses and a Mercury retrograde, you may feel exhausted before the month even begins! Be sure to get plenty of rest and to take time out for yourself to do what you enjoy.

The solar eclipse in Cancer on July 2 brings new financial opportunities. You might sell a novel, screenplay or some other artistic creation or find an excellent mortgage or insurance rate. Since Cancer is involved, the new opportunity may relate to home and family. Thanks to a beneficial angle from Uranus, the opportunities may occur suddenly and without warning.

The lunar eclipse in Capricorn on July 16 falls in your financial area. Pluto is closely conjunct the eclipse degree, suggesting that whatever you're feeling is powerful and perhaps all consuming. It may be related to your career, which directly impacts your finances.

Before either of the eclipses occur, Mars enters Leo on July 1 and for the next six weeks, until August 18, you're a swirling dervish of activity and forward momentum. You feel as though nothing can stop you, that no obstacle is too large to overcome. Even though Mercury will be retrograde in Leo for part of this Mars transit, from July 7 to 31, you'll have so much thrust built up that it won't slow you down by much!

Before the retro begins, read over the Mercury retrograde section in the introduction. Following the suggested guidelines will enable you to navigate this period more successfully. Since Leo is such a creative sign, try not to start new projects; dust off the old ones, and dive in. It's an excellent time to research and study topics that interest you, particularly spiritual traditions and philosophy.

On the 27th, Venus joins Mars in Leo, and these cosmic lovers travel together until August 18. Venus remains in Leo until August 21. During the time they're traveling together, you and a romantic partner are completely into each other. You might say the relationship approaches near bliss!

On the same day Mercury turns direct in Cancer, the 31st, there's a new moon in Leo, and Venus is still close enough to this new moon that it should be a very good day! New opportunities surface in creativity and international travel. Pack your bag, Sadge. You're in for an adventure.

AT A GLANCE
July 1—Mars goes into Leo
July 2—Solar eclipse in Cancer
July 3—Venus enters Cancer
July 7—Mercury turns retrograde in Leo
July 16—Lunar eclipse in Capricorn
July 27—Venus enters Leo
July 31—Mercury turns direct, new moon in Leo

August 2019
Career focus

The last few weeks of August are all about earth energy—specifically, Virgo—and about your career. But let's start with August 11, when Jupiter turns direct and Mercury enters Leo once again. Jupiter now moves forward once more toward its appointment with Capricorn on December 2. You can now enjoy its expansive energy in the outer world again. It won't be back to your sign for another twelve years, so make these months count!

On August 12, Uranus turns retrograde in Taurus and stays that way until January 6, 2020. Periodically through these months, you may feel restless and have a greater need for independence. If and when it gets to be too much, take to the open road!

The full moon in Aquarius on August 15 brings news about some facet of your daily life. It could be a writing project, a change in your neighborhood, something about a sibling or neighbor or even news about a project you have pitched.

On the 18th, 21st and 29th, Mars, Venus and then Mercury enter Virgo and your career area. Wow. Now your conscious focus turns fully to your professional life. Both the Mercury and Venus transits last until September 14, and the Mars transit lasts until November 19. The combination indicates that you communicate exceptionally well. You're the right person in the right place at the right time, and your peers and bosses recognize it. You could land a bonus or raise, be promoted or find a new career path altogether. Remember that Mars is the planet that makes stuff happen, Mercury is the communicator and Venus is the attractor and facilitator.

As if this isn't enough, there's a new moon in Virgo on August 30, the exclamation point at the end of the month. It may deliver everything you've been working toward professionally.

AT A GLANCE
August 11—Jupiter turns direct, Mercury enters Leo
August 12—Uranus turns retrograde
August 15—Full moon in Aquarius
August 18—Mars enters Virgo
August 21—Venus goes into Virgo
August 29—Mercury enters Virgo
August 30—New moon in Virgo

September 2019
Networking

It's a calmer month, and the emphasis is on compatible air sign Libra—and relationships.

Circle the 14th on your calendar, with three astrological events occurring that day. Both Mercury and Venus enter Libra, and there's a full moon in Pisces. Mercury remains in Libra until October 3, and Venus stays there until the 8th. With these two planets traveling together once again you're in a sociable mood and spend a lot more time with friends, networking and perhaps brainstorming as well. If you're involved in any legal proceedings, things should shake out in your favor. Venus rules Libra and functions well here, so there may be a new romance or artistic project in the offing. It's also possible that a new source of income comes out of all your networking.

The full moon in Pisces highlights the home and family area of your chart. You may hear news about a family member or, since Pisces is involved, about a creative endeavor. With retrograde Neptune conjunct within 4 degrees of this moon and retrograde Pluto sending friendly beams to it, the news may be initially confusing. Once you find out the full details, though, Pluto assures that you're in a more powerful spot.

Saturn turns direct in Capricorn on September 18—good news for your finances. You now have a much clearer idea about which financial structures need bolstering.

The new moon in Libra on September 29 brings in new opportunities in friendships, networking and publicity. Enjoy this one! Libra brings an awareness of the importance of balance in all your relationships.

AT A GLANCE
September 14—Mercury and Venus enter Libra, full moon in Pisces
September 18—Saturn turns direct in Capricorn
September 29—New moon in Libra

October 2019
Rapidly shifting energies

October is a mix of astrological energies that includes the last Mercury retrograde of the year, which begins on October 31. But before we get there, let's start earlier in the month. Mercury enters Scorpio on October 3, and from then until the retro begins, the transit favors research, psychological counseling and exploring your own psyche. Consider getting a past-life regression or attending a workshop or seminar on something that sheds light on who you are. Sign contracts and make your travel plans before the retrograde begins.

Also on the 3rd, Pluto turns direct in Capricorn, good news for your finances and your career. You can now move forward with certainty that your ambition won't become unbridled!

Between October 4 and November 19, Mars transits Libra and forms a beneficial angle to your sun sign. During these six weeks, your people skills are heightened, and you use all the social media at your disposal to publicize a product or service for the company where you work or for your own company. In some way, the events that unfold during this transit move you closer to attaining a dream.

On October 8, Venus joins Mercury in Scorpio. These two planets have traveled together several times this year, and now that both are in such an emotionally intense sign, you may be swept up into a romantic intrigue. It could be a fictional intrigue or something that occurs in a dream. If it's a dream, note the details. It may be referring to something in the future. If a romance does begin during this transit, it will be passionate and sexual. The Venus transit lasts until November 1.

The full moon in Aries on October 13 brings news about a romantic relationship, a creative endeavor or one of your children. Jupiter is friendly to this full moon, so the news should be positive. Since Aries is a trailblazing sign, there may be a certain unpredictable wildness to the day's energy.

With the new moon in Scorpio on the 27th, you may have a chance to conduct research into an esoteric area that intrigues you—and get paid for it! Any opportunity that unfolds on or around the time of this new moon is likely to do so suddenly because retrograde Uranus in Taurus is opposed to it.

On the 31st, Mercury turns retrograde in Scorpio and stays that way until November 20. Look over the Mercury retrograde section in the introduction, and follow the general guidelines for navigating this period more successfully. Specifically, it's a good idea to avoid confrontation and to not take anything personally!

AT A GLANCE

October 3—Mercury goes into Scorpio, Pluto turns direct
October 4—Mars enters Libra
October 8—Venus goes into Scorpio
October 13—Full moon in Aries
October 27—New moon in Scorpio
October 31—Mercury turns retrograde

November 2019
5-star month

Lucky you, Sadge! November has two stellar events that you'll love. From November 1–25, Venus transits your sign. In spite of the Mercury retrograde, this period should be pleasant for you. You feel more self-confident, optimistic and in tune with who you are. Your personal magnetism attracts others, and women are especially helpful. Your partner just can't get enough of you. Your muse is also attentive and eager to help, and it's to your advantage to work on your creative endeavors. Just don't start anything new until after Mercury turns direct on November 20.

The other event you'll love is the new moon in your sign on November 26. This moon comes along only once a year and sets the tone for the next twelve months. Make a wish list about what you would like to experience and accomplish during the next year, and post it where you'll see it often. Possible opportunities surface in publishing, international travel, higher education, romance, finances and your career. Take your pick. Wherever you have placed your attention and intentions this year will now blossom.

The full moon in Taurus on November 12 highlights your daily work area and, because Taurus is involved, possibly your finances as well. What's interesting about this full moon is that both Saturn and Pluto in Capricorn are friendly to it. Any news you hear has a long-term impact and should put you in a more powerful position. Retrograde Neptune in Pisces is also friendly, indicating a spiritual and intuitive component to the day's events.

From November 19 to January 4, 2020, Mars transits Scorpio, a sign it co-rules. You may be spending more time alone during a good part of this transit, perhaps tying up work projects so you can enter the new year with a clean slate. Once Mars enters your sign early in January 2020, you'll want to have things in your life lined up so you can take full advantage of the transit that launches the new year.

Mercury turns direct in Scorpio on November 20 and moves toward its appointment with your sign on December 9. Now you can move forward once again with everything you put on a back burner during the retrograde.

With Venus transiting Capricorn from November 25 to December 20, your expenses may spike, perhaps due to holiday shopping. Just try to pay cash for what you buy so you don't go into shock in January when the bills come due! Your income could rise during this transit, too, perhaps through freelance work.

On the 27th, Neptune turns direct in Pisces. This shifts feeds your imagination and deepens your spirituality, and it's easier to implement your ideas into your work.

AT A GLANCE
November 1—Venus goes into Sagittarius
November 12—Full moon in Taurus
November 19—Mars enters Scorpio
November 20—Mercury turns direct
November 25—Venus enters Capricorn
November 26—New moon in Sagittarius
November 27—Neptune turns direct

December 2019
Jupiter shift

Give some thought to the new year—what you would like to experience, explore and achieve. If you already did this for the new moon in your sign last month, then add to the list. Brainstorm with yourself. Be as wild and imaginative as possible, and post the list where you'll see it often.

On December 2, Jupiter makes a major shift when it moves into earth sign Capricorn, joining Saturn and Pluto in your financial area. This transits lasts until December 27, 2020. Take a look at your natal chart to see where Capricorn falls. That will be the area that expands and grows during the next year. In a solar chart, Capricorn is on the cusp of your financial area, and with this lineup of planets, your income should rise significantly. Saturn in Capricorn advises you to invest wisely and live within your means, and Pluto here is a powerful reminder that money is simply a form of energy. Use it wisely.

Mercury transits your sign from December 9 to 29, taking you through the Christmas holidays. It's an ideal transit for enjoying yourself with friends and family and seeing the larger picture of the year ahead. On the 29th, Mercury enters Capricorn and stays until January 17, 2020, adding to all the Capricorn earth energy that's already in your financial area. Your focus will be extraordinary, and you'll be able to accomplish a lot during this transit.

The full moon in Gemini on December 12 lights up your partnership area and heightens your communication skills. If you and a partner disagree about something on or around the time of this moon, be aware that you don't have the full details. This also goes for any news you hear. Don't make any rash decisions.

From December 20 to January 14, 2020, Venus transits compatible air sign Aquarius, a perfect transit for getting together with neighbors and siblings to celebrate the holidays. You may need more freedom and independence than usual, and as long as you indulge that feeling without hurting anyone else, you'll enjoy this transit. It's a nice one to take you into 2020.

A solar eclipse in Capricorn on December 26 really revs up the earth energy in your chart now. New financial opportunities surface that increase your earnings. You can thank Jupiter in Capricorn for that expansion!

AT A GLANCE
December 2—Jupiter enters Capricorn
December 9—Mercury enters Sagittarius
December 12—Full moon in Gemini
December 20—Venus goes into Aquarius
December 26—Solar eclipse in Capricorn
December 29—Mercury enters into Capricorn

Reflection
How did the year measure up for you? In what ways did Jupiter expand your life? Are you pleased with the way the year turned out? What, if anything, would you change? Jot your thoughts below.

_____
_____
_____
_____
_____

Happy New Year!

Capricorn 2019

Saturn rules your sign, and it's one of the reasons you're the hardest worker in the zodiac. In late December 2017, it entered Capricorn and will continue to transit it until March 22, 2020. It functions well here, so you're comfortable with its energy. Saturn governs discipline, responsibility, restrictions and the structures in our lives. This year, it will be retrograde from April 29 to September 18, and during this period, you may be more serious than usual and will scrutinize the structures you've built in relationships, your career, finances and in all areas of your life.

In the monthly roundups, you'll find information on which transiting planets are impacting your sun sign or Saturn, retrogrades, new and full moon, eclipses, planets that are entering new signs and what it all may mean for you.

2019 may bring about profound changes in your life, Capricorn, because Pluto and Saturn are traveling together. Pluto helps us to transform at the deepest levels, and Saturn makes those changes long-lasting. This year, you're setting the groundwork for expansion, and from December 2 into the new year, Jupiter in your sign helps to make that expansion a reality.

January 2019
Business

Welcome to 2019! The year begins with Mars transiting Aries and the home/family area of your chart—i.e. your place is the hub of post-holiday activity! It entered Aries on December 31 and will be there until February 14. You may be finishing up renovation projects on your home, getting your kids ready to return to school and preparing your own agenda for the next few months.

Mercury enters your sign on January 4, and between then and January 24, your intellect is keenly focused on your goals and ambitions. You're eager to embrace everything 2019 has to offer and are ready to move forward. Mercury moves into Aquarius and your financial area on January 24, and now your conscious awareness shifts to earning money. In fact, one of your goals for this year may be to increase your income significantly. Until February 10, you're a wheeler and dealer and stubborn in your strategies.

On the 5th, there's a solar eclipse in your sign, and this one should be positive for you. New opportunities flow into your life that are personally satisfying. Thanks to a conjunction with Pluto and a friendly beam from Neptune to the eclipse degree, the opportunities may involve the arts or your spirituality and put you in a more powerful position.

This eclipse is followed two weeks later by a lunar eclipse in Leo. Something may surface that makes you feel off or annoyed. It could involve your creativity or resources you share with others—a partner, child, parent or roommate. If possible, avoid conflict and drama. Keep your opinion to yourself, and move forward.

Once Uranus turns direct in Aries on January 6, it fuels Mars, also in Aries, with plenty of energy. Unusual people once again enter your life.

Venus transits Sagittarius from January 7 to February 3 and makes it easier for you to see the bigger picture in romance, your creative endeavors and even in your finances. If a romance starts during this transit, it may be kept under wraps until Venus enters your sign next month.

January 4—Mercury enters into Capricorn
January 5—Solar eclipse in Capricorn
January 6—Uranus turns direct in Aries
January 7—Venus goes into Sagittarius
January 21—Lunar eclipse in Leo
January 24—Mercury goes into Aquarius

February 2019
5 stars

In 2019, you have at least three beautiful periods when your love life is near bliss, your muse is at your beck and call and life in general feels so perfect you wonder why it can't always be like this. The first of these periods falls between February 3 and March 1, when Venus transits your sign. You're really in your element now. Your self-confidence is high, and your personal magnetism attracts the right people at the right time. If you're not involved in a relationship when this transit starts, you may be by the time it ends. Be sure to carve out time daily during this period for your creative activities.

The new moon in Aquarius on February 4 is a beauty for bringing in new sources of income. Jupiter is friendly to it, and Mercury is closely conjunct. You're able to talk your way through anything, with anyone, and that helps you to land the project or freelance gig or make the sale.

Mercury enters Pisces on February 10, and until it turns retrograde on March 5, you're exceptionally intuitive, and your imagination works overtime. This transit favors all sorts of communication—blogging, websites, social media and even good, old-fashioned, face-to-face communication! If you're a writer or work in the arts, be sure to submit your products before the retrograde begins. To prepare yourself for it, reread the Mercury retrograde section in the introduction. We'll talk more in depth about this retro in next month's roundup.

You'll enjoy the period from February 14 to March 31. Mars, the planet that makes stuff happen, will be in Taurus, in the area of your chart that governs love/romance and creativity. Despite the fact that Mercury will be retro for part of this transit, you'll still be able to accomplish a lot because Mars now forms a terrific angle to your sun sign. It brings patience, resoluteness and stubbornness. It gets the job done!

On February 19, the full moon in Virgo, a fellow earth sign, highlights your communication ability and your attention to detail (Virgo). There could be news about a publishing project, a trip overseas or something connected to your worldview and spiritual beliefs.

February 3—Venus enters Capricorn
February 4—New moon in Aquarius
February 10—Mercury goes into Pisces
February 14—Mars enters into Taurus
February 19—Full moon in Virgo

March 2019
Uranus shift

In addition to a Mercury retrograde in Pisces that runs from March 5–28, Uranus makes a major shift. For the last seven years, the planet of sudden, unexpected change has been transiting Aries. On March 6, it will enter Taurus once again. It was in that sign for a brief time in 2018, then turned retrograde, slipped back into Aries and now the transit continues until 2026.

During this lengthy transit, Uranus will be forming a terrific angle to your sun sign, so you're going to benefit tremendously from this transit. Life will be more exciting and all sorts of opportunities will open up for you, many of them sudden and unforeseen. Your capacity for self-expression will grow and evolve. By embracing change, you will find that your interests are expanding. It's a great time to study esoteric topics and to delve into areas like quantum physics, science and astronomy.

Between March 1 and 26, Venus transits Aquarius and your financial area. Although Mercury will be retrograde for most of this transit, you should see some improvement in what you earn. Your expenses could rise as well, but you should have the money to cover them. Unusual ideas may occur to you during this transit. Be sure to jot them down. They may come in handy later on.

From March 5 to 28, Mercury is moving retrograde through Pisces. Follow the general guidelines suggested in the introduction's section on Mercury retrograde. Since this one occurs in your communication area, be sure to think before you speak and to say what you mean. The potential for misunderstandings are greater during Mercury retrogrades.

On the 6th, in addition to Uranus changing signs, there's a new moon in Pisces. This could bring an opportunity for a writing or speaking project. Just be sure, though, that you don't sign any contracts until after Mercury turns direct. Otherwise, you may be revisiting the terms.

On the 20th, the full moon in Libra lights up your career area. You become more aware of the need for balance between your professional and personal life and realize you may have to start carving out more time for yourself. Career news may necessitate a slight adjustment in your attitude.

On the 26th, two days before Mercury turns direct, Venus enters Pisces and what fun this transit will be for you. From now until April 20, your imagination slams into overdrive, and you may be brainstorming with fiends and family on how to implement some of your ideas into your daily life. You're more intuitive now and are able to feel what others feel. In a sense, you become a psychic sponge during this transit, particularly after Mercury turns direct in this sign, so it's important you hang out with upbeat, positive people!

From March 31 to May 15, Mars transits Gemini, and suddenly, you're able to get things done at the speed of light. This transit benefits not only your daily work routine, but your career as well. You may be networking more frequently through social media and in person.

AT A GLANCE
March 1—Venus enters into Aquarius
March 5—Mercury turns retrograde in Pisces
March 6—New moon in Pisces, Uranus enters Taurus
March 20—Full moon in Libra
March 26—Venus goes into Pisces
March 28—Mercury turns direct
March 31—Mars enters Gemini

April 2019
Unsettled

It may feel like a weird month, sort of off, and it's not because you're coming down with a cold! Three planets turn retrograde, and two of those retros occur in your sign. On April 10, Jupiter turns retrograde in Sagittarius, and on April 25 and 29, Pluto and then Saturn turn retrograde in Capricorn.

Jupiter's retro lasts until August 11, and its expansive energy now turns inward. You'll be looking deep within your own psyche and mining it to better understand your motives, core beliefs and wishes and desires. You could become a kind of dream archaeologist whose dreams are vivid and hold information and insights that can provide guidance and confirmation. You may also be taking a deeper look at your spirituality and perhaps sampling other spiritual traditions. It's an ideal time to begin a meditation practice.

Pluto's retrograde lasts until October 3. Your shadow side may surface more strongly now, and you, better than anyone, know what that shadow is. When you see it creeping into your interactions with others, open a dialogue with it. Learn what you can, and then do something that brings light to the shadow.

Saturn's retrograde enables you to examine the structures in your life—finances, career, family and friendships—and to determine which ones work well and which ones need bolstering. This retro lasts until September 18.

Before any of these planets turn retrograde, a new moon in Aries on April 5 brings an opportunity to move, find a new roommate or renovate your home in some way. Someone may move out of your place—an adult child, for example—which frees up a room you can turn into an office.

Mercury enters Aries on April 17, and from then until May 6, you're in a pioneering mindset. You come up with new, different ideas about how to do something. You may launch your home-based business, start a blog, build a website or research a particular topic. On the 20th, Venus joins Mercury in Aries, and these two travel together until May 6, feeding off of each other and bringing more excitement into your home life. You may want to beautify your home in some way or start a garden. You and your partner may decide to start a family. The Venus transit lasts until May 15.

In between, there's a second full moon in Libra, which brings positive news about professional matters—a raise, promotion or larger office. There's no telling how this may develop. One thing is for sure, though. With retrograde Jupiter so friendly to this full moon, your career expands.

AT A GLANCE
April 5—New moon in Aries
April 10—Jupiter turns retrograde in Sagittarius
April 17—Mercury enters Aries
April 19—Full moon in Libra
April 20—Venus enters Aries
April 25—Pluto turns retrograde in Capricorn
April 29—Saturn turns retrograde in Capricorn

May 2019
Nearly perfect

You'll enjoy May. There's an emphasis on earth energy planets and a full moon in a compatible water sign. Let's take a look.

The new moon in Taurus on May 4 could bring a new romantic interest whose spiritual ideals and beliefs are similar to your own. It's also possible that you're commissioned for a creative endeavor or that one of your projects sells. If you're self-employed, you may sign up a new client or land a gig that that thrills you.

On the 6th, Mercury enters Taurus, and on the 15th, Venus follows. The planet of communication and the planet of romance and love are traveling together frequently this year. This time, they're together until May 21, when Mercury moves on. Since Venus rules Taurus, it functions well here, deepening your sensuality, conferring greater patience, resilience and even a hint of mysticism. The Venus transit last until June 8 and marks one of the most enjoyable periods for you all year. Your partner is attentive, your muse is eager to help and your relationship with children runs smoothly.

Also on the 15th, Mars enters Cancer, your opposite sign, where it will be until July 1. This transit deepens your intuition and your appreciation for your family and enables you to find a business partner quite easily, if you're looking for one. If you're married or in a committed relationship, this transit is marked by greater emotional closeness and intimacy.

Then there's a full moon in Scorpio on May 18 that you'll enjoy. Your social calendar gets crowded during the several days leading up to this date, and you recognize the opportunity to network and connect with friends. Pluto is friendly to this full moon, indicating that any news you hear puts you in a more powerful position.

On May 21, Mercury enters Gemini, which it rules, and between then and June 4, you're quite the chatterbox, able to talk to anyone about anything. You may be using social media more frequently—for both business and pleasure—and could decide to upgrade your phone or computer.

AT A GLANCE
May 4—New moon in Taurus
May 6—Mercury enters Taurus
May 15—Venus goes into Taurus, Mars enters Cancer
May 18—Full moon in Scorpio
May 21—Mercury goes into Gemini

June 2019
Mixed

June is a mix of energies. If you have a moon or rising in an air or fire sign, you'll love this month. Otherwise, maybe not so much.

The new moon in Gemini on June 3 ushers in new opportunities in your daily work routine and in the maintenance of your health. You might be promoted or tapped to head up a team, or if you've been looking for employment, you get the job you want. If you're self-employed, a new client or project comes your way. You may have a stab at a writing project or could be hired for a publicity or merchandising campaign.

Mercury transits Cancer from June 4 to 26 and joins Mars in your partnership area. The combination indicates that you aggressively pursue goals with a romantic or business partner. You may be working from home, and perhaps you've taken time off from your regular employment to do this. Once Mercury enters Leo, where it will be moving direct until July 7, your flair for the dramatic comes out in various ways—the way you talk and interact with others, the way you dress and even in the places to which you travel. Resort, anyone? Club Med?

On June 8, Venus enters Gemini, and now you're the person everyone at work comes to for answers. If a romance is sparked between now and July 3, when the transit ends, the flow of conversation will be excellent, and the attraction may initially begin as a mental connection. You've read the same books, have the same political beliefs and share similar spiritual beliefs.

The full moon in Sagittarius on June 17 enjoys a friendly beam from retrograde Jupiter. By now you know that means any news you hear will be positive and will expand your life in some way. You may feel more restless around, or on, this date and may have to satisfy it by taking a few days off!

From June 20 to January 17, 2020, Neptune will be retrograde in Pisces. The impact is subtle. Think of this period as a reality check, where things you have been ignoring or pushing aside to deal with later are seen now for what they are.

AT A GLANCE
June 3—New moon in Gemini
June 4—Mercury enters into Cancer
June 8—Venus goes into Gemini
June 17—Full moon in Sagittarius
June 20—Neptune turns retrograde
June 26—Mercury enters Leo

July 2019
Challenging

There's a lot going on this month, and the events include two eclipses, one of them in your sign and a Mercury retrograde. Be sure to get plenty of rest!

On July 2, the solar eclipse occurs in your opposite sign, Cancer. Potential opportunities with this one have a wide range: you move to a neighborhood or house that suits you and your family; you and your romantic partner make a deeper commitment to each other by moving in together, getting married or starting a family; or you start your own business. Since Uranus is friendly to the degree of this eclipse, opportunities unfold suddenly and without warning.

The lunar eclipse in your sign on July 16 should be positive for you. Pluto is friendly to this eclipse, and that means that whatever you experience emotionally and internally puts you in a more powerful position. This one could involve an important female in your life—mother, sister or close friend.

Before either of these eclipses occur, on July 1, Mars enters fire sign Leo and remains there until August 18. During this transit, you make great strides in your creativity and may delve into metaphysical topics—hauntings and ghosts, life after death and reincarnation. You may be able to use what you discover in some tangible way that produces income.

Between July 3 and 27, Venus transits Cancer. This should be another pleasant period for you. You feel self-confident and happy with where your life is right now and where it's headed. Your intuition is especially strong now, so be sure to listen to that inner voice and let it guide you. On the 27th, Venus enters Leo, joining Mars, and these two travel together until August 18, when Mars moves on. Think of this duo as the cosmic lovers. The chemistry with a romantic interest is ideal, and just watch how things unfold during this period!

On July 31, Mercury turns direct in Cancer and moves forward toward its second appointment with Leo next month. Also on the 31st, the new moon in Leo promises to be a romantic time because Venus is closely conjunct. And if you're not involved yet in a relationship, this new moon could make it happen.

AT A GLANCE
July 1—Mars goes into Leo
July 2—Solar eclipse in Cancer
July 3—Venus enters Cancer
July 7—Mercury turns retrograde in Leo
July 16—Lunar eclipse in Capricorn
July 27—Venus enters Leo
July 31—Mercury turns direct, new moon in Leo

August 2019
Connecting all the dots

The latter part of the month will be pleasing for you, with a concentration of planets and a new moon in fellow earth sign Virgo. Before we get there, though, Jupiter turns direct on August 11, and Mercury enters Leo once again. The shift in Jupiter's movement means that its expansive nature moves out into the external world again. You may be traveling overseas, get involved in a publishing project or have a chance to teach a class or workshop.

On August 12, Uranus turns retrograde in Taurus, and between now and January 6, 2020, you may feel more restless and have a need for greater independence and freedom. Since Uranus is now in the romance/creativity sector of your chart, this impacts not only your love life, but anything connected to your creativity.

The full moon in Aquarius on August 15 highlights your financial area. Thanks to a positive angle from retrograde Jupiter and Pluto, any news you hear is good news and puts you in a stronger position.

On the 18th, 21st and 29th, Mars, Venus and Mercury enter Virgo. Then, on the 30th, there's a new moon in Virgo. The planets all form terrific angles to your sun sign, so you're the beneficiary of all this earth energy. The Mars transit lasts until it October 4 and brings excellent physical energy. You may want to join a gym or take up some other regular form of physical exercise. You're better able to connect the dots in all your activities and have an excellent grasp of details.

The Venus transit lasts until September 14, and with Venus now traveling with Mars, your love life and creativity should pick up in a major way. Your communication skills are stellar during these three transits, so you may want to dust off an old manuscript, go through it and submit it. Don't hesitate to take any freelance jobs, particularly if they involve communication.

Once Mercury joins the other planets in Virgo, you're really a happy camper and feel very much in your element. Any challenge that surfaces can be easily overcome through attention to details, your communication skills and your wit and charm. The Mercury transits lasts until September 14.

The new moon in Virgo on August 30 is a beauty. You may have a chance to show off your writing and speaking skills—and get paid for it!—start a blog, build a website and use social media in a new way to publicize a product or your services.

AT A GLANCE
August 11—Jupiter turns direct, Mercury enters Leo
August 12—Uranus turns retrograde
August 15—Full moon in Aquarius
August 18—Mars enters Virgo
August 21—Venus goes into Virgo
August 29—Mercury enters Virgo
August 30—New moon in Virgo

September 2019
Career matters

The emphasis in September is on Libra and your career. Circle September 14, when both Mercury and Venus enter Libra, and there's a full moon in Pisces.

Once again, Mercury and Venus travel together until October 3, when Mercury moves into Scorpio. The Venus transit lasts until October 8. This period should be favorable for your professional life. You get along well with co-workers and bosses who look to you for answers and insights. Your artistic sense is greatly heightened, and you may change your appearance in some way—new hairstyles or clothing—or beautify your professional surroundings. With Venus here, a promotion and raise is possible.

The full moon in Pisces should be pleasant. Retrograde Neptune is closely conjunct, and retrograde Pluto is friendly to it. News you hear may involve the arts or your spirituality or could appeal to your ideals. It puts you in a solid and powerful position.

Saturn turns direct in your sign on the 19th, certainly a shift that benefits you in many ways. You can now bolster the various structures in your life that need it and move forward, confident that all is well!

The new moon in Libra on the 29th is the exclamation point that accompanies the transits of Mercury and Venus through Libra. This one may bring a promotion and raise or a new career path altogether.

AT A GLANCE
September 14—Mercury and Venus enter Libra, full moon in Pisces
September 18—Saturn turns direct in Capricorn
September 29—New moon in Libra

October 2019
Powerful

October is busy and includes the final Mercury retrograde of the year. It doesn't begin until October 31, so you have plenty of time this month to tie up loose ends at work, sign contracts, make travel plans and do everything you're advised *not to do* during a retrograde.

October 3 features two events: Mercury enters Scorpio, so it's forming a beneficial angle to your sun sign, and Pluto turns direct in your sign. While Mercury is moving direct in Scorpio (until Halloween) your mind is deeply attuned to other realms. You may have psychic experiences, synchronicity may happen more frequently and you might even see a ghost. Your dreams should be especially vivid, and if you're feeing really adventurous, try waking up inside a dream and manipulating it to a desired outcome.

Pluto's change in direction means its power and punch is working in your favor again. Your shadow self fades away, and you feel as if you're on more solid ground.

From October 4 to November 19, Mars transits Libra and your career area. This powerhouse enables you to get things done at the speed of light. Even if things slow down during the Mercury retrograde, you should be able to complete important projects and meet deadlines by the time the retrograde begins. After that, until November 20, revise, review and reconsider older projects and activities.

On the 8th, Venus joins Mercury in Scorpio, so these two are traveling companions once again until November 1, when Venus moves on. Your sexuality and intuition are greatly heightened during this transit, and any romance that begins is likely to be passionate and perhaps a bit possessive as well. There could also be an element of secrecy.

The full moon in Aries on October 13 lights up your home and family life, and due to the fiery nature of Aries, things at home could be a little wild on or around this date. Any news you hear should be positive, thanks to a friendly beam from Jupiter.

On October 27, the new moon in Scorpio is likely to bring in new friends and contacts. Through these individuals new opportunities surface and new doors swing open. If any of these opportunities require a contract, sign it immediately or wait until after Mercury turns direct on November 20.

Be sure to look over the Mercury retrograde section in the introduction and follow the general guidelines. Since this one occurs in Scorpio, in your friendship area, be sure that your communications with people in your immediate environment are clear. Otherwise you may have trouble with a friend. Double check all your facts and appointments.

AT A GLANCE
October 3—Mercury goes into Scorpio, Pluto turns direct
October 4—Mars enters Libra
October 8—Venus goes into Scorpio
October 13—Full moon in Aries
October 27—New moon in Scorpio
October 31—Mercury turns retrograde

November 2019
Mixed

The latter half of November, after Mercury has turned direct, should be more pleasing to you than the beginning of the month. That said, let's take a look at November 1, when Venus enters Sagittarius and remains there until it enters your sign on November 25. Now *that* is a transit to anticipate.

While Venus is in Sagittarius, Jupiter is also there, and that usually spells luck, serendipity, growth and increase. Even though you may feel a need for a greater independence and freedom now, your heart still yearns for intimacy, companionship and love. Any romance that begins during this transit will be passionate, fun and will in some way make you more aware of the bigger picture of your life, needs, desires and ambitions.

On the 9th, the full moon in Taurus should bring news about a romantic relationship, creative endeavor, finances or one of your kids. Despite Mercury's mischief, this full moon receives such friendly beams from Saturn, Pluto and retrograde Neptune that the news should be positive. Besides, the earth energy of this moon is comfortable for you.

Mars enters Scorpio, a sign it co-rules, on November 19, and this dynamic transit takes you into the new year, to January 4, 2020. You may feel like you're on a speeding train headed toward an unknown destination, but you certainly enjoy the ride and the excitement. Because Scorpio is such an emotionally intense sign, you'll be feeling everything more deeply.

Once Mercury turns direct on the 20th, it travels with Mars until December 9. Your psychic antenna may be twitching nonstop during this period. Your insight into others is sharp, and if you follow your inner voice, you won't make a misstep.

Once Venus enters your sign on November 25, you're feeling wonderful about your life, future and all the possibilities ahead. This is the second time this year that Venus has transited your sign, so you should be familiar with how everything seems to run more smoothly and effortlessly. Between now and December 20, when the transit ends, be sure to carve out time for you and your muse to brainstorm! And, of course, make plenty of room for romance and love, an area that will flow beautifully.

The new moon in Sagittarius on November 26 could bring an opportunity for international travel and an exploration of your spirituality. It's also a wonderful time to invite friends over for dinner or a party and to indulge this gregarious Sagittarius moon.

Neptune turns direct in Pisces on the 27th, a call to your creative side. Now your imagination can once again roam the universe of ideas and bring back gifts that you can use in your daily life.

AT A GLANCE
November 1—Venus goes into Sagittarius
November 12—Full moon in Taurus
November 19—Mars enters Scorpio
November 20—Mercury turns direct
November 25—Venus enters Capricorn
November 26—New moon in Sagittarius
November 27—Neptune turns direct

December 2019
Jupiter enters your sign

You'll experience a certain excitement this month when Jupiter enters your sign, a cycle that happens every twelve years. It begins on December 2 and ends on December 20, 2020. During this period, Jupiter is the equivalent of Santa Clause for you, Capricorn. Anything in your life that can expand, will, and the growth may start immediately, the first day of the transit.

Some possibilities: a significant increase in your income, a promotion and raise at work, a new career, a marriage, the birth of a child, a move, the purchase a house or property, acceptance into graduate or law school or the chance to live and work overseas. In other words, pivotal life events can occur during this transit. It's best if you check your natal chart to see where Capricorn falls; that area will experience the most growth. You may also want to make a wish list about what you like to experience and achieve in the year ahead. Post it where you'll see it frequently.

From December 9 to 29, Mercury transits Sagittarius. This transit favors the holiday season, when people tend to be in upbeat moods: office parties, home parties, festivities galore, surprises wrapped in pretty paper and good food and company. Enjoy yourself. Once Mercury enters your sign on the 29th, you usher in the new year with your goals and dreams, and everything you wish for seems attainable. That transit ends on January 17, 2020.

The full moon in Gemini on December 12 is ideal for getting your work-related projects completed before the holidays. You may be networking and socializing more around this time. If there's news of any kind, it may initially be confusing. Once you have the full details, you'll know how to proceed. That's due to a challenging angle from Neptune.

Venus enters Aquarius and your financial area on December 20, and this transit takes you into the new year with unusual ideas about how to earn more money. The only thing you have to figure out is how best to implement the ideas. This transit ends on January 14, 2020.

The solar eclipse in your sign the day after Christmas should bring some surprising opportunities in terms of your personal life, career and any other area where you've placed your focus and intentions. Jupiter is conjunct the eclipse degree, and that means you're in the right place at the right time—growth and increase. You've got so much energy packed into your sign by the end of the year that it may not get any better than this!

AT A GLANCE
December 2—Jupiter enters Capricorn
December 9—Mercury enters Sagittarius
December 12—Full moon in Gemini
December 20—Venus goes into Aquarius
December 26—Solar eclipse in Capricorn
December 29—Mercury enters into Capricorn

Reflection
Take a few minutes to look back at 2019. What did you like about it? Are you pleased with the way things turned out? Are you happier or more prosperous? Did you achieve your dreams? What pivotal life events did you experience?

_____

_____

_____

_____

_____

Happy New Year!

Aquarius 2019

Your sign is ruled by Uranus, the planet that governs, among other areas, sudden, unexpected change. Its job is to turn the status quo on its head, and it does this by shaking up those areas of your life where you have become habitual and routine. It gets rid of the dead wood so that the new can move in.

Since March 2011, it has been transiting fire sign Aries and forming a beneficial angle to your sun sign. It's likely that the changes you've been experiencing are exciting and fun. It's also likely that you've been a magnet for cutting edge ideas that you have been able to use in your work and creative endeavors and to generally improve the quality of your life.

In 2018, Uranus entered Taurus but stayed only several months, then turned retrograde and slipped back into Aries. On March 6, 2019, Uranus enters it again. It will be there for the next seven years, until April 28, 2026. If you have a copy of your natal chart, check it to see where Taurus falls. That area of your life will undergo the most change.

In a solar chart, where your sun sign is placed on the ascendant, Taurus falls in the home/family area of your chart. This isn't as accurate, of course, as your natal chart, but it's the way astrologers make predictions that pertain to all people of a certain sign. Some possible changes you may experience during this transit? A move, a change in financial or marital status, a move out of or into your home by someone, a career change or a birth or death. In other words, pivotal life events. The best way to deal with any Uranus transit is to embrace change rather than resist it.

In these monthly roundups, you'll find information on the signs the transiting planets are entering and the angles they are making to your sun sign, which planets are retrograde, the new and full moons, eclipses and just about anything else you should know to successfully navigate the month.

January 2019
Wow!

Welcome to 2019! The year starts off with a proverbial bang for you, with Mars having entered Aries on December 31, joining Uranus in that area of your chart that governs communication, travel, siblings and your conscious mind. You're eager to start the year off on the right track and have plenty of drive and ambition. You may be doing a lot of writing and public speaking between now and February 14, when the transit ends. Others are attracted to your unusual ideas and appreciate that you allow them to be who they are. You aren't into pretenses.

On January 4, Mercury enters earth sign Capricorn, which both Saturn and Pluto are transiting. Your conscious mind is goal-oriented and may be focused on a particular project or creative endeavor that you hope to launch or nurture along to greater growth and expansion. Saturn provides the structure, and Pluto confers the power.

The solar eclipse in Capricorn on January 5 triggers new opportunities to achieve your goals. Since Mercury, Saturn and Pluto are also in this area of your chart, you're grounded and determined to make the abstract tangible. This eclipse gives you a chance to do that. Neptune is friendly to the eclipse degree, indicating that the opportunity appeals to your ideals and spirituality.

The lunar eclipse in Leo that follows two weeks later, on January 21, falls in your partnership area. Since lunar eclipses concern inner events and our emotional world, you may feel as if you've been unfairly criticized or that your creativity is being eclipsed in some way. Rather than creating drama, just let whatever it is roll away from you. It's not worth a battle.

Uranus turns direct in Aries on January 6, a definite benefit! Now you can take advantage of all the edgy energy and of the idiosyncratic and unusual ideas you have. It now moves toward its appointment with Taurus on March 6.

From January 7 to February 3, Venus transits compatible fire sign Sagittarius. What fun these few weeks will be for you! Your social calendar heats up, friends vie for your attention and company and you're able to network with ease. You may travel internationally during this transit or become involved in some facet of the publishing industry. If a romance begins, it may be with someone you meet through friends.

From January 24 to February 10, Mercury transits your sign, and now you're really in your element! You're primarily a mental person and this transit heightens your communication abilities, your capacity to generate ideas and the way you interact with others.

AT A GLANCE
January 4—Mercury enters into Capricorn
January 5—Solar eclipse in Capricorn
January 6—Uranus turns direct in Aries
January 7—Venus goes into Sagittarius
January 21—Lunar eclipse in Leo
January 24—Mercury goes into Aquarius

February 2019
New opportunities

The best news this month is the new moon in your sign on February 4, Aquarius. This moon comes along just once a year and sets the tone for the next twelve months. Take some time to think about what you would like to achieve and experience in the next year. Make a list. Post it where you'll see it frequently. Visualize, and back the visualizations with powerful emotion. Then step out of the way, and let the universe do its job.

This is the new moon that can help you gain your desires. With Jupiter forming a beautiful angle to it and Mercury conjunct, any opportunities that surface should please you immensely and broaden your world in some significant way.

Before the new moon, on February 3, Venus enters Capricorn, joining Saturn and Pluto. Any romance that starts during this transit will be serious and could be long range. As an Aquarian, your freedom and independence in any relationship are paramount, but don't dismiss this relationship just because the other person is serious about it. Or conversely, you could be the one who is serious! The transit ends March 1, when Venus enters your sign, a time to anticipate!

Mercury enters Pisces and your financial area on February 10 and moves direct until March 5. Take advantage of your increased intuition and accelerated imagination to come up with creative ideas about how to increase your income. If you're artistic, how can you make your talent commercially viable? You may be questioning whether you're happy doing what you're doing, and Mercury in Pisces gives you a chance to brainstorm with yourself and others about possible options.

Mars transits Taurus from February 14 to March 31, and your home hums with activity and becomes the center of the universe! If you have kids, then they and their friends all congregate at your place. You may be inspired to refurbish your home in some way—by building an addition, turning a basement into a living space or knocking down a wall to create a larger space. This transit increases your physical energy, and it's a good idea to start a regular physical exercise routine if you don't have one already. Take on projects that require patience and resolve.

The full moon in Virgo on February 19 highlights resources you share with others—a partner, parent, child or roommate. If you've applied for a mortgage, then you may hear news that you've been approved for an excellent interest rate. There could also be news that your partner has gotten a bonus or raise. Mars is friendly to this full moon, so whatever news you hear should move events forward.

AT A GLANCE
February 3—Venus enters Capricorn
February 4—New moon in Aquarius
February 10—Mercury goes into Pisces
February 14—Mars enters into Taurus
February 19—Full moon in Virgo

March 2019
Mixed

It's a month of mixed energies for you, some great and some not so much!

On March 1, Venus enters your sign, marking the beginning of one of the most romantic and creative periods for you all year. Your head and your heart are now in complete agreement, and you feel compelled to dive into your various creative endeavors with renewed optimism and enthusiasm. Your partner is enormously attentive and goes out of the way to make you happy. The transit lasts until March 26, and the only problem with it is that Mercury is retrograde for most of it.

That said, you can make the Venus transit work best for you by doing everything you need to do before March 5, when Mercury turns retro. Sign contracts, pitch ideas, brainstorm with your muse, submit manuscripts, start new projects, move in with your lover or get married. But between March 5 and 28 do none of the above.

Read over the Mercury retro section in the introductions (pages 9 and 185) and follow the general guidelines for navigating this period with less stress. Since the retro is in Pisces, in your financial area, take precautions with your money—check and double check bank and investment accounts, and safeguard passwords if you do online banking. If payments to you are delayed, pursue the person/company about where the check is.

On the 6th, two events occur: Uranus enters Taurus for its seven-year run in that sign, and there's a new moon in Pisces. Reread the introduction to your sign for 2019 to get a sense of the kinds of things that may occur during Uranus's transit through Taurus. The early part of the transit may be the most jarring. Just try to go with the flow, Aquarius.

The new moon in Pisces should bring in a new source of income (perhaps through something in the arts), but it may not happen until after Mercury turns direct. Neptune is conjunct this new moon, and Saturn is friendly to it, so the opportunities that surface have long-range effects.

The full moon in fellow air sign Libra on March 20 brings news about a publishing or academic activity or about a long distance trip you're planning. Your artistic sense is heightened, and so is your understanding that your closest relationships are in need of greater balance. In other words, Aquarius, strive not to be so self-involved. Reach out to the people you love.

Between March 26 and April 20, Venus transits Pisces and your financial area. Except for the two days when Mercury is still retrograde in this area, Venus compensates for everything that may have gone haywire during the retro. It may bring on the opportunities promised by the new moon in Pisces earlier this month. Even if your expenses rise during this transit, so will your income. This transit also favors any creative work where imagination and intuition are essential to success.

Finally, on the 28th, Mercury turns direct again. Now move forward and embrace everything that got delayed during the retrograde. On the 31st, Mars enters fellow air sign Gemini, and between now and May 15, you're a dervish of mental activity. Your communication skills are greatly enhanced, and you're blogging, writing and networking. If you're traveling or doing something else you enjoy, you're filled with a sense of adventure and the feeling that life is now flowing your way. Mars in this area of your chart heightens your sexuality, but for you, any sexual attraction begins first in the mind, with a similarity in beliefs.

AT A GLANCE
March 1—Venus enters into Aquarius
March 5—Mercury turns retrograde in Pisces
March 6—New moon in Pisces, Uranus enters Taurus
March 20—Full moon in Libra
March 26—Venus goes into Pisces
March 28—Mercury turns direct
March 31—Mars enters Gemini

April 2019
Challenging

April may be an odd month. Three planets turn retrograde—Jupiter, Pluto and Saturn. But the other astrological events should please you. Let's take a closer look.

The new moon in Aries on April 5 brings new opportunities to exhibit your trailblazing qualities. This is the time to implement one or several of the unusual ideas that come so easily to you. You may feel more restless on or around this time, but also more driven.

Jupiter turns retrograde in Sagittarius on April 10. Between now and August 11, when it turns direct again, your focus is on your spiritual beliefs and intellectual growth and how these things fit into the rest of your life. If you travel overseas during this time, you'll combine business and pleasure with a quest for greater knowledge or understanding. You may brainstorm with several friends who have the same questions you do about the nature of reality.

Between April 17 and May 6, Mercury transits Aries and the same area of your chart where the new moon occurred. You're comfortable with this position for Mercury. It fires you up mentally, kicking you into high gear to launch projects, pitch ideas and to generally get things rolling.

The full moon in fellow air sign Libra on April 19 is a beauty. It illuminates that part of your chart that represents the higher mind. Jupiter retrograde is friendly to it, indicating that any news you hear should be positive and will lead to spiritual growth.

From April 20 to May 15, Venus transits Aries. For part of this time, it travels with Mercury and enhances your communication abilities and your relationship with siblings and neighbors. Any romance that begins during this transit will be passionate, exciting and unpredictable. Your need for independence and freedom in any relationship won't be a problem with this one.

On the 25th and 29th, Pluto and then Saturn turn retrograde in Capricorn, in that part of your chart that governs the personal unconscious. The Pluto retro lasts until October 3, and during this transit, your shadow side may surface now and then. But Pluto enables you to dive to the depths of your own psyche, so as soon as the shadow appears, you can take steps to mitigate its impact. You have an opportunity now to better understand your inner being.

Saturn's retrograde lasts until September 18. It enables you to reevaluate the various structures in your life—family, career, finances, romance, creativity—and to grasp which ones no longer serve your best interest and to bolster the ones that do.

AT A GLANCE
April 5—New moon in Aries
April 10—Jupiter turns retrograde in Sagittarius
April 17—Mercury enters Aries
April 19—Full moon in Libra
April 20—Venus enters Aries
April 25—Pluto turns retrograde in Capricorn
April 29—Saturn turns retrograde in Capricorn

May 2019
One step at a time

Compared to April, May is a more evenly paced month, with an emphasis on earth energy. It's a good month to tackle projects that require patience and resilience.

The new moon in Taurus on May 4 should bring new opportunities to your home and family life. You might put your home on the market, sell your home or launch a home-based business. Or, also possible, someone moves in or out. Neptune in Pisces is friendly to this new moon, indicating that opportunities may have artistic or spiritual aspects to them.

From May 6 to 21, Mercury moves through Taurus. This transit reinforces your innate stubbornness and enables you to take abstract ideas and make them tangible and comprehensible to others. You set more realistic goals and work patiently toward achieving them.

On the 15th, Venus enters Taurus and travels with Mercury until the 21st. The Venus transit lasts until June 8 and brings a smoothness and ease to your home life. Your sensuality is deepened and so is your appreciation for beauty and art. You may decide to refurbish and beautify your personal space in some way. You might start a garden or bring the outdoors inside with a fountain, fresh flowers or potted plants.

Also on the 15th, Mars enters Cancer, and between now and July 1, you're focused on a work project that benefits from your deepened intuition and your ability to nurture an idea from birth to completion. Your family may figure into this transit, too, because Cancer represents home and family.

The full moon in Scorpio on May 18 highlights your professional life. You feel everything more intensely now and are able to see all the connecting pieces of your career with greater clarity. Pluto is friendly to this full moon, an indication that news you hear puts you in a stronger position to negotiate and bargain.

You'll enjoy Mercury's transit through fellow air sign Gemini from May 21 to June 4. As it moves through the romance and creativity area of your chart, you talk and think about your partner and your various creative projects and should carve out time daily to indulge in both. If you're not involved with anyone at the moment, you may meet someone special during Venus's transit of this area next month.

AT A GLANCE
May 4—New moon in Taurus
May 6—Mercury enters Taurus
May 15—Venus goes into Taurus, Mars enters Cancer
May 18—Full moon in Scorpio
May 21—Mercury goes into Gemini

June 2019
5 stars

June may be one of your best months all year, and it starts on June 3, with a new moon in Gemini, in the romance/creative area of your chart. If you aren't involved in a romantic relationship, this moon may change the status quo, particularly once Venus transits Gemini and this same area of your chart from June 8 to July 3. The new moon and this Venus transit also facilitates all your creative endeavors. Whatever your skill or talent, you may sell a project this month or be invited to exhibit your products. If you and your partner are considering starting a family, then this new moon and the Venus transit may bring it about. This part of your chart also governs children.

Between June 4–26, Mercury transits Cancer and forms a friendly angle to the career area of your chart. You should be able to take an idea and nurture it through birth to completion. Your intuition is powerful during this transit, but you may feel more vulnerable emotionally and take other people's remarks personally even when they aren't meant that way.

The full moon in Sagittarius on June 17 means you are primed and ready for a party! You're in a festive mood and may want to plan a summer solstice celebration for friends and family. Retrograde Jupiter is widely conjunct this moon, suggesting that any news you hear is positive and broadens your perspective in some way. Friends are helpful on or around this date.

Neptune turns retrograde in Pisces on June 20, and until November 27, it's reality check time, Aquarius. It's more difficult to gloss over certain aspects of your life or to pretend these areas are something other than what they are. Since Neptune is in your financial area, money may be the part you have to honestly appraise.

Mercury enters Leo, your opposite sign, on June 26 and moves in direct motion until July 7, when it turns retrograde. It will slip back into Cancer and turn direct in that sign on July 31. While it's direct in Leo, you and your partner may be talking about the ebb and flow of your relationship and what works and what doesn't. Focus on what's positive. Your creative flair during this period will be superb.

AT A GLANCE
June 3—New moon in Gemini
June 4—Mercury enters into Cancer
June 8—Venus goes into Gemini
June 17—Full moon in Sagittarius
June 20—Neptune turns retrograde
June 26—Mercury enters Leo

July 2019
Bumpy

With two eclipses and another Mercury retrograde this month, July may be a bit rough at times. Just remember, this too shall pass!

On July 1, Mars enters Leo, your opposite sign, and between then and August 18, you're driven by your passions—sexual, creative and mental. With Mercury retro and Venus traveling with Mars for at least part of the time, you're in for a treat. This transit also enables you to get stuff done with such dramatic flair that you attract the attention of the people around you. Your magnetism is indisputable.

Before we get to Venus's transit and the Mercury retrograde, let's talk about this month's eclipses. On July 2, the solar eclipse in Cancer ushers in new opportunities related to your family and home life and to your daily work. You might, for example, be able to work more from home on a flexible schedule that suits your lifestyle and need for independence. You could be tapped to spearhead a team that markets a new product, or perhaps you and a partner decide to launch your own business. Uranus is friendly to the eclipse degree, usually an indication that there's a suddenness to events. Just be vigilant and ready to seize the opportunities as they surface.

The lunar eclipse in Capricorn on July 16 may bring up issues from the past that you never resolved or that you simply pushed aside, perhaps in the hopes the issues would disappear. They could involve your career, childhood, a failed relationship or virtually anything. Pluto is widely conjunct the eclipse degree, so regardless of what comes up, you're able to resolve it, and that puts you in a better position.

Venus transits Cancer and the same area of your chart in which the solar eclipse occurred between July 3 and 27. It should facilitate any of the opportunities that surfaced on or around the eclipse. If a romance begins during this transit, you may keep it under wraps for some reason. That won't last once Venus enters your sign on July 27 and begins traveling with Mars.

The cosmic lovers make sure that you and your romantic partner have plenty of time alone to explore your attraction to each other. The chemistry is good. If you've been in a relationship for awhile, then you and your partner may deepen your commitment to each other by moving in together, getting married or starting a family. Venus transits Leo until August 21, and Mars separates from that sign on August 18.

Mercury is retro in Leo from July 7 to 31. Okay, this could be a little painful because it occurs in your partnership area. However, read over the Mercury retrograde section in the introduction, and follow the general guidelines. In addition, be clear and succinct in how you communicate with business and personal partners. If you disagree with them, avoid drama and confrontation. Wait until after Mercury turns direct to make any decisions about relationships.

July 31 marks the end of Mercury retrograde, and there's a new moon in Leo. This new moon should be terrific for you. Venus is closely conjunct, and that means your creativity reaches new heights. Money may flow in through a new business partnership, and your love life hums along at a perfect pitch.

AT A GLANCE
July 1—Mars goes into Leo
July 2—Solar eclipse in Cancer
July 3—Venus enters Cancer
July 7—Mercury turns retrograde in Leo
July 16—Lunar eclipse in Capricorn
July 27—Venus enters Leo
July 31—Mercury turns direct, new moon in Leo

August 2019
Not your favorite

It's another one of those months where the astrological energy is mixed. From the 18th to the end of the month, the emphasis is on earth sign Virgo, which will enable you to tend to details you may have overlooked.

On August 11, Jupiter turns direct in Sagittarius, and Mercury enters Leo for the second time. Jupiter's motion is a bonus. Its expansive energy now turns to the external world again, and you may discover new people entering your life and new opportunities for overseas travel. On December 2, Jupiter enters Capricorn.

Mercury's transit lasts until August 29 and allows you to complete whatever you were doing before Mercury turned retrograde on July 7. You and your partner may cook up a new strategy for your business or choose to market a product/service in a different way. This transit energizes your creative drive and passion.

On the 12th, Uranus turns retrograde in Taurus and remains that way until January 6, 2020. This retro doesn't have the punch of a Mercury retrograde, but may accentuate your need for freedom and independence and lead to feelings of restlessness.

The full moon in your sign on August 15 should be a beauty. It highlights that area of your chart that is all about *you*—as opposed to co-workers, family or friends. Jupiter in Sagittarius is friendly to it, so any news you hear should be positive and lead to growth and expansion.

On August 18, 21 and 29, Mars, then Venus and then Mercury all enter Virgo. The Mars transit lasts until October 4 and galvanizes the area of your chart that governs resources you share with others. This includes your partner's income, mortgages, loans, insurance payments, royalties and inheritances. Your partner may be working longer hours in anticipation of a bonus or a raise. Since this house also rules everything that goes bump in the night, it's possible that you have experiences with ghosts or spirits.

Both the Venus and Mercury transits end on September 14. With this trio traveling together, your sexuality is heightened, and your communication skills are excellent. If you're involved in a relationship, you and your partner should be on the same page in terms of your needs and expectations.

On the 30th, the new moon in Virgo is an exclamation point for the end of the month. Thanks to a friendly beam from retrograde Uranus, opportunities unfold suddenly, and the only thing required of you is to be ready! The possibilities? You have a chance to refinance your home for a lower interest rate or sign up a new client, or you're tapped for a freelance project.

AT A GLANCE
August 11—Jupiter turns direct, Mercury enters Leo
August 12—Uranus turns retrograde
August 15—Full moon in Aquarius
August 18—Mars enters Virgo
August 21—Venus goes into Virgo
August 29—Mercury enters Virgo
August 30—New moon in Virgo

September 2019
Calmer

September is calmer than August, and the transits are more beneficial for you. On the 14th, Mercury and Venus enter fellow air sign Libra, and a full moon in Pisces lights up your financial area. The Mercury and Venus transits make you more aware of the importance of balance in your closest relationships. Your artistic sense is heightened, and you may take in a concert, attend the theater or even travel overseas to some beautiful exotic spot that speaks to your soul. Since Venus rules Libra, it functions well in this sign and deepens your capacity for love and compassion. The Mercury transit ends on October 3, and the Venus transit ends on October 8.

The full moon in Pisces brings news about your finances or a creative endeavor. With retrograde Neptune and retrograde Pluto friendly to this full moon, the news appeals to your ideals and spirituality and puts you in a more powerful position to call the shots.

On the 18th, Saturn turns direct in Capricorn. Now you can bolster the structures in your life that need it and shed the structures that no longer serve your best interest. For instance, you might change jobs, end a relationship, move or find new ways to invest your money.

The new moon in Libra on September 29 brings new opportunities in the arts, publishing or academia or overseas travel. Plan something special with the one you love—a weekend getaway or tickets for a concert or art exhibit you've both wanted to see.

AT A GLANCE
September 14—Mercury and Venus enter Libra, full moon in Pisces
September 18—Saturn turns direct in Capricorn
September 29—New moon in Libra

October 2019
Career focus

Each month possesses its own unique texture and tone, and October's energy emphasizes your career and professional life.

On October 3, Mercury moves into Scorpio and your career area, and Pluto turns direct in Capricorn. Five days later, Venus joins Mercury in Scorpio and, on the 27th, the new moon in Scorpio is the bonus. Let's take a closer look.

Mercury is moving direct until the 31st. That means you should do all the things now that are best to avoid during the retrograde—sign contracts, make travel plans and submissions, pitch ideas, hire employees and upgrade your computer and phone. You get the idea. With Pluto now in direct motion and in a friendly angle to your career area, your professional activities have a deep and lasting impact.

From October 4 to November 19, Mars transits Libra, and this galvanizes you to research and study philosophy, various spiritual traditions and political ideologies. You may travel overseas in pursuit of specific knowledge or insight, and the people you meet on these travels will be instrumental in your finding what you're seeking.

Venus joins Mercury in Scorpio on the 8th, and between then and November 1, the people you work with regard you as the one with the answers. You're recognized as the tour de force you are. A promotion and raise may be part of this transit, too. Your creativity is powerful now, and so is your need for intimacy. If you get involved romantically, it may be with someone you meet through your work.

The full moon in Aries on October 13 receives a friendly beam from Jupiter in Sagittarius and should bring good news in any area where you've been placing your focus and attention.

On the 27th, the new moon in Scorpio brings new professional and career opportunities. You might change jobs, be promoted, move to a more spacious office or be assigned a new territory. If you're self-employed, your client base may be expanding, you're offered freelance projects that pay well or you have a chance to expand what you're doing.

Mercury turns retrograde in Scorpio on October 31, and from then until November 20, things slow down. Look over the Mercury retrograde section in the introduction and follow the general guidelines for navigating this retro period more successfully and with less stress. Since it occurs in your career area, definitely follow the rule of the three Rs: revise, review and reconsider rather than starting something new.

AT A GLANCE
October 3—Mercury goes into Scorpio, Pluto turns direct
October 4—Mars enters Libra
October 8—Venus goes into Scorpio
October 13—Full moon in Aries
October 27—New moon in Scorpio
October 31—Mercury turns retrograde

November 2019
Mostly enjoyable

Since Mercury doesn't turn direct until November 20, you've got a couple of weeks where things continue to be slow. But there are some other things going on that should delight you.

From November 1 to 25, Venus moves through Sagittarius, an ideal transit for the Thanksgiving holidays. You're in a festive mood, your self-confidence soars and you have such personal magnetism that people seek out your company. Your social calendar quickly fills up, and you have your choice of parties and dinners to attend.

On the 12th, the full moon in Taurus lights up the home and family area of your chart. There's news about a family member, your home sells, you buy a home or you hear that you and your partner are going to become parents. With Saturn, Pluto and retrograde Neptune friendly to this full moon, the news has lasting impact.

From November 19 to January 4, 2020, Mars transits Scorpio, a sign it co-rules, and your career area. This transit enables you to complete projects and clear your desk so that you enter the new year with a clean slate. You're after the bottom line in everything you tackle, and Mars in Scorpio pushes you to dig deeper and deeper until you find what you need.

On the 20th, Mercury turns direct in Scorpio, and from now until December 9, it travels with Mars. This adds to your resolve to get things done. Your intuition is deeper, and you're able to see the truth about other people.

Venus transits Capricorn from November 25 to December 20, and brings a quiet focus to something you're doing behind the scenes or in solitude. If a romance begins during this transit, the two of you may be spending most of your time alone together rather than with friends. Once Venus enters your sign on December 29, then you head out into the larger world together to announce that you're a couple.

The new moon in Sagittarius on November 26 should result in new opportunities in networking, international travel or publishing. Think big with this new moon, Aquarius. The bigger you think, the more likely it is that a wish or desire you have will unfold.

On the 27th, Neptune turns direct in Pisces, a bonus for your finances in that you're more clear-headed about what you earn and spend.

AT A GLANCE
November 1—Venus goes into Sagittarius
November 12—Full moon in Taurus
November 19—Mars enters Scorpio
November 20—Mercury turns direct
November 25—Venus enters Capricorn
November 26—New moon in Sagittarius
November 27—Neptune turns direct

December 2019
Varied

December is busy and the emphasis is on earth sign Capricorn. However, the best part of the month begins on December 20, when Venus enters your sign. More on that shortly.

On December 2, Jupiter enters Capricorn after spending thirteen months in Aries. This planet's role is to expand your life and prompt inner growth. Look at your natal chart to see where Capricorn falls; that will be the area that experiences the most growth. In a solar chart, with your sun sign on the ascendant, Capricorn falls in your twelfth house of the personal unconscious. In this area, the growth is in your own psyche, but because it forms a beneficial angle to your career area, your work life will benefit as well.

You might be hired to work in some new capacity that uses your talents in a different way. You might have a past-life regression or begin remembering some of your previous lives. Your dreams may be precognitive or offer insights and information that guide you. During these months, you're going to enjoy yourself, Aquarius.

Between December 9 and 29, Mercury transits Sagittarius, a wonderful transit for the holidays. Your spirits, like those of the people around you, will be high and festive, and you'll feel at the top of your game. From December 29 to January 17, 2020, Mercury joins Jupiter in Capricorn, a good way to enter the new year.

The full moon in Gemini on December 12 occurs in the romance and creativity section of your chart. News that you hear may be confusing at first but only because you don't have all the information. Once you do, you'll know how to proceed,

Now we come to the magical date, December 20, when Venus enters your sign. From now until January 14, 2020, you enjoy the third period this year—which takes you into the new year—when your love life and creativity are at a peak. Your partner is eager to spend as much time with you as possible, and although you may feel a bit smothered now and then, you secretly bask in all the attention. Your muse is ever so attentive as well and really wants to help! This transit is a terrific way to end one year and begin another.

Jupiter is widely conjunct the solar eclipse in Capricorn that happens on December 26. That means that the goods this eclipse delivers will have your heart singing.

AT A GLANCE
December 2—Jupiter enters Capricorn
December 9—Mercury enters Sagittarius
December 12—Full moon in Gemini
December 20—Venus goes into Aquarius
December 26—Solar eclipse in Capricorn
December 29—Mercury enters into Capricorn

Reflection

It's smart to look back at the year and evaluate the events and how you feel about them. Did 2019 measure you to your expectations? What pivotal life events did you experience? Are you happier now? How can you use what you learned to make 2020 a fabulous year? Record your thoughts below.

_____

_____

_____

_____

_____

Happy new year!

Pisces 2019

Neptune rules your sign, and Jupiter is the co-ruler. Neptune has been transiting your sign since early February 2012. It will be there until March 2025, when it enters Aries. However, due to a retrograde, it slips back into Pisces in October 2025 and then enters Aries once again in January 2026. Neptune's long transit through your sign heightens your imagination and intuition, your ideals and idealism and all of your other traits and qualities. Neptune is happy here and functioning at optimum capacity.

2019 should be an interesting year for you. Jupiter begins the year in Sagittarius, where it has been since November 2018, and will be there until December 2, when it enters Capricorn. While it has been transiting your career area, your professional life has grown and expanded. You may be traveling more or handling foreign clients for your company or both. Other possibilities with this transit: you're promoted, given a significant raise, find a new career path altogether, move to a more spacious office or launch your own business. Expansion and growth are Jupiter's keywords.

In the monthly roundups, take special note of transits any planets are making to Neptune or Jupiter. You'll also find information on when the plants are retrograde, new and full moons, eclipses and when the transiting planets enter new signs.

January 2019
Energetic start

Welcome to 2019! The year springs into action with energetic Mars in Aries moving through your financial area until February 14. This transit galvanizes your pursuit to earn more money, and you find innovative ways to do so. You might take on a part-time job, land a freelance project or start the new year with that substantial raise that Jupiter promises. Uranus retrograde is also in Aries and attracts unusual encounters with idiosyncratic people.

Mercury enters Capricorn, a sign compatible with yours, on January 4. Between then and January 24, you may be brainstorming with friends, networking in new ways or using social media more frequently. You have specific goals and a strategy for achieving them. You're also more practical and grounded and less indecisive.

The solar eclipse on January 5 is in Capricorn and should bring in new opportunities in friendships and with networking for business and pleasure. Some of the contacts you make as a result of the eclipse will be helpful in your achieving your wishes and dreams. Neptune and Pluto are both friendly to the eclipse degree, indicating that events appeal to your artistic and creative side and place you in a better position.

On January 6, Uranus turns direct in Aries, in your financial area, and you can once again take advantage of this planet's quirky and unusual energy. Jot down ideas that occur to you and synchronicities you experience. You may even notice signs and symbols in your environment. All can act as guidance and confirmation.

Between January 7 and February 3, Venus joins Jupiter in Sagittarius and your career area. Wow! The two most enjoyable planets traveling together like this indicates that your professional life should move along with smoothness and ease. Your co-workers regard you as the one with the insights and answers, and your boss appreciates you and the artistic touches you bring with you to work. This period could be one in which a promotion and raise occur. If you're self-employed, business should be terrific on all fronts—things suddenly take off with little or no effort on your part, clients are beating down your door and your inbox fills with accolades and opportunities.

As a result of the lunar eclipse in Leo on January 21, there may be changes in your daily work or in your creative endeavors. You may decide to change your health routine in some way—hit the gym more often, try a different nutritional program or alter your sleeping habits. You'll feel a surge of emotions that can be put to a positive use.

Between January 24 and February 20, Mercury transits Aquarius and the part of your chart that rules the personal unconscious. Your dreams are more vivid during this transit and may contain insights and information that are useful to you. Some of these dreams could be about future events—precognition—so it's to your advantage to keep a journal. You may want to treat yourself to a past-life regression or give therapy a try. You're priming yourself for when Mercury enters your sign next month.

January 4—Mercury enters into Capricorn
January 5—Solar eclipse in Capricorn
January 6—Uranus turns direct in Aries
January 7—Venus goes into Sagittarius
January 21—Lunar eclipse in Leo
January 24—Mercury goes into Aquarius

February 2019
Nearly perfect

February should be a good month for you!

Between February 3 and March 1, Venus transits Capricorn and creates a beneficial angle to your sun sign. Your friends and acquaintances vie for your company and people are drawn to your magnetism and air of mystery. If a romantic relationship begins during this transit, you and your new love interest may decide to join forces on a creative endeavor or even a sideline business. Capricorn usually has a laser focus on work, career and business and is goal-oriented.

The new moon in Aquarius on February 4 may result in a chance to put your imagination and unusual ideas to work. Mercury is still in Aquarius, too, stirring up your unconscious, urging you to question the status quo and not to shy away from the strange and idiosyncratic. Jupiter is friendly to this new moon and that means the opportunities broaden your life in some way.

Mercury enters your sign on February 10, and between then and March 5, when it turns retrograde, you're in a very good place. Your intuition is so sharp now you can size up a stranger or unfamiliar situation in seconds flat. You may be a bit more indecisive than usual, but that won't be an issue if you simply heed the advice of that inner voice. We'll talk about the retrograde in next month's roundup.

Mars enters Taurus on February 14 and forms a harmonious angle with your sun. You're a powerhouse of physical energy until March 31. You may be working longer hours—but love every second of it—and should tackle challenging projects that require patience and resilience. Your communication skills are greatly enhanced. You're able to take abstract ideas and make them tangible. You feel more grounded. If you don't have a regular exercise routine yet, now is the time to start something you know you'll stick to.

The full moon on February 19 is in Virgo, your opposite sign, and enjoys a friendly beam from Mars in Taurus. With this combination, you're able to connect the dots in a partnership, either business or romantic, and to immediately tell what's working and what's not. There may be news about a partnership or a writing project, and the news should be good.

AT A GLANCE
February 3—Venus enters Capricorn
February 4—New moon in Aquarius
February 10—Mercury goes into Pisces
February 14—Mars enters into Taurus
February 19—Full moon in Virgo

March 2019
Surreal at times

Even though Mercury, Venus and a new moon are in your sign this month, the energy in March may feel strange at times. The Mercury retrograde in your sign puts a damper on things between March 5 to 28. But before you decide to hide in a cave, read the Mercury retrograde section in the introduction and follow the general guidelines to emerge on the other side of the period without losing your mind! Since it's in your sign, be sure you communicate clearly with everyone in your environment and that you don't take anything someone else says personally. Funnel your imagination into your creative endeavors.

From March 1 to 26, Venus moves through Aquarius and your twelfth house, the area of the personal unconscious. This transit stirs your compassion and concern about the larger family of humanity, the planet and things over which you have no control. You may have frequent psychic experiences, perhaps with a partner or friend, or you may experience a spontaneous past-life experience. Synchronicities flourish.

March 6 features a new moon in your sign, and Uranus enters Taurus. This new moon happens only once a year and sets the tone for the next twelve months. Prepare for it by creating a list of what you would like to achieve and experience in the next year. Let your imagination play with these desires by seeing yourself involved in the experiences. *Feel it happening.* Few signs are as proficient as you are in actualizing desires.

The shift in signs for Uranus is significant because these transits last about seven years. Uranus transited Taurus for several months in 2018, then turned retro and slipped back into Aries.

In a solar chart, where your sun sign is placed on the ascendant, Taurus falls in your third house, the communication area. Take a look at your natal chart to see where Taurus is; that's the area that will experience the most sudden and unexpected change. You may move, change jobs, get married or divorced, immerse yourself in a particular area of study, lose and gain friends or change careers. It all depends on where you have become rigid or habitual in your life. Uranus sweeps in, shakes out the stuff that's no longer working and makes space for the new.

The full moon in Libra on March 20 brings news about a legal matter, a relationship or your spouse's income. If you recently applied for a mortgage or loan, you hear the verdict. Make sure your credit is in good shape regardless; creditors also fall in this area.

On March 26, you enter one of the most romantic and creative times for you all year: Venus enters your sign. You may not benefit immediately, but once Mercury turns direct on March 28, you're in your groove, Pisces, and the universe is right there with you. From then until April 20, your romantic partner worships you, and your relationship moves at a pace that suits you both. Your muse is knocking softly at the door, offering to help you in any way he or she can. Accept the offer. Dive into the ocean of your creative self. The only other period that equals this one occurs between July 3 to 27, when Venus transits Cancer and the romance/creativity section of your chart.

March 28 is party time! Mercury turns direct in your sign, and the best way to honor it is to have some fun. Now you can pack your bags and take off for parts unknown, sign contracts, pitch ideas, make submissions and move forward with confidence.

Between March 31 and May 15, Mars moves through Gemini and the family/home area of your chart. It's possible you'll be working from home and making new contacts through social media and in person. Your place is the hub of activity. You're able to talk to anyone about anything, may be reading voraciously and are eager to share what you know.

AT A GLANCE
March 1—Venus enters into Aquarius
March 5—Mercury turns retrograde in Pisces
March 6—New moon in Pisces, Uranus enters Taurus
March 20—Full moon in Libra
March 26—Venus goes into Pisces
March 28—Mercury turns direct
March 31—Mars enters Gemini

April 2019
Challenging

It's a month of mixed energies, with three planets turning retrograde, two planets entering new signs and the usual new and full moon. Let's starts with the retrogrades.

From April 10 to August 11, Jupiter is retrograde in Sagittarius, your career area. It means that the planet's expansive energy now turns inward, promoting spiritual and intellectual growth. You might delve into the study of ancient mythologies and spiritual traditions by traveling to sacred sites on other continents. You might take workshops or attend seminars on topics that intrigue you. If you've ever wanted to write a novel or book, this would be a good time to start.

On April 25 and April 29, Pluto and then Saturn turn retrograde in Capricorn. Pluto's retro lasts until October 3, and during this time, your shadow side may emerge more strongly. For you, this could entail greater indecisiveness as your head and your heart battle it out or a tendency to become possessive in a romantic relationship. But you'll have signs to guide you away from this kind of behavior.

Saturn's retro period lasts until September 18. These months may be introspective in the sense that you'll be scrutinizing the kind of structures you have built—with friends, family, finances, career and your partner and kids. You'll be able to see how certain areas need bolstering and how others aren't worth your time and effort.

Before the retrogrades begin, there's a new moon in Aries on April 5. This one should bring a new financial opportunity of some kind. You might strike out on your own in some capacity, for example, or perhaps a hobby now becomes a commercial commodity.

On the 17th, Mercury enters Aries and on the 20th, Venus follows. These two planets travel together until May 6, when Mercury changes signs. The Venus transit lasts until May 15. Your intellect is focused on making more money or bringing in a new source of income, and Venus is the facilitator that enables you to do this. With Venus in your financial area, your expenses may rise, but so does your income, and you have the means to meet the expenses. When any planet transits Aries, there's a restless, trailblazing component to it. Any romance that begins during these transits will stoke your passions.

The full moon in Libra on April 19 highlights resources you share with others—a partner, child, parent or roommate. News you hear about finances generally should be quite favorable, thanks to a friendly beam from Jupiter and from Pluto.

AT A GLANCE
April 5—New moon in Aries
April 10—Jupiter turns retrograde in Sagittarius
April 17—Mercury enters Aries
April 19—Full moon in Libra
April 20—Venus enters Aries
April 25—Pluto turns retrograde in Capricorn
April 29—Saturn turns retrograde in Capricorn

May 2019
Ideal

You'll enjoy May. Most of the transits are in signs compatible with yours and so are the new and full moon.

On May 4, the new moon in earth sign Taurus may bring an uptick in your finances. A communication opportunity of some kind may surface, too. It could be a freelance job that involves writing or teaching, perhaps as part of a team, or maybe you finally get going on that book you want to write. Neptune is friendly to this new moon, so whatever unfolds could have a spiritual or artistic component to it.

Between May 6 and 21, Mercury transits Taurus. You feel on solid ground during these few weeks, focused and intent on completing something you've started. You're able to make the abstract tangible and practical. This transit favors any kind of work that requires patience and diligence. From May 21 to June 4, Mercury transits Gemini, a sign it rules. Mercury is happy in this sign and is likely to stir up laughter and great discussions while it's moving through the home/family section of your chart. If you have kids, your place becomes the hub of activity and networking.

May 15 features two transits: Venus enters Taurus, and Mars enters Cancer and the creativity/romance section of your chart. The first transit lasts until June 8, and because Venus rules this sign, it functions at optimum capacity. Your aesthetic sensibilities deepen, and your sensuality is heightened. Taurus enjoys beauty, and you may feel compelled to start a garden or spiff up your home or neighborhood in some way. You get along well with siblings and neighbors, and overall, feel good during this transit.

The Mars transit through fellow water sign Cancer from May 15 to July 1 revs up your love life and stirs your muse into action. Your intuition is greatly heightened during this transit, and if you listen to that soft inner voice, you won't make a wrong move. Your capacity for enjoyment, particularly with your family, expands. It's a good idea to dive into any creative endeavor about which you're passionate.

The full moon in fellow water sign Scorpio on May 18 highlights that part of your chart that rules the higher mind—your worldview and deeper spiritual and philosophic beliefs, higher education and international travel. Thanks to a friendly beam from Pluto, news you hear about any of these areas is profound and powerful.

AT A GLANCE
May 4—New moon in Taurus
May 6—Mercury enters Taurus
May 15—Venus goes into Taurus, Mars enters Cancer
May 18—Full moon in Scorpio
May 21—Mercury goes into Gemini

June 2019
Kick back & relax

For the most part, June is a laid-back month. The only possible glitch is when Neptune turns retrograde on June 20. You may feel somewhat disoriented then and for the first several days after the retro begins. But because it doesn't turn direct again until November 27, your energy will adjust to it. You may notice, though, that it's more difficult to gloss over stuff you don't want to deal with at the moment. Think of this retro as a reality check.

If you're planning the family's summer vacation, then the day to do it is on June 3, when the new moon in Gemini brings in new opportunities for your family/home. Unless your kids are very young, engage the entire family in the decision about where to go this year. If you have been going to the same areas year after year, be more adventurous now and choose a spot where none of you have been. Just don't travel between July 7–31, when Mercury will be retrograde for the second time this year.

Mercury enters Cancer on June 4 and travels with Mars until June 26. This period should be terrific, with an ebb and flow that suits you. You and your partner are able to discuss things openly, and at times, you're so in tune with each other you complete each other's thoughts and sentences. The telepathic connection is powerful. Your creative drive is strong now, too, and you may be indulging it frequently.

Between June 8 and July 3, Venus transits Gemini, in the home and family section of your chart. This period would be ideal for that family vacation. You're all in sociable moods and eager to explore some place new. Conversations are spirited, information is exchanged freely and eagerly and really, what's not to like about any of it?

On June 17, the full moon in Sagittarius highlights your career area. You may hear that your book or novel has sold, that you're being sent overseas for a conference or workshop or to work with foreign clients or that you're being promoted. Whatever the news, it's positive, and you have retrograde Jupiter to thank for that.

Mercury enters fire sign Leo on June 26, and from then until July 7, when it turns retrograde, your focus is on your daily work and the way you maintain your health. Your thoughts are especially dramatic now, and if you work in the arts, this flair serves you well. But regardless of where you work or what you do to earn your daily bread, allow your innate creativity to shine.

AT A GLANCE
June 3—New moon in Gemini
June 4—Mercury enters into Cancer
June 8—Venus goes into Gemini
June 17—Full moon in Sagittarius
June 20—Neptune turns retrograde
June 26—Mercury enters Leo

July 2019
New opportunities

Months that feature eclipses can be exciting or tense. It depends on the issues that surface and where the eclipse falls in your chart. The solar eclipse in Cancer on July 2 should be positive for you. Opportunities surface in romance and in your creative endeavors. You could meet your soul mate, your company is featured prominently in social media or your novel or book sells. Thanks to a friendly beam from Uranus, these opportunities surface suddenly, and you just have to be ready to seize them.

The lunar eclipse in Capricorn on July 16 may prompt you to recognize that the work you do isn't your passion. Perhaps you've known this for some time, but just didn't want to acknowledge it. You may feel that your creative talents are "eclipsed" by the work you're doing. The good news is that the realization urges you to take steps to rectify the situation. Start sending out resumes or figuring how out you can do what you love. It's also possible that you recognize the truth about a particular friendship, that the person isn't who you thought.

Mars enters Leo on July 1 and from then until August 18, you're a spinning dervish of action and forward momentum. You meet deadlines, sign up new clients, pitch ideas, make submissions, hire new employees and land auditions. From July 27 to August 18, Mars and Venus travel together, and whenever the cosmic lovers do that, it's terrific for your love life and your creative drive. But before Venus enters Leo, it transits Cancer from July 3–27, marking one of the most romantic and creative times for you all year. During these few weeks, you're more self-confident and optimistic. Your magnetism attracts the right people at the right time. Your partner is especially attentive, and your relationship with your kids is smoother. Life generally feels good, and you're pleased with where you are and where you're headed.

Mercury's retrograde begins on July 7 in Leo, and yes, things will slow down between then and July 31, when it turns direct in Cancer. Look over the section in the introduction on Mercury retrograde and follow the suggestions for navigating this period without losing your mind! Since it occurs in your work area, be particularly diligent about following directions, being on time and communicating clearly. If you're self-employed, work with the clients and projects you have.

On July 31, Mercury turns direct in Cancer, and there's a new moon in Leo. You know what to do now that Mercury is direct—everything that was placed on a back burner during the retrograde! This new moon is one to anticipate. Thanks to Venus's close conjunction, you can expect new romance, a new job, a new boss and perhaps even a promotion.

July 1—Mars goes into Leo
July 2—Solar eclipse in Cancer
July 3—Venus enters Cancer
July 7—Mercury turns retrograde in Leo
July 16—Lunar eclipse in Capricorn
July 27—Venus enters Leo
July 31—Mercury turns direct, new moon in Leo

August 2019
Partnership emphasis

The latter half of this month is all about earth sign Virgo, your opposite sign. It means your emphasis will be on partnerships, communication and connecting the dots. But let's take a look first at what happens earlier in August.

On August 11, Jupiter turns direct in Sagittarius—your career area—and Mercury enters Leo again. Jupiter's motion is a welcome event. It means its expansiveness now extends into the outer world once again, enhancing your professional growth. Between now and December 2, when Jupiter enters Capricorn, you can expect new career opportunities to pop up. So set your sights and your intentions, make your career wish list and then step aside and let the universe make it all happen.

Once Mercury enters Leo again on the 11th, it travels with Venus until the 21st, and your focus is very much on how to integrate your creative talents more readily into your daily work. An office flirtation could turn into a romance and will prove to be dramatic and passionate, with emotional highs and lows.

Uranus turns retrograde in Taurus on August 12 and that takes you into the new year, to January 6. During these months you may be more restless than usual and have a greater need for freedom and independence in your daily life. To people around you, your behavior may seem erratic and confusing at times, but don't worry about it. You're discovering your outermost boundaries, delving into new interests and exploring new ideas.

The full moon in Aquarius on August 15 enjoys a wide conjunction with Jupiter and that means growth and expansion for you. Since this moon occurs in the area of your chart that rules your personal unconscious, you may have an epiphany about an issue or relationship that you haven't understood.

Now we arrive at the Virgo part of the month. On August 18, Mars enters Virgo, followed by Venus on the 21st, Mercury on the 29th and a new moon in Virgo on the 30th. The Mars transit ends on October 4, and during these weeks, you're able to bring people and details together so that a business deal culminates. You and your romantic partner may be sparring over small things. It may not be due to problems in the relationship so much as Virgo's tendency to nitpick and criticize. Avoid that!

Once Venus joins Mars, the cosmic lovers are together once again, and your love life, sex life and creative life improve. Venus also facilities dealings with business partners and with communication generally. When Mercury joins Venus and Mars, things really get interesting. You're able to take abstract and complex ideas and connect them in a way that others understand. These transits favor writing, learning and teaching. Mercury and Venus both change signs on September 14.

The new moon in Virgo on August 30 brings in a sudden opportunity to team up with someone who provides a terrific balance for your imagination and intuition. What you can imagine, this person can make real. What you can intuit and sense, this person can grasp logically. Right brain, left brain.

AT A GLANCE
August 11—Jupiter turns direct, Mercury enters Leo
August 12—Uranus turns retrograde
August 15—Full moon in Aquarius
August 18—Mars enters Virgo
August 21—Venus goes into Virgo
August 29—Mercury enters Virgo
August 30—New moon in Virgo

September 2019
News

This month's emphasis is on air sign Libra—relationships, legal matters and resources you share with others. There's also a full moon in your sign, and that one should be a beauty.

September 14 features three astrological events: Mercury and Venus enter Libra, and there's that full moon in your sign. The Mercury transit ends on October 3, and the Venus transit ends on October 8, so these two planets spend quite a bit of time together this month. Your conscious focus is relationships, particularly with people to whom you are the closest. You become aware of the importance of balance—that you shouldn't be the one who constantly bends over backward to accommodate others. If you're involved in any legal matters, things should shake out in your favor. In terms of romance and creativity, Venus also rises to the occasion. It rules Libra, so it's happy here and does its best to keep things moving smoothly.

Your psychic antenna is apt to be quite active because of the full moon in your sign on the same day the Mercury and Venus transits begin, and it's wise to heed whatever your gut tells you. With both Jupiter and retrograde Pluto forming beneficial angles to this full moon, any news you hear should be positive and have a profound impact.

On the 18th, Saturn turns direct in Capricorn. You now have a much clearer picture of the various structures in your life and know which ones work, which ones need bolstering and which ones you may have to release.

On the 29th, the new moon in Libra could bring a raise for your partner and an increase in income from an insurance rebate, a refinancing of your home for a better interest rate, royalties or repayment of a loan.

AT A GLANCE
September 14—Mercury and Venus enter Libra, full moon in Pisces
September 18—Saturn turns direct in Capricorn
September 29—New moon in Libra

October 2019
Diverse

For the most part, October is a wild mix of energies, some that are terrific for you, others that may challenge you. Let's get the bad news out of the way first. The Mercury retrograde that begins on October 31 is in fellow water sign Scorpio. By now, you know the drill for these retrogrades. But here are the reminders: sign contracts before the retro starts or after it ends on November 20. Make your travel plans now for travel on either side those dates. Pitch your ideas and submit manuscripts, resumes and portfolios. Read over the Mercury retrograde sections in the introduction, and follow the general guidelines for getting through this period with less stress and worry.

Mercury enters Scorpio on October 3, and your conscious awareness turns to the deeper part of life, an area with which you are intimately familiar. Psychic and synchronistic experiences may occur frequently during this transit—ghosts, past life memories, vivid dreams, out of body experiences or spirit communication. Any or all of these things can happen with Mercury in Scorpio. Your intuition deepens, and you're able to size up people within moments of meeting them. You usually can do this on your own, on any given day, but often doubt your impressions. With this transit, you won't have any doubt. If you're a writer, this transit urges you to dig deeply within yourself and write from the inside out.

Also on October 3, Pluto turns direct in Capricorn. If you've resolved the shadow elements in your personality, great. If not, the shadow retreats to a back room, and you can bolt the door and be done with it for a while. Now Pluto is its most powerful self, attracting people whose knowledge and insights help you to achieve what you desire.

Between October 4 and November 19, Mars transits Libra and travels for several days with Venus. The chemistry with the one you love is strong and powerful during the four days before Venus enters Scorpio. Enjoy it, and create memories from it. Once Mars travels alone in Libra, you're networking, blogging and using social media to connect with others. If you're looking for better health care insurance, mortgage rates and royalty cuts, this transit facilitates your search.

Venus transits Scorpio from October 8 to November 1 and travels with Mercury. With your mind and your heart in the same place, you may feel somewhat overwhelmed at times by the emotional and mental intensity of Scorpio, but by pacing yourself and disengaging from negative people, you do just fine. It's an ideal time to enjoy your sexuality and creativity and to allow your psychic ability to shine. Any romantic relationships that begin during this transit will be passionate and emotional and could be a soul connection.

The full moon in Aries on October 13 highlights your finances and values. With Jupiter so friendly to this moon, any news you hear will be positive and lead to growth and expansion. If you've been job hunting, this full moon could bring the job that pays you more for doing something you enjoy.

October 27 features a new moon in Scorpio, and thanks to a close angle from Uranus, the opportunities that unfold will be sudden and unforeseen. You might have a chance to travel overseas, your book or novel could sell or you may be invited to teach a workshop or seminar.

Then, on Halloween, Mercury turns retro in Scorpio, and things slow down.

AT A GLANCE
October 3—Mercury goes into Scorpio, Pluto turns direct
October 4—Mars enters Libra
October 8—Venus goes into Scorpio
October 13—Full moon in Aries
October 27—New moon in Scorpio
October 31—Mercury turns retrograde

November 2019
Moments that shine

It's another mixed month, but there are also some nice gems for you, Pisces. On November 1, Venus enters Sagittarius and your career area, and what a terrific transit this should be! Until the 25th, you're the apple of everyone's eye at work. You land a promotion and raise, learn that you'll be traveling internationally for work or that your company or office are moving. Sagittarius rules the publishing industry, and if you're interested in working in that field, then this transit could make it happen. You feel confident about your skills and talents, and others sense it and come to you for insights and answers.

If a romance beings during this transit, it will be with someone you meet through your profession or who is part of your work world. Your creative drive is strong now, and you're able to grasp the larger picture of whatever you're working on.

From November 25 to December 20, Venus transits compatible earth sign Capricorn, and your social calendar quickly fills up. Most people are in festive moods around the holidays, so this transit is perfect for hanging out with friends, networking and generally enjoying yourself. Since the transit is in ambitious Capricorn, it favors your professional activities, too.

The full moon in Taurus on November 12 should be a beauty! All communications are highlighted. There could be unexpected news about a writing or teaching project, and the news looks good. Thanks to beneficial angles from Saturn and Pluto and from your ruler, Neptune, the news has a long-lasting impact and could involve some facet of the arts.

From November 19 to January 4, 2020, Mars transits Scorpio, a sign it co-rules. During this period, you're highly motivated to explore hidden terrains—ghosts, past lives, communication with the dead or psychic phenomena—and to expand your general knowledge about spiritual traditions and other cultures. You may be traveling abroad on a quest of some kind, perhaps with a small group of like-minded individuals. You might be taking a workshop or course in an area that interests you.

Mars finally turns direct on November 20, just in time for the Thanksgiving holidays. Now you can get busy doing whatever you delayed during the retrograde.

The new moon in Sagittarius on November 26 highlights your career area. Here come the promotion and raise, Pisces, and an acknowledgment from your boss that your work and creativity are greatly appreciated.

When Neptune turns direct on November 27, you undoubtedly feel it, a kind of inward relief. Now you can move forward again, confident that your creative endeavors are born within your higher mind rather than from your ego.

AT A GLANCE
November 1—Venus goes into Sagittarius
November 12—Full moon in Taurus
November 19—Mars enters Scorpio
November 20—Mercury turns direct
November 25—Venus enters Capricorn
November 26—New moon in Sagittarius
November 27—Neptune turns direct

December 2019
Onward

After thirteen months in Aries, Jupiter enters Capricorn on December 2 and stays there until December 20, 2020. What can you expect? Plenty of positive experiences, growth and expansion. Take a look at your natal chart to see where Capricorn falls. That area will be the one where you experience the greatest growth. Regardless of its exact place, though, it forms a beneficial angle to your sun for more than a year, and that aspect brings a greater optimism and self-expression, expansion in your career and personal life and perhaps increased prosperity as well. You feel so upbeat about your life that it's easier to achieve what you desire.

From December 9 to 29, Mercury transits Sagittarius and your career area, an ideal spot for office parties, gift-exchanges with co-workers and just generally enjoying yourself. You should be able to clear off your desk before the end of the year, and once Mercury enters Capricorn on December 29, it carries you into the new year with new resolve and clear goals. It lasts until January 17, 2020.

The full moon in Gemini on December 12 highlights your home and family life. You're gearing up for the holidays, and there may be some confusing news about who is staying at your place. Once you have the full details, you'll be able to adjust your plans accordingly.

From December 20 to January 14, 2020, Venus transits Aquarius. You're planting seeds for Venus's transit into your sign early in the new year, an event to anticipate, and you're doing it by exploring your own psyche. What motivates you? How can you integrate your creative skills more fully into your daily life? What insights and information do your dreams hold?

The solar eclipse in Capricorn on December 26 ushers in new friendships, new career opportunities and new ways to achieve your wishes and dreams. With Jupiter closely conjunct, these opportunities broaden and expand your life.

AT A GLANCE
December 2—Jupiter enters Capricorn
December 9—Mercury enters Sagittarius
December 12—Full moon in Gemini
December 20—Venus goes into Aquarius
December 26—Solar eclipse in Capricorn
December 29—Mercury enters into Capricorn

Reflection
How did the year unfold for you? Did your spirituality change? Your core beliefs? What pivotal events did you experience? Are you happier and more prosperous? What, if anything, would change about this year? Jot your thoughts below.

_____
_____
_____
_____
_____

Happy New Year!

Acknowledgments

I'd like to thank Al Zuckerman, my terrific agent, and both Will Kiester and Sarah Monroe.

About the Author

Trish MacGregor has been a professional astrologer and writer for more than thirty years. She's the author of several dozen astrology books and, for a decade, she and her husband, Rob, co-authored the Sydney Omarr series of astrology books. Her most recent astrology book is *Unlocking the Secrets to Scorpios.* She has also written on dreams, the tarot and synchronicity.

As TJ MacGregor, she is the author of 40 novels that have been translated into fifteen languages. She won an Edgar Allan Poe Award for her novel *Out of Sight.*

Trish lives in South Florida with her husband and daughter, Megan, along with a noble golden retriever and two cats. She can be contacted at: blog.synchrosecrets.com.

Index

A

air element, 13

April

  Aquarius

    in 2017, 159–160

    in 2018, 321

    in 2019, 486–487

  Aries

    in 2017, 26–27

    in 2018, 189–190

    in 2019, 350–351

  Cancer

    in 2017, 66–67

    in 2018, 228–229

    in 2019, 391–392

  Capricorn

    in 2017, 145–146

    in 2018, 307

    in 2019, 472–473

  Gemini

    in 2017, 53–54

    in 2018, 216

    in 2019, 377–378

  Leo

    in 2017, 79–80

    in 2018, 241–242

    in 2019, 405–406

  Libra

    in 2017, 105–106

    in 2018, 267

    in 2019, 432–433

  Pisces

    in 2017, 172–174

    in 2018, 334

    in 2019, 500–501

  Sagittarius

    in 2017, 132–133

    in 2018, 294

    in 2019, 459–460

  Scorpio

    in 2017, 119–120

    in 2018, 280

    in 2019, 446–447

  Taurus

    in 2017, 40–41

    in 2018, 203–204

    in 2019, 363–364

  Virgo

    in 2017, 92–93

    in 2018, 254

    in 2019, 418–419

Aquarius, generally

  air element, 13

  characteristics of, 12

  fixed modality, 13

  Neptune and, 14

  Pluto and, 14

  symbol, dates, and

    archetype theme of, 10

  Uranus and, 15

Aquarius, in 2017, 155–169

  January, 156

  February, 157

  March, 158

  April, 159–160

  May, 160

  June, 161–162

  July, 162–163

  August, 163–164

  September, 164–165

  October, 165–166

  November, 166–167

  December, 167–168

Aquarius, in 2018, 317–330

  January, 317–318

  February, 318–319

  March, 319–321

  April, 321

  May, 322–323

  June, 323–324

  July, 324–325

  August, 325

  September, 326–327

  October, 327–328

  November, 328–329

  December, 329–330

Aquarius, in 2019, 482–496

  January, 482–483

  February, 483–484

  March, 485–486

  April, 486–487

  May, 487–488

  June, 488–489

  July, 489–490

  August, 490–491

  September, 492

  October, 492–493

  November, 493–494

  December, 495

archetype themes, of sun

  signs, 10

Aries, generally

  cardinal modality, 13

  characteristics of, 10

  fire element, 12

  Mars and, 14, 23

  symbol, dates, and

    archetype theme of, 10

Aries, in 2017, 23–36

  January, 23–24

  February, 24–25

  March, 25–26

  April, 26–27

  May, 27–28

  June, 28–29

July, 30
August, 31–32
September, 32–33
October, 33–34
November, 34–35
December, 35–36
Aries, in 2018, 186–199
    January, 186–187
    February, 187–188
    March, 188–189
    April, 189–190
    May, 190–191
    June, 192
    July, 193
    August, 194
    September, 195
    October, 196
    November, 197–198
    December, 198
Aries, in 2019, 346–359
    January, 346–347
    February, 348
    March, 348–349
    April, 350–351
    May, 351–352
    June, 352–353
    July, 353–354
    August, 354–355
    September, 355
    October, 356
    November, 357–358
    December, 358–359
ascendant. *See* houses and
    rising signs
August
    Aquarius
        in 2017, 163–164
        in 2018, 325
        in 2019, 490–491
    Aries
        in 2017, 31–32
        in 2018, 194

        in 2019, 354–355
Cancer
    in 2017, 70–71
    in 2018, 232–233
    in 2019, 395–396
Capricorn
    in 2017, 149–150
    in 2018, 311–312
    in 2019, 476–477
Gemini
    in 2017, 57–58
    in 2018, 220–221
    in 2019, 382–383
Leo
    in 2017, 83–84
    in 2018, 245–246
    in 2019, 409–410
Libra
    in 2017, 110
    in 2018, 271–272
    in 2019, 436–437
Pisces
    in 2017, 177–178
    in 2018, 338
    in 2019, 505–506
Sagittarius
    in 2017, 136–137
    in 2018, 298
    in 2019, 463–464
Scorpio
    in 2017, 123–124
    in 2018, 284–285
    in 2019, 450–451
Taurus
    in 2017, 44–45
    in 2018, 207–208
    in 2019, 368–369
Virgo
    in 2017, 96–97
    in 2018, 258–259
    in 2019, 422–424

C
Cancer, generally
    cardinal modality, 13
    characteristics of, 11
    Moon and, 14
    symbol, dates, and
        archetype theme of, 10
    water element and, 13
Cancer, in 2017, 62–75
    January, 63
    February, 64–65
    March, 65–66
    April, 66–67
    May, 67
    June, 68–69
    July, 69–70
    August, 70–71
    September, 71–72
    October, 72–73
    November, 73–74
    December, 74–75
Cancer, in 2018, 225–237
    January, 225–226
    February, 226–227
    March, 227–228
    April, 228–229
    May, 229–230
    June, 230–231
    July, 231–232
    August, 232–233
    September, 233–234
    October, 234–235
    November, 235–236
    December, 236–237
Cancer, in 2019, 387–400
    January, 387–388
    February, 389
    March, 390–391
    April, 391–392
    May, 392–393
    June, 393–394
    July, 394–395

August, 395–396
September, 396–397
October, 397–398
November, 398–399
December, 399–400
Capricorn, generally
cardinal modality, 13
characteristics of, 11
earth element, 12
Pluto and, 14
Saturn and, 15
symbol, dates, and
archetype theme of, 10
Capricorn, in 2017, 142–155
January, 142–143
February, 143–144
March, 144–145
April, 145–146
May, 147
June, 147–148
July, 148–149
August, 149–150
September, 150–151
October, 152
November, 153
December, 154–155
Capricorn, in 2018, 303–316
January, 304
February, 305
March, 305–306
April, 307
May, 307–309
June, 309–310
July, 310–311
August, 311–312
September, 312–313
October, 313–314
November, 314–315
December, 315–316
Capricorn, in 2019, 468–481
January, 469–470
February, 470–471
March, 471–472

April, 472–473
May, 472–474
June, 474–475
July, 475–476
August, 476–477
September, 477–478
October, 478–479
November, 479–480
December, 480–481
cardinal modality, of sun
signs, 13
career. See professional life
communication skills
Aquarius
in 2017, 156, 158,
159–160, 162–163,
167–168
in 2018, 319–323,
325, 327–329
in 2019, 482–483,
485–487, 490–491
Aries
in 2017, 27–28, 30,
35–36
in 2018, 190–191,
192, 193, 195, 198
in 2019, 346–351,
358–359
Cancer
in 2017, 65–72
in 2018, 227–228,
230–234
in 2019, 389, 391–
394, 397–398
Capricorn
in 2017, 142–146
in 2018, 305–309,
314–315
in 2019, 470–474,
476–477, 478–479
Gemini
in 2017, 50–51,
53–54, 56–57

in 2018, 218–224
in 2019, 374–383,
386
Leo
in 2017, 76–77,
79–80, 82–87
in 2018, 240–241,
244–245, 247–248
in 2019, 403–406,
410–412
Libra
in 2017, 105–106,
107, 110, 111, 114
in 2018, 263–264,
268–275
in 2019, 429–430,
433–437, 438,
440–441
Pisces
in 2017, 172,
173–174, 180
in 2018, 332–337,
340, 341, 342
in 2019, 499–500,
505–506, 508–509
Sagittarius
in 2017, 129–138,
140–141
in 2018, 292, 294–
297, 298, 301–302
in 2019, 457–459,
461–462, 467–468
Scorpio
in 2017, 119–125
in 2018, 276–279,
282–288, 289
in 2019, 443,
447–451, 454
Taurus
in 2017, 37–39,
42–43
in 2018, 203–204,
208–212

in 2019, 362–367
Virgo
  in 2017, 93–94,
    97–101
  in 2018, 252–260,
    262
  in 2019, 420–426
creativity
Aquarius
  in 2017, 156, 162–
    165, 167–168
  in 2018, 317–319,
    321, 322–327
  in 2019, 482–483,
    485–486, 492–493
Aries
  in 2017, 24–25, 30,
    31–32
  in 2018, 187–190,
    192, 193, 194
  in 2019, 348–349,
    351–355, 357–358
Cancer
  in 2017, 66–67,
    72–74
  in 2018, 226–237
  in 2019, 387–388,
    389, 394–397
Capricorn
  in 2017, 143–150
  in 2018, 305–314
  in 2019, 469–471,
    475–477
Gemini
  in 2017, 50–52,
    55–56, 59–60
  in 2018, 214, 216,
    220–221, 223–224
  in 2019, 374–377,
    380–381, 383
Leo
  in 2017, 80–81, 87
  in 2018, 238–249

in 2019, 401–402,
    406–414
Libra
  in 2017, 103–109,
    112, 113
  in 2018, 263–266,
    269–275
  in 2019, 430–431,
    434–435, 440
Pisces
  in 2017, 170,
    173–176
  in 2018, 332, 335–
    338, 339, 341
  in 2019, 500–501,
    505–508
Sagittarius
  in 2017, 129–134,
    138–141
  in 2018, 292–296,
    299, 300, 301–302
  in 2019, 456,
    457–464
Scorpio
  in 2017, 115–117,
    121–122, 125–128
  in 2018, 278–279,
    283–288, 289
  in 2019, 444,
    445–446, 448
Taurus
  in 2017, 38–40,
    43–46
  in 2018, 202–204,
    206–209
  in 2019, 360–372
Virgo
  in 2017, 88–89,
    91–92, 95–96,
    100–101
  in 2018, 250–261
  in 2019, 415–419,
    421–428

D
date ranges, of sun signs, 10
December
Aquarius
  in 2017, 167–168
  in 2018, 329–330
  in 2019, 495
Aries
  in 2017, 35–36
  in 2018, 198
  in 2019, 358–359
Cancer
  in 2017, 74–75
  in 2018, 236–237
  in 2019, 399–400
Capricorn
  in 2017, 154–155
  in 2018, 315–316
  in 2019, 480–481
Gemini
  in 2017, 61–62
  in 2018, 224
  in 2019, 386
Leo
  in 2017, 87
  in 2018, 249
  in 2019, 413–414
Libra
  in 2017, 114
  in 2018, 275
  in 2019, 440–441
Pisces
  in 2017, 181–182
  in 2018, 342
  in 2019, 509–510
Sagittarius
  in 2017, 140–141
  in 2018, 302
  in 2019, 467–468
Scorpio
  in 2017, 127–128
  in 2018, 289
  in 2019, 454

Taurus
in 2017, 48–49
in 2018, 211–212
in 2019, 372–373
Virgo
in 2017, 100–101
in 2018, 262
in 2019, 427–428

E
earth element, sun signs of,
12
eclipses. *See* lunar eclipses;
solar eclipses
E-Cubed (Grout), 94
eighth house
(transformation), 18
elements, of sun signs, 12–13
eleventh house (ideals and
dreams), 19

F
February
Aquarius
in 2017, 157
in 2018, 318–319
in 2019, 483–484
Aries
in 2017, 24–25
in 2018, 187–188
in 2019, 348
Cancer
in 2017, 64–65
in 2018, 226–227
in 2019, 389
Capricorn
in 2017, 143–144
in 2018, 305
in 2019, 470–471
Gemini
in 2017, 51–52
in 2018, 214
in 2019, 375–376

Leo
in 2017, 76–77
in 2018, 239
in 2019, 402–403
Libra
in 2017, 103–104
in 2018, 265
in 2019, 430–431
Pisces
in 2017, 171
in 2018, 332
in 2019, 498–499
Sagittarius
in 2017, 130–131
in 2018, 292
in 2019, 457
Scorpio
in 2017, 116–117
in 2018, 278
in 2019, 444
Taurus
in 2017, 38–39
in 2018, 201
in 2019, 361–362
Virgo
in 2017, 90–91
in 2018, 252
in 2019, 416–417
fifth house (children and
creativity), 17
finances
Aquarius
in 2017, 156, 158,
163–165
in 2018, 318–321,
324–329
in 2019, 483–486,
488–491, 492
Aries
in 2017, 23–29,
33–35
in 2018, 188–191,
193, 196, 198

in 2019, 348–349,
351–355, 356,
357–358
Cancer
in 2017, 63, 66–67,
69–75
in 2018, 225–235
in 2019, 387–388,
389, 390–391,
393–396, 399–400
Capricorn
in 2017, 142–145,
148–150
in 2018, 304,
307–313
in 2019, 469–472,
476–477, 479–481
Gemini
in 2017, 50–53,
55–56, 60
in 2018, 213,
214–221, 224
in 2019, 374–376,
378–381, 385, 386
Leo
in 2017, 76, 78–80,
83–86
in 2018, 238–248
in 2019, 402–406,
409–410
Libra
in 2017, 104–108,
112, 113, 114
in 2018, 265–271,
273–275
in 2019, 431–434,
438–439, 440
Pisces
in 2017, 171, 172,
173–176, 178–180
in 2018, 332–336,
338, 339, 340, 341,
342

in 2019, 497–501,
502, 506–508
Sagittarius
in 2017, 129–130,
132–136, 139–144
in 2018, 290–297,
299, 300, 302
in 2019, 456, 457–
463, 464, 465–468
Scorpio
in 2017, 115–116,
119–124, 126–128
in 2018, 276–277,
280–283, 286–288,
289
in 2019, 443, 444,
447–448, 450–451,
453–454
Taurus
in 2017, 37–44,
47–49
in 2018, 203–206,
209–212
in 2019, 360–366,
371–373
Virgo
in 2017, 88–94,
97–101
in 2018, 252–253,
254, 258–262
in 2019, 415–419,
421–422, 424,
425–427
fire elements, sun signs of, 12
first house (personality), 16
cusp, 15, 16
fixed modality, of sun signs,
13
fourth house (roots), 17
IC cusp, 15, 16

G
Gemini, generally
air element, 13
characteristics of, 11
Mercury and, 14
mutable modality, 13
symbol, dates, and
archetype theme of, 10
Gemini, in 2017, 50–62
January, 50–51
February, 51–52
March, 52–53
April, 53–54
May, 54–55
June, 55–56
July, 56–57
August, 57–58
September, 58–59
October, 59–60
November, 60
December, 61–62
Gemini, in 2018, 212–225
January, 213–214
February, 214
March, 214–216
April, 216
May, 217–218
June, 218–219
July, 219–220
August, 220–221
September, 221–222
October, 222–223
November, 223–224
December, 224
Gemini, in 2019, 373–387
January, 374–375
February, 375–376
March, 376–377
April, 377–378
May, 378–379
June, 379–380
July, 380–381

August, 382–383
September, 383
October, 384
November, 385
December, 386
Grout, Pam, 94

H
home and family life
Aquarius
in 2017, 158,
159–160
in 2018, 322–325,
328–330
in 2019, 483–484,
487–490, 493–494
Aries
in 2017, 28–29, 30
in 2018, 190–191,
192
in 2019, 351–354
Cancer
in 2017, 64–67,
68–69, 71–73
in 2018, 232–236
in 2019, 390–392,
396–398
Capricorn
in 2017, 142–146,
150–151, 152
in 2018, 305–313
in 2019, 469–470,
472–473, 478–481
Gemini
in 2017, 57–59
in 2018, 214–216,
219–220
in 2019, 382–383
Leo
in 2017, 80–82,
85–87

in 2018, 241–242,
244–249
in 2019, 406–407,
411–413
Libra
in 2017, 102–103,
108–109, 114
in 2018, 263–266,
267, 272–274
in 2019, 429–433,
440–441
Pisces
in 2017, 173–174,
181–182
in 2018, 336–337
in 2019, 499–500,
503, 509–510
Sagittarius
in 2017, 129–130,
132–135, 137–138
in 2018, 290–293,
298, 301–302
in 2019, 457–459,
462–463, 464
Scorpio
in 2017, 115–117,
121–123, 127–128
in 2018, 276–277,
280–281, 283–284
in 2019, 443, 444,
445–446, 449–451,
454
Taurus
in 2017, 43–44
in 2018, 204–208
in 2019, 365–369
Virgo
in 2017, 92–100
in 2018, 259–261,
262
in 2019, 415–416,
418–421, 426–428

houses and rising signs
basics and critical angles
of, 15–16
meanings of, 16–19

I

Internet resources
birth chart, 15
natal chart, 19

J

January
Aquarius
in 2017, 156
in 2018, 317–318
in 2019, 482–483
Aries
in 2017, 23–24
in 2018, 186–187
in 2019, 346–347
Cancer
in 2017, 63
in 2018, 225–226
in 2019, 387–388
Capricorn
in 2017, 142–143
in 2018, 304
in 2019, 469–470
Gemini
in 2017, 50–51
in 2018, 213–214
in 2019, 374–375
Leo
in 2017, 76
in 2018, 238–239
in 2019, 401–402
Libra
in 2017, 102–103
in 2018, 263–264
in 2019, 429–430
Pisces
in 2017, 170
in 2018, 331–332

in 2019, 497–498
Sagittarius
in 2017, 129–130
in 2018, 290–291
in 2019, 456
Scorpio
in 2017, 115–116
in 2018, 276–277
in 2019, 443
Taurus
in 2017, 37–38
in 2018, 200–201
in 2019, 360–361
Virgo
in 2017, 88–89
in 2018, 250–251
in 2019, 415–416
July
Aquarius
in 2017, 162–163
in 2018, 324–325
in 2019, 489–490
Aries
in 2017, 30
in 2018, 193
in 2019, 353–354
Cancer
in 2017, 69–70
in 2018, 231–232
in 2019, 394–395
Capricorn
in 2017, 148–149
in 2018, 310–311
in 2019, 475–476
Gemini
in 2017, 56–57
in 2018, 219–220
in 2019, 380–381
Leo
in 2017, 82–83
in 2018, 244–245
in 2019, 408–409

Libra
    in 2017, 108–109
    in 2018, 270–271
    in 2019, 435–436
Pisces
    in 2017, 176–177
    in 2018, 337–338
    in 2019, 504–505
Sagittarius
    in 2017, 135–136
    in 2018, 297–298
    in 2019, 462–463
Scorpio
    in 2017, 122–123
    in 2018, 283–284
    in 2019, 449–450
Taurus
    in 2017, 43–44
    in 2018, 206–207
    in 2019, 366–367
Virgo
    in 2017, 95–96
    in 2018, 257–258
    in 2019, 421–422
June
  Aquarius
    in 2017, 161–162
    in 2018, 323–324
    in 2019, 488–489
  Aries
    in 2017, 28–29
    in 2018, 192
    in 2019, 352–353
  Cancer
    in 2017, 68–69
    in 2018, 230–231
    in 2019, 393–394
  Capricorn
    in 2017, 147–148
    in 2018, 309–310
    in 2019, 474–475
  Gemini
    in 2017, 55–56

in 2018, 218–219
in 2019, 379–380
Leo
  in 2017, 81–82
  in 2018, 243–244
  in 2019, 407–408
Libra
  in 2017, 107–108
  in 2018, 269–270
  in 2019, 434–435
Pisces
  in 2017, 175–176
  in 2018, 336–337
  in 2019, 503
Sagittarius
  in 2017, 134–135
  in 2018, 296–297
  in 2019, 461–462
Scorpio
  in 2017, 121–122
  in 2018, 282–283
  in 2019, 448
Taurus
  in 2017, 42–43
  in 2018, 205–206
  in 2019, 365–366
Virgo
  in 2017, 94–95
  in 2018, 256–257
  in 2019, 420–421
Jung, Carl, 111, 116, 363, 378
Jupiter
  length of transit of signs, 14
  signs ruled by, 14

L
Leo, generally
  characteristics of, 11
  fire element, 12
  fixed modality, 13

Sun and, 14
symbol, dates, and
  archetype theme of, 10
Leo, in 2017, 75–88
  January, 76
  February, 76–77
  March, 78–79
  April, 79–80
  May, 80–81
  June, 81–82
  July, 82–83
  August, 83–84
  September, 84–85
  October, 85–86
  November, 86–87
  December, 87
Leo, in 2018, 238–250
  January, 238–239
  February, 239
  March, 240–241
  April, 241–242
  May, 242–243
  June, 243–244
  July, 244–245
  August, 245–246
  September, 246–247
  October, 247–248
  November, 248–249
  December, 249
Leo, in 2019, 401–414
  January, 401–402
  February, 402–403
  March, 403–405
  April, 405–406
  May, 406–407
  June, 407–408
  July, 408–409
  August, 409–410
  September, 410–411
  October, 411–412
  November, 412–413
  December, 413–414
  air element, 13

Libra
  cardinal modality, 13
  characteristics of, 11
  symbol, dates, and
    archetype theme of, 10
  Venus and, 14
Libra, in 2017, 102–115
  January, 102–103
  February, 103–104
  March, 104–105
  April, 105–106
  May, 107
  June, 107–108
  July, 108–109
  August, 110
  September, 111
  October, 112
  November, 113
  December, 114
Libra, in 2018, 263–276
  January, 263–264
  February, 265
  March, 265–266
  April, 267
  May, 268–269
  June, 269–270
  July, 270–271
  August, 271–272
  September, 272–273
  October, 273–274
  November, 274–275
  December, 275
Libra, in 2019, 428–442
  January, 429–430
  February, 430–431
  March, 431–432
  April, 432–433
  May, 433–434
  June, 434–435
  July, 435–436
  August, 436–437
  September, 438
  October, 438–439

November, 440
December, 440–441
lunar eclipses, 22
  Aquarius
    in 2017, 163–164,
      167
    in 2018, 317–318,
      324–325
    in 2019, 482–483,
      489–490
  Aries
    in 2017, 25, 31
    in 2018, 193
    in 2019, 346–347,
      353–354
  Cancer
    in 2017, 64–65,
      70–71
    in 2018, 225–226,
      231–232
    in 2019, 387–388,
      394–395
  Capricorn
    in 2017, 143–144,
      149–150
    in 2018, 304,
      310–311
    in 2019, 469–470,
      475–476
  Gemini
    in 2017, 51–52,
      57–58
    in 2018, 213,
      219–220
    in 2019, 374–375,
      380–381
  Leo
    in 2017, 76–77,
      83–84
    in 2018, 238–239,
      244–245
    in 2019, 401–402,
      408–409

Libra
  in 2017, 103–104,
    110
  in 2018, 263–264,
    270–271
  in 2019, 429–430,
    435–436
Pisces
  in 2017, 171,
    177–178
  in 2018, 331–332,
    337–338
  in 2019, 497–498,
    504–505
Sagittarius
  in 2017, 130–131,
    136–137
  in 2018, 290–291,
    297–298
  in 2019, 456,
    462–463
Scorpio
  in 2017, 116–117,
    123–124
  in 2018, 276–277,
    283–284
  in 2019, 443,
    449–450
Taurus
  in 2017, 38–39,
    44–45
  in 2018, 200–201,
    206–207
  in 2019, 360–361,
    366–367
Virgo
  in 2017, 90–91,
    96–97
  in 2018, 250–251,
    258
  in 2019, 415–416,
    421–422

M

March
  Aquarius
    in 2017, 158
    in 2018, 319–321
    in 2019, 485–486
  Aries
    in 2017, 25–26
    in 2018, 188–189
    in 2019, 348–349
  Cancer
    in 2017, 65–66
    in 2018, 227–228
    in 2019, 390–391
  Capricorn
    in 2017, 144–145
    in 2018, 305–306
    in 2019, 471–472
  Gemini
    in 2017, 52–53
    in 2018, 214–216
    in 2019, 376–377
  Leo
    in 2017, 78–79
    in 2018, 240–241
    in 2019, 403–405
  Libra
    in 2017, 104–105
    in 2018, 265–266
    in 2019, 431–432
  Pisces
    in 2017, 172
    in 2018, 332–334
    in 2019, 499–500
  Sagittarius
    in 2017, 131–132
    in 2018, 292–293
    in 2019, 457–459
  Scorpio
    in 2017, 118
    in 2018, 278–279
    in 2019, 445–446
  Taurus
    in 2017, 39–40
    in 2018, 202–203
    in 2019, 362–363
  Virgo
    in 2017, 91–92
    in 2018, 252–253
    in 2019, 417–418
Mars
  length of transit of signs, 14
  signs ruled by, 14, 23
Maslow, Abraham, 368
May
  Aquarius
    in 2017, 160
    in 2018, 322–323
    in 2019, 487–488
  Aries
    in 2017, 27–28
    in 2018, 190–191
    in 2019, 351–352
  Cancer
    in 2017, 67
    in 2018, 229–230
    in 2019, 392–393
  Capricorn
    in 2017, 147
    in 2018, 307–309
    in 2019, 472–474
  Gemini
    in 2017, 54–55
    in 2018, 217–218
    in 2019, 378–379
  Leo
    in 2017, 80–81
    in 2018, 242–243
    in 2019, 406–407
  Libra
    in 2017, 107
    in 2018, 268–269
    in 2019, 433–434
  Pisces
    in 2017, 174
    in 2018, 335–336
    in 2019, 502
  Sagittarius
    in 2017, 133–134
    in 2018, 294–296
    in 2019, 460–461
  Scorpio
    in 2017, 120
    in 2018, 280–281
    in 2019, 447–448
  Taurus
    in 2017, 41–42
    in 2018, 204–205
    in 2019, 364–365
  Virgo
    in 2017, 93–94
    in 2018, 254–256
    in 2019, 419–420
Mercury
  length of transit of signs, 14
  signs ruled by, 14
Mercury retrograde
  in 2017, 20–21
  in 2018, 184
  in 2019, 344
  stories about, 9, 185, 345
  three Rs of (revise, review, and revisit), 9
modalities, of sun signs, 13
moon
  length of transit of signs, 14
  sign ruled by, 14
mutable modality, of sun signs, 13

N

Neptune
  length of transit of signs, 14

sign ruled by, 15
new and full moons
    in 2017, 21
    in 2018, 183–184
    in 2019, 343–344
ninth house (worldview), 18
November
    Aquarius
        in 2017, 166–167
        in 2018, 328–329
        in 2019, 493–494
    Aries
        in 2017, 34–35
        in 2018, 197–198
        in 2019, 357–358
    Cancer
        in 2017, 73–74
        in 2018, 235–236
        in 2019, 398–399
    Capricorn
        in 2017, 153
        in 2018, 314–315
        in 2019, 479–480
    Gemini
        in 2017, 60
        in 2018, 223–224
        in 2019, 385
    Leo
        in 2017, 86–87
        in 2018, 248–249
        in 2019, 412–413
    Libra
        in 2017, 113
        in 2018, 274–275
        in 2019, 440
    Pisces
        in 2017, 180
        in 2018, 341
        in 2019, 508–509
    Sagittarius
        in 2017, 139–140
        in 2018, 301–302
        in 2019, 466–467

    Scorpio
        in 2017, 126–127
        in 2018, 287–288
        in 2019, 453–454
    Taurus
        in 2017, 47–48
        in 2018, 210–211
        in 2019, 371–372
    Virgo
        in 2017, 99–100
        in 2018, 261–262
        in 2019, 426–427

O

October
    Aquarius
        in 2017, 165–166
        in 2018, 327–328
        in 2019, 492–493
    Aries
        in 2017, 33–34
        in 2018, 196
        in 2019, 356
    Cancer
        in 2017, 72–73
        in 2018, 234–235
        in 2019, 397–398
    Capricorn
        in 2017, 152
        in 2018, 313–314
        in 2019, 478–479
    Gemini
        in 2017, 59–60
        in 2018, 222–223
        in 2019, 384
    Leo
        in 2017, 85–86
        in 2018, 247–248
        in 2019, 411–412
    Libra
        in 2017, 112
        in 2018, 273–274
        in 2019, 438–439

    Pisces
        in 2017, 179–180
        in 2018, 340
        in 2019, 507–508
    Sagittarius
        in 2017, 138–139
        in 2018, 300
        in 2019, 465–466
    Scorpio
        in 2017, 125–126
        in 2018, 286–287
        in 2019, 452–453
    Taurus
        in 2017, 46–47
        in 2018, 209–210
        in 2019, 370–371
    Virgo
        in 2017, 98–99
        in 2018, 260–261
        in 2019, 425–426

P

partnerships and romance
    Aquarius
        in 2017, 156, 158,
          159–168
        in 2018, 317–325,
          327–329
        in 2019, 483–484,
          486–491, 493–494,
          495
    Aries
        in 2017, 23–28,
          31–35
        in 2018, 186–189,
          192, 193, 194, 195,
          196, 197–198
        in 2019, 346–355,
          357–358
    Cancer
        in 2017, 63, 64–65,
          67, 68–70, 72–75
        in 2018, 225–237

in 2019, 387–388, 389, 392–400

Capricorn
in 2017, 142–150, 152, 153, 154–155
in 2018, 304, 305–316
in 2019, 469–471, 473–480

Gemini
in 2017, 50–62
in 2018, 214–224
in 2019, 374–380, 382–383, 384, 385

Leo
in 2017, 76–77, 79–84, 86–87
in 2018, 238–239, 241–245, 248–249
in 2019, 401–414

Libra
in 2017, 102–106, 107, 108–109, 110, 111, 114
in 2018, 263–266, 267, 269–274, 275
in 2019, 429–433, 435–437, 438–439

Pisces
in 2017, 170, 171, 172, 173–182
in 2018, 331–338, 339, 340, 342
in 2019, 498–500, 502, 503, 504–508

Sagittarius
in 2017, 130–134, 136–141
in 2018, 290–293, 294–297, 299, 300, 301–302
in 2019, 456, 457–462, 465–468

Scorpio
in 2017, 115–117, 118, 121–128
in 2018, 278–288, 289
in 2019, 444, 445–447, 448, 449–451, 453–454

Taurus
in 2017, 38–43, 46–49
in 2018, 200–212
in 2019, 360–372

Virgo
in 2017, 88–91, 94–101
in 2018, 250–251, 252, 254–261, 262
in 2019, 415–424, 426–428

personal unconscious
Aquarius, in 2019, 486–487, 495
Aries
in 2018, 187–188
in 2019, 348–349
Cancer
in 2017, 74
in 2019, 392–393
Gemini
in 2017, 60–61
in 2018, 217–218
in 2019, 376–377
Leo
in 2017, 76
in 2018, 406–407, 408–409
Libra
in 2017, 110
in 2019, 430–431, 436–437
Pisces
in 2017, 177

in 2019, 497–498, 499–500, 505–506
Sagittarius, in 2017, 138–139
Scorpio
in 2017, 119–120, 125–126
in 2018, 278–279
in 2019, 451
Taurus, in 2019, 360–361, 363–364, 370–371
Virgo
in 2017, 90
in 2019, 421–422

Pisces, generally
characteristics of, 12
Jupiter and, 14
mutable modality, 13
Neptune and, 14, 15
symbol, dates, and archetype theme of, 10
water element and, 13
Pisces, in 2017, 169–182
January, 170
February, 171
March, 172
April, 172–174
May, 174
June, 175–176
July, 176–177
August, 177–178
September, 178–179
October, 179–180
November, 180
December, 181–182
Pisces, in 2018, 330–342
January, 331–332
February, 332
March, 332–334
April, 334
May, 335–336
June, 336–337

July, 337–338
August, 338
September, 339
October, 340
November, 341
December, 342
Pisces, in 2019, 489–510
    January, 497–498
    February, 498–499
    March, 499–500
    April, 500–501
    May, 502
    June, 503
    July, 504–505
    August, 505–506
    September, 506–507
    October, 507–508
    November, 508–509
    December, 509–510
planets, signs ruled by, 14–15
Pluto
    length of transit of signs,
      14
    sign ruled by, 15
profession and career (tenth
    house), 18
professional life
    Aquarius
      in 2017, 156, 160,
        161–168
      in 2018, 317–330
      in 2019, 487–495
    Aries
      in 2017, 23–24,
        26–27, 30, 33–36
      in 2018, 186–189,
        192, 194, 195, 196,
        197–198
      in 2019, 346–347,
        348, 350–351,
        354–355, 356,
        357–359

Cancer
    in 2017, 63, 64–66,
      67
    in 2018, 225–231,
      235–237
    in 2019, 387–388,
      391–400
Capricorn
    in 2017, 143–152,
      154–155
    in 2018, 304,
      305–316
    in 2019, 471–475,
      477–481
Gemini
    in 2017, 50–51,
      54–55, 58–62
    in 2018, 213,
      214–224
    in 2019, 374–377,
      379–380, 383, 384,
      385
Leo
    in 2017, 76–84, 87
    in 2018, 238–248
    in 2019, 402–407,
      409–410, 412–414
Libra
    in 2017, 102–104,
      107–108, 112, 113,
      114
    in 2018, 263–266,
      267, 268–272,
      274–275
    in 2019, 430–436,
      438–441
Pisces
    in 2017, 170, 171,
      172, 173–178,
      181–182
    in 2018, 331–332,
      335–338, 340, 341,
      342

    in 2019, 497–500,
      502, 503, 504–505,
      508–510
Sagittarius
    in 2017, 131–141
    in 2018, 290–298,
      299, 300
    in 2019, 457, 459–
      461, 463–467
Scorpio
    in 2017, 116–117,
      118, 120, 122–127
    in 2018, 276–286
    in 2019, 443, 444
Taurus
    in 2017, 37–38,
      44–47
    in 2018, 200–211
    in 2019, 360–363,
      365–366, 368–370
Virgo
    in 2017, 88–89,
      92–96, 100–101
    in 2018, 250–259,
      261–262
    in 2019, 415–424,
      426–428

R

retrograde planets, 8–9. *See
    also* Mercury retrograde
romance. *See* partnerships
    and romance

S

Sagittarius, generally
    characteristics of, 11
    fire element, 12
    Jupiter and, 14
    mutable modality, 13
    symbol, dates, and
      archetype theme of, 10

Sagittarius, in 2017, 128–141
  January, 129–130
  February, 130–131
  March, 131–132
  April, 132–133
  May, 133–134
  June, 134–135
  July, 135–136
  August, 136–137
  September, 137–138
  October, 138–139
  November, 139–140
  December, 140–141
Sagittarius, in 2018, 290–303
  January, 290–291
  February, 292
  March, 292–293
  April, 294
  May, 294–296
  June, 296–297
  July, 297–298
  August, 298
  September, 299
  October, 300
  November, 301–302
  December, 302
Sagittarius, in 2019, 455–468
  January, 456
  February, 457
  March, 457–459
  April, 459–460
  May, 460–461
  June, 461–462
  July, 462–463
  August, 463–464
  September, 464
  October, 465–466
  November, 466–467
  December, 467–468
Saturn
  length of transit of signs, 14
  sign ruled by, 15

Scorpio, generally
  characteristics of, 11
  fixed modality, 13
  Mars and, 14
  Pluto and, 15
  symbol, dates, and archetype theme of, 10
  water element and, 13
Scorpio, in 2017, 115–128
  January, 115–116
  February, 116–117
  March, 118
  April, 119–120
  May, 120
  June, 121–122
  July, 122–123
  August, 123–124
  September, 124–125
  October, 125–126
  November, 126–127
  December, 127–128
Scorpio, in 2018, 276–289
  January, 276–277
  February, 278
  March, 278–279
  April, 280
  May, 280–281
  June, 282–283
  July, 283–284
  August, 284–285
  September, 285–286
  October, 286–287
  November, 287–288
  December, 289
Scorpio, in 2019, 442–455
  January, 443
  February, 444
  March, 445–446
  April, 446–447
  May, 447–448
  June, 448
  July, 449–450
  August, 450–451

  September, 451
  October, 452–453
  November, 453–454
  December, 454
second house (personal values), 16
September
  Aquarius
    in 2017, 164–165
    in 2018, 326–327
    in 2019, 492
  Aries
    in 2017, 32–33
    in 2018, 195
    in 2019, 355
  Cancer
    in 2017, 71–72
    in 2018, 233–234
    in 2019, 396–397
  Capricorn
    in 2017, 150–151
    in 2018, 312–313
    in 2019, 477–478
  Gemini
    in 2017, 58–59
    in 2018, 221–222
    in 2019, 383
  Leo
    in 2017, 84–85
    in 2018, 246–247
    in 2019, 410–411
  Libra
    in 2017, 111
    in 2018, 272–273
    in 2019, 438
  Pisces
    in 2017, 178–179
    in 2018, 339
    in 2019, 506–507
  Sagittarius
    in 2017, 137–138
    in 2018, 299
    in 2019, 464

Scorpio
  in 2017, 124–125
  in 2018, 285–286
  in 2019, 451
Taurus
  in 2017, 45–46
  in 2018, 208–209
  in 2019, 369–370
Virgo
  in 2017, 97–98
  in 2018, 259–260
  in 2019, 424
seventh house (partnerships and marriage), 18
  cusp, 15, 17
sexuality. *See* partnerships and romance
sixth house (work and responsibility), 17
solar eclipses, 22
  Aquarius
    in 2017, 163–164, 167
    in 2018, 318–319, 324–325
    in 2019, 482–483, 489–490, 495
  Aries
    in 2017, 25, 31
    in 2018, 187–188, 193, 194
    in 2019, 346–347, 353–354
  Cancer
    in 2017, 64–65, 70–71
    in 2018, 226–227, 231–232
    in 2019, 394–395, 399–400
  Capricorn
    in 2017, 143–144, 149–150

    in 2018, 305, 310–311
    in 2019, 311–312, 469–470, 475–476
  Gemini
    in 2017, 51–52, 57–58
    in 2018, 214, 219–221
    in 2019, 374–375, 380–381
  Leo
    in 2017, 76–77, 83–84
    in 2018, 239, 244–246
    in 2019, 401–402, 408–409, 413–414
  Libra
    in 2017, 103–104, 110
    in 2018, 265, 271–272
    in 2019, 429–430, 435–436, 440–441
  Pisces
    in 2017, 171, 177–178
    in 2018, 332, 337–338
    in 2019, 497–498, 504–505, 509–510
  Sagittarius
    in 2017, 130–131, 136–137
    in 2018, 292, 298
    in 2019, 456, 462–463
  Scorpio
    in 2017, 116–117, 123–124
    in 2018, 278, 283–285

    in 2019, 443, 449–450
  Taurus
    in 2017, 38–39, 44–45
    in 2018, 201, 206–208
    in 2019, 360–361, 366–367, 372–373
  Virgo, 427–428
    in 2017, 90–91, 96–97
    in 2018, 252, 257–259
    in 2019, 415–416, 421–422
Sun
  length of transit of signs, 14
  sign ruled by, 14
sun signs
  characteristics of, 10–12
  elements and modes of, 12–13
  symbols of, 10
synchronicity
  Aries, in 2017, 23–24, 34
  Cancer
    in 2018, 234–235
    in 2019, 395–396
  Capricorn
    in 2018, 307
    in 2019, 478–479
  Gemini
    in 2017, 55–56, 59–60
    in 2019, 382–383
  Leo, in 2019, 407–408, 413–414
  Libra
    in 2017, 102–103, 110–111, 113
    in 2018, 274–275

in 2019, 429–430
Pisces, in 2019, 497–498,
   499–500, 507–508
Sagittarius, in 2018, 292
Taurus
   in 2017, 39–40,
     44–45
   in 2018, 201,
     210–211
   Virgo
     in 2017, 94–95
     in 2018, 256–257

T

Taurus, generally
   earth element, 12
   fixed modality, 13
   symbol, dates, and
     archetype theme of, 10
   Venus and, 14
Taurus, in 2017, 36–49
   January, 37–38
   February, 38–39
   March, 39–40
   April, 40–41
   May, 41–42
   June, 42–43
   July, 43–44
   August, 44–45
   September, 45–46
   October, 46–47
   November, 47–48
   December, 48–49
Taurus, in 2018, 199–212
   January, 200–201
   February, 201
   March, 202–203
   April, 203–204
   May, 204–205
   June, 205–206
   July, 206–207
   August, 207–208
   September, 208–209

October, 209–210
November, 210–211
December, 211–212
Taurus, in 2019, 359–373
   January, 360–361
   February, 361–362
   March, 362–363
   April, 363–364
   May, 364–365
   June, 365–366
   July, 366–367
   August, 368–369
   September, 369–370
   October, 370–371
   November, 371–372
   December, 372–373
tenth house (profession and
   career), 18
   MC cusp of, 15, 18
third house (communication
   and learning), 16
travel
   Aquarius
     in 2017, 156, 159–
       160, 165–168
     in 2018, 327–329
     in 2019, 482–483,
       485–487, 493–494
   Aries
     in 2017, 28–29, 34
     in 2018, 188–189,
       197–198
     in 2019, 346–347,
       354–355, 358–359
   Cancer
     in 2017, 63, 67,
       71–75
     in 2018, 226–227,
       234–237
     in 2019, 390–391,
       393–394
   Capricorn
     in 2017, 147–148,

150–151, 154–155
     in 2018, 305–306,
       311–315
     in 2019, 476–477,
       479–480
   Gemini
     in 2017, 58–59
     in 2018, 214–219,
       221–222, 224
     in 2019, 375–376,
       382–383, 385, 386
   Leo
     in 2017, 79–80,
       83–86
     in 2018, 240–242,
       246–247
     in 2019, 401–402,
       411–413
   Libra
     in 2017, 107–109,
       113
     in 2018, 263–264,
       267, 272–275
     in 2019, 436–437
   Pisces
     in 2017, 174,
       175–180
     in 2018, 332–334,
       337–338, 340
     in 2019, 499–500,
       508–509
   Sagittarius
     in 2017, 129–130,
       135–137
     in 2018, 294, 297–
       298, 301–302
     in 2019, 466–467
   Scorpio
     in 2017, 120, 121–
       123, 127–128
     in 2018, 278–279,
       283–284, 289
     in 2019, 452–453

Taurus
    in 2017, 41–44,
        47–48
    in 2018, 200–203,
        207–208, 210–212
    in 2019, 360–362,
        365–366, 371–373
Virgo
    in 2017, 88–89,
        92–94, 96–97,
        99–100
    in 2018, 252–256,
        258–259, 261–262
    in 2019, 416–420,
        425–426
twelfth house (personal
unconscious), 19
2017, 20
    eclipses during, 22
    Mercury retrogrades
        during, 20–21
    new and full moons
        during, 21
    see also specific signs or
        months
2018, 183
    eclipses during
    Mercury retrogrades
        during, 184
    new and full moons
        during, 183–184
    see also specific signs or
        months
2019, 343
    eclipses during
    Mercury retrograde, 344
    new and full moons
        during, 343–344
    see also specific signs or
        months

U
Uranus
    length of transit of signs,
        14
    sign ruled by, 15

V
Venus
    length of transit of signs,
        14
    signs ruled by, 14
Virgo, generally
    characteristics of, 11
    earth element, 12
    Mercury and, 14
    mutable modality, 13
    symbol, dates, and
        archetype theme of, 10
Virgo, in 2017, 88–101
    January, 88–89
    February, 90–91
    March, 91–92
    April, 92–93
    May, 93–94
    June, 94–95
    July, 95–96
    August, 96–97
    September, 97–98
    October, 98–99
    November, 99–100
    December, 100–101
Virgo, in 2018, 250–263
    January, 250–251
    February, 252
    March, 252–253
    April, 254
    May, 254–256
    June, 256–257
    July, 257–258
    August, 258–259
    September, 259–260
    October, 260–261

November, 261–262
December, 262
Virgo, in 2019, 415–428
    January, 415–416
    February, 416–417
    March, 417–418
    April, 418–419
    May, 419–420
    June, 420–421
    July, 421–422
    August, 422–424
    September, 424
    October, 425–426
    November, 426–427
    December, 427–428

W
water element, sun signs of,
    13